textbook*plus⁺*

Equipping Instructors and Students with
FREE RESOURCES for Core Zondervan Textbooks

Available Resources for Basics of Biblical Hebrew Grammar

Teaching Resources

- Chapter quizzes
- Presentation slides
- Tests
- Exams
- Alternative grammar presentations

Study Resources

- Workbook answer key
- Scriptures indices

*How To Access Resources

- Go to www.ZondervanAcademic.com
- Click "Sign Up" button and complete registration process
- Find books using search field or categories navigation feature
- Click "Teaching Resources" or "Study Resources" tab once you get to book page to access resources

→ *www.ZondervanAcademic.com*

Also by Gary D. Pratico and Miles V. Van Pelt

Basics of Biblical Hebrew Workbook: Second Edition

Basics of Biblical Hebrew Vocabulary Audio

Biblical Hebrew (Zondervan Get an A! Study Guide)

Old Testament Hebrew Vocabulary Cards

Biblical Hebrew Survival Kit

Charts of Biblical Hebrew

Vocabulary Guide to Biblical Hebrew

Graded Reader of Biblical Hebrew

Other Books/Resources by Miles V. Van Pelt

English Grammar to Ace Biblical Hebrew

Basics of Biblical Hebrew Video Lectures

Old Testament Hebrew Vocabulary Cards App

Biblical Hebrew: A Compact Guide

Basics of Biblical Aramaic

Basics of Biblical Aramaic Video Lectures

Second Edition

Basics
of
Biblical
Hebrew

GRAMMAR

Gary D. PRATICO
and
Miles V. VAN PELT

ZONDERVAN

ZONDERVAN

Basics of Biblical Hebrew Grammar
Copyright © 2001, 2007 by Gary D. Pratico and Miles V. Van Pelt

Requests for information should be addressed to:
Zondervan, 3900 *Sparks Dr. SE, Grand Rapids, Michigan 49546*

This edition: ISBN 978-0-310-52067-2

The Library of Congress cataloged the previous editions as follows:

    Pratico, Gary Davis.
        Basics of biblical Hebrew grammar / Gary D. Pratico and Miles V. Van Pelt. — 2nd ed.
           p. cm.
        Includes bibliographical references and index.
        ISBN 978-0-310-27020-1
        1. Hebrew language — Grammar. 2. Bible. O.T. — Language, style. I. Van Pelt, Miles V., 1969— II. Title.
    PJ4567.3.P73 2007
    492.4 — dc22   2006032091

Interior design: Miles V. Van Pelt

Printed in China

17 18 19 20 /ASC/ 22 21 20 19 18 17 16 15 14 13 12 11 10 9 8 7 6 5

To Mary my Beloved

הִנָּךְ יָפָה רַעְיָתִי הִנָּךְ יָפָה

Song 4:1

To Aaron, Martha, and Jon
with my love

וְאָנֹכִי וּבֵיתִי נַעֲבֹד אֶת־יְהוָה

Josh 24:15

To Laurie for her love

רְשָׁפֶיהָ רִשְׁפֵּי אֵשׁ שַׁלְהֶבֶתְיָה

Song 8:6

To Ben, Kacie, Madie, and Max

לְכוּ־בָנִים שִׁמְעוּ־לִי יִרְאַת יְהוָה אֲלַמֶּדְכֶם

Ps 34:12 [11]

גַּל־עֵינַי וְאַבִּיטָה נִפְלָאוֹת מִתּוֹרָתֶךָ

Open my eyes that I may see wonderful
things from your law.

Psalm 119:18

Table of Contents

Section 4: Introduction to the Derived Stems

Section 5: Reading and Studying Your Hebrew Bible

Appendices

Preface

As the title indicates, this grammar represents the "basics" of biblical Hebrew. From the perspective of its authors, it represents the basics in the categories of phonology, morphology, and syntax. Some will want more; others will want less. Nevertheless, this is our best judgment as what should constitute a basic, one year course in biblical Hebrew. By design, we have minimized the introduction of issues related to the historical development of the language and to the area of comparative Semitic philology. While these issues are interesting and at times helpful, they are often distracting and confusing to the beginning student and should be studied at the intermediate level.

We recognize that a large percentage of those who study biblical Hebrew do so in preparation for some type of pastoral or teaching ministry. For most of us, therefore, the study of Hebrew is not only an academic exercise, but also an act of obedience in the fulfillment of a calling to the ministry of God's Word. We have been entrusted with the preaching and teaching of God's Word and thereby with the oversight of his people, and thus the study of biblical languages should constitute a fundamental and significant part of our training. In general, the design of this grammar reflects both its scope (basic) and its primary audience (those training for biblical ministry). Some of the more notable features of its presentation are detailed below.

1. There are two parts to *Basics of Biblical Hebrew*: a grammar and a workbook. All practice exercises have been located in a separate workbook, *Basics of Biblical Hebrew: Workbook* (Grand Rapids: Zondervan, 2007). The workbook contains exercises for each chapter in the grammar. Located on Zondervan's resource website is the full answer key to the workbook exercises and Scripture indices. The answer key has been stored in PDF format so that it may be printed and used as needed (**www.TextbookPlus.Zondervan.com**).

2. Toward the end of each chapter, vocabulary words are listed for memorization. The Hebrew words and their definitions were based on Larry A. Mitchel's *A Student's Vocabulary for Biblical Hebrew and Aramaic* (Grand Rapids: Zondervan, 1984). The vocabulary of this grammar includes all words occurring seventy times or more in the Hebrew Bible, excluding most proper names. Proper names have been identified for the student in the workbook exercises. Several words that occur fewer than seventy times are included because of their appearance in the grammar or workbook.

3. Throughout the grammar, frequent reference is made to statistical information in order to illustrate the significance or distribution of the counted item. For example, after each vocabulary word and its definition, we identify how many times that particular word occurs in the Hebrew Bible. Statistical information is also provided for certain inflected forms, grammatical constructions, and other similar items. Our statistical information is derived from the Accordance module BHS-W4. We acknowledge our indebtedness to this software and its developers (www.accordancebible.com). We have used this invaluable resource extensively in the production of both the grammar and the workbook. We recognize, however, that this database is not without error and have corrected infrequent errors, being careful to check results whenever possible. We also recognize that discrepancies with other statistical sources do exist but have utilized the Accordance statistics throughout for the sake of consistency.

4. After the vocabulary section of each chapter, we have included a brief study that is intended to encourage students in their study of Hebrew. Many of these studies are "exegetical insights" or "biblical-theological reflections" with reference to specific Hebrew texts. A few are devoted to observations on Hebrew words or phraseology; others explore various aspects of Hebrew language that contribute to our understanding or interpretation of specific biblical passages. These studies will often emphasize a point of grammar or vocabulary that has been studied in a particular chapter. A few are readings that will highlight selected Hebrew verses of a biblical text with a view to grammatical, theological, and exegetical commentary. These studies have been written by pastors, youth leaders, graduate students, and professors; to them we express our gratitude for their contributions (see the following "Table of Insights"). This mix of contributors, with different levels of exposure to the language, should be an encouragement that any level of competence with the language can provide a better understanding of the Old Testament and enhance one's effectiveness in the communication of biblical truth.

5. We have been parsimonious with regard to the use of English punctuation so as not to clutter or confuse the appearance of the Hebrew script, especially the vowels and accent marks. This is most notable in our diminished use of commas, which would frequently obscure certain vowels. Additionally, we have chosen not to follow certain standard scholarly conventions with regard to capitalization and the use of italics and parentheses so as to present the components and concepts of the grammar with greater emphasis and clarity for the beginning student.

6. Zondervan's resource website, Textbook Plus, has been established to provide additional resources to complement the grammar and workbook. The address for this site is **www.TextbookPlus.Zondervan.com**.

7. The *Old Testament Hebrew Vocabulary Cards App* has been created for use on iOS devices. The app includes the following features: Over 1,000 of the most common biblical Hebrew words; pronunciation; sortable (by chapter, frequency, and part of speech); viewable alphabetically, by frequency, or randomly. Test your knowledge with a "Quiz Mode" that tracks your progress. Go to **zndr.vn/hebrewapp** to get more details or to purchase the app.

There are a number of people we wish to thank: Jim Jumper, Filip Vukosavovic, Jason DeRouchie, Becky Josberger, Jun Kawashima, Mary Lewis, and Alan Tischler. We wish to express a word of special gratitude to Jonathan Kline for his significant contribution to the production of this volume and to John Beckman for his writing of sections 9.20 and 23.9. We are also indebted to those who tested the grammar in its earlier stages: Donna Petter, Jason Bembry, Jack Klem, Alice Via, Keith Bodner, and Frank Wheeler. We are grateful to Zondervan for their assistance in the production and publication of this grammar. We especially want to recognize Verlyn Verbrugge, Jack Kragt, Bob Buller, Jody DeNeef, and Lee Fields. Finally, we recognize and thank Bill Mounce for his encouragement and significant contributions to this project.

Gary Pratico wishes to thank the trustees and academic administration of Gordon-Conwell Theological Seminary for their many levels of support and encouragement, including the sabbatical year that was devoted exclusively to this publication.

Miles Van Pelt would like to thank Professor John Hartley of Azusa Pacific University for his profound investments in an unlikely student. I would also like to thank Larry and Martha Armitstead for all of their support and help. But most of all, I especially thank my wife, Laurie, for her countless sacrifices and enduring support of my calling.

Gary D. Pratico
Miles V. Van Pelt
September 2006

Table of Insights

The Hebrew Alphabet

1.1 The Hebrew alphabet consists of twenty-three consonants or letters. It is written from right to left. The first step in learning Hebrew requires that you memorize the alphabet in order. You will also want to learn the names of the Hebrew letters, how each letter is pronounced, and the transliterated value of each.

Hebrew Letter	Name	Pronunciation	Transliteration
א	Alef	(silent)	$^{\prime}$
ב	Bet	b as in boy	b
ג	Gimel	g as in God	g
ד	Dalet	d as in day	d
ה	He	h as in hay	h
ו	Waw	w as in way	w
ז	Zayin	z as in Zion	z
ח	Ḥet	ch as in Bach	ḥ
ט	Tet	t as in toy	ṭ
י	Yod	y as in yes	y
כ	Kaf	k as in king	k
ל	Lamed	l as in lion	l
מ	Mem	m as in mother	m
נ	Nun	n as in now	n
ס	Samek	s as in sin	s
ע	Ayin	(silent)	ʿ
פ	Pe	p as in pastor	p
צ	Tsade	ts as in boots	ṣ
ק	Qof	k as in king	q
ר	Resh	r as in run	r
שׂ	Sin	s as in sin	ś
שׁ	Shin	sh as in ship	š
ת	Taw	t as in toy	t

1.2   **Pronouncing א and ע.** You have just learned that א and ע are silent, lacking any phonetic value. While א is indeed silent, the consonant ע does have some phonetic value. For English speakers, however, the pronunciation of ע is so subtly nuanced that, for all practical purposes, we are considering it too as silent. When these two consonants are encountered in a word, neither consonant will have a phonetic value; only their assigned vowels will be pronounced. This means that if an א or ע is assigned an "a" vowel, only that vowel will be pronounced. At this point, therefore, it is only important to know that א and ע are silent and only their assigned vowels will have a phonetic value.

1.3   As mentioned above, Hebrew is written from right to left, *not* left to right as in English. In the following order, beginning on the right, carefully study and memorize the twenty-three consonants of the Hebrew alphabet.

אבגדהוזחטיכלמנסעפצקרשׂשׁת

1.4   **Final Forms.** Five of the Hebrew letters have final forms. That is to say, when one of these letters occurs at the end of a word, it is written differently than when it appears at the beginning or in the middle of a word. *The changing of a letter's form, however, does not change its pronunciation or transliteration.* The five final forms are listed below. These final forms must also be memorized. Remember that the Hebrew examples are written from right to left, whereas the transliteration of the Hebrew examples is written from left to right.

Regular Form	Final Form	Example	Transliteration	Translation
כ	ך	דרך	*drk*	road, way
מ	ם	עם	*ʿm*	nation, people
נ	ן	זקן	*zqn*	old man, elder
פ	ף	כסף	*ksp*	money, silver
צ	ץ	ארץ	*ʾrṣ*	earth, land

1.5   *Begadkephat* **Letters.** Six of the Hebrew consonants have two possible, but closely related, pronunciations. Collectively, these are known as the *begadkephat* consonants. This term is simply a mnemonic device allowing for the easy memorization of these six letters (בגדכפת). To distinguish between the two pronunciations, a dot called a Daghesh

Lene was inserted into the consonantal character (בגדכפת). The presence of the Daghesh Lene indicates a hard pronunciation and its absence denotes a soft pronunciation. *A Daghesh Lene will only appear in the begadkephat letters.* The student should learn the different pronunciations indicated below. You will also notice that each letter without the Daghesh Lene is transliterated with a small horizontal line either below or above the English character. Memorize both the pronunciation and the transliteration.

Begadkephat Letter	*Pronunciation*	*Transliteration*
בּ	b as in boy	*b*
ב	v as in vine	*b̲*
גּ	g as in God	*g*
ג	gh as in aghast	*ḡ*
דּ	d as in day	*d*
ד	dh as in the	*d̲*
כּ	k as in king	*k*
כ	ch as in Bach	*k̲*
פּ	p as in pastor	*p*
פ	ph as in alphabet	*p̲*
תּ	t as in toy	*t*
ת	th as in thin	*t̲*

1.6   **Gutturals**. Four of the Hebrew letters are called *gutturals*. They are called gutturals because they are pronounced in the back of the throat. The guttural consonants are א, ע, ה and ח. Sometimes ר will also behave like a guttural. For now, you only need to memorize which of the consonants are gutturals. Later you will learn certain rules that govern the use of these consonants.

1.7   **Easily Confused Letters**. For the beginning student, certain pairs or groups of consonants can sometimes look alike and become confused (just as in English with the capital I and lowercase l in the word "Idol"). You have probably observed also that different Hebrew letters can sound alike (just as in English with the *c* in *cat* and the *k* in *kite*). In order to avoid any confusion, it is sometimes helpful to compare the following characters and carefully note their distinguishing features. There is no need to memorize these consonant groups. It is only important that you are able to distinguish between the different letters and sounds.

Hebrew consonants that look alike:

1. בּ (Bet) and כּ (Kaf)
2. גּ (Gimel) and נ (Nun)
3. ה (He) and ח (Ḥet) and ת (Taw)
4. שׂ (Sin) and שׁ (Shin)
5. ם (final Mem) and ס (Samek)
6. ד (Dalet) and ר (Resh)
7. צ (Tsade) and ע (Ayin)
8. ו (Waw) and ז (Zayin)
9. ו (Waw) and ן (final Nun)
10. ך (final Kaf) and ן (final Nun)

Hebrew consonants that sound alike:

1. ט (Tet) and תּ (Taw with Daghesh Lene)
2. כּ (Kaf with Daghesh Lene) and ק (Qof)
3. ס (Samek) and שׂ (Sin)

1.8   Transliteration. It is important to learn the system of transliteration presented above, not for the purpose of pronouncing or reading biblical Hebrew, but for studying other books that refer to Hebrew words without using Hebrew characters. Many commentaries, word study books, theological dictionaries, and other language tools do not use Hebrew font characters but a transliteration system whereby Hebrew letters are assigned equivalent letters from the English alphabet. In most instances, these books will list their system of transliteration somewhere at the beginning, usually between the table of contents and the first chapter or section. Some transliteration values are easily confused, so study the following transliterations carefully and observe the distinctions.

1. ʾ (א) and ʿ (ע). These are the most unusual transliteration symbols.

2. *h* (ה) and *ḥ* (ח)

3. *ṭ* (ט) and *t* (ת) and *t̲* (ת)

4. *s* (ס) and *ṣ* (צ) and *ś* (שׂ) and *š* (שׁ)

5. You will also want to review the different transliteration symbols for the *begadkephat* letters listed in 1.5. Remember that the consonants *without the Daghesh Lene*, with the soft pronunciation, have a horizontal line above or below the letter.

1.9 **Numerical Values.** Hebrew does not have a separate set of characters to represent numbers (like the English 1, 2, 3, etc.). Rather, each letter of the Hebrew alphabet represents a numerical value. The consonants א through ט represent the numbers 1-9. Consonants י through צ represent numbers 10-90 in multiples of 10 (10, 20, 30, etc.). And ק through ת represent the numbers 100, 200, 300 and 400 (שׂ and שׁ both represent 300). For a full presentation of the Hebrew numerical system, see chapter 11 (Hebrew Numbers).

1.10 **Summary.** Before you move on to the exercises for this chapter, be sure that you are comfortable with the following summary. When possible, treat the exercises like a quiz, not using your book to answer the questions. Then go back and make corrections with your book. This will give you an idea of the material you have mastered and the material you need to study further.

1. Memorize the twenty-three consonants of the Hebrew alphabet in order. Be able to write out the alphabet completely from right to left. You should also know the name, pronunciation, and transliteration value of each letter.

2. Five letters of the Hebrew alphabet (כ, מ, נ, פ and צ) have final forms (ך, ם, ן, ף and ץ). These must be memorized. Note that a final ך (Kaf) will frequently appear with two dots (ךְ).

3. Six Hebrew consonants are known as *begadkephat* letters (בגדכפת). They are capable of two different pronunciations, hard and soft. These pronunciations are distinguished by the presence or absence of a Daghesh Lene. The distinction in pronunciation and transliteration must be memorized.

4. Four Hebrew consonants are called gutturals: א, ע, ה and ח. Remember that ר may also behave like a guttural.

1.11   **The Hebrew Acrostic.** Knowledge of the Hebrew alphabet opens the door of understanding to the Hebrew acrostic or alphabetical psalms. These are biblical poems in which consecutive units (either lines, verses, or groups of verses) begin with sequential letters of the Hebrew alphabet. No doubt such a linguistic device provides a simple memory aid to the listener while still communicating the intensity and passion of the poet. For instance, the individual verses of Ps 9-10, 25, 34, and 145 begin with words whose first letters are, consecutively, the letters of the Hebrew alphabet. In Ps 37, the opening letters of alternate verses are arranged according to the sequence of the alphabet. Another variation occurs in Ps 111 and 112, where each line (rather than each verse) begins with successive letters of the Hebrew alphabet. The most elaborate acrostic biblical poem is Ps 119. This artistically shaped poem consists of twenty-two sections, each comprised of eight verses. These units feature twenty-two letters of the Hebrew alphabet, with all eight verses of a given unit beginning with the same letter of the alphabet.

As an artistic device, the acrostic uses both structure and content to express totality and completeness. Thus, everything from A to Z (or א to ת) is praised regarding the qualities of God (Ps 111 and 145), the just man (Ps 112), the virtuous woman (Prov 31:10-31), or the beauty of the law (Ps 119). Conversely, the writer of the book of Lamentations uses the acrostic to communicate the complete sense of grief over Jerusalem's fall. What is notable about the acrostic is that such an artificial scheme did not stand in the way of producing literature of a high order full of passion and thoughtfulness.

Roger Valci
Executive Pastor, Harbor Light Church
Fremont, California

1.12 **Advanced Information: Traditional and Modern Pronunciation.**[1] The pronunciation of modern or Israeli Hebrew differs in a number of ways from what is considered to be the traditional or ancient pronunciation. Though many differences could be observed, the most notable differences involve the pronunciation of ג, ד, ת and ו. In Modern Hebrew, the three *begadkephat* consonants ג, ד, and ת without Daghesh Lene are pronounced just like the forms with Daghesh Lene.

Consonant	*Traditional Pronunciation*	*Modern Pronunciation*
ג	gh as in aghast	g as in God
ד	dh as in the	d as in day
ת	th as in thin	t as in toy
ו	w as in way	v as in vine

---

[1] Periodically, throughout the chapters of this grammar, you will come across a section like this one entitled "Advanced Information." This material is not required but often helpful and interesting.

Chapter 2

The Hebrew Vowels

2.1   **Hebrew Vowels**. You might be surprised to learn that originally the Hebrew language had no *written* system of vowels. This does not mean, however, that Hebrew vowels did not exist. While they did not exist in written form, they had always been present in the *spoken* form of the language. If we were to take the vowels out of the English writing system, these vowels would still be present in the spoken form. An English translation of Deut 6:5 serves as an example: "Love the Lord your God with all your heart." Without the vowels, we are left with a series of consonants, much like the ancient written form of Hebrew: Lv th Lrd yr Gd wth ll yr hrt. In order to read this sentence out loud, you would need to rely on your knowledge of English and supply the necessary vowels. In the same way, when Joshua read the entire law of Moses to the Israelites (Josh 8), he had before him a consonantal text with no vowels. This required Joshua to supply from memory the necessary vowels when reading. Fortunately for us, this is not the case today. In the second half of the first millennium A.D., a group of dedicated scribes called *Masoretes* became concerned with preserving the oral tradition or spoken form of Hebrew. They developed an elaborate system of vowel notation called *pointing*. This pointing system was designed to preserve the spoken system of vowels in the written text. Because the Masoretic scribes considered the biblical text to be sacred, their vowel symbols were designed in such a way as never to alter the original consonantal text. To do this, the Masoretes developed vowel symbols that were placed under, inside (to the left) or above the consonantal characters. Let us look once again at Deut 6:5 but this time in Hebrew. You will notice that the consonants are exactly the same in both examples. In the second example, however, the Masoretic vowel pointing system has been added. Notice that the majority of symbols exist below the consonants with occasional symbols inside (to the left) or over the consonants.

וְאָהַבְתָּ אֵת יְהוָה אֱלֹהֶיךָ בְּכָל לְבָבְךָ   ואהבת את יהוה אלהיך בכל לבבך   (without vowels)

(with vowels)   וְאָהַבְתָּ אֵת יְהוָה אֱלֹהֶיךָ בְּכָל לְבָבְךָ

2.2 **Hebrew Vowel Charts.** In the following charts, Hebrew vowels are presented in three major categories: long, short, and reduced. Within these vowel types, there are five vowel classes (a, e, i, o, u), though not all are attested in each of the vowel types. Each vowel will appear with the consonant בּ in order to show the position of the vowel with respect to its consonant. It is important to note that the vowel is pronounced after the consonant with which it is associated. For example, בַּ is pronounced *ba* and not *ab* and בֹּ is pronounced *bo* and not *ob*. Remember that while Hebrew is written from right to left, English transliteration is written from left to right.

Study each of the following vowel charts with care. For each vowel, you should be able to give its vowel class, vowel type, vowel name, and transliteration. The transliteration system is fairly simple for vowels. All a-class vowels, for example, are transliterated with some form of the letter a. This is the same for each subsequent class of vowels. In transliteration, long vowels have a horizontal line (macron) over the letter: *ā, ē, ō*. Short vowels are unaltered: *a, e, i, o, u*. Reduced vowels exhibit what looks like a small "u" placed above the letter: *ă, ĕ, ŏ*.

For now, do not be concerned about the physical similarity between the Qamets (בָּ, long *ā*) and the Qamets Hatuf (בָּ, short *o*). You will learn how to distinguish between them in the next chapter. Finally, you should begin the process of becoming familiar with the pronunciation value of each vowel. Learning the sound for each vowel will take some time. Be patient.

2.3 **Hebrew Vowel Chart 1: Long Vowels.** In this type, i-class and u-class vowels are not attested. These vowels are often called "changeable" long vowels.

	Symbol	*Vowel Name*	*Pronunciation*	*Transliteration*
a-class	בָּ	Qamets	a as in father	*ā*
e-class	בֵּ	Tsere	e as in they	*ē*
o-class	בֹּ	Holem	o as in role	*ō*

2.4   **Hebrew Vowel Chart 2: Short Vowels**. In this type, all five classes of vowels (a, e, i, o, u) are attested.

	Symbol	Vowel Name	Pronunciation	Transliteration
a-class	בַ	Pathach	a as in bat	*a*
e-class	בֶ	Seghol	e as in better	*e*
i-class	בִ	Hireq	i as in bitter	*i*
o-class	בָ	Qamets Hatuf	o as in bottle	*o*
u-class	בֻ	Qibbuts	u as in ruler	*u*

2.5   **Hebrew Vowel Chart 3: Reduced Vowels**. In this type, i-class and u-class vowels are not attested.

	Symbol	Vowel Name	Pronunciation	Transliteration
a-class	בֲ	Hateph Pathach	a as in amuse	*ă*
e-class	בֱ	Hateph Seghol	e as in metallic	*ě*
o-class	בֳ	Hateph Qamets	o as in commit	*ŏ*

2.6   **Summary Vowel Chart: Long, Short and Reduced Vowels.**

	a	*e*	*i*	*o*	*u*
Long	בָ Qamets	בֵ Tsere		בֹ Holem	
Short	בַ Pathach	בֶ Seghol	בִ Hireq	בָ Qamets Hatuf	בֻ Qibbuts
Reduced	בֲ Hateph Pathach	בֱ Hateph Seghol		בֳ Hateph Qamets	

2.7   **Hebrew Vowel Letters**. In the charts below, you will encounter what are called "vowel letters." The ancient Hebrew scribe was well aware of the difficulties associated with reading texts without vowels. To this end, as early as the tenth century B.C., the innovative scribes would occasionally use certain Hebrew consonants to indicate different vowel sounds. The consonant ה was generally used to indicate the *a* vowels (but others also). The consonant י was used to indicate the *i* and *e* vowels and the consonant ו was used to indicate *u* and *o* vowels. A good example of this phenomenon is the variable spelling of David's name. Originally it was spelled דוד (*dwd*). But later, it was spelled דויד (*dwyd*). In the second example, you will notice the insertion of י to indicate the *i* vowel in the second half of the name. The י is not functioning as a consonant but as a vowel. In other words, certain Hebrew letters can be either consonantal or vocalic. In general, vowel letters are written with a combination of a vowel (long or short) and a consonant (ה, ו, or י). The most common vowel letters are Hireq Yod (יִ), Holem Waw (וֹ) and Shureq (וּ).

2.8 **Hebrew Vowel Letter Charts**. In other standard Hebrew grammars, these vowels may be referred to as "historically" long vowels.

1. **Vowel Letters Written with ה (He)**. Note that ה is used as a vowel letter only at the end of a word, as in תּוֹרָה (law) and יִבְנֶה (he will build). The name of each is a combination of the name of the vowel (e.g., "Qamets") and the name of the consonant (e.g., "He").

	Symbol	Vowel Name	Pronunciation	Transliteration
a-class	בָּה	Qamets He	a as in father	*â*
e-class	בֵּה	Tsere He	e as in they	*ê*
	בֶּה	Seghol He	e as in better	*ê*
o-class	בֹּה	Holem He	o as in role	*ô*

2. **Vowel Letters Written with ו (Waw)**. These vowels are often referred to as *unchangeable long vowels* because they do not reduce or "change." Note that the name of the u-class vowel in this type is unique. Its name is not a combination of any vowel or consonant as is the case with all other vowel letters.

	Symbol	Vowel Name	Pronunciation	Transliteration
o-class	בּוֹ	Holem Waw	o as in role	*ô*
u-class	בּוּ	Shureq	u as in ruler	*û*

3. **Vowel Letters Written with ׳ (Yod)**. These vowels are also referred to as *unchangeable long vowels* because they do not reduce or "change." The name of each is a combination of the name of the vowel (e.g., "Hireq") and the name of the consonant (e.g., "Yod"). Some grammarians consider Qamets Yod and Pathach Yod to be vowel letters; others consider them diphthongs (see 3.10).

	Symbol	Vowel Name	Pronunciation	Transliteration
e-class	בֵּי	Tsere Yod	e as in they	*ê*
	בֶּי	Seghol Yod	e as in better	*ê*
i-class	בִּי	Hireq Yod	i as in machine	*î*

2.9 **Summary Vowel Chart: Hebrew Vowel Letters**.

	a	*e*	*i*	*o*	*u*
With ה	בָה בָּה Qamets He	בֵּה/בֶּה Seghol He / Tsere He		בֹּה Holem He	
With ו				בֹּו Holem Waw	בּוּ Shureq
With ׳		בֵּי/בֶּי Seghol Yod / Tsere Yod	בִּי Hireq Yod		

2.10 **Defective Writing**. You have just learned that certain vowels use a consonant in the formation of their symbol and that these vowels are called *vowel letters*. Sometimes, certain vowel letters are written without their consonant. This phenomenon, known as *defective writing*, occurs with some frequency. It should also be noted that when these vowels are written with their consonants it is called *full writing*. The full or defective spelling of a word makes no difference in the meaning of the word. There are three patterns of defective writing to be learned.

	Full Writing		*Defective Writing*	
Example	בּוֹ	➤	בֹּ	Holem Waw to Holem
	שׁוֹפָר	➤	שֹׁפָר	ram's horn
Example	בּוּ	➤	בֻּ	Shureq to Qibbuts
	מַדּוּעַ	➤	מַדֻּעַ	why?
Example	בִּי	➤	בִּ	Hireq Yod to Hireq
	דָּוִיד	➤	דָּוִד	David

There is no certain way to always predict when a vowel will be written defectively. Familiarity with vocabulary and frequent exposure to this phenomenon will help you in the identification of defectively spelled words. Study a few more examples.

תּוֹרוֹת	➤	תֹּרֹת	laws
מוֹעֵד	➤	מֹעֵד	meeting place
עַמּוּד	➤	עַמֻּד	pillar
שְׁבוּעָה	➤	שְׁבֻעָה	oath

2.11 **Shewa.** You will notice in Hebrew Vowel Chart 3 (2.5) that each reduced vowel (בֲ, בֱ, בֳ) exhibits a pair of vertical dots on the right side of the vowel symbol. These vertical dots also occur without an accompanying vowel (בְ). This vowel sign is called *Shewa*. The Shewa is not listed in the above vowel charts because it is not like any other vowel. The Shewa does not belong to any vowel class (a, e, i, o, u) nor does it belong to any vowel type (long, short, reduced). There are two basic types of Shewa in Hebrew: *Silent Shewa* and *Vocal Shewa*. The Silent Shewa has a zero value and is never pronounced and never transliterated. The Vocal Shewa maintains a *hurried* pronunciation and sounds like the *a* in *amuse*. It is transliterated either as an upside-down *e* (בְ, bə) or as a superscript *e* (בְ, b^e). In the next chapter, you will learn how to distinguish between Silent and Vocal Shewa.

2.12 **Holem over the שׂ and שׁ.** In some instances, when the vowel symbol Holem (בֹ) is used with שׂ (Sin) or שׁ (Shin), the two dots combine into one dot over the consonant. For example, we would expect to see something like יֹשְׁבִים (yōš^{e}ḇîm) with two distinct dots. But the two dots will sometimes combine into a single dot (יֹשְׁבִים) which will serve two purposes. It distinguishes between שׁ (*š*) and שׂ (*ś*) and it also serves as the long o-class vowel (Holem). You will learn in the next chapter that *all initial consonants must be followed by a vowel*. Given this rule, the dot over the שׁ in the above example must also function as the Holem vowel. For a different variation, the dot over the Sin in שֹׂנֵא (*śōnēʾ*) distinguishes between שׁ (*š*) and שׂ (*ś*) and it also serves as the Holem vowel.

2.13 **Daghesh Forte**. There is another pointing symbol to be discussed at this point, the *Daghesh Forte*. You know his brother, the Daghesh Lene. In chapter 1, you learned that six Hebrew consonants (the *begadkephat* letters) have two different pronunciations. In order to distinguish between the two pronunciations, a small dot (Daghesh Lene) was inserted into the consonant (בּ for the hard *b* and ב for the soft *v*). The Daghesh Forte looks exactly like the Daghesh Lene. The effect of the Daghesh Forte, however, is to *double the consonant in which it occurs*. For example, the Hebrew word הַשָּׁמַיִם (the heavens) has a Daghesh Forte located in the Shin (שּׁ). When pronouncing or transliterating this word, therefore, it should be rendered with two Shins (שּׁשׁ), *haššāmayim*. The Daghesh Forte can occur in any consonant except the gutturals (א, ע, ה, ח) and ר. The gutturals and ר, therefore, will never take a Daghesh Lene or Forte. Like the Daghesh Lene, the Daghesh Forte can occur in a *begadkephat* consonant. It is important to note that when a Daghesh Forte occurs in a *begadkephat* consonant, it doubles the hard pronunciation and not the soft. In the next chapter, you will learn how to tell the difference between the Daghesh Lene and the Daghesh Forte when they appear in *begadkephat* letters.

2.14 **Summary**. After working through this chapter, you should be able to identify the Hebrew vowels by name. You should also be able to write, pronounce, and transliterate the vowels (including the Shewa, בְּ). In other words, make sure that you master the information in the summary below before moving on to the exercises.

1. **Summary Vowel Chart: Long, Short and Reduced Vowels.**

	a	*e*	*i*	*o*	*u*
Long	בָּ Qamets	בֵּ Tsere		בֹּ Holem	
Short	בַּ Pathach	בֶּ Seghol	בִּ Hireq	בָּ Qamets Hatuf	בֻּ Qibbuts
Reduced	בֲּ Hateph Pathach	בֱּ Hateph Seghol		בֳּ Hateph Qamets	

2. **Summary Vowel Chart: Vowel Letters.**

	a	*e*	*i*	*o*	*u*
With ה	בָה בָּה Qamets He	בֵה/בֶה Seghol He/ Tsere He		בֹה Holem He	
With ו				בוֹ Holem Waw	בוּ Shureq
With י		בֵי/בֶי Seghol Yod/ Tsere Yod	בִי Hireq Yod		

3. Vowel letters written with ה (He) occur only at the end of a word, as in תּוֹרָה (law) and יִבְנֶה (he will build).

4. Vowel letters written with ו (Waw) and י (Yod) are often referred to as *unchangeable long vowels* because, as you will learn later, they do not reduce or "change."

5. Defective writing is that phenomenon in which certain vowel letters are written without their consonant. There are three patterns of defective writing to be learned.

בּוֹ ➤ בֹּ   Holem Waw to Holem

בּוּ ➤ בֻּ   Shureq to Qibbuts

בִּי ➤ בִּ   Hireq Yod to Hireq

6. The Daghesh Forte (בּ) doubles the consonant in which it appears. It can occur in any consonant except the gutturals and ר.

2.15 **The Languages and Pastoral Ministry.** "No second hand knowledge of the revelation of God for the salvation of a ruined world can suffice the needs of a ministry whose function it is to convey this revelation to men, commend it to their acceptance and apply it in detail to their needs–to all their needs, from the moment they are called into participation in the grace of God, until the moment when they stand perfect in God's sight, built up by his Spirit into new men. For such a ministry as this the most complete knowledge of the wisdom of the world supplies no equipment; the most fervid enthusiasm of service leaves without furnishing. Nothing will suffice for it but to know; to know the book; to know it at first hand; and to know it through and through. And what is required first of all for training men for such a ministry is that the book should be given them in its very words [Hebrew, Aramaic, and Greek] as it has come from God's hand and in the fullness of its meaning, as that meaning has been ascertained by the labors of generations of men of God who have brought to bear upon it all the resources of sanctified scholarship and consecrated thought."

B. B. Warfield
Selected Shorter Writings–I
"Our Seminary Curriculum"

2.16 **Advanced Information: Alternative Vowel Classification**. Originally, there were only three vowel classes in Hebrew: a-class, i-class, and u-class. The other vowel classes (e-class and o-class) developed later. The e-class developed from the original i-class and the o-class developed from the original u-class. For this reason, most grammarians prefer to divide Hebrew vowels into three (a, i, u) rather than five (a, e, i, o, u) classes. By doing this, e-class vowels are considered to be a subset of the i-class and o-class vowels are considered to be a subset of the u-class. Other grammarians, however, divide Hebrew vowels into the five classes with which most students are familiar from their study of English. In this grammar, we have adopted the five-class system. For your reference, the following chart shows both categorization systems together. Note that this information is not presented for memorization but so that you might be familiar with other grammar presentations.

	a-class	*i-class*		*u-class*	
	a	*e*	*i*	*o*	*u*
Long	בָ	בֵ		בֹ	
Short	בַ	בֶ	בִ	בָ	בֻ
Reduced	בֲ	בֱ		בֳ	

Chapter 3

Syllabification and Pronunciation

3.1   Now that we have covered the Hebrew system of consonants and vowels, it becomes important to refine our ability to pronounce Hebrew words correctly. To do so, it is necessary to work on the issue of syllabification.[1] Syllabification is simply the process of dividing words into syllables, the basic sounds of each word. In most English dictionaries, entries are commonly syllabified to aid with pronunciation. Examples include bib-li-cal, gram-mar and in-tro-duc-tion. Some words have only one syllable (monosyllabic) and, therefore, they have no syllable divider: dog, cat, friend. In English, we syllabify words instinctively. But since we are not native speakers of Hebrew, we will not have the instincts needed to correctly syllabify Hebrew words. For this reason, we will have to rely on certain rules and principles to aid us in this process.

3.2   **Two Rules of Syllabification.** In order to divide Hebrew words into syllables, you must begin with two simple rules.

1. *Every syllable must begin with one consonant and have only one vowel.* In Hebrew, therefore, a syllable does not begin with a vowel (with one exception to be discussed in 5.7.2). The Hebrew word for "word" is דָּבָר and is syllabified as דָּ|בָר (dā-ḇār). This example has two syllables, each beginning with a consonant and each having only one vowel.

2. *There are only two types of syllables: open and closed.* Open syllables end with a vowel and closed syllables end with a consonant. These two types of syllables are present in the above example, דָּ|בָר (dā-ḇār). The first syllable, דָּ (dā), is open because it ends in a vowel. The second syllable, בָר (ḇār), is closed because it ends in a consonant. It is that simple!

These two rules are the essence of this chapter. The remainder of the chapter will discuss more specific issues and potential difficulties with the application of these rules to Hebrew words.

---

[1] Your pronunciation of Hebrew will improve with an understanding of syllabification. These issues are important because proper pronunciation will enhance your ability to memorize and retain elements of the language.

3.3   **Hebrew Accents**. *Hebrew words are usually accented (stressed) on the last syllable*. What this means is that the force of pronunciation is usually given to the last syllable. Using דָּבָר as an example, the stress or force of pronunciation falls on the last syllable, בָר (*ḇār*). Cultivating the ability to stress the last syllable in Hebrew words will be difficult for most of us since we typically stress the first syllable in English. You should also note that there are some Hebrew words that are not stressed on the last syllable. The stress in these words will be indicated by an accent mark over the stressed syllable. For example, the Hebrew word for "book" is סֵפֶר (סֵ|פֶר, *sē-p̄er*). This word happens to be stressed on the first syllable. This is indicated by the accent mark over the Samek (סֵ). If a Hebrew word is stressed on the last syllable, however, no accent mark is used. As a general rule, if the stress falls to any other syllable, it is indicated with the accent mark.

3.4   **Syllable Classification**. In Hebrew, syllables are classified by their proximity to the accent.[2]

1.   *Tonic*. The accented syllable is called the tonic (or tone) syllable. Once again, using the example דָּבָר, the syllable בָר (*ḇār*) is the tonic syllable because it is the accented syllable. In the example סֵפֶר, the syllable סֵ (*sē*) is the tonic syllable because it is the accented syllable.

2.   *Pretonic*. Syllables in the pretonic position occur *before the tonic syllable*. In the example דָּבָר, the syllable דָּ (*dā*) is pretonic because it occurs *before* the tonic syllable.

3.   *Propretonic*. The syllable occurring *before the pretonic syllable* is called the *propretonic* syllable. In the examples דְּבָרִים (דְּ|בָ|רִים, transliterated *dᵉ-ḇā-rîm*) and סְפָרִים (סְ|פָ|רִים, transliterated *sᵉ-p̄ā-rîm*), the syllables דְּ (*dᵉ*) and סְ (*sᵉ*) are propretonic syllables because they occur before the pretonic syllable.

3.5   **The Daghesh and Syllabification**. You will remember from chapter 2 that the *begadkephat* consonants can take a Daghesh Lene (hardening the sound of the consonant) and all consonants, except the gutturals and ר, can take a Daghesh Forte (doubling the consonant). The *Daghesh Lene* does not affect syllabification. The *Daghesh Forte*, however, does

---

[2]   An alternative system of syllable classification also exists for which the location of the accent is not determinative. In this system, the *ultima* is the last syllable of a word. The *penultima* is the next-to-last syllable and the *antepenultima* is the syllable before the penultima.

affect syllabification because it doubles the value of the consonant. For example, one of the Hebrew words for "you" is אַתָּה. Inside the second letter of this word is a *Daghesh Forte* (תּ). Because the *Daghesh Forte* doubles the value of a consonant, it must be rendered twice in transliteration, *ʾattāh* (note the double "t"). Since the Taw (תּ) is doubled, it functions *both* as the final consonant of the first syllable and the first consonant of the second syllable, *ʾat-tāh*. In order to syllabify the Hebrew word, you would need to draw a vertical line through the Daghesh Forte in the Taw (תּ). In this grammar, however, syllabification of words with a *Daghesh Forte* is rendered in the following manner, אַת|תָה. Note that the gray character (ת) does not really exist, except to demonstrate the doubling power of the *Daghesh Forte*. The following examples are intended to illustrate further the syllabification of the Daghesh Forte.

חֻקָּה	⪢	חֻק|קָה
יַבָּשָׁה	⪢	יַב|בָ|שָׁה
אוּרִיָּה	⪢	או|רִי|יָה
תְּפִלָּה	⪢	תְּ|פִל|לָה

So far, things are relatively simple. There is, however, one potentially confusing issue. The *begadkephat* letters can take either a *Daghesh Forte* or a *Daghesh Lene*. How can you tell which Daghesh is being used in a *begadkephat* letter? Here are a few simple rules.

1. *The Daghesh in a begadkephat is a Forte if preceded by a vowel* (אַתָּה, תּ preceded by the Pathach vowel).

2. *The Daghesh in a begadkephat is a Lene if preceded by a consonant* (מַלְכָּה, כּ preceded by ל with Silent Shewa). You will learn how to distinguish between Vocal and Silent Shewa in the next section.

3. *A begadkephat letter at the beginning of a word takes a Daghesh Lene unless the previous word ends in a vowel* (דָּבָר, דּ with Daghesh Lene begins the word).

3.6   **The Shewa and Syllabification.** In section 2.7, you learned that there are two types of Shewas in Hebrew: *Silent Shewa* and *Vocal Shewa*. The Silent Shewa has a zero value and is never pronounced or transliterated. The Vocal Shewa maintains a hurried pronunciation and sounds like the *a* in *amuse*. It is transliterated either as an upside-down *e* (בְּ, *bə*) or as a superscript *e* (בְּ, *bᵉ*). *The Vocal Shewa will always occur in an open* *syllable*. A Silent Shewa will always come at the end of a closed syllable, that is, after a short vowel (or an accented long vowel).

We now need to learn how to distinguish between a Vocal Shewa and a Silent Shewa. There are two simple rules.

1. *The Shewa is silent if the previous vowel is short.* This is just a different way of saying, as above, that a Silent Shewa will always come at the end of a closed syllable. Consider the Shewa in the word מַלְכָּה (*malkāh*), meaning "queen." It is immediately preceded by a short vowel (Pathach under the מ) and it comes at the end of a closed syllable. Consider the following applications of this first rule.

   a. A Shewa is silent when immediately preceded by a short vowel. For example, in פַּרְעֹה (*par-ʿōh*), the Shewa under the ר is preceded by the short *a* vowel and, therefore, is silent.

   b. The first of two contiguous (side-by-side) Shewas within a word is silent. For example, the Shewa under the שׁ of מִשְׁפְּטֵי is silent and the Shewa under the פ is vocal (3.6.2b). The word is syllabified מִשְׁ|פְּ|טֵי (*miš-pᵉ-ṭê*).

   c. A Shewa at the end of a word is silent, as in כָּתַבְתְּ. Both Shewas in this form are silent. The word is syllabified as כָּ|תַבְתְּ (*kā-taḇt*). This is the only exception to the above principle.

2. *The Shewa is vocal if not immediately preceded by a short vowel.* That is to say, in all other circumstances, the Shewa is vocal. Consider the following applications of this second rule:

   a. Initial Shewa is always vocal as in בְּרָכָה (*bᵉ-rā-ḵāh*).

   b. The second of two contiguous (side-by-side) Shewas within a word is vocal as in מִשְׁפְּטֵי (*miš-pᵉ-ṭê*). The Shewa under the פ is vocal because it is preceded by the consonant שׁ and not a short vowel. The Shewa under the שׁ is silent.

   c. A Shewa under any consonant with Daghesh Forte is vocal as in הַמְּלָכִים (*ham-mᵉ-lā-ḵîm*). The Daghesh in the מ must be Forte because it is not a *begadkephat* letter.

   d. A Shewa after an unaccented long vowel is vocal, as in כֹּתְבִים (*kō-ṯᵉ-ḇîm*). The Shewa is preceded by the changeable long *ō* vowel and, therefore, is vocal.

It is important, at this point, to note that the gutturals cannot take a Vocal Shewa but they can take a Silent Shewa as in שָׁמַעְתָּ (*šā-maʿ-tā*). The Shewa under the ע comes at the end of a closed syllable and it is immediately preceded by a short vowel. It is, therefore, silent.

When dealing with the Shewa in Hebrew, remember to keep it simple. *A Shewa is silent if the previous vowel is short. In most other circumstances, it is vocal.*

3.7   **Qamets and Qamets Hatuf**. You already know from section 2.2 that two vowels look exactly alike, the Qamets (בָ, changeable long *ā*) and the Qamets Hatuf (בָ, short *o*). How do you tell the difference? In general, the Qamets occurs much more frequently than the Qamets Hatuf. So when in doubt, defer to the Qamets. Since, however, this method is not error free, the following rules are given.

1. The Qamets Hatuf (בָ, short *o*) occurs only in a *closed and unaccented syllable*. In חָכְמָה (*ḥok̲-māh*), the vowel under the ח is a Qamets Hatuf since it occurs in a closed syllable that is unaccented. The vowel under the מ is a Qamets since it occurs in an accented syllable. The word occurring most frequently with the Qamets Hatuf is כָּל (*kol*), which means "all of," "each of," or "every."

2. The Qamets (בָ, changeable long *ā*) prefers an open, pretonic syllable or a closed, accented syllable. In the example דָּבָר, both vowels are Qamets. The first is in an open, pretonic syllable. The second is in a closed, accented syllable (see 3.14 for further discussion of syllable preferences).

3. A small symbol called *Metheg* may also be used to distinguish between Qamets and Qamets Hatuf.[3] The Metheg is a small vertical line that is placed beneath a consonant and to the left of a vowel, as in בָּתִּים (*bāt-tîm*). In this word, the Metheg is the vertical line to the left of the Qamets under the ב. In terms of vowel identification, the Metheg occurs with the Qamets and not with the Qamets Hatuf. For example, in the word בָּתִּים (houses), the vowel symbol under the ב could be taken either as Qamets or Qamets Hatuf. The appearance of the Metheg to the left of the vowel (בָּתִּים) identifies it as Qamets and not Qamets Hatuf. In the word חָכְמָה (wisdom), however, the vowel under

---

[3] Though there are other uses of the Metheg, the symbol will be used in this grammar only to distinguish between Qamets and Qamets Hatuf in ambiguous circumstances.

the ה is Qamets Hatuf (short *o*) and, therefore, is not marked with Metheg. The Shewa under the כ is silent because it comes at the end of a closed syllable that contains a short vowel.

3.8 **Furtive Pathach**. You have learned that Hebrew vowels are pronounced after the consonant with which they are associated (בַ is rendered *ba* and not *ab*). There is, however, one minor exception to this rule. *When a word ends in ח or ע, a Pathach may appear beneath this consonant and must be pronounced and transliterated before the guttural.* This special use of the Pathach is called the *Furtive Pathach*. In terms of syllabification, the Furtive Pathach is not considered to be a full vowel, nor is it counted in syllabification. Note the following examples.

בֹּרֵחַ	*bōrēaḥ*	➤	בֹּ|רֵחַ	*bō-rēaḥ*
נֹטֵעַ	*nōṭēaʿ*	➤	נֹ|טֵעַ	*nō-ṭēaʿ*
רָקִיעַ	*rāqîaʿ*	➤	רָ|קִיעַ	*rā-qîaʿ*
רוּחַ	*rûaḥ*	➤	רוּחַ	*rûaḥ* (monosyllabic)

3.9 **Quiescent א**. When א occurs without a vowel, it is *quiescent* as in חַטָּאת (sin). When the א is quiescent, it is not considered to be a consonant with reference to the rules of syllabification. This word should be divided as חַטּ\|טָאת.

3.10 **Hebrew Diphthong**. In Hebrew, there is a cluster of consonants and vowels that always act together as a unit. Technically, this phenomenon is called a *diphthong*. *Diphthong* is a grammatical term used to identify sounds normally distinct but now functioning as a single unit. The most common Hebrew diphthong is יַ (*ayi*).[4] Syllables that contain this diphthong are considered to be closed because they end with a consonant. Note the following examples for syllabification.

שָׁמַיִם	*šāmayim*	➤	שָׁ|מַיִם	*šā-mayim*
בַּיִת	*bayiṯ*	➤	בַּיִת	*bayiṯ* (monosyllabic)

3.11 **Summary**. In the following summary, all the major rules for syllabification are listed. These rules are not to be rigorously memorized, but rather should be understood and applied to the syllabification and pronunciation of Hebrew words.

---

[4] Some grammarians consider Pathach Yod (and Qamets Yod) to be a vowel letter; others consider it a diphthong. The status of this combination remains disputed and uncertain.

1. Every syllable must begin with a consonant and have only one vowel (with very few exceptions).

2. There are only two types of syllables: open and closed. Open syllables end with a vowel and closed syllables end with a consonant.

3. A *Daghesh Forte* doubles the consonant in which it occurs and must be divided in syllabification.

4. A *Daghesh* in a *begadkephat* consonant is a *Lene* if preceded by a consonant and a *Forte* if preceded by a vowel.

5. A *Daghesh Forte* in a *begadkephat* consonant doubles the hard sound and never the soft sound.

6. The gutturals and ר cannot take *Daghesh Lene* or *Daghesh Forte*.

7. A Shewa is *vocal* in the following circumstances: if it occurs under the first consonant of a word; if it is the second of two contiguous Shewas within a word; if it is under any consonant with a Daghesh Forte; if it is after any unaccented long vowel.

8. A Shewa is *silent* in the following circumstances: if the previous vowel is short; if it is the first of two contiguous Shewas within a word; if it is at the end of a word.

9. A guttural cannot take a Vocal Shewa but it can take a Silent Shewa as in שָׁ|מָ|עְ|תָּ (שָׁמָעְתָּ).

10. Unlike the gutturals, the consonant ר can take Vocal Shewa.

11. The reduced vowels (בֲ, בֱ, בֳ) always occur in open syllables. They are never silent.

12. The Metheg may be used to distinguish between Qamets and Qamets Hatuf. The Metheg occurs with Qamets (בָּתִּים) and not with Qamets Hatuf.

13. Furtive Pathach is not considered to be a full vowel, nor is it counted in syllabification. It must, however, be pronounced and transliterated before the guttural.

14. When א occurs without a vowel, it is *quiescent* as in חַטָּאת (sin).

15. Syllables that contain the *diphthong* (יִ֫) are considered to be closed because they always end with a consonant.

3.12 **Vocabulary**. The numbers in parentheses indicate how many times that word occurs in the Hebrew Bible.

אָדָם	man, mankind, Adam (562)
אֶרֶץ	land, earth, ground (2,505); feminine
אֱלֹהִים	God, gods (2,602)
אָב	father, ancestor (1,211)
אֵל	God, god (317)
בֵּן	son (4,941)
בַּיִת	house, household (2,047)
דָּבָר	word, matter, thing (1,454)
יוֹם	day (2,301)
יִשְׂרָאֵל	Israel (2,507)
יְרוּשָׁלַ͏ִם	Jerusalem (643); יְרוּשָׁלַיִם (alternate form)
יְהוָה	Yahweh, Lord (6,828) *Adonai*
מִצְרַיִם	Egypt (682)
מֹשֶׁה	Moses (766)
מֶלֶךְ	king, ruler (2,530)
סוּס	horse (138)
עֶבֶד	slave, servant (803)
פַּרְעֹה	Pharaoh (274)
שָׁנָה	year (878)
שֵׁם	name, reputation (864)

3.13 **The Imperative Summons to Praise.** Of the many names and descriptive titles by which God is called in the Old Testament, only one is his personal name. He is called יהוה (commonly translated as "Lord" or rendered as "Yahweh"). The name is composed of four consonants and thus known as the *tetragrammaton* (Greek: "having four letters"). The divine name may also appear as a shortened independent form as in Ex 15:2: עָזִּי וְזִמְרָת יָהּ (the Lord is my strength and my song). The form יָהּ is the shortened form of the *tetragrammaton*. The name is also attested in shortened forms that are commonly used in the formation of personal names such as יְהוֹנָתָן (Jonathan, "Yahweh has given"), יְהוֹשָׁפָט (Jehoshaphat, "Yahweh has judged"), יוֹאֵל (Joel, "Yahweh is God") or יְהוֹרָם (Jehoram, "Yahweh is exalted").

The shortened independent form occurs primarily in poetry and is perhaps most common in the spelling of "hallelujah," as in Ps 135:3, הַלְלוּ־יָהּ כִּי־טוֹב יְהוָה (Praise the Lord for he is good!). The verse begins with a verbal form that will not be studied until chapter 27. It is a Piel Imperative 2mp verb from the root הָלַל which means "to praise." As an Imperative form, it translates "you praise" or simply "praise." You recognize the shortened form of the divine name (יָהּ) attached to the Imperative with the raised horizontal line that is known as Maqqef. You now understand the etymology of "hallelujah" (the imperative summons to praise). The call to praise may also appear without a Maqqef, as in the first verse of Ps 106: הַלְלוּיָהּ (Praise the Lord!). This grammatical form is the same as that in Ps 135:3.[5]

As you might expect, the most frequent use of the verbal root הָלַל in expression of praise to God is in the book of Psalms, especially in the so-called Hallelujah Psalms that are found in several groups (Ps 104-106; 111-113; 115-117; 135; 146-150). Here, the imperative summons to praise may appear as an integral part of the psalm (135:3), or it may serve as a liturgical introduction[6] and/or conclusion[7] with either of the spellings detailed above. It is significant to note that most of these occurrences are plural, emphasizing (though not uniquely) the congregational and communal dimension of praise. Praise can manifest itself in speaking (Jer 31:7) and singing (Ps 69:30) and with dancing and musical instruments (Ps 149:3). However offered, corporately or individually, praise is a vital response to God. The book of Psalms concludes:

> Let everything that breathes praise the Lord.
> Praise the Lord!
> (Ps 150:6)

Gary D. Pratico
Professor of Old Testament
Gordon-Conwell Theological Seminary
South Hamilton, Massachusetts

---

[5] Note also that the call to praise may be phrased with the full spelling of the tetragrammaton and the accusative marker: הַלְלוּ אֶת־יְהוָה (Praise the Lord!) as in Ps 117:1.

[6] Ps 106:1; 111:1; 112:1; 113:1; 117:1; 135:1; 146:1; 147:1; 148:1; 149:1; 150:1.

[7] Ps 104:35; 105:45; 106:48; 113:9; 115:18; 116:19; 135:21; 146:10; 147:20; 148:14; 149:9; 150:6.

3.14 **Advanced Information: Vowels and Their Syllable Preferences.** As you know from chapter 2, Hebrew vowels are grouped into three basic categories: long, short, and reduced. The vowels of each category prefer to be in certain types of syllables. A vowel's preference for a particular type of syllable is determined by two primary factors: the type of syllable (open or closed) and the proximity of the syllable to the accent. Awareness of a vowel's syllable preference will help with syllabification and pronunciation, and will enable you to identify and explain changes in a word's spelling.

1. *Short Vowels.* Short vowels prefer either *closed, unaccented* syllables or *open, accented* syllables.

   עֹ|בֵד   short vowel in a closed, unaccented syllable (בֵד)

   עֹ|בֵד   short vowel in an open, accented syllable (עֹ)

2. *Long Vowels.* Long vowels (changeable or unchangeable) prefer either *closed, accented* syllables or *open, pretonic* syllables.

   דְּ|בַר   long vowel in a closed, accented syllable (בַר)

   דְּ|בַר   long vowel in an open, pretonic syllable (דְּ)

3. *Vocal Shewa and Reduced Vowels.* Vocal Shewa and reduced (Hateph) vowels prefer *open, propretonic* syllables. The reduced vowels appear with guttural consonants in the open, propretonic position.[8]

   דְּ|בָ|רִים   Vocal Shewa in an open, propretonic syllable (דְּ)

   אֱ|לֹ|הִים   reduced vowel in an open, propretonic syllable (אֱ)

---

[8] Of course, there are exceptions to this general rule, for example, with the stem vowel of certain forms of the Imperfect verb (see 15.4.7).

Chapter 4

Hebrew Nouns

4.1   **Introduction**. Hebrew nouns function just like English nouns. They are used to indicate a person, place, thing, or idea. Like nouns in English, Hebrew nouns can be either *singular* or *plural* in number. But unlike English nouns, they can also be *dual* in number, indicating a plurality of two (i.e., two eyes, two hands, etc.). Hebrew nouns also have gender. They are either *masculine* or *feminine*.

In English, most nouns are pluralized with the addition of an "s" or "es." For example, when the noun *prophet* is pluralized it becomes *prophets*. The letter "s" was added to make the singular into a plural. Hebrew nouns pluralize in much the same way. Different endings are added to singular nouns in order to indicate the plural and dual forms. In Hebrew, however, the plural ending for a masculine noun is different from the plural ending for a feminine noun. The following noun chart illustrates how masculine and feminine nouns are pluralized.

4.2   **Plural and Dual Endings on Masculine and Feminine Nouns**.

	Masculine Noun	*Feminine Noun*
Singular	סוּס horse	תּוֹרָה law
Plural	סוּסִים horses	תּוֹרוֹת laws
Dual	סוּסַׂיִם two horses	תּוֹרָתַיִם two laws

4.3   **Gender and Number**. Hebrew nouns are *masculine* or *feminine*, though a few nouns are both masculine and feminine. With regard to a noun's number, it may be *singular*, indicating one; *plural*, indicating more than one; or *dual*, indicating two.

Masculine singular nouns are *endingless* nouns; that is, they have *no distinctive endings*. The plural and dual masculine endings are very distinct and, for this reason, easy to identify. Masculine plural nouns usually end in ים ָ as in סוּסִים (horses) or דְּבָרִים (words). Masculine dual nouns end in יִ ַ ם as in סוּסַׂיִם (two horses) or עֵינַיִם (two eyes).

28

In contrast to endingless masculine singular nouns, feminine singular nouns are *usually* marked with distinctive endings. The most common ending is הָ as in תּוֹרָה (law). Additionally, the endings תַ (בַּת, daughter), תֶ (תִּפְאֶרֶת, glory), ית (בְּרִית, covenant) and וּת (מַלְכוּת, kingdom) are distinctly feminine. Feminine plural nouns end in וֹת as in מְלָכוֹת (queens) or תּוֹרוֹת (laws). Feminine dual nouns end in יִם as in יָדַיִם (two hands) or תַיִם as in תּוֹרָתַיִם (two laws). You will notice that *the dual ending is the same for both masculine and feminine nouns.* Usually words for paired body parts (hands, feet, eyes, ears) utilize the dual ending.

It is important to understand that feminine nouns (grammatical gender) do not refer only to feminine things (natural gender) or masculine nouns only to masculine things. For example, the Hebrew word for "law" is תּוֹרָה and it is feminine. This does not mean, however, that laws apply only to women. What the gender of a Hebrew noun indicates is the *pattern of inflection* it will usually follow. In other words, masculine nouns take one set of endings for pluralization and feminine nouns take another. But, of course, grammatical gender and natural gender do correspond in most Hebrew nouns. For example, the word for "daughter" (בַּת) in Hebrew is feminine and, therefore, grammatical and natural gender correspond. Likewise, the Hebrew word for "son" (בֵּן) is masculine, so natural and grammatical gender once again correspond. The following chart summarizes all possible endings for the pluralization of masculine and feminine nouns.

4.4   Summary of Noun Endings.

	Masculine Noun	*Feminine Noun*
Singular	endingless	וּת/ ית/ תֶ/ תַ/ הָ
Plural	ים	וֹת
Dual	יִם	יִם or תַיִם

4.5   The following word lists contain examples of singular, plural, and dual nouns. You will quickly realize how simple it is to identify the gender and number of most nouns by learning the few endings in the above chart.

Masculine Singular (ms)	Masculine Plural (mp)	Feminine Singular (fs)	Feminine Plural (fp)	Mas/Fem Dual
סוּס	סוּסִים	מַלְכָּה	מְלָכוֹת	יוֹמַ֫יִם
מֶ֫לֶךְ	מְלָכִים	תּוֹרָה	תּוֹרוֹת	תּוֹרָתַ֫יִם
דָּבָר	דְּבָרִים	חוֹמָה	חוֹמוֹת	רַגְלַ֫יִם
יֶ֫לֶד	יְלָדִים	בַּת	בָּנוֹת	יָדַ֫יִם
יוֹם	יָמִים	קֶ֫שֶׁת	קְשָׁתוֹת	עֵינַ֫יִם

4.6 **Lexical Form.** When in doubt with regard to a word's meaning or form, you will have to look it up in what is called a Hebrew lexicon (Hebrew dictionary). When looking up a noun in the lexicon, you must search for its lexical form. *The lexical form for any noun is the singular form.* For example, if you were to search for the definition of סוּסִים or סוּסַ֫יִם, you would have to look under סוּס, the masculine singular form. Likewise, if you were to search for the feminine plural תּוֹרוֹת, you would find it listed in its singular or lexical form, תּוֹרָה. In almost every instance, the lexical form of a noun will be the form you have memorized as vocabulary.

4.7 **Exceptions to the Rules.** As with every set of rules or patterns, there are always exceptions. Some of the most common exceptions are listed below.

1. *Endingless Feminine Nouns.* You have learned that all masculine singular nouns are endingless. Not all endingless nouns, however, are masculine singular. In a few instances, feminine singular nouns are also endingless. For example, the nouns אֶ֫רֶץ (land), עִיר (city), and אֶ֫בֶן (stone) are endingless but also feminine. The only way to be certain of any noun's gender is to look it up in the lexicon (dictionary). But do not be confused by this irregularity. As a general observation, the gender of a noun does not affect its meaning, only its pattern of pluralization. Whether a noun like יָד (hand) is masculine or feminine, pluralized with יִם (masculine) or וֹת (feminine), makes absolutely no difference with regard to its meaning.

2. *Exception to Normal Pluralization.* In very few instances, singular nouns of one gender take the plural ending of the other gender. For example, the Hebrew word for "father" is אָב and it is

masculine. We would expect, therefore, that this masculine singular noun would take the masculine plural ending. This is not the case, however, as the plural of אָב is אָבוֹת. But again, such irregularity is no cause for confusion. If you know that the Hebrew word for "father" is אָב and that וֹת is a plural ending, then אָבוֹת must mean "fathers." Similarly, even though שָׁנָה (year) is a feminine noun, it is commonly pluralized as שָׁנִים (years) with the masculine plural ending. All such irregularities will be noted in the vocabulary sections throughout the grammar.

3. *Special Dual Nouns.* You know that Hebrew nouns can be *dual* in number and as such indicate a plurality of two, as in יָדַיִם, meaning "*two* hands." There are three special Hebrew words, however, that are *always dual in form.* They are שָׁמַיִם (heaven, heavens), מִצְרַיִם (Egypt), and מַיִם (water). These three nouns occur frequently and should be memorized.

4. *Irregular Stem Change.* Some Hebrew nouns will alter their actual (consonantal) stem when they add their plural endings. The *stem* of a noun refers to the *original combination of consonants* that make up a particular word. This type of irregularity is the most difficult to identify. For example, the plural of אִישׁ (man) is אֲנָשִׁים (men) and the plural of אִשָּׁה (woman) is נָשִׁים (women).[1] In some instances, letters are lost when forming the plural; in others they are added. There are not many Hebrew words that undergo this type of change, and all such irregularities will be identified in the vocabulary sections throughout the grammar.

5. *Defective Spelling of* וֹת. Occasionally, the feminine plural ending וֹת will be spelled תֹ, with a Holem rather than a Holem Waw. For example, the Hebrew word for "congregation" is עֵדָה. The ending clearly indicates that this is a feminine noun. Normally we would expect to see עֵדוֹת in the plural. Sometimes, however, the feminine plural form appears as עֵדֹת. This shorter spelling is called "defective spelling" or "defective writing." The longer or full form is called the *plene* (Latin for "full") spelling. Defective spelling is that spelling which does not use the vowel letters (see 2.14.4). Once again, the change is minor. Both spellings have the same type of vowel and are pronounced exactly the same.

---

[1] The noun אִשָּׁה (woman) pluralizes with the masculine plural ending (נָשִׁים).

4.8   **Basic Patterns of Noun Pluralization.** You have probably noticed that most nouns undergo significant vowel changes with the addition of plural endings. For example, observe the vowel changes from the singular מֶלֶךְ (king) to the plural מְלָכִים (kings). In fact, relatively few nouns pluralize without altering the vowels of the noun stem in some way. These changes are occasioned by a shift in accent and a change in syllable structure when plural endings are added. Carefully study the following basic patterns of noun pluralization.

1.   *Pluralization with No Change.* There are a number of nouns that are pluralized simply with the addition of the masculine or feminine plural ending. In other words, there are no changes in the vocalization (vowel pattern) of the noun itself. Nouns of this type may be monosyllabic with an unchangeable long vowel.

שִׁיר song   ➤   שִׁירִים songs

אוֹת sign   ➤   אוֹתוֹת signs

Nouns of this type may also be composed of two syllables with Shewa or Hateph Pathach in the first syllable and an unchangeable long vowel in the second syllable.

חֲלוֹם dream   ➤   חֲלוֹמוֹת dreams

רְחוֹב street   ➤   רְחוֹבוֹת streets

2.   *Pluralization with Propretonic Reduction.* Two-syllable nouns that are accented on the final syllable and have either Qamets or Tsere in the first or pretonic syllable will experience what is called "propretonic reduction" with the addition of plural endings. With the addition of the plural endings, the Qamets or Tsere is placed in an open, propretonic syllable. In an open, propretonic syllable, the Qamets or the Tsere will *reduce to Shewa*. This is called *propretonic reduction* (3.14.3).

דָּבָר word   ➤   דְּבָרִים words

לֵבָב heart   ➤   לְבָבוֹת hearts

Nouns with an initial guttural consonant cannot take a Vocal Shewa but prefer Hateph Pathach.

עָנָן cloud   ➤   עֲנָנִים clouds

חָצֵר courtyard   ➤   חֲצֵרוֹת courtyards

Note that nouns with a vowel letter (unchangeable long vowel) in the first syllable will *not* experience propretonic reduction.

כּוֹכָב star ➤ כּוֹכָבִים stars

3. *Pluralization of Segholate Nouns.* All two-syllable nouns that are *accented on the first syllable* are classified as Segholate nouns. Both masculine and feminine nouns appear in this class. They are called Segholate nouns because they typically have two Seghol vowels as in the following examples: מֶלֶךְ (king), אֶרֶץ (earth, land), דֶּרֶךְ (road, way), פֶּסֶל (idol), and חֶרֶב (sword). Other vowel patterns also appear in this class, usually with at least one Seghol vowel as in the following examples: סֵפֶר (book), בֹּקֶר (morning), and זֶרַע (seed). The nouns בַּעַל (lord) and נַעַר (young man) are also Segholate nouns because they are accented on the first syllable even though they exhibit a vowel pattern without a Seghol vowel. While the vowel pattern of Segholate nouns will vary in the singular, they will *always have the same vowel pattern in the plural*. Carefully study the following plural forms of Segholate nouns and note that each plural form has the same vowel pattern with Vocal Shewa or a Hateph vowel under the first consonant and Qamets under the second consonant.

מֶלֶךְ	king	➤	מְלָכִים	kings
נֶפֶשׁ	life	➤	נְפָשׁוֹת	lives
חֶרֶב	sword	➤	חֲרָבוֹת [2]	swords
סֵפֶר	book	➤	סְפָרִים	books
בֹּקֶר	morning	➤	בְּקָרִים	mornings
זֶרַע	seed	➤	זְרָעִים	seeds
נַעַר	boy	➤	נְעָרִים	boys

4. *Pluralization of Geminate Nouns.* Geminate nouns appear to have only two root consonants as in עַם (people). Actually, Geminate nouns originally had three consonants. For example, the Hebrew word for "people" (עַם) was originally spelled עמם. There are still a few Geminate nouns in biblical Hebrew that occasionally preserve both Geminate consonants, such as לֵבָב (heart). What makes this noun class unique is that the last two consonants of

---

[2] Gutturals cannot take a Vocal Shewa (3.6.2). In such instances, they will take a reduced vowel, usually Hateph Pathach.

the original stem are identical. The term "Geminate" comes from the Latin *gemini*, meaning "twins." With most Geminate nouns, however, only one geminate consonant appears in the spelling of the singular form. When nouns of this type are pluralized, *the consonant that originally appeared twice will now be written once with Daghesh Forte*. The Daghesh Forte represents the lost Geminate consonant. The "twin" has reappeared, not as a consonant, but as a Daghesh Forte.[3] Observe the following examples.

עַם	people	➤	עַמִּים	peoples (original root עמם)
חֵץ	arrow	➤	חִצִּים	arrows (original root חצץ)
חֹק	statute	➤	חֻקִּים	statutes (original root חקק)

5. *Irregular Pluralization*. Finally, there are numerous nouns that are irregular and unpredictable in their pluralization. Below are some of the most common examples.

אִישׁ	man	➤	אֲנָשִׁים	men
אִשָּׁה	woman	➤	נָשִׁים	women
עִיר	city	➤	עָרִים	cities
אָב	father	➤	אָבוֹת	fathers
בַּיִת	house	➤	בָּתִּים	houses
בַּת	daughter	➤	בָּנוֹת	daughters
בֵּן	son	➤	בָּנִים	sons
יוֹם	day	➤	יָמִים	days

4.9   Summary.

1. Hebrew nouns have both *gender* and *number*. With regard to gender, a noun will be either *masculine* or *feminine*, rarely both. With regard to number, a noun will be *singular*, *plural*, or *dual*.

---

[3] Note, however, that not all Biconsonantal nouns were originally Geminate nouns. For example, the nouns אָב (father), בֵּן (son), and שֵׁם (name) are Biconsonantal but not Geminate. When these nouns pluralize, there is no Daghesh Forte: אָבוֹת (fathers), בָּנִים (sons), and שֵׁמוֹת (names).

2. Masculine singular nouns are endingless. Masculine plural nouns have the ים ָ ending. Masculine dual nouns have the ﬦִי ַ ending.

3. The most common feminine singular ending is ה ָ but others are attested (ות/ית ִ /ת ֶ /ת ַ). Feminine singular nouns may also be endingless. Feminine plural nouns have the ות ending. Feminine dual nouns have the ﬦִי ַ or תַים ָ ending. Feminine singular nouns that end in ה ָ will not be identified as feminine in the vocabulary sections or in the grammar's lexicon.

4. Exceptions to these standard rules or patterns include:

   a. *Endingless Feminine Nouns.* All masculine singular nouns are endingless but a few feminine singular nouns are also endingless. Examples include עִיר (city) and אֶבֶן (stone).

   b. *Exception to Normal Pluralization.* A few singular nouns of one gender take the plural endings of the other gender. For example, אָב (father) is a masculine singular noun but takes a feminine plural ending, אָבוֹת (fathers).

   c. *Special Dual Nouns.* A few nouns are always dual in form but usually singular in meaning (מַיִם, dual in form but translated as singular, "water").

   d. *Irregular Stem Change.* A few nouns change their (consonantal) stem when forming the plural. For example, אִישׁ (man) becomes אֲנָשִׁים (men) in the plural.

   e. *Defective Spelling of* וֹת. Sometimes, the feminine plural ending וֹת will be spelled תֹ, with a Holem rather than a Holem Waw. For example, עֵדָה (congregation) is usually spelled עֵדֹת in the plural, with Holem rather than Holem Waw.

5. Most nouns undergo a change in vowel pattern with the addition of plural endings. Be certain that you understand the patterns of noun pluralization that are discussed in section 4.8.

6. A Hebrew dictionary is called a *lexicon*. When looking up words you must search for them by their *lexical form*. The lexical form of a Hebrew noun is the *singular form*.

4.10   **Vocabulary.** Endingless feminine nouns will be identified in the vocabulary sections throughout the grammar.

אֲדֹנָי	Lord; אָדוֹן lord, master (774)
אָח	brother (629); אַחִים (irregular plural)
אִישׁ	man, husband (2,198); אֲנָשִׁים (irregular plural)
אִשָּׁה	woman, wife (779); נָשִׁים (irregular plural)
בַּת	daughter (603); בָּנוֹת (irregular plural)
גּוֹי	nation, people (567)
דֶּרֶךְ	way, road, journey (712); masculine / feminine
הַר	mountain, hill, hill country (558); הָרִים (plural)
כֹּהֵן	priest (750)
לֵב	heart, mind, will (854); לֵבָב (alternate form)
מַיִם	water (586)
נֶפֶשׁ	soul, life, person, neck, throat (757); feminine
נָבִיא	prophet (317)
סֵפֶר	book, scroll, document (191)
עַיִן	eye, spring (900); עֵינַיִם (dual); feminine
עִיר	city, town (1095); עָרִים (irregular plural); feminine
צָבָא	host, army, war, service (487); צְבָאוֹת (plural)
קוֹל	voice, sound, noise (505)
רֹאשׁ	head, top, chief (600)
תּוֹרָה	law, instruction, teaching, custom (223)

4.11   **Kinship Terms and God's Relationship with His People.** Some of the first vocabulary words a student learns in Hebrew are some of the richest theological terms in the Old Testament. Several of these words are kinship terms that provide the conceptual framework for understanding Israel's relationship with Yahweh and with each other. אָב is the common word for "father" but one that also means, by extension, "ancestor." The "children of Israel" (בְּנֵי־יִשְׂרָאֵל) were literally the *sons* of Jacob, also named Israel. Jacob was the grandson of Abraham whose name was changed from "Father is lofty" (Abram) to "Father of multitudes" (Abraham). Metaphorically, אָב may refer to the originator or leader of a group. The head of a tribal unit (Deut 26:5), a musical guild (Gen 4:21), or a religious group (2 Kgs 6:21) may be a "father." Abraham becomes, in the New Testament, the father of the faithful (Gal 3:7, 29; Rom 4:11-16). Most significantly, God is seen as the spiritual father of his people.

Israel is sometimes described as Yahweh's firstborn "son" (בֵּן). "When Israel was a child," writes Hosea (11:1), "I loved him. And out of Egypt I called my son" (בְּנִי). In Ezek 16, Israel is allegorically pictured as God's adopted daughter (born originally to Amorite and Hittite parents), who eventually becomes his wife. The most common way that God refers to corporate Israel is as "my people." In almost 250 cases (concentrated in Exodus and in the prophets), God uses the term עַמִּי. Implicit in this term is a covenant relationship. Yahweh brought Israel out of bondage and at Mt. Sinai presented her with the terms for this relationship. Exodus records the inauguration of the covenant; the prophets describe its breakdown and hope for renewal.

The fatherhood of God for Israel is, from a theological perspective, inseparably bound to the fraternal relationship between the members of the community. אַחִים (brothers) are not simply those with whom there are blood ties; they are all those who share in the covenant God made with the "extended family" called Israel. The community of Israel was to be understood, fundamentally, as the family of God. Misunderstanding and abusing the rights and privileges of another member of the community was a capital crime. In Deut 24:7 we read, "If a man is caught kidnapping one of his fellow Israelites [אֶחָיו] and treats him as a slave or sells him, the kidnapper must die" (cf. Lev 25:46).

Interestingly, Israel's neighbors were viewed as אַחִים as well. Tyre was condemned for ignoring a "treaty of *brotherhood*" and Edom was to be judged for mistreating *brother* Israel (Amos 1:9, 11). These statements are likely the result of real treaties made between the parties. But they also hint at a perspective on God's universal relationship with all nations as vassals. Amos, quoting the Lord, asks, "Are not you Israelites the same to me as the Cushites? ... Did I not bring Israel up from Egypt, the Philistines from Caphtor, and the Arameans from Kir?" (Amos 9:7). In similarly explicit covenant language, Isaiah predicts a time when "The LORD Almighty will bless them, saying, 'Blessed be Egypt my people, Assyria my handiwork, and Israel my inheritance'" (Isa 19:25).

Tim Laniak
Associate Professor of Old Testament
Gordon-Conwell Theological Seminary
Charlotte, North Carolina

4.12 **Advanced Information: Rules of Shewa**. In various sections of this grammar, we will refer to the Rules of Shewa. Here, the two basic Rules of Shewa and two exceptions are presented.

1. *The First Rule of Shewa*. Hebrew will not allow two contiguous (side-by-side) Vocal Shewas. When two side-by-side Shewas occur within a word, you have learned that the first is silent and the second is vocal. What happens, however, when two side-by-side Shewas would occur at the beginning of a word? In such a circumstance, the first of two Vocal Shewas becomes Hireq in a closed syllable. In other words, two Vocal Shewas become a single syllable in which there are no Vocal Shewas. For example, the prefixing of the preposition לְ (to, for) to נְבִיאִים (prophets) would produce לְנְבִיאִים but two Vocal Shewas are not allowed at the beginning of a word. The application of the first Rule of Shewa produces לִנְבִיאִים (for prophets).

2. *Exception to the First Rule of Shewa*. The application of the first Rule of Shewa produces a different spelling if the word begins with the syllable יְ as in יְהוּדָה (Judah). Again, the prefixing of the preposition לְ (to) to יְהוּדָה (Judah) would produce לְיְהוּדָה but two Vocal Shewas at the beginning of a word are not allowed. In the case of a word that begins with the יְ syllable, the application of the Rule of Shewa produces לִיהוּדָה (to Judah) with Hireq Yod. Remember that this spelling is only with a word that begins with the יְ syllable.

3. *The Second Rule of Shewa*. A second Rule of Shewa applies to syllables that have a guttural consonant followed by a reduced or Hateph vowel. For example, the prefixing of the preposition בְ (in) to חֲלוֹם (dream) would produce בְּחֲלוֹם but this combination of syllables is not allowed. A Vocal Shewa cannot precede a guttural with a reduced vowel. Application of this second Rule of Shewa produces בַּחֲלוֹם (in a dream). With this spelling, the preposition takes the corresponding short vowel (Pathach) of the reduced vowel (Hateph Pathach).

4. *Exception to the Second Rule of Shewa.* There is one very important exception to the second Rule of Shewa. When a preposition like לְ is prefixed to אֱלֹהִים (God), the result is לֵאלֹהִים (to God). The appearance of the Tsere under the לֹ is occasioned by the quiescing (silencing) of the א. This exception occurs frequently with אֱלֹהִים. After a few encounters, this spelling will be recognized immediately.

Chapter 5
Definite Article and Conjunction Waw

5.1   **Introduction.** In English, a noun will be either *definite* or *indefinite*. Nouns are definite when they appear with the definite article "the" as in *the* student, *the* book and *the* teacher. Nouns are indefinite when they appear either without the definite article or with the indefinite article "a" or "an" as in *a* student, *a* book or *an* instructor. In Hebrew, there is no indefinite article (see 5.12 below). Therefore, מֶלֶךְ may be translated as either "king" or "a king." For this reason, words occurring without the definite article should be considered indefinite unless otherwise indicated. There are three types of definite nouns in Hebrew. The most common definite nouns are those occurring with the Hebrew definite article. Proper nouns (Egypt) and nouns with possessive pronouns (your book) are also considered to be definite. In this chapter, we will concentrate on nouns with the Hebrew definite article. In general, the Hebrew definite article functions much like the English definite article.

5.2   **Form of the Hebrew Definite Article.** The Hebrew word for "king" or "a king" is מֶלֶךְ. As it appears, the noun is indefinite. In Hebrew, a noun is made definite by *prefixing the definite article, which consists of* הַ *plus a Daghesh Forte in the first consonant of the noun.*

Definite Article

הַמֶּלֶךְ

Thus מֶלֶךְ (a king) becomes הַמֶּלֶךְ (*the* king). You can see how easy it is to identify the definite article in the following examples.

Indefinite Noun		*Definite Noun*	
נָבִיא	a prophet	הַנָּבִיא	the prophet
זָקֵן	an elder	הַזָּקֵן	the elder
סוּס	a horse	הַסּוּס	the horse
שֹׁפֵט	a judge	הַשֹּׁפֵט	the judge

5.3   **The Article and Initial *Begadkephat* Consonants.** You know that words with an initial *begadkephat* consonant will appear with a Daghesh Lene as in בַּיִת (house), דֶּרֶךְ (road, way), and גִּבּוֹר (warrior). When the definite article is added to these words, the Daghesh Lene is replaced by a Daghesh Forte. The following examples show that nothing really changes in the spelling, though the original Daghesh Lene is now a Daghesh Forte with the addition of the article.

Indefinite Noun		*Definite Noun*	
בַּיִת	a house	הַבַּיִת	the house
דֶּרֶךְ	a road	הַדֶּרֶךְ	the road
גִּבּוֹר	a warrior	הַגִּבּוֹר	the warrior

5.4   **The Article and Initial Guttural Consonants.** An important part of the definite article is the Daghesh Forte that is inserted into the first consonant of the noun. But you know that the gutturals and ר cannot take a Daghesh Forte. They reject it. What happens, then, when the initial consonant of a noun is a guttural or ר?

1. *Compensatory Lengthening.* With the initial gutturals א, ר and ע, the rejection of the Daghesh Forte results in what is called *compensatory lengthening*. This means that the Pathach (short *a*) vowel of the definite article הַ lengthens to a Qamets (long *ā*) as in הָ.[1] In this way, the definite article *compensates* for the loss of the Daghesh Forte by the *lengthening* of its vowel (short *a* to long *ā*), thus *compensatory lengthening*. The definite article is still easy to identify, as the following examples illustrate.

Indefinite Noun		*Definite Noun*	
אִישׁ	a man	הָאִישׁ	the man
אִשָּׁה	a woman	הָאִשָּׁה	the woman
רֹאשׁ	a head	הָרֹאשׁ	the head
עִיר	a city	הָעִיר	the city

2. *Virtual Doubling.* When ה or ח is the first consonant of a noun, the rejection of the Daghesh Forte results in what is called *virtual*

---

[1] There are three patterns of compensatory lengthening with which you need to become familiar. Each pattern involves the lengthening of a short vowel to a changeable long vowel: Pathach lengthens to Qamets (בַּ ﹥ בָּ), Hireq lengthens to Tsere (בִּ ﹥ בֵּ), and Qibbuts lengthens to Holem (בֻּ ﹥ בֹּ).

doubling. Virtual doubling is the *rejection of the Daghesh Forte without the lengthening of the Pathach* (short *a*) vowel. For example, the Hebrew word for "palace" is הֵיכָל. With the addition of the definite article, it is rendered הַהֵיכָל, "*the* palace." Another example is חוֹמָה (wall) and it is rendered as הַחוֹמָה (*the* wall). Notice how the ה and the ח reject the Daghesh Forte but the Pathach vowel *does not lengthen* in either example. This is virtual doubling.

3. *Irregular Seghol Vowel*. Before nouns that begin with an unaccented עָ, הָ or חָ (חָ may also be accented), the definite article appears with Seghol (short *e*) and without the Daghesh Forte (הֶ). Observe, for example, how the word חָכָם (wise man) becomes הֶחָכָם (*the* wise man).

5.5 **The Article with Initial י and מְ**. With few exceptions, words that begin with י or מְ give up the Daghesh Forte that is associated with the definite article. For example, יְלָדִים (boys) becomes הַיְלָדִים (*the* boys) and מְרַגְּלִים (spies) becomes הַמְרַגְּלִים (*the* spies). In both instances, the Daghesh Forte is given up but the Pathach vowel (short *a*) is not lengthened. This is similar to the issue of virtual doubling with gutturals mentioned above. Note that the Shewa under the first consonant of the noun remains a Vocal Shewa by analogy to the basic form of the article with Daghesh Forte.

5.6 **Vowel Changes**. You now know that a Hebrew noun is rendered definite by the prefixing of the definite article (ה plus a Daghesh Forte in the first consonant of the noun). You also know that there are some minor variations to this standard construction, especially with initial guttural consonants. There are a few nouns that deviate from these rules. But none of these changes should concern you too much. It is good to be aware of exceptions and variations to the standard pattern. But it is more important for you to *concentrate on what does not change*. The presence of the prefixed ה never changes. That is, no matter what the vowels or the Daghesh Forte do or do not do, the ה is unaltered. Second, the stem of the noun will rarely change with the addition of the definite article. Therefore, if you know your vocabulary and understand that a prefixed ה indicates the definite article, you will rarely have any trouble identifying nouns with the definite article in Hebrew.

In a small group of words, the prefixing of the definite article occasions slight changes in the vocalization of the noun. In the following examples, note that *the vowel under the first consonant of each noun has changed to Qamets* with the prefixing of the definite article.

אֶ֫רֶץ	earth	➤	הָאָ֫רֶץ	the earth
עַם	people	➤	הָעָם	the people
גַּן	garden	➤	הַגָּן	the garden
הַר	mountain	➤	הָהָר	the mountain
אֲרוֹן	ark	➤	הָאָרוֹן	the ark

5.7 **The Conjunction וְ.** In the vocabulary for this lesson, you are given the basic form of the conjunction וְ (and, but, also, even). This word occurs more frequently than any other word in the Hebrew Bible, with over 50,000 occurrences. On average, therefore, the conjunction וְ occurs about 2.5 times per verse. It is always prefixed to another word and so never occurs independently. For example, "and a man" is written in Hebrew as וְאִישׁ with the conjunction וְ prefixed to אִישׁ (man). This conjunction has four basic spelling possibilities, depending on the vocalization of the word to which it is prefixed.

1. Before most consonants, the conjunction will appear as וְ (the way it is spelled in the lexicon). It occurs this way about fifty percent of the time. Note the following examples.

וְעֶ֫בֶד	and a servant
וְאִשָּׁה	and a woman
וְהָאִשָּׁה	and the woman
וְאִישׁ	and a man
וְהָאִישׁ	and the man

2. There are two circumstances in which the conjunction will appear as וּ (Shureq).

   a. It is spelled with Shureq (וּ) before the consonants בּ, מ or פ (the so-called labial consonants). This is sometimes referred to as the "bump" rule because the word "bump" contains the transliterated values of בּ, מ and פ. Note the following examples and observe that initial *begadkephat* consonants (for example, the בּ in בַּ֫יִת) will lose the Daghesh Lene when the conjunction is prefixed (וּבַ֫יִת).

וּבֵין   and between   ⟩   בֵּין + וְ

וּבַיִת   and a house   ⟩   בַּיִת + וְ

וּמֶלֶךְ   and a king   ⟩   מֶלֶךְ + וְ

וּפַרְעֹה   and Pharaoh   ⟩   פַּרְעֹה + וְ

b. The conjunction וְ is also spelled as Shureq (וּ) before most consonants having a Vocal Shewa. Note the following examples.

וּנְעָרִים   and young men   ⟩   נְעָרִים + וְ

וּזְרָעִים   and seeds   ⟩   זְרָעִים + וְ

וּסְפָרִים   and books   ⟩   סְפָרִים + וְ

וּשְׁמוּאֵל   and Samuel   ⟩   שְׁמוּאֵל + וְ

There is an exception to this rule. If the conjunction וְ is prefixed to a word that begins with the syllable יְ then these two syllables contract to וִי as illustrated by the following example.

וִיהוּדָה   and Judah   ⟩   יְהוּדָה + וְ

3. Before a reduced or Hateph vowel, the conjunction is spelled with the corresponding short vowel of the Hateph vowel. For example, the Hebrew word for "dream" is חֲלוֹם and with the conjunction it is וַחֲלוֹם (and a dream). The conjunction is spelled with *Pathach* (וַ) because it is prefixed to a word beginning with the reduced vowel *Hateph Pathach* (חֲ). Note the following additional examples.

וַאֲנָשִׁים   and men   ⟩   אֲנָשִׁים + וְ

וֶאֱמֶת   and truth   ⟩   אֱמֶת + וְ

וָחֳלִי   and sickness   ⟩   חֳלִי + וְ

There is one important exception to this rule. When אֱלֹהִים (God) occurs with the conjunction וְ it is spelled וֵאלֹהִים (and God).

4. The conjunction וֹ may also be spelled with a Qamets (וָ) before monosyllabic words and certain words with an initial accent.

וְ + צֹאן   ➤   וָצֹאן   and sheep

וְ + לֶ֫חֶם   ➤   וָלֶ֫חֶם   and bread

Let us end our discussion of the conjunction וֹ with a final point of encouragement. In addition to this conjunction, there are only six words in the Hebrew Bible that begin with the consonant ו (three proper nouns, two common nouns, and one adjective). These six words occur only eighteen total times in the Hebrew Bible. Therefore, when you see the consonant ו at the beginning of a Hebrew word, you should expect the conjunction over ninety-nine percent of the time. In other words, regardless of the vowel occurring under an initial וֹ, you know that it is the Hebrew conjunction.

5.8   **Summary**.

1. In general, the Hebrew definite article *functions* much like the English definite article. There is no indefinite article in Hebrew.

2. A noun is made definite by prefixing the definite article, which consists of הַ plus the Daghesh Forte in the first consonant of the noun.

3. The Daghesh Lene of an initial *begadkephat* consonant is replaced by a Daghesh Forte with the prefixing of the definite article.

4. Gutturals and ר reject the Daghesh Forte of the definite article.

     a. *Compensatory Lengthening*. With initial א, ר and ע, the rejection of the Daghesh Forte results in the lengthening of the Pathach (short *a*) to a Qamets (changeable long *ā*): הַ changes to הָ (הָאִישׁ).

     b. *Virtual Doubling*. With initial ה and ח, the Daghesh Forte is rejected but the Pathach vowel *does not lengthen* (הַהֵיכָל).

    c. *Irregular Seghol Vowel.* When nouns begin with unaccented עָ, הָ or חָ (חָ may also be accented), the definite article appears with Seghol and without the Daghesh Forte (הֶחָכָם).

5. Despite the variation of vowels beneath the ה of the definite article, *concentrate on what does not change*. The ה of the article will never change and the spelling of the noun will rarely change.

6. The Hebrew conjunction וְ (and, but, also, even) is the most frequently occurring word in the Hebrew Bible. This conjunction has four basic spelling possibilities.

    a. Before most consonants, the conjunction will appear as וְ.

    b. Before ב, מ or פ ("bump" rule) and syllables beginning with Vocal Shewa, the conjunction will appear as וּ (Shureq).

    c. Before a Hateph vowel, the conjunction is spelled with the corresponding short vowel of the Hateph vowel.

    d. Before monosyllabic words and certain words with initial accent, the conjunction is spelled with Qamets (וָ).

5.9   Vocabulary.

אֵשׁ	fire (376); feminine
הֵיכָל	temple, palace (80)
וְ	and, but, also, even, then (50, 524)
זָהָב	gold (392)
חֶרֶב	sword (413); feminine
חַי	(adj) living, alive (254); (noun) חַיִּים life, lifetime (140)
יֶלֶד	child, boy, youth (89)
יָם	sea (396)
כֶּסֶף	silver, money (403)
כֹּה	thus, here (577)
מָקוֹם	place, location (401)
מִשְׁפָּט	judgment, decision, ordinance, law, custom, manner (425)
מִזְבֵּחַ	altar (403)
נְאֻם	utterance, announcement, revelation (376)
עוֹלָם	forever, everlasting, ancient (439)

עָנָן   clouds, cloud mass (87)

רוּחַ   spirit, wind, breath (378); usually feminine

שַׂר   chief official, ruler, prince (421)

שַׁעַר   gate (373)

שָׁמַיִם   heaven, sky (421)

5.10   **The Long Nose of God.** Of the many wonders to be found in the Word of God, few surpass the revelation of the character of God. For example, we know that God is the creator of all things (Gen 1:1-2:3; Isa 45:6) and the redeemer of his people (Ex 14; Isa 43:1) and that by these actions he has demonstrated his immeasurable and unparalleled power. Another way we learn about the character of God is by certain divinely inspired descriptions of God, such as "majestic in holiness" or "awesome in glory" (Ex 15:11). Yet, perhaps the most remarkable way in which we learn about the character of God is when God describes himself. For example, in Scripture God has described himself as compassionate (רַחוּם in Ex 34:6), gracious (חַנּוּן in Ex 34:6), and holy (קָדוֹשׁ in Lev 11:45; 19:2). These are some of the most well-known attributes of God's character. However, you might be surprised to discover that God has also described himself as having a "long nose."

This unique description of God's character is first found in Exodus 34:6, when God came and stood with Moses to proclaim his name. We read in the text, "And he passed in front of Moses, proclaiming, 'The Lord, the Lord, the compassionate and gracious God, slow to anger, abounding in love and faithfulness'" (NIV). What is translated as "slow to anger" in English is the Hebrew expression אֶרֶךְ אַפַּיִם, literally "long of nose." This expression may also be translated as "patient" or "longsuffering" (KJV). In Hebrew, the idiom "long of nose" was used to describe someone who was patient or slow to anger (Prov 14:29). Conversely, a person "short of nose" (קְצַר־אַפַּיִם as in Prov 14:17) was considered to be impatient or quick-tempered, much like the modern English idioms "hothead" or "short fuse."

The theological significance of God's long nose is not to be underestimated. Because God is patient, his people do not perish. Because God's nose is long, he has not treated us as we deserve. In the New Testament we are encouraged to "bear in mind that God's patience means salvation" (2 Peter 3:15; cf. 3:9). Reflecting on these realities, the psalmist has put it this way (Ps 103:8-10, NIV):

> The LORD is compassionate and gracious,
>> slow to anger [long of nose], abounding in love.
> He will not always accuse,
>> nor will he harbor his anger forever;
> he does not treat us as our sins deserve
>> or repay us according to our iniquities.

Miles V. Van Pelt
Associate Professor of Old Testament
Reformed Theological Seminary
Jackson, Mississippi

5.11 **Advanced Information: Special Uses of the Definite Article.** There are a few special uses of the Hebrew article that do not correspond to English usage. Below are a few of the most common special uses.

1. *Demonstrative Adjective.* The definite article may, at times, be used like a demonstrative adjective (this, that).

   אָנֹכִי מְצַוְּךָ הַיּוֹם   I am commanding you *the* day (literally).
   I am commanding you *this* day (today).

2. *Vocative Use. Vocative* is a term used to indicate *direct address.* This means that a definite article can be used on names or titles when a speaker is referring to the person with whom he or she is talking (usually translated "O king," "O man," "O Lord," etc.).

   וַיִּקְרָא לֵאמֹר הַמֶּלֶךְ   And he called saying, *"the* king" (literally).
   And he called saying, "O king."

3. *Superlative Use.* The definite article may be used to indicate the superlative use of adjectives (good/best or high/highest).

   הַטּוֹב וְהַיָּשָׁר   the good and the upright (literally)
   the *best* and the *most* upright

4. *Possessive Pronoun.* The definite article may, at times, be used like a possessive pronoun (my, his, her, your, etc.).

   וְלָקַח דָּוִד הַכִּנּוֹר   And David took *the* harp (literally).
   And David took *his* harp.

5.12 **Advanced Information: Indefinite Article**. Hebrew has no indefinite article. Sometimes, however, the Hebrew words for "one," אֶחָד (ms) and אַחַת (fs), are used like the English indefinite article *to mark indefinite nouns*.

אִישׁ אֶחָד *one* man (literally)
a man or *a certain* man

אִשָּׁה אַחַת *one* woman (literally)
a woman or *a certain* woman

Chapter 6
Hebrew Prepositions

6.1   **Introduction.** The study of prepositions in Hebrew is straightforward and uncomplicated. Hebrew prepositions function like English prepositions. They are used to describe relationships between words. For example, these relationships can be spatial as in *under* the book, *on* the book, *over* the book. These relationships can also be temporal as in *before* class, *during* class, *after* class. Many other relationships also exist. The word following the preposition is called the *object* of the preposition. In Hebrew, there are three types of prepositions, to be studied: independent prepositions, Maqqef prepositions, and inseparable prepositions. This classification is based on a preposition's form and relationship to its object, not its meaning.

6.2   **Independent Prepositions.** The majority of Hebrew prepositions *stand alone* and, for this reason, are called *independent*. This is just like the English preposition. The following examples illustrate how simple it is to work with this type of preposition.

לִפְנֵי הַמֶּֽלֶךְ	*before* the king
תַּֽחַת הָעֵץ	*under* the tree
אַחַר הַמַּבּוּל	*after* the flood
בֵּין הַמַּֽיִם	*between* the water(s)

6.3   **Maqqef Prepositions.** Prepositions of this type are almost always joined to their objects by a raised horizontal stroke called a *Maqqef*. Among the most common prepositions of this type are עַל־ (on, upon, concerning), אֶל־ (to, toward), עַד־ (until, as far as) and מִן־ (from). In the following examples, you will see the Maqqef used to join these prepositions with their objects.

עַל־הָאֶֽבֶן	*upon* the stone
אֶל־הַהֵיכָל	*to* the temple
עַד־הַנָּהָר	*as far as* the river
מִן־הָאָֽרֶץ	*from* the land

6.4   **Inseparable Prepositions.** These prepositions are prefixed directly to their objects and never occur independently. In other words, they are *inseparable* from their objects. There are only three inseparable prepositions to be learned.[1]

בְּ	in, by, with
לְ	to, for
כְּ	like, as, according to

1. Before most consonants, the inseparable prepositions will appear with Vocal Shewa as בְּ, לְ or כְּ (the way each is spelled in the lexicon). The following examples illustrate how these prepositions are prefixed to their objects.

בְּשָׂדֶה	*in* a field
לְנַעַר	*for* a young man
כְּמֶלֶךְ	*like* a king

2. Before a reduced or Hateph vowel, the inseparable prepositions take the corresponding short vowel of the Hateph vowel. This is the same type of rule that you have already learned for the conjunction וַ (5.7.3).[2]

כַּאֲנָשִׁים	*like* men
בֶּאֱמֶת	*in* truth
לָחֳלִי	*for* sickness

3. Before consonants with Vocal Shewa, the inseparable prepositions are spelled with Hireq. This is because two contiguous (side-by-side) Vocal Shewas cannot stand at the beginning of a word (4.12.1) and so the Rule of Shewa applies.[3]

לִנְבִיאִים	*for* prophets
לִבְרִית	*for* a covenant

---

[1] Though there are only three inseparable prepositions, together they occur 38,932 times in the Hebrew Bible: בְּ occurs 15,559 times; כְּ occurs 3,053 times; and לְ occurs 20,321 times. Due to their frequency, it is important that students become familiar with these prepositions.

[2] When an inseparable preposition is prefixed to אֱלֹהִים (God), it is spelled לֵאלֹהִים. This spelling follows the exception to the second Rule of Shewa (4.12).

[3] If an inseparable preposition (בְּ, for example) is prefixed to a word beginning with יְ then it will contract to בִּי as in בִּיהוּדָה (in Judah). In other words, בְּ plus יְהוּדָה becomes בִּיהוּדָה. This is similar to what you learned for Rule of Shewa (4.12.2) and the conjunction וַ (5.7.2b).

4. In nouns *with the definite article*, the prefixing of the preposition is somewhat unusual. The vowel and Daghesh Forte of the definite article are retained but the consonant of the preposition replaces the ה of the definite article. The following examples illustrate this process.

שָׂדֶה	a field	➤	הַשָּׂדֶה	the field
		➤	בַּשָּׂדֶה	*in the* field
אֵשׁ	a fire	➤	הָאֵשׁ	the fire
		➤	בָּאֵשׁ	*in the* fire
נַעַר	a boy	➤	הַנַּעַר	the boy
		➤	לַנַּעַר	*for the* boy
מֶלֶךְ	a king	➤	הַמֶּלֶךְ	the king
		➤	כַּמֶּלֶךְ	*like the* king

6.5   The Form of the Preposition מִן. This preposition deserves special consideration because it may occur as a Maqqef preposition or as an inseparable preposition.

1. Frequently, the preposition מִן is simply joined to its object by the Maqqef as in מִן־הַבַּיִת (from the house) or מִן־הַמַּלְכָּה (from the queen).

2. The preposition מִן can also occur as an inseparable preposition. When this happens, the נ of the preposition assimilates into the first consonant of the noun to which it is prefixed. The assimilated נ is subsequently represented by a Daghesh Forte. For example:

מִן־מֶלֶךְ from a king ➤ מִמֶּלֶךְ from a king

The Daghesh Forte in the second מ of מִמֶּלֶךְ represents the assimilated נ of the original preposition. The Daghesh Forte that results from the assimilated נ behaves in the same way as the Daghesh Forte of the definite article construction. The following explanations show how the Daghesh Forte interacts with *begadkephat* and guttural consonants.

a. When מִן is inseparably prefixed to a word beginning with a *begadkephat* consonant, the Daghesh Lene of the *begadkephat* consonant becomes a Daghesh Forte as in בַּיִת (a house) ➤ מִבַּיִת (from a house). The Daghesh Forte in the ב of מִבַּיִת represents the assimilated נ of the preposition.

b. When מִן is inseparably prefixed to a word beginning with a guttural consonant, the guttural rejects the Daghesh Forte of the assimilating נ with the result that the Hireq (short *i*) under the מ of the preposition lengthens to Tsere (long *ē*) as in מֵאִישׁ (from a man) or מֵעִיר (from a city). The lengthening of Hireq to Tsere is another example of *compensatory lengthening.*[4] When מִן is prefixed to words with the definite article, the ה of the article is retained as in מֵהָאָרֶץ (from the land).

c. When מִן is inseparably prefixed to a word beginning with ח, the Daghesh Forte is often rejected by the guttural but without compensatory lengthening as in מְחוּץ (from outside). This is called *virtual doubling* (see 5.4.2). In some instances, however, compensatory lengthening will occur, as in מֵחֶרֶב (from a sword).

6.6 **The Use of the Preposition מִן.** Because of the frequency with which the preposition מִן occurs (7,592 times), it is worth studying a few of its special uses.

1. *Comparative Use.* In English, adjectives are used to express the comparative and superlative ideas: *big* becomes *bigger* (comparative) or *biggest* (superlative) and *good* becomes *better* or *best.* In Hebrew, the preposition מִן is often used to indicate the comparative or "better than" idea. The following examples illustrate this usage.

טוֹבָה חָכְמָה מִזָּהָב

Literally: Wisdom is *good from* gold.

Comparatively: Wisdom is *better than* gold.

טוֹב הַסֵּפֶר הַזֶּה מִן־הַסֵּפֶר הַהוּא

Literally: This book is *good from* that book.

Comparatively: This book is *better than* that book.

---

[4] This is your second encounter with compensatory lengthening. The first occurrence appeared with the definite article: Pathach to Qamets (5.4.1). A second pattern of compensatory lengthening now occurs with the prefixing of the preposition מִן: Hireq to Tsere.

The comparative use of מִן can also communicate the nuance of "too ... for" as in the following example.

קָשָׁה הָעֲבוֹדָה מֵהָאֲנָשִׁים

> Literally: The work is difficult *from* the men.
>
> Comparatively: The work is *too* difficult *for* the men.

2. *Superlative Use.* In Hebrew, the preposition מִן may be used with כֹּל (all, each, every) in the formation of a superlative מִכֹּל, literally "from every." The following example illustrates this usage.

עָרוּם מִכֹּל חַיַּת הַשָּׂדֶה

> Literally: *clever from every* living thing of the field
>
> Superlatively: *the most clever* living thing of the field

3. *Partitive Use.* The partitive use of מִן is the way that Hebrew expresses a part or portion of something. The following examples illustrate this usage.

מִפְּרִי

> Literally: *from* a fruit
>
> Partitively: *some* (of the) fruit

מֵהָאֲנָשִׁים

> Literally: *from* the men
>
> Partitively: *some of* the men

6.7   The Definite Direct Object Marker. In Hebrew prose, definite direct objects are usually marked with אֵת/אֶת־. The direct object is the word that receives the action of the verb. For example, in the sentence "God created the earth," the word "earth" is the direct object of the verb "created." The direct object "earth" is also a *definite* direct object because it has the *definite* article, "the earth." In Hebrew, the definite direct object marker, also called the accusative marker, is often spelled exactly the same as the preposition אֵת/אֶת־ which translates "with." In most instances, context will enable you to distinguish between these two forms. Consider the following sentence.

כָּתַב אֶת־הַדְּבָרִים בַּסֵּפֶר   He wrote the words in the book.

The masculine plural noun דְּבָרִים (words) is the direct object of the verb כָּתַב (he wrote). This direct object is definite, that is, it has the definite article (הַדְּבָרִים). As the definite direct object of the verb, it is marked with אֵת־. Note that the definite direct object marker is not translated. It is a word that has a grammatical function but no translation value. A few more examples will help to illustrate the use of the object marker.

בָּרָא אֱלֹהִים אֵת הַשָּׁמַיִם	God created the heavens.
נָתַן הַנָּבִיא אֶת־הַסֵּפֶר לַמֶּלֶךְ	The prophet gave the book to the king.
בָּנָה הַמֶּלֶךְ אֶת־הַהֵיכָל הַגָּדוֹל	The king built the great temple.

In each of the examples above, the direct object is considered to be definite because it has the definite article. Proper nouns (שְׁמוּאֵל, Samuel) and nouns with pronominal suffixes (סוּסִי, my horse) are also considered to be definite. Therefore, direct objects that are proper nouns or nouns with pronominal suffixes will also be marked with אֶת/אֵת־. Study the following sentences and be certain that you understand why the object marker is present.

שָׁמַר הַמֶּלֶךְ אֶת־הַמִּצְוָה וְאֶת־הַתּוֹרוֹת	The king observed the commandment and the laws.
שָׁלַח הַנָּבִיא אֶת־הַמַּלְאָךְ אֶל־הָעִיר	The prophet sent the messenger to the city.
אָהַב דָּוִד אֶת־יְהוֹנָתָן	David loved Jonathan.
נָתַן הַמֶּלֶךְ אֶת־תּוֹרוֹתָיו לָעָם	The king gave his laws to the people.

If the direct object of a verb is not definite, then the definite direct object marker is not used. In the following examples, the direct objects are indefinite and, therefore, the definite direct object marker is not present.

בָּנָה הַמֶּלֶךְ הֵיכָל גָּדוֹל	The king built a great temple.
בָּנָה הַנַּעַר בַּיִת קָטֹן בָּעִיר	The young man built a small house in the city.

6.8   Summary.

1. Hebrew prepositions function like English prepositions. The word following the preposition is called the *object* of the preposition. There are three types of Hebrew prepositions: independent, Maqqef, and inseparable.

2. Independent prepositions stand alone. Maqqef prepositions are joined to their objects by a raised horizontal stroke called a *Maqqef*. Inseparable prepositions are prefixed directly to their objects.

3. The inseparable prepositions בְּ (in, by, with), לְ (to, for), and כְּ (like, as, according to) are prefixed directly to their objects and never occur independently.

   a. Before most consonants, the inseparable prepositions will appear with Vocal Shewa as בְּ, לְ or כְּ.

   b. Before a reduced or Hateph vowel, the inseparable prepositions are spelled with the corresponding short vowel of the Hateph vowel.

   c. Before consonants with Vocal Shewa, the inseparable prepositions are spelled with Hireq because of the application of Rule of Shewa (4.12.1).

   d. In nouns with the definite article, the vowel and Daghesh Forte of the definite article are retained but the consonant of the preposition replaces the ה of the definite article.

4. The preposition מִן occurs both as a Maqqef preposition and as an inseparable preposition. When occurring as an inseparable preposition, the נ assimilates into the following consonant and appears as a Daghesh Forte. This Daghesh Forte is rejected by gutturals, resulting in either compensatory lengthening or virtual doubling.

5. The preposition מִן can be used *comparatively* (as in "better than"); *superlatively* with כֹּל (מִכֹּל, as in "the most"); and *partitively* (as in "some of").

6. In Hebrew prose, definite direct objects are usually marked with אֵת/אֶת־ (the accusative marker). The definite direct object marker is never translated. It is a word that has a grammatical function but no translation value.

6.9 **Vocabulary**.

אַחַר	after, behind (718); also as אַחֲרֵי
אֵת	with, beside (890); also as אֶת־
אֵת	definite direct object marker, not translated (10,978); also as אֶת־
אֶל	to, toward, in, into (5,518); also as אֶל־
בֵּין	between (409); וּבֵין with the conjunction וְ
בְּ	in, at, with, by, against (15,559)
בְּתוֹךְ	in the midst (middle) of, inside; (n) תָּוֶךְ middle, center (420)
חָכְמָה	wisdom, skill (153); note that the vowel under the ח is Qamets Hatuf
כְּ	as, like, according to (3,053)
כֹּל	all, each, every (5,415); also as כָּל־
לִפְנֵי	before, in front of (1,102)
לְ	to, toward, for (20,321)
לְמַעַן	on account of, for the sake of (272)
מִן	from, out of (7,592); also as מִן־
מַעַל	above, upward, on top of (140); often with מִן (מִמַּעַל)
מִצְוָה	commandment (184); מִצְוֹת (irregular plural)
עַד	until, as far as, during (1,263)
עַל	on, upon, on account of, according to (5,777)
עַל־דְּבַר	because of, on account of (49)
עִם	with, together with (1,048)
פֶּה	mouth, opening (498)
שָׂדֶה	field, pasture land (329)
תַּחַת	under, below, instead of (510)

6.10 **Who Is Like You?** Of the so-called Minor Prophets, Micah is one of the better known to modern readers. He was a contemporary of Isaiah in the latter half of the eighth century B.C. and he prophesied to both Judah and Israel. He delivers a direct and powerful message of judgment upon each nation and its political and religious leadership. The language of judgment is graphic and startling (3:1-12), mediated with conviction and moral outrage (3:8). God's judgment is just (1:3-5; 2:1-2; 3:9-12). The sins of the people demand it. Micah is a purveyor of judgment to be sure, but amidst the prediction of certain doom, the prophet mediates the divine promise of restoration and the coming of God's kingdom through the appearance of a Saviour (4:1-4; 5:2). With reference to this unique blend of divine justice (we get what we deserve) and divine mercy (we don't get what we deserve), the prophet declares מִי־אֵל כָּמוֹךָ toward the end of the book (7:18). A simple grammatical construction, the question is composed of the interrogative pronoun מִי, the divine title אֵל and the preposition כְּ with a 2ms pronominal suffix (Who is a God like you?). Despite the use of the interrogative pronoun, the question neither demands nor expects a response. It is rhetorical. Micah expects no raised hand in the gallery of his readership. Though deities abound in the pantheons of ancient Israel's neighbors, no candidates will be identified as God's equal because the God of Israel and the attributes of his character are unique, especially his mercy – justice tempered with mercy, a portrait consistent with the divine self-revelation in Ex 34:5-7.

The consummate expression of divine mercy with which the book of Micah ends (7:18-20) finds its expression at the beginning of the composition (1:1) with the identification of the prophet's name. In Hebrew, the name Micah is spelled מִיכָה (Micah 1:1) or מִיכָיְהוּ (Judg 17:1, 4). The name is composed of the interrogative pronoun מִי, the preposition כְּ and a shortened form of the divine name (Who is like Yahweh?). In Hebrew, the link between the prophet's name (1:1) and his message of divine mercy in 7:18 (מִי־אֵל כָּמוֹךָ) is unmistakable. The question without an answer, which stands as a declaration and affirmation of the unique and merciful character of God, echoes throughout the Old Testament.

> Who is like you, O Lord, among the gods?
> Who is like you, majestic in holiness,
> terrible in glorious deeds, doing wonders?
> (Ex 15:11)
>
> All my bones say, "O Lord, who is like you?"
> (Ps 35:10)

Gary D. Pratico
Professor of Old Testament
Gordon-Conwell Theological Seminary
South Hamilton, Massachusetts

6.11 **Advanced Information: Compound Prepositions.** Some Hebrew prepositions are formed by combining two different prepositions (or a preposition and a noun) in order to make a new preposition.

1. Several high frequency prepositions are formed from the noun פָּנֶה (face), which is attested only in the plural (פָּנִים). The following are among the most important forms.

   לִפְנֵי before, in the presence of (לְ + פָּנִים)

   מִפְּנֵי away from, out from, from the presence of, from before, on account of, because of (מִן + פָּנִים)

   מִלִּפְנֵי away from, from before, from the presence of, on account of (מִן + לְ + פָּנִים)

   עַל־פְּנֵי in the face of, in the sight of, in front of, before, up against, opposite to (עַל־ + פָּנִים)

2. The following are some common prepositions that are created by the compounding of two different prepositions.

   מֵעַל from upon ➤ מִן is prefixed to עַל

   מִתַּחַת from under ➤ מִן is prefixed to תַּחַת

   מֵאֵת from with ➤ מִן is prefixed to אֵת

3. The following prepositions are created by the compounding of a noun with a preposition.

   עַל־דְּבַר on account of ➤ עַל is prefixed to דְּבָר

   בְּתוֹךְ in the midst of ➤ בְּ is prefixed to תָּוֶךְ

   מִתּוֹךְ from the midst of ➤ מִן is prefixed to תָּוֶךְ

Chapter 7

Hebrew Adjectives

7.1   **Introduction**. Hebrew adjectives function just like English adjectives. They are used to modify, describe, characterize, or classify nouns. In other words, adjectives give nouns a certain amount of increased specificity. For example, the noun "king" can be modified by any number of different adjectives, such as *"righteous* king" or *"wicked* king." Whatever you want to say about a king, you can say it with adjectives.

7.2   **The Inflection of Adjectives**. Hebrew adjectives inflect (change their form) in order to indicate gender and number. They are inflected in four forms: masculine singular and masculine plural, feminine singular and feminine plural. The good news is that the inflectional endings for adjectives are the same endings that you have already learned for nouns. Observe how the Hebrew adjective טוֹב (good) is inflected.

	Inflected Adjective		*Inflectional Endings*	
	Masculine	*Feminine*	*Masculine*	*Feminine*
Singular	טוֹב	טוֹבָה		הָ
Plural	טוֹבִים	טוֹבוֹת	ים	וֹת

7.3   **Notes on the Inflection of Adjectives**. There are a few additional things that you should know about Hebrew adjectives.

1.   *Hebrew adjectives agree in gender and number with the nouns they modify.* This means that an adjective modifying a feminine noun will take a feminine ending. Similarly, an adjective modifying a masculine noun will take a masculine ending. For example, סוּס טוֹב is translated "good horse" or "a good horse." The noun סוּס is masculine and so the adjective טוֹב must also be masculine in form. Similarly, מַלְכָּה טוֹבָה is translated "good queen" or "a good queen." The noun מַלְכָּה is feminine and so the adjective טוֹבָה must also be feminine in form because adjectives modifying feminine nouns take feminine endings. *The gender of an adjective does not change the meaning of an adjective.*

2. *Adjectives that are plural in form are singular in translation value.* In other words, they do not translate with any kind of plural meaning. For example, מְלָכוֹת טוֹבוֹת is translated *"good* queens." The reason the adjective טוֹבוֹת is plural *in form* is because the noun it is modifying is plural. In Hebrew, the number of an adjective does not change the meaning of an adjective, unless the adjective is used substantively (7.4.3).

3. Unlike טוֹב, *most adjectives undergo vowel changes when the inflectional endings are added.* These patterns of change are similar to those that occur in nouns (see 7.10 for various patterns of adjectival inflection).

7.4 **The Use of Adjectives.** We now turn our attention to adjectival usage. In other words, how do adjectives modify or relate to nouns? Adjectival usage falls into three categories: attributive, predicative, and substantive.

1. *Attributive Use.* When an adjective modifies a noun, it is being used attributively. In the examples *"good* student" and *"big* book," the adjectives modify the nouns. In Hebrew, attributive adjectives follow, or come after, the noun they are modifying. The modifying adjective must also agree with the noun in gender, number, and definiteness. The term "definiteness" refers to the presence (definiteness) or absence (indefiniteness) of the definite article. The following examples illustrate the attributive use of the adjective.

אִישׁ טוֹב	good man *or* a good man
הָאִישׁ הַטּוֹב	the good man
אִשָּׁה טוֹבָה	good woman *or* a good woman
הָאִשָּׁה הַטּוֹבָה	the good woman
אֲנָשִׁים טוֹבִים	good men
הָאֲנָשִׁים הַטּוֹבִים	the good men
נָשִׁים טוֹבוֹת[1]	good women
הַנָּשִׁים הַטּוֹבוֹת	the good women

---

[1] The plural of אִשָּׁה is נָשִׁים. This is an example of irregular pluralization (4.7.4). Even though נָשִׁים takes the masculine plural ending, the noun is still feminine and so the adjective agrees with natural gender (fp) and not grammatical gender (mp).

In each of the examples above, be certain that you understand the agreement between noun and adjective in the categories of gender, number, and definiteness (or indefiniteness).

2. *Predicative Use.* This use of the adjective does not modify a noun but rather asserts something about it. In the examples "the student is *good*" or "the book is *big*," the adjectives assert something about the nouns so as to create a predication. In English, a form of the verb "to be" is used to indicate the predicative relationship. In Hebrew, the predicative relationship is indicated when an adjective matches the noun in gender and number *but not definiteness*. The predicate adjective never takes the definite article. With regard to word order, the adjective may either precede or follow the noun. The following examples illustrate the predicative use of the adjective.

הָאִישׁ טוֹב / טוֹב הָאִישׁ	The man is good.
הָאִשָּׁה טוֹבָה / טוֹבָה הָאִשָּׁה	The woman is good.
הָאֲנָשִׁים טוֹבִים / טוֹבִים הָאֲנָשִׁים	The men are good.
הַנָּשִׁים טוֹבוֹת / טוֹבוֹת הַנָּשִׁים	The women are good.

In the examples above that illustrate the predicate usage, there is no form of the Hebrew verb "to be." The "is" or "are" translations are supplied because of the predicative relationship between the noun and the adjective. In this usage, a predication is created with a noun and with an adjective without the definite article. The noun can also be a proper name as in יָשָׁר שְׁמוּאֵל (Samuel is upright) or יָפָה רוּת (Ruth is beautiful). Verbless clauses with predicate adjectives should usually be translated only with the English present tense of the verb "to be," as in צַדִּיק הַנָּבִיא (the prophet *is* righteous) or צַדִּיקִים הַנְּבִיאִים (the prophets *are* righteous). Apart from context, you should not supply the English past tense of the verb "to be." A verbless clause can be translated with the past tense ("was" or "were") but only if a past tense verbal form is present or if warranted by context.

Given that the predicate adjective never takes the definite article, certain constructions may pose ambiguity. For example, אִישׁ טוֹב can be translated either as "a good man" or as "a man is good." In such instances, only context will suggest whether the usage is attributive or predicative.

3. *Substantive Use.* Adjectives may be used independently as nouns. In such cases, there will be no noun for the adjective to modify. The Hebrew adjective meaning "wise" is חָכָם. Used substantively, by itself, it means "a wise one" or "a wise man." Similarly, with the definite article, הֶחָכָם is translated "the wise one" or "the wise man."

7.5   **Lexical Form.** The lexical form of a Hebrew adjective is always the *masculine singular* form. This is different than a noun, for which the lexical form is masculine *or* feminine singular, depending on the gender of the noun.

7.6   **The Directional Ending.** In Hebrew, a special ending may be added to a word in order to express the idea of *motion toward someone or something*. This special ending is the *directional ending* הָ (it is always unaccented). In terms of meaning, the use of the directional ending הָ is the same as a prepositional phrase with אֶל־ (to, toward). Compare the following examples.

אֶל־הָאָרֶץ   to (toward) the land

אַרְצָה   to (toward) [the] land

In the second example above, the noun אֶרֶץ (land) appears with the directional ending and is translated just like the first example with the preposition אֶל־ (to, toward). This directional ending occurs 1,119 times in the Hebrew Bible. In the examples below, the directional ending has been added to words that occur frequently with this ending. You will also note in the following examples that vowel changes are clearly observable in some words. It is better, however, to master recognition through frequency of encounter rather than attempting to memorize all the spelling changes. Note also that a Daghesh Forte is sometimes added to the last consonant of the word when the directional ending is attached (for example, יָמָּה and שָׁמָּה).

בַּיִת	house	➤	הַבַּיְתָה	to (toward) the house
עִיר	city	➤	הָעִירָה	to (toward) the city
שָׁמַיִם	heaven	➤	הַשָּׁמַיְמָה	to heaven, heavenward
מִצְרַיִם	Egypt	➤	מִצְרַיְמָה	to (toward) Egypt

הַר	mountain	➤	הָהָרָה	to (toward) the mountain
שָׁם	there	➤	שָׁמָּה	to there, to that place
יָם	sea, west	➤	יָמָּה	toward the sea, toward the west, westward

Now that you have studied the Hebrew directional ending (הָ ָ), it might be helpful to review the other הָ ָ endings that you have encountered.

1. Feminine singular *nouns* often end in הָ ָ as in תּוֹרָה (law). The ending is accented.

2. Feminine singular *adjectives* end in הָ ָ as in גְּדוֹלָה (great). The ending is accented.

3. In later chapters, you will learn that prepositions, nouns, and the definite direct object marker may take a 3fs pronominal suffix that consists of הָ ָ as in לָהּ (to her) or סוּסָהּ (her horse). Note, however, that the הּ of the 3fs pronominal suffix has a dot within it that is called *Mappiq*.

7.7   Summary.

1. Hebrew adjectives inflect in order to indicate gender and number. They are inflected in four forms: masculine singular and masculine plural, feminine singular and feminine plural. The inflectional endings for adjectives are the same endings that you have already learned for nouns.

2. Hebrew adjectives agree in gender and number with the nouns they modify. The gender of an adjective does not change the meaning of an adjective.

3. Adjectives that are plural in form are singular in translation value. The number of an adjective does not change the translation value of an adjective.

4. Adjectival usage falls into three categories: attributive, predicative and substantive.

   a. *Attributive* adjectives follow the noun they modify and agree in gender, number, and definiteness (or indefiniteness).

   b. *Predicative* adjectives either precede or follow the noun they modify and agree in gender and number only. Predicative adjectives never take the definite article.

    c. *Substantive* adjectives are used independently as nouns. In such cases, there will be no noun for the adjective to modify.

5. In Hebrew, the directional ending הָ may be added to the end of a word in order to express the idea of motion toward someone or something. The directional ending is always unaccented and is translated "to" or "toward."

7.8   Vocabulary.

אֶחָד	one (976)
גָּדוֹל	great, big, large (527)
דַּל	poor, weak, needy (48)
זָקֵן	(adjective) old; (noun) elder (180)
חָכָם	wise, skillful, experienced (138) *similar to wisdom*
טוֹב	good, pleasant (535)
יָפֶה	beautiful (43)
יָשָׁר	upright, just, level, straight (119)
כֵּן	so, thus; עַל־כֵּן or לָכֵן therefore (741)
מְאֹד	very, exceedingly (300)
מְעַט	little, few (101)
עַתָּה	now, after all, at last, then (435)
צַדִּיק	righteous, just, innocent (206)
קֹדֶשׁ	holiness, something that is holy (470)
קָדוֹשׁ	holy, set apart (117)
קָטֹן	small, young, insignificant (74) *little carton*
קָרוֹב	near, close (75)
קָשֶׁה	difficult, hard, severe (36) *car sharing → difficult*
רָחוֹק	distant, remote, far away (84)
רַב	great, many (419)
רַע	bad, evil, wicked (312)
רָשָׁע	wicked, guilty (264)
שִׁיר	song (78) *Ed Sheeran*

7.9   **Theological Motivation.**[2] Shortly after I began the study of Hebrew, over forty years ago now, I became motivated to comprehend the biblical languages when I realized that most of my knowledge of God was derived from Holy Scripture, and the accuracy of that knowledge was contingent upon the correctness with which I handled its languages. God incarnated himself in those languages, not only in the body of Jesus Christ to whom they point. Instructively, in the closing letters of Paul, the apostle to the Gentiles, and of Peter, the apostle to the Jews, just prior to their deaths, they both wed their Christian teachings with the God-breathed Old Testament. In his letter with the famous closing line, "I have fought the good fight, I have finished the race, I have kept the faith" (2 Tim 4:7), Paul wrote:

> But as for you, *continue in what you have learned* and have become convinced of, because you know those from whom you learned it, *and how from infancy you have known the holy Scriptures,* which are able to make you wise for salvation through faith in Christ Jesus. All Scripture is God-breathed and is useful for teaching, rebuking, correcting and training in righteousness, so that the man of God may be thoroughly equipped for every good work (2 Tim 3:14-17).

Likewise Peter, immediately after writing, "I think it is right to refresh your memory as long as I live in the tent of this body, because I know that I will soon put it aside, as our Lord Jesus Christ has made clear to me," added:

> And I will make every effort to see that after my departure you will always be able to remember these things. We did not follow cleverly invented stories when we told you about the power and coming of our Lord Jesus Christ, but we were eyewitnesses of his majesty . . . And we have the word of the prophets made more certain, and you will do well to pay attention to it, as to a light, shining in a dark place, until the day dawns and the morning star rises in your hearts. Above all, you must understand no prophecy of Scripture came about by the prophet's own

---

[2]   Bruce K. Waltke, "How I Changed My Mind About Teaching Hebrew (or Retained it)," *Crux* 29.4 (1993): 10-11. Reprinted with author's permission.

interpretation. For prophecy never had its origin in the will of man, but men spoke from God, as they were carried along by the Holy Spirit (2 Pet 1:12-21).

The logic of this Christian theology, that God revealed himself through the Scripture, inescapably led me to the conclusion that the authenticity of that knowledge rested on a precise understanding of the biblical languages. That conviction led me to earn my first doctorate in Greek and New Testament and the second in the Ancient Near Eastern languages and literatures with a major in Old Testament. From the beginning of my formal theological education it remained my purpose, by God's grace, to be in God's house an article of gold and silver, not of wood and clay, for noble purposes, not ignoble, so as to be "an instrument for noble purposes, made holy, useful to the Master and prepared to do any good work" (2 Tim 2:20-21). I must confess that I find it difficult to engage theological presentations that have not been purged through the fire of careful exegesis.

Bruce K. Waltke
Professor of Old Testament
Reformed Theological Seminary
Orlando, Florida

7.10 Advanced Information: Basic Patterns of Adjectival Inflection. For the most part, those changes that occur with adjectives are the same as those that occur with nouns (4.8). Below are some of the most common patterns of adjectival inflection. These patterns demonstrate how an adjective's vowels will change when inflected for gender and number.

1. *Adjectival Inflection with No Change.* Certain adjectives, like the monosyllabic adjective טוֹב, do not change with the addition of inflectional endings.

	Masculine	*Feminine*
Singular	טוֹב	טוֹבָה
Plural	טוֹבִים	טוֹבוֹת

2. *Adjectival Inflection with Propretonic Reduction.* Review 4.8.2 for discussion of propretonic reduction. In adjectives, with the addition of inflectional endings, a (changeable) long vowel (Qamets or Tsere) in an open, propretonic syllable will reduce to Vocal Shewa. This type of change occurs when the open, pretonic

syllable of the masculine singular adjective becomes propretonic with the addition of inflectional endings. Study the following examples with propretonic reduction.

a. Adjectives with the vowel pattern of גָּדוֹל (great)

	Masculine	Feminine
Singular	גָּדוֹל	גְּדוֹלָה
Plural	גְּדוֹלִים	גְּדוֹלוֹת

b. Adjectives with the vowel pattern of זָקֵן (old)

	Masculine	Feminine
Singular	זָקֵן	זְקֵנָה
Plural	זְקֵנִים	זְקֵנוֹת

c. Adjectives with the vowel pattern of יָשָׁר (upright, right)

	Masculine	Feminine
Singular	יָשָׁר	יְשָׁרָה
Plural	יְשָׁרִים	יְשָׁרוֹת

d. Adjectives with an initial guttural consonant cannot take a Vocal Shewa but prefer Hateph Pathach.

	Masculine	Feminine
Singular	חָכָם	חֲכָמָה
Plural	חֲכָמִים	חֲכָמוֹת

3. *Inflection of Adjectives Ending in* הָ *.* Adjectives like קָשֶׁה (difficult) can be difficult to recognize because the הָ ending is dropped when the inflectional endings are added. It must be recognized, for example, that קָשִׁים derives from קָשֶׁה before a form like this can be located in the lexicon.

	Masculine	Feminine
Singular	קָשֶׁה	קָשָׁה
Plural	קָשִׁים	קָשׁוֹת

4. *Inflection of Geminate Adjectives.* Like Geminate nouns (4.8.4), Geminate adjectives such as רַב (many) will take a Daghesh Forte in the second consonant with the addition of inflectional endings.

	Masculine	*Feminine*
Singular	רַב	רַבָּה
Plural	רַבִּים	רַבּוֹת

Note that Geminate adjectives like רַע (evil), with a guttural for the second consonant, cannot take the Daghesh Forte. Because the guttural rejects the Daghesh Forte, the Pathach under the ר undergoes compensatory lengthening.

	Masculine	*Feminine*
Singular	רַע	רָעָה
Plural	רָעִים	רָעוֹת

Chapter 8

Hebrew Pronouns

8.1   **Introduction**. A pronoun is a word that replaces a noun. The noun that a pronoun refers back to is called the *antecedent*. Stated differently, the antecedent of a pronoun is the word or words for which the pronoun stands. In the example, "Moses was one hundred and twenty years old when he died," the word "he" is a pronoun that refers back to "Moses," the antecedent. In Hebrew, there are personal, demonstrative, relative, and interrogative pronouns. Hebrew pronouns function much like their English counterparts.

8.2   **Independent Personal Pronouns**. In Hebrew, the independent personal pronoun is labeled "independent" because it stands alone and is not prefixed or suffixed to another word. Personal pronouns can be first, second, or third person and either singular or plural. First person pronouns refer to the person speaking (I, we). Second person pronouns refer to the person being spoken to (you). Third person pronouns refer to the person or thing spoken of (he, she, it, they). The second and third person pronouns have both masculine and feminine forms. First person pronouns, however, are *common*, meaning that they may refer to either masculine or feminine nouns (they are not inflected for gender). In Hebrew, independent personal pronouns are *subjective*, meaning they are used as the subject of a verb, never as the object of the verb. Personal pronouns may also appear as the subject of a verbless clause. For this reason, they are sometimes called *subject pronouns*. The Hebrew independent personal pronouns are listed below. Note that some pronouns have more than one form or spelling.

8.3 **Independent Personal Pronoun Paradigm.**

	Singular		Plural	
1 Common	אֲנִי ,אָנֹכִי	I	אֲנַ֫חְנוּ[1]	we
2 Masculine	אַתָּה	you	אַתֶּם	you
2 Feminine	אַתְּ	you	אַתֵּ֫נָה[2]	you
3 Masculine	הוּא	he/it	הֵם ,הֵ֫מָּה	they
3 Feminine	הִיא ,הִוא[3]	she/it	הֵן ,הֵ֫נָּה	they

8.4 **The Use of the Independent Personal Pronoun.** The independent personal pronouns and their translations should be memorized as vocabulary. Hebrew personal pronouns often occur in conjunction with verbs. They may also be used, however, in a predicative relationship with nouns or adjectives in verbless clauses. The following examples illustrate how the independent personal pronouns are used with nouns, adjectives, or a prepositional phrase in a predicative relationship.

אֲנִי יְהוָה	I am the LORD.
הוּא נָבִיא צַדִּיק	He is a righteous prophet.
אַתָּה מֶ֫לֶךְ טוֹב	You (2ms) are a good king.
אַחִים אֲנַ֫חְנוּ	We are brothers.
הִיא אִשָּׁה חֲכָמָה	She is a wise woman.
אַתֶּם בָּעִיר הַגְּדוֹלָה	You (2mp) are in the great city.

In terms of normal word order in a verbless clause, the independent personal pronoun may precede or follow the noun or adjective. As with the predicative use of the adjective (7.4.2), a form of the verb "to be" in the present tense must be supplied.

8.5 **Demonstrative Pronouns and Adjectives.** The English demonstratives are "this," "these," "that" and "those." They may be used either as adjectives (*this* man, *those* women) or as pronouns (*this* is the man, *those* are the women). Demonstratives increase the level of a word's specificity beyond that of the definite article. The level of specific reference increases from "*a* man," to "*the* man," to "*this* man." Hebrew demonstratives function like English demonstratives.

---

[1] The alternate forms אֲנוּ and נַחְנוּ occur only seven total times.

[2] The alternate form אַתֵּן occurs only one time.

8.6   **Demonstrative Paradigm.**

	Singular		Plural	
Masculine	זֶה	this	אֵלֶּה	these
Feminine	זֹאת	this	אֵלֶּה	these
Masculine	הוּא	that	הֵם, הֵמָּה	those , *them*
Feminine	הִיא	that	הֵן, הֵנָּה	those

1. The masculine and feminine singular forms הוּא and הִיא are identical to the third person masculine and feminine independent personal pronouns. In most instances where ambiguity exists, the larger context of the sentence will enable you to make the correct choice. Note the ambiguity in the following examples.

הוּא הָאִישׁ	He is the man.	(personal pronoun)
	That is the man.	(demonstrative pronoun)

הִיא הָאִשָּׁה	She is the woman.	(personal pronoun)
	That is the woman.	(demonstrative pronoun)

2. The demonstrative אֵלֶּה (these) is both masculine and feminine plural. Remember that the designation for this phenomenon is "common," meaning *not inflected for gender*. In other words, this common form can modify either masculine or feminine nouns.

3. There are a few variant or alternative forms for some of the demonstratives. These forms should not be memorized because of their infrequency.

זֶה	➤	הַלָּזֶה and הַלָּז
זֹאת	➤	הַלֵּזוּ and זוֹ, זֹה
אֵלֶּה	➤	אֵל

8.7   **The Use of the Hebrew Demonstratives.** Hebrew demonstratives may be used either as adjectives (*this* man, *those* women) or as pronouns (*this* is the man, *those* are the women).

1. *Demonstrative Adjectives.* When a Hebrew demonstrative is functioning as an adjective, it will *follow* the noun it modifies and agree in gender, number, *and definiteness*. This is just like

---

[3] The alternate 3fs form הוּא is found only in the first five books of the Old Testament.

the attributive use of adjectives as explained in 7.4.1. The following examples illustrate the use of demonstrative adjectives.

הָאִישׁ הַזֶּה	this man
הָאִשָּׁה הַזֹּאת	this woman
הָאִישׁ הַהוּא	that man
הָאִשָּׁה הַהִיא	that woman
הָאֲנָשִׁים הָאֵלֶּה	these men
הַנָּשִׁים הָאֵלֶּה	these women
הָאֲנָשִׁים הָהֵם	those men
הַנָּשִׁים הָהֵנָּה	those women

In each of these examples, be certain that you understand the agreement between the noun and demonstrative adjective in the categories of gender, number, and definiteness. Note that the demonstrative follows the noun in every instance. You should also note that when an attributive adjective is introduced, it is placed between the noun and demonstrative adjective. It must also agree in gender, number, and definiteness.

הָאִישׁ הַטּוֹב הַזֶּה	this good man
הָאִשָּׁה הַטּוֹבָה הַזֹּאת	this good woman
הָאִישׁ הַטּוֹב הַהוּא	that good man
הָאִשָּׁה הַטּוֹבָה הַהִיא	that good woman
הָאֲנָשִׁים הַטּוֹבִים הָאֵלֶּה	these good men
הַנָּשִׁים הַטּוֹבוֹת הָאֵלֶּה	these good women
הָאֲנָשִׁים הַטּוֹבִים הָהֵם	those good men
הַנָּשִׁים הַטּוֹבוֹת הָהֵנָּה	those good women

2. *Demonstrative Pronouns.* When a Hebrew demonstrative is functioning as a pronoun, it will *precede* the noun and agree in gender and number *but not definiteness*. This is just like the predicative use of adjectives (7.4.2). The following examples illustrate the use of demonstrative pronouns.

זֶה הָאִישׁ	This is the man.
זֹאת הָאִשָּׁה	This is the woman.
הוּא הָאִישׁ	That is the man.

הִיא הָאִשָּׁה	That is the woman.
אֵלֶּה הָאֲנָשִׁים	These are the men.
אֵלֶּה הַנָּשִׁים	These are the women.
הֵם הָאֲנָשִׁים	Those are the men.
הֵנָּה הַנָּשִׁים	Those are the women.

When an attributive adjective is introduced, it is placed after the noun it modifies. It will agree in gender, number, and definiteness with the noun it is modifying.

זֶה הָאִישׁ הַטּוֹב	This is the good man.
אֵלֶּה הָאֲנָשִׁים הַטּוֹבִים	These are the good men.
הִיא הָאִשָּׁה הַטּוֹבָה	That is the good woman.
הֵנָּה הַנָּשִׁים הַטּוֹבוֹת	Those are the good women.

8.8   **Relative Pronoun.** The major relative pronouns in English are "who," "whom," "whose," "that," and "which." A relative pronoun introduces a relative clause that modifies a noun. A relative clause is composed of the relative pronoun and the clause that it introduces. In the sentence "happy is the person *who studies Hebrew*," the clause "who studies Hebrew" is a relative clause modifying the noun "person." In Hebrew, the word אֲשֶׁר functions as the relative pronoun.[4] The form of this word never changes. In other words, it does not inflect to indicate the gender and number of its antecedent (the noun it is modifying). The relative pronoun אֲשֶׁר may appear either with or without the Maqqef. In the following examples, you will notice that when אֲשֶׁר functions as a relative pronoun introducing a relative clause, it immediately follows the noun it is modifying.

הָעֵץ אֲשֶׁר בְּתוֹךְ־הַגָּן	the tree *that* (is) in the middle of the garden
הֶהָרִים אֲשֶׁר־תַּחַת הַשָּׁמָיִם	the mountains *that* (are) under the heavens
הַמֶּלֶךְ אֲשֶׁר בְּחַרְתֶּם	the king *whom* you chose

---

[4] In addition to אֲשֶׁר, the particle שֶׁ also functions as a relative pronoun, occurring 139 times in the Hebrew Bible (mostly in poetry). Like the definite article, it is prefixed to a word with a Daghesh Forte in the first consonant (where possible), as in שֶׁטּוֹב (who is good).

דָּוִד אֲשֶׁר בְּבֵית יְהוָה   David, *who* (is) in the house of the LORD

8.9   **Interrogative Pronouns.** Interrogative pronouns are used to ask a question. In Hebrew, the main interrogative pronouns are מִי (who? whom?) and מָה (what?). These pronouns do not inflect and can appear with or without the Maqqef. The vocalization of מִי does not change. The vocalization of מָה, however, may change slightly. In addition to מָה, this interrogative is also spelled מַה and מֶה. When spelled as מַה, a Daghesh Forte will usually appear in the first consonant of the following word (unless that consonant is a guttural). It is not essential to know what causes these vocalization changes. It is easier simply to be aware of the three spelling options. The following examples illustrate how these interrogative pronouns are used.

מַה־שְּׁמוֹ	What (is) his name?
מֶה־עָשִׂיתָ	What have you done?
מָה הַחֲלוֹם הַזֶּה	What (is) this dream?
מִי־אַתָּה	Who (are) you?
מִי־הָאִישׁ הַזֶּה	Who (is) this man?
מִי הָאֲנָשִׁים הָאֵלֶּה	Who (are) these men?

8.10   **The Interrogative Particle הֲ.** In addition to the interrogative pronouns above, Hebrew also has an interrogative particle.[5] In Hebrew, questions are not created with punctuation as in English (?). Rather, interrogative clauses (those that ask a question) are created with the use of certain interrogative pronouns or with a form of the particle הֲ prefixed to the first word of the sentence. Consider the following examples.

שָׁלַח הַמֶּלֶךְ אֶת־הַנָּבִיא	The king sent the prophet.
הֲשָׁלַח הַמֶּלֶךְ אֶת־הַנָּבִיא	Did the king send the prophet?

The first example is a statement; the second is a question. In the second example, the sentence begins with a verb to which the interrogative particle הֲ has been prefixed. The question has been created by the prefixing of the interrogative particle. The spelling of the particle will change, depending on the spelling of the form to which it is prefixed. The rules are quite simple.

---

[5] The interrogative particle הֲ occurs 664 times in the Hebrew Bible.

1. Prefixed to most consonants, it is הַ as in the example above.

2. Prefixed to a guttural consonant or any consonant with Shewa, it is normally הַ.

3. Prefixed to a guttural consonant followed by Qamets, the spelling of the particle is הֶ.

There is the possibility of confusing the interrogative particle with the definite article. To avoid confusion, it will be helpful to remember the following clues.

1. The interrogative particle does not normally have an associated Daghesh Forte as does the definite article.[6]

2. With some frequency, the interrogative particle will be prefixed to a verbal form or another particle. Verbs and particles, of course, will not take the definite article.

3. The Hateph Pathach (הֲ) of the interrogative particle (as it appears with most consonants) is not one of the spellings of the definite article.

8.11   Summary.

1. A pronoun is a word that replaces a noun. The noun that the pronoun refers back to is called the *antecedent*.

2. A *personal pronoun* is a pronoun that replaces a noun referring to a person or thing. It can be first, second, or third person and either singular or plural. First person pronouns are labeled "common," meaning that they may refer to either masculine or feminine nouns (they are not inflected for gender). Second and third person pronouns have both masculine and feminine forms.

	Singular		*Plural*	
1 Common	אֲנִי, אָנֹכִי	I	אֲנַ֫חְנוּ	we
2 Masculine	אַתָּה	you	אַתֶּם	you
2 Feminine	אַתְּ	you	אַתֵּ֫נָה	you
3 Masculine	הוּא	he/it	הֵם, הֵ֫מָּה	they
3 Feminine	הִיא, הִוא	she/it	הֵן, הֵ֫נָּה	they

---

[6] Infrequently, the prefixing of the interrogative particle may occasion the doubling of the following consonant but this is anomalous.

3. The Hebrew demonstratives may be used either as adjectives (*this* man, *those* women) or as pronouns (*this* is the man, *those* are the women).

	Singular		*Plural*	
Masculine	זֶה	this	אֵ֫לֶּה	these
Feminine	זֹאת	this	אֵ֫לֶּה	these
Masculine	הוּא	that	הֵם, הֵ֫מָּה	those
Feminine	הִיא	that	הֵן, הֵ֫נָּה	those

a. When a Hebrew demonstrative is functioning as an adjective, it will *follow* the noun it modifies and agree in gender, number, *and definiteness* (הָאִישׁ הַזֶּה, this man).

b. When a Hebrew demonstrative is functioning as a pronoun, it will *precede* the noun it modifies and agree in gender and number *but not definiteness* (זֶה הָאִישׁ, this is the man).

4. The word אֲשֶׁר (who, whom, whose, which, that) functions as the Hebrew relative pronoun. The form of this word never changes.

5. In Hebrew, the most common interrogative pronouns are מִי (who? whom?) and מָה (what?). These words do not inflect and can appear with or without Maqqef.

6. Another way Hebrew asks a question is with the interrogative particle הֲ. This particle is prefixed to the first word of the interrogative clause (those that ask a question). Usually, it is spelled הֲ. However, it also occurs as הַ (before most guttural consonants and consonants with Shewa) and הֶ (before guttural consonants with Qamets).

8.12 Vocabulary.

אֹ֫הֶל	tent (348)
אַחֵר	other, another, foreign (166)
אֵיךְ	how? (61); also as אֵיכָה (17)
אֶ֫לֶף	thousand (496)
אֲשֶׁר	who, whom, that, which; כַּאֲשֶׁר as, when (5,503)
בְּהֵמָה	animal(s), beast(s), cattle (190)

גַּם	also, even (769)
דָּם	blood (361)
הֲ	interrogative particle (664)
טָהוֹר	clean, pure (96)
כִּי	that, because; (adversative) but, except; (emphatic) indeed, truly; כִּי־אִם but, except, only (4,487)
כְּסִיל	fool, shameless person (70)
לָמָּה	why? (178); also as לָמָה
מָה	what? (571)
מַדּוּעַ	why? (72)
מִי	who? (424)
עָנִי	poor, humble, afflicted (80)
שֶׁמֶן	oil, fat (193)
שֹׁפֵט	one who judges, a judge (68)

8.13 I Myself Have Given. In English, the subject of the verb and the verb itself are two separate words, e.g., "I (subject) wrote (verb)" or "he (subject) spoke (verb)." In Hebrew, however, the subject and the verb are one word as in כָּתַבְתִּי (I wrote) or אָמַר (he said). Thus Hebrew uses one word where English uses two words. But when a biblical writer wanted to emphasize the subject, he would place an independent personal pronoun just before the verb, as in אֲנִי כָּתַבְתִּי (I *myself* wrote). The first word, אֲנִי, is not necessary but serves to emphasize the subject's involvement in the action of the verb.

An example of the emphatic use of the independent personal pronoun is found in Lev 17:11, one of the clearest verses in the Old Testament on the theology of sacrifice. Here the Lord says, "For the life of the flesh is in the blood, and I *myself* have given it [וַאֲנִי נְתַתִּיו] to you upon the altar to make atonement for your lives, for it is the blood, by means of the life, that makes atonement." On the one hand, God says that sacrificial blood is for the purpose of making atonement. On the other hand, however, he emphasizes that *he himself* is the one who provides the means for atonement in the first place. This is an important reversal of how we normally think about sacrifice, namely, as something *we* give to God. This verse turns that idea completely on its head. It is God who has given to us! As in the New Testament, then, God shows his grace not only by granting forgiveness, but by providing sinners with the means of forgiveness to begin with. This is the same idea expressed in Rom 5:8, "But God demonstrates his own love for us in this way: while we were still sinners, Christ died for us."

Jay A. Sklar
Assistant Professor of Old Testament
Covenant Theological Seminary
St. Louis, Missouri

8.14 **Advanced Information: More Interrogative Pronouns.** In addition to מָה (what?), מִי (who? whom?), and the interrogative particle הֲ, Hebrew possesses a number of other interrogative words as well. Some of the more common interrogatives are listed below for your reference.

1. לָמֶה or לָמָה (why?)

אֵלִי אֵלִי לָמָה עֲזַבְתָּנִי
My God, my God, *why* have you forsaken me?
(Ps 22:2 [English 22:1])

לָמָּה תַעֲשֶׂה כֹה לַעֲבָדֶיךָ
Why are you doing thus to your servants?
(Ex 5:15)

2. אֵיכָה or אֵיךְ (how?)

וְאֵיךְ אֶעֱשֶׂה הָרָעָה הַגְּדֹלָה הַזֹּאת וְחָטָאתִי לֵאלֹהִים
How could I do this great evil
and sin against God?
(Gen 39:9)

אֵיכָה נֵדַע אֶת־הַדָּבָר
How may we know the word?
(Deut 18:21)

3. אֵי or אַיֵּה (where?)

וַיֹּאמֶר יְהוָה אֶל־קַיִן אֵי הֶבֶל אָחִיךָ
And the Lord said to Cain,
"*Where* is Abel your brother?"
(Gen 4:9)

אַיֵּה שָׂרָה אִשְׁתֶּךָ
Where is Sarah your wife?
(Gen 18:9)

Chapter 9

Hebrew Pronominal Suffixes

9.1 **Introduction**. In the last chapter, we studied the *subjective* (he, she, we) independent personal pronouns. In this chapter, we will study pronouns that can be either *possessive* (his, her, our) or *objective* (him, her, us). In Hebrew, these possessive and objective pronouns appear as *suffixes* on nouns, prepositions, and the definite direct object marker. For this reason, they are called *pronominal suffixes*. When appearing on nouns, they are possessive as in "his book" or "her wisdom." When appearing on prepositions or the definite direct object marker, they are objective as in "to them," "for them," or "them."

9.2 **The Pronominal Suffixes.** In Hebrew, there are two sets of pronominal suffixes to be learned, Type 1 and Type 2. Both types have the same possessive and objective translation values. As suffixes, these pronouns are attached to the end of a word.

	Type 1 Suffixes	*Type 2 Suffixes*	*Translation Possessive/Objective*
1cs	יִ	יִ	my / me
2ms ^{masculine}	ךָ	יךָ	your / you
2fs ^{feminine}	ךְ	יִךְ	your / you
3ms ^{masculine}	וֹ	יו	his (its) / him (it)
3fs ^{feminine}	הָ	יהָ	her (its) / her (it)
1cp	נוּ	ינוּ	our / us
2mp	כֶם	יכֶם	your / you
2fp	כֶן	יכֶן	your / you
3mp	הֶם	יהֶם	their / them
3fp	הֶן	יהֶן	their / them

80

9.3 **Notes on the Pronominal Suffixes.** The chart with Type 1 and Type 2 suffixes constitutes the essence of this chapter. The remainder of the chapter simply illustrates *how* these pronominal suffixes appear on different words.

1. With few exceptions, Type 1 suffixes occur with singular nouns and Type 2 suffixes occur with plural nouns.

2. All pronominal suffixes have person, gender, and number. Gender is distinguished in all second and third person forms, both singular and plural. The first person singular and plural forms are common, meaning not inflected for gender.

3. In general, there are many similarities in form between Type 1 and Type 2 suffixes, especially in the plural. All Type 2 suffixes have ◌ as part of their spelling. It is the presence of this ◌ that will enable you to distinguish between the two types.

4. Note the dot in the ה of the Type 1 3fs suffix (הּ). This is not a Daghesh Lene or a Daghesh Forte. The Daghesh Lene occurs only in a *begadkephat* consonant and the Daghesh Forte cannot occur in the gutturals or ר. This dot in a final ה is called *Mappiq* and frequently marks the 3fs suffix.

5. A few alternate forms exist for the Type 1 pronominal suffixes. They should not give you too much trouble but are important forms to memorize. You will encounter these alternate forms on selected nouns and prepositions below.

	Type 1 Suffix		Alternate Form
1cs	◌ִי	>	נִי
3ms	וֹ	>	הוּ
3fs	הָ	>	ָהָ
3mp	הֶם	>	ָם
3fp	הֶן	>	ָן

9.4   **Masculine Nouns with Pronominal Suffixes.**[1] It has already been explained that pronominal suffixes on nouns express possession (9.1). Singular nouns use Type 1 suffixes and plural nouns use Type 2 suffixes. The following paradigms use the masculine noun סוּס (horse) to illustrate how masculine nouns receive their pronominal suffixes.

	Type 1 Suffixes		*Type 2 Suffixes*	
	Noun ms	*Translation*	*Noun mp*	*Translation*
1cs	סוּסִי	my horse	סוּסַי	my horses
2ms	סוּסְךָ	your horse	סוּסֶיךָ	your horses
2fs	סוּסֵךְ	your horse	סוּסַיִךְ	your horses
3ms	סוּסוֹ	his horse	סוּסָיו	his horses
3fs	סוּסָהּ	her horse	סוּסֶיהָ	her horses
1cp	סוּסֵנוּ	our horse	סוּסֵינוּ	our horses
2mp	סוּסְכֶם	your horse	סוּסֵיכֶם	your horses
2fp	סוּסְכֶן	your horse	סוּסֵיכֶן	your horses
3mp	סוּסָם	their horse	סוּסֵיהֶם	their horses
3fp	סוּסָן	their horse	סוּסֵיהֶן	their horses

9.5   **Notes on Masculine Nouns with Pronominal Suffixes.**

1. It is important to understand that singular nouns can take both singular and plural pronominal suffixes. In the same way, plural nouns can take both singular and plural pronominal suffixes. For example, the singular noun סוּס can take both a singular suffix as in סוּסִי (*my* horse) or a plural suffix as in סוּסֵנוּ (*our* horse). In these two examples, the noun is singular in both instances but the pronominal suffix is singular in the first example and plural in the second example.

2. When pronominal suffixes are added to masculine plural nouns, the masculine plural ending (◌ִים) is dropped. With the absence of this ending, a masculine noun is often recognizable as plural only by the use of Type 2 pronominal suffixes.

3. If a feminine noun takes a masculine plural ending (4.7), then it will also follow the masculine plural pattern above. For example, the feminine noun עִיר (city) takes the masculine plural ending,

עָרִים (cities). When a pronominal suffix is added, this feminine noun continues to act like a masculine noun, עָרֵיכֶם (your cities).

4. Be careful to note the important distinction between the 1cs suffixes on singular and plural nouns: סוּסִי (my horse) and סוּסַי (my horses). With the singular noun, the suffix is Hireq Yod. With the plural noun, the suffix is Pathach Yod.

5. In the masculine singular noun paradigm above, the alternate endings appear in the forms סוּסָם (with 3mp suffix) and סוּסָן (with 3fp suffix). Once again, it is important to memorize the Type 1 alternate suffixes.

6. Nouns ending in הָ will frequently drop this ending before adding pronominal suffixes. For example, שָׂדֶה (field) becomes שָׂדְךָ (your field) or שָׂדִי (my field). In order to locate these nouns in a lexicon, you must be able to recognize that the הָ ending has been dropped.

9.6   Feminine Nouns with Pronominal Suffixes.[2] Feminine nouns also take Type 1 suffixes in the singular and Type 2 suffixes in the plural. The following chart uses the feminine noun תּוֹרָה (law) to illustrate how feminine nouns ending in הָ receive their pronominal suffixes.

	Type 1 Suffixes		Type 2 Suffixes	
	Noun fs	Translation	Noun fp	Translation
1cs	תּוֹרָתִי	my law	תּוֹרוֹתַי	my laws
2ms	תּוֹרָתְךָ	your law	תּוֹרוֹתֶיךָ	your laws
2fs	תּוֹרָתֵךְ	your law	תּוֹרוֹתַיִךְ	your laws
3ms	תּוֹרָתוֹ	his law	תּוֹרוֹתָיו	his laws
3fs	תּוֹרָתָהּ	her law	תּוֹרוֹתֶיהָ	her laws
1cp	תּוֹרָתֵנוּ	our law	תּוֹרוֹתֵינוּ	our laws
2mp	תּוֹרַתְכֶם	your law	תּוֹרוֹתֵיכֶם	your laws
2fp	תּוֹרַתְכֶן	your law	תּוֹרוֹתֵיכֶן	your laws
3mp	תּוֹרָתָם	their law	תּוֹרוֹתֵיהֶם	their laws
3fp	תּוֹרָתָן	their law	תּוֹרוֹתֵיהֶן	their laws

---

[1]   Endingless feminine singular nouns are also included in this category.

[2]   This category covers feminine singular nouns that end in הָ.

9.7   Notes on Feminine Nouns with Pronominal Suffixes.

1. When a feminine singular noun ending in ה ָ (as in תּוֹרָה) receives a pronominal suffix, the ה is replaced by ת. In other words, the feminine singular noun תּוֹרָה becomes תּוֹרָת before receiving a pronominal suffix.[3] Note the presence of this ת in every form of the feminine singular paradigm above. The inability to recognize this ת as indicative of feminine singular nouns ending in ה ָ will prevent the identification of its lexical form.

2. Unlike masculine plural nouns, feminine plural nouns retain their plural ending (וֹת). In this case, both the feminine plural ending and the use of Type 2 pronominal suffixes identify these nouns as plural.

9.8   Vowel Changes in Nouns with Pronominal Suffixes. In the above discussion, the nouns סוּס and תּוֹרָה were selected because their vowels almost never change with the addition of pronominal suffixes. The majority of nouns, however, will experience vowel changes with the addition of suffixes. Note the following examples.

Lexical Form		Suffix Form	Translation
דָּבָר	➤	דְּבָרִי	my word
דָּבָר	➤	דִּבְרֵיהֶן	their (fp) words
בַּיִת	➤	בֵּיתְךָ	your (ms) house
מָוֶת	➤	מוֹתוֹ	his death

Some of these vowel changes are predictable and follow prescribed rules, but many will deviate from expected patterns. Rather than focus on the changing vowels, however, it is preferable to concentrate on what does not change. Notice that in each of the above forms, the basic consonants do not change. The pronominal suffixes will also remain unchanged. You should be able to identify most nouns with pronominal suffixes in the Hebrew Bible with three capabilities: (1) the memorization of all Type 1 and Type 2 pronominal suffixes, (2) reasonable recall of vocabulary and (3) the use of a standard lexicon.

---

[3] It must be understood that this is a descriptive analysis of how this feminine singular noun receives pronominal suffixes.

9.9 **Monosyllabic Nouns with Pronominal Suffixes.** There are a number of high-frequency monosyllabic nouns that will add י to their stem before a pronominal suffix. This occurs only when the noun is singular. As you will observe from the following paradigms, the addition of this י to singular nouns with Type 1 suffixes may cause them to be confused with plural nouns having Type 2 suffixes. With regard to consonants, both paradigms are identical. The singular noun paradigm, however, has Hireq Yod throughout (אָחִיךָ, your brother). The plural noun paradigm varies its vowel but never has Hireq Yod (אַחֶיךָ, your brothers). Recognizing this distinction now will prevent confusion later. The singular noun אָח (brother) and its plural אַחִים (brothers) are presented below with Type 1 and Type 2 suffixes.

	Type 1 Suffixes		*Type 2 Suffixes*	
	Noun ms	*Translation*	*Noun mp*	*Translation*
1cs	אָחִי	my brother	אַחַי	my brothers
2ms	אָחִיךָ	your brother	אַחֶיךָ	your brothers
2fs	אָחִיךְ	your brother	אַחַיִךְ	your brothers
3ms	אָחִיו[4]	his brother	אֶחָיו	his brothers
3fs	אָחִיהָ	her brother	אַחֶיהָ	her brothers
1cp	אָחִינוּ	our brother	אַחֵינוּ	our brothers
2mp	אֲחִיכֶם	your brother	אֲחֵיכֶם	your brothers
2fp	אֲחִיכֶן	your brother	אֲחֵיכֶן	your brothers
3mp	אֲחִיהֶם	their brother	אֲחֵיהֶם	their brothers
3fp	אֲחִיהֶן	their brother	אֲחֵיהֶן	their brothers

9.10 **Prepositions with Pronominal Suffixes.** In Hebrew, prepositions also take pronominal suffixes. When doing so, the pronominal suffixes are objective rather than possessive. In other words, they function as the object of the preposition as in "to *him*," "for *her*," "with *me*," etc. Some prepositions take Type 1 suffixes and others take Type 2. You need not concern yourself with a preposition's suffix preference. On prepositions, the translation value is the same for both types. The following charts illustrate how certain prepositions receive their pronominal suffixes.

---

[4] This form also occurs with the alternate 3ms ending הוּ, אָחִיהוּ (his brother).

The inseparable preposition לְ (to, for) takes Type 1 suffixes. The preposition עַל (on, upon) takes Type 2 suffixes.

	Type 1	Translation	Type 2	Translation
1cs	לִי	to me	עָלַי	on me
2ms	לְךָ	to you	עָלֶיךָ	on you
2fs	לָךְ	to you	עָלַיִךְ	on you
3ms	לוֹ	to him (it)	עָלָיו	on him (it)
3fs	לָהּ	to her (it)	עָלֶיהָ	on her (it)
1cp	לָנוּ	to us	עָלֵינוּ	on us
2mp	לָכֶם	to you	עֲלֵיכֶם	on you
2fp	לָכֶן	to you	עֲלֵיכֶן	on you
3mp	לָהֶם	to them	עֲלֵיהֶם	on them
3fp	לָהֶן	to them	עֲלֵיהֶן	on them

9.11   Notes on Prepositions with Pronominal Suffixes.

1. The presentation of prepositions with pronominal suffixes is straightforward. Some variation in the spelling of the pronominal suffixes will be observed with certain prepositions. With relatively few exceptions, however, these variations should not occasion much difficulty in terms of recognizing the person, gender, and number of the suffix. The emphasis must be on recognition and not on the ability to produce these forms in Hebrew.

2. Once again, some prepositions will take Type 1 suffixes. The prepositions לְ (to, for), בְּ (in, on), עִם (with), and אֵת (with) all take Type 1 suffixes. Prepositions that take Type 2 suffixes include: עַל (on, upon), אֶל (to, for), תַּחַת (under), and אַחֲרֵי (after). With regard to translation, a preposition's suffix preference is of little importance. You should be comfortable identifying prepositions with either type of pronominal suffix.

9.12 **The Prepositions כְּ and מִן with Pronominal Suffixes**. These two prepositions are spelled differently when pronominal suffixes are added.

	כְּ	Translation	מִן	Translation
1cs	כָּמֹֽונִי	like me	מִמֶּֽנִּי	from me
2ms	כָּמֹֽוךָ	like you	מִמְּךָ	from you
2fs	כָּמֹֽוךְ	like you	מִמֵּךְ	from you
3ms	כָּמֹֽוהוּ	like him (it)	מִמֶּֽנּוּ	from him (it)
3fs	כָּמֹֽוהָ	like her (it)	מִמֶּֽנָּה	from her (it)
1cp	כָּמֹֽונוּ	like us	מִמֶּֽנּוּ	from us
2mp	כָּכֶם	like you	מִכֶּם	from you
2fp	כָּכֶן	like you	מִכֶּן	from you
3mp	כָּהֶם	like them	מֵהֶם	from them
3fp	כָּהֶן	like them	מֵהֶן[5]	from them

9.13 **Notes on כְּ and מִן with Pronominal Suffixes**.

1. With the preposition כְּ, the forms with singular and 1cp suffixes exhibit a longer, alternate spelling of the preposition, כְּמֹו. In the forms with second and third person plural suffixes, the spelling of the preposition exhibits the shorter form. Note the presence of the alternate endings in the forms with 1cs (כָּמֹֽונִי), 3ms (כָּמֹֽוהוּ), and 3fs (כָּמֹֽוהָ) suffixes.

2. With the preposition מִן, the forms with singular and 1cp suffixes also exhibit a longer, alternate spelling of the preposition. In the forms with second and third person plural suffixes, the spelling of the preposition has the shorter form. Note the presence of alternate endings throughout the paradigm. Special attention should be given to the forms with 3ms (מִמֶּֽנּוּ) and 1cp (מִמֶּֽנּוּ) suffixes since they are identical. When confronted by this form, context should enable you to make the correct choice.

9.14 **The Definite Direct Object Marker and the Preposition אֵת/אֶת־ with Pronominal Suffixes**. The object marker אֵת/אֶת־ takes Type 1 pronominal suffixes. The combination of the object marker and a pronominal

---

[5] The 3fp suffix on מִן may also be written as מֵהֵֽנָּה (3 times). It occurs only two times in the form written above in the paradigm.

suffix is translated as a personal pronoun in the objective or accusative case. Be careful not to confuse the object marker with the preposition אֶת/אֵת־ meaning "with." While sharing the same lexical form, these two words can be distinguished by their vowels after pronominal suffixes have been added. The object marker is distinguished by a Holem vowel after the initial consonant (אֹתִי). It is Seghol in the 2mp and 2fp forms (אֶתְכֶם). The preposition is distinguished by the presence of a Hireq vowel under the initial consonant (אִתִּי). The preposition also has a Daghesh Forte in the ת. These are important distinctions to remember. Both paradigms are listed below for comparison.

	Object Marker	Translation	Preposition	Translation
1cs	אֹתִי	me	אִתִּי	with me
2ms	אֹתְךָ	you	אִתְּךָ	with you
2fs	אֹתָךְ	you	אִתָּךְ	with you
3ms	אֹתוֹ	him (it)	אִתּוֹ	with him (it)
3fs	אֹתָהּ	her (it)	אִתָּהּ	with her (it)
1cp	אֹתָנוּ	us	אִתָּנוּ	with us
2mp	אֶתְכֶם	you	אִתְּכֶם	with you
2fp	אֶתְכֶן	you	אִתְּכֶן	with you
3mp	אֹתָם	them	אִתָּם	with them
3fp	אֹתָן	them	אִתָּן	with them

9.15 **עַם and עִם with Pronominal Suffixes.** The preposition עִם (with)[6] and the noun עַם (people) with pronominal suffixes can be easily confused. Both are listed below for comparison. The most significant difference between the two words is the vowel that appears under the first consonant. The preposition has Hireq (עִמִּי, with me) and the noun has Pathach (עַמִּי, my people). Both words take a Daghesh Forte in the מ when pronominal suffixes are added.

---

[6] The Hebrew prepositions עִם and אֶת/אֵת־ are both translated "with."

	Preposition	Translation	Noun	Translation
1cs	עִמִּי	with me	עַמִּי	my people
2ms	עִמְּךָ	with you	עַמְּךָ	your people
2fs	עִמֵּךְ	with you	עַמֵּךְ	your people
3ms	עִמּוֹ	with him (it)	עַמּוֹ	his people
3fs	עִמָּהּ	with her (it)	עַמָּהּ	her people
1cp	עִמָּ֫נוּ	with us	עַמֵּ֫נוּ	our people
2mp	עִמָּכֶם	with you	עַמְּכֶם	your people
2fp	עִמָּכֶן	with you	עַמְּכֶן	your people
3mp	עִמָּם	with them	עַמָּם	their people
3fp	עִמָּן	with them	עַמָּן	their people

9.16 Summary.

1. Pronominal suffixes are *possessive* (my, his, her) when appearing on nouns and *objective* (me, him, her) when appearing on prepositions.

2. All pronominal suffixes have person, gender, and number.

3. There are two sets of pronominal suffixes to be learned, Type 1 (for singular nouns and selected prepositions) and Type 2 (for plural nouns and selected prepositions). Both types have the same possessive and objective translation values. As a general observation, Type 2 suffixes are distinguished by the presence of י throughout their spelling.

4. The dot in the Type 1 3fs suffix is called *Mappiq* (הּ). It is neither the Daghesh Forte nor the Daghesh Lene.

5. Singular nouns can take both singular and plural pronominal suffixes. Plural nouns can also take both singular and plural pronominal suffixes.

6. Singular nouns take Type 1 pronominal suffixes; plural nouns take Type 2.

7. With masculine plural nouns, the plural ending (ים) is lost when pronominal suffixes are added (סוּסַי, my horses). Feminine nouns retain their plural inflectional ending (תּוֹרוֹתַי, my laws).

8. When a feminine singular noun ending in ה (תּוֹרָה) receives a pronominal suffix, the ה is replaced by ת (תּוֹרָתִי, my law).

9. When a noun ending in הֶ ָ (שָׂדֶה) receives a pronominal suffix, the final ה simply drops off and is *not* replaced by ת (שָׂדִי, my field).

10. Certain singular monosyllabic nouns will add י (appears as Hireq Yod with Type 1 suffixes) to their stem before a pronominal suffix (אָח, "brother" becomes אָחִיךָ, "your brother").

11. Prepositions may take either Type 1 or Type 2 pronominal suffixes. Which type of suffix a preposition prefers is of little significance because the translation value is the same for both types.

12. With the addition of pronominal suffixes, the prepositions כְּ (like, as, according to) and מִן (from) exhibit longer, alternate spellings in all forms with singular and 1cp suffixes (כָּמֹוךָ and מִמְּךָ).

13. The object marker אֶת־/אֵת takes Type 1 pronominal suffixes. It is translated as a personal pronoun in the objective or accusative case. Be careful not to confuse the object marker with the preposition אֶת־/אֵת meaning "with."

14. The Type 1 and Type 2 pronominal suffix paradigms are presented below. The alternate Type 1 suffixes are also included and must be memorized.

	Type 1 Suffixes	Type 1 Alternate	Type 2 Suffixes	Translation
1cs	ִי	נִי	ִי	my/me
2ms	ךָ		יךָ	your/you
2fs	ךְ		יִךְ	your/you
3ms	וֹ	הוּ	יו	his (its)/him (it)
3fs	הָ	הָ	יהָ	her (its)/her (it)
1cp	נוּ		ינוּ	our/us
2mp	כֶם		יכֶם	your/you
2fp	כֶן		יכֶן	your/you
3mp	הֶם	ָם	יהֶם	their/them
3fp	הֶן	ָן	יהֶן	their/them

9.17 Vocabulary.

אוֹ	or (321)
אַ֫יִן	there is not, there are not (791); also as אֵין (construct)
אַף	nostril, nose; (metaphorically) anger (277); אַפַּ֫יִם (dual)
בֹּ֫קֶר	morning (213)
בָּקָר	cattle, herd (183)
בְּרָכָה	blessing, gift (71)
הֵן	behold, if (107)
הִנֵּה	behold (1,061)
חַטָּאת	sin, sin offering (298); feminine
יֵשׁ	there is, there are (138)
כָּבוֹד	glory, splendor, honor, abundance (200)
כְּלִי	vessel, implement, weapon (325)
לֶ֫חֶם	bread, food (340)
לְבַד	alone, by oneself (161)
מִשְׁפָּחָה	family, clan (304)
מִלְחָמָה	war, battle, struggle (319)
סָבִיב	around, about, surroundings, circuit (338)
עַם	people (1,869)
עֵץ	tree, wood (329)

9.18 A Cherished Name of God. God is called by many names, titles, and epithets throughout the Old Testament. He is called אֵל (God), a designation that is frequent in poetical literature (especially Psalms and Job). This name is commonly compounded with other descriptive titles (Gen 14:18-21; 16:13; 17:1; 21:33; 31:13; Ps 29:3; Isa 12:2). Each is expressive of some aspect of God's person and character, though none can encompass the fullness of his being. A common designation for God in the Hebrew Bible is אֱלֹהִים (God), a plural form with singular meaning that implies the fullness of deity.[7]

---

[7] The designation אֱלֹהִים occurs 2,602 times in the Hebrew Bible.

As revealed in Ex 3:13-15 and 6:2-8, there is only one personal name for God in the Old Testament. That name is יהוה ("Yahweh" or "Lord"), a form composed of four consonants and called the *tetragrammaton. The* name יהוה is also the covenant name for God in the faith of ancient Israel.[8] This name is also attested in shortened forms that are commonly used in the formation of personal names such as Elijah (אֵלִיָּהוּ or אֵלִיָּה), which translates "(My) God is Yahweh."

But one of the most cherished names of God in the Old Testament is עִמָּנוּ אֵל ("Immanuel" or "Emmanuel"). Most readers will be familiar with the name and its meaning but now you can understand its etymology in Hebrew. It is composed of two words in its three occurrences in Isaiah (7:14; 8:8, 10). The name is composed of the preposition עִם (with) to which has been affixed the 1cp pronominal suffix (us).[9] The divine name אֵל comes at the end of the form. The name עִמָּנוּ אֵל means "God (is) with us." The etymology is easy; the theology of the name is profound. The name is cherished because it bespeaks the depth of God's grace and mercy that he gives his presence, and even himself (Matt 1:23), to his human creation. Beyond its specific context in Isa 7:14, the name עִמָּנוּ אֵל has come to symbolize and summarize the story of biblical revelation. It is a narrative through time that documents the promise of divine presence and the relentless movement of redemption, by divine initiative, from heaven to earth. This is sometimes called the "Immanuel theme" in covenant theology. The theme begins in Eden with the intimate and unhindered fellowship between God and his human creation, and it concludes with the restoration of that fellowship in the events of Rev 21:1-4.

Behold, the dwelling of God is with men.
He will dwell with them,
and they shall be his people,
and God himself will be with them.
(Rev 21:3)

Gary D. Pratico
Professor of Old Testament
Gordon-Conwell Theological Seminary
South Hamilton, Massachusetts

---

[8] The name יהוה occurs 6,828 times in the Hebrew Bible. Given that this is God's covenant name, it is instructive that it occurs with the greatest frequency in Jeremiah (726 times), Psalms (695 times), and Deuteronomy (550 times).

[9] You learned this form (עִמָּנוּ) in section 9.15 of this lesson.

9.19 **Advanced Information**. The following prepositions occur frequently with pronominal suffixes. You should not have any trouble identifying these forms but they are listed for your reference.

	בְּ	*Translation*	אֶל	*Translation*
1cs	בִּי	in me	אֵלַי	to me
2ms	בְּךָ	in you	אֵלֶיךָ	to you
2fs	בָּךְ	in you	אֵלַיִךְ	to you
3ms	בּוֹ	in him (it)	אֵלָיו	to him (it)
3fs	בָּהּ	in her (it)	אֵלֶיהָ	to her (it)
1cp	בָּנוּ	in us	אֵלֵינוּ	to us
2mp	בָּכֶם	in you	אֲלֵיכֶם	to you
2fp	בָּכֶן	in you	אֲלֵיכֶן	to you
3mp	בָּהֶם	in them	אֲלֵיהֶם	to them
3fp	בָּהֶן	in them	אֲלֵיהֶן	to them

	תַּחַת	*Translation*	אַחֲרֵי	*Translation*
1cs	תַּחְתַּי	under me	אַחֲרַי	after me
2ms	תַּחְתֶּיךָ	under you	אַחֲרֶיךָ	after you
2fs	תַּחְתַּיִךְ	under you	אַחֲרַיִךְ	after you
3ms	תַּחְתָּיו	under him (it)	אַחֲרָיו	after him (it)
3fs	תַּחְתֶּיהָ	under her (it)	אַחֲרֶיהָ	after her (it)
1cp	תַּחְתֵּינוּ	under us	אַחֲרֵינוּ	after us
2mp	תַּחְתֵּיכֶם	under you	אַחֲרֵיכֶם	after you
2fp	תַּחְתֵּיכֶן	under you	אַחֲרֵיכֶן	after you
3mp	תַּחְתֵּיהֶם	under them	אַחֲרֵיהֶם	after them
3fp	תַּחְתֵּיהֶן	under them	אַחֲרֵיהֶן	after them

9.20 **Advanced Information: Resumptive Pronouns.** As discussed previously (8.8), a relative clause modifies the noun that it follows. In the expression "the king *whom you chose*," the clause "whom you choose" is a relative clause modifying the noun "king." In Hebrew, a relative clause may have a resumptive pronoun. *A resumptive pronoun is a pronoun within the relative clause that refers back to the noun that the relative clause modifies.* In "the king whom you chose *him*," the word "him" is a resumptive pronoun referring back to "king." Similarly, in the sentence "This is the book that I read *it*," the word "it" is a resumptive pronoun referring back to "book." Although resumptive pronouns are common in Hebrew, they are improper in English, so they should be omitted from an English translation.

הַמָּקוֹם אֲשֶׁר אַתָּה עוֹמֵד עָלָיו

the place which you are standing on *(it)*

(Exod 3:5)

הַבָּתִּים אֲשֶׁר־יֹאכְלוּ אֹתוֹ בָּהֶם

the houses which they eat it in *(them)*

(Exod 12:7)

וַיִּשְׁמְרֵנוּ בְּכָל־הַדֶּרֶךְ אֲשֶׁר הָלַכְנוּ בָהּ

(And) he guarded us in all the way that we walked in *(it)*.

(Josh 24:17)

Chapter 10

Hebrew Construct Chain

10.1 **Introduction.** There is no word for "of" in biblical Hebrew. Rather, Hebrew expresses the "of" (possessive) relationship between two nouns by what is called the *construct chain*. For those who have studied Greek, the construct chain is Hebrew's rough equivalent of the genitive case. This grammatical relationship is created by placing two or more nouns side by side. Observe the following examples.

קוֹל הָאִישׁ	the voice *of* the man
מֶלֶךְ הָאָרֶץ	the king *of* the land
עֶבֶד הַמֶּלֶךְ	the servant *of* the king

In the above examples, there is no explicit Hebrew word for "of." Rather, it is implied because each set of nouns is side by side, that is, in a construct chain. In most instances, two different translations are possible. For example, קוֹל הָאִישׁ may be translated as either "the voice of the man" or "the man's voice." Similarly, עֶבֶד הַמֶּלֶךְ may be translated as either "the servant of the king" or "the king's servant." While studying the construct chain in this chapter, the "of" translation is used throughout.

10.2 **Basic Grammar of the Hebrew Construct Chain.**

1. *Construct and Absolute States.* If we use the imagery of a chain, there are two links in the Hebrew construct chain, the *construct* link and the *absolute* link. The first of the two nouns in the construct chain is called the *construct noun* and is said to be in the *construct state*. The second of the two nouns is called the *absolute noun* and is said to be in the *absolute state*. The absolute form of a noun is also its lexical form.

Absolute Noun   **Construct Noun**

In a construct chain, there is only one absolute noun and the absolute noun is always the last noun in the chain. However, multiple construct nouns may appear in a construct chain. You should also note that when two nouns are "in construct," no other words or particles may separate them. In other words, the "chain" cannot be broken.

2. *Definiteness and Indefiniteness.* Construct chains are either entirely definite (*the … of the …*) or entirely indefinite (*a … of a …*) but the construct noun will not take the definite article. The definiteness or indefiniteness of a construct chain is determined by the definiteness or indefiniteness of the absolute noun. Therefore, a construct chain is definite if the absolute noun is definite and indefinite if the absolute noun is indefinite. If the absolute noun is definite, so are all the construct nouns linked to it. If the absolute noun is indefinite, so are all the construct nouns linked to it. In the following examples, the construct chains are indefinite because the absolute nouns are indefinite.

קוֹל אִישׁ   *a* voice of *a* man

מֶלֶךְ אֶרֶץ   *a* king of *a* land

עֶבֶד מֶלֶךְ   *a* servant of *a* king

Using the same nouns, notice how the following construct chains are entirely definite because the absolute nouns are definite.

קוֹל הָאִישׁ   *the* voice of *the* man

מֶלֶךְ הָאָרֶץ   *the* king of *the* land

עֶבֶד הַמֶּלֶךְ   *the* servant of *the* king

Even though the construct nouns lack the definite article, they are considered to be definite because the absolute nouns are definite. Remember that a noun is considered to be definite under three circumstances: (1) if it has the definite article, as in הַמַּלְכָּה (the queen); (2) if it has a pronominal suffix, as in סוּסוֹ (his horse); or (3) if it is a proper noun, as in שְׁמוּאֵל (Samuel). Note how the following construct chains are definite. In the first two examples, the construct chain is definite because the absolute noun is a proper noun. In the last two examples, the construct chain is definite because the absolute noun has a pronominal suffix.

אֲבִי אַבְרָהָם   *the* father of *Abraham*

עֶבֶד שְׁמוּאֵל   *the* servant of *Samuel*

בֵּית מַלְכִּי   *the* house of *my* king

סֵפֶר אָבִיהוּ   *the* book of *his* father

3. *Multiple Construct Nouns.* It has already been explained that *multiple construct nouns may appear in a given construct chain* but there is only one absolute noun for each construct chain. In other words, a train may have many cars but only one caboose. In instances where multiple construct nouns appear, each construct noun is translated with the key word "of" and they all depend on the absolute noun for definiteness. In the following examples, the construct chains contain more than one noun in the construct state.

עֶבֶד אֲחִי הַמֶּלֶךְ   the servant of the brother of the king

עֶבֶד בֵּית הַמֶּלֶךְ   the servant of the house of the king

דִּבְרֵי מֶלֶךְ הָאָרֶץ   the words of the king of the land

כָּל־מִשְׁפַּחַת בֵּית־אֲבִי אִמּוֹ[1]   all of the family of the house of the father of his mother (Judg 9:1)

4. *Construct Chains Linked with Maqqef.* The nouns of a construct chain are sometimes joined by Maqqef.[2]

בֶּן־דָּוִד   the son of David

כָּל־הָעָם   all of the people

10.3 Construct Chains with Adjectives.

1. *Attributive Adjectives.* It has already been explained that the nouns of a construct chain cannot be separated by other words. For this reason, when an adjective modifies either the construct or absolute noun, it must follow the entire chain. Like any attributive adjective, it must agree with the noun it modifies in gender, number, and definiteness. In the following examples, דְּבַר is the

---

[1] The form כָּל־ (with Qamets Hatuf) is the construct of כֹּל (all, each, every).

[2] The use of the Maqqef indicates that the two joined words form a single accented unit. In other words, the first word gives up its primary accent to the second word and the entire chain is pronounced as if it were a single word. This process is known technically as "proclisis," whereby the first word becomes "proclitic" to the second word.

construct form of דָּבָר and מֶלֶךְ is both the construct and absolute (lexical) form of this noun.

דְּבַר הַמַּלְכָּה הַטּוֹב	the *good word* of the queen The adjective is masculine singular, modifying the construct noun.
דְּבַר הַמַּלְכָּה הַטּוֹבָה	the word of the *good queen* The adjective is feminine singular, modifying the absolute noun.
מֶלֶךְ הָאָרֶץ הַטּוֹב	the *good king* of the land The adjective is masculine singular, modifying the construct noun. The noun אֶרֶץ is feminine singular.
מֶלֶךְ הָאָרֶץ הַטּוֹבָה	the king of the *good land* The adjective is feminine singular, modifying the absolute noun.

In the following construct chains, the adjective may modify either the construct or the absolute noun. In ambiguous constructions like these, context must be your guide. Note that דִּבְרֵי is the construct form of דְּבָרִים and עֶבֶד is both the construct and absolute (lexical) form of this noun.

דְּבַר הַמֶּלֶךְ הַטּוֹב	the *good word* of the king *or* the word of the *good king*
דִּבְרֵי הַמְּלָכִים הַטּוֹבִים	the *good words* of the kings *or* the words of the *good kings*
עֶבֶד הַנָּבִיא הָרַע	the *evil servant* of the prophet *or* the servant of the *evil prophet*

2. *Demonstrative Adjectives.* Just like attributive adjectives, demonstrative adjectives must follow the construct chain. The following examples illustrate this point. Note that אֵשֶׁת is the construct form of אִשָּׁה (woman, wife).

אֵשֶׁת הָאִישׁ הַזֶּה	the wife of *this man*
אֵשֶׁת הָאִישׁ הַטּוֹב הַזֶּה	the wife of *this good man*
דִּבְרֵי הַנָּבִיא הָאֵלֶּה	*these words* of the prophet
דִּבְרֵי הַנָּבִיא הַזֶּה	the words of *this prophet*
דִּבְרֵי הַנָּבִיא הַטּוֹב הַזֶּה	the words of *this good prophet*

דְּבַר הַנָּבִיא הַזֶּה   the word of *this prophet or*
this word of the prophet

דִּבְרֵי הַנְּבִיאִים הָאֵלֶּה   *these words* of the prophets *or*
the words of *these prophets*

3. *Adjectives in the Construct State.* You have already learned that an adjective may be used substantively, like a noun. As such, a substantival adjective can appear, just like a noun, in the construct state. The following examples illustrate this point.

יְפַת מַרְאֶה   beautiful of appearance
(יְפַת is the fs construct of יָפֶה)

חֲכַם־לֵב   wise of heart
(חֲכַם is the ms construct of חָכָם)

קְדוֹשׁ יִשְׂרָאֵל   the Holy One of Israel
(קְדוֹשׁ is the ms construct of קָדוֹשׁ)

10.4 **Construct Nouns with Inseparable Prepositions.** Although a construct noun cannot take the definite article, a construct noun may appear with one of the inseparable prepositions (בְּ, לְ, כְּ) as in בְּבֵית דָּוִד, meaning "*in* the house of David." In this example, the construct noun בֵּית has the prefixed preposition בְּ. The entire chain is definite because the absolute noun is a proper noun. Note the loss of the Daghesh Lene in the second ב of בְּבֵית because this *begadkephat* consonant is now preceded by a vowel (Vocal Shewa).

10.5 **The Spelling of Nouns in the Construct State.** In many instances, the singular construct noun and its lexical form are identical in spelling. Examples include סוּס (horse or horse of), קוֹל (voice or voice of), and מֶלֶךְ (king or king of). Most construct nouns, however, are spelled differently than their lexical form. *These changes are occasioned because a construct noun surrenders its primary accent. Therefore, only the absolute noun has the primary accent and the entire construct chain is pronounced as though it were a single word.* The changes in spelling that occur with nouns in the construct state are similar to those changes that a noun undergoes when taking a pronominal suffix. Although a standard lexicon will provide the construct form for most nouns, a few rules will enable you to identify most of the changes on your own.

1. *Vowel Reduction.* Because the construct noun loses its primary accent, the vowels of the construct noun will often reduce or change their length. The following rules apply to endingless nouns, either masculine or feminine (excluding Segholate nouns).

a. In the construct state, *Qamets (and sometimes Tsere) changes to Pathach in a final closed syllable.*

Absolute			Construct	
מִשְׁפָּט	judgment	➤	מִשְׁפַּט	judgment of
מִדְבָּר	wilderness	➤	מִדְבַּר	wilderness of
מַלְאָךְ	angel	➤	מַלְאַךְ	angel of

In certain words, Tsere may also change to Pathach in a final closed syllable. For example, מִזְבֵּחַ (altar) becomes מִזְבַּח (altar of) in the construct state.

b. In the construct state, *Qamets or Tsere changes to Vocal Shewa in an open, unaccented syllable.*

Absolute			Construct	
נָבִיא	prophet	➤	נְבִיא	prophet of
שָׁלוֹם	peace	➤	שְׁלוֹם	peace of
מָקוֹם	place	➤	מְקוֹם	place of

c. Frequently, both of the rules in 1a-b will apply to the formation of a noun in the construct state. In other words, the vowels in both syllables will reduce. Note that in the last example (חָצֵר), the guttural takes a Hateph Pathach, not a Vocal Shewa as in the other example.

Absolute			Construct	
דָּבָר	word	➤	דְּבַר	word of
לֵבָב	heart	➤	לְבַב	heart of
קָהָל	assembly	➤	קְהַל	assembly of
זָקֵן	elder	➤	זְקַן	elder of
חָצֵר	court	➤	חֲצַר	court of

d. The monosyllabic nouns כֹּל (all) and בֵּן (son) occur more frequently in the construct state than any other nouns in the Hebrew Bible.[3] In the construct state, these nouns (and others like them) will experience reduction of the changeable long vowel to its corresponding short vowel.

Absolute			Construct	
בֵּן	son	➤	בֶּן	son of
כֹּל	all	➤	כָּל	all of
יָד	hand	➤	יַד	hand of

2. The masculine plural ◌ִים and dual ◌ַיִם endings change to ◌ֵי in the construct state and then rule 1b above is applied to produce the construct form. This is an important type of change to memorize.

Absolute			Construct	
אֱלֹהִים	God	➤	אֱלֹהֵי	God of
בָּנִים	sons	➤	בְּנֵי	sons of
עֵינַיִם	two eyes	➤	עֵינֵי	(two) eyes of
דְּבָרִים	words	➤	דִּבְרֵי[4]	words of

3. Feminine singular nouns with the ◌ָה ending change this ending to ◌ַת and then rule 1b above is applied to produce the construct form.[5] This is an important type of change to memorize.

Absolute			Construct	
תּוֹרָה	law	➤	תּוֹרַת	law of
מַלְכָּה	queen	➤	מַלְכַּת	queen of
שָׁנָה	year	➤	שְׁנַת	year of

4. Feminine plural nouns ending in וֹת retain this diagnostic ending and then rule 1b above is applied to produce the construct form.

---

[3] In the construct state, בֶּן occurs 4,649 times and כָּל occurs 4,556 times. Together, these two words constitute almost 20% of all construct nouns in the Hebrew Bible.

[4] Both propretonic reduction and the application of Rule of Shewa (4.12) apply.

[5] As in section 9.7, it must be understood that this is a descriptive analysis of how certain feminine singular absolute nouns become constructs.

Absolute		*Construct*	
מַמְלָכוֹת	kingdoms	⮞ מַמְלְכוֹת	kingdoms of
שֵׁמוֹת	names	⮞ שְׁמוֹת	names of
שָׂדוֹת	fields	⮞ שְׂדוֹת	fields of
בְּרָכוֹת	blessings	⮞ בִּרְכוֹת[6]	blessings of

5. Certain singular monosyllabic nouns add Hireq Yod to their stem in the construct state. You will recall that this also occurs when these same nouns take pronominal suffixes. You must be careful not to confuse this Hireq Yod with the 1cs pronominal suffix.

Absolute		*Construct*	
אָב	father	⮞ אֲבִי	father of
אָח	brother	⮞ אֲחִי	brother of

Compare the above construct forms with אָבִי (my father) and אָחִי (my brother).

6. A small group of nouns that occur with some frequency in the construct state are characterized by the diphthong יַ (3.10). Two such nouns are בַּיִת (house) and עַיִן (eye, spring). In the construct state this diphthong changes to Tsere Yod (יַ changes to יֵ). The construct forms of these nouns are much more common than their absolute or lexical forms.[7] For this reason, it is important to memorize both the absolute and construct forms as vocabulary. All such construct forms will be listed in the vocabulary sections throughout the grammar.

Absolute		*Construct*	
בַּיִת	house	⮞ בֵּית	house of
עַיִן	spring	⮞ עֵין	spring of

---

[6] This last example involves application of the Rule of Shewa (4.12). The Qamets under the ר in בְּרָכוֹת changes to Shewa according to 1b above (בְּרְכוֹת) in the construct state. Two initial, side-by-side Vocal Shewas are not permitted and so Rule of Shewa is applied, producing בִּרְכוֹת (blessings of).

[7] The noun בַּיִת occurs a total of 2,047 times in the Hebrew Bible. In 477 instances (23%), it appears in the absolute state or lexical form. It appears 1,570 times (77%) in the construct state (בֵּית). Likewise, עַיִן occurs 83 times (9%) in the absolute state but 817 times (91%) in the construct state (עֵין).

7. *Segholate Nouns.* The singular absolute or lexical form of a Segholate noun is identical to its singular construct form. For example, מֶ֫לֶךְ may be translated as either "king" in the absolute state or "king of" in the construct state. The plural construct form follows the pattern of מַלְכֵי (kings of).[8]

	Absolute			Construct	
מֶ֫לֶךְ	king	>	מֶ֫לֶךְ	king of
עֶ֫בֶד	servant	>	עֶ֫בֶד	servant of
מְלָכִים	kings	>	מַלְכֵי	kings of
עֲבָדִים	servants	>	עַבְדֵי	servants of

8. Nouns ending in הָ have a singular construct form with an הַ ending.

	Absolute			Construct	
שָׂדֶה	field	>	שְׂדֵה	field of
מַחֲנֶה	camp	>	מַחֲנֵה	camp of

10.6 Summary.

1. Hebrew expresses the "of" (possessive) relationship between two nouns by placing them side by side, in a *construct chain*.

2. A construct chain may have one or more nouns in the construct state but only one noun in the absolute state. The absolute noun is always last in the construct chain.

3. Construct chains are either definite (*the … of the …*) or indefinite (*a … of a …*). The definiteness or indefiniteness of a construct chain is determined by the definiteness or indefiniteness of the absolute noun. The construct noun will not take the definite article. Therefore, a construct chain is definite if the absolute noun is definite and indefinite if the absolute noun is indefinite.

4. Nouns in a construct chain may be linked by Maqqef as in בֶּן־דָּוִד (the son of David).

---

[8] Frequently, in the construct plural of Segholate nouns (such as מַלְכֵי and עַבְדֵי in this section), the Daghesh Lene that is expected in the *begadkephat* consonant after the Silent Shewa is given up. This loss of Daghesh Lene (in a *begadkephat* consonant) after a closed syllable will be encountered in other circumstances (18.7).

5. When two or more nouns are "in construct," no other words or particles may separate them. For this reason, attributive adjectives must follow the construct chain as in מֶ֫לֶךְ הָאָ֫רֶץ הַטּוֹב (the good king of the land).

6. Although a construct noun cannot take the definite article, a construct noun may appear with one of the inseparable prepositions as in בְּבֵית דָּוִד (*in* the house of David).

7. Most construct nouns change their spelling in comparison to their absolute or lexical forms. This is because the construct noun surrenders its primary accent or stress to the absolute noun in the construct chain. The most significant changes are listed below.

   a. In the construct form of endingless nouns (except for Segholate nouns), Qamets (and sometimes Tsere) changes to Pathach in a final closed syllable. Qamets and Tsere change to Vocal Shewa (or a reduced vowel with gutturals) in an open, unaccented syllable.

   b. The masculine plural (ים) and dual (יִם) endings are replaced by י in the construct state and the rules of vowel reduction are applied.

   c. The ה ending of a feminine singular noun changes to ת in the construct state and the rules of vowel reduction are applied.

   d. Feminine plural nouns ending in וֹת retain this diagnostic ending in the construct and the rules of vowel reduction are applied.

   e. Certain singular monosyllabic nouns add Hireq Yod to their stem as in אֲבִי (father of).

   f. The singular absolute or lexical form of a Segholate noun is identical to its singular construct form. The plural construct form follows the pattern of מַלְכֵי (kings of).

   g. Nouns ending in ה have a singular construct ending in ה as in שְׂדֵה (field of).

10.7   Vocabulary.

אֶבֶן	stone (276); feminine
אֲדָמָה	ground, land, earth (222)
אֹיֵב	enemy (285)
בָּשָׂר	flesh, meat, skin (270)
בְּרִית	covenant (287); feminine
גְּבוּל	border, boundary, territory (251)
חַיִל	strength, wealth, army (246)
חֶסֶד	loyalty, faithfulness, steadfast love, lovingkindness (249)
חֹדֶשׁ	month, new moon (283)
יָד	hand; (metaphorically) side, power (1,627); יָדוֹת (plural); feminine
מָוֶת	death, dying (153); מוֹת (irregular construct form)
מַטֶּה	staff, rod, tribe (252)
מִדְבָּר	wilderness, desert, pasture (269)
עוֹד	again, still, as long as (491)
עֵת	time, point of time (296); feminine
עֹלָה	whole burnt offering (286)
פָּנִים	face, front (2,126); פְּנֵי (construct)
צֹאן	flock(s), flock of sheep and goats (274)
רֶגֶל	foot (251); feminine

10.8   Bitzer Was a Banker![9] In 1982, Baker Book House reissued a 1969 book of daily Scripture readings in Hebrew and Greek called *Light on the Path*. The readings were short, and vocabulary helps were given with the Hebrew verses. The aim of the editor, who died in 1980, was to help pastors preserve and improve their ability to interpret the Bible from the original languages.

His name was Heinrich Bitzer. He was a banker.

---

[9] John Piper, *Brothers, We are Not Professionals: A Plea to Pastors for Radical Ministry* (Nashville: Broadman & Holman, 2002): 81-88. Reprinted with author's permission.

A banker! Brothers, must we be admonished by the sheep as to what our responsibility is as shepherds? Evidently so. For we are surely not admonishing and encouraging each other to press on in Greek and Hebrew. And most seminaries, evangelical as well as liberal, have communicated by their curriculum emphases that learning Greek and Hebrew may have some value for a few rare folks but is optional for the pastoral ministry.

I have a debt to pay to Heinrich Bitzer, and I would like to discharge it by exhorting all of us to ponder his thesis: "The more a theologian detaches himself from the basic Hebrew and Greek text of Holy Scripture, the more he detaches himself from the source of real theology! And real theology is the foundation of a fruitful and blessed ministry."[10]

What happens to a denomination when a useful knowledge of Greek and Hebrew is not cherished and encouraged for the pastoral office? I don't mean simply offered and admired. I mean cherished, promoted, and sought.

Several things happen as the original languages fall into disuse among pastors. First, the confidence of pastors to determine the precise meaning of Biblical texts diminishes. And with the confidence to interpret rigorously goes the confidence to preach powerfully. It is difficult to preach week in and week out over the whole range of God's revelation with depth and power if you are plagued with uncertainty when you venture beyond basic gospel generalities.

Second, the uncertainty of having to depend on differing translations – which always involve much interpretation – will tend to discourage careful textual analysis in sermon preparation. For as soon as you start attending to crucial details like tenses, conjunctions, and vocabulary repetitions, you realize the translations are too diverse to provide a sure basis for such analysis. For example, most of the modern English translations (RSV, NIV, NASB, NLT) do not enable the expositor to see that "have fruit" in Romans 6:22 links with "bear fruit" five verses later in Romans 7:4.[11] They all translate Romans 6:22 without the word *fruit*.

---

[10] Heinrich Bitzer, ed., *Light on the Path: Daily Scripture Readings in Hebrew and Greek* (Grand Rapids: Baker, 1982), 10.

[11] Of modern translations, the ESV is one of the few that gets it right.

So the preacher often contents himself with the general focus or flavor of the text, and his exposition lacks the precision and clarity which excite a congregation with the Word of God. Boring generalities are a curse in many pulpits.

Expository preaching, therefore, falls into disuse and disfavor. I say disfavor because we often tend to protect ourselves from difficult tasks by minimizing or ignoring their importance. So what we find in groups where Greek and Hebrew are not cherished and pursued and promoted is that expository preaching – which devotes a good bit of the sermon to explaining the meaning of the text – is not much esteemed by the preachers or taught in the seminaries.

Sometimes this is evident in outright denunciation of exposition as pedantic and schoolish. More often there is simply a benign neglect; and an emphasis on sermonic features like order, diction, illustration, and relevance crowds out the need for careful textual exposition.

Another result when pastors do not study the Bible in Greek and Hebrew is that they, and their churches with them, tend to become second-handers. The harder it is for us to get at the original meaning of the Bible, the more we will revert to the secondary literature. For one thing, it is easier to read. It also gives us a superficial glow that we are "keeping up" on things. And it provides us with ideas and insights which we can't dig out of the original for ourselves.

We may impress one another for a while by dropping the name of the latest book we've read, but secondhand food will not sustain and deepen our people's faith and holiness.

Weakness in Greek and Hebrew also gives rise to exegetical imprecision and carelessness. And exegetical imprecision is the mother of liberal theology.

Where pastors can no longer articulate and defend doctrine by a reasonable and careful appeal to the original meaning of Biblical texts, they will tend to become close-minded traditionalists who clutch their inherited ideas, or open-ended pluralists who don't put much stock in doctrinal formulations. In both cases the succeeding generations will be theologically impoverished and susceptible to error.

Further, when we fail to stress the use of Greek and Hebrew as valuable in the pastoral office, we create an eldership of professional academicians.

We surrender to the seminaries and universities essential dimensions of our responsibility as elders and overseers of the churches. I am deeply grateful for seminaries and for Bible-believing, God-centered, Christ-exalting scholars. But did God really intend that the people who interpret the Bible most carefully be one step removed from the weekly ministry of the Word in the church?

Acts 20:27 charges *us* with the proclamation of "the whole counsel of God." But we look more and more to the professional academicians for books which fit the jagged pieces of revelation into a unified whole. Acts 20:28 charges *us* to take heed for the flock and guard it from wolves who rise up in the church and speak perverse things. But we look more and more to the linguistic and historical specialists to fight our battles for us in books and articles. We have, by and large, lost the Biblical vision of a pastor as one who is mighty in the Scriptures, apt to teach, competent to confute opponents, and able to penetrate to the unity of the whole counsel of God. Is it healthy or biblical for the church to cultivate an eldership of pastors (weak in the Word) and an eldership of professors (strong in the Word)?

One of the greatest tragedies in the church today is the depreciation of the pastoral office. From seminaries to denominational headquarters, the prevalent mood and theme is managerial, organizational, and psychological. And we think thereby to heighten our professional self-esteem! Hundreds of teachers and leaders put the mastery of the Word first *with their lips* but by their curriculums, conferences, seminars, and personal example, show that it is not foremost.

One glaring example is the nature of the doctor of ministry programs across the country.

The theory is good: continuing education makes for better ministers. But where can you do a D.Min. in Hebrew language and exegesis? Yet what is more important and more deeply *practical* for the pastoral office than advancing in Greek and Hebrew exegesis by which we mine God's treasures?

Why then do hundreds of young and middle-aged pastors devote years of effort to everything but the languages when pursuing continuing education? And why do seminaries not offer incentives and degrees to help pastors maintain the most important pastoral skill – exegesis of the original meaning of Scripture?

No matter what we say about the inerrancy of the Bible, our actions reveal our true convictions about its centrality and power.

We need to recover our vision of the pastoral office – which embraces, if nothing else, the passion and power to understand the original revelation of God. We need to pray for the day when pastors can carry their Greek Testaments to conferences and seminars without being greeted with one-liners – the day when the esteem of God's Word and its careful exposition is so high among pastors that those who do not have the skill will humbly bless and encourage those who do and will encourage younger men to get what they never got. Oh, for the day when prayer and grammar will meet each other with great spiritual combustion!

In 1829, twenty-four-year-old George Mueller, famous for his faith and prayer and orphanages, wrote:

> I now studied much, about 12 hours a day, chiefly Hebrew
> . . . [and] committed portions of the Hebrew Old Testament
> to memory; and this I did with prayer, often falling on my
> knees . . . I looked up to the Lord even whilst turning over
> the leaves of my Hebrew dictionary.[12]

In the Methodist Archives of Manchester you can see the two-volume Greek Testament of the evangelist George Whitefield liberally furnished with notes on the interleaved paper. He wrote of his time at Oxford, "Though weak, I often spent two hours in my evening retirements and prayed over my Greek Testament, and Bishop Hall's most excellent Contemplations, every hour that my health would permit."[13]

Luther said, "If the languages had not made me positive as to the true meaning of the word, I might have still remained a chained monk, engaged in quietly preaching Romish errors in the obscurity of a cloister; the pope, the sophists, and their anti-Christian empire would have remained unshaken."[14] In other words, he attributes the breakthrough of the Reformation to the penetrating power of the original languages.

---

[12] George Mueller, *Autobiography of George Mueller* (London: J. Nisbet and Co., 1906), 31.

[13] Arnold Dallimore, *George Whitefield*, vol. 1 (Edinburgh: The Banner of Truth Trust, 1970), 77.

[14] W. Carlos Martyn, *The Life and Times of Martin Luther* (New York: American Tract Society, 1866), 474.

Luther spoke against the backdrop of a thousand years of church darkness without the Word when he said boldly, "It is certain that unless the languages remain, the Gospel must finally perish."[15] He asks, "Do you inquire what use there is in learning the languages...? Do you say, 'We can read the Bible very well in German?'" And he answers:

> Without languages we could not have received the Gospel. Languages are the scabbard that contains the sword of the Spirit; they are the casket which contains the priceless jewels of antique thought; they are the vessel that holds the wine; and as the gospel says, they are the baskets in which the loaves and fishes are kept to feed the multitude.

> If we neglect the literature we shall eventually lose the gospel . . . No sooner did men cease to cultivate the languages than Christendom declined, even until it fell under the undisputed dominion of the pope. But no sooner was this torch relighted, than this papal owl fled with a shriek into congenial gloom . . . In former times the fathers were frequently mistaken, because they were ignorant of the languages and in our days there are some who, like the Waldenses, do not think the languages of any use; but although their doctrine is good, they have often erred in the real meaning of the sacred text; they are without arms against error, and I fear much that their faith will not remain pure.[16]

Brothers, perhaps the vision can grow with your help. It is never too late to learn the languages. There are men who began after retirement! It is not a question of time but of values. John Newton, the author of "Amazing Grace" and former sea captain, was a pastors' pastor with a winsome, gentle love for people who, nevertheless, thought it important to pursue the languages. He once counseled a younger minister, "The original Scriptures well deserve your pains, and will richly repay them."[17] Concerning the early years of studying the languages he says:

---

[15] Hugh T. Kerr, *A Compend of Luther's Theology* (Philadelphia: The Westminster Press, 1943), 17.

[16] Martyn, *The Life and Times of Martin Luther*, 474-75.

[17] John Newton, *The Works of the Rev. John Newton*, vol. 1 (Edinburgh: The Banner of Truth Trust, 1985), 143.

> You must not think that I have attained, or ever aimed at, a critical skill in any of these: . . . In the Hebrew, I can read the Historical Books and Psalms with tolerable ease; but, in the Prophetical and difficult parts, I am frequently obliged to have recourse to lexicons, etc. However, I know so much as to be able, with such helps as are at hand, to judge for myself the meaning of any passage I have occasion to consult.[18]

Continuing education is being pursued everywhere. Let's give heed to the word of Martin Luther: "As dear as the gospel is to us all, let us as hard contend with its language." Bitzer did. And Bitzer was a banker!

John Piper
Pastor of Preaching, Bethlehem Baptist Church
Minneapolis, Minnesota

10.9 **Advanced Information: The Superlative.** In section 6.6.2, you learned that the preposition מִן may be used with כֹּל (all, each, every) in the formation of a superlative construction (מִכֹּל). This is only one of several ways that Hebrew can express the superlative idea. Two additional superlative constructions in Hebrew are detailed below.

1. Perhaps the most common superlative construction is created by the use of an adjective that has been made definite by the definite article, a pronominal suffix, or the construct state. Of course, not all "definite" adjectives will translate as superlatives but context will suggest the possibility.

   מִן־הַקָּטֹן וְעַד־הַגָּדֹול (literally) "from the small one to the great one" or (superlatively) "from the *smallest* one to the *greatest* one" (1 Sam 30:19)

   מִגְּדֹולָם וְעַד־קְטַנָּם (literally) "from the great one of them to the small one of them" or (superlatively) "from the *greatest* of them to the *least* of them" (Jonah 3:5)

---

[18] Richard Cecil, *Memoirs of the Rev. John Newton, In The Works of the Rev. John Newton*, vol. 1, 49-50. For the story of Newton's life and ministry see John Piper, *The Roots of Endurance: Invincible Perseverance in the Lives of John Newton, Charles Simeon, and William Wilberforce* (Wheaton: Crossway, 2002).

הַקָּטֹן אֶת־אָבִינוּ הַיּוֹם   (literally) "the young one is with our father today" or (superlatively) "the *youngest* one is with our father today" (Gen 42:13)

הַיָּפָה בַּנָּשִׁים   (literally) "the beautiful one among (the) women" or (superlatively) "the *most beautiful* one among (the) women" (Song 1:8)

בְּנוֹ הַקָּטָן   (literally) "his young son" or (superlatively) "his *youngest* son" (Gen 9:24)

קְטֹן בָּנָיו   (literally) "the young one of his sons" or (superlatively) "the *youngest* one of his sons" (2 Chr 21:17)

2. Another superlative construction consists of two nouns in a construct chain where the construct noun is singular and the absolute noun is plural and definite. In this construction, the two nouns must be the same.

קֹדֶשׁ הַקֳּדָשִׁים   "the holy of holies," meaning the *most* holy place (Ex 26:33)

אֲדֹנֵי הָאֲדֹנִים   "the Lord of lords," meaning the *greatest* Lord (Deut 10:17)

שִׁיר הַשִּׁירִים   "the song of songs," meaning the *greatest* song (Song 1:1)

Chapter 11

Hebrew Numbers

11.1 **Introduction.** Biblical Hebrew does not have a separate set of numerical symbols (1, 2, 3, etc.) as we do in English. Rather, Hebrew numbers are written out (see chart below). In Hebrew, there are both cardinal and ordinal numbers. Cardinal numbers are used for counting (one, two, three, etc.) and ordinal numbers are used to indicate position in a series (first, second, third, etc.).

11.2 **Cardinal Numbers: One through Ten.** In Hebrew, cardinal numbers have masculine and feminine forms. They also occur in both the absolute and construct states. It is not necessary to memorize all of the following forms. Instead, memorize only the masculine absolute forms and then note the types of changes that occur in the remaining forms. Those changes indicating gender and state should be familiar to you from your study of previous chapters. You will need to give special attention to the spelling of numbers *one* and *two*.

	Masculine		Feminine	
	Absolute	*Construct*	*Absolute*	*Construct*
One	אֶחָד	אַחַד	אַחַת	אַחַת
Two	שְׁנַ֫יִם	שְׁנֵי	שְׁתַּ֫יִם	שְׁתֵּי
Three	שָׁלֹשׁ	שְׁלֹשׁ	שְׁלֹשָׁה	שְׁלֹ֫שֶׁת
Four	אַרְבַּע	אַרְבַּע	אַרְבָּעָה	אַרְבַּ֫עַת
Five	חָמֵשׁ	חֲמֵשׁ	חֲמִשָּׁה	חֲמֵ֫שֶׁת
Six	שֵׁשׁ	שֵׁשׁ	שִׁשָּׁה	שֵׁ֫שֶׁת
Seven	שֶׁ֫בַע	שְׁבַע	שִׁבְעָה	שִׁבְעַת
Eight	שְׁמֹנֶה	שְׁמֹנֶה	שְׁמֹנָה	שְׁמֹנַת
Nine	תֵּ֫שַׁע	תְּשַׁע	תִּשְׁעָה	תִּשְׁעַת
Ten	עֶ֫שֶׂר	עֶ֫שֶׂר	עֲשָׂרָה	עֲשֶׂ֫רֶת

1. With number *one*, the masculine form is spelled with ד (אֶחָד) and the feminine form with ת (אַחַת). The number *one* is used like an *adjective*. As such, it follows the noun it modifies and

113

agrees in gender and definiteness. When used in the construct state, it will precede an absolute noun that is usually plural.

בֵּן אֶחָד one son	בַּת אַחַת one daughter
הַבֵּן הָאֶחָד the one son	הַבַּת הָאַחַת the one daughter
אַחַד הַבָּנִים one of the sons	אַחַת הַבָּנוֹת one of the daughters

2. With number *two*, the masculine form is spelled with נ (שְׁנַיִם) and the feminine with ת (שְׁתַּיִם). Note that both forms are dual in number. The number *two* is classified as a *noun* and agrees in gender with the other noun to which it is related. The absolute and construct forms are used interchangeably without any apparent change in meaning.

בָּנִים שְׁנַיִם two sons	בָּנוֹת שְׁתַּיִם two daughters
שְׁנַיִם בָּנִים two sons	שְׁתַּיִם בָּנוֹת two daughters
שְׁנֵי בָּנִים two sons	שְׁתֵּי בָּנוֹת two daughters

3. With numbers *three* through *ten*, there is no change in spelling, except to indicate gender and state. Like number *two*, these numbers are classified as nouns but they *do not agree in gender* with the other nouns to which they are related. In other words, masculine numbers can be used with feminine nouns and feminine numbers can be used with masculine nouns. Note also that while the numbers are singular in form, the nouns are plural.

שְׁלֹשָׁה בָּנִים three sons	שָׁלוֹשׁ בָּנוֹת three daughters
בָּנִים שְׁלֹשָׁה three sons	בָּנוֹת שָׁלוֹשׁ three daughters
שְׁלֹשֶׁת בָּנִים three sons	שְׁלֹשׁ בָּנוֹת three daughters

4. Numbers *two* through *ten* may also occur with pronominal suffixes. These suffixes are added to the construct forms of the number.

שְׁנֵיהֶם two of them	שְׁתֵּיהֶן two of them
שְׁנֵיכֶם two of you	שְׁתֵּיכֶן two of you
שְׁנֵינוּ two of us	שְׁתֵּינוּ two of us

11.3 Cardinal Numbers: Eleven through Nineteen. Numbers *eleven* through *nineteen* are formed with a combination of the number *ten* and *one* through *nine*. For example, the Hebrew number *eleven* is אַחַד עָשָׂר, a combination of *one* (אֶחָד) and *ten* (עָשָׂר).

	With Masculine Nouns	With Feminine Nouns
Eleven	אַחַד עָשָׂר	אַחַת עֶשְׂרֵה
	עַשְׁתֵּי עָשָׂר	עַשְׁתֵּי עֶשְׂרֵה
Twelve	שְׁנֵי עָשָׂר	שְׁתֵּי עֶשְׂרֵה
	שְׁנֵים עָשָׂר	שְׁתֵּים עֶשְׂרֵה
Thirteen	שְׁלֹשָׁה עָשָׂר	שְׁלֹשׁ עֶשְׂרֵה
Fourteen	אַרְבָּעָה עָשָׂר	אַרְבַּע עֶשְׂרֵה
Fifteen	חֲמִשָּׁה עָשָׂר	חֲמֵשׁ עֶשְׂרֵה
Sixteen	שִׁשָּׁה עָשָׂר	שֵׁשׁ עֶשְׂרֵה
Seventeen	שִׁבְעָה עָשָׂר	שְׁבַע עֶשְׂרֵה
Eighteen	שְׁמֹנָה עָשָׂר	שְׁמֹנֶה עֶשְׂרֵה
Nineteen	תִּשְׁעָה עָשָׂר	תְּשַׁע עֶשְׂרֵה

1. Note that *eleven* and *twelve* have alternate forms. The alternate forms for *eleven* (with עַשְׁתֵּי) occur only nineteen times in the Hebrew Bible.

2. Most of the time, these numbers occur with plural nouns. A few nouns, however, appear regularly in the singular. When singular nouns of this type occur with these numbers, they are translated as plural nouns.

שְׁנֵי עָשָׂר אִישׁ	twelve men (Josh 3:12)
שְׁלֹשׁ עֶשְׂרֵה שָׁנָה	thirteen years (1 Kgs 7:1)
אַרְבָּעָה עָשָׂר יוֹם	fourteen days (Ex 12:6)
חֲמִשָּׁה עָשָׂר שָׁקֶל	fifteen shekels (Lev 27:7)

11.4   Cardinal Numbers: Twenty through Ninety Nine.

Twenty	עֶשְׂרִים	*Plural ending*
Thirty	שְׁלֹשִׁים	
Forty	אַרְבָּעִים	
Fifty	חֲמִשִּׁים	
Sixty	שִׁשִּׁים	
Seventy	שִׁבְעִים	
Eighty	שְׁמֹנִים	
Ninety	תִּשְׁעִים	

1. עֶשְׂרִים (twenty) is the masculine plural form of עֶשֶׂר (ten). Numbers *thirty* through *ninety* (by ten) are the masculine plural forms of *three* through *nine*. For example, שִׁשִּׁים (sixty) is the plural form of שֵׁשׁ (six).

2. In Hebrew, *twenty-one* and other such numbers occur either as "twenty and one" or, less frequently, as "one and twenty."

עֶשְׂרִים וְאַחַת	twenty-one (2 Kgs 24:18)
שִׁבְעִים וְשִׁבְעָה	seventy-seven (Gen 4:24)
תִּשְׁעִים וָתֵשַׁע	ninety-nine (Gen 17:24)
שְׁנַיִם וּשְׁלֹשִׁים	thirty-two (Num 31:40)

11.5   Cardinal Numbers: One Hundred and Higher.

One Hundred	מֵאָה	(construct מְאַת; plural מֵאוֹת)
Two Hundred	מָאתַיִם	(dual form of מֵאָה)
Three Hundred	שְׁלֹשׁ מֵאוֹת	
One Thousand	אֶלֶף	(plural אֲלָפִים)
Two Thousand	אַלְפַּיִם	(dual form of אֶלֶף)
Three Thousand	שְׁלֹשֶׁת אֲלָפִים	
Ten Thousand	רְבָבָה	
Twenty Thousand	רִבּוֹתַיִם	(dual form of רְבָבָה)
Thirty Thousand	שְׁלֹשׁ רִבּוֹת	

1. The numbers *one hundred* (מֵאָה), *one thousand* (אֶלֶף), and *ten thousand* (רְבָבָה) should be memorized.

2. Note that *two hundred* (מָאתַיִם) is the dual form of *one hundred* (מֵאָה), *two thousand* (אַלְפַּיִם) is the dual form of *one thousand* (אֶלֶף) and *twenty thousand* (רִבּוֹתַיִם) is the dual form of *ten thousand* (רְבָבָה).

3. The remaining numerical sequences (*three hundred, four hundred, five hundred, six hundred,* etc.) follow the pattern exhibited by *three hundred* (שְׁלֹשׁ מֵאוֹת), *three thousand* (שְׁלֹשֶׁת אֲלָפִים) and *thirty thousand* (שְׁלֹשׁ רִבּוֹת).

11.6 Ordinal Numbers. The ordinal numbers are used to express position in a series (first, second, third, etc.). In Hebrew, ordinal numbers have both masculine and feminine forms.

	Masculine	*Feminine*
First	רִאשׁוֹן	רִאשׁוֹנָה
Second	שֵׁנִי	שֵׁנִית
Third	שְׁלִישִׁי	שְׁלִישִׁית
Fourth	רְבִיעִי	רְבִיעִית
Fifth	חֲמִישִׁי	חֲמִישִׁית
Sixth	שִׁשִּׁי	שִׁשִּׁית
Seventh	שְׁבִיעִי	שְׁבִיעִית
Eighth	שְׁמִינִי	שְׁמִינִית
Ninth	תְּשִׁיעִי	תְּשִׁיעִית
Tenth	עֲשִׂירִי	עֲשִׂירִית

1. The ordinal רִאשׁוֹן (first) is derived from the noun רֹאשׁ (head, chief, beginning). The remaining ordinals share a common root with their corresponding cardinal number. For example, שֵׁשׁ (six) and שִׁשִּׁי (sixth) share a common root.

2. With ordinals *second* through *tenth*, the masculine form is distinguished from the feminine form by a final ת in the feminine. In other words, masculine ordinals end with יִ as in שְׁלִישִׁי and feminine ordinals end with ית as in שְׁלִישִׁית.

3. Ordinal numbers are classified as *adjectives*. When attributive, they follow the noun they modify and usually agree in gender and definiteness.

בַּיּוֹם הָרִאשׁוֹן	on the first day (Lev 23:7)
בַּיּוֹם הַשְּׁבִיעִי	on the seventh day (Gen 2:2)
יוֹם הַשִּׁשִּׁי	the sixth day (Gen 1:31)

4. For ordinals greater than *tenth*, cardinal numbers are used.

וּשְׁלֹשׁ־עֶשְׂרֵה שָׁנָה	and the thirteenth year (Gen 14:4)
בִּשְׁלֹשִׁים וָשֶׁבַע שָׁנָה	in the thirty-seventh year (Jer 52:31)
בִּשְׁנַת הָאַרְבָּעִים	in the fortieth year (1 Chr 26:31)

11.7   Summary.

1. Cardinal numbers are used for counting (one, two, three, etc.) and ordinal numbers are used to indicate position in a series (first, second, third, etc.).

2. In Hebrew, cardinal numbers have both masculine and feminine forms. They also occur in the absolute and construct states. In most instances, you need only to memorize the masculine absolute forms.

3. While cardinal number *one* functions like an adjective, numbers *two* and higher function like nouns. Note that numbers *three* through *ten* do not agree in gender with the noun with which they are associated.

4. Cardinal numbers *eleven* through *nineteen* are formed with a combination of the number *ten* and *one* through *nine*. For example, the Hebrew number *eleven* is אַחַד עָשָׂר, a combination of *one* (אַחַד) and *ten* (עָשָׂר).

5. In Hebrew, the number *twenty-one* and other such numbers occur as either "twenty and one" or, less frequently, as "one and twenty."

6. Ordinal numbers are classified as adjectives and have both masculine and feminine forms. Masculine ordinals end in ִי as with שְׁלִישִׁי (third) and feminine ordinals end in ִית as with שְׁלִישִׁית (third).

11.8 (Vocabulary.

אַמָּה	cubit (distance between elbow and tip of middle finger), forearm (249)
אֵם	mother (220); feminine
בֶּגֶד	clothing, garment, covering (216)
זֶרַע	seed, offspring, descendants (229)
חָצֵר	courtyard, village, settlement (192)
לַיְלָה	night (234)
לָכֵן	therefore (200)
מוֹעֵד	appointed time (of feast), meeting place, assembly (223)
מַחֲנֶה	camp, army (215)
מַלְאָךְ	messenger, angel (213)
מַעֲשֶׂה	work, deed, act (235)
נַעַר	boy, youth, servant (240)
נַחֲלָה	inheritance, property, possession (222)
עָוֹן	transgression, iniquity, guilt, punishment (of sin) (233)
קֶרֶב	inner part(s), organ(s), body; (prep) בְּקֶרֶב in the middle of, among (227)
רַק	only, still, but, however (109)
שָׁלוֹם	peace, welfare, wholeness, deliverance (237)
שָׁם	there, then, at that time (835)
תָּמִיד	continually (104)

11.9 **Martin Luther (1483-1546): On the Importance of the Biblical Languages**. Martin Luther was the German leader of the Protestant Reformation, who, by the study of the Scriptures in their original languages, found the grace of God and the freedom from sin that only comes by that grace. On this ground, he became convinced that reading Greek and Hebrew was one of the greatest privileges and responsibilities of the Reformation preacher. Few arguments for the importance of biblical languages are clearer than Luther's 1524 treatise, "To the Councilmen of All Cities in Germany That They Establish and Maintain Christian Schools." The following is an excerpt from this work.

And let us be sure of this we will not long preserve the gospel without the languages. The languages are the sheath in which this sword of the Spirit is contained; they are the casket in which this jewel is enshrined; they are the vessel in which this wine is held; they are the larder in which this food is stored; and, as the gospel itself points out, they are the baskets in which are kept these loaves and fishes and fragments. If through our neglect we let the languages go (which God forbid!), we shall ... lose the gospel ...

Experience too has proved this and still gives evidence of it. For as soon as the languages declined to the vanishing point, after the apostolic age, the gospel and faith and Christianity itself declined more and more ... On the other hand, now that the languages have been revived, they are bringing with them so bright a light and accomplishing such great things that the whole world stands amazed and has to acknowledge that we have the gospel just as pure and undefiled as the apostles had it, that it has been wholly restored to its original purity, far beyond what it was in the days of St. Jerome and St. Augustine ...

Yes, you say, but many of the fathers were saved and even became teachers without the languages. That is true. But how do you account for the fact that they so often erred in the Scriptures?... Even St. Augustine himself is obliged to confess... that a Christian teacher who is to expound the Scriptures must know Greek and Hebrew in addition to Latin. Otherwise, it is impossible to avoid constant stumbling; indeed, there are plenty of problems to work out even when one is well versed in the languages.

There is a vast difference therefore between a simple preacher of the faith and a person who expounds Scripture, or, as St. Paul puts it, a prophet. A simple preacher (it is true) has so many clear passages and texts available through translations that he can know and teach Christ, lead a holy life, and preach to others. But when it comes to interpreting Scripture, and working with it on your own, and disputing with those who cite it incorrectly, he is unequal to the task; that cannot be done without languages. Now there must always be such prophets in the Christian church who can dig into Scripture, expound it, and carry on disputations. A saintly life and right doctrine are not enough. Hence languages are absolutely and altogether necessary in the Christian church, as are the prophets or interpreters; although it is not necessary that every Christian or every preacher be such a prophet, as St. Paul points out in I Corinthians 12 and Ephesians 4 …

Since it becomes Christians then to make good use of the Holy Scriptures as their one and only book and it is a sin and a shame not to know our own book or to understand the speech and words of our God, it is a still greater sin and loss that we do not study languages, especially in these days when God is offering and giving us men and books and every facility and inducement to this study, and desires his Bible to be an open book. O how happy the dear fathers would have been if they had had our opportunity to study the languages and come thus prepared to the Holy Scriptures! What great toil and effort it cost them to gather up a few crumbs, while we with half the labor—yes, almost without any labor at all—can acquire the whole loaf! O how their effort puts our indolence to shame! Yes, how sternly God will judge our lethargy and ingratitude!

Here belongs also what St. Paul calls for in I Corinthians 14, namely, that in the Christian church all teachings must be judged. For this a knowledge of the language is needful above all else. The preacher or teacher can expound the Bible from beginning to end as he pleases, accurately or inaccurately, if there is no one there to judge whether he is doing it right or wrong. But in order to judge, one must have a knowledge of the languages; it cannot be done in any other way. Therefore, although faith and the gospel may indeed be proclaimed by simple preachers without a knowledge of languages, such preaching is flat and tame; people finally become weary and bored with it, and it falls to the ground. But where the preacher is versed in the languages, there is a freshness and vigor in his preaching, Scripture is treated in its entirety, and faith finds itself constantly renewed by a continual variety of words and illustrations. Hence, Psalm 129 likens such scriptural studies to a hunt, saying to the deer God opens the dense forests; and Psalm 1 likens them to a tree with a plentiful supply of water, whose leaves are always green.[1]

---

[1] Martin Luther, "To the Councilmen of All Cities in Germany That They Establish and Maintain Christian Schools," in *Luther's Works*, ed. W. Brandt and H. Lehman (Philadelphia: Muhlenberg, 1962) 357-366.

Chapter 12

Introduction to Hebrew Verbs

12.1 **Introduction.** At this point in your study of Hebrew, you have hopefully mastered the essential elements of Hebrew nouns and nominals. It is now time to study the Hebrew verbal system. Verbs are those words used to describe an action (he *studied*) or state of being (she *is wise*). In the Hebrew Bible, there are just over 23,000 verses. In the midst of these verses are found almost 72,000 verbs. This means that, on average, there are approximately three verbs in each verse. These statistics demonstrate that you must understand the Hebrew verbal system in terms of form, function, and meaning to succeed in the language. In this chapter, you will learn about the basic grammatical issues relating to verbs. *However, there is no need to memorize the Hebrew verbal forms in this chapter.* They are simply examples that illustrate the topics under discussion.

12.2 **Roots and Stems.** You are about to discover that many of the nouns you have memorized as vocabulary have verbal counterparts. The following nouns, for example, are listed with their verbal counterparts.

מֶלֶךְ	king	➤	מָלַךְ	to reign
דָּבָר	word	➤	דִּבֶּר	to speak
מִשְׁפָּט	judgment	➤	שָׁפַט	to judge

Notice how each pair shares a common set of consonants and related definitions. The reason for this relationship is due to the fact that they share a common root. It is very important to understand the distinction between a root and those words derived from that root. It is a distinction between root and stem. Hebrew roots are typically composed of three consonants (triconsonantal), occasionally two (biconsonantal). *A root represents the origin or simplest form from which any number of Hebrew words are derived.* From a root, therefore, any number of nouns or verbs may be derived. *A stem is the most basic form of any word derived from a root.* For example, from the triconsonantal root מלך come the noun stems מֶלֶךְ (king), מַלְכָּה (queen), מַלְכוּת (kingdom), and the verb stem מָלַךְ (to reign, be king). Once again, notice how each different word shares a common set of consonants and related definitions. This relationship is based upon the sharing of a common root. The system of deriving different words or stems from a common root should be a point of encouragement for students since it can take some of the pain out of vocabulary memorization. For additional examples of Hebrew words sharing a common root, see our *Vocabulary Guide to Biblical Hebrew* (Grand Rapids: Zondervan, 2003), pages 90-137.

12.3 **Person, Gender, and Number**. In English, a verb by itself does not have person, gender, or number (study). It must be supplied by the addition of a personal pronoun (she studied). In Hebrew, however, most verbs have person, gender, and number. These verbal characteristics are indicated in Hebrew verbs by certain patterns of inflection. For example, the verb כָּתַב means "he wrote" and the verb כָּתְבָה means "she wrote." The different endings indicate person, gender, and number. In Hebrew, therefore, a verb's person, gender, and number are usually indicated in the verbal form itself. These endings will be discussed in the following chapters. Even though most Hebrew verbs are capable of indicating person, gender, and number by themselves, they may also occur with independent personal pronouns. For example, both כָּתַבְתִּי and אֲנִי כָּתַבְתִּי are translated "I wrote." Because most Hebrew verbs by themselves can indicate person, gender, and number, the addition of an independent personal pronoun is not usually required. With regard to person, Hebrew verbs can be first person (I, we), second person (you), or third person (he, she, it, they). With regard to number, Hebrew verbs will be either singular (I, you, he, she, it) or plural (we, you, they). And with regard to gender, Hebrew verbs will be either masculine (he), feminine (she), or common, meaning either masculine or feminine (I, we).

12.4 **Chart: Summary of Person, Gender, and Number**.

Person		
	First	I, we
	Second	you
	Third	he, she, it, they
Gender	*Masculine*	referring to *masculine* subjects
	Feminine	referring to *feminine* subjects
	Common	referring to *masculine or feminine* subjects
Number	*Singular*	referring to *one* person or thing
	Plural	referring to *more than one* person or thing

12.5   **Introduction to Verbal Stems.** In the Hebrew verbal system, there are seven major stems: the Qal stem, Niphal stem, Piel stem, Pual stem, Hiphil stem, Hophal stem, and Hithpael stem. The Qal stem is the basic or simple verbal stem. From the Qal stem all other verbal stems are formed. For this reason, *the Niphal through Hithpael stems are called "derived stems" because their forms are derived or based on the Qal stem.* Verbal stems tell us two things about the action or meaning of a verb: the *type of verbal action* and the *voice of verbal action.*

In Hebrew, there are three basic categories of verbal action: simple action (to break), intensive action (to smash into pieces) and causative action (to cause to break). There are also three basic categories of verbal voice: active, passive, and reflexive. *The voice of a verb indicates the relationship between the subject of a verb and the action of the verb.* Stated differently, voice indicates whether the subject acts or is acted upon. With the active voice, the subject of the verb is performing the action of the verb. In the example "David defeated the enemy," *David* is the subject of the verb "defeated" and he is performing the action. With the passive voice, the subject of the verb is receiving the action of the verb. In the example "David *was* defeated by the enemy," David is no longer performing the action of the verb but receiving the verbal action. With the reflexive voice, the subject of the verb is both doing and receiving the action of the verb. In the example "David dressed *himself,*" David is both performing and receiving the verbal action. Notice that the sentence was rendered reflexive by using an English "reflexive" pronoun (himself).

12.6   **English and Hebrew Spelling of the Verbal Stems with Diagnostics.** The names of the Hebrew verbal stems might seem strange at first. They sound strange to us because they are the traditional Hebrew names. The Qal (קַל) is the basic verbal stem. The term "Qal" means "simple," with reference to the fact that the root is unaugmented, nothing has been added to it. The six derived stems have names that are constructed on the verbal root פעל, inflecting each in its Perfect, third masculine singular (3ms) form. You should carefully study how the names are constructed because their spelling preserves certain diagnostic points of vocalization. Note that in the following chart, you will see references to what is called a "stem vowel." In Hebrew, *the stem vowel is that vowel which is associated with the second consonant of the verbal root.*

Verb first in a clause

English Spelling		Hebrew Spelling	Spelling Diagnostics
Qal	➤	קַל	unaugmented
Niphal	➤	נִפְעַל	נִ prefix; Pathach stem vowel
Piel	➤	פִּעֵל	Hireq-Tsere vowel pattern
Pual	➤	פֻּעַל	Qibbuts-Pathach vowel pattern
Hiphil	➤	הִפְעִיל	הִ prefix; Hireq Yod stem vowel
Hophal	➤	הָפְעַל	הָ prefix;[1] Pathach stem vowel
Hithpael	➤	הִתְפַּעֵל	הִתְ prefix; Tsere stem vowel

[handwritten: Simple passive] (Niphal)
[handwritten: passive intensive] (Pual)
[handwritten: Causative verb / made something to...] (Hiphil)
[handwritten: reflexive action] (Hithpael)

12.7 **The Hebrew Verbal Stems.** In this section, we will briefly discuss the significance of the Qal and derived stems in terms of their verbal action and voice. Please note that what follows is a simple preview of basic information. These issues will receive further attention in subsequent chapters.

1. **Qal.** The Qal is the simple or basic verbal stem. Qal verbs are **Simple Active** *active* in voice, though a few passive forms do exist. The Qal stem exhibits the *simple* or unnuanced type of action. An example of a verb in the Qal stem is שָׁמַע meaning "he heard."

2. **Niphal.** The Niphal stem is used to express *simple* action with either a *passive* or *reflexive* voice. In other words, whatever a verb means in the Qal stem, it becomes passive or reflexive in the Niphal stem. An example of a verb in the Niphal stem is **Simple Passive/ Reflexive** נִשְׁמַע meaning "he *was* heard" (passive) or "he heard *himself*" (reflexive). Notice the change in spelling from שָׁמַע (Qal) to נִשְׁמַע (Niphal). The most notable difference between the two forms is the prefixing of נ to the Niphal stem. The name "Niphal" *will remind you* that every verb in the Niphal stem takes a נ prefix. This prefix is unique to the Niphal stem and so distinguishes it from the other verbal stems.

---

[1] The vowel under the ה prefix of the Hophal stem is Qamets Hatuf.

Intensive Active

3. **Piel**. The Piel stem is sometimes used to express an *intensive* type of action with an *active* voice.[2] In other words, the simple action of the Qal stem will take on some type of intensive nuance in the Piel stem. For example, the verb שָׁבַר means "he broke" in the Qal stem. The Piel form, however, is שִׁבֵּר and means "he smashed into pieces." Notice the change in spelling from שָׁבַר (Qal) to שִׁבֵּר (Piel). The distinguishing characteristics of the Piel stem are a unique vowel pattern and the presence of a Daghesh Forte in the second root consonant.

Intensive Passive

4. **Pual**. The Pual is the passive form of the Piel. The Pual stem, therefore, is used to express an *intensive* type of action with a *passive* voice. For example, the Piel verb שִׁבֵּר means "he smashed into pieces." The Pual form, however, would be שֻׁבַּר and is translated "he (it) *was* smashed into pieces." Notice how a form of the English verb "to be" (was) is used to make the translation passive. Like the Piel, the Pual stem is distinguished by the presence of a Daghesh Forte in the second consonant of the verbal root. Notice also the Qibbuts-Pathach vowel pattern in the Pual form of the verb. This vowel pattern will distinguish the Pual stem from the corresponding Piel stem form.

Causative Active

5. **Hiphil**. The Hiphil stem is used to express *causative* action with an *active* voice. For example, the verb מָלַךְ means "he was king" or "he reigned" in the Qal stem. The Hiphil form, however, is הִמְלִיךְ and means "he *caused* to reign" or "he *made* (someone) king." Notice the change in spelling from מָלַךְ (Qal) to הִמְלִיךְ (Hiphil). The most notable differences between the two forms are the prefixing of הַ to the first root consonant and the Hireq Yod stem vowel. The presence of הַ and the Hireq Yod stem vowel make identifying the Hiphil stem very easy.

---

[2] We recognize the difficulty of characterizing the varieties of action denoted by the Piel stem (also Pual and Hithpael) with a single designation like "intensive." Such a designation is, however, a helpful starting point for the beginning student. Additionally, it is legitimate to think of the factitive and iterative as "types" of intensive action.

Causative Passive

6. **Hophal**. The Hophal is the passive form of the Hiphil. The Hophal stem, therefore, is used to express *causative* action with a *passive* voice. For example, the Hiphil verb הִמְלִיךְ means "he made (someone) king." The Hophal form is הָמְלַךְ and it is translated "he *was* made king." Notice how ה is prefixed to both the Hiphil and Hophal, clearly distinguishing them from the previous stems. The Hiphil and Hophal are distinguished from one another by their prefix and stem vowels.

Intensive Reflexive

7. **Hithpael**. The Hithpael stem is used to express an *intensive* type of action with a *reflexive* (or sometimes passive) voice. For example, the verb חָבָא means "he hid" in the Qal stem. The Hithpael form is הִתְחַבֵּא and it means "he hid *himself*." Notice the drastic change in spelling from חָבָא (Qal) to הִתְחַבֵּא (Hithpael). The most notable differences between the two forms are the prefixing of הִתְ to the first root consonant and the Daghesh Forte in the second root consonant. At this point, it is helpful to note that all verbs exhibiting an intensive type of action (Piel, Pual, and Hithpael) insert a Daghesh Forte into the second consonant of the verbal root. This is a "diagnostic" feature of the intensive stems. The term "diagnostic" means that the presence of the Daghesh Forte in the second root consonant is a feature that identifies or diagnoses the intensive verbal stems. When you examine a Hebrew verb and see this diagnostic feature, you will be able to successfully identify or diagnose the verbal stem being used.

12.8 Chart: Summary of Basic Verbal Stem Meaning.

	Simple Action	*Intensive Action*	*Causative Action*
Active Voice	**Qal**	**Piel**	**Hiphil**
Passive Voice	**Niphal**	**Pual**	**Hophal**
Reflexive Voice	**Niphal**	**Hithpael**	

12.9 Summary of Verbal Translation Values. Once again, there is no need to memorize the Hebrew forms. They appear only for the sake of illustration. Review the spelling patterns and the translation values for each of the verbal stems.

Verbal Stem	Verbal Form	Translation Value
Qal	שָׁמַע	he heard
Niphal	נִשְׁמַע	he was heard
Piel	שִׁבֵּר	he smashed into pieces
Pual	שֻׁבַּר	he (it) was smashed into pieces
Hiphil	הִמְלִיךְ	he made king
Hophal	הָמְלַךְ	he was made king
Hithpael	הִתְחַבֵּא	he hid himself

It is important to note that most Hebrew verbs are not attested in each of the basic verbal stems. Some verbs are not even attested in the Qal stem. For example, the Hebrew verb meaning "to love" is אָהַב and it does not occur in the Hophal stem. Similarly, the Piel verb דִּבֶּר (to speak) does not occur in the Hiphil or Hophal stems.

12.10   Verbal Stems and Verbal Meaning. The meaning of a verb in the Qal may be different when that same verb appears in another stem. This is one of the major reasons why it is important to understand the verbal stems as presented above. For example, the Hebrew verb שָׁבַר in the Qal means "to break." This same verb in the Piel stem (שִׁבֵּר) means "to smash into pieces." In this and many other instances, the relationship between the two meanings is apparent in light of the discussion above. In other instances, however, the reason for the change in verbal meaning between the different stems is not as apparent. For example, the verb בָּרַךְ means "to kneel" in the Qal. This same verbal root in the Piel stem means "to bless." Always consult a lexicon to be certain of a verb's meaning in a given stem.

Having studied verbal stems and how they affect verbal meaning, we now turn to verbal conjugations and how they denote verbal function. In other words, *verbal stems are used to indicate verbal meaning* and *verbal conjugations are used to denote verbal function.*

12.11   Introduction to the Verbal Conjugations. In English, verbs are conjugated in order to express different verbal functions. The term "conjugation" is used to describe the inflected verbal forms that express particular verbal functions. Some verbal conjugations also express what is called "tense." The term "tense" indicates the relationship between the time of the verbal action and the time of speaking. For example, an

English verb may be conjugated in the present tense in order to express action taking place but not yet complete, that is, incomplete or *imperfective* action.

Singular: I study, you study, he/she/it studies
Plural: we study, you study, they study

This same verb may also be conjugated in the past tense in order to express action that has been completed, that is, *perfective* action.

Singular: I studied, you studied, he/she/it studied
Plural: we studied, you studied, they studied

This verb may also be conjugated in the future tense in order to express action not yet begun but expected in the future.

Singular: I will study, you will study, he/she/it will study
Plural: we will study, you will study, they will study

English verbs may also be conjugated as Participles (studying), Infinitives (to study), or Imperatives (study!). Each English verb takes on a different form (study, studies, studied, studying, to study) in order to express a different verbal function. In Hebrew, there are eight basic verbal conjugations: Perfect, Imperfect, Imperative, Cohortative, Jussive, Infinitive Construct, Infinitive Absolute, and Participle. This means that a verb in the Qal may be conjugated any one of eight different ways, depending on what verbal function the author intends. In most cases, the change in verbal function will be identifiable by a change in verbal form. Each of the derived stems (Niphal, Piel, Pual, etc.) may also be conjugated in any one of these eight different conjugations. In Hebrew, therefore, there are seven verbal stems (Qal and the derived stems) and eight verbal conjugations (Perfect, Imperfect, etc.). For example, the Qal verb שָׁמַע may be conjugated in any one of eight different ways depending on the intended function of the verb (Qal Participle, Qal Infinitive, Qal Imperative, etc.). This same verb in the Niphal stem may also be conjugated in any one of the eight different Hebrew conjugations (Niphal Participle, Niphal Infinitive, Niphal Imperative, etc.). The following chapters will take you step by step through each verbal stem and each verbal conjugation. At this point, however, it will be helpful to briefly define the function of each Hebrew verbal conjugation.

1. **Perfect.** The Perfect conjugation is used to express a *completed action* or a *state of being*. When used to describe a completed action (either in reality or in the mind of the speaker), the Hebrew Perfect may be translated by the English past tense (he studied), present perfect (he has studied), past perfect (he had studied), or future perfect (he will have studied). When used to describe a state of being, it will often be translated with the English present **Completed** tense (he is wise). The Hebrew Perfect may also be translated by **Action** the English present tense with verbs of perception or attitude (he knows, he loves). It must be emphasized that the Hebrew Perfect does not have tense (time of action) apart from context and issues of syntax. Rather, it primarily signifies aspect (type of action). The Perfect aspect designates a verbal action with its conclusion envisioned in the mind of the speaker or writer. To state it differently, *the Perfect aspect denotes completed action, whether in the past, present, or future.*

2. **Imperfect.** The Imperfect conjugation is used to express *incomplete action* and is usually translated by the English present tense (I study) or future tense (I will study). The action of the verb occurs either at the time of speaking or after the time of speaking. The Hebrew Imperfect is also used to denote habitual or customary action, whether in the past, present, or future (he prays regularly, **Incomplete** he used to pray). The Imperfect may also be rendered by one of **Action** several modal values (would, could, should, may, might, can, etc.). These modal translation values are suggested by various contextual considerations. It must also be emphasized that, like the Perfect, the Hebrew Imperfect does not have tense (time of action) apart from context and issues of syntax. It too primarily signifies aspect (type of action). The Imperfect aspect designates a verbal action for which, in the mind of the speaker or writer, the conclusion is not in view. To state it differently, *the Imperfect aspect denotes incomplete action, whether in the past, present, or future.*

3. **Imperative.** The next three conjugations (Imperative, Cohortative, and Jussive) are *volitional* conjugations, meaning they are used **2nd Person** *to express some type of command, wish, or desire.* The Imperative **Command** conjugation is used primarily to express direct commands, demanding immediate action from the one being addressed. It can also be used to request permission or communicate a request.

The Hebrew Imperative occurs only in the second person. For example, "(You) *defend* the cause of the weak!"

1st Person Volitional

4. **Cohortative.** This second volitional conjugation is used much like the Imperative, to express a wish, request, or command. It may also be used, however, to express purpose (in order to) or result (resulting in). The Cohortative conjugation occurs in the first person, for example, "*Let* me (first person singular) *honor* the Lord!" or "*Let* us (first person plural) *honor* the Lord!"

3rd Person Volitional

5. **Jussive.** The Jussive conjugation is also used to express either some type of mild command or strong wish. Strictly speaking, it occurs only in the third person, singular and plural. For example, "*May* the Lord (third person) *give* to me another son." To sum up the volitional conjugations, all three are used to express some type of command, request, or desire. Context will help determine which volitional nuance is intended by the author. The Cohortative occurs in the first person (I, we), the Imperative in the second person (you), and the Jussive in the third person (he, she, it, they).

Verbal Noun

6. **Infinitive Construct.** An Infinitive is a verbal noun. In Hebrew, there are two Infinitive forms: the Infinitive Construct and the Infinitive Absolute. The Infinitive Construct may function much like an English Infinitive, usually translated with the preposition "to" plus a verb, as in "to study" or "to learn." Like a noun, it can be used as the subject (*to study* is hard work) or object of a verb (I want *to study*). It may also be used in a number of other ways that will be detailed in chapter 20.

Verbal Noun

7. **Infinitive Absolute.** The Hebrew Infinitive Absolute has no real English counterpart. It may be used in conjunction with other verbs to emphasize or intensify the verbal action. It may also be used in the place of an Imperative to express a command. In special instances, it can be used with other verbs to express two verbal actions occurring at the same time, that is, contemporaneous action.

Verbal Adjective

8. **Participle.** A Participle is a verbal adjective. As such, it has both verbal and adjectival characteristics. Verbally, it expresses some type of verbal action such as "studying" or "learning." Adjectivally, it is used much like a Hebrew adjective: attributively, predicatively, or substantively.

12.12 **Strong and Weak Verbs**. Hebrew verbs are classified as either strong or weak. Strong verbs have no weak consonants. Weak verbs, however, have at least one weak root consonant. The weak principal consonants are the gutturals and ר. For example, the verbs כָּתַב, קָטַל and קָבַץ are strong verbs and שָׁמַע, מָצָא and עָלָה are weak verbs. The consonants י and נ are also considered weak *but only when they appear as the first consonant of the verbal root*, as in יָשַׁב and נָפַל and only in certain conjugations. Biconsonantal and Geminate verbal roots are also considered to be weak. Biconsonantal roots have two rather than three root consonants, as in קָם (he arose). Geminate roots are those in which the second and third root consonants are identical, as in סָבַב (he surrounded). When studying the various Hebrew conjugations, you will first learn the strong verb forms and then the weak verb forms. The following chart provides you with examples of weak verbal roots and their system of classification. The roman numerals that are used in their classification indicate which root letter is weak: "I" indicates the first root position; "II" the second root position; and "III" the third root position.

12.13 **The Classification of Weak Verbal Roots**.

	Verb	Description
I-Guttural	עָמַד	guttural in first root position
II-Guttural	גָּאַל	guttural in second root position
III-ח/ע	בָּרַח	ח or ע in third root position
III-א	מָצָא	א in third root position
III-ה	בָּנָה	ה in third root position
I-י	יָשַׁב	י in first root position
I-נ	נָפַל	נ in first root position
Doubly Weak	עָלָה	I-Guttural *and* III-ה (for one example)
Biconsonantal	קָם	only two root consonants[3]
Geminate	סָבַב	identical second and third consonants

12.14 **Word Order in the Hebrew Verbal Sentence**. In English, the ordering of words in a sentence helps to identify the function of those words. For example, in the sentence "Jacob loved Rachel," *Jacob* is the subject of the verb because his name precedes the verb. Additionally, *Rachel* is

---

[3] Biconsonantal verbs are also called "Hollow" or II-י/ו verbs (see 14.12).

the object of the verb because her name follows the verb. If the sentence was "Rachel loved Jacob," then *Rachel* would be the subject and *Jacob* the object because of their positions in the sentence. In English, normal word order is subject-verb-object. In Hebrew, however, normal word order for a verbal sentence is *verb-subject-object* as the following example illustrates.

$$\text{בָּרָא אֱלֹהִים אֵת הַשָּׁמַיִם וְאֵת הָאָרֶץ}$$
God created the heavens and the earth (Gen 1:1).

In this example, the verb is in first position (בָּרָא), the subject in second position (אֱלֹהִים) and the two objects follow the subject (הַשָּׁמַיִם and הָאָרֶץ). It must be acknowledged, however, that there are frequent variations and exceptions to this "normal" ordering of words in a Hebrew sentence. For example, it is not uncommon for the direct object to stand at the beginning of a Hebrew sentence for the purpose of emphasis as the following example illustrates.

$$\text{אֶת־יְהוָה אֱלֹהֶיךָ תִּירָא}$$
The Lord your God you shall fear (Deut 10:20).

In this example, observe how the direct object (אֶת־יְהוָה אֱלֹהֶיךָ) precedes the verb (תִּירָא) for the purpose of emphasis. A discussion of issues related to sentence syntax is presented in chapter 23.

12.15 Parsing Hebrew Verbs. In the following chapters, you will learn how to "parse" Hebrew verbs. Parsing is the process whereby you will identify a verb's stem, conjugation, person, gender, number, and lexical form. For example, the verb נִשְׁמַע is parsed as a Niphal Perfect third masculine singular (3ms) from שָׁמַע. You will get plenty of practice parsing verbs in the following chapters.

12.16 Lexical Form for Hebrew Verbs. The lexical form of a triconsonantal verbs is the *Qal Perfect 3ms*. This is also the form of the verb that you will be memorizing as vocabulary. With Biconsonantal verbs, however, you will memorize a different lexical form (14.12).

12.17 Summary.

1. Verbs are those words used to describe an action or state of being.

2. A *root* represents the origin or simplest form from which any number of Hebrew words are derived. Most Hebrew verbs are triconsonantal.

3. Hebrew verbs can indicate person, gender, and number by certain patterns of *inflection*.

4. Hebrew verbs may appear in seven different *stems*: the Qal and six derived stems (Niphal, Piel, Pual, Hiphil, Hophal, Hithpael). These stems indicate verbal action (simple, intensive, causative) and verbal voice (active, passive, reflexive).

5. Hebrew verbs may be inflected in eight different conjugations: Perfect, Imperfect, Imperative, Cohortative, Jussive, Infinitive Construct, Infinitive Absolute, and Participle. The term "conjugation" is used to describe the inflected verbal forms that express particular verbal functions.

6. At the end of this chapter, we have included an illustration that attempts to represent graphically the relationship between Hebrew roots, stems, and conjugations.

7. Hebrew verbs are classified as either *strong* or *weak*. Weak verbs are those verbs having at least one weak root consonant. Strong verbs have no weak consonants.

8. Though frequent exceptions and variations do exist, the normal word order for a Hebrew verbal sentence is *verb-subject-object*.

9. The process of "parsing" a verb involves the identification of the verbal stem, conjugation, person, gender, number, and lexical form.

10. The lexical form of a triconsonantal verbs is the *Qal Perfect 3ms*.

12.18 Vocabulary.

Verbs *caloky*

אָכַל	to eat, consume (820)
אָמַר	to say, mention, think (5,316)
הָלַךְ	to go, walk (metaphorically, behave), die, pass away (1,554)
הָיָה	to be, become, happen, occur (3,576)
יָצָא	to go out, go forth, come out, come forth (1,076)
יָשַׁב	to sit (down), remain, dwell, inhabit (1,088)
נָתַן	to give, put, set (2,014)
עָשָׂה	to do, make, create (2,632)
רָאָה	to see, perceive, understand (1,311)
שָׁבַת	to stop, cease, rest (71)
שָׁמַע	to hear, listen to, understand, obey (1,165)

Nouns

אָרוֹן	ark, chest, coffin (202)
מִנְחָה	gift, offering, tribute (211)
שַׁבָּת	Sabbath, period of rest (111)

Other

אַךְ	only, surely, nevertheless (161)
אַל	no, not (729)
אִם	if (1,070)
לֹא	no, not (5,189)

12.19 Ulrich Zwingli (1484-1531): Languages are Gifts of the Holy Ghost. The beginning of the Reformation in Switzerland dates from the New Testament lectures of Ulrich Zwingli in 1519, just three years after his own study of the Scriptures led him to question and finally renounce the teaching of the Roman Church. Foundational to all of Zwingli's ministry was his conviction that the Scriptures bear sole authority in the life of the Christian.

Zwingli wrote a treatise on the proper godly education of youth, within which he emphasizes the necessity for the biblical languages. The following is an excerpt from this treatise.

Once a young man is instructed in the solid virtue which is formed by faith, it follows that he will regulate himself and richly adorn himself from within: for only he whose whole life is ordered finds it easy to give help and counsel to others.

But a man cannot rightly order his own soul unless he exercises himself day and night in the Word of God. He can do that most readily if he is well versed in such languages as Hebrew and Greek, for a right understanding of the Old Testament is difficult without the one, and a right understanding of the New is equally difficult without the other.

But we are instructing those who have already learned the rudiments, and everywhere Latin has the priority. In these circumstances I do not think that Latin should be altogether neglected. For an understanding of Holy Scripture it is of less value than Hebrew and Greek, but for other purposes it is just as useful. And it often happens that we have to do the business of Christ amongst those who speak Latin. No Christian should use these languages simply for his own profit or pleasure: for languages are gifts of the Holy Ghost.

After Latin we should apply ourselves to Greek. We should do this for the sake of the New Testament, as I have said already. And if I may say so, to the best of my knowledge the Greeks have always handled the doctrine of Christ better than the Latins. For that reason we should always direct our young men to this source. But in respect of Greek as well as Latin we should take care to garrison our souls with innocence and faith, for in these tongues there are many things which we learn only to our hurt: wantonness, ambition, violence, cunning, vain philosophy and the like. But the soul … can steer safely past all these if it is only forewarned, that is, if at the first sound of the voices it pays heed to the warning: Hear this in order to shun and not to receive.

I put Hebrew last because Latin is in general use and Greek follows conveniently. Otherwise I would willingly have given Hebrew precedence, for in many places even amongst the Greeks those who are ignorant of Hebrew forms of speech have great difficulty in attempting to draw out the true sense of Scripture. But it is not my purpose to speak exhaustively of these languages.

If a man would penetrate to the heavenly wisdom, with which no earthly wisdom ought rightly to be considered, let alone compared, it is with such arms that he must be equipped. And even then he must still approach with a humble and thirsting spirit.[4]

---

[4] Ulrich Zwingli, "On the Education of Youth," in *Zwingli and Bullinger*, The Library of Christian Classics: Ichthus Edition, ed. G. W. Bromiley (Philadelphia: Westminster, 1953) 108-9.

Verbal Root, Stems & Conjugations

Root
קטל

Qal Stem
קָטַל

Derived Stems

Niphal	Piel	Pual	Hiphil	Hophal	Hithpael
נִקְטַל	קִטֵּל	קֻטַּל	הִקְטִיל	הָקְטַל	הִתְקַטֵּל

Verbal Conjugations

Perfect
Imperfect
Imperative
Cohortative
Jussive
Inf Construct
Inf Absolute
Participle

Chapter 13

Qal Perfect - Strong Verbs

13.1 **Introduction.** Of the almost 72,000 verbs in the Hebrew Bible, over two-thirds (50,699 verbs) occur in the Qal stem. For this reason, in the following chapters, significant attention will be given to the various forms of the Qal stem. Only after the Qal stem has been mastered will the derived stems be studied. In this grammar, memorization of paradigms will be kept to a minimum. Only in your study of the Qal stem will paradigm memorization be required. Once we move into the derived stems, no further paradigm memorization is required. Instead, you will learn a system of *diagnostic* indicators whereby identification of the derived stems and their conjugations is made possible without the burden of memorizing paradigms. The use of *diagnostic* indicators is an important and unique feature of this grammar. It should make learning the Hebrew verbal system much easier than the traditional method of paradigm memorization for the conjugations of the derived stems.

13.2 **The Qal Stem.** The Qal is the simple or basic verbal stem. Qal verbs are *active* in voice, though a few passive forms do exist. The Qal stem also exhibits a *simple* or unnuanced type of action. An example of a verb in the Qal stem is קָטַל meaning "he killed." The simple action of the Qal stem is further divided into transitive, intransitive, and stative.

1. *Transitive.* Transitive verbs may take a direct object. In the example "the prophet wrote the book," the word "book" is the direct object of the verb "wrote" because it receives the verbal action.

2. *Intransitive.* Intransitive verbs cannot take a direct object. The English verb "perish," for example, as in "the king perished in the battle," cannot take a direct object. Other examples of intransitive verbs include "to live," "to die," and "to fast."

3. *Stative.* Stative verbs are used to describe a state of being. In the example, "the priest is old," the verbal construction "is old" describes the state or condition of the subject (the priest). In English, a stative (or state-of-being) idea is expressed with a form of the verb "to be" (is) and an adjective (old). In Hebrew, a stative idea may be expressed through various verbs themselves,

such as כָּבֵד (to be heavy) and קָטֹן (to be small). Most stative verbs are considered to be intransitive because they cannot take a direct object.

13.3   **The Perfect Conjugation.** The Perfect conjugation is used to express a *completed action* or *state of being.* When used to describe a completed action (either in reality or in the mind of the speaker), the Hebrew Perfect may be translated by the English past tense (he studied), present perfect (he has studied), past perfect (he had studied), or future perfect (he will have studied). When used to describe a state of being, it will be translated with the English present tense (he is wise) or past tense (he was wise). The Hebrew Perfect may also be translated by the English present tense with verbs of perception or attitude (he knows, he loves). It must be emphasized that the Hebrew Perfect does not have tense (time of action) apart from context and issues of syntax. Rather, it primarily signifies aspect (type of action). The Perfect aspect designates a verbal action with its conclusion envisioned in the mind of the speaker or writer. To state it differently, *the Perfect aspect denotes completed action, whether in the past, present, or future.*

13.4   **Introduction to Qal Perfect Strong Verbs.** The Perfect conjugation is sometimes called the "suffix conjugation." It has been called the suffix conjugation because different inflectional endings or *sufformatives* are added to the verbal root in order to indicate person, gender, and number. *The following Qal Perfect paradigm must be memorized with a view to both writing and oral recitation.* When writing out the paradigm, exact spelling of all consonants, vowels, and accent marks is required. When practicing oral recitation, be as clear and precise as possible. Be sure to make a distinction in pronunciation, for example, between the Qamets and Pathach. This type of precision will aid in the spelling of subsequently encountered verbal forms. In the following paradigm, both the complete verbal paradigm and the Perfect sufformatives are listed together. This should help you to identify the distinctive endings used to indicate person, gender, and number. In every Perfect conjugation of the Qal and derived stems (Niphal, Piel, etc.), the sufformatives are the same. For this reason, it is important to memorize these endings now.

13.5   The Qal Perfect Paradigm of the Strong Verb.

	Sufformative	*Perfect*	*Translation*
3ms		קָטַל	he killed
3fs	ה ָ	קָטְלָה	she killed
2ms	תָּ	קָטַלְתָּ	you killed
2fs	תְּ	קָטַלְתְּ	you killed
1cs	תִּי	קָטַלְתִּי	I killed
3cp	וּ	קָטְלוּ	they killed
2mp	תֶּם	קְטַלְתֶּם	you killed
2fp	תֶּן	קְטַלְתֶּן	you killed
1cp	נוּ	קָטַלְנוּ	we killed

13.6   Notes on the Qal Perfect Paradigm of the Strong Verb.

1. The ordering of this paradigm might seem a bit unusual. The presentation of forms moves from third person to second and first person, singular then plural. Notice how the paradigm begins with the third masculine singular (3ms) form, קָטַל. This is the *lexical form.* Because the third masculine singular form is also the lexical form, its definition may be listed as "to kill" in the lexicon. It is, however, never translated this way when used in a sentence. In a sentence, קָטַל translates "he killed." This is also the only Perfect form that does not have a sufformative. Most strong triconsonantal verbal roots follow this same vowel pattern in the third masculine singular form. The following graphic illustrates the common vowel pattern of the Qal Perfect 3ms strong verb.

Qal Perfect 3ms
Strong Verb
קָטַל

2. With regard to gender, three forms of the Perfect conjugation are listed as *common, meaning not inflected for gender.* The common forms are first person singular (קָטַלְתִּי) and plural (קָטַלְנוּ) and

third person plural (קָטְלוּ). As common forms, these verbs may be used with either masculine or feminine subjects.

3. Once you have mastered the spelling and pronunciation of the Qal Perfect paradigm listed above, you are encouraged to practice the Perfect inflection with other strong verbs. The following verbs are given as examples for practice: יָשַׁב (to sit, dwell, inhabit), זָכַר (to remember), כָּתַב (to write), שָׁמַר (to keep, observe), and קָבַץ (to gather). Remember, both the vocalization (vowel pattern) and sufformatives (inflectional endings) will remain the same for these verbs. Only the root consonants will change as you work with the different verbs. In order to show the uniformity of these verbal forms, their full paradigms are presented in the next section.

4. Note the presence of the Metheg in the 3fs (קָטְלָה) and 3cp (קָטְלוּ) forms, which serves to identify the vowel as Qamets and *not* Qamets Hatuf.

13.7 The Qal Perfect Paradigm of Other Strong Verbs. Based on your memorization of the קָטַל paradigm above, you should be able to generate the full Qal Perfect paradigm for each of the following strong verbs. Only the verbal root consonants will change.

	יָשַׁב *to dwell*	זָכַר *to remember*	כָּתַב *to write*	שָׁמַר *to keep*	קָבַץ *to gather*
3ms	יָשַׁב	זָכַר	כָּתַב	שָׁמַר	קָבַץ
3fs	יָשְׁבָה	זָכְרה	כָּתְבה	שָׁמְרה	קָבְצה
2ms	יָשַׁבְתָּ	זָכַרְתָּ	כָּתַבְתָּ	שָׁמַרְתָּ	קָבַצְתָּ
2fs	יָשַׁבְתְּ	זָכַרְתְּ	כָּתַבְתְּ	שָׁמַרְתְּ	קָבַצְתְּ
1cs	יָשַׁבְתִּי	זָכַרְתִּי	כָּתַבְתִּי	שָׁמַרְתִּי	קָבַצְתִּי
3cp	יָשְׁבוּ	זָכְרוּ	כָּתְבוּ	שָׁמְרוּ	קָבְצוּ
2mp	יְשַׁבְתֶּם	זְכַרְתֶּם	כְּתַבְתֶּם	שְׁמַרְתֶּם	קְבַצְתֶּם
2fp	יְשַׁבְתֶּן	זְכַרְתֶּן	כְּתַבְתֶּן	שְׁמַרְתֶּן	קְבַצְתֶּן
1cp	יָשַׁבְנוּ	זָכַרְנוּ	כָּתַבְנוּ	שָׁמַרְנוּ	קָבַצְנוּ

13.8 Verbal Roots Ending in ת. When a verbal root ending in ת receives a sufformative beginning with ת, the two identical consonants become one consonant with a Daghesh Forte. In other words, תת is written as

תּ. As you have observed from the above paradigms, five of the Perfect sufformatives begin with תּ. These five Perfect forms of the Hebrew verb כָּרַת (to cut) illustrate this point.

כָּרַ֫תָּ	2ms	you cut
כָּרַתְּ	2fs	you cut
כָּרַ֫תִּי	1cs	I cut
כְּרַתֶּם	2mp	you cut
כְּרַתֶּן	2fp	you cut

As you can see, the two identical consonants have become one consonant. The final תּ of the verbal root has assimilated into the initial תּ of the Perfect sufformatives. The presence of the first (assimilated) תּ is indicated by the placement of the Daghesh Forte in the תּ of the sufformatives; תתּ is written as תּ.

13.9   **Verbal Roots Ending in נ.** Similar to the discussion in the preceding section, when a verbal root ending in נ receives a Perfect sufformative beginning with נ, the two identical consonants become one consonant with Daghesh Forte. The only sufformative that begins with נ is the 1cp (נוּ). Observe, therefore, that the 1cp form of שָׁכַן (to dwell) is written as שָׁכַ֫נּוּ. You would expect to see two Nuns in this form, the last letter of the verbal root and the first letter of the 1cp sufformative. The two identical consonants, however, become one consonant; ננ is written as נּ.

This process of assimilation of נ in the 1cp form is also observable in those Perfect forms that have sufformatives beginning with תּ. In other words, נת can also become תּ. For example, the 1cs form of the verb נָתַן (to give) is נָתַ֫תִּי. The final נ of the verbal root has assimilated into the תּ of the sufformative and its presence is represented by the Daghesh Forte (see 14.18 for the Qal Perfect paradigm of נָתַן).

13.10   **Stative Verbs: Perfect.** You learned above that stative verbs describe a state of being. More specifically, they describe the state or condition of the subject (he is old, she is wise) rather than describing a verbal action (he wrote, she observed).[1] Stative verbs are classified by their stem vowel. *The stem vowel is the vowel that is associated with the second root consonant.* For example, in the strong verb paradigms above, the stem

---

[1] Most stative verbs are intransitive, that is, they do not take a direct object. Though rare, certain verbs that are spelled like a stative may be transitive, as illustrated by שָׂנֵא (to hate). This verb can take a direct object.

3. With the Holem-Stative, an o-class stem vowel appears throughout the paradigm (except in the 3fs and 3cp). The only change in this paradigm, therefore, is the o-class stem vowel. In every other way, it is vocalized just like the regular strong verb. Note the o-class vowel Qamets Hatuf in the 2mp (קְטָנְתֶּם) and 2fp (קְטָנְתֶּן) forms. You should also note that in the 1cp form (קָטֹנּוּ), the נ of the verbal root has assimilated into the נ of the Perfect sufformative and is represented by the Daghesh Forte.

4. Stative verbs are closely related to their corresponding adjectives. For example, the form זָקֵן is either the Qal Perfect 3ms stative verb (he is old) or the masculine singular adjective (old). Note the following additional examples.

Stative Verb *Qal Perfect 3ms*		*Adjective* *Masculine Singular*	
כָּבֵד	to be heavy	כָּבֵד	heavy
מָלֵא	to be full	מָלֵא	full
טָמֵא	to be unclean	טָמֵא	unclean
רָעֵב	to be hungry	רָעֵב	hungry

The difference, however, between a stative verb and its corresponding adjective is that one is inflected as a verb (above) and the other as an adjective: כָּבֵד (ms), כְּבֵדִים (mp), כְּבֵדָה (fs), כְּבֵדוֹת (fp). Note that identical forms exist only in the Qal Perfect 3ms and masculine singular adjective (כָּבֵד). In this case, you will need to rely on context in order to correctly identify the form. The Qal Perfect 3fs (כָּבְדָה) and feminine singular adjective (כְּבֵדָה) are similar but should not be confused.

13.11 Parsing. The parsing of Perfect verbs involves the identification of the verbal stem, conjugation, person, gender, number, and verbal root. When parsing, give the appropriate information in the proper order as the following examples illustrate. Though it is given below, translation is not a required part of parsing information.

זָכַרְתִּי	Qal Perfect 1cs	זָכַר	I remembered
שָׁמַרְתְּ	Qal Perfect 2fs	שָׁמַר	you observed

13.12 The Negative Particle לֹא. Perfect (and Imperfect) verbs are negated with the particle לֹא, usually translated "not." It may also be spelled לוֹא.[2] The negative particle is always placed immediately before the verb. The following examples illustrate how this particle is used.

לֹא שְׁמַרְתֶּם אֶת־הַתּוֹרוֹת   You did *not* observe the laws.

לֹא זָכַרְתָּ אֶת־הַבְּרִית   You did *not* remember the covenant.

13.13 The Particle הִנֵּה. The word הִנֵּה (also as הֵן and הֶן־) is commonly translated "behold" in many, often older, translations. In vocabulary, this is the translation value that is to be memorized and it is the basic meaning given in most standard lexicons. Translated in this way, הִנֵּה could be called a demonstrative interjection, but this is only one of its many uses and nuances. This particle has no exact equivalent in English.

הִנֵּה appears over 1,000 times in the Hebrew Bible. It can stand alone or take Type 1 pronominal suffixes (those attached to singular nouns). The attested forms with pronominal suffixes are presented in the following chart.

1cs	הִנֶּנִּי/הִנְנִי	*1cp*	הִנֶּנּוּ/הִנְנוּ
2ms	הִנְּךָ	*2mp*	הִנְּכֶם
2fs	הִנֵּךְ	*2fp*	
3ms	הִנּוֹ	*3mp*	הִנָּם

While the particle הִנֵּה is used in a number of different ways, three common uses are detailed below.

1. The particle הִנֵּה may be used to add emphasis or to stress the importance of something (demonstrative interjection).

וַיַּרְא אֱלֹהִים אֶת־כָּל־אֲשֶׁר עָשָׂה וְהִנֵּה־טוֹב מְאֹד

And God saw all that he had made, and
behold, (it was) very good (Gen 1:31).

הִנֵּה עֵין יְהוָה אֶל־יְרֵאָיו

Behold, the eye of the Lord is upon
the ones who fear him (Ps 33:18).

---

[2] The negative particle לֹא occurs 5,193 times in the Hebrew Bible. It appears with the full spelling לוֹא 188 times.

2. The particle הִנֵּה may be used to indicate the immediate presence of someone or something with an emphasis on immediacy and urgency (predicator of existence).

וְהִנֵּה אָנֹכִי עִמָּךְ

And *behold*, I am with you (Gen 28:15).

וַיֹּאמֶר הִנֵּנִי

And he said, "*I am here*" (Gen 22:1). The form הִנֵּנִי (literally, "behold me") is the particle הִנֵּה with 1cs pronominal suffix.

3. The particle הִנֵּה may be used to introduce a fact or situation on which a subsequent statement is based.

וַיֹּאמֶר שְׁמוּאֵל אֶל־כָּל־יִשְׂרָאֵל הִנֵּה שָׁמַעְתִּי בְקֹלְכֶם
לְכֹל אֲשֶׁר־אֲמַרְתֶּם לִי וָאַמְלִיךְ עֲלֵיכֶם מֶלֶךְ

And Samuel said to all of Israel, "*Behold,* I have listened to all that you have said to me and (therefore) I have caused a king to reign over you" (1 Sam 12:1).

הִנֵּה־נָא יָדַעְתִּי כִּי אִשָּׁה יְפַת־מַרְאֶה אָתְּ וְהָיָה כִּי־יִרְאוּ
אֹתָךְ הַמִּצְרִים . . . וְהָרְגוּ אֹתִי וְאֹתָךְ יְחַיּוּ

Behold, I know that you are a woman with a beautiful appearance and (so) when the Egyptians see you . . . they will kill me but let you live (Gen 12:11-12).

13.14 Summary.

1. The Qal stem is the simple or basic verbal stem. It is used to express *simple action* with an *active voice*.

2. The simple action of the Qal stem may be *transitive* (may take a direct object), *intransitive* (cannot take a direct object), or *stative* (describing a state of being).

3. The Perfect conjugation is used to express a *completed action* and is translated with the English past tense (also with the English present perfect, past perfect, and future perfect tenses). It may also be used to describe a *state of being* and, as such, will be translated with the English past or present tense.

4. The Perfect conjugation is also called the "suffix conjugation" because different inflectional endings or *sufformatives* are added to the verbal root in order to indicate person, gender, and number.

5. You must memorize the Qal Perfect paradigm of the strong verb. You must also memorize the Perfect sufformatives.

6. When a verbal root ending in תּ receives a sufformative beginning with תּ, the two identical consonants become one consonant with a Daghesh Forte; תת is written as תּ (כָּרַֽתָּ).

7. When a verbal root ending in נ receives a Perfect sufformative beginning with נ, the two identical consonants become one consonant with Daghesh Forte; ננ is written as נּ (שָׁכַ֫נּוּ). This final נ of the verbal root may also assimilate into the initial תּ of those sufformatives that begin with תּ, that is, נת is written as תּ (נָתַ֫תִּי).

8. Stative verbs are classified by their stem vowel. *The stem vowel is the vowel that is associated with the second root consonant.* The Pathach-Stative (גָּדַל) is conjugated just like the regular strong verb. The Tsere-Stative has a Tsere stem vowel only in the Qal Perfect 3ms (כָּבֵד). The Holem-Stative has an o-class stem vowel in all forms (קָטֹן), except the 3fs and 3cp.

9. Perfect (and Imperfect) verbs are negated with the particle לֹא. This particle is always placed immediately before the verb.

10. The particle הִנֵּה is commonly translated as "behold." It may be used to add emphasis (demonstrative interjection), to indicate the immediate presence of someone or something (predicator of existence), or to introduce a fact or situation upon which a subsequent statement is based.

13.15 Vocabulary.

Verbs

בָּרַךְ	to bless (327)
זָכַר	to remember, recall, call to mind, mention (235)
זָקֵן	to be(come) old (26)
חָזַק	to be(come) strong, grow firm, have courage (290)
יָדַע	to know, have understanding, know sexually (956)
כָּבֵד	to be heavy, be honored (114)
כָּתַב	to write (upon), register, record (225)
מָלֵא	to be full, fill (252)

מָלַךְ   to be(come) king or queen, reign, rule (350)

מָצָא   to find (out), reach, obtain (457)

פָּקַד   to attend, pay attention to, take care of, number, appoint, visit (304)

שָׁכַב   to lie down, have sexual intercourse (213)

שָׁלַח   to send, stretch out (854)

שָׁמַר   to watch (over), guard, keep, observe, protect (469)

13.16 At Your Service. הִנֵּה is a particle that may mark temporal and spatial immediacy. Typically found in direct discourse, this particle often appears with a pronominal suffix to emphasize the subject who is available *here and now*. The traditional translation "behold" is not only outdated in modern English but it fails to convey the full freight of meaning this common particle carries. For example, הִנֵּנִי may be translated "Here I am" or "I'm ready now" or, more colloquially, "At your service."

This simple response is a motif in the story of the binding of Isaac. When God prepares to test Abraham, he calls his covenant partner by name. The respectful response is הִנֵּנִי (Gen 22:1). When Isaac wants an explanation for their journey, he calls his father and gets the same response: הִנֵּנִי (22:7). At the point in the story when the angel calls to Abraham, his answer again is הִנֵּנִי (22:11). Abraham is rewarded for his unqualified availability and unhesitating readiness to obey, qualities implicit in the simple response הִנֵּנִי. This is the response Samuel gives first to Eli and then to the Lord when he is called in the night (1 Sam 3). It is also the response Isaiah gives to the question "Whom shall I send?" in Isa 6:8: *"Here I am. Send me!"*

For a sense of immediacy, an author will often use the construction הִנֵּה (often with a suffix) plus a Participle. For example, Yahweh says to Noah in Gen 6:17, *"I am about to* bring the flood" (וַאֲנִי הִנְנִי מֵבִיא אֶת־הַמַּבּוּל). No prophet uses this form more than Jeremiah (some 150 times), who is intent on emphasizing the *imminence* of God's judgment. For example, Jer 11:11 reads, *"Surely I am about to* bring upon them evil" (הִנְנִי מֵבִיא אֲלֵיהֶם רָעָה). The most common use of this construction in Jeremiah (and throughout the Old Testament) is with the verb בּוֹא. Jeremiah says twenty-one times, "The days are approaching when ..." (הִנֵּה יָמִים בָּאִים). Although this phrase typically introduces the threat of judgment, the good news in Jeremiah is that *God's grace is also imminent.* In 23:5 God promises the coming of a Righteous Branch; in 30:3, the restoration of their fortunes; and in 31:31, a new covenant. In each of these verses, הִנֵּה is also used.

Tim Laniak
Associate Professor of Old Testament
Gordon-Conwell Theological Seminary
Charlotte, North Carolina

Chapter 14

Qal Perfect - Weak Verbs

14.1 **Introduction.** Now that you have studied the Qal Perfect forms of the strong verb, we turn to the Qal Perfect inflection of various weak verb types. In chapter 12, you learned that weak verbs are those verbs having one or more weak root consonants. The presence of a weak consonant in a verbal root can cause changes in the vocalization or consonantal spelling of the verb. In order to identify or parse weak verb forms successfully, these changes must be studied and, in many cases, memorized. All such weak variations are identifiable only in comparison with the strong verb form. You should not work through this chapter of the grammar, therefore, until you have mastered the Qal Perfect strong verb paradigm in the previous chapter.

14.2 **I-Guttural, II-Guttural and III-ח/ע Weak Verbs.** I-Guttural verbs have a guttural for the first root consonant, as in עָמַד meaning "to stand." II-Guttural weak verbs have a guttural for the second root consonant, as in בָּחַר meaning "to choose." III-ח/ע weak verbs have either ח or ע for the third root consonant, as in לָקַח meaning "to take" or שָׁמַע meaning "to hear." These weak verbs are studied together because they exhibit a similar type of change compared to the strong verb paradigm. The changes in the I-Guttural and II-Guttural paradigms are minor and you have already learned the rule that governs them. It has to do with the relationship between gutturals and the Vocal Shewa. You will recall from section 3.6 that *a guttural cannot take a Vocal Shewa but prefers the reduced a-vowel, Hateph Pathach.* For this reason, the few Vocal Shewas that occur in the strong verb paradigm will change to a Hateph Pathach when the strong consonant associated with these Shewas is replaced by a guttural consonant. In the three weak paradigms listed below, there are only five total changes. The strong verb paradigm is also included for comparison. *Please note that, despite any changes in vocalization because of the presence of a guttural consonant, the Perfect sufformatives do not change.*

	I-Guttural	*II-Guttural*	*III-ח/ע*	*Strong*
3ms	עָמַד	בָּחַר	שָׁמַע	קָטַל
3fs	עָמְדָה	בָּחֲרָה	שָׁמְעָה	קָטְלָה
2ms	עָמַ֫דְתָּ	בָּחַ֫רְתָּ	שָׁמַ֫עְתָּ	קָטַ֫לְתָּ
2fs	עָמַדְתְּ	בָּחַרְתְּ	שָׁמַעַתְּ	קָטַלְתְּ
1cs	עָמַ֫דְתִּי	בָּחַ֫רְתִּי	שָׁמַ֫עְתִּי	קָטַ֫לְתִּי
3cp	עָמְדוּ	בָּחֲרוּ	שָׁמְעוּ	קָטְלוּ
2mp	עֲמַדְתֶּם	בְּחַרְתֶּם	שְׁמַעְתֶּם	קְטַלְתֶּם
2fp	עֲמַדְתֶּן	בְּחַרְתֶּן	שְׁמַעְתֶּן	קְטַלְתֶּן
1cp	עָמַ֫דְנוּ	בָּחַ֫רְנוּ	שָׁמַ֫עְנוּ	קָטַ֫לְנוּ

14.3   I-Guttural, II-Guttural and III-ח/ע Weak Notes. The following notes and observations will help as you work through these paradigms.

1. In the I-Guttural and II-Guttural paradigms, the Vocal Shewas have changed to the reduced a-vowel, Hateph Pathach, because of the presence of the guttural consonants (עֲמַדְתֶּם, עֲמַדְתֶּן, בָּחֲרָה, בָּחֲרוּ). Because the changes in vocalization are minor and follow a standard rule, there is no need to memorize the I-Guttural and II-Guttural paradigms listed above. You should memorize, however, the rule governing these changes. Once again, it is important to have first memorized the Qal Perfect strong verb paradigm. If you know the strong verb paradigm and the rule governing the gutturals and Vocal Shewa, then you will not have to memorize these weak verb paradigms.

2. In the III-ח/ע paradigm, the Silent Shewa under the guttural of the 2fs form שָׁמַעַתְּ has changed to Pathach. This is the only change that occurs in this weak verb class. There is no need to memorize the full paradigm on account of this minor change. You should simply be aware of the anomaly.

14.4   III-א Weak Verbs. These weak verbs have א for the third root consonant, as in מָצָא meaning "to find." The changes in this type of weak verb are considerable compared to the last three weak verb classes. You will recall from section 3.9 that an א is silent when there is no vowel under it, as in the noun חַטָּאת (sin). With III-א weak verbs, the א is silent in almost every inflected form. For this reason, the changes in vocalization are significant when compared to the strong verb paradigm. Because these changes are so pronounced, *memorization of the III-א paradigm is required.*

	III-א	Strong
3ms	מָצָא	קָטַל
3fs	מָצְאָה	קָטְלָה
2ms	מָצָ֫אתָ	קָטַ֫לְתָּ
2fs	מָצָאת	קָטַלְתְּ
1cs	מָצָ֫אתִי	קָטַ֫לְתִּי
3cp	מָצְאוּ	קָטְלוּ
2mp	מְצָאתֶם	קְטַלְתֶּם
2fp	מְצָאתֶן	קְטַלְתֶּן
1cp	מָצָ֫אנוּ	קָטַ֫לְנוּ

14.5   III-א Weak Notes. The following notes and observations will help as you work through the III-א weak verb paradigm.

1. The differences begin with the first form in the paradigm. The 3ms form (מָצָא) does not have the standard vowel pattern previously illustrated for all strong triconsonantal verbal forms. All III-א and III-ה weak verbs (which will be studied in the next section) exhibit the following pattern in their 3ms or lexical form.

Qal Perfect 3ms
III-א/ III-ה
בָּנָה/ מָצָא

2. The stem vowel (the vowel under the second root consonant) has changed from Pathach to Qamets in every form in the above paradigm except in the two forms whose stem vowel is Vocal Shewa (3fs and 3cp).

3. Because of the quiescent א, the expected Silent Shewa under the third root consonant of many of the inflected forms is no longer necessary.

4. You will notice that the Daghesh Lene normally in the initial consonant of the five sufformatives beginning with a תָּ, is absent. For example, the 1cs sufformative תִּי has become תִי, losing the Daghesh Lene. This loss is occasioned by the quiescing of the א in pronunciation. When this happens, the ת is preceded by a vowel sound and, therefore, loses the Daghesh Lene. Remember, however, that though the א is not pronounced, it is essential to the spelling of the word.

5. The changes in this paradigm are significant enough to warrant memorization of the entire paradigm. Be certain that you can recite and write the full Qal Perfect paradigm of מָצָא (to find).

14.6 **III-ה Weak Verbs**. These weak verbs have ה for the third root consonant, as in בָּנָה meaning "to build." As with III-א weak verbs, the changes in this weak class are considerable compared to the strong verb paradigm. The most significant change in this paradigm is the loss of the final ה root consonant in every form. For this reason, and because of the frequency of III-ה verbs, *memorization of the following paradigm is required*.

	III-ה	*Strong*
3ms	בָּנָה	קָטַל
3fs	בָּנְתָה	קָטְלָה
2ms	בָּנִיתָ	קָטַׄלְתָּ
2fs	בָּנִית	קָטַלְתְּ
1cs	בָּנִֽיתִי	קָטַׄלְתִּי
3cp	בָּנוּ	קָטְלוּ
2mp	בְּנִיתֶם	קְטַלְתֶּם
2fp	בְּנִיתֶן	קְטַלְתֶּן
1cp	בָּנִֽינוּ	קָטַׄלְנוּ

14.7 III-ה Weak Notes.

1. The vowel pattern learned for III-א weak verbs is the same for III-ה weak verbs in the 3ms.

2. The irregularities of this weak verb class are occasioned by the loss of the final ה *in every form of the paradigm*. The ה in the 3ms form (בָּנָה) is not a root consonant but rather a vowel letter (also called a *mater lectionis*) used for the final vowel of this form (2.7).

3. Another unusual feature of this paradigm is the ת in the 3fs form (בָּנְתָה). This ת will distinguish the 3fs form from the 3ms form.

4. It is important to observe that all second and first person forms, both singular and plural, have a distinctive or diagnostic stem vowel. In each of these forms, the stem vowel is Hireq Yod (for example, בָּנִיתָ). It is helpful to understand that III-ה verbs were originally III-י and that the stem vowel of a form like בָּנִיתָ is reminiscent of the original consonant in third root position (see also 22.8.4). In the Qal Perfect, the diagnostic Hireq Yod stem vowel will help you to identify the III-ה class of verbs.

5. Lastly, as in the III-א paradigm, the Daghesh Lene in the sufformatives beginning with ת is absent. This loss of the Daghesh Lene is due to the fact that the *begadkephat* consonant ת is now preceded by a vowel, the distinctive Hireq Yod stem vowel.

14.8 Doubly Weak Verbs. Verbs of this type have more than one weak consonant as part of their verbal root. Most of the verbs in this weak class are both III-ה and I-Guttural or II-Guttural.[1] The Perfect paradigm of a doubly weak verb will combine the spelling variations occassioned by its two weak consonants. Therefore, once you have mastered the

---

[1] Examples include רָעָה (to feed, graze, tend flocks), עָשָׂה (to do, make), חָרָה (to become angry), and הָרָה (to conceive, become pregnant). However, not all doubly weak verbs are III-ה. For example, the verbs אָהַב (to love), אָחַז (to seize), and חָטָא (to sin) are doubly weak but not III-ה.

types of changes that occur in the weak verbs presented in 14.2-7, you should have little difficulty identifying the Qal Perfect forms of doubly weak verbs. Because of their frequency, two doubly weak III-ה verbs will be studied here: רָאָה (to see) and עָלָה (to go up). The first is III-ה/II-Guttural and the second is III-ה/I-Guttural.

	III-ה/ II-Gutt	III-ה/ I-Gutt	*Strong Verb*
3ms	רָאָה	עָלָה	קָטַל
3fs	רָאֲתָה	עָלְתָה	קָטְלָה
2ms	רָאִ֫יתָ	עָלִ֫יתָ	קָטַ֫לְתָּ
2fs	רָאִית	עָלִית	קָטַלְתְּ
1cs	רָאִ֫יתִי	עָלִ֫יתִי	קָטַ֫לְתִּי
3cp	רָאוּ	עָלוּ	קָטְלוּ
2mp	רְאִיתֶם	עֲלִיתֶם	קְטַלְתֶּם
2fp	רְאִיתֶן	עֲלִיתֶן	קְטַלְתֶּן
1cp	רָאִ֫ינוּ	עָלִ֫ינוּ	קָטַ֫לְנוּ

14.9   Doubly Weak Notes.

1. In both doubly weak paradigms, the changes learned for III-ה verbs are fully present: (1) the loss of final consonantal ה in every form; (2) the insertion of ת in the 3fs form; (3) the presence of the diagnostic Hireq Yod stem vowel; and (4) the loss of the Daghesh Lene in the sufformatives beginning with ת.

2. In these doubly weak verbal roots, the changes occasioned by the ה in third root position are combined with the changes caused by the presence of additional guttural consonants. These types of changes should be familiar to you by now. In the 3fs form רָאֲתָה, the expected Vocal Shewa under the guttural א has changed to Hateph Pathach because a guttural cannot take a Vocal Shewa but rather prefers the vowel Hateph Pathach. For the same reason, the 2mp (עֲלִיתֶם) and 2fp (עֲלִיתֶן) forms have a Hateph Pathach under the initial guttural consonant. Although the full memorization of these paradigms might be helpful, it is not considered essential if you have already memorized the paradigm of the III-ה weak verb and remember that gutturals reject Vocal Shewa.

14.10 Geminate Verbs. Verbs of this class have identical second and third root consonants, as in סָבַב meaning "to go around." Other examples include אָרַר (to curse) and תָּמַם (to be finished). Verbs of this type exhibit two distinctive features. In most forms, the first Geminate consonant assimilates into the second Geminate consonant and is represented as a Daghesh Forte. Secondly, there is the insertion of a "connecting" vowel, the Holem Waw (וֹ), between the verbal root and the sufformative. The presence of the Holem Waw connecting vowel is a helpful way to identify the Qal Perfect of Geminate verbs. In the following paradigms, three Geminate verbs are presented for study. Only the first paradigm, using סָבַב, needs to be memorized.

	Geminate Strong	Geminate Weak 1	Geminate Weak 2	Strong Verb
3ms	סָבַב	אָרַר	תַּם	קָטַל
3fs	סָבְבָה	אָרְרָה	תַּמָּה	קָטְלָה
2ms	סַבּׄוֹתָ	אַרׄוֹתָ	תַּמּׄוֹתָ	קָטַׄלְתָּ
2fs	סַבּוֹת	אַרוֹת	תַּמּוֹת	קָטַלְתְּ
1cs	סַבּׄוֹתִי	אַרׄוֹתִי	תַּמּׄוֹתִי	קָטַׄלְתִּי
3cp	סָבְבוּ	אָרְרוּ	תַּׄמּוּ	קָטְלוּ
2mp	סַבּוֹתֶם	אַרוֹתֶם	תַּמּוֹתֶם	קְטַלְתֶּם
2fp	סַבּוֹתֶן	אַרוֹתֶן	תַּמּוֹתֶן	קְטַלְתֶּן
1cp	סַבּׄוֹנוּ	אַרׄוֹנוּ	תַּמּׄוֹנוּ	קָטַׄלְנוּ

14.11 Geminate Notes. All initial observations are directed primarily toward the forms of the Geminate verb סָבַב.

1. Note that in all first and second person forms, both singular and plural, the first Geminate consonant assimilates into the second Geminate consonant with a resulting Daghesh Forte. In other words, בב is written as בּ in the first and second person forms, singular and plural. This Daghesh Forte is a diagnostic feature of the Qal Perfect Geminate verb.

2. Additionally, all first and second person forms, both singular and plural, exhibit the Holem Waw (וֹ) connecting vowel, as in the example סַבּׄוֹתָ. The presence of Holem Waw between the verbal root and the Perfect sufformative is a diagnostic feature of the Qal Perfect Geminate verb.

3. By now, you should expect the loss of Daghesh Lene in the initial ת of a sufformative when preceded by a vowel.

4. The verb אָרַר differs from סָבַב in one way. In the second and first person forms, singular and plural, the Geminate consonant rejects the Daghesh Forte and the Pathach under the א becomes Qamets due to compensatory lengthening.

5. Finally, with regard to the paradigm of תָּמַם, the Geminate consonants have assimilated in all forms and remain as a Daghesh Forte (except in the 3ms). Unlike the 3fs and 3cp forms of many Geminate verbs, note the presence of the Daghesh Forte in the Geminate consonant of these two forms (תַּמָּה and תַּמּוּ).

14.12 Biconsonantal Verbs. The study of verb forms to this point has been concerned with triconsonantal verbal roots, that is, roots composed of three consonants. The verbs have been either strong or weak but all of them have been composed of three consonants. We now begin the study of the so-called "Biconsonantal" class of weak verbs. As the name indicates, these verbs are composed of two consonants. Examples include קָם (to rise), שָׂם (to set, put) and בָּא (to enter).

Biconsonantal verbs are also called "Hollow" or II-י/ו verbs. These designations reflect the fact that Biconsonantal verbs, in some conjugations, exhibit a medial vowel letter. In the Perfect conjugation, however, these vowel letters are not present. Only in the Imperfect and related conjugations do they appear. It is important to note, at this point, that the lexical or dictionary form of a Biconsonantal verb is *not* the Qal Perfect 3ms form as in most verbs. These verbs are listed in the lexicon under their Infinitive Construct forms and, as such, appear with their vowel letters. In other words, קָם is listed under קוּם, שָׂם under שִׂים and בָּא under בּוֹא.

Carefully study the Qal Perfect paradigms of these three Biconsonantal verbs. The Perfect of קוּם should be memorized.

| | Biconsonantal Paradigms | | | Strong |
	Strong²	Strong	Weak	Verb
3ms	קָם	שָׂם	בָּא	קָטַל
3fs	קָמָה	שָׂמָה	בָּאָה	קָטְלָה
2ms	קַמְתָּ	שַׂמְתָּ	בָּאתָ	קָטַלְתָּ
2fs	קַמְתְּ	שַׂמְתְּ	בָּאת	קָטַלְתְּ
1cs	קַמְתִּי	שַׂמְתִּי	בָּאתִי	קָטַלְתִּי
3cp	קָמוּ	שָׂמוּ	בָּאוּ	קָטְלוּ
2mp	קַמְתֶּם	שַׂמְתֶּם	בָּאתֶם	קְטַלְתֶּם
2fp	קַמְתֶּן	שַׂמְתֶּן	בָּאתֶן	קְטַלְתֶּן
1cp	קַמְנוּ	שַׂמְנוּ	בָּאנוּ	קָטַלְנוּ

14.13 Biconsonantal Notes.

1. In the strong Biconsonantal paradigms (קוּם and שִׂים), *all third person forms* have Qamets under the first root consonant, while all other forms (first and second person) have Pathach.

2. In the weak paradigm (בוֹא), *all forms* have Qamets under the first root consonant.

3. In the weak Biconsonantal paradigm, the א is quiescent as in III-א triconsonantal verbs. For this reason, the expected Daghesh Lene in the initial ת of selected Perfect sufformatives is absent.

14.14 Summary. At this point, you might feel a bit overwhelmed. All of the changes and variations presented in these weak verb paradigms can be intimidating at first. With time and continued exposure to weak verb forms, you will become more and more familiar with these changes. Actually, the variations observed in weak verbs are based upon only a few standard rules or patterns.

1. Of first importance is the need to memorize the strong verb paradigm and the Perfect sufformatives (chapter 13). The Perfect sufformatives will not change, despite any weakness in the verbal root.

2. Guttural consonants cannot take a Vocal Shewa and will prefer some type of a-vowel, usually Hateph Pathach. This accounts for changes in I-Guttural, II-Guttural and doubly weak verbs.

3. With III-א weak verbs, the א is quiescent. This causes the loss of the Daghesh Lene in the ת of the Perfect sufformatives because the ת is now preceded by a vowel.

4. With III-ה weak verbs, the final ה of the verbal root is lost in all forms of the Qal Perfect paradigm. All second and first person forms of this paradigm, both singular and plural, have the diagnostic Hireq Yod stem vowel (בָּנִיתָ). Additionally, the Daghesh Lene that is expected in the ת of the Perfect sufformatives is lost because this *begadkephat* consonant is preceded by a vowel (the Hireq Yod stem vowel).

5. With Geminate verbs like סָבַב (to go around), expect the assimilation of the first Geminate consonant into the second Geminate consonant with a resulting Daghesh Forte in all first and second person forms (סַבּוֹתָ). The Holem Waw (וֹ) connecting vowel is also a diagnostic feature of this weak verb class. As with III-א and III-ה verbs, the Daghesh Lene that is expected in the ת of the Perfect sufformatives is lost because the ת is preceded by a vowel.

14.15 Qal Perfect Paradigms: Strong and Weak Verbs. The III-א, III-ה, Geminate and Biconsonantal paradigms must be memorized. You should be able to identify the forms of other weak verbs, given your knowledge of certain rules or patterns of inflection learned in this chapter.

---

[2] Though Biconsonantal verbs are considered weak, a "strong" Biconsonantal verb is one without a guttural consonant (קוּם). The verb בּוֹא, however, is considered to be a "weak" Biconsonantal verb because of the presence of the guttural א.

Strong	I-Gutt	II-Gutt	III-ח/ע	III-א	III-ה	Doubly Weak	Gem Verbs	Bicon Verbs
קָטַל	עָמַד	בָּחַר	שָׁמַע	מָצָא	בָּנָה	עָלָה	סָבַב	קָם
קָטְלָה	עָמְדָה	בָּחֲרָה	שָׁמְעָה	מָצְאָה	בָּנְתָה	עָלְתָה	סָבְבָה	קָמָה
קָטַלְתָּ	עָמַדְתָּ	בָּחַרְתָּ	שָׁמַעְתָּ	מָצָאתָ	בָּנִיתָ	עָלִיתָ	סַבּוֹתָ	קַמְתָּ
קָטַלְתְּ	עָמַדְתְּ	בָּחַרְתְּ	שָׁמַעַתְּ	מָצָאת	בָּנִית	עָלִית	סַבּוֹת	קַמְתְּ
קָטַלְתִּי	עָמַדְתִּי	בָּחַרְתִּי	שָׁמַעְתִּי	מָצָאתִי	בָּנִיתִי	עָלִיתִי	סַבּוֹתִי	קַמְתִּי
קָטְלוּ	עָמְדוּ	בָּחֲרוּ	שָׁמְעוּ	מָצְאוּ	בָּנוּ	עָלוּ	סָבְבוּ	קָמוּ
קְטַלְתֶּם	עֲמַדְתֶּם	בְּחַרְתֶּם	שְׁמַעְתֶּם	מְצָאתֶם	בְּנִיתֶם	עֲלִיתֶם	סַבּוֹתֶם	קַמְתֶּם
קְטַלְתֶּן	עֲמַדְתֶּן	בְּחַרְתֶּן	שְׁמַעְתֶּן	מְצָאתֶן	בְּנִיתֶן	עֲלִיתֶן	סַבּוֹתֶן	קַמְתֶּן
קְטַלְנוּ	עָמַדְנוּ	בָּחַרְנוּ	שָׁמַעְנוּ	מָצָאנוּ	בָּנִינוּ	עָלִינוּ	סַבּוֹנוּ	קַמְנוּ

14.16 Vocabulary.

Verbs

בּוֹא	to go in, enter, come to (2,592)
בָּנָה	to build (up), build (establish) a family (377)
יָלַד	to bring forth, bear (499)
יָרֵא	to fear, be afraid, be in awe of (317)
יָרַד	to go down, come down, descend (382)
לָקַח	to take, grasp, capture, seize, lay hold of (967)
מוּת	to die (854)
נָפַל	to fall, fall prostrate, fall upon (435)
נָשָׂא	to lift, carry, raise, bear (load or burden), take away (659)
עָלָה	to go up, ascend (894)
עָבַר	to pass over, pass through, pass by, cross (553)
עָמַד	to stand (up), take one's stand, stand still (524)

קוּם	to rise, arise, get up, stand (627)
קָרָא	to call, summon, proclaim, announce, read aloud (739)
שִׂים	to set (up), put, place, lay (upon), establish (588)
שׁוּב	to turn back, return, go back (1,075)

Other

פֹּה	here, at this place (82)

14.17 **Train Up a Child.** Students who are preparing for youth ministry or pastoral counseling sometimes wonder about the benefit of investing the time and effort required to gain a working knowledge of Hebrew. In reality, however, the biblical texts that are most relevant for these areas of ministry are often the very ones where a knowledge of the original language is of greatest advantage. Prov 22:6 is a case in point.

חֲנֹךְ לַנַּעַר עַל־פִּי דַרְכּוֹ גַּם כִּי־יַזְקִין לֹא־יָסוּר מִמֶּנָּה

The Authorized Version translates it, "Train up a child in the way he should go: and when he is old, he will not depart from it." As desirable as such a promise would be, experience contradicts it far too often to be attributable solely to deficient parenting. Indeed, in spite of the best parenting in the universe, namely God's own, many of his children departed from the way they should have gone, and they continued in their rebellion to the bitter end (cf. Isa 1:2, "I reared children and brought them up, but they have rebelled against me").

A second difficulty with the traditional understanding of Prov 22:6 is the likelihood that the final clause, which begins in Hebrew with גַּם כִּי, rather than merely כִּי, should be rendered "*even* when he is old he will not depart from it," as in many recent translations (NASB; cf. ASV, NEB, JPS, NAB). If this is correct, it implies not just an eventual return, perhaps after a period of waywardness as illustrated by the prodigal son in Luke 15, but a lifelong adherence to the way one should go.

The most serious difficulty with the traditional rendering of Prov 22:6, however, is the startling fact that in the Hebrew text there is virtually no basis to justify the all-important qualifier "should" in the phrase, "the way he *should* go." The Hebrew merely has עַל־פִּי דַרְכּוֹ, which is literally, "according to *his way*," as is correctly indicated in the margin of the *New American Standard Bible*. Although in theory, דַרְכּוֹ (his way) could be an elliptical means for expressing "the way *he should go*," there are, in fact, no biblical examples that support this interpretative expansion. Forms of דֶּרֶךְ with a pronominal suffix, such as דַּרְכּוֹ (his way), are well attested in the Bible; there are 25 examples in the book of Proverbs alone. None of these requires a rendering similar to "the way he should go." Instead, in each case, "his way" (8:22; 11:5; 14:8; 16:9, 17; 19:3; 20:24; 21:29), "his ways" (3:31; 10:9; 14:2, 14; 19:16), "her ways" (3:17; 6:6; 7:25), "their way" (1:31), etc., refer to the way these persons actually go. The evidence is similar for analogous expressions, such as "the way of wicked men" (2:12), "a man's ways" (5:21), "the way of a fool" (12:15), etc.

Accordingly, Prov 22:6 is not so much a promise, as it is a solemn warning. Parents, if you train up your child "according to *his* way" – in other words, if you quit the hard work of loving discipline and just give in and let your child have his own way – you will reinforce his sinful proclivities to such a degree that, apart from supernatural intervention, "even when he is old he will not depart from it." The book of Proverbs elsewhere places similar urgency on the discipline of children and the danger of being left to follow one's own way.

> Discipline your son, for in that there is hope;
> do not be a willing party to his death (19:18).

> Folly is bound up in the heart of a child,
> but the rod of discipline will drive it far from him (22:15).

> The rod of correction imparts wisdom,
> a child left to himself disgraces his mother (29:15).

It is likely that earlier translators missed this understanding of the text as a warning not because of any difficulty in the Hebrew, but because it construes the first clause as an ironic command. It tells the reader to do something he should not do: "train up a child according to his way." Actually, such a rhetorical device is entirely at home in wisdom literature such as Proverbs, which uses sarcasm to good effect. Compare Prov 19:27, "Stop listening to instruction, my son, and you will stray from the words of knowledge."

Gordon P. Hugenberger
Senior Pastor, Park Street Church
Boston, Massachusetts

14.18 Advanced Information: הָיָה and נָתַן. Both נָתַן (to give) and הָיָה (to be) occur frequently throughout the Hebrew Bible. The multiple weaknesses of these verbal roots can, in certain forms, make their identification difficult. Their Qal Perfect forms are listed below.

	נָתַן *to give*	הָיָה *to be*	*Strong Verb*
3ms	נָתַן	הָיָה	קָטַל
3fs	נָתְנָה	הָיְתָה	קָטְלָה
2ms	נָתַׄתָּ	הָיִׄתָ	קָטַׄלְתָּ
2fs	נָתַׄתְּ	הָיִית	קָטַלְתְּ
1cs	נָתַׄתִּי	הָיִׄיתִי	קָטַׄלְתִּי
3cp	נָתְנוּ	הָיוּ	קָטְלוּ
2mp	נְתַתֶּם	הֱיִיתֶם	קְטַלְתֶּם
2fp	נְתַתֶּן	הֱיִיתֶן	קְטַלְתֶּן
1cp	נָתַׄנּוּ	הָיִׄינוּ	קָטַׄלְנוּ

Notes: הָיָה and נָתַן.

1. In the Perfect conjugation of נָתַן, the final נ of the verbal root has assimilated into the consonant at the beginning of the Perfect sufformative in all first and second person forms.

2. With one minor deviation, the verb הָיָה inflects just like other III-ה verbs in the Qal Perfect. Note the presence of the Hateph Seghol in the 2mp (הֱיִיתֶם) and 2fp (הֱיִיתֶן) forms. The guttural ה cannot take a Vocal Shewa and, therefore, takes a reduced vowel (Hateph Seghol with הָיָה).

14.19 Advanced Information: יָרֵא **and** מוּת. The following verbs are both weak *and* stative. The verb יָרֵא (to be afraid) is III-א and מוּת (to die) is Biconsonantal.

	יָרֵא *to be afraid*	מוּת *to die*	*Strong Verb*
3ms	יָרֵא	מֵת	קָטַל
3fs	יָרְאָה	מֵ֫תָה	קָטְלָה
2ms	יָרֵ֫אתָ	מַ֫תָּה³	קָטַ֫לְתָּ
2fs	יָרֵאת	מַתְּ	קָטַלְתְּ
1cs	יָרֵ֫אתִי	מַ֫תִּי	קָטַ֫לְתִּי
3cp	יָרְאוּ	מֵ֫תוּ	קָטְלוּ
2mp	יְרֵאתֶם	מַתֶּם	קְטַלְתֶּם
2fp	יְרֵאתֶן	מַתֶּן	קְטַלְתֶּן
1cp	יָרֵ֫אנוּ	מַ֫תְנוּ	קָטַ֫לְנוּ

---

³ Note the assimilation of the final root consonant into the sufformative. This occurs in the 2ms, 2fs, 1cs, 2mp and 2fp forms.

Chapter 15

Qal Imperfect - Strong Verbs

15.1 **Introduction**. The Imperfect is the second major Hebrew verbal conjugation to be studied. Of the over 50,000 occurrences of the Qal stem in the Hebrew Bible, the Imperfect conjugation occurs 21,951 times, approximately forty-three percent of Qal stem occurrences.[1] Like the Perfect conjugation, the Imperfect inflects, or changes its form, in order to indicate person, gender and number.

15.2 **The Meaning of the Qal Imperfect**. The Imperfect conjugation is used to express *incomplete action* and is usually translated by the English present tense (I study) or future tense (I will study). The action of the verb occurs either at the time of speaking or after the time of speaking. The Hebrew Imperfect is also used to denote habitual or customary action, whether in the past, present or future (he prays regularly, he used to pray). The Imperfect may also be rendered by one of several modal values (would, could, should, may, might, can, etc.). These modal translation values are suggested by context and various issues of syntax. It must also be emphasized that, like the Perfect, the Hebrew Imperfect does not have tense (time of action) apart from context and issues of syntax. It too primarily signifies aspect (type of action). The Imperfect aspect designates a verbal action for which, in the mind of the speaker or writer, the conclusion is not in view. To state it differently, *the Imperfect aspect denotes incomplete action, whether in the past, present, or future.*

15.3 **The Form of the Qal Imperfect**. Recall that the Perfect conjugation is called the *suffix* conjugation because inflectional suffixes called *sufformatives* are attached to the verbal root in order to indicate person, gender and number. The Imperfect conjugation is called the *prefix* conjugation because inflectional prefixes called *preformatives* are added to all Imperfect verbal forms. These preformatives distinguishes the Imperfect conjugation from all other conjugations. It should also be noted, however, that half of the Imperfect verbal forms also take their own Imperfect sufformatives. The Imperfect paradigm must be

---

[1] The Imperfect conjugation in the remaining derived stems totals 9,303 occurrences. These statistics count both the regular Imperfect and the Imperfect with Waw Conversive.

memorized with a view to both writing and oral recitation. When writing out the paradigm, exact spelling of all consonants, vowels, and accent marks is required. The preformatives and sufformatives of the Qal Imperfect are the same for all Imperfect forms in the derived stems, strong and weak verbs.

	Suffor- mative	Imperfect Paradigm	Prefor- mative	Translation
3ms		יִקְטֹל	יִ	he will kill
3fs		תִּקְטֹל	תִּ	she will kill
2ms		תִּקְטֹל	תִּ	you (ms) will kill
2fs	יִ	תִּקְטְלִי	תִּ	you (fs) will kill
1cs		אֶקְטֹל	אֶ	I will kill
3mp	וּ	יִקְטְלוּ	יִ	they (mp) will kill
3fp	נָה	תִּקְטֹלְנָה	תִּ	they (fp) will kill
2mp	וּ	תִּקְטְלוּ	תִּ	you (mp) will kill
2fp	נָה	תִּקְטֹלְנָה	תִּ	you (fp) will kill
1cp		נִקְטֹל	נִ	we will kill

15.4 Notes on the Qal Imperfect Strong Verb Paradigm.

1. Once again, precise memorization of this paradigm is essential. The careful memorization of this Qal Imperfect paradigm will prevent the need to memorize other Imperfect paradigms in subsequent chapters. All Imperfect verbs in the derived stems use these same preformatives and sufformatives.

2. As in the Perfect, the Imperfect paradigm moves from third person to first person, singular then plural.

3. In the Qal stem, only the Imperfect conjugation has a verbal preformative. Knowing this fact will make identification of Imperfect forms much easier. In the Qal strong verb, all preformative consonants have the Hireq vowel, except the 1cs form, which has Seghol (אֶקְטֹל).

4. You have probably already noticed that two sets of forms are identical in the Imperfect paradigm. In each instance, context must provide the proper identification. Having duplicate forms, however, does make paradigm memorization easier!

תִּקְטֹל   both 3fs and 2ms (she will kill *or* you will kill)

תִּקְטֹלְנָה   both 3fp and 2fp (they will kill *or* you will kill)

5. In the Perfect, the third person plural form קָטְלוּ (they killed) is common in gender. In the Imperfect, the third person plural is inflected for gender and so there are two third person plural forms: יִקְטְלוּ (3mp) and תִּקְטֹלְנָה (3fp).

6. The Imperfect prefix תּ is a *begadkephat* letter. An initial *begadkephat* letter will normally have a Daghesh Lene, as is seen in the above paradigm.

7. The stem vowel is Holem, except in those forms that have suf-formatives that consist of a vowel (2fs, 3mp, and 2mp), wherein the Holem stem vowel is reduced to Vocal Shewa.

8. With some frequency in the Hebrew Bible (325 times), the 3mp and the 2mp forms will be written with a final ן as in יִקְטְלוּן or תִּקְטְלוּן. This final ן is called *Nun Paragogicum*. Verbs with this final Nun may also be spelled defectively (meaning that the vowel letter Shureq is written as Qibbuts), as in תִּקְטְלֻן or יִקְטְלֻן.

9. The following graphic identifies the prefix and stem vowels that are diagnostic of the Qal Imperfect. These diagnostics must be memorized. Note that the Silent Shewa under ק is not considered to be diagnostic.

> *Qal Imperfect*
> *Strong Verb*
>
> יִקְטֹל

15.5 **The Qal Imperfect Paradigm of Other Strong Verbs.** The paradigms below are not to be memorized. You should be able to reproduce them once you have memorized the forms of קָטַל listed above. Note the Daghesh Lene in the second root consonant of the Imperfect forms of כָּתַב, זָכַר and קָבַץ. The presence of the Daghesh Lene is due to the fact that these *begadkephat* letters are preceded by a consonant and not a vowel (see 3.5).

	זָכַר to remember	כָּתַב to write	שָׁמַר to keep	קָבַץ to gather
3ms	יִזְכֹּר	יִכְתֹּב	יִשְׁמֹר	יִקְבֹּץ
3fs	תִּזְכֹּר	תִּכְתֹּב	תִּשְׁמֹר	תִּקְבֹּץ
2ms	תִּזְכֹּר	תִּכְתֹּב	תִּשְׁמֹר	תִּקְבֹּץ
2fs	תִּזְכְּרִי	תִּכְתְּבִי	תִּשְׁמְרִי	תִּקְבְּצִי
1cs	אֶזְכֹּר	אֶכְתֹּב	אֶשְׁמֹר	אֶקְבֹּץ
3mp	יִזְכְּרוּ	יִכְתְּבוּ	יִשְׁמְרוּ	יִקְבְּצוּ
3fp	תִּזְכֹּרְנָה	תִּכְתֹּבְנָה	תִּשְׁמֹרְנָה	תִּקְבֹּצְנָה
2mp	תִּזְכְּרוּ	תִּכְתְּבוּ	תִּשְׁמְרוּ	תִּקְבְּצוּ
2fp	תִּזְכֹּרְנָה	תִּכְתֹּבְנָה	תִּשְׁמֹרְנָה	תִּקְבֹּצְנָה
1cp	נִזְכֹּר	נִכְתֹּב	נִשְׁמֹר	נִקְבֹּץ

15.6 **Stative Verbs: Imperfect.** In chapter 13, you studied the inflection of stative verbs in the Qal Perfect. You will recall that stative verbs are classified by their stem vowel: Pathach (גָּדַל), Tsere (כָּבֵד), or Holem (קָטֹן). This variation in stem vowel caused differences in the spelling of certain Perfect forms. For example, the Tsere-Stative has a Tsere stem vowel in the Qal Perfect 3ms (כָּבֵד). Additionally, the Holem-Stative has an o-class stem vowel throughout (קָטֹנְתָּ). With the Imperfect inflection of stative verbs, however, the stem vowel is Pathach regardless of the stem vowel in the Perfect.

	Perfect		Imperfect
Pathach-Stative	גָּדַל	➤	יִגְדַּל
Tsere-Stative	כָּבֵד	➤	יִכְבַּד
Holem-Stative	קָטֹן	➤	יִקְטַן

As you can see, the stem vowel is Pathach in each of the above Imperfect forms. Note that the Pathach stem vowel of the Imperfect stative is distinct from the Holem stem vowel of the regular Imperfect strong verb form (יִקְטֹל). Apart from this change in stem vowel, however, the Imperfect conjugation of the stative verb follows the regular strong verb pattern. Note, however, the assimilation of the third consonant of the verbal root (נ) into the נ of the Imperfect sufformative in the 3fp and 2fp forms of קָטֹן (תִּקְטַנָּה)

	גָּדַל Pathach- Stative	כָּבֵד Tsere- Stative	קָטֹן Holem- Stative
3ms	יִגְדַּל	יִכְבַּד	יִקְטַן
3fs	תִּגְדַּל	תִּכְבַּד	תִּקְטַן
2ms	תִּגְדַּל	תִּכְבַּד	תִּקְטַן
2fs	תִּגְדְּלִי	תִּכְבְּדִי	תִּקְטְנִי
1cs	אֶגְדַּל	אֶכְבַּד	אֶקְטַן
3mp	יִגְדְּלוּ	יִכְבְּדוּ	יִקְטְנוּ
3fp	תִּגְדַּלְנָה	תִּכְבַּדְנָה	תִּקְטַנָּה
2mp	תִּגְדְּלוּ	תִּכְבְּדוּ	תִּקְטְנוּ
2fp	תִּגְדַּלְנָה	תִּכְבַּדְנָה	תִּקְטַנָּה
1cp	נִגְדַּל	נִכְבַּד	נִקְטַן

15.7   **Lexical Form.** The lexical form for most Imperfect verbs is the Qal Perfect 3ms. The Qal Perfect 3ms is the standard lexical form for most verbs regardless of stem or conjugation.

15.8   **Parsing.** When asked to parse Qal Imperfect verbs, you will be required to identify the verbal stem, conjugation, person, gender, number, and verbal root. When parsing, give the required information in the proper order as the following examples illustrate. Though given below, translation is not a required part of the parsing information.

יִשְׁמְעוּ   Qal Imperfect 3mp   שָׁמַע   they will hear

יִמְלֹךְ   Qal Imperfect 3ms   מָלַךְ   he will reign (be king)

15.9   **Negation of the Imperfect: The Particles לֹא and אַל.**

1.   Like the Perfect, the Imperfect is also negated with לֹא.[2] This negative particle is always placed immediately before the verb. In addition to the use of the negative particle to simply negate the verb, there is a special use of לֹא before an Imperfect. In the Ten Commandments (Decalogue), the combination of לֹא plus the Imperfect is used for an absolute or permanent prohibition.

---

[2] The combination of לֹא plus the Imperfect occurs 2,654 times in the Hebrew Bible.

לֹא תַעֲשֶׂה   you shall not make (Ex 20:4)

לֹא תִשָּׂא   you shall not take (Ex 20:7)

לֹא תִּרְצָח   you shall not kill (Ex 20:13)

לֹא תִּנְאָף   you shall not commit adultery (Ex 20:14)

לֹא תִגְנֹב   you shall not steal (Ex 20:15)

לֹא תַעֲנֶה   you shall not answer (Ex 20:16)

לֹא תַחְמֹד   you shall not covet (Ex 20:17)

2. The negative particle אַל is also used with an Imperfect verb[3] to express an immediate, specific, and non-durative prohibition.[4] In other words, prohibitions with לֹא are permanent and absolute; prohibitions with אַל are immediate and specific. The particle אַל is often prefixed to the verb with Maqqef (אַל־).

אַל־תִּכְתֹּב בַּסֵּפֶר   Do not write in the book!

אַל־תִּירָא   Do not fear! (Gen 15:1)

אַל־תִּשְׁמְעוּ אֶל־דִּבְרֵי   Do not listen to the words of your

נְבִיאֵיכֶם   prophets! (Jer 27:16)

15.10 Summary.

1. The Qal stem is used to express *simple action* with an *active voice*. The Imperfect conjugation is used to express an *incomplete action*, which may be translated with either the English present or future tense.

2. The Imperfect conjugation is also called the *prefix* conjugation because every form takes a verbal prefix, hereafter called a *preformative*. The preformatives are unique to the Imperfect conjugation in the Qal and derived stems.

3. The following graphic identifies the preformative and stem vowels that are diagnostic of the Qal Imperfect. These diagnostics must be memorized.

---

[3] See also the discussion of the Jussive in 18.15.

[4] The combination of אַל plus the Imperfect occurs 678 times in the Hebrew Bible.

*Qal Imperfect
Strong Verb*

יִקְטֹל

4. With the Imperfect inflection of stative verbs, the stem vowel is Pathach (יִכְבַּד) and not Holem (יִקְטֹל).

5. The Qal Perfect 3ms is the standard lexical form for most verbs, regardless of stem or conjugation.

6. Imperfect verbs are usually negated with the negative particle לֹא. In addition to this use, the negative particle לֹא may be used before an Imperfect verb to express an absolute or permanent prohibition. The negative particle אַל before an Imperfect is used to express an immediate and specific prohibition (see 18.5, 15).

15.11 Vocabulary.

Verbs

חָיָה	to live, be alive, stay alive, revive, restore to life (282)
יָכֹל	to be able, be capable of, endure, prevail, be victorious (193)
כָּרַת	to cut off, cut down, make a covenant (289)
סוּר	to turn aside, turn off, leave (298)
עָבַד	to work, serve, toil, till, cultivate (289)
עָנָה	to answer, respond, reply, testify (316)

Nouns

אֹזֶן	ear (188); feminine
אַיִל	ram, ruler; (adj) mighty (171)
גִּבּוֹר	(adj) mighty, valiant, heroic; (n) hero (160)
זֶבַח	sacrifice (162)
צְדָקָה	righteousness, righteous act, justice (159)
צָפוֹן	north, northern (153); feminine

Other

אָז	then, since, before (141)
אַף	also, indeed, even (133)
פֶּן־	lest, otherwise (133)

15.12 The Feast of Cover-over.[5] "The first metaphor we meet with in the Bible," writes M. G. Kline, "likens the Creator-Spirit to a bird hovering over the deep-and-darkness (Gen 1:2)."[6] In fact, we are confronted throughout Scripture with avian (bird) metaphors for God. For example, the Lord tells Israel with reference to the Exodus: "You have seen what I did to the Egyptians, *and how I bore you on eagles' wings* and brought you to myself" (Exod 19:4). The Glory theophany that overshadowed the תֹהוּ וָבֹהוּ (formlessness and emptiness) in the beginning, and which also guided the Israelites out of Egypt and through the wilderness, manifested itself in the form of a pillar of cloud. The aptness of avian imagery for the divine Glory may be seen in the fact that clouds, like birds, are said to fly across the sky (cf. Isa 60:8). Additionally, there are often associated with the Lord winged angelic creatures (such as the winged cherubim that guarded God's Presence in the tabernacle), who also are said to fly through the celestial regions (Isa 6:6; Dan 9:21; Rev 14:6).

The avian imagery that first appeared in Gen 1:2, and which reemerges in the description of the theophanic Glory-cloud that attends Israel's exodus from Egypt and subsequent wilderness wanderings, is prominent also in Exod 12. This fact has gone largely unnoticed, however, primarily because of the long-standing mistranslation of the verb פָּסַח.

Exod 12 contains two Hebrew verbs – עָבַר and פָּסַח – that have traditionally been translated "pass over." "Pass over (or through)" is in fact a good rendering of עָבַר, which in Exod 12 denotes the action undertaken by the "destroyer" who passes through the land of Egypt on a mission of judgment. "Pass over" is not, however, a satisfactory translation for the verb פָּסַח here, nor is the nominal equivalent "Passover" an adequate rendering of the noun פֶּסַח. Two streams of lexical evidence – from Hebrew and Egyptian – explain the meaning of פָּסַח in Exod 12. Here we will consider the former.[7]

There are two פסח roots in Hebrew, one meaning "limp" and the other meaning "cover, hover." Evidence of the latter is found in Isa 31:5,

---

[5] The present essay is a summary of an article of the same name written by Meredith G. Kline and published in *Journal of the Evangelical Theological Society* (37.4 [December 1994]: 497-510). Dr. Kline (my grandfather) has kindly granted me permission to summarize his arguments and to borrow freely from his language without acknowledging the many cases where my mode of expression imitates his.

[6] *Cover-over*, 497.

[7] The Egyptian evidence is given in *Cover-over*, 503-7.

where פָּסַח parallels the verb עוּף (which in the context means "to hover") as well as גָּנַן ("to cover" or "to surround"):

> As birds hovering (עוּף),
>> So Yahweh of hosts will cover (גָּנַן) Jerusalem;
>> Covering (גָּנַן), he will deliver it,
> Hovering (פָּסַח), he will save it.

A verb פָּסַח also occurs in 1 Kgs 18:21, where Elijah, likening the people assembled on Mt. Carmel to hovering birds hesitant to land on a tree, says to them: "How long will you hover (פָּסַח) between two branches?" (the implicit exhortation being, "Land on one bough or the other!").[8] פָּסַח appears again a few verses later, in 1 Kgs 18:26, where the prophets of Baal are said to flutter (פָּסַח) in a frenzy around their altar.

Throughout the history of biblical interpretation, it has been assumed that פָּסַח in 1 Kgs 18:21, 26 is related to the frequently attested adjective פִּסֵּחַ, "lame." (For the verb פָּסַח, "to be lame," see 2 Sam 4:4.) When this understanding is brought to bear on the interpretation of פָּסַח in Exod 12, the image then emerges of God hopping or hobbling over the homes of the Israelites in order not to destroy them along with the Egyptians. "That would be a lame metaphor indeed," writes Kline with a touch of humor, "and there is . . . another root פָּסַח that yields a far more apt image for the Exodus 12 context."[9]

This other פסח root is the one we have seen in Isa 31:5 and 1 Kgs 18:21, 26, which means "hover" or "cover." The Egyptian linguistic evidence confirms this understanding of פָּסַח, and, what is more, indicates that the Hebrew noun פֶּסַח denotes a sort of shielding shelter. Returning now to Exod 12, we perceive that the situation that obtained on the night before the Exodus was not that of God *passing by* the homes of the Israelites. Rather, during that dark night of death the Lord protectively *hovered over* his people as an abiding, shielding presence.

Such an understanding leads us to conclude that "Passover" (despite its well-established use) is not an entirely accurate designation for the eve of the Exodus or for the feast that commemorates it. More appropriate (even if it sounds slightly odd) would be the name "Cover-over," which

---

[8] An appropriate metaphor emerges when it is recognized that the noun סְעִפִּים, usually translated "opinions" in this verse, should be rendered "branches" here, and that פָּסַח means "hover." See *Cover-over*, 500.

[9] *Cover-over*, 499.

reflects the glorious reality that the Lord protected his people from the coming wrath by personally covering over them and interposing himself between them and the wrath of the destroyer.

"The wonder of grace deepens when we recall that by reason of his personal Presence hovering (פָּסַח) over the Israelite houses, the Lord himself was their shielding shelter (פֶּסַח). The lamb is the פֶּסַח and the Lord is the פֶּסַח. Both are true because the Lord becomes the lamb."[10]

The original "Passover" event, glorious though it was, was but a type pointing forward to the realities of the new covenant. In the fullness of time, the Lamb of God would come and interpose himself between the wrath of God and his people, thereby freeing them for all time from the power of death and the devil and securing for them (as a reward for his victorious death and resurrection) the promised Paraclete, that same Spirit-Presence who abided with and protected his people by hovering over and covering them in the days of the Exodus.

J. Bergman Kline
M.A., Biblical Languages
Gordon-Conwell Theological Seminary
South Hamilton, Massachusetts

---

[10] *Cover-over*, 507.

Chapter 16

Qal Imperfect - Weak Verbs

16.1 **Introduction.** Compared to the Perfect, the Imperfect conjugation of weak verbs exhibits significant variation. The addition of both preformatives *and* sufformatives to weak verbal roots increases the likelihood of spelling variation. Regardless of a verb's weakness, however, the preformative consonants and the sufformatives of the Imperfect conjugation do not change. For this reason, it is important to have first memorized the Imperfect forms of the strong verb before working through this chapter. In this chapter, you are not required to memorize every weak verb paradigm. Rather, you will be required to memorize only four weak paradigms: II-Guttural verbs (16.2), III-ע/ח verbs (16.2), III-א verbs (16.4), and III-ה verbs (16.6). Only recognition of the remaining weak verb forms will be emphasized.

16.2 **II-Guttural and III-ח/ע Verbs.** Both II-Guttural and III-ח/ע weak verbs differ from the strong verb primarily in the stem vowel. Strong verbs have a Holem stem vowel (יִקְטֹל), but these two classes have Pathach (יִבְחַר).

	II-Guttural	III-ע/ח	Strong
3ms	יִבְחַר	יִשְׁלַח	יִקְטֹל
3fs	תִּבְחַר	תִּשְׁלַח	תִּקְטֹל
2ms	תִּבְחַר	תִּשְׁלַח	תִּקְטֹל
2fs	תִּבְחֲרִי	תִּשְׁלְחִי	תִּקְטְלִי
1cs	אֶבְחַר	אֶשְׁלַח	אֶקְטֹל
3mp	יִבְחֲרוּ	יִשְׁלְחוּ	יִקְטְלוּ
3fp	תִּבְחַרְנָה	תִּשְׁלַחְנָה	תִּקְטֹלְנָה
2mp	תִּבְחֲרוּ	תִּשְׁלְחוּ	תִּקְטְלוּ
2fp	תִּבְחַרְנָה	תִּשְׁלַחְנָה	תִּקְטֹלְנָה
1cp	נִבְחַר	נִשְׁלַח	נִקְטֹל

16.3   II-Guttural and III-ח/ע Notes.

1. Like the Qal Imperfect stative verbs studied in the last chapter, II-Guttural and III-ח/ע verbs take a Pathach stem vowel. This shift in stem vowel is due to the fact that guttural consonants prefer a-type vowels. Note that the vocalization of the Qal Imperfect stative (15.6) is identical to the vocalization of the Qal Imperfect III-ח/ע verb.

2. In the II-Guttural class, note the Hateph Pathach under the guttural in the 2fs (תִּבְחֲרִי), 3mp (יִבְחֲרוּ) and 2mp (תִּבְחֲרוּ) forms. You understand that the guttural in second root position cannot take the expected Vocal Shewa.

16.4   III-א Verbs. Most of the changes that take place in this weak class result from the fact that the א in third root position is quiescent in most forms. This quiescent א changes the stem vowel in most forms of the paradigm when compared to the strong verb. Other than changes in the stem vowel, III-א verbs inflect just like the strong verb. Because the III-א class of weak verbs boasts some high frequency vocabulary, it is important to memorize the following paradigm.

	III-א	Strong
3ms	יִמְצָא	יִקְטֹל
3fs	תִּמְצָא	תִּקְטֹל
2ms	תִּמְצָא	תִּקְטֹל
2fs	תִּמְצְאִי	תִּקְטְלִי
1cs	אֶמְצָא	אֶקְטֹל
3mp	יִמְצְאוּ	יִקְטְלוּ
3fp	תִּמְצֶאנָה	תִּקְטֹלְנָה
2mp	תִּמְצְאוּ	תִּקְטְלוּ
2fp	תִּמְצֶאנָה	תִּקְטֹלְנָה
1cp	נִמְצָא	נִקְטֹל

16.5   III-א Notes.

1. In those forms without a sufformative, the stem vowel is Qamets (יִמְצָא). Recall that the stem vowel of the strong verb is Holem (יִקְטֹל).

2. Those forms with sufformatives that consist of a vowel (2fs, 3mp, and 2mp) are identical to their corresponding strong verb forms.

3. The twin 3fp and 2fp forms (תִּמְצֶּאנָה) exhibit an unexpected Seghol stem vowel. This variation is unusual but will pose no difficulty for the identification of these two forms.

16.6   **III-ה Verbs.** The changes in this class of weak verb are considerable. As with the Perfect, the most significant change is the loss of the final ה root consonant in every form. For this reason, memorization of the following paradigm is required.

	III-ה	*Strong*
3ms	(יִבְנֶה)	יִקְטֹל
3fs	תִּבְנֶה	תִּקְטֹל
2ms	תִּבְנֶה	תִּקְטֹל
2fs	תִּבְנִי	תִּקְטְלִי
1cs	אֶבְנֶה	אֶקְטֹל
3mp	יִבְנוּ	יִקְטְלוּ
3fp	תִּבְנֶׁינָה	תִּקְטֹלְנָה
2mp	תִּבְנוּ	תִּקְטְלוּ
2fp	תִּבְנֶׁינָה	תִּקְטֹלְנָה
1cp	נִבְנֶה	נִקְטֹל

16.7   **III-ה Notes.**

1. Imperfect forms *without a sufformative* have an ה ending. This makes it seem as though the stem vowel of this weak class has shifted from Holem (יִקְטֹל) to Seghol (יִבְנֶה). The final ה in these forms is not, however, the original third root consonant but rather a vowel letter or *mater lectionis*. While this final ה is not the original consonant, it does make identification of the verbal root easier in these forms. Even in the derived stems, the ה ending will be diagnostic of most III-ה Imperfect forms.

2. Imperfect forms *with a sufformative* appear without the הֶ ending. This is an important feature to recognize. When you are confronted by such a form, you will have only two of the three original root consonants. In order to determine the lexical form, therefore, you will have to reconstruct the original root consonants based upon your understanding of how III-ה verbal roots inflect.

3. In the twin 3fp and 2fp forms, the stem vowel is Seghol Yod (תִּבְנֶ֫ינָה). This is similar to the Hireq Yod stem vowel found in the Perfect conjugation of this weak verb class (compare the Perfect 2ms form בָּנִ֫יתָ). The similarity is in the fact that both the Perfect and Imperfect have unchangeable long stem vowels that include a Yod.

4. You will learn below that the Imperfect 3ms form of III-ה verbs (יִבְנֶה) may also occur without the final ה vowel letter (יִ֫בֶן). This form has a special use that will be treated in chapters 17 and 18.

16.8 I-Guttural Verbs. There are two types of I-Guttural weak verbs. Each type is classified by the stem vowel. Type 1 has a Pathach stem vowel (יֶחֱזַק) and Type 2 has a Holem stem vowel (יַעֲמֹד). Recognition rather than memorization of these weak verbal forms is required. That is, you will not be required to reproduce these paradigms in Hebrew but you will need to be able to identify and parse each form.

	I-Guttural Type 1	I-Guttural Type 2	Strong
3ms	יֶחֱזַק	יַעֲמֹד	יִקְטֹל
3fs	תֶּחֱזַק	תַּעֲמֹד	תִּקְטֹל
2ms	תֶּחֱזַק	תַּעֲמֹד	תִּקְטֹל
2fs	תֶּחֶזְקִי	תַּעַמְדִי	תִּקְטְלִי
1cs	אֶחֱזַק	אֶעֱמֹד	אֶקְטֹל
3mp	יֶחֶזְקוּ	יַעַמְדוּ	יִקְטְלוּ
3fp	תֶּחֱזַ֫קְנָה	תַּעֲמֹ֫דְנָה	תִּקְטֹ֫לְנָה
2mp	תֶּחֶזְקוּ	תַּעַמְדוּ	תִּקְטְלוּ
2fp	תֶּחֱזַ֫קְנָה	תַּעֲמֹ֫דְנָה	תִּקְטֹ֫לְנָה
1cp	נֶחֱזַק	נַעֲמֹד	נִקְטֹל

16.9   I-Guttural Notes.

1. Type 1 verbs with the Pathach stem vowel exhibit a *Seghol preformative vowel* followed by a Hateph Seghol under the guttural in first root position (יֶחֱזַק). Note that in those forms having a sufformative consisting of a vowel (2fs, 3mp, 2mp), the vowel under the guttural is just Seghol in a closed syllable (תֶּחֶזְקוּ).

2. Type 2 verbs with the Holem stem vowel generally exhibit a *Pathach preformative vowel* and a Hateph Pathach under the guttural in first root position (יַעֲמֹד). The only exception to this pattern is the 1cs form אֶעֱמֹד with Seghol under the preformative and Hateph Seghol under the guttural. Note that the vowel under the guttural is just Pathach in a closed syllable in the 2fs (תַּעַמְדִי), 3mp (יַעַמְדוּ), and 2mp (תַּעַמְדוּ).

16.10   I-א Verbs. Although verbs with א in the first root position are to be classified as I-Guttural, weak verbs of this type require additional comment. While most I-א verbs inflect in a silimar fashion to חָזַק in the Imperfect (see 16.8 above), there are five I-א verbs that follow a different pattern.[1] This alternate pattern is represented by the Type 2 paradigm below. Recognition rather than memorization of these weak verb forms is required.

	I-א *Type 1*	*I-א* *Type 2*	*Strong*
3ms	יֶאֱסֹר	יֹאמַר	יִקְטֹל
3fs	תֶּאֱסֹר	תֹּאמַר	תִּקְטֹל
2ms	תֶּאֱסֹר	תֹּאמַר	תִּקְטֹל
2fs	תַּאַסְרִי	תֹּאמְרִי	תִּקְטְלִי
1cs	אֶאֱסֹר	אֹמַר	אֶקְטֹל
3mp	יַאַסְרוּ	יֹאמְרוּ	יִקְטְלוּ
3fp	תֶּאֱסֹרְנָה	תֹּאמַרְנָה	תִּקְטֹלְנָה
2mp	תַּאַסְרוּ	תֹּאמְרוּ	תִּקְטְלוּ
2fp	תֶּאֱסֹרְנָה	תֹּאמַרְנָה	תִּקְטֹלְנָה
1cp	נֶאֱסֹר	נֹאמַר	נִקְטֹל

---

[1] The five I-א verbs that follow this Type 2 pattern are אָמַר (to say), אָכַל (to eat), אָבַד (to perish), אָפָה (to bake), and אָבָה (to be willing).

16.11 I-א Notes.

1. It has already been noted that I-א verbs of the Type 1 class inflect just like the Type 1 verbs of the I-Guttural class (compare, for example, יֶחֱזַק with יֶאְסֹר). This should be easy to remember since א is a guttural consonant. Note the shift to a-type vowels in the 2fs (תַּאַסְרִי), 3mp (יַאַסְרוּ), and 2mp (תַּאַסְרוּ) Imperfect forms of אָסַר. These vowel changes and the differences in stem vowel should occasion no difficulty for identifying these forms.

2. Type 2 verbs of this class are very different in their inflection. The preformative vowel is Holem and the א is quiescent (יֹאמַר). While this pattern occurs in only five verbs, some of these verbs occur with a high frequency. For example, the Qal Imperfect forms of אָמַר (to say) occur 2,973 times and the forms of אָכַל (to eat) occur 382 times.

3. Note the unusual 1cs form of the Type 2 paradigm, אֹמַר (I will say). You would expect the א to be written twice, once for the Imperfect preformative and once for the first consonant of the verbal root. Observe, however, that it is written only once. The א that is present is the 1cs Imperfect preformative. The first consonant of the verbal root is not written.

16.12 Geminate Verbs. You have already learned that a Geminate verb is one in which the second and third root consonants of the verbal root are identical, as in סָבַב (to go around) or תָּמַם (to be complete). Recognition rather than memorization of these weak verbal forms is required.

	Geminate Type 1	*Alternate Type 1*	*Geminate Type 2*	*Strong*
3ms	יָסֹב	יִסֹּב	יֵתַם	יִקְטֹל
3fs	תָּסֹב	תִּסֹּב	תֵּתַם	תִּקְטֹל
2ms	תָּסֹב	תִּסֹּב	תֵּתַם	תִּקְטֹל
2fs	תָּסֹבִּי	תִּסֹּבִי	תֵּתַּמִּי	תִּקְטְלִי
1cs	אָסֹב	אֶסֹּב	אֵתַם	אֶקְטֹל
3mp	יָסֹבּוּ	יִסֹּבוּ	יֵתַּמּוּ	יִקְטְלוּ
3fp	תְּסֻבֶּינָה	תִּסֹּבֶינָה	תִּתַּמֶּינָה	תִּקְטֹלְנָה
2mp	תָּסֹבּוּ	תִּסֹּבוּ	תֵּתַּמּוּ	תִּקְטְלוּ
2fp	תְּסֻבֶּינָה	תִּסֹּבֶינָה	תִּתַּמֶּינָה	תִּקְטֹלְנָה
1cp	נָסֹב	נִסֹּב	נֵתַם	נִקְטֹל

16.13 Geminate Notes.

1. There are two types of Geminate verbs. Type 1 has a Holem stem vowel in most forms (יָסֹב). Type 2 has a Pathach stem vowel (יֵתַם). Note also that Type 1 Geminate verbs have an alternate form that also has a Holem stem vowel (יִסֹּב). Each type is further distinguished by its preformative vowel. Type 1 verbs have a Qamets (יָסֹב) or the alternate Hireq preformative vowel (יִסֹּב). Type 2 verbs exhibit a Tsere preformative vowel (יֵתַם). Other minor variations also exist for which a lexicon will provide information.

2. In every form of the Geminate paradigms above, only one of the Geminate consonants remains. In those forms with a sufformative, the presence of a Daghesh Forte in the remaining Geminate consonant should help you to identify the verbal root. In those forms without a sufformative, there is no Daghesh Forte in the Geminate consonant. This will make identification of the verbal root more difficult, as you will simply have to recognize the Geminate root as a possibility.

16.14 Biconsonantal Verbs.
You learned in 14.12 that Biconsonantal verbs are composed of two rather than three root consonants (קָם, he rose up). You will also recall that Biconsonantal verbs are sometimes designated as II-י/ו verbs. It should be clear from the paradigms below

why this weak class has been called II-י/ו. With the Imperfect and related conjugations, a medial vowel letter is found in every form. In the Imperfect, these Biconsonantal or II-י/ו verbs are further classified by their medial vowel letter.

Class	Qal Perfect 3ms	Qal Imperfect 3ms	Lexical Entry
Shureq	קָם he arose	יָקוּם he will arise	קוּם to arise
Hireq Yod	שָׂם he placed	יָשִׂים he will place	שִׂים to place
Holem Waw	בָּא he entered	יָבוֹא he will enter	בּוֹא to enter

The vowel letters are an important feature of these verbs and should be memorized as a part of your vocabulary. Biconsonantal verbs are listed in the lexicon and vocabulary sections in the Infinitive Construct form (קוּם, שִׂים and בּוֹא).[2] Recognition rather than memorization of the following Imperfect weak verb forms is suggested.

	ו Class קוּם	י Class שִׂים	ו Class בּוֹא	Strong
3ms	יָקוּם	יָשִׂים	יָבוֹא	יִקְטֹל
3fs	תָּקוּם	תָּשִׂים	תָּבוֹא	תִּקְטֹל
2ms	תָּקוּם	תָּשִׂים	תָּבוֹא	תִּקְטֹל
2fs	תָּקֹוּמִי	תָּשִׂוֹמִי	תָּבוֹאִי	תִּקְטְלִי
1cs	אָקוּם	אָשִׂים	אָבוֹא	אֶקְטֹל
3mp	יָקֹוּמוּ	יָשִׂימוּ	יָבוֹאוּ	יִקְטְלוּ
3fp	תָּקוּמֶ֫ינָה	תְּשִׂימֶ֫ינָה	תָּבוֹאנָה[3]	תִּקְטֹ֫לְנָה
2mp	תָּקֹוּמוּ	תָּשִׂימוּ	תָּבוֹאוּ	תִּקְטְלוּ
2fp	תָּקוּמֶ֫ינָה	תְּשִׂימֶ֫ינָה	תָּבוֹאנָה	תִּקְטֹ֫לְנָה
1cp	נָקוּם	נָשִׂים	נָבוֹא	נִקְטֹל

16.15 Biconsonantal Notes.

1. In all forms (except 3fp and 2fp) and in every class, the preformative vowel is Qamets (יָבוֹא/יָשִׂים/יָקוּם).

---

[2] The Infinitive Construct of Biconsonantal verbs will be studied in 20.7 below.

[3] The alternate spellings תְּבֹאֶ֫ינָה and תָּבֹאנָה are also attested.

2. The stem vowel of every form is determined by the Biconsonantal sub-class: Shureq (יָקוּם), Hireq Yod (יָשִׂים), or Holem Waw (יָבוֹא).

3. It should be noted that some mixing of the diagnostic stem vowel does occur. For example, יָשִׂים is sometimes rendered יָשׂוּם (Ex 4:11). It should also be noted that sometimes the stem vowel may be written defectively. For example, יָקוּם may appear as יָקֻם (Gen 27:31).

16.16 I-י Verbs. In terms of the Imperfect, I-י verbs inflect in one of two ways. With Type 1 verbs, the first consonant of the verbal root drops off in every form. With Type 2 verbs, the first root consonant is seemingly preserved as a vowel letter. We have also included the verb הָלַךְ (to walk) in the following paradigms because it inflects just like I-י (Type 1) weak verbs. Recognition rather than memorization of these weak verbal forms is suggested.

	I-י Type 1	הָלַךְ	I-י Type 2	Strong
3ms	יֵשֵׁב	יֵלֵךְ	יִירַשׁ	יִקְטֹל
3fs	תֵּשֵׁב	תֵּלֵךְ	תִּירַשׁ	תִּקְטֹל
2ms	תֵּשֵׁב	תֵּלֵךְ	תִּירַשׁ	תִּקְטֹל
2fs	תֵּשְׁבִי	תֵּלְכִי	תִּירְשִׁי	תִּקְטְלִי
1cs	אֵשֵׁב	אֵלֵךְ	אִירַשׁ	אֶקְטֹל
3mp	יֵשְׁבוּ	יֵלְכוּ	יִירְשׁוּ	יִקְטְלוּ
3fp	תֵּשַׁבְנָה	תֵּלַכְנָה	תִּירַשְׁנָה	תִּקְטֹלְנָה
2mp	תֵּשְׁבוּ	תֵּלְכוּ	תִּירְשׁוּ	תִּקְטְלוּ
2fp	תֵּשַׁבְנָה	תֵּלַכְנָה	תִּירַשְׁנָה	תִּקְטֹלְנָה
1cp	נֵשֵׁב	נֵלֵךְ	נִירַשׁ	נִקְטֹל

16.17 I-י Notes.

1. In every form of the Type 1 paradigm, the initial י root consonant has dropped and the Imperfect preformative vowel is Tsere throughout. You should also note that the stem vowel is Tsere in all forms without a sufformative. Verbs of this type can be difficult to recognize because the initial consonant (י) is lost,

leaving only the second and third consonants of the verbal root. You should understand that the ' in the 3ms and 3mp forms is the Imperfect preformative and not the first consonant of the verbal root. It is helpful to think of the Tsere preformative vowel as characteristic of this class of I-' verbs. Recognizing this feature should help you to accurately reconstruct the full verbal root.

2. In the Type 2 paradigm, the initial ' of the verbal root is seemingly preserved as the vowel letter Hireq Yod. The stem vowel is Pathach (יִירַשׁ), except in those forms that have a sufformative consisting of a vowel. Identification of the verbal root in this class should not be as difficult as Type 1 verbs because of the additional ' in the preformative vowel.

3. The verb הָלַךְ (to walk) inflects just like the Type 1 verb above with a loss of the initial root consonant. This verb occurs frequently and so it is important to be able to recognize these forms.

16.18 I-נ Verbs. As with I-' verbs, there are two types of I-נ verbs. Type 1 verbs have a Holem stem vowel (יִפֹּל). Type 2 verbs have the Pathach stem vowel (יִסַּע). An additional doubly weak paradigm is also included for study (I-נ and II-Guttural). Recognition rather than memorization of these weak verbal forms is suggested.

	I-נ Type 1	I-נ Type 2	לָקַח	Doubly Weak	Strong
3ms	יִפֹּל	יִסַּע	יִקַּח	יִנְחַל	יִקְטֹל
3fs	תִּפֹּל	תִּסַּע	תִּקַּח	תִּנְחַל	תִּקְטֹל
2ms	תִּפֹּל	תִּסַּע	תִּקַּח	תִּנְחַל	תִּקְטֹל
2fs	תִּפְּלִי	תִּסְעִי	תִּקְחִי	תִּנְחֲלִי	תִּקְטְלִי
1cs	אֶפֹּל	אֶסַּע	אֶקַּח	אֶנְחַל	אֶקְטֹל
3mp	יִפְּלוּ	יִסְעוּ	יִקְחוּ	יִנְחֲלוּ	יִקְטְלוּ
3fp	תִּפֹּלְנָה	תִּסַּעְנָה	תִּקַּחְנָה	תִּנְחַלְנָה	תִּקְטֹלְנָה
2mp	תִּפְּלוּ	תִּסְעוּ	תִּקְחוּ	תִּנְחֲלוּ	תִּקְטְלוּ
2fp	תִּפֹּלְנָה	תִּסַּעְנָה	תִּקַּחְנָה	תִּנְחַלְנָה	תִּקְטֹלְנָה
1cp	נִפֹּל	נִסַּע	נִקַּח	נִנְחַל	נִקְטֹל

16.19   I-נ Notes.

1. Type 1 verbs are distinguished from Type 2 verbs by their stem vowel. Type 1 has the Holem stem vowel and Type 2 exhibits the Pathach stem vowel. With both Type 1 and Type 2 verbs, the initial root consonant (נ) has assimilated into the second consonant of the verbal root and is represented by a Daghesh Forte. For example, יִנְפֹּל has become יִפֹּל with the assimilation of the נ. The presence of this Daghesh Forte should enable you to identify the verbal root as I-נ. Note, however, that the assimilated נ may be given up in the 2fs, 3mp, and 2mp forms of the Type 2 class.

2. The verb לָקַח (to take) inflects just like the Type 2 verb above with assimilation of the first root consonant (ל) into the second root consonant with a resulting Daghesh Forte (יִקַּח). This verb occurs frequently and so it is important to be able to recognize its Imperfect forms.

3. In the above doubly weak paradigm (I-נ and II-Guttural), you will notice that the נ which is the first root consonant does *not* assimilate into the second root consonant. The expected assimilation does not occur because the second root consonant is a guttural and, therefore, rejects the assimilation of the נ because it cannot take a Daghesh Forte.

16.20   Doubly Weak Verbs. As you know, some verbal roots have more than one weak root consonant. For example, the verb יָצָא (to go or come out) is both I-י and III-א. When this occurs, the verb will exhibit the weak features of both weak verbal categories. Several doubly weak verbs that occur frequently are listed below for your study. You should not try to memorize these paradigms. Rather, work through the forms of each paradigm and identify the weak features. In other words, use the information that you have already learned in this chapter to analyze the following weak verbs.

familiar

	עָשָׂה	רָאָה	הָיָה	יָצָא	נָשָׂא	נָתַן
3ms	יַעֲשֶׂה	יִרְאֶה	יִהְיֶה	יֵצֵא	יִשָּׂא	יִתֵּן
3fs	תַּעֲשֶׂה	תִּרְאֶה	תִּהְיֶה	תֵּצֵא	תִּשָּׂא	תִּתֵּן
2ms	תַּעֲשֶׂה	תִּרְאֶה	תִּהְיֶה	תֵּצֵא	תִּשָּׂא	תִּתֵּן
2fs	תַּעֲשִׂי	תִּרְאִי	תִּהְיִי	תֵּצְאִי	תִּשְׂאִי	תִּתְּנִי
1cs	אֶעֱשֶׂה	אֶרְאֶה	אֶהְיֶה	אֵצֵא	אֶשָּׂא	אֶתֵּן
3mp	יַעֲשׂוּ	יִרְאוּ	יִהְיוּ	יֵצְאוּ	יִשְׂאוּ	יִתְּנוּ
3fp	תַּעֲשֶׂינָה	תִּרְאֶינָה	תִּהְיֶינָה	תֵּצֶאנָה	תִּשֶּׂאנָה	תִּתֵּנָּה
2mp	תַּעֲשׂוּ	תִּרְאוּ	תִּהְיוּ	תֵּצְאוּ	תִּשְׂאוּ	תִּתְּנוּ
2fp	תַּעֲשֶׂינָה	תִּרְאֶינָה	תִּהְיֶינָה	תֵּצֶאנָה	תִּשֶּׂאנָה	תִּתֵּנָּה
1cp	נַעֲשֶׂה	נִרְאֶה	נִהְיֶה	נֵצֵא	נִשָּׂא	נִתֵּן

16.21 Doubly Weak Notes.

1. In the three III-ה paradigms (עָשָׂה, רָאָה and הָיָה), note the הֶ ending, except in those forms with sufformatives. The הֶ ending is diagnostic of III-ה Imperfect verbs in both the Qal and derived stems.

2. The verb עָשָׂה is both III-ה and I-Guttural. Note the vowel pattern of Pathach under the Imperfect preformative and Hateph Pathach under the guttural in first root position. This is the expected pattern in the Type 2 class of I-Guttural verbs (16.8). Even the Seghol/Hateph Seghol pattern is preserved in the 1cs form (אֶעֱשֶׂה).

3. Study the Imperfect forms of הָיָה with care. You will observe that this doubly weak verb inflects exactly like the Imperfect of בָּנָה (16.6). Careful study is required, however, because the presence of י in second root position creates certain forms that appear to be irregular in their inflection such as תִּהְיִי (2fs), יִהְיוּ (3mp), תִּהְיוּ (2mp) and even תִּהְיֶינָה (3fp and 2fp). In fact, these forms are inflected exactly like their counterparts in the בָּנָה paradigm above.

4. In the Imperfect of נָשָׂא, most forms preserve a Daghesh Forte in the second consonant of the verbal root as in יִשָּׂא (3ms). This Daghesh Forte represents the assimilated נ that is the first root

consonant. Observe, however, that the Daghesh Forte is given
up in the 2fs, 3mp, and 2mp forms.

5. The Imperfect forms of נָתַן need careful study as did those of
    הָיָה above. In every form, the first consonant of the verbal root
    (נ) has assimilated into the second root consonant and remains
    as a Daghesh Forte. But there is another process of assimilation
    to be observed in this paradigm. In the two feminine plural
    forms that are identical (תִּתֵּנָּה), the final נ that is the third
    consonant of the verbal root has assimilated into the נ of the
    sufformative (נָה) and is represented as a Daghesh Forte.

16.22 Reconstructing Verbal Roots. As you know by now, some weak verbs
may lose one or more of their original root consonants. For example,
in the above paradigm of נָתַן (to give), the Imperfect 3ms form יִתֵּן (he
will give) exhibits the loss of the first root consonant. This type of loss
can make identification of the full verbal root a difficult task. How,
therefore, do you identify a verbal root when one or more of the original
root consonants is missing? The first step is to know your options.
With the Imperfect, there are four major weak verb classes that drop a
root consonant: I-י, I-נ, III-ה and Geminate. Secondly, after all else fails
and if you are still lost in one of the standard lexicons, an analytical or
computerized lexicon will provide the verbal root for any inflected
form in the Hebrew Bible. There are, however, clues or diagnostic
features for certain weak verbal roots that will make their identification
easier.

1. With certain I-י verbs, the Yod consonant drops off in every
    form. For example, the Imperfect 3ms form of יָשַׁב (to sit, dwell)
    is יֵשֵׁב (he will sit, dwell). This weak form preserves only two of
    the three original root consonants. If you are unfamiliar with the
    verbal root, how do you know what has dropped off? Is this
    verb Biconsonantal (שָׁב or שׁוּב), Geminate (שָׁבַב), III-ה (שָׁבָה),
    I-י (יָשַׁב), or I-נ (נָשַׁב)? In this case, the key to identifying the
    verbal root is the Tsere preformative vowel (יֵשֵׁב). The Tsere
    preformative vowel is a diagnostic feature of the I-י Imperfect
    conjugation. By knowing this, you will be able to correctly identify
    the verbal root without having to look up numerous other verbal
    roots in a lexicon.

2. Most I-נ verbs (and לָקַח) assimilate their first root consonant into the second root consonant with a resulting Daghesh Forte. For example, the Imperfect 3ms form of נָפַל (to fall) is יִפֹּל (he will fall). In this case, the Daghesh Forte in the second root consonant (יִפֹּל) should alert you to the fact that this is a I-נ weak verbal root.

3. With III-ה weak verbal roots, the loss of the final ה root consonant occurs in every Imperfect form. In those forms without an Imperfect sufformative, a final ה vowel letter is present (יִבְנֶה). This is not, however, the third consonant of the verbal root. Fortunately, the presence of this vowel letter makes reconstructing the original verbal root much easier. In the remaining forms of the Imperfect having a sufformative, the final ה is altogether absent. For example, the Imperfect 3mp form of בָּנָה (to build) is יִבְנוּ (they will build). Note the absence of the final root consonant. In this case, it is helpful to use a process of elimination: (1) there is no Daghesh Forte in the בּ of this form and so it is not I-נ; (2) the preformative vowel is not Tsere and so it is not I-י; and (3) it could be Geminate but the preformative vowel of a Geminate verb is usually Qamets or Tsere. The only other option is III-ה. This might seem like a complicated process at first, but it is better than trying to look up numerous, possibly nonexistent, forms in a Hebrew lexicon in an attempt to discover the original root consonants.

4. With Geminate verbs, only one Geminate consonant remains in the Imperfect conjugation. For example, the Imperfect 3ms form of סָבַב (to surround) is יָסֹב (he will surround), with only one בּ. Some Geminate forms of the Imperfect exhibit a Daghesh Forte in the remaining Geminate consonant. In such instances, this clue should enable you to identify the weak verbal form as Geminate. In those forms without the Daghesh Forte, you will want to use the same process of elimination as with III-ה verbs, though it is more difficult with Geminate verbs because they exhibit considerable variation.

16.23 Summary.

1. Verbal paradigms to be memorized.

Strong	*II-Gutt*	*III-ע/ח*	*III-א*	*III-ה*
יִקְטֹל	יִבְחַר	יִשְׁלַח	יִמְצָא	יִבְנֶה
תִּקְטֹל	תִּבְחַר	תִּשְׁלַח	תִּמְצָא	תִּבְנֶה
תִּקְטֹל	תִּבְחַר	תִּשְׁלַח	תִּמְצָא	תִּבְנֶה
תִּקְטְלִי	תִּבְחֲרִי	תִּשְׁלְחִי	תִּמְצְאִי	תִּבְנִי
אֶקְטֹל	אֶבְחַר	אֶשְׁלַח	אֶמְצָא	אֶבְנֶה
יִקְטְלוּ	יִבְחֲרוּ	יִשְׁלְחוּ	יִמְצְאוּ	יִבְנוּ
תִּקְטֹלְנָה	תִּבְחַרְנָה	תִּשְׁלַחְנָה	תִּמְצֶאנָה	תִּבְנֶינָה
תִּקְטְלוּ	תִּבְחֲרוּ	תִּשְׁלְחוּ	תִּמְצְאוּ	תִּבְנוּ
תִּקְטֹלְנָה	תִּבְחַרְנָה	תִּשְׁלַחְנָה	תִּמְצֶאנָה	תִּבְנֶינָה
נִקְטֹל	נִבְחַר	נִשְׁלַח	נִמְצָא	נִבְנֶה

2. All other weak verbs that have been studied above are for recognition only. This means that you are not required to reproduce their paradigms in Hebrew. You must be able, however, to identify and parse these weak verb forms.

3. Here are verbal features to be memorized for reconstructing missing root consonants.

    a. I-י verbs normally drop their first root consonant but will be identifiable by the Tsere preformative vowel (and Tsere stem vowel) for Type 1 verbs. Type 2 verbs have the Hireq Yod preformative vowel and Pathach stem vowel (16.16). The verb הָלַךְ (to walk) also inflects like a I-י verb of the Type 1 class.

    b. I-נ verbs frequently assimilate the נ of the first root consonant into the second root consonant. The resulting Daghesh Forte will enable you to identify the missing consonant as I-נ. The verb לָקַח (to take) also inflects like a I-נ verb with assimilation of the ל.

    c. III-ה verbs drop their final root consonant but are identifiable by their distinctive ה ֶ ending (in those forms without a sufformative).

d. Geminate verbs retain only one Geminate consonant in the Imperfect conjugation. In some forms, this weak class is identifiable by a Daghesh Forte in the remaining Geminate consonant. In those forms without a Daghesh Forte, it is identifiable by a process of elimination and a Qamets or Tsere preformative vowel in most forms.

16.24 Vocabulary.

Verbs

גָּאַל	to redeem, deliver, act as kinsman, avenge (104)
חָטָא	to miss (a goal or mark), sin, commit a sin (240)
יָסַף	to add, continue (213)
יָרַשׁ	to inherit, take possession of, dispossess, take away someone's property (232)
כָּפַר	to cover, atone, make atonement (102)
נָטָה	to spread out, stretch out, extend, pitch (a tent) (216)
עָזַב	to leave, forsake, abandon, set free, let go (214)
קָרַב	to approach, draw near, come near (280)
רָבָה	to be(come) numerous, be(come) great, increase (229)
שָׁתָה	to drink (217)
תָּמַם	to be(come) complete, come to an end, cease, be consumed, be spent, be burned out (64)

Nouns

כַּף	hand, palm, sole of the foot (195); feminine
רֵעַ	friend, companion, neighbor (188)

Other

נֶגֶד	opposite, in front of (151)

16.25 **The Covenant Donkey.**[4] Gen 49:10-12 contains a prophecy of Messiah that describes both his sufferings and glory (cf. Luke 24:25-27, 45-48; Acts 26:22-23; 1 Pet 1:10-11). (The dual theme of Messiah's sufferings and glory is also present, for example, in Gen 3:15.) One suggestion of Messiah's sufferings in Gen 49:11 is found in the particular terms used to describe the animal that is bound to the vine. The first half of this verse reads as follows:

אֹסְרִי לַגֶּפֶן עִירוֹ   He [Shiloh] ties to the vine his foal

וְלַשֹּׂרֵקָה בְּנִי אֲתֹנוֹ   And to the choice vine the son of his female donkey

The general import of this language (and of the surrounding context) is that in the messianic era the grapevines will be so luxuriant and fruitful that one can simply hitch his donkey to them without concern for their being damaged. The two terms used to describe the donkey here, עַיִר and בְּנִי אֲתֹנוֹ (the Hireq Yod on בְּנִי here is a genitive ending), are picked up in Zechariah 9 (see further below), the primary Old Testament background for the Gospel accounts of Jesus' triumphal entry on a donkey into Jerusalem (Matt 21:1-9; Mark 11:1-10; Luke 19:28-38; John 12:12-16).

There is a text from Mari, a city on the upper Euphrates, dating from about the eighteenth century B.C., that describes a situation in which a suzerain has sent his lieutenant to supervise a covenant ratification ceremony between two of the suzerain's vassals. The royal servant has done his duty and is now reporting back to his lord. The lieutenant recounts in particular that in this covenant ceremony he took a certain kind of animal and killed it to seal the covenant and, specifically, to symbolize the curse that would overtake anyone who would break the covenant. The term he uses for this animal is cognate to Hebrew עַיִר בֶּן אָתוֹן. Evidently, this special breed of donkey was specifically stipulated for use in covenant ratification ceremonies (cf. *NIDOTTE* 1:575-577). The shedding of the blood of the עַיִר בֶּן אָתוֹן would ratify the covenant. It was the covenant donkey.

It is against this background that the significance of the donkey in Gen 49:11 can be appreciated. The covenant donkey also sheds light on Zech 9 and the Gospel accounts of the triumphal entry, which associate Messiah with this particular donkey known for its role in the shedding of blood in order to ratify a covenant. In particular, Messiah's association with the covenant donkey hints that the way to glory will be achieved through the shedding of blood. Jesus is qualified to be grantee and guarantor of the new covenant through the shedding of the blood of the covenant.

Zech 9:9-12 speaks in figurative terms of Messiah, the cross, and the preaching of the gospel, the speaking of peace to the nations. V. 9bc reads as follows:

הִנֵּה מַלְכֵּךְ יָבוֹא לָךְ	Behold, your king will come to you.
צַדִּיק וְנוֹשָׁע הוּא	He is [declared] righteous and vindicated,
עָנִי וְרֹכֵב עַל־חֲמוֹר	afflicted and riding on a donkey,
וְעַל־עַיִר בֶּן־אֲתֹנוֹת	and on a foal, son of a female donkey.

The coming king is righteous and victorious in the accomplishment of salvation for his people (this is Messiah's glory), but he is also afflicted and he comes riding on the covenant donkey (this is Messiah's suffering). Here the עַיִר and בֶּן אָתוֹן of Gen 49:11 come together again. By means of this terminological convergence, Zech 9:9 ties the Gen 49:11 prophecy to the triumphal entry of Jesus. Jesus' riding on a donkey on that occasion signifies, more than his humility, that he comes as the one who sheds the blood of the covenant. This was his primary purpose as he rode into Jerusalem on that day, and this is signalized by his arrival on the covenant donkey.

Much more evidence could be adduced in support of this interpretation. One further support is found in the fact that the context of Zech 9:9 (particularly vv. 10-12) speaks (symbolically) of Christ's work on the cross. By emerging justified from the sufferings of the cross Christ the glorified Messiah wins the right to offer reconciliation to those who are in rebellion against the heavenly suzerain, to speak the peace of the gospel to the nations.

J. Bergman Kline
M.A., Biblical Languages
Gordon-Conwell Theological Seminary
South Hamilton, Massachusetts

---

[4] This exegetical insight is based on the content of a lecture delivered by Meredith G. Kline as part of a course on the prophets given at Westminster Seminary California. Dr. Kline (my grandfather) has kindly granted me permission to summarize his arguments and throughout to use his own language freely.

16.26 **Advanced Information**. The Qal Imperfect of the stative verb יָכֹל (to be able) is irregular and occurs with some frequency.

	יָכֹל	Translation
3ms	יוּכַל	he is able
3fs	תּוּכַל	she is able
2ms	תּוּכַל	you are able
2fs	תּוּכְלִי	you are able
1cs	אוּכַל	I am able
3mp	יוּכְלוּ	they are able
3fp	תּוּכַלְנָה	they are able
2mp	תּוּכְלוּ	you are able
2fp	תּוּכַלְנָה	you are able
1cp	נוּכַל	we are able

Chapter 17

Waw Consecutive

17.1 **Introduction.** For the Qal stem, you have now completed the study of the Perfect and Imperfect verbal conjugations. You know that the Perfect conjugation is used to express a *completed action* and is usually translated by the English past tense (see 12.11.1; 13.3). You also know that the Imperfect conjugation is used to express *incomplete action* and is usually translated by the English future or present tenses (see 12.11.2; 15.2).

In this chapter, you will study a special and complementary use of the Perfect and Imperfect conjugations. When used in the context of biblical narrative (and sometimes in poetry), an Imperfect verb may be prefixed with a distinctive form of the conjunction וֹ and translated with the values of the Perfect. This special form of the conjunction is called *Waw Consecutive*. When prefixed with Waw Consecutive, the Imperfect verb may be called a "consecutive" Imperfect. Similarly, when a Waw Consecutive is prefixed to a Perfect verbal form, it may be called a "consecutive" Perfect.

The Waw Consecutive and the consecutive verbal forms are used primarily in narrative sequences to denote consecutive actions, that is, actions occurring in sequence. For example, the sentence "I sat down, and then I opened my book, and then I studied Hebrew" describes a sequence of consecutive actions occurring in the past. Similarly, the sentence "I will sit down, and I will open my book, and I will study Hebrew" describes consecutive or sequentially related actions occurring in the future. Below you will study both the form and function of the Waw Consecutive and the consecutive verbal forms.

17.2 **Form and Translation of the Consecutive Imperfect.**[1] When an Imperfect is prefixed with Waw Consecutive, *it will be translated with the values of a Perfect verbal form*. A few examples illustrate its form and basic translation value.

---

[1] The Hebrew Imperfect verbal form occurs 15,966 times in the Hebrew Bible. The consecutive Imperfect (Imperfect with Waw Consecutive) occurs 15,034 times.

Qal Imperfect without Waw Consecutive		*Qal Imperfect with Waw Consecutive*	
יִשְׁמֹר	he will observe	וַיִּשְׁמֹר	and he observed
יִזְכֹּר	he will remember	וַיִּזְכֹּר	and he remembered

The consecutive Imperfect is commonly translated with the English past tense (he killed) or present perfect tense (he has killed). With the Imperfect, the Waw Consecutive is spelled with the conjunction וֹ with Pathach and a Daghesh Forte in the Imperfect preformative.

Imperfect with Waw Consecutive

וַיִּקְטֹל

The pointing of the Waw Consecutive with the Imperfect should remind you of the definite article (הַ·). Now study the full Qal Imperfect paradigm of the strong verb with Waw Consecutive.

Imperfect with Waw Consecutive

3ms	וַיִּקְטֹל	and he killed
3fs	וַתִּקְטֹל	and she killed
2ms	וַתִּקְטֹל	and you killed
2fs	וַתִּקְטְלִי	and you killed
1cs	וָאֶקְטֹל	and I killed
3mp	וַיִּקְטְלוּ	and they killed
3fp	וַתִּקְטֹלְנָה	and they killed
2mp	וַתִּקְטְלוּ	and you killed
2fp	וַתִּקְטֹלְנָה	and you killed
1cp	וַנִּקְטֹל	and we killed

Notes:

1. With the prefixing of the Waw Consecutive, the spelling of the Imperfect verbal forms is unchanged. Be certain to note how these forms are translated. Each is Imperfect in form but Perfect

in translation. With Waw Consecutive, therefore, Imperfect verbs are translated like Perfect verbs.

2. Note the spelling of the Waw Consecutive in the 1cs וָאֶקְטֹל (and I killed). Because the א preformative is a guttural, it rejects the Daghesh Forte and the Pathach under the Waw becomes Qamets as a result of compensatory lengthening.

3. Imperfect verbs may also appear with the regular conjunction וְ as in וְיִכְתֹּב (and he will write). The regular conjunction וְ has neither the form nor the function of the Waw Consecutive. With the regular conjunction וְ, the Imperfect retains its normal translation values. Compare the two paradigms below and note how the spelling of the Waw Consecutive on the Imperfect is distinct from that of the regular conjunction וְ on the Imperfect.

	Qal Imperfect with Waw Consecutive		*Qal Imperfect with Regular Conjunction*	
3ms	וַיִּקְטֹל	and he killed	וְיִקְטֹל	and he will kill
3fs	וַתִּקְטֹל	and she killed	וְתִקְטֹל	and she will kill
2ms	וַתִּקְטֹל	and you killed	וְתִקְטֹל	and you will kill
2fs	וַתִּקְטְלִי	and you killed	וְתִקְטְלִי	and you will kill
1cs	וָאֶקְטֹל	and I killed	וְאֶקְטֹל	and I will kill
3mp	וַיִּקְטְלוּ	and they killed	וְיִקְטְלוּ	and they will kill
3fp	וַתִּקְטֹלְנָה	and they killed	וְתִקְטֹלְנָה	and they will kill
2mp	וַתִּקְטְלוּ	and you killed	וְתִקְטְלוּ	and you will kill
2fp	וַתִּקְטֹלְנָה	and you killed	וְתִקְטֹלְנָה	and you will kill
1cp	וַנִּקְטֹל	and we killed	וְנִקְטֹל	and we will kill

17.3 **Changes in the Spelling of the Consecutive Imperfect Verb.** In most verb classes, the prefixing of the Waw Consecutive does not change the spelling of the Imperfect. There are some weak verbs, however, that do experience minor changes. In terms of recognition, these changes should not give you too much trouble.

1. In I-א verbs of the אָמַר type (16.10) and certain I-י verbs (as well as הָלַךְ), the stem vowel normally changes to Seghol.[2] Note the following examples:

יֹאמַר	he will say	⟩	וַיֹּאמֶר	and he said
יֵשֵׁב	he will dwell	⟩	וַיֵּשֶׁב	and he dwelt
יֵלֵךְ	he will go	⟩	וַיֵּלֶךְ	and he went

2. With the prefixing of the Waw Consecutive, Biconsonantal and III-ה verbs are usually "shortened" in those Imperfect forms without a sufformative.[3] In Biconsonantal verbs, the medial vowel letter is lost. In III-ה verbs, the final הָ drops off. Note the following examples (see also 18.14):

יָקוּם	he will rise up	⟩	[4]וַיָּקָם	and he rose up
יָשִׂים	he will set	⟩	וַיָּשֶׂם	and he set
יִבְנֶה	he will build	⟩	וַיִּבֶן	and he built
יִגְלֶה	he will reveal	⟩	וַיִּגֶל	and he revealed

17.4 **The Use of the Consecutive Imperfect**. In the context of Hebrew narrative, the consecutive Imperfect is normally used for the *past tense narrative sequence*.[5] In other words, when an author wanted to write about a series of actions in the past, he would use the Imperfect with Waw Consecutive.

1. Frequently, a past tense narrative sequence will begin with a Perfect verb followed by any number of consecutive Imperfect verbs. The Perfect verb that begins the sequence serves to signal the past tense narration. In this past tense narration, each consecutive Imperfect verb may be temporally, logically, sequentially, or consequentially related to the preceding verb.

---

[2] This type of change is occasioned by the retraction of the accent that occurs with the prefixing of the Waw Consecutive to forms without a sufformative (except for the 1cs).

[3] This type of change is also occasioned by retraction of the accent.

[4] Note that the vowel under the ק is Qamets Hatuf and not Qamets.

[5] Though the terminology "past tense narrative sequence" is not commonly used, the term is descriptive of how the Imperfect with Waw Consecutive functions in biblical narration. The language will be used throughout because it is easily understood by the beginning student.

וְהָאָדָם יָדַע אֶת־חַוָּה אִשְׁתּוֹ וַתַּהַר וַתֵּלֶד אֶת־קַיִן

And Adam knew Eve his wife, *and then she
conceived, and then she bore* Cain (Gen 4:1).

וּמֹשֶׁה עָלָה אֶל־הָאֱלֹהִים וַיִּקְרָא אֵלָיו יְהוָה מִן־הָהָר

And Moses went up to God, *and then* the LORD
called to him from the mountain (Ex 19:3).

2. It is not uncommon for a past tense narrative sequence to begin
with the consecutive Imperfect (and not with a Perfect as above).

וַיִּקְרָא אֶל־מֹשֶׁה וַיְדַבֵּר יְהוָה אֵלָיו מֵאֹהֶל מוֹעֵד

And he *called* to Moses and the LORD *spoke* to him
from the tent of meeting (Lev 1:1).

וַיִּפְשַׁע מוֹאָב בְּיִשְׂרָאֵל אַחֲרֵי מוֹת אַחְאָב

Moab *rebelled* against Israel after the
death of Ahab (2 Kgs 1:1).

3. A past tense narrative sequence may begin with the temporal
modifier וַיְהִי followed by Imperfect verbs with Waw Consecutive.
The form וַיְהִי is the Qal Imperfect 3ms form of הָיָה (to be) with
Waw Consecutive. The temporal modifier stands at the beginning
of the sequence in which it appears.

וַיְהִי אַחֲרֵי מוֹת אַבְרָהָם וַיְבָרֶךְ אֱלֹהִים אֶת־יִצְחָק בְּנוֹ

And after the death of Abraham
God *blessed* Isaac his son (Gen 25:11).

4. You now understand that the past tense narrative sequence is
composed of a string of consecutive Imperfect verbs, that is,
Imperfect verbs with Waw Consecutive. Occasionally, this
sequence of consecutive Imperfect verbs may be interrupted by
a Perfect in the place of an expected Imperfect with Waw
Consecutive. This interruption in the narrative sequence can
happen for a number of reasons, as for example when a negative
clause appears in the sequence. The negated verb interrupts the
sequence with the result that the verb is no longer an Imperfect
with Waw Consecutive but now appears as a Perfect following
the negative particle. Note that the regular conjunction וְ is often
prefixed to this negative particle (וְלֹא). After this interruption,

the sequence may return to the string of consecutive Imperfect verbs. The following example illustrates a past tense narrative sequence which begins with a consecutive Imperfect (וַיֶּחֱזַק). Note that the sequence is interrupted by a negative clause (beginning with וְלֹא־שָׁמַע) and thereafter returns to consecutive Imperfect verbs (וַיִּפֶן and וַיָּבֹא).

$$\text{וַיֶּחֱזַק לֵב־פַּרְעֹה וְלֹא־שָׁמַע אֲלֵהֶם כַּאֲשֶׁר דִּבֶּר יְהוָה}$$
$$\text{וַיִּפֶן פַּרְעֹה וַיָּבֹא אֶל־בֵּיתוֹ}$$

And Pharaoh's heart *became hard* and *he did not listen* to them just as the Lord had said. And (so) Pharaoh *turned* and *went* to his house (Ex 7:22-23).

17.5 Form and Translation of the Consecutive Perfect.[6] When a Perfect verb is prefixed with Waw Consecutive, *it will be translated with the values of the Imperfect.* A few examples will illustrate its form and basic translation value.

Qal Perfect without Waw Consecutive		*Qal Perfect with Waw Consecutive*	
שָׁמַר	he observed	וְשָׁמַר	and he will observe
זָכַר	he remembered	וְזָכַר	and he will remember

Note that the Waw Consecutive with the Perfect is spelled differently than the Waw Consecutive with the Imperfect.

Perfect with Waw Consecutive	*Imperfect with Waw Consecutive*
וְקָטַל	וַיִּקְטֹל

With the Perfect, it is important to observe that there is no difference in spelling between the Waw Consecutive and the regular conjunction וְ (both are prefixed according to the rules of 5.7). Later in this chapter, we will discuss how to distinguish between the Waw Consecutive and

---

[6] The Hebrew Perfect verb occurs 20,829 times in the Hebrew Bible. The Perfect prefixed with וְ (Waw Consecutive or regular conjunction וְ) occurs 6,463 times. As you can see, the Imperfect with Waw Consecutive, which occurs 15,034 times, is much more common than the Perfect with Waw Consecutive.

the regular conjunction וְ on the Perfect. For now, study both the form and translation value of the Perfect with Waw Consecutive.

Perfect with Waw Consecutive

3ms	וְקָטַל	and he will kill
3fs	וְקָטְלָה	and she will kill
2ms	וְקָטַלְתָּ	and you will kill
2fs	וְקָטַלְתְּ	and you will kill
1cs	וְקָטַלְתִּי	and I will kill
3cp	וְקָטְלוּ	and they will kill
2mp	וּקְטַלְתֶּם	and you will kill
2fp	וּקְטַלְתֶּן	and you will kill
1cp	וְקָטַלְנוּ	and we will kill

Notes:

1. The spelling of the Perfect verb is not changed by the prefixing of the Waw Consecutive.

2. On most forms, the Waw Consecutive is spelled with Shewa (וְ). In the 2mp (וּקְטַלְתֶּם) and 2fp (וּקְטַלְתֶּן), the Waw Consecutive is spelled as Shureq (וּ) because it occurs before a consonant with Vocal Shewa (see 5.7).

3. In the Perfect with Waw Consecutive, the accent usually shifts to the final syllable in the 2ms and 1cs forms. For example, קָטַלְתִּי (I killed) is accented on the second syllable but וְקָטַלְתִּי (and I will kill) is usually accented on the final syllable because it is prefixed with the Waw Consecutive. This shift in accent does not occur, however, when the Perfect verb is prefixed with the regular conjunction וְ as in וְקָטַלְתִּי (and I killed). The shift in accent can help to distinguish between the Waw Consecutive and the regular conjunction וְ in the 2ms and 1cs forms. This point is illustrated in the beginning of Gen 9:15, which reads: וְזָכַרְתִּי אֶת־בְּרִיתִי. Given that the Waw Consecutive and the regular conjunction וְ are spelled the same with a Perfect verb, is the conjunction prefixed to זָכַרְתִּי the Waw Consecutive or the regular conjunction? Should this text be translated as "I

remembered my covenant" (with the regular conjunction וְ) or "I will remember my covenant" (with Waw Consecutive)? Because the Hebrew Bible locates the accent on the final syllable (וְזָכַרְתִּ֫י), the Waw should be identified as the Waw Consecutive and the clause translated, "I will remember my covenant." Other contextual considerations, to be studied in the next section, will further help you to distinguish between the Waw Consecutive and the regular conjunction וְ on the Perfect.

17.6   **The Use of the Consecutive Perfect.** Like the consecutive Imperfect, the consecutive Perfect is used in narrative sequences. The consecutive Perfect is used for the *future tense narrative sequence*[7] (and also to express habitual-durative action). For example, Hebrew may use the consecutive Perfect for prophetic revelations that look to the future or for legal instruction that regulates future conduct.

1. Normally, the future tense narrative sequence begins with an Imperfect verb followed by any number of consecutive Perfect verbs. The Imperfect verb that begins this narrative sequence signals the future tense narration.

    שֵׁשֶׁת יָמִים תַּעֲבֹד וְעָשִׂיתָ כָּל־מְלַאכְתֶּ֑ךָ

    Six days *you will labor and (you will) do*
    all your work (Deut 5:13).

    לְמַעַן תִּזְכְּרוּ וַעֲשִׂיתֶם אֶת־כָּל־מִצְוֹתָי
    וִהְיִיתֶם קְדֹשִׁים לֵאלֹהֵיכֶם

    In order that *you may remember and (you may) do* all my
    commandments *and (you may) be holy* to your God (Num 15:40).

2. The consecutive Perfect may follow an Imperative verb and be translated with the full force of the initial Imperative. Even though you have not yet studied the Imperative verb, the following examples should be clear. The forms עֲמֹד (stand!) and שִׁמְעוּ (hear!) are both Imperatives.

---

[7] Though the terminology "future tense narrative sequence" is not commonly used, the term is descriptive of how the Perfect with Waw Consecutive functions in biblical narration. As with the designation "past tense narrative sequence" above, this language will also be used throughout the discussion because it is easily understood by the beginning student.

עֲמֹד בְּשַׁעַר בֵּית יְהוָה וְקָרֵאתָ שָּׁם אֶת־הַדָּבָר הַזֶּה
וְאָמַרְתָּ שִׁמְעוּ דְבַר־יְהוָה

Stand (Imperative) in the gate of the Lord's house
and proclaim there this word *and say*, "Hear
the word of the Lord" (Jer 7:2).

שִׁמְעוּ אֶת־דִּבְרֵי הַבְּרִית הַזֹּאת וַעֲשִׂיתֶם אוֹתָם

Hear (Imperative) the words of this
covenant *and do* them (Jer 11:6).

3. A future tense narrative sequence may begin with the temporal
modifier וְהָיָה followed by Perfect verbs with Waw Consecutive.
The form וְהָיָה is the Qal Perfect 3ms of הָיָה with Waw Consecutive.
The temporal modifier stands at the beginning of the sequence
in which it appears.

וְהָיָה בַיּוֹם הַהוּא וְשָׁבַרְתִּי אֶת־קֶשֶׁת יִשְׂרָאֵל

And in that day *I will break* the
bow of Israel (Hos 1:5).

4. Infrequently, the Perfect may appear with the regular conjunction
וְ and not the Waw Consecutive. In these instances, the verbal
construction is translated with "and" plus the past (or present)
tense of the verb, as in וְקָטַל (and he killed). There are two basic
contexts in which the Perfect with the regular conjunction וְ may
appear.

a. The Perfect with the regular conjunction וְ may occur in a
series of Perfect verbs. In this context, the first verb in the
series will be the regular Perfect. The Perfect verbs that
follow may be joined by the regular conjunction וְ and
should be translated with the temporal value of the first
Perfect verb.[8]

וַאֲנִי זָקַנְתִּי וָשַׂבְתִּי

But as for me, *I am old* and *I am gray* (1 Sam 12:2).

---

[8] Note that similar constructions exist in which a Perfect verb may be followed
by consecutive Perfects. In these cases, the verbal forms are separated by one of the
major disjunctive accents (36.2.3). For examples, see Deut 6:11; Jer 28:13; Ezek 18:21.

אָבִיךָ הֲלוֹא אָכַל וְשָׁתָה וְעָשָׂה מִשְׁפָּט

As for your father, did he not *eat*
and *drink* and *do* justice? (Jer 22:15)

> b. The Perfect with the regular conjunction וְ may occur in a series of short (syntactically) parallel clauses. In this context, both clauses contain a Perfect verb, the second of which is prefixed with the regular conjunction וְ and not the Waw Consecutive.

הִנֵּה נָגַע זֶה עַל־שְׂפָתֶיךָ וְסָר עֲוֺנֶךָ

Behold, he *touched* this upon your lips
and he *removed* your iniquity (Isa 6:7).

כִּי־פָדָה יְהוָה אֶת־יַעֲקֹב וּגְאָלוֹ מִיַּד חָזָק מִמֶּנּוּ

For the Lord *ransomed* Jacob and he *redeemed* him
from a hand of one stronger than he (Jer 31:11).

17.7 Translating Temporal Modifiers. Because of their frequency in certain contexts, the temporal modifiers וַיְהִי and וְהָיָה are best not translated, though the conjunction may still be translated as "and." Some will suggest that וַיְהִי be translated, "and it came to pass that" and that וְהָיָה be translated, "and it will be that." Given the frequency of these temporal modifiers in narrative, it is preferable to avoid these translations in the interest of good English style.

17.8 Parsing. The parsing of consecutive verbal forms is just like the parsing of regular Perfect or Imperfect verbs except that you must identify the presence of the Waw Consecutive, as the following examples illustrate.

וַיִּשְׁמֹר Qal Imperfect 3ms   שָׁמַר with Waw Consecutive

וְזָכַר Qal Perfect 3ms   זָכַר with Waw Consecutive

17.9 Summary.

1. Perfect and Imperfect verbs with Waw Consecutive are used primarily in narrative sequences to denote consecutive actions, that is, actions occurring in logical or temporal sequence.

2. When an Imperfect verb is prefixed with Waw Consecutive, it will be translated with the values of the Perfect. The Waw Consecutive on the Imperfect consists of the conjunction וְ with Pathach and a Daghesh Forte in the Imperfect preformative (וַיִּקְטֹל).

3. Some weak verb classes experience minor spelling changes with the prefixing of the Waw Consecutive to the Imperfect. In I-א verbs of the אָמַר type and certain I-י verbs (as well as הָלַךְ), the stem vowel usually changes to Seghol. Biconsonantal and III-ה consecutive verbs are usually "shortened" in those forms without a sufformative (except the 1cs).

4. The consecutive Imperfect is commonly used for the past tense narrative sequence. This narrative sequence may begin with a Perfect verb followed by any number of consecutive Imperfects.

5. When a Perfect verb is prefixed with Waw Consecutive, it will be translated with the values of the Imperfect. The Waw Consecutive with the Perfect is spelled just like the regular conjunction וְ (וְקָטַל).

6. The consecutive Perfect is commonly used for the future tense narrative sequence (and also to express habitual-durative action). This narrative sequence may begin with an Imperfect verb followed by any number of consecutive Perfects.

7. Rarely, the Perfect may appear with the regular conjunction וְ and not the Waw Consecutive. In these instances, the verbal construction is translated with "and" plus the past tense. There are two basic contexts in which the Perfect with the regular conjunction וְ may appear: (1) in a series of Perfect verbs and (2) in a series of short (syntactically) parallel clauses with Perfect verbs.

8. A past tense narrative sequence may begin with the temporal modifier וַיְהִי (Qal Imperfect 3ms form of הָיָה with Waw Consecutive) followed by Imperfect verbs with Waw Consecutive. A future tense narrative sequence may begin with the temporal modifier וְהָיָה (Qal Perfect 3ms הָיָה with Waw Consecutive) followed by Perfect verbs with the Waw Consecutive.

17.10 Vocabulary.

Verbs

אָבַד	to perish, vanish, be(come) lost (185)
אָהַב	to love (217)
אָסַף	to gather (in), take in, take away, destroy (200)
בָּעַר	to burn (up), consume (60)

גָּלָה	to uncover, reveal, disclose (187)
טָהֵר	to be clean, be pure (94)
כָּלָה	to (be) complete, be finished, come to an end (207)
רוּם	to be high, be exalted, rise (197)
שָׁפַט	to judge, decide (204)

Nouns

אֱמֶת	truth, fidelity (127); feminine
כִּסֵּא	seat, chair, throne (135)
מִסְפָּר	number (134)
עֶשֶׂר	ten (492)
שֶׁמֶשׁ	sun (134)

17.11 Believing is Seeing. When Abraham was called in Gen 12, he was expected to trust God to take him "to a land *I will show you*" (אַרְאֶךָּ, Hiphil Imperfect 1cs of רָאָה with 2ms pronominal suffix). This was a radical call, to leave everything familiar without any knowledge of where he was going. His only source of confidence could be the promise of God "to show him." In a second episode of testing (Gen 22), Abraham was called to sacrifice his beloved son in "the land of Moriah" or הַמֹּרִיָּה (a name likely playing on the same root, רָאָה). Abraham set out promptly and on the third day he lifted up his eyes and *saw* (וַיַּרְא Qal Imperfect 3ms of רָאָה with Waw Consecutive) the place to which God was leading him (22:4). In 22:8, when Isaac asked his father where the offering was, the answer was simply: "God will *reveal* it" אֱלֹהִים יִרְאֶה־לּוֹ (Qal Imperfect 3ms of רָאָה). As Abraham was about to slay his son, the angel's voice stopped him. The patriarch lifted up his eyes (again) and *saw* (וַיַּרְא Qal Imperfect 3ms of רָאָה with Waw Consecutive) a ram caught in the thicket (22:13).

As a result of this divine provision, Abraham named the place יְהוָה יִרְאֶה (The LORD *will see*). In 22:13, the verb is again a Qal Imperfect of רָאָה. To this day, we are told in 22:14, the name is retained because, "on the mount of the LORD it shall be revealed" יֵרָאֶה Niphal Imperfect 3ms of רָאָה).

Most of us know the name from this story as "Jehovah Jireh," which translates "The LORD [my] Provider." The root רָאָה certainly carries the nuance of providing in this context. But it is helpful to bear in mind its primary meaning, that of sight: The Lord "revealed" the sacrifice to Abraham.

In the Old Testament, faith is sometimes described as a form of sight. In 2 Chr 26:5, the faithful king Uzziah was commended for, literally, "learning how *to see* God" (רְאֹת Qal Infinitive Construct from רָאָה). One of the most common designations for an Old Testament prophet is רֹאֶה, a *seer*. A prophet was a person who could see divine things, and could see earthly things from God's perspective. Abraham would one day be honored in Hebrews 11 for a faith defined as the "conviction of things *not yet seen*."

Tim Laniak
Associate Professor of Old Testament
Gordon-Conwell Theological Seminary
Charlotte, North Carolina

17.12 **Advanced Information: Waw Consecutive**. Hebrew grammars will refer to Perfect and Imperfect verbs prefixed with the Waw Consecutive in a number of different ways. A brief summary of this varied terminology can help to explain some of the nuances of the consecutive forms.

1. *Waw Consecutive.* Perfect and Imperfect verbal forms prefixed with the conjunction Waw are used primarily in narrative sequences to denote consecutive actions, that is, actions occurring in logical or temporal sequence. For example, the sentence "I sat down, and then I opened my book, and then I studied Hebrew" describes a sequence of consecutive actions occurring in the past. Similarly, the sentence "I will sit down, and I will open my book, and I will study Hebrew" describes consecutive or sequentially related actions occurring in the future. The terminology "Waw Consecutive" is descriptive of the function of this special form of the conjunction.

2. *Waw Conversive.* Because the Perfect and Imperfect conjugations appear to switch values when prefixed with this special form of the conjunction Waw, the designation "Waw Conversive" is descriptive of the fact that the prefixing of the conjugation appears to "convert" the value of the verbal form – Imperfect to Perfect or Perfect to Imperfect. Those forms that appear with the Waw Conversive are often called "converted" verbal forms. It should

be noted, however, that the presence of the conjunction does not "convert" the verb, but rather marks its special function. However, the "converted" and "conversive" terminology is helpfully descriptive of what appears to occur in terms of basic translation value.

3. *Waw Relative.* When prefixed to the Perfect or Imperfect conjugations, the conjunction "relates" the verb to a previous verb. In other words, the function of the "Waw Relative" is to relate verbs one to another, especially in terms of temporal succession. Therefore, the terminology "Waw Relative" is descriptive of the function of this conjunction at the level of sentence syntax.

4. *Wayyiqtol and Weqatal.* These terms are simply the English transliterations of וַיִּקְטֹל (*wayyiqtol*) and וְקָטַל (*weqatal*). This terminology is descriptive of the verbal construction without reference to either its translation value or its function.

5. *Preterite.* The term "preterite" is a grammatical term describing a verb that refers to a simple action in the past. This is the primary value of the Imperfect conjugation when prefixed with the Waw Consecutive. Because of this, the consecutive Imperfect verb is often referred to as the "preterite." The term "preterite" does not, however, refer to the *weqatal* form.

Chapter 18

Qal Imperative, Cohortative, and Jussive

18.1 **Introduction.** In this chapter, we will study the Hebrew *volitional* conjugations known as Imperative, Cohortative and Jussive. The term "volitional" describes those conjugations used, as a general rule, *to express some type of command, wish, or desire.* The various forms of the volitional conjugations are related to corresponding Imperfect forms. For this reason, you will want to have mastered the Imperfect forms of strong and weak verbs before working through this chapter.

18.2 **Imperative Conjugation.** The Imperative is the most frequently occurring volitional conjugation in the Hebrew Bible.[1] It is used primarily to express direct commands, demanding (immediate) action from the one being addressed. It can also be used to grant permission or to communicate a request. The Hebrew Imperative *occurs only in the second person, singular and plural.* For example, "*You* (second person) *defend* the cause of the weak!"

18.3 **Imperative Paradigm: Strong Verbs.** Because the Imperative conjugation occurs exclusively in the second person, there are only four forms to study: masculine singular and plural and feminine singular and plural. These forms will be easy to memorize because they are derived from their corresponding Imperfect forms. You should think of the Imperative verbal form as an Imperfect without the preformative. The following Imperative paradigm must be memorized.

	Imperative	*Sufformative*	*Translation*
2ms	קְטֹל		(you) kill!
2fs	קִטְלִי	ִי	(you) kill!
2mp	קִטְלוּ	וּ	(you) kill!
2fp	קְטֹלְנָה	נָה	(you) kill!

---

[1] The Imperative conjugation occurs 4,288 times in the Hebrew Bible. In the Qal stem it occurs 2,896 times, 68% of all Imperatives.

18.4   Imperative Paradigm Notes.

1. The most important observation to make is that the above forms of the Imperative are related to their corresponding Imperfect forms. Remove the Imperfect preformative (consonant and vowel) from the four second person forms, singular and plural, and you have the Imperative paradigm. This means that if you have memorized the Imperfect paradigm, then you already know the forms of the Imperative.

	Imperfect Form		Subtract Preformative		Imperative Form
2ms	תִּקְטֹל	＞	תִּ׀קְטֹל	＞	קְטֹל
2fs	תִּקְטְלִי	＞	תִּ׀קְטְלִי	＞	קִטְלִי
2mp	תִּקְטְלוּ	＞	תִּ׀קְטְלוּ	＞	קִטְלוּ
2fp	תִּקְטֹלְנָה	＞	תִּ׀קְטֹלְנָה	＞	קְטֹלְנָה

2. Both the 2fs and 2mp forms undergo a minor change based upon the rule that two Vocal Shewas cannot stand together at the beginning of a word (4.12). For example, begin with the Imperfect form תִּקְטְלוּ and subtract the preformative (consonant and vowel) for the Imperative and you are left with קְטְלוּ. Because two Vocal Shewas cannot stand together at the beginning of a word, the Imperative form is subsequently rendered קִטְלוּ after applying Rule of Shewa (4.12).

3. Frequently (309 times), the 2ms Imperative appears with an הָ ending as in קָטְלָה (kill!).[2] Note that the vowel in the first syllable is Qamets Hatuf and not Qamets. Be careful not to confuse this alternate Imperative form with the Qal Perfect 3fs קָטְלָה. Context (and the Metheg) will enable you to distinguish between the two forms. The alternate form with הָ does not necessarily translate differently than the regular 2ms form. Below are three more examples of the 2ms Imperative with the הָ ending.

---

[2] The הָ ending also appears with the consecutive Imperfect (104 times) and with the Cohortative (525 times), to be studied later in this chapter.

Verbal Root	Regular 2ms Form	Alternate Form (הָ)	Translation
שָׁמַר	שְׁמֹר	שָׁמְרָה	you (2ms) observe!
שָׁפַט	שְׁפֹט	שָׁפְטָה	you (2ms) judge!
שָׁמַע	שְׁמַע	שִׁמְעָה³	you (2ms) listen!

18.5 **Negation of the Imperative.** To produce a negative command, Hebrew does not negate an Imperative form. Prohibitions (negative commands) are expressed with the negative particles לֹא or אַל with the Imperfect (see 15.9). For review, the particle לֹא before the Imperfect can express an absolute and permanent prohibition. The particle אַל before an Imperfect expresses an immediate and specific prohibition (see also 18.15).

18.6 **The Particle נָא.** Frequently (191 times), Imperatives are followed by the particle נָא which may be translated as "please" or simply left untranslated. This particle may or may not be connected to the Imperative with a Maqqef. For example, both שְׁמֹר נָא and שְׁמָר־נָא occur and may be translated as either "observe!" or "please observe!" Note that when the Imperative is connected to the particle with a Maqqef, there is a vowel change in the Imperative (Holem to Qamets Hatuf). Do not be concerned about this change, however, since the presence of the נָא particle is often an indication of the Imperative (though it may signal other forms as well).

18.7 **Translating the Imperative.** When translating the Hebrew Imperative, it is not always necessary to use the second person pronoun (you). For example, שְׁמֹר may be translated as either "you observe!" or simply "observe!" English style normally prefers the shorter translation without the pronoun. Please note, however, that the Imperative is always second person even if you choose not to use the second person pronoun in your translation.

עִבְדוּ אֶת־יְהוָה⁴

"You (2mp) serve the Lord!"

or

"Serve the Lord!" (Ps 100:2)

---

³ With relative frequency, the vowel under the first root consonant in these alternate Imperative forms will be Hireq instead of Qamets Hatuf.

⁴ Frequently, in the 2fs and 2mp Imperative forms (such as עִבְדִי and עִבְדוּ), the Daghesh Lene that is expected in the *begadkephat* consonant after the Silent Shewa is given up.

18.8 Weak Forms of the Imperative: Part 1. You have learned that strong verb Imperative forms are related to strong Imperfect forms. This also holds true for the weak verb forms of the Imperative. There are, however, some weak Imperative forms that do not correspond exactly to their Imperfect counterparts. The changes in these forms are minor and should not present any great difficulty in terms of recognizing the forms of the paradigm. It is important to note that in the following weak verb Imperatives no root consonants are lost and all of the expected sufformatives remain unchanged.

	I-Guttural				II-Guttural		
	Imperfect		*Imperative*		*Imperfect*		*Imperative*
2ms	תֶּחֱזַק	≻	חֲזַק		תִּבְחַר	≻	בְּחַר
2fs	תֶּחֶזְקִי	≻	חִזְקִי		תִּבְחֲרִי	≻	בַּחֲרִי
2mp	תֶּחֶזְקוּ	≻	חִזְקוּ		תִּבְחֲרוּ	≻	בַּחֲרוּ
2fp	תֶּחֱזַקְנָה	≻	חֲזֹקְנָה		תִּבְחַרְנָה	≻	בְּחַרְנָה

	I-א Type 1[5]				I-א Type 2		
	Imperfect		*Imperative*		*Imperfect*		*Imperative*
2ms	תֶּאֱסֹר	≻	אֱסֹר		תֹּאמַר	≻	אֱמֹר
2fs	תַּאַסְרִי	≻	אִסְרִי		תֹּאמְרִי	≻	אִמְרִי
2mp	תַּאַסְרוּ	≻	אִסְרוּ		תֹּאמְרוּ	≻	אִמְרוּ
2fp	תֶּאֱסֹרְנָה	≻	אֱסֹרְנָה		תֹּאמַרְנָה	≻	אֱמֹרְנָה

	III-ע/ח				III-א		
	Imperfect		*Imperative*		*Imperfect*		*Imperative*
2ms	תִּשְׁלַח	≻	שְׁלַח		תִּמְצָא	≻	מְצָא
2fs	תִּשְׁלְחִי	≻	שִׁלְחִי		תִּמְצְאִי	≻	מִצְאִי
2mp	תִּשְׁלְחוּ	≻	שִׁלְחוּ		תִּמְצְאוּ	≻	מִצְאוּ
2fp	תִּשְׁלַחְנָה	≻	שְׁלַחְנָה		תִּמְצֶאנָה	≻	מְצֶאנָה

---

[5] You will recall that there are two types of I-א Imperfects. Type 1 has a Seghol preformative vowel as in יֶאֱסֹר and Type 2 has a Holem preformative vowel as in יֹאמַר. In the Imperative conjugation, however, only one type exists. Regardless of the Imperfect pattern, the Imperative conjugation follows only one pattern of vocalization.

18.9 **Weak Forms of the Imperative: Part 2.** In the above triconsonantal weak verb classes (18.8), you studied Imperative forms in which no root consonants were lost. Compared to the strong verb paradigm, some minor vowel changes were observed. Now we will study four triconsonantal weak verb classes in which a root consonant is lost. When encountering such a form, you will need to recover the missing consonant in order to identify the verbal root. Once again, the best way to begin reconstructing verbal roots is to know your options. As you will see from the following discussion, there are four major classes that drop a root consonant in the Imperative conjugation: III-ה, I-נ, I-י and Geminate. When you are attempting to reconstruct a triconsonantal verbal root from only two remaining consonants, use the order provided above. For example, if you were to encounter שַׁל־נְעָלֶיךָ (…your shoes!) in Exodus 3:5, you would need to reconstruct the verbal root of the Imperative שַׁל in order to determine its meaning. Begin with the III-ה option, שָׁלָה (be quiet) and you will find from the lexicon that this does not work (Be quiet your shoes!). Next, try the I-נ option, נָשַׁל (to remove) and you will discover that this is the correct option (Remove your shoes!). Once you have correctly identified the full verbal root, you may want to check the other options in order to confirm your selection. In this case, neither the I-י form יָשַׁל (unattested) or the Geminate form שָׁלַל (Plunder your shoes!) provides a better option.

	III-ה				**Geminate**		
	Imperfect		*Imperative*		*Imperfect*		*Imperative*
2ms	תִּבְנֶה	➤	בְּנֵה [6]		תָּסֹב	➤	סֹב
2fs	תִּבְנִי	➤	בְּנִי		תָּסֹבִּי	➤	סֹבִּי [7]
2mp	תִּבְנוּ	➤	בְּנוּ		תָּסֹבּוּ	➤	סֹבּוּ
2fp	תִּבְנֶינָה	➤	בְּנֶינָה		תָּסֻבֶּינָה	➤	סֹבְנָה

---

[6] The final ה in this form is a vowel letter and not the third root consonant. This vowel letter, however, does make identification of the verbal root a little easier. The ה ֵ ending is diagnostic of III-ה ms Imperative forms in the Qal and derived stems.

[7] The Daghesh Forte in the remaining Geminate consonant of the Imperative 2fs and 2mp forms is diagnostic of the Geminate class.

I-נ Type 1[8]

	Imperfect		Imperative
2ms	תִּפֹּל	>	נְפֹל
2fs	תִּפְּלִי	>	נִפְלִי
2mp	תִּפְּלוּ	>	נִפְלוּ
2fp	תִּפֹּלְנָה	>	נְפֹלְנָה

I-נ Type 2[9]

	Imperfect		Imperative
2ms	תִּסַּע	>	סַע
2fs	תִּסְעִי	>	סְעִי
2mp	תִּסְעוּ	>	סְעוּ
2fp	תִּסַּעְנָה	>	סַעְנָה

I-י Type 1

	Imperfect		Imperative
2ms	תֵּשֵׁב	>	שֵׁב
2fs	תֵּשְׁבִי	>	שְׁבִי
2mp	תֵּשְׁבוּ	>	שְׁבוּ
2fp	תֵּשַׁבְנָה	>	שֵׁבְנָה

I-י Type 2[10]

	Imperfect		Imperative
2ms	תִּירַשׁ	>	רַשׁ
2fs	תִּירְשִׁי	>	רְשִׁי
2mp	תִּירְשׁוּ	>	רְשׁוּ
2fp	תִּירַשְׁנָה	>	רַשְׁנָה

18.10 Biconsonantal Imperative Forms. Biconsonantal Imperatives are quite easy to recognize with only minor variation in the 2fp. Carefully study the Imperative forms of the three Biconsonantal classes. Note that the Imperatives, for the most part, retain the distinctive vowel letters of the corresponding Imperfect forms.

---

[8] In the Imperfect of this I-נ class, the נ (first consonant of the verbal root) has assimilated into the second root consonant and remains as a Daghesh Forte. It does not assimilate, however, in the Imperative forms of this type. In this type of I-נ verb, the Imperative preserves all three consonants of the verbal root, including the נ in first root position.

[9] In the 2ms and 2fp Imperfect forms of this I-נ class, the second root consonant exhibits the Daghesh Forte, representing the assimilated נ that is the first consonant of the verbal root. The Imperative forms of this I-נ type (Type 2) simply drop the נ that is the first consonant of the verbal root. These are called short Imperative forms because only two root consonants remain.

[10] In the Imperfect of both I-י types, the first consonant of the verbal root has been lost (though the Hireq Yod preformative vowel in Type 2 is helpfully reminiscent of this lost consonant). Both Type 1 and Type 2 have short Imperative forms, preserving only the second and third root consonants.

קוּם

	Imperfect		Imperative
2ms	תָּקוּם	➤	קוּם[11]
2fs	תָּקֹ֫ומִי	➤	קֹ֫ומִי
2mp	תָּקֹ֫ומוּ	➤	קֹ֫ומוּ
2fp	תְּקוּמֶ֫ינָה	➤	קֹ֫מְנָה

שִׂים

	Imperfect		Imperative
2ms	תָּשִׂים	➤	שִׂים
2fs	תָּשִׂ֫ימִי	➤	שִׂ֫ימִי
2mp	תָּשִׂ֫ימוּ	➤	שִׂ֫ימוּ
2fp	תְּשִׂימֶ֫ינָה		

בּוֹא

	Imperfect		Imperative
2ms	תָּבוֹא	➤	בּוֹא
2fs	תָּבֹ֫ואִי	➤	בֹּ֫ואִי
2mp	תָּבֹ֫ואוּ	➤	בֹּ֫ואוּ
2fp	תְּבֹ֫ואנָה		

18.11 Irregular or Doubly Weak Imperatives. The following six paradigms represent irregular or doubly weak verbs. For the most part, each Imperative form is related to its Imperfect counterpart. If you have mastered the Imperfect of these verbs, then the Imperative forms will present no significant difficulty.

נָתַן (to give)

	Imperfect		Imperative
2ms	תִּתֵּן	➤	תֵּן[13]
2fs	תִּתְּנִי	➤	תְּנִי
2mp	תִּתְּנוּ	➤	תְּנוּ
2fp	תִּתֵּ֫נָּה	➤	תֵּ֫נָּה

לָקַח[12] (to take)

	Imperfect		Imperative
2ms	תִּקַּח	➤	קַח
2fs	תִּקְּחִי	➤	קְחִי
2mp	תִּקְּחוּ	➤	קְחוּ
2fp	תִּקַּ֫חְנָה	➤	קַ֫חְנָה

---

[11] The alternate form קוּמָה occurs 16 times (see 18.4.3).

[12] This verb behaves just like the Type 2 verb of the I-נ class listed above (נָסַע); that is, the ל behaves just like the נ and is assimilated in selected Imperfect forms. There is no assimilation of the ל in the Imperative forms. It simply drops.

[13] The alternate form תְּנָה occurs 24 times.

	הָלַךְ[14] (to walk)			הָיָה (to be)		
	Imperfect		*Imperative*	*Imperfect*		*Imperative*
2ms	תֵּלֵךְ	⪼	לֵךְ[15]	תִּהְיֶה	⪼	הֱיֵה
2fs	תֵּלְכִי	⪼	לְכִי	תִּהְיִי		
2mp	תֵּלְכוּ	⪼	לְכוּ	תִּהְיוּ	⪼	הֱיוּ
2fp	תֵּלַכְנָה	⪼	לֵכְנָה	תִּהְיֶ֫ינָה		

	עָלָה (to go up)			נָטָה (to extend)		
	Imperfect		*Imperative*	*Imperfect*		*Imperative*
2ms	תַּעֲלֶה	⪼	עֲלֵה	תִּטֶּה	⪼	נְטֵה
2fs	תַּעֲלִי	⪼	עֲלִי	תִּטִּי	⪼	נְטִי
2mp	תַּעֲלוּ	⪼	עֲלוּ	תִּטּוּ	⪼	נְטוּ
2fp	תַּעֲלֶ֫ינָה	⪼	עֲלֶ֫ינָה	תִּטֶּ֫ינָה	⪼	נְטֶ֫ינָה

18.12 **Frequently Confused Forms.** Some forms of the Imperative are easily confused with other verb and noun forms. Five sets of the most commonly confused words are listed below. In some instances, the different words are identical in form. In such cases, context will enable you to make the correct choice.

1. כָּתְבָה Qal Perfect 3fs from כָּתַב meaning "she wrote"

   כָּתְבָה Qal Imperative 2ms from כָּתַב (with the הָ ending) meaning "(you) write!"

2. כָּתְבוּ Qal Perfect 3cp from כָּתַב meaning "they wrote"

   כִּתְבוּ Qal Imperative 2mp from כָּתַב meaning "(you) write!"

3. בְּנִי Qal Imperative 2fs from בָּנָה meaning "(you) build!"

   בְּנִי Masculine singular noun בֵּן with 1cs pronominal suffix meaning "my son"

---

[14] This verb behaves just like the Type 1 verb of the I-י class discussed above (16.16).

[15] The alternate form לְכָה occurs 33 times.

4. בָּנוּ Qal Perfect 3cp from בָּנָה meaning "they built"

בָּ֫נוּ Preposition בְּ with 1cp pronominal suffix meaning "against us"

בְּנוּ Qal Imperative 2mp from בָּנָה meaning "(you) build!"

5. עָלוּ Qal Perfect 3cp from עָלָה meaning "they went up"

עֲלוּ Qal Imperative 2mp from עָלָה meaning "(you) go up!"

18.13 Cohortative. Like the Imperative (second person), the Cohortative is used to express a wish, request, or command. The Cohortative *occurs only in the first person, singular and plural.* For example, "*Let* me (1cs) *honor* the Lord!" or "*May* we (1cp) *honor* the Lord!" When translating the Cohortative, use the key words "let" or "may" as in these two examples. The particle נָא may also occur with the Cohortative.

The simple form of the Cohortative is the same as the Imperfect 1cs and 1cp forms, אֶקְטֹל and נִקְטֹל. What identifies the Cohortative or volitional use of the first person Imperfect is the position of the Imperfect verb in its clause. In general, when the Imperfect (not consecutive) 1cs or 1cp verb is first in its clause, it is Cohortative. Conversely, when the Imperfect 1cs or 1cp verb is not first in its clause, it is not Cohortative but the regular Imperfect (though there are exceptions). The following sets of examples illustrate both the Cohortative and the regular use of the Imperfect. Note that what distinguishes usage in the following examples is the position of the Imperfect verb in its clause.

נַעֲשֶׂה אָדָם בְּצַלְמֵנוּ

Let us make man in our image (Gen 1:26).

כֹּל אֲשֶׁר־דִּבֶּר יְהוָה נַעֲשֶׂה

Everything that the Lord has spoken *we will do* (Exod 19:8).

אֶעֱבֹר בְּכָל־צֹאנְךָ

Let me pass through all of your flocks (Gen 30:32).

כִּי־אֶעֱבֹר בְּקִרְבְּךָ

For *I will pass* through your midst (Amos 5:17).

While the simple form of the Cohortative is the same as the regular Imperfect, the most common form of the Cohortative (approximately sixty-five percent of the time) appears with an הָ ending, as in אֶקְטְלָה

(may I kill) or נִקְטְלָה (let us kill).[16] Because of the frequency with which the Cohortative appears with the הָ ending, it may be helpful to think of this ending as a diagnostic indicator of the Cohortative on the Imperfect 1cs or 1cp. Note that with the addition of the הָ ending, the stem vowel reduces to Vocal Shewa. Finally, note that the lengthened Cohortative does not necessarily translate differently than the form without it. The following Cohortative examples appear with the הָ ending.

אֶשְׁמְרָה תוֹרָתְךָ

May I observe your law (Ps 119:44).

נִכְרְתָה בְרִית

Let us make (cut) a covenant (Gen 26:28).

נֵלְכָה דֹּתָיְנָה

Let us go to Dothan (Gen 37:17).

אֶעְבְּרָה בְאַרְצֶךָ

Let me pass through your land (Deut 2:27).

18.14 Jussive. Like the Imperative (second person) and the Cohortative (first person), the Jussive is used to express a wish, request, or command. The Jussive *occurs in the third person* (3ms, 3fs, 3mp, 3fp). When translating the Jussive, you can use the same key words "let" or "may" as with the Cohortative. The particle נָא also occurs with the Jussive.

The basic form of the Jussive is the same as the Imperfect (3ms, 3fs, 3mp, 3fp). Like the Cohortative, the Jussive or volitional use of the third person Imperfect is identified by the position of the Imperfect verb in its clause.[17] In general, when the third person Imperfect (not consecutive) verb is first in its clause, it is Jussive. Conversely, when the third person Imperfect verb is not first in its clause, it is not Jussive but the regular Imperfect (though there are exceptions). The following sets of examples illustrate both the Jussive and the regular use of the Imperfect. Note that what distinguishes usage in the following examples is the position of the verb in its clause.

---

[16] Recall from above that the הָ ending also appears with the consecutive Imperfect (104 times) and with the Imperative 2ms (309 times).

יִזְכָּר־נָא הַמֶּלֶךְ אֶת־יְהוָה

Let the king *remember* the LORD (2 Sam 14:11).

עַתָּה יִזְכֹּר עֲוֺנָם

Now *he will remember* their iniquity (Jer 14:10).

יִשְׁפֹּט יְהוָה בֵּינִי וּבֵינֶיךָ

May the LORD *judge* between me and between you (Gen 16:5).

וְהוּא יִשְׁפֹּט־תֵּבֵל בְּצֶדֶק

And *he will judge* the world with righteousness (Ps 9:9 [8]).

יִסְלַח־נָא יְהוָה לְעַבְדֶּךָ

May the LORD *forgive* your servant (2 Kgs 5:18).

וַיהוָה יִסְלַח־לָהּ

And the LORD *will forgive* her (Num 30:6 [5]).

With certain weak verbs (and the Hiphil), the spelling of the Jussive may be a shortened (or apocopated) form of the Imperfect (approximately twenty-three percent of verbs identified as Jussive are short forms). These shortened forms are most common in the III-ה class of weak verbs.[18] Study the following chart listing III-ה Perfect, Imperfect and (short) Jussive forms. All forms are 3ms.

---

[17] Alviero Niccacci states, "First, I think that morphology is not a sufficient criterion to identify volitive or jussive *yiqtol* forms because, on the one hand, in many cases such verbal forms are not distinguishable from the indicative ones and, on the other, morphology is not always rigorously respected even where distinctive verbal forms are possible. Second, sentence-initial position alone identifies a *yiqtol* as jussive, although second-place jussive *x-yiqtol* are also clearly attested." Alviero Niccacci, "The Biblical Hebrew Verbal System in Poetry," in *Biblical Hebrew in Its Northwest Semitic Setting: Typological and Historical Perspectives*, eds. Steven E. Fassberg and Avi Hurvitz (Jerusalem: The Hebrew University Magnes Press and Winona Lake: Eisenbrauns, 2006), 252 (cf. p. 261 and especially footnote 24). Cf. Peter J. Gentry, "The System of the Finite Verb in Classical Biblical Hebrew," *Hebrew Studies* 39 (1998): 7-39; Elisha Qimron, "A New Approach Toward Interpreting the Imperfect Verbal Forms in Early Hebrew," *Leshonenu* 41 (1998): 31-43 (Hebrew).

[18] Shortened forms are also attested with Biconsonantal roots. For example, יָרֶב בּוֹ הַבַּעַל translates, "*Let* Baal *contend* against him" (Judg 6:32). The form יָרֶב is the short or apocopated form of the Qal Imperfect 3ms יָרִיב from רִיב (to strive, contend).

Perfect	*Imperfect*	*Jussive (short)*
בָּנָה he built	יִבְנֶה he will build	יִבֶן let him build
עָשָׂה he made	יַעֲשֶׂה he will make	יַעַשׂ let him make
עָלָה he went up	יַעֲלֶה he will go up	יַעַל let him go up
רָאָה he saw	יִרְאֶה he will see	יֵרֶא let him see

With III-ה verbs, it is obvious that the regular Imperfect and the Jussive forms are spelled differently. The regular Imperfect forms have an ה ֶ ending. The Jussive forms *do not* have the ה ֶ ending. These distinctive Jussive forms are attested only in the singular (3ms, 3fs). They are not attested in the plural (3mp, 3fp) because the plural Imperfect forms have sufformatives that cannot be dropped.

Below study two sets of examples of III-ה Jussive and regular Imperfect verbs. Note that in the following examples, the Jussive verbs are short and first in their clause. The regular Imperfect verbs are not short and not first in their clause.

וְיִבֶן אֶת־בֵּית יְהוָה

And *let him build* the house of the LORD (Ezra 1:3).

הוּא יִבְנֶה־בַּיִת לִשְׁמִי

He will build a house for my name (2 Sam 7:13).

יְהִי אוֹר

Let there be light (Gen 1:3).

יְהִי is a shortened form of the Qal Imperfect 3ms יִהְיֶה from הָיָה.

עֶבֶד עֲבָדִים יִהְיֶה לְאֶחָיו

A servant of servants *he will be* to his brothers (Gen 9:25).

The Jussive form in each text is translated with the volitional nuance ("let him build" and "let there be"). Note that the short Jussive form is the same form that occurs when prefixed with the Waw Consecutive (וַיִּבֶן and וַיְהִי; see 17.3.2). It is important to remember that when prefixed with the Waw Consecutive, the short Imperfect form will not be translated with a volitional nuance.

18.15 Negation of the Cohortative and Jussive. In general, Jussive and Cohortative verbs are negated with אַל (15.9; 18.5). This construction expresses a negative wish or a milder form of prohibition than that expressed by לֹא plus the Imperfect. The particle נָא is sometimes attached to אַל with the Maqqef (אַל־נָא). In most instances, you do not need to translate the particle נָא.

אַל־נָא נֹאבְדָה	Do not let us perish (Jonah 1:14).
וְאַל־יִחַר אַפְּךָ בְּעַבְדֶּךָ	Do not let your anger burn against your servant (Gen 44:18).

18.16 Summary.

1. In Hebrew, the volitional conjugations are the Imperative (second person), Cohortative (first person), and Jussive (third person). A volitional conjugation is used to express a command, wish, or desire. The Imperative is the most frequent volitional conjugation in the Hebrew Bible.

2. In terms of basic form, each of the volitional conjugations is related to the corresponding Imperfect forms.

3. Memorization of the Qal Imperative paradigm is required (18.3).

4. In the strong verb, the Qal Imperative forms are related to their corresponding Imperfect forms. Remove the Imperfect preformative from the four second person forms and you have the Imperative paradigm. Some variation in spelling does occur in certain weak verb classes.

5. The Cohortative occurs in the first person, singular and plural. The basic form of the Cohortative is the same as the Imperfect 1cs and 1cp forms. Often, what identifies the Cohortative or volitional use of the first person Imperfect is the position of the Imperfect verb in its clause. In general, when the 1cs or 1cp Imperfect (not consecutive) is first in its clause, it is Cohortative. Frequently, the Cohortative appears with an הָ ending, as in אֶקְטְלָה (may I kill) or נִקְטְלָה (let us kill).

6. The Jussive occurs in the third person, singular and plural. The basic form of the Jussive is the same as the regular Imperfect. In general, when the third person Imperfect (not consecutive) is first in its clause, it is Jussive. The Jussive may also be a shortened form of the Imperfect. This is the case with III-הָ and Biconsonantal verbal roots.

7. To produce a negative command, the Imperative is not negated. Prohibitions (negative commands) are expressed with the negative particles לֹא and אַל followed by the Imperfect.

8. The particle of entreaty נָא occurs with all three volitional forms, and it is a helpful marker of the volitional conjugations. It may be translated as "please" or simply left untranslated. This particle may occur with or without the Maqqef (נָא־).

18.17 Vocabulary.

Verbs

בָּחַר	to choose, test, examine (172)
בִּין	to understand, perceive, consider (171)
דָּרַשׁ	to seek, inquire, investigate, ask for, require, demand (165)
הָרַג	to kill, slay (167)
חָפֵץ	to delight in, take pleasure in, desire, be willing (74)
טוֹב	to be good, be pleasing, be pleasant, be joyful, be well with (44)
קָדַשׁ	to be holy, set apart or consecrated (171)
רָעָה	to pasture, tend (flocks), shepherd, feed (167)
שָׁאַל	to ask (of), inquire (of), request, demand (176)

Nouns

בַּעַל	owner, master, husband, (divine title) Baal (161)
שֵׁבֶט	rod, staff, scepter, tribe (190)

Other

בַּעַד	behind, through (104); also as בְּעַד
יַעַן	on account of (100)
נָא	please, now, surely (405); particle often not translated

18.18 Yes, I Will Remember. Measuring the emotional and volitional intensity of a writer can be a tricky matter. Unfortunately, it can degenerate into a wholly subjective exercise if we try to read our own feelings or volition into the text in order to wring something from the text. Yet this is precisely where the presence of the Cohortative verb assists the exegete and expositor. It signals the express direction and clear intention of the author's will. By it we can discern some of the emotional and volitional freight laden on the text.

For instance, in Ps 77 there are no less than eight Cohortative verbs. These are most strikingly conveyed in verses 12-13 (English 77:11-12) in two pairs of first common singular verbs, with the second in each set being Cohortative.

אַזְכִּיר מַעַלְלֵי־יָהּ כִּי־אֶזְכְּרָה מִקֶּדֶם פִּלְאֶךָ
וְהָגִיתִי בְכָל־פָּעֳלֶךָ וּבַעֲלִילוֹתֶיךָ אָשִׂיחָה

I will remember the deeds of the Lord; *yes, I will remember* your wonders
of old. *I will meditate* on all of your works and
I will consider all of your deeds.

The positioning of these Cohortative verbs emphasizes the author's personal intensity and intentionality as he wrestles with his faith amid trying circumstances.

"I will remember"	אַזְכִּיר	Hiphil Imperfect 1cs	זָכַר
"Yes, I will remember"	אֶזְכְּרָה	Qal Imperfect 1cs	זָכַר
"I will meditate"	וְהָגִיתִי	Qal Perfect 1cs	הָגָה
"I will consider"	אָשִׂיחָה	Qal Imperfect 1cs	שִׂיחַ

The piling up of such verbs is not superfluous verbiage. Rather, in the context of the psalm, this is how the author communicates his own deliberate action with respect to God's actions on behalf of his people. He will remember and he will muse on what God has done. This intentional, upward incline of his will is how he battles his own downward decline into depression and doubt. This is a tactic both for himself and for his audience. The use of Cohortative verbs underscores his desire to let God dominate his view, first and foremost. The author knows that only then will he be able to correctly assess his situation without numbing fear. This is the way faith fights.

Dorington G. Little
Senior Pastor, First Congregational Church of Hamilton
Hamilton, Massachusetts

Chapter 19

Pronominal Suffixes on Verbs

19.1 **Introduction.** In chapter 9, you learned how to identify pronominal suffixes on nouns, prepositions, and the definite direct object marker. In this chapter, you will learn how to identify pronominal suffixes on Qal Perfect, Imperfect, and Imperative verbs. You already know that when a pronoun is the direct object of a verb, it is commonly attached to the definite direct object marker אֵת or אֶת־ (9.14), as in the following examples.

יִשְׁמֹר אֹתָ֫נוּ   he will keep us

שָׁפַט אֹתְךָ   he judged you

In each of these examples, the direct object is a pronoun and it is attached to the accusative particle. There is, however, another way of indicating this grammatical construction. Instead of adding the pronominal suffix to the definite direct object marker, it may be added directly to the verb.

יִשְׁמְרֵ֫נוּ   he will keep us
(Qal Imperfect 3ms שָׁמַר with 1cp suffix)

שְׁפָטְךָ   he judged you
(Qal Perfect 3ms שָׁפַט with 2ms suffix)

Note that both grammatical constructions are translated in the same way. In this chapter, you will learn how to identify pronominal suffixes on verbs and some of the spelling changes that take place in the verbal stem with the addition of these suffixes.

19.2 **The Pronominal Suffixes.** The suffixes added to the definite direct object marker are the same suffixes that you will see on verbs. In general, verbs use Type 1 pronominal suffixes with an objective translation value. For your review, Type 1 pronominal suffixes with their objective translation values are listed below. Carefully study both the form and translation value for each suffix before continuing in this chapter.

	Type 1 Suffixes	Type 1 Alternate	Objective Translation
1cs	יָ	נִי	me
2ms	ךָ		you
2fs	ךְ		you
3ms	וֹ	הוּ	him (it)
3fs	הָ	הָ	her (it)
1cp	נוּ		us
2mp	כֶם		you
2fp	כֶן		you
3mp	הֶם	ם	them
3fp	הֶן	ן	them

19.3 **Pronominal Suffixes on the Perfect**. In the following chart, the Qal Perfect 3ms verb קָטַל (he killed) is listed with the full range of pronominal suffixes. Observe how the suffix is added to the verb and translated as the direct object of that verb.

	Qal Perfect 3ms	Translation
1cs	קְטָלַנִי	he killed me
2ms	קְטָלְךָ	he killed you
2fs	קְטָלֵךְ	he killed you
3ms	קְטָלוֹ	he killed him (it)
3fs	קְטָלָהּ	he killed her (it)
1cp	קְטָלָנוּ	he killed us
2mp	קְטָלְכֶם	he killed you
2fp	קְטַלְכֶן	he killed you
3mp	קְטָלָם	he killed them
3fp	קְטָלָן	he killed them

Notes:

1. The spelling of the Qal Perfect 3ms verbal stem has changed from קָטַל to קְטָל with the addition of pronominal suffixes. You should already be familiar with this type of change. The addition of a pronominal suffix to the verbal stem causes a shift in accent and syllable structure, resulting in a spelling change. The spelling קְטָל is due, therefore, to propretonic reduction in the first syllable (קְ) and lengthening of the pretonic vowel to Qamets (טָ).

2. In the Perfect conjugation, the alternate Type 1 pronominal suffixes are preferred for the 1cs (קְטָלַּנִי), 3mp (קְטָלָם), and 3fp (קְטָלָן). Both forms of the 3ms suffix appear with some frequency (קְטָלָהוּ or קְטָלוֹ).

3. The 2mp, 2fp, and 3fp pronominal suffixes appear infrequently or are not attested with the Perfect.

19.4 **Spelling of the Perfect Conjugation with Pronominal Suffixes**. It was noted above that the spelling of the Qal Perfect 3ms changed with the addition of pronominal suffixes (קָטַל to קְטָל). Unfortunately, similar types of changes occur in all forms of the Perfect conjugation. The changes in spelling depend on whether the suffix is added to a Perfect form that ends in a consonant or one that ends in a vowel. In the 3ms, for example, the suffixes are added to a form that ends in a consonant (קְטָל). The following chart shows how the various forms of the Qal Perfect strong verb are spelled before pronominal suffixes. Be especially careful to note any change in the spelling of the Perfect sufformative.

	Qal Perfect Without Suffixes	Qal Perfect Before Suffixes
3ms	קָטַל	קְטָל[1]
3fs	קָטְלָה	קְטָלַת
2ms	קָטַלְתָּ	קְטַלְתְּ
2fs	קָטַלְתְּ	קְטַלְתִּי
1cs	קָטַלְתִּי	קְטַלְתִּי
3cp	קָטְלוּ	קְטָלוּ
2mp[2]	קְטַלְתֶּם	
2fp	קְטַלְתֶּן	
1cp	קָטַלְנוּ	קְטַלְנוּ

Notes:

1. In the 3fs, the הָ sufformative is replaced by either תָ or תַ before a pronominal suffix (קְטָלַת). The suffix is then added to the תָ or תַ ending. This type of change in feminine forms should be familiar by now.

$$קְטָלַתְהוּ \quad \succ \quad הוּ \; + \; (קְטָלַת) \; קָטְלָה \quad \text{she (it) killed him}$$

$$אֲכָלַתְנִי \quad \succ \quad נִי \; + \; (אֲכָלַת) \; אָכְלָה \quad \text{she (it) devoured me}$$

$$מְצָאַתְנוּ \quad \succ \quad נוּ \; + \; (מְצָאַת) \; מָצְאָה \quad \text{she (it) found us}$$

2. When suffixes are added to the 2ms form (קָטַלְתָּ), the sufformative is simply תָּ before the suffix (קְטַלְתָּ).

$$קְטַלְתָּהוּ \quad \succ \quad הוּ \; + \; (קְטַלְתָּ) \; קָטַלְתָּ \quad \text{you killed him}$$

$$יְדַעְתּוֹ \quad \succ \quad וֹ \; + \; (יְדַעְתָּ) \; יָדַעְתָּ \quad \text{you knew him}$$

$$עֲבַדְתַּנִי \quad \succ \quad נִי \; + \; (עֲבַדְתָּ) \; עָבַדְתָּ \quad \text{you served me}$$

3. The spelling of the 2fs and 1cs forms are identical before pronominal suffixes (קְטַלְתִּי). Note, however, that the 2fs form of the Perfect conjugation with a pronominal suffix occurs only sixteen times in the Hebrew Bible. In other words, when you encounter a form like קְטַלְתִּי with a pronominal suffix, you should

---

[1] It is important to note that the vowel under the ט is Qamets and not Qamets Hatuf.

expect the 1cs form. Note also that the Hireq Yod ending is frequently written defectively as Hireq before the pronominal suffix.

קְטַלְתִּי (קְטַלְתִּ֫י)	+	וּ	>	קְטַלְתִּיו	I killed him
נָתַתִּי (נְתַתִּ֫י)	+	הָ	>	נְתַתִּ֫יהָ	I gave her (it)
עָשִׂיתִי (עֲשִׂיתִ֫י)	+	ם	>	עֲשִׂיתִם	I made them

4. The spelling of the 3cp before a pronominal suffix (קְטָל֫וּ) should be easy to recognize because the sufformative (וּ) is retained. The Shureq sufformative of the Perfect 3cp may be written defectively as Qibbuts before a pronominal suffix.

קָטְלוּ (קְטָל֫וּ)	+	הוּ	>	קְטָל֫וּהוּ	they killed him
סָבְבוּ (סְבָב֫וּ)	+	נִי	>	סְבָב֫וּנִי	they surrounded me
יָדְעוּ (יְדָע֫וּ)	+	ם	>	יְדָע֫וּם	they knew them

5. The Perfect 1cp form (קָטַ֫לְנוּ) is spelled קְטַלְנוּ before a pronominal suffix, preserving the spelling of the sufformative (נוּ). It may also be spelled defectively (קְטַלְנֻ).

קְטַלְנ֫וּ (קְטַלְנֻ֫הוּ)	+	הוּ	>	קְטַלְנ֫וּהוּ	we killed him
דָּרַשְׁנוּ (דְּרַשְׁנֻ֫)	+	הוּ	>	דְּרַשְׁנֻ֫הוּ	we sought him
יָדַ֫עְנוּ (יְדַעֲנ֫וּ)	+	ם	>	יְדַעֲנ֫וּם	we knew them

6. Though infrequent (52 times), in the Perfect conjugation of III-ה verbs, the 3ms form drops the ה before the pronominal suffix as in the following example: רָאָה + הוּ > רָאָ֫הוּ (he saw him).

19.5 Changes in the Spelling of a Suffix on the Perfect. To this point, our study has focused on how the verbal stem is spelled before a pronominal suffix. Additionally, there are slight variations in how the pronominal suffixes themselves are spelled when added to a Perfect form.

1. Some suffixes are spelled differently, depending on whether they are being added to a Perfect form that ends in a consonant (3ms, 3fs, or 2ms) or one that ends in a vowel (all other Perfect forms). For example, the alternate form of the 3fs suffix (הָ) is used if the verbal stem ends in a vowel as in קְטַלְתִּ֫יהָ (I killed her). The 3ms suffix also exhibits some variation in spelling. Frequently, the 3ms suffix וֹ is spelled ו after a vowel as in נְתַתִּיו (I gave him). These types of changes are relatively minor and should not give you too much trouble.

2. The addition of certain pronominal suffixes to verb forms that end in a consonant will frequently require some type of *connecting vowel* between the verbal stem and pronominal suffix. For example, the form שְׁלָחֲךָ (he sent you [2fs]) requires a connecting vowel (Tsere) between the verbal stem and suffix. A form like קְטַלְתִּיךָ (I killed you), however, does not require a connecting vowel because the verb form already ends in a vowel. You are not required to learn all the possible connecting vowels for each form. Rather, you simply must be aware that connecting vowels are used when required (see 19.13).

19.6   **Pronominal Suffixes on the Imperfect.** Like the Perfect, Type 1 pronominal suffixes are used with the Imperfect. There are, however, three additional suffixes that occur on the Imperfect with some frequency. These additional suffixes may be called Nun-suffixes because of their distinctive form.

	Type 1 Suffix	Nun- Suffix	Example	Translation
2ms	ךָ	ךֶּ	יִלְכְּדֶךָ	he will capture *you*
3ms	הוּ/וֹ	נּוּ	יִלְכְּדֶנּוּ	he will capture *him*
3fs	הָ ֶ/ךָ	נָּה	יִלְכְּדֶנָּה	he will capture *her*

Notes:

1. As you can see, these suffixes are distinguished by the presence of a נ (Nun).[3] Note that in the 2ms form (ךֶּ), the נ has been assimilated and appears as Daghesh Forte in the consonant of the pronominal suffix.

2. Despite the variety of forms for a particular type of suffix, its translation value is the same. For example, the 3ms suffixes וֹ, הוּ and נּוּ are all translated with the same objective value, "him."

19.7   **Spelling of the Imperfect Conjugation with Pronominal Suffixes.** The changes that take place in the Imperfect with the addition of pronominal suffixes are minor compared to those in the Perfect. The changes are

---

[2] The 2mp occurs only 3 times with a pronominal suffix. It is spelled קְטַלְתּוּ before a suffix. The 2fp is not attested in the Hebrew Bible with a pronominal suffix.

[3] Though infrequent, Nun-suffixes are also attested in the 1cs (נִי ֶ/נִּי ֶ) and 1cp (נוּ ֶ).

minor for two reasons: (1) the spelling of the Imperfect preformative is unchanged in every form; and (2) most Imperfect forms that take a pronominal suffix do not have a sufformative. Compare below the regular spelling of the Qal Imperfect with its spelling before most pronominal suffixes.

	Qal Imperfect Without Suffixes	*Qal Imperfect Before Suffixes*
3ms	יִקְטֹל	יִקְטְל
3fs	תִּקְטֹל	תִּקְטְל
2ms	תִּקְטֹל	תִּקְטְל
2fs	תִּקְטְלִי	תִּקְטְלִי
1cs	אֶקְטֹל	אֶקְטְל
3mp	יִקְטְלוּ	יִקְטְלוּ
3fp	תִּקְטֹלְנָה	
2mp	תִּקְטְלוּ	תִּקְטְלוּ
2fp	תִּקְטֹלְנָה	
1cp	נִקְטֹל	נִקְטְל

Notes:

1. There is only one basic change in the spelling of the strong Imperfect verb before pronominal suffixes. This change is the reduction of the stem vowel (pretonic reduction) from Holem (יִקְטֹל) to Shewa (יִקְטְל). Of course, this reduction has already taken place in the 2fs, 3mp, and 2mp Imperfect forms. Note the following examples.

יִקְטֹל	+	הוּ	➣	יִקְטְלֵהוּ	he will kill him
יִקְטְלוּ	+	נוּ	➣	יִקְטְלוּנוּ	they will kill us
וַיִּקְבְּרוּ	+	הוּ	➣	וַיִּקְבְּרֻהוּ	and they buried him

2. The reduction of the stem vowel from Holem to Shewa does not take place with the addition of the 2ms suffix (ךְ). In this case, the Holem is *shortened* to Qamets Hatuf.[4]

| יִשְׁמֹר | + | ךְ | ➣ | יִשְׁמָרְךָ | he will observe you |
| יִקְטֹל | + | ךְ | ➣ | יִקְטָלְךָ | he will kill you |

---

[4] If the original Imperfect stem vowel is Tsere, then it is shortened to Seghol with the addition of the 2ms pronominal suffix.

If the verb has a Pathach stem vowel, the Pathach is not reduced but *lengthened* to Qamets before the 2ms pronominal suffix.

יִשְׁלַח	+	דְּ	➤	יִשְׁלָחֲךָ	he will send you
יִשְׁמַע	+	דְּ	➤	יִשְׁמָעֲךָ	he will hear you

3. If the Imperfect form ends in a consonant, a connecting vowel may be used between the verb and pronominal suffix, as in יִקְטְלֵהוּ (Tsere) and יִשְׁמְרֶהָ (Seghol). If the Imperfect form ends in a vowel, no connecting vowels are necessary (as in יִקְטְלוּנוּ and יִשְׁמְרוּם). As with the Perfect, you are not required to learn all the possible connecting vowels for each form.[5] Rather, you must be aware that connecting vowels are used when required (see 19.14).

4. In the Imperfect conjugation of III-ה verbs, forms that end in הֶ drop this ending before the pronominal suffix, as in the following example: יִרְאֶה + נָה ➤ יִרְאֶנָּה (he will see her).

5. The Imperfect forms of the weak verbs נָתַן (to give), לָקַח (to take), and שִׂים (to put, place) occur frequently with pronominal suffixes. These verbs can be difficult to identify at first and so we have included some examples below.

וַיִּתֵּן	+	ם	➤	וַיִּתְּנֵם	and he gave them
וַיִּקַּח	+	הָ	➤	וַיִּקָּחֶהָ	and he took her (it)
יָשִׂים	+	דְּ	➤	יְשִׂימְךָ	he will place you

19.8 Pronominal Suffixes on the Imperative. The suffixes used on the Imperative are the same as those used on the Imperfect. A few observations will be helpful, however, in terms of understanding some of the minor spellings changes that take place in the verb stem.

1. The Qal Imperative 2ms form קְטֹל is spelled קָטְל before a pronominal suffix. The vowel beneath the ק is Qamets Hatuf.

שְׁמֹר	+	ם	➤	שָׁמְרֵם	(You) observe them!
שְׁפֹט	+	נִי	➤	שָׁפְטֵנִי	(You) judge me!

---

[5] In general, Perfect verbs prefer a-class connecting vowels (Pathach and Qamets) and Imperfect verbs prefer e-class connecting vowels (Seghol and Tsere).

2. The Imperative 2fs (קָטְלִי) and 2mp (קָטְלוּ), both ending in a vowel, do not change before a pronominal suffix.[6]

תִּפְשׂוּ + ם > תִּפְשׂוּם (You) seize them!

דִּרְשׁוּ + נִי > דִּרְשׁוּנִי (You) seek me!

3. Like the Imperfect, Imperatives with a Pathach stem vowel (שְׁמַע) lengthen the Pathach to Qamets before the pronominal suffix.

שְׁמַע + נִי > שְׁמָעֵנִי (You) hear me!

גְּאַל + הָ > גְּאָלָהּ (You) redeem her (it)!

19.9 **Parsing**. When parsing verbs with pronominal suffixes, you will need to identify the verb and also the person, gender and number of the suffix.

נְתַתִּיךָ   Qal Perfect 1cs   נָתַן   with 2ms suffix

יִלְכְּדֶנּוּ   Qal Imperfect 3ms   לָכַד   with 3ms suffix

19.10 **Summary**.

1. When a pronoun is the direct object of a verb, it may be attached to either the definite direct object marker (נְתַתִּי אֹתְךָ) or directly to the verb (נְתַתִּיךָ).

2. In general, Perfect, Imperfect, and Imperative verbs use Type 1 pronominal suffixes with an objective translation value. With the Imperfect, three additional suffixes must be memorized: ךָ (2ms), נּוּ (3ms), and נָּה (3fs). These are the so-called Nun-suffixes. You must be able to recognize and identify the person, gender and number of all pronominal suffixes.

3. You will need to become familiar with the spelling changes that occur in the verb stem with the addition of pronominal suffixes to the Perfect, Imperfect, and Imperative.

4. The addition of certain pronominal suffixes to verbal forms that end in a consonant will frequently require some type of connecting vowel between the verbal stem and pronominal suffix. In general,

---

[6] Pronominal suffixes occurring on the Imperative 2fs form occur only in the Hiphil stem (8 times). Pronominal suffixes are not attested on the Imperative 2fp form.

Perfect verbs prefer a-class connecting vowels (Pathach or Qamets), whereas Imperfect and Imperative verbs prefer e-class connecting vowels (Seghol or Tsere).

19.11 Vocabulary.

Verbs

בָּטַח	to trust, be confident, rely (upon) (118)
בָּכָה	to weep (in grief or joy), weep for (114)
לָבַשׁ	to put on a garment, clothe, be clothed (112)
שָׂרַף	to burn (completely), destroy; שָׂרָף fiery serpent (117)
שָׁלֵם	to be complete, be finished (116)

Nouns

דּוֹר	generation (167)
חוּץ	outside, street (164)
מְלָאכָה	work, occupation, service (167)
פַּר	bull, ox, steer (133)
פֶּתַח	opening, entrance, doorway (164)
רֹב	multitude, abundance, greatness (150)
שָׂפָה	lip, language, edge, shore (178)

19.12 The Wife of Uriah the Hittite. Often the narrator's emphasis or viewpoint concerning a certain event(s) is expressed by the various ways that individuals are designated in the text, for example, "Bathsheba" or "wife of Uriah the Hittite." Likewise, the order of designations when clustered together and the repetition or preference of one designation over another is also important. These designations, in conjunction with other grammatical and narrative features, often signal the main idea driving the story line. When applying some of these observations to Bathsheba in 2 Sam 11-12, "The David and Bathsheba Tragedy," we can gain insight on the author's perspective and point(s) of emphasis.

The narrator uses five separate designations for Bathsheba in these chapters. On one occasion, her kinship tie as the "daughter of Eliam" is expressed (11:3). At the beginning and the end of the story, the proper name "Bathsheba" is used (11:3; 12:24). The common female designation "woman" occurs in four places (11:2 [2 times], 3, 5). The 3fs pronominal suffix (she/her) is used eight times (11:4 [3 times], 26 [2 times], 27; 12:24 [2 times]). And her rank in society as either Uriah's or David's "wife" appears ten times (11:3, 11, 26, 27; 12:9 [2 times], 10 [2 times], 15, 24).

These numbers reveal two important factors. First, the author favors her classification as "wife" above all other designations in the passage. Of the ten instances of אִשָּׁה, six speak of Uriah's wife and four refer to David taking as a wife someone who rightfully belonged to another. The narrator deliberately keeps the woman's intimate relationship with Uriah constantly before the reader. Secondly, generic designations feature strongly. This results in a limited use of the proper name "Bathsheba." In other words, a somewhat depersonalized individual continually appears before the reader. As a result of this, her social standing is emphasized while the person Bathsheba is not a point of emphasis. Bathsheba as a person is truly peripheral in the story. The author's choice of designations, especially "the wife of Uriah the Hittite," magnifies David's gross misconduct and undeniable guilt. This expressive choice in designation helps direct the narrative and serves to underscore David's sin and weakness as a man in contrast to his known strength(s) as king of Israel. As a result, David appears rather human to the reader. In this manner, the narrator exposes purpose and viewpoint simply by the choice of a dominating designation and its repetition in the narrative.

Donna Petter
Assistant Professor of Old Testament
Gordon-Conwell Theological Seminary
South Hamilton, Massachusetts

19.13 Advanced Information: Pronominal Suffixes on the Perfect. The following chart is given for your reference. It includes the basic and most frequently attested spellings of pronominal suffixes on Perfect verbs. In this chart, the connecting vowels are included and the suffixes are placed in one of two categories: (1) those attached to Perfect forms ending in a consonant; and (2) those attached to Perfect forms that end in a vowel.

	Suffixes after Consonant	*Suffixes after Vowel*	*Objective Translation*
1cs	נִי/ָנִי/ַ֫נִי	נִי	me
2ms	ָךְ/ְךָ/ךָ	ךָ	you
2fs	ֵךְ/ָךְ	ךְ	you
3ms	ו/הוּ/ָ֫הוּ	הוּ/ו	him (it)
3fs	הָ/ָהּ	הָ	her (it)
1cp	נוּ/ָ֫נוּ	נוּ	us
2mp	כֶם	כֶם	you
2fp	–	–	you
3mp	ָם/ַם	ם	them
3fp	ָן	ן	them

19.14 Advanced Information: Pronominal Suffixes on the Imperfect. The following chart is given for your reference. It includes the basic and most frequently attested spellings of pronominal suffixes on Imperfect verbs. In this chart, the connecting vowels are included.

	Type 1 Suffixes with Imperfect	Nun-Suffixes with Imperfect	Objective Translation
1cs	נִי ֵ/נִי ֵ/נִי ִ	נִי ֶ	me
2ms	ךָ ֶ/ךָ ְ/ךָ ֱ/ךָ	ךָ ֶ	you
2fs	ךְ ֵ/ךְ		you
3ms	הוּ ֵ/הוּ	נּוּ ֶ	him (it)
3fs	הָ ֵ/הָ ֶ/הָ ָ	נָּה ֶ	her (it)
1cp	נוּ ֵ/נוּ	נּוּ ֶ	us
2mp	כֶם ְ		you
2fp			you
3mp	ם ֵ/ם		them
3fp	ן ָ		them

Chapter 20

Qal Infinitive Construct

20.1 **Introduction.** In Hebrew, there are two Infinitive forms, the Infinitive Construct and the Infinitive Absolute. Infinitives are *verbal nouns* and, as such, have features in common with both verbs and nouns. The Infinitive Construct can function much like the English Infinitive, commonly translated with the preposition "to" plus a verb as in "to study" or "to learn." In this chapter, we will study both the form and function of the Qal Infinitive Construct. In the next chapter, we will cover the Qal Infinitive Absolute.

20.2 **The Form of the Infinitive Construct.** The Infinitive Construct form is not inflected for person, gender, or number. There is one basic form and, therefore, no paradigm to memorize. The following graphic represents the standard vowel pattern for the Qal Infinitive Construct strong verb.

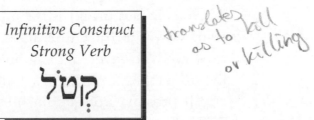

Infinitive Construct Strong Verb

קְטֹל

translates as to kill or killing

Note that the Infinitive Construct form of the strong verb is identical to the Qal Imperative 2ms (also קְטֹל). There are, therefore, two possible identifications for קְטֹל (Qal Infinitive Construct or Qal Imperative 2ms). Context will likely resolve this ambiguity.

The vowel pattern for the Qal Infinitive Construct is consistent for all strong verbs and even for most weak verbs. Carefully study the following strong and weak verb Infinitive Constructs and note the consistency of this vowel pattern. Give special attention to how the Qal Infinitive Construct compares to the Qal Imperative 2ms, especially with the weak verbs.

	Imperative 2ms	Infinitive Construct	Translation
Strong	כְּתֹב	כְּתֹב	to write, writing
Strong	זְכֹר	זְכֹר	to remember, remembering
Strong	שְׁמֹר	שְׁמֹר	to keep, keeping
I-Gutt	עֲזֹב	עֲזֹב	to abandon, abandoning
I-א	אֱמֹר	אֱמֹר	to say, saying
II-Gutt	בְּחַר	בְּחֹר	to choose, choosing
III-ח	שְׁלַח	שְׁלֹחַ	to send, sending
III-ע	שְׁמַע	שְׁמֹעַ	to hear, hearing
III-א	קְרָא	קְרֹא[1]	to call, calling

20.3   Notes on the Form of the Infinitive Construct.

1. You will recall that Imperfect verbs with a-class stem vowels (such as II-Guttural, III-ח/ע and III-א) will preserve that same stem vowel in the Imperative. This a-class stem vowel is not preserved, however, in the Infinitive Construct form. For example, the Imperative 2ms of the II-Guttural verb בָּחַר is בְּחַר (choose!), and it preserves the Pathach stem vowel of the Imperfect 2ms תִּבְחַר (you will choose). The Infinitive Construct form of this verb (בְּחֹר) does not preserve, however, the Pathach stem vowel. Rather, it follows the standard Shewa-Holem vowel pattern as in the strong verb. This same observation also applies to the III-ח/ע and III-א weak verbs as seen in the chart above.

2. I-Guttural and I-א verbal roots have a reduced vowel under the guttural in first root position (אֱמֹר and עֲזֹב). This should come as no surprise because you know that guttural consonants cannot take Vocal Shewa.

3. Note the Furtive Pathach in שְׁלֹחַ and שְׁמֹעַ (III-ח/ע verbs). Do not confuse this with the stem vowel. The stem vowel in these forms is still Holem.

---

[1] The alternate form קְרֹאת also occurs, especially with the לְ preposition as לִקְרֹאת (2 times with קָרָא, "to call" and 119 times with קָרָא, "to encounter").

20.4 **III-ה Infinitive Construct Forms.** The Infinitive Construct form of III-ה verbs ends in וֹת. For this class of weak verb, you will recall that Imperfect forms end in ה֟ (except in those forms with sufformatives) and that Imperative forms end in ה֟ (2ms). Now you must learn that the Infinitive Constructs of III-ה verbs end in וֹת.

Summary of III-ה Verbal Endings

	Ending	Example	Translation
Imperfect	ה֟	יִבְנֶה	he will build
Imperative	ה֟	בְּנֵה	you (2ms) build!
Infinitive Construct	וֹת	בְּנוֹת	to build, building

In the following chart, several III-ה verbs are listed in their Infinitive Construct form. Note that every form begins with a Vocal Shewa (or a Hateph vowel with gutturals) under the first root consonant. Additionally, every form ends in וֹת, the characteristic ending of III-ה Infinitive Constructs.

Verbal Root	*Infinitive Construct*	*Translation*
בָּנָה	בְּנוֹת	to build, building
בָּכָה	בְּכוֹת	to weep, weeping
עָלָה	עֲלוֹת	to go up, going up
עָנָה	עֲנוֹת	to answer, answering
עָשָׂה	עֲשׂוֹת	to do, doing
הָיָה	הֱיוֹת	to be, being
רָאָה	רְאוֹת	to see, seeing

20.5 **I-נ Infinitive Construct Forms.** Many verbs with נ in the first root position have Infinitive Constructs that conform to the strong verb pattern with preservation of the נ as in נְפֹל or נְסֹעַ. A number of I-נ verbs, however, have an alternate Infinitive Construct form in which the initial נ is lost and a ת is added to the end as in סַעַת (from נָסַע meaning "to depart"). As seen in the chart below, there are other vocalization possibilities for the alternate form of the Infinitive Construct with ת. Recognizing the diagnostic final ת on these verbs is essential for identification of the verbal form and reconstruction of the verbal root.

Verbal Root	Infinitive Construct *with* נ	Alternate Form *with* ת
נָסַע	נְסֹעַ	סַ֫עַת
נָגַע	נְגֹעַ	גַּ֫עַת
נָטַע	נְטֹעַ	טַ֫עַת
נָשָׂא	נְשֹׂא	(שְׂאֵת) שֵׂאת
נָגַשׁ		גֶּ֫שֶׁת
נָתַן	נְתֹן	תֵּת[2]

20.6 I-י Infinitive Construct Forms. A few verbs of this class preserve the standard vowel pattern as in יְשֹׁן from יָשֵׁן (to sleep). Most I-י verbs, however, drop the initial י and add a final ת (similar to the alternate form of I-נ verbs above). The vowel pattern of these Infinitives with ת is generally reminiscent of Segholate nouns (with accent on the first syllable). There are, therefore, two weak verb classes that drop the initial weak consonant and add a final ת: I-י and I-נ weak verbs. The following examples illustrate the I-י weak class.

Verbal Root	Infinitive Construct
יָשַׁב	שֶׁ֫בֶת
יָרַשׁ	רֶ֫שֶׁת
יָדַע	דַּ֫עַת[3]
יָצָא	צֵאת[4]
הָלַךְ	לֶ֫כֶת[5]

---

[2] This alternate Infinitive Construct form has lost both its first and third root consonants and it is very difficult to identify. Because this form occurs over 150 times in the Hebrew Bible, it is best to memorize it as a separate vocabulary word.

[3] Variation in vowel pattern (Pathach instead of Seghol) is occasioned by the guttural consonant in third root position.

[4] Variation in vowel pattern is occasioned by the quiescent א in third root position.

[5] As you know by now, הָלַךְ inflects like a I-י verb.

20.7 **Biconsonantal Infinitive Construct Forms**. Recall that Biconsonantal verbs are divided into three classes based on the medial vowel letter: קוּם with Shureq, בּוֹא with Holem Waw, and שִׂים with Hireq Yod. The forms that you have been memorizing for vocabulary (lexical form) are, in fact, the Infinitive Construct forms. These forms are also identical to the Biconsonantal Imperative 2ms verbal form. Once again, when confronted by one of these identical forms, context should enable you to distinguish between the Imperative and Infinitive Construct. The following examples illustrate the Infinitive Construct of this weak class.

Verbal Root	Infinitive Construct
שׁוּב	שׁוּב
מוּת	מוּת
בּוֹא	בּוֹא
בּוֹשׁ	בּוֹשׁ
דִּין	דִּין

20.8 **Parsing the Infinitive Construct**. The Infinitive Construct form is *not* inflected for person, gender, or number. When parsing, therefore, you will be required to identify only stem, conjugation, and lexical form. The following examples illustrate how you should parse the Qal Infinitive Construct.

כְּתֹב   Qal Infinitive Construct   כָּתַב

אֱמֹר   Qal Infinitive Construct   אָמַר

20.9 **The Infinitive Construct with Pronominal Suffixes.**[6] Though the Infinitive Construct is not inflected, the form frequently appears with a pronominal suffix that can function as either the subject or object of the verbal idea.

The Infinitive Construct of the strong verb קָטַל with the full range of suffixes is listed below. Notice how the vocalization changes with the addition of pronominal suffixes. Each form now begins with a Qamets Hatuf in a closed syllable. This initial closed syllable with Qamets Hatuf is diagnostic of the strong verb Infinitive Construct with pronominal suffixes (variations can occur with the 2ms and 2mp suffixes). Note that two different translations are given below. The first represents the

---

[6] Pronominal suffixes occur on the Infinitive Construct 1,519 times, that is, on 23% of all Infinitive Construct forms.

pronominal suffix functioning as the subject of the verbal idea. The second translation renders the suffix as the object of the verbal action.

	Suffix PGN	Suffix As Subject	Suffix As Object
קָטְלִי	1cs	my killing	killing me
קָטְלְךָ [7]	2ms	your killing	killing you
קָטְלֵךְ	2fs	your killing	killing you
קָטְלוֹ	3ms	his killing	killing him
קָטְלָהּ	3fs	her killing	killing her
קָטְלֵנוּ	1cp	our killing	killing us
קָטְלְכֶם [8]	2mp	your killing	killing you
קָטְלְכֶן	2fp	your killing	killing you
קָטְלָם	3mp	their killing	killing them
קָטְלָן	3fp	their killing	killing them

20.10 The Infinitive Construct with Inseparable Prepositions. The inseparable prepositions בְּ, כְּ and לְ may be prefixed to the Infinitive Construct with a range of uses and translation values. In general, however, the Infinitive Construct with לְ is used to express purpose or result, as in לִזְכֹּר (*in order to* remember). When prefixed to an Infinitive Construct, the inseparable prepositions בְּ and כְּ are used temporally and either preposition may translate as "when" or "while," as in בִּשְׁמֹר or כִּשְׁמֹר (*when* or *while* observing). Of all the verbal conjugations studied so far, only the Infinitive Construct will take a prepositional prefix. This means that whenever you encounter a verbal form with a prepositional prefix, you can be confident that it is an Infinitive Construct. In addition, note that the Infinitive Construct form with a prefixed preposition can also take a pronominal suffix, as in כְּשָׁמְעוֹ. This form should be parsed as a Qal Infinitive Construct of שָׁמַע with prefix כְּ and 3ms pronominal suffix.

---

[7] The alternate spelling קָטָלְךָ is also attested.

[8] The alternate spelling קְטָלְכֶם is also attested.

20.11 Negation of the Infinitive Construct. The negative particles לֹא and אַל are not used to negate the Infinitive Construct. Rather, the Hebrew Infinitive is negated with בִּלְתִּי meaning "not" or "in order not." More frequently, it occurs as לְבִלְתִּי.[9] There is, however, no difference in meaning between the two forms. In other words, both בִּלְתִּי קְטֹל and לְבִלְתִּי קְטֹל mean the same thing ("in order not to kill" or "not to kill").

20.12 The Use of the Infinitive Construct. Of all the Hebrew conjugations, the Infinitive Construct poses the most difficulty in terms of translation. As noted earlier, it may occur with pronominal suffixes that can function as either the subject or the object, depending on context (20.9). In addition, the inseparable prepositions בְּ, כְּ or לְ may be prefixed to an Infinitive Construct with a range of uses and translation values (20.10). Though surely not the equivalent of an Infinitive in English, the Hebrew Infinitive Construct does share the essential characteristic of having both noun and verbal functions. Some of its more common uses are detailed below.

1. *Purpose, Intention, or Result.* When prefixed with the preposition לְ,[10] the Infinitive Construct may denote purpose, intention or result. When used in this way, the key words "to" or "in order to" may be used in your translation.

לִרְאוֹת אֶת־עֶרְוַת הָאָרֶץ בָּאתֶם

(In order) *to see* the nakedness of the land
you have come (Gen 42:9).

לִרְאוֹת Qal Infinitive Construct רָאָה with prefix לְ

וַיִּקַּח אֶת־הַמַּאֲכֶלֶת לִשְׁחֹט אֶת־בְּנוֹ

And he took the knife (in order)
to slaughter his son (Gen 22:10).

לִשְׁחֹט Qal Infinitive Construct שָׁחַט with prefix לְ

וַיֵּשְׁבוּ לֶאֱכָל־לֶחֶם

And they sat down (in order) *to eat* bread (Gen 37:25).

לֶאֱכָל Qal Infinitive Construct אָכַל with prefix לְ

---

[9] This negative particle occurs 112 times, 26 times without לְ (בִּלְתִּי) and 86 times with לְ (לְבִלְתִּי).

[10] The Infinitive Construct occurs 6,610 times in the Hebrew Bible. It appears with the preposition לְ 4,529 times (69%).

וְלֹא־נָתַן יְהוָה לָכֶם לֵב לָדַעַת וְעֵינַיִם לִרְאוֹת
וְאָזְנַיִם לִשְׁמֹעַ עַד הַיּוֹם הַזֶּה

But the LORD has not given to you a heart *to know* or eyes
to see or ears *to hear* until this day (Deut 29:3 [English 29:4]).

לָדַעַת Qal Infinitive Construct יָדַע with prefix לְ

לִרְאוֹת Qal Infinitive Construct רָאָה with prefix לְ

לִשְׁמֹעַ Qal Infinitive Construct שָׁמַע with prefix לְ

כִּי הָאָרֶץ אֲשֶׁר אַתָּה בָא־שָׁמָּה לְרִשְׁתָּהּ לֹא כְאֶרֶץ מִצְרַיִם

For the land which you are entering *to take possession of it* (to
possess it) is not like the land of Egypt (Deut 11:10).

לְרִשְׁתָּהּ Qal Infinitive Construct יָרַשׁ with prefix לְ
and 3fs pronominal suffix functioning as the object

2. *Inceptive.* When prefixed with the preposition לְ, the Infinitive
   Construct may denote an action about to take place. This construction frequently involves the use of הָיָה (to be) and an Infinitive Construct prefixed with the preposition לְ. When used in
   this way, the key words "about to" may be used in your translation.

וַיְהִי הַשֶּׁמֶשׁ לָבוֹא

The sun was *about to set* (Gen 15:12).

לָבוֹא Qal Infinitive Construct בּוֹא with prefix לְ

וַיְהִי הַשַּׁעַר לִסְגּוֹר

The gate was *about to shut* (Josh 2:5).

לִסְגּוֹר Qal Infinitive Construct סָגַר with prefix לְ

3. *Verbal Noun.* In this use, the Infinitive Construct functions like a
   noun, often as the subject or object of the verbal idea. It may or
   may not be prefixed with the preposition לְ when used in this
   way.

הִנֵּה שְׁמֹעַ מִזֶּבַח טוֹב

Behold, *to obey* (obeying) is better than sacrifice (1 Sam 15:22).

שְׁמֹעַ Qal Infinitive Construct שָׁמַע

טוֹב לְהֹדוֹת לַיהוָה

It is good to praise the Lord, or Praising
the Lord is good (Ps 92:2).

לְהֹדוֹת Hiphil Infinitive Construct יָדָה with prefix לְ

4. *Complementary.* Another use of the Infinitive Construct is to explain, clarify, or complement a preceding action or statement. It may or may not be prefixed with the preposition לְ.[11] When used in this way, you can translate the Infinitive Construct with "by" plus the "-ing" form of the verb as in the following examples.

וְשָׁמְרוּ בְנֵי־יִשְׂרָאֵל אֶת־הַשַּׁבָּת לַעֲשׂוֹת
אֶת־הַשַּׁבָּת לְדֹרֹתָם בְּרִית עוֹלָם

The people of Israel shall observe the Sabbath *by doing*
the Sabbath throughout their generations as an
everlasting covenant (Ex 31:16).

לַעֲשׂוֹת Qal Infinitive Construct עָשָׂה with prefix לְ

וְלֹא־הָיִיתָ כְּעַבְדִּי דָוִד אֲשֶׁר שָׁמַר מִצְוֹתַי וַאֲשֶׁר־הָלַךְ
אַחֲרַי בְּכָל־לְבָבוֹ לַעֲשׂוֹת רַק הַיָּשָׁר בְּעֵינָי

You were not (have not been) like my servant David
who observed my commandments and who walked
after me with all his heart *by doing* only what was
right in my eyes (1 Kgs 14:8).

לַעֲשׂוֹת Qal Infinitive Construct עָשָׂה with prefix לְ

וְשָׁמַרְתָּ אֶת־מִצְוֹת יְהוָה אֱלֹהֶיךָ לָלֶכֶת בִּדְרָכָיו

And you shall observe the commandments of the Lord
your God *by walking* in his ways (Deut 8:6).

לָלֶכֶת Qal Infinitive Construct הָלַךְ with prefix לְ

5. *Temporal.* All of the above uses relate to the construction of the Infinitive Construct with prefixed לְ. Now we turn to another common use of the Infinitive Construct. When prefixed with the

---

[11] In addition to these four uses of the Infinitive Construct with לְ, there are several other less frequent uses. When prefixed with the preposition לְ, the Infinitive Construct may also (1) complement a preceding verb and be translated like a finite (Perfect or Imperfect) verb, (2) denote consecution of verbal action(s), or (3) denote obligation or necessity.

prepositions בְּ or כְּ, the Infinitive Construct may be used in a temporal clause. When used in this way, the prepositions בְּ and כְּ are translated either "when" or "while." Frequently, in this construction, the Infinitive Construct will also have a pronominal suffix.[12]

The operative phrase in the preceding paragraph is "temporal clause." Given that the Infinitive Construct is a form *without tense*, the temporal value (i.e., past, present, or future) assigned to the Infinitive must be taken from context. For example, the form כְּשָׁמְעוֹ (Qal Infinitive Construct of שָׁמַע with prefix כְּ and 3ms pronominal suffix) may be translated as either "when he heard" or "when he hears (will hear)." Note the two possible translation values: one denoting action completed (when he heard) and the other indicating action not completed (when he hears or when he will hear). In the absence of context, the phrase can be translated either way. However, in the constructions וַיְהִי כְּשָׁמְעוֹ (and when he heard) or וְהָיָה כְּשָׁמְעוֹ (and when he hears [will hear]), the temporal modifiers provide the context for determining the temporal value of the Infinitive Construct. Remember that the temporal modifier וַיְהִי signals past tense narration (17.4.3) and the temporal modifier וְהָיָה signals future tense narration (17.7). Of course, there are other contextual considerations that will determine tense value such as recognition of the narrative sequence in which the Infinitive Construct appears. Study the following biblical examples of how the Infinitive Construct is used in a temporal clause, especially with וַיְהִי and וְהָיָה.

וַיְהִי בִּשְׁכֹּן יִשְׂרָאֵל בָּאָרֶץ הַהִוא

When (while) Israel *dwelt* in that land ... (Gen 35:22)

בִּשְׁכֹּן Qal Infinitive Construct שָׁכַן with prefix בְּ

וַיְהִי בִּהְיוֹתָם בַּשָּׂדֶה

When they were in the field ... (Gen 4:8)

בִּהְיוֹתָם Qal Infinitive Construct הָיָה with prefix בְּ and 3mp pronominal suffix

---

[12] The Infinitive Construct is prefixed with the prepositions בְּ or כְּ 989 times in the Hebrew Bible. In 557 instances (56%), this construction appears with a pronominal suffix.

וְהָיָה כְּצֵאת מֹשֶׁה אֶל־הָאֹהֶל יָקוּמוּ כָּל־הָעָם
וְנִצְּבוּ אִישׁ פֶּתַח אָהֳלוֹ

Whenever Moses *went out* to the tent, all the people rose up
and every man stood at the door of his tent (Ex 33:8).

כְּצֵאת Qal Infinitive Construct יָצָא with prefix כְּ

וְהָיָה בְּעָבְרְכֶם אֶת־הַיַּרְדֵּן תָּקִימוּ אֶת־הָאֲבָנִים הָאֵלֶּה

And *when you pass* (have passed) over the Jordan,
you shall set up these stones (Deut 27:4).

בְּעָבְרְכֶם Qal Infinitive Construct עָבַר with prefix בְּ
and 2mp pronominal suffix

וְהָיָה כְשִׁבְתּוֹ עַל כִּסֵּא מַמְלַכְתּוֹ וְכָתַב לוֹ אֶת־מִשְׁנֵה
הַתּוֹרָה הַזֹּאת עַל־סֵפֶר

And *when he sits* on the throne of his kingdom, he will write
for himself a copy of this law in (upon) a book (Deut 17:18).

כְשִׁבְתּוֹ Qal Infinitive Construct יָשַׁב with prefix כְּ
and 3ms pronominal suffix

אֵלֶּה הָעֵדֹת וְהַחֻקִּים וְהַמִּשְׁפָּטִים אֲשֶׁר דִּבֶּר מֹשֶׁה אֶל־בְּנֵי
יִשְׂרָאֵל בְּצֵאתָם מִמִּצְרָיִם

These are the testimonies and the statutes and the
judgments which Moses spoke to the people of Israel
when they came out from Egypt (Deut 4:45).

בְּצֵאתָם Qal Infinitive Construct יָצָא with prefix בְּ and 3mp
pronominal suffix functioning as the subject

20.13 Summary.

1. The Infinitive Construct is not inflected for person, gender, or
   number. In strong and many weak verbal roots, its basic form is
   identical to the Qal Imperative 2ms.

> *Infinitive Construct*
> Strong Verb
>
> קְטֹל

2. Three weak verb classes have Infinitive Construct forms that vary significantly from the vowel pattern of the strong verb.

   a. The Infinitive Construct of III-ה verbs drops the final ה and adds וֹת as in בְּנוֹת from בָּנָה.

   b. The Infinitive Construct of some I-נ verbs drops the initial נ and adds ת as in סַ֫עַת from נָסַע.

   c. The Infinitive Construct of some I-י verbs drops the initial י and adds ת as in שֶׁ֫בֶת from יָשַׁב.

3. The Infinitive Construct may occur with prepositional prefixes, pronominal suffixes, or both. In other words, you must be familiar with the following four options:

קְטֹל	basic form
קָטְלִי	basic form with pronominal suffix (1cs)
לִקְטֹל	basic form with prepositional prefix (לְ)
כְּקָטְלוֹ	basic form with prepositional prefix (כְּ) and pronominal suffix (3ms)

4. The Infinitive Construct may occur with a pronominal suffix that can function as either the subject or object of the verbal idea.

5. The Infinitive Construct is negated with בִּלְתִּי or לְבִלְתִּי ("not" or "in order not").

6. There are five common uses of the Infinitive Construct.

   a. Occurring with לְ to express purpose, intention, or result.

   b. Occurring with לְ to denote an action about to take place.

   c. Occurring with or without לְ as a verbal noun.

   d. Occurring with or without לְ to explain, clarify, or complement a preceding action or statement.

   e. Occurring with בְּ or כְּ in a temporal clause with or without pronominal suffixes.

20.14 Vocabulary.

Verbs

אָחַז	to seize, grasp, take (63)
טָמֵא	to be(come) unclean (162)
יָצַר	to form, fashion, shape, create (63)
נוּס	to flee, escape (160)
נָגַע	to touch, strike, reach (150)
סָבַב	to turn, go around, march around, surround (163)
סָפַר	to count (107)
שָׂמַח	to rejoice, be joyful, be glad (156)
שָׁבַר	to break (up), break in pieces, smash, shatter (148)

Nouns

יַחְדָּו	together, at the same time (96); יַחַד together, along with (46)
יַיִן	wine (141)
עֲבֹדָה	work, labor, service, worship (145); also spelled עֲבוֹדָה
עֵדָה	congregation, assembly (171)

Other

בִּלְתִּי	not, except (112); usually appears as לְבִלְתִּי with the Infinitive Construct

20.15 A Life Centered on Torah. The priest/scribe Ezra was a man whose life provided a model of godly leadership to a people in desperate need of hearing God's Word and seeing God's will lived out in practical ways.

You have learned that the Infinitive Construct with the preposition לְ often complements the main verb by expressing the purpose, goal, or result to which the main verb points. In Ezra 7:10, there are three Infinitive Construct forms that are used in this way in a verse that highlights Ezra's personal commitments.

The narrator has already introduced Ezra as a minister with the right pedigree (7:1-5) and the right professional abilities: he was a סֹפֵר, a "scribe," "skilled in the Torah of Moses" (7:6; cf. 7:11). Ezra's every request was granted him by the Persian king and his ministry flourished "because the (good) hand of Yahweh his God was on him" (7:6, 9). Ezra 7:10 then provides the reason for this divine favor.

כִּי עֶזְרָא הֵכִין לְבָבוֹ לִדְרוֹשׁ אֶת־תּוֹרַת יְהוָה
וְלַעֲשֹׂת וּלְלַמֵּד בְּיִשְׂרָאֵל חֹק וּמִשְׁפָּט

For Ezra set his heart *to study* the Torah of Yahweh,
and *to practice* (it), and *to teach* (its) statutes
and ordinances in Israel.

Here we find the main verb הֵכִין (to set, establish)[13] followed by three Infinitive Construct verbs with the preposition לְ (לִדְרוֹשׁ, לַעֲשֹׂת, לְלַמֵּד)[14], each of which clarifies the purpose to which Ezra committed himself: study → practice → teach. This progression of action, grounded in God's Word, characterized Ezra's life and ministry and we are perhaps wise to follow his example. Sound study of the Scriptures must give rise to personal practice. Only then can we have a basis for effective teaching. But as Daniel I. Block emphasizes, far too often preachers and teachers either lose the centrality of the Word in their ministry or confuse the order of Ezra's resolve. Some focus on teaching technique at the expense of quality time in the Word, thus substituting the shape of the message for its essence. Others are quick to proclaim God's truth but are slow to apply it to their own lives, resulting in hypocritical leaders who have forgotten that only the pure in heart will see God (Matt 5:8; cf. Ps 24:3-5; Heb 12:13). Still others apply before having studied, allowing their own definitions of right and wrong to guide conduct rather than the revealed divine will in the Scriptures.[15]

Ezra was serious about understanding God's Word, applying it, and proclaiming it - in that order! This personal commitment generated a ministry blessed by God. We would do well to follow the pattern of Ezra today. "The hand of our God works for good on all who seek him, but his powerful wrath is against all who forsake him" (Ezra 8:22).

Jason S. DeRouchie
Assistant Professor of Old Testament Studies
Northwestern College, Saint Paul, Minnesota

---

[13] Hiphil Perfect 3ms of כּוּן

[14] Piel Infinitive Construct of לָמַד with לְ preposition

[15] Daniel I. Block, "Training Scribes and Pastors in the Tradition of Ezra," *Southern Seminary Magazine* (June, 1999) 6.

Chapter 21

Qal Infinitive Absolute

21.1 **Introduction.** The Infinitive Absolute occurs less frequently than any other Hebrew conjugation, with only 872 total occurrences. Like the Infinitive Construct, the Infinitive Absolute is also a verbal noun. With regard to function, however, there is no precise English equivalent to the Hebrew Infinitive Absolute.

21.2 **Qal Infinitive Absolute of the Strong Verb.** The Infinitive Absolute is not inflected for person, gender, or number. There is, therefore, only one form to memorize. This form is easy to identify and varies little with weak verbal roots. The following graphic represents the Qal Infinitive Absolute form for the strong verb.

Infinitive Absolute
Strong Verb
קָטוֹל

21.3 **Notes on the Form of the Qal Infinitive Absolute.**

1. The vowel pattern of the strong verb also occurs in most weak verb types (see 21.4 below).

2. Frequently, the Holem Waw stem vowel is written defectively as Holem. In other words, קָטוֹל is also spelled קָטֹל. This variation in spelling should not present any difficulty.

3. Be careful not to confuse the alternate form of the Infinitive Absolute (קָטֹל) with the Imperative 2ms or Infinitive Construct verb forms (קְטֹל). The Qamets under the first root consonant will distinguish the Infinitive Absolute from these two forms.

4. Unlike the Infinitive Construct, the Infinitive Absolute does not occur with prepositional prefixes or pronominal suffixes.

21.4 **Weak Forms of the Qal Infinitive Absolute**. Most weak verb forms follow the strong verb pattern as the following examples illustrate.

	Qal Perfect *3ms*	*Infinitive* *Absolute*
I-Guttural	הָלַךְ	הָלוֹךְ
I-Guttural	עָבַר	עָבוֹר
I-א	אָכַל	אָכוֹל
II-Guttural	גָּאַל	גָּאוֹל
II-Guttural	בָּחַר	בָּחוֹר
III-ח	שָׁכַח	שָׁכוֹחַ
III-ע	שָׁמַע	שָׁמוֹעַ
III-א	יָצָא	יָצוֹא
I-נ	נָפַל	נָפוֹל
I-י	יָדַע	יָדוֹעַ
Geminate	סָבַב	סָבוֹב

As you can see, the weak verbs above follow the standard pattern of vocalization. Despite this consistency, however, a few weak verb forms deserve comment.

1. Note the Furtive Pathach in שָׁכוֹחַ, שָׁמוֹעַ, and יָדוֹעַ (III-ח/ע verbs). Do not confuse this with the stem vowel. The stem vowel in these forms is still Holem Waw.

2. With III-ה verbs, the Infinitive Absolute may appear in one of two forms.

Verbal Root	*Infinitive Absolute*
עָשָׂה ➢	עָשֹׂה or עָשֹׂו
שָׁתָה ➢	שָׁתֹה or שָׁתֹו
רָאָה ➢	רָאֹה or רָאֹו
חָיָה ➢	חָיֹה or חָיֹו

3. With Biconsonantal verbs, the Infinitive Absolute appears with a Holem Waw (or Holem) stem vowel in every class. In other words, שִׂים (with Hireq Yod) and קוּם (with Shureq) appear as שׂוֹם and קוֹם in the Infinitive Absolute.

Verbal Root		*Infinitive Absolute*
בּוֹא	➤	בּוֹא or בֹּא
שִׂים	➤	שׂוֹם
קוּם	➤	קוֹם
מוּת	➤	מוֹת

Note the similarity between the Infinitive Absolute of מוּת and the construct form of מָוֶת (מוֹת).

21.5 **Parsing the Infinitive Absolute**. The Infinitive Absolute form is *not* inflected for person, gender, or number. When parsing, therefore, you will be required to identify only stem, conjugation, and lexical form. The following examples illustrate how you should parse the Qal Infinitive Absolute.

הָלוֹךְ	Qal Infinitive Absolute	הָלַךְ
מוֹת	Qal Infinitive Absolute	מוּת

21.6 **The Use of the Infinitive Absolute**. The Infinitive Absolute is a verbal noun. With regard to function, however, there is no precise English equivalent to the Hebrew Infinitive Absolute. It may be used in conjunction with other verbs to emphasize or intensify the verbal meaning. It may also be used in the place of an Imperative to express a command. In special instances, it can be used with other verbs to express two verbal actions occurring at the same time. Once again, remember that the Infinitive Absolute does not occur with prepositional prefixes or pronominal suffixes. The four most common uses are detailed below.

1. *Emphatic*. Frequently, the Infinitive Absolute will immediately precede (or rarely follow) a Perfect or Imperfect verbal form of the same root in order to emphasize the verbal meaning. Study the following examples and note how the translations give emphasis to the verbal meaning.

שָׁמוֹעַ תִּשְׁמְעוּ   you (2mp) will *indeed* listen (Ex 19:5)

מוֹת תָּמוּת   you (2ms) will *certainly* die (2 Kgs 1:16)

אָמוֹר אָמַרְתִּי	I have *surely* said (1 Sam 2:30)
יָדֹעַ תֵּדַע כִּי מוֹת תָּמוּת	know *for certain* that you (2ms) will *surely* die (1 Kgs 2:37)

2. *Imperatival.* The Infinitive Absolute can stand by itself and function as an Imperative.

זָכוֹר אֶת־הַיּוֹם הַזֶּה	*Remember* this day! (Ex 13:3)
שָׁמוֹר אֶת־יוֹם הַשַּׁבָּת	*Observe* the sabbath day! (Deut 5:12)

3. *Contemporaneous Action.* With some frequency, two Infinitive Absolutes may be used together with a Perfect or Imperfect verb for the purpose of expressing two verbal actions occurring simultaneously.

וַיֵּלֶךְ הָלוֹךְ וְאָכֹל	(literally) and he walked, *walking* and *eating*; (idiomatically) and he walked, *eating as he went* (Judg 14:9)
וְעָלוּ עָלֹה וּבָכֹה	(literally) and they went up, *going up* and *weeping*; (idiomatically) and they went up, *weeping as they went* (2 Sam 15:30)

4. *Complementary.* An Infinitive Absolute may complement the main verb of a sentence and carry the temporal value of that main verb. In this usage, the Infinitive will translate just like a Perfect or Imperfect even though it is not an inflected form.

רָגוֹם אֹתוֹ בָאֲבָנִים כָּל־הָעֵדָה	All of the congregation *shall stone him* with stones (Num 15:35).
נָתוֹן אֹתוֹ עַל כָּל־אֶרֶץ מִצְרָיִם	*He set him* over all the land of Egypt (Gen 41:43).

21.7   **The Particles יֵשׁ and אַיִן.** Hebrew may express *the existence of someone or something* by using the particle יֵשׁ (also spelled יֶשׁ־), which translates either "(there) is" or "(there) are." This particle does not change its spelling to indicate gender or number.

יֵשׁ מֶלֶךְ	"there is a king" or "a king is"
יֵשׁ מְלָכִים	"there are kings" or "kings are"
אָכֵן יֵשׁ יְהוָה בַּמָּקוֹם הַזֶּה	Surely the Lord is in this place (Gen 28:16).

The particle יֵשׁ may also be used to express possession when followed by the preposition לְ (to).

יֶשׁ־לִי תִקְוָה	Literally: There is to me hope. Idiomatically: I have hope (Ruth 1:12).
הֲיֵשׁ לָכֶם אָח	Literally: Is there to you a brother? Idiomatically: Do you have a brother? (Gen 43:7)
יֶשׁ־לָנוּ אָב זָקֵן	Literally: There is to us an elderly father. Idiomatically: We have an elderly father (Gen 44:20).

Hebrew may express *the non existence or absence of someone or something* by using the particle אֵין (also spelled אַיִן), which translates either "(there) is not" or "(there) are not." This particle is the negative counterpart of יֵשׁ and it also is not inflected for gender or number.

אֵין־יוֹסֵף בַּבּוֹר	Joseph was not in the cistern (Gen 37:29).
וְאֵין־דַּעַת אֱלֹהִים בָּאָרֶץ	(And) there is no knowledge of God in the land (Hos 4:1).
אֵין לוֹ בֵּן	He did not have a son (Num 27:4).

With some frequency, the particle אֵין will appear with pronominal suffixes as in אֵינֶנּוּ (3ms or 1cp) and אֵינָם (3mp).[1] Finally, the particle אֵין may be used to negate a verbless clause or sentences with Participles used predicatively.

אֵינָם יְרֵאִים אֶת־יְהוָה	They do not fear the Lord (2 Kgs 17:34).
אָמַר נָבָל בְּלִבּוֹ אֵין אֱלֹהִים	(The) fool says in his heart, "There is no God" (Ps 53:2 [English 53:1]).
אֵין עֹשֵׂה־טוֹב אֵין גַּם־אֶחָד	There is no one who does good, there is not even one (Ps 53:4 [English 53:3]).
אֲנִי יְהוָה וְאֵין עוֹד זוּלָתִי אֵין אֱלֹהִים	I am the Lord and there is no other; apart from me there is no God (Isa 45:5).

---

[1] Pronominal suffixes on יֵשׁ (9 times) are rare by comparison with the frequency of their appearance on אֵין (104 times).

21.8 Summary.

1. The Infinitive Absolute is not inflected for person, gender, or number. The following graphic represents the Qal Infinitive Absolute form for the strong verb.

*Infinitive Absolute
Strong Verb*
קָטוֹל

2. The stem vowel of the Infinitive Absolute may be written defectively as Holem (קָטֹל).

3. Most weak verb forms follow the standard קָטוֹל pattern. Remember, however, that III-ע/ח verbs have Furtive Pathach (שָׁמוֹעַ), III-ה verbs occur in one of two forms (בָּכֹה or בָּכוֹ), and Biconsonantal verbs typically have the Holem Waw (or Holem) stem vowel (קוֹם or שׂוֹם).

4. The Infinitive Absolute is a verbal noun with a variety of uses. The four most common uses are: (1) emphatic; (2) imperatival; (3) contemporaneous action; and (4) complementary.

5. Hebrew may express the existence of someone or something by using the particle יֵשׁ (also spelled יֶשׁ־), which translates either "(there) is" or "(there) are." Hebrew may express the non-existence or absence of someone or something by using the particle אַיִן (also spelled אֵין), which translates either "(there) is not" or "(there) are not."

21.9 Vocabulary.

Verbs

זָבַח	to slaughter, sacrifice (134)
חָנָה	to decline, camp, encamp, lay seige to (143)
נוּחַ	to rest, settle down (140)
נָסַע	to pull (out or up), set out, start out, depart, journey, march (146)
פָּנָה	to turn (134)
פָּתַח	to open (136)

רָדַף	to pursue, follow after, chase, persecute (144)
שָׂנֵא	to hate (148)
שָׁאַר	to remain, be left over, survive (133)

Nouns

בָּמָה	(cultic) high place, hill (106)
חֻקָּה	statute, ordinance (104); חֻקֹּת or חֻקּוֹת (plural)
יָמִין	right hand, south (141); feminine
מִשְׁכָּן	dwelling place, tabernacle (139)
נַחַל	stream, brook, wadi (137)
רָעָב	famine, hunger; רָעֵב (adj) hungry (101)

21.10 What a Difference a Pronoun Makes. You know that, in addition to functioning as the subject of a non verbal sentence, the independent personal pronoun can also be used with (finite) verbs for a number of reasons, one of which is to emphasize the subject. If the author places no particular stress on the subject, he would simply state: יָשַׁב בָּעִיר (He lived in the city). But if the author wanted to indicate that it was *he*, and not someone else who lived in the city, the 3ms independent personal pronoun could be added: יָשַׁב הוּא בָּעִיר or הוּא יָשַׁב בָּעִיר (He or He himself lived in the city). This particular use of the independent personal pronoun is referred to as the "emphatic use." Although it may seem to be a minor grammatical point, the emphatic use of the independent personal pronoun is employed by the authors of the Old Testament at various points to make important theological statements. For example, in Deut 4:35, Moses asserts:

יְהוָה הוּא הָאֱלֹהִים אֵין עוֹד מִלְבַדּוֹ

Yahweh (Yahweh himself) is God; there is none beside him.

Similarly, in 1 Kgs 18:39, when the people witnessed the power of the Lord in contrast to the power of Baal, they cried out:

יְהוָה הוּא הָאֱלֹהִים יְהוָה הוּא הָאֱלֹהִים

Yahweh (Yahweh, he) is God! Yahweh (Yahweh, he) is God!

As a final example, the emphatic use of the independent personal pronoun appears in Isa 46 to make the same claim to the Lord's supremacy and matchlessness. The chapter opens in Isa 46:1-2 with a description of the idols of two Babylonian deities:

Bel has bowed down, Nebo stoops over;
  their images are assigned to the beasts and to the cattle.
The things that you carry are burdensome,
  a load for the weary beast.
They stoop over, they have bowed down together,
  they could not rescue the burden,
  but have themselves gone into captivity.

In striking contrast, verses 3-4 emphasize that Israel has been carried not by animals, but *by Yahweh himself*, from the very beginning of her existence. She has been lifted up *by Yahweh* from birth. The theme continues, with an intentional emphasis on Yahweh as the means of Israel's support:

Until old age, *I* am he.	אֲנִי הוּא
Until your hair is grey, *I myself* will bear you.	אֲנִי אֶסְבֹּל
I myself have done (it),	אֲנִי עָשִׂיתִי
and *I myself* will lift (you) up,	אֲנִי אֶשָּׂא
and *I myself* will bear (you),	אֲנִי אֶסְבֹּל
and I will deliver you.	

With the emphatic use of the personal pronoun, Isaiah asserts one of the most important theological concepts in the Bible, that there is no God but Yahweh. Tragically, this emphatic sense is often lost in English translations. It is not missed, however, by those who read biblical Hebrew! These subtle, but significant, features of Hebrew are the very reasons why we learn to read the Bible in its original languages. What a difference a pronoun makes!

Catherine Beckerleg
PhD Candidate
Harvard University
Cambridge, Massachusetts

Chapter 22

Qal Participle

22.1 **Introduction.** In English, Participles are formed by adding "-ing" to a verb as in "walking," "eating" or "sleeping." Because a Participle is a verbal adjective, it shares the characteristics of both verbs and adjectives. As a verb, the Participle has stem (Qal) and voice (active or passive) and expresses some type of verbal action, such as "running" or "studying." As an adjective, the Participle has gender (masculine or feminine) and number (singular or plural) and is used much like an adjective: attributively ("the *sleeping* student"), predicatively ("the student is *sleeping*"), and substantively ("*the one who studies*"). When translating the Hebrew Participle, begin by using the "-ing" form of the verb as in the above examples.

22.2 **The Qal Active Participle Paradigm: Strong Verbs.** The Participle inflects like an adjective, with both gender and number. It is not inflected for person. Having already memorized the endings for nouns and adjectives, the inflection of the Participle should look familiar. The following paradigm must be memorized. Note that there are two feminine singular forms.

	Active Participle		Inflectional Endings	
	Singular	*Plural*	*Singular*	*Plural*
Masculine	קֹטֵל	קֹטְלִים		ים ָ
Feminine	קֹטֶלֶת	קֹטְלוֹת	ת ֶ	וֹת
Feminine	קֹטְלָה		ה ָ	

22.3 **Notes on the Qal Active Participle Paradigm: Strong Verbs.**

1. As you can see from the paradigm above, Participles are not inflected for person, only for gender and number. The inflectional endings for the Participle are the same as those you have memorized for adjectives and nouns. Note, however, that there are two feminine singular forms.

2. In terms of inflection, the feminine singular קֹטֶ֫לֶת is more irregular than קֹטְלָה but it occurs more frequently. Nevertheless, both forms must be memorized.

3. The Holem vowel in the first syllable of all Participle forms is diagnostic of the Qal active Participle (קֹטֵל). Recognition of this diagnostic vowel is important. Do not be surprised to see this vowel written as Holem Waw (קוֹטֵל). The Holem-Tsere vowel pattern is distinctive of the masculine singular Qal active Participle.

Qal Active Participle
Strong Verb

קֹטֵל

22.4   The Qal Active Participle: Weak Verbs. In the Qal stem, all I-Guttural, I-נ, I-י and Geminate weak verbs follow the strong verb pattern as the following paradigms illustrate:

	Singular	*Plural*	*Singular*	*Plural*
Masculine	עֹמֵד	עֹמְדִים	נֹפֵל	נֹפְלִים
Feminine	עֹמֶ֫דֶת	עֹמְדוֹת	נֹפֶ֫לֶת	נֹפְלוֹת
Feminine	עֹמְדָה		נֹפְלָה	

	Singular	*Plural*	*Singular*	*Plural*
Masculine	יֹשֵׁב	יֹשְׁבִים	סֹבֵב	סֹבְבִים
Feminine	יֹשֶׁ֫בֶת	יֹשְׁבוֹת	סֹבֶ֫בֶת	סֹבְבוֹת
Feminine	יֹשְׁבָה		סֹבְבָה	

Other weak verb roots, however, deviate from this strong verb pattern. Note below that in every weak verb class except one (Biconsonantal), the diagnostic Holem vowel and inflectional endings are unchanged.

1. *II-Guttural Verbal Roots.* The presence of a guttural consonant in second root position will create only minor spelling differences compared to the strong verb. In one of the feminine singular and both plural forms, Vocal Shewa is expected under the second

root consonant (קְטְלָה). With II-Guttural verbal roots, however, the Vocal Shewa cannot stand under the guttural consonant and so the guttural takes Hateph Pathach (בֹּחֲרָה or שֹׁאֲלִים). This minor change should not pose any problem as the diagnostic Holem vowel is preserved in every form. Note the Holem-Tsere vowel pattern in the masculine singular form of both weak verb types.

	Singular	*Plural*	*Singular*	*Plural*
Masculine	בֹּחֵר	בֹּחֲרִים	שֹׁאֵל	שֹׁאֲלִים
Feminine	בֹּחֶרֶת	בֹּחֲרוֹת	שֹׁאֶלֶת	שֹׁאֲלוֹת
Feminine	בֹּחֲרָה		שֹׁאֲלָה	

2. III-ח/ע *Verbal Roots*. In this weak verb class, only the feminine singular form, שֹׁלַחַת or שֹׁמַעַת, varies from the strong verb pattern (קֹטֶלֶת). As you know, this change in vowel pattern is due to the fact that gutturals prefer a-class vowels. Note the Furtive Pathach in the masculine singular form.

	Singular	*Plural*	*Singular*	*Plural*
Masculine	שֹׁלֵחַ	שֹׁלְחִים	שֹׁמֵעַ	שֹׁמְעִים
Feminine	שֹׁלַחַת	שֹׁלְחוֹת	שֹׁמַעַת	שֹׁמְעוֹת
Feminine	שֹׁלְחָה		שֹׁמְעָה	

3. III-א *Verbal Roots*. Once again, it is only the feminine singular מֹצֵאת that varies from the strong verb pattern. In this form, the א is quiescent. The remaining III-א forms follow the strong verb pattern.

	Singular	*Plural*
Masculine	מֹצֵא	מֹצְאִים
Feminine	מֹצֵאת	מֹצְאוֹת
Feminine	מֹצְאָה	

4. *III-ה Verbal Roots.* In this weak class, the final root consonant (ה) is lost in every form. In the singular forms, however, the presence of the vowel letter ה (a *mater lectionis*) helps with identification. Be careful to distinguish between the masculine singular בֹּנֶה and the feminine singular בֹּנָה. Note also that the feminine singular בֹּנִיָּה is not well-attested, occurring only ten times. It has been included to complete the paradigm but not for memorization. Like the singular forms, only two root consonants remain in the masculine and feminine plural forms. There is no ה vowel letter, however, with either plural form to help with identification. Only mastery of the paradigm will enable you to recognize these forms, though it helps to remember that III-ה verbs will drop the final consonant in all forms of the Participle.

	Singular	Plural
Masculine	בֹּנֶה	בֹּנִים
Feminine	בֹּנָה	בֹּנוֹת
Feminine	בֹּנִיָּה	

5. *Biconsonantal Verbal Roots.* This weak class is the only one without a diagnostic Holem vowel. For this reason, memorization of the following paradigm is required. Note that the masculine singular Participle קָם (rising) is identical to the Qal Perfect 3ms form קָם (he rose). Likewise, the feminine singular Participle קָמָה (rising) is distinguished from the Qal Perfect 3fs form קָמָה (she rose) only by the accent. In both cases, context (and accent) will enable you to make the correct choice.

	Singular	Plural
Masculine	קָם	קָמִים
Feminine	קָמָה	קָמוֹת

22.5 **The Use of the Qal Active Participle.** In Hebrew, Participles function just like adjectives. As such, the three uses of the Participle are attributive, predicative, and substantive.

1. *Attributive Use.* When a Participle directly modifies a noun, it is being used attributively. In the examples, *"sleeping* giant" and *"running* water," the Participle directly modifies a noun. In the

attributive usage, the Participle follows, or comes after, the noun that it modifies. The modifying Participle must also match the noun in gender, number, *and definiteness*. As with nouns and adjectives, the term "definiteness" refers to the presence (definite) or absence (indefinite) of the definite article. Note that the attributive Participle may also be translated with a relative clause as in "the giant *who is sleeping*" or "the water *that is running*." The following examples illustrate the attributive use of the Participle.

agree in def. → dwelling

הָעָם הַיֹּשֵׁב בָּאָרֶץ	the people *who dwell* (who are dwelling) in the land (Num 13:28)
הַמַּלְאָךְ הַדֹּבֵר בִּי	the angel *who was speaking* with me (Zech 2:2 [English 2:3])
יְהוָה אֱלֹהֶיךָ אֵשׁ אֹכְלָה	The Lord your God is a *consuming* fire (Deut 4:24).

2. *Predicative Use.* This use of the Participle does not directly modify a noun but rather asserts something about it and creates a predication, as in "the giant *is sleeping*" or "the water *is running*." In English, a form of the verb "to be" is used to indicate the predicative relationship. In Hebrew, the predicative relationship is indicated when an adjective matches the noun in gender and number *but not definiteness*. In this usage, the Participle never takes the definite article. With regard to word order, the Participle usually follows the noun. Finally, note that the Participle is a "tenseless" verb form and so must take its tense from context (past tense, present tense, future tense, etc.). The following examples illustrate the predicative use of the Participle.

וְהָהָר בֹּעֵר בָּאֵשׁ	And the mountain *was burning* with fire (Deut 4:11).
וּשְׁמוּאֵל שֹׁכֵב בְּהֵיכַל	And Samuel *was lying down* in (the) temple (1 Sam 3:3).

3. *Substantive Use.* A Participle may be used independently as a noun, indicating the "one who" performs a certain action. In Hebrew, when a Participle is used substantively, it behaves just like a noun. As such it may function as the subject or object of a verb, take a definite article, appear in a construct chain or take

pronominal suffixes and prepositional prefixes. In fact, several
Hebrew Participles are used with such frequency as substantives *noun*
that they are commonly listed as nouns. For example, the nouns
כֹּהֵן (priest), אֹיֵב (enemy), and שֹׁפֵט (judge) are technically
masculine singular Participles functioning substantively (each
noun retains the Holem-Tsere vowel pattern of the masculine
singular Participle). A similar phenomenon occurs in English as
well. For example, the "one who teaches" is called a "teacher"
and the "one who studies" is called a "student." The following
examples illustrate the substantive use of the Participle.

הַיּוֹשֶׁבֶת בַּגַּנִּים   *the one who dwells* in the gardens
(Song 8:13)

וְלֹא יִישָׁן שׁוֹמֵר יִשְׂרָאֵל   and *the one who keeps* Israel will
not sleep (Ps 121:4)

22.6   **The Qal Passive Participle.** In addition to the active Participle that you
have just studied, there is also a passive Participle in Hebrew. The
terms *active* and *passive* (voice) are used to describe the relationship
between subject and verb. With verbs having an active voice, the subject
of the verb performs the action of the verb (David killed Goliath). With
verbs having a passive voice, the subject of the verb receives or is the
object of the verbal action (Goliath was killed by David). When translating
a passive Participle, the "-ing" ending appears on the helping verb as
in "*being* killed" or "*being* written." Additionally, an English form like
"blessed" may be used as in "*Blessed* is the person who studies Hebrew."

22.7   **The Qal Passive Participle Paradigm.** The passive Participle, like the
active Participle, is inflected in four forms. Unlike the active Participle,
however, there is only one feminine singular form. Remember that
neither Participle (active or passive) is inflected for person, only gender
and number.

	Passive Participle		Inflectional Endings	
	Singular	*Plural*	*Singular*	*Plural*
Masculine	קָטוּל	קְטוּלִים		ים ָ
Feminine	קְטוּלָה	קְטוּלוֹת	ה ָ	וֹת

22.8 Notes on the Qal Passive Participle Paradigm.

1. The diagnostic feature of the Qal passive Participle is the Qamets-Shureq vowel pattern (קָטוּל). It may also be spelled defectively with Qibbuts, as in קָטֻל.

Qal Passive Participle
Strong Verb
קָטוּל

blessed be

2. In those forms with inflectional endings (fs, mp, fp), a Vocal Shewa appears under the first root consonant, as in קְטוּלָה.[1] With I-Guttural verbal roots, this Vocal Shewa changes to Hateph Pathach, as in עֲזוּבָה (from עָזַב, to leave, forsake, abandon). As you know, this occurs because gutturals cannot take Vocal Shewa but take reduced vowels, usually Hateph Pathach.

3. You should be able to recognize the passive Participle of most weak verbs without difficulty. In the following weak verb examples, the strong verb vowel pattern is present in every form. Only the masculine singular forms are given.

עָזוּב	abandoned	פָּתוּחַ	opened
שָׂנוּא	hated	יָדוּעַ	known
שָׁאוּל	asked	נָטוּעַ	planted
שָׁחוּט	slaughtered	אָרוּר	cursed
אָכוּל	eaten	יָעוּץ	advised

4. The form of the III-ה passive Participle is quite unusual at first glance. In every form, the consonant י stands in the place of the third root consonant, reminiscent of the fact that III-ה verbs were originally III-י (see 14.7.4). For example, נְטוּיָה is the feminine singular Qal passive Participle from נָטָה (to stretch out). You should think of this י as indicative of the III-ה class of weak verbs. Knowing this will help you to reconstruct the lexical form of these weak verbs.

---

[1] With the addition of inflectional endings (fs, mp, fp), the Qamets under the first root consonant reduces to Shewa according to the principle of propretonic reduction (קְטוּלָה ◁ ָה + קָטוּל).

	Singular	Plural
Masculine	בָּנוּי בְּנוּיִים	
Feminine	בְּנוּיָה בְּנוּיוֹת	

22.9   The Use of the Qal Passive Participle. The passive Participle is used just like the active Participle: attributively, predicatively, or substantively.

1. *Attributive Use.* The passive Participle follows the noun it modifies and agrees in gender, number and definiteness.

    הַבְּרִית הַכְּתוּבָה בְּסֵפֶר הַתּוֹרָה הַזֶּה   the covenant *written* in this book of the law (Deut 29:20 [English 29:21])

    וַיִּבֶן אֶת־כָּל־הַחוֹמָה הַפְּרוּצָה   (And) he (re)built all of the *broken* wall (2 Chr 32:5).

2. *Predicative Use.* The passive Participle either precedes or follows the noun it modifies and agrees in gender and number only (not definiteness).

    בָּרוּךְ יְהוָה לְעוֹלָם   *Blessed* is the Lord forever (Ps 89:53 [English 89:52]).

    בָּרוּךְ הַגֶּבֶר אֲשֶׁר יִבְטַח בַּיהוָה   *Blessed* is the man who trusts (will trust) in the Lord (Jer 17:7).

    בָּרוּךְ הַבָּא בְּשֵׁם יְהוָה   *Blessed* is he who comes in the name of the Lord (Ps 118:26).

    אֲרוּרָה הָאֲדָמָה בַּעֲבוּרֶךָ   *Cursed* is the ground because of you (Gen 3:17).

3. *Substantive Use.* In the examples below, the passive Participles are used independently as nouns, indicating the "one who" performs a certain action. When a Participle is used substantively, it behaves just like a noun.

    וְהֶחָלוּץ יַעֲבֹר לִפְנֵי אֲרוֹן יְהוָה   And *the one equipped* (for battle) will pass before the ark of the Lord (Josh 6:7).

    וְתַחַת הֲרוּגִים יִפֹּלוּ   And they will fall among *the slain ones* (Isa 10:4).

22.10 **Parsing the Participle.** Like a verb, the Participle has stem and voice. Like an adjective, it is inflected for gender and number. When parsing, therefore, you will be required to identify stem, conjugation (with voice), gender, number, and lexical form. The following examples illustrate how you should parse Qal Participles.

יָשַׁב	Qal Active Participle	ms	יֹשֵׁב
בָּרַךְ	Qal Passive Participle	ms	בָּרוּךְ

22.11 **Participles with Prefixes and Suffixes.** Because Participles behave like nouns, they may take the definite article, prepositional prefixes, or pronominal suffixes. They may also be found in the construct state. Study the following examples and be certain that you understand how each Participle is used.

הַהֹלֵךְ בַּשָּׂדֶה — *"the one who walks* in the field" (Gen 24:65). Note the definite article on the Participle.

לְשֹׁמְרֵי בְרִיתוֹ — *"to those who keep (who are keeping)* his covenant" (Ps 103:18). Literally, the phrase translates "to the keepers of his covenant." Note the לְ preposition that is prefixed to the Participle. Observe also that the Participle is in the construct state.

אֲנִי יְהוָה רֹפְאֶךָ — "I am the Lord *who heals you*" (Ex 15:26). Note the 2ms object suffix (ךָ) on the Participle.

יֹדְעֵי טוֹב וָרָע — *"knowing* good and evil" (Gen 3:5). The Participle is in the construct state. Note the diagnostic construct ending (ֵי), as in Ps 103:18 above.

22.12 **Summary.**

1. Participles are verbal adjectives. Like a verb, Participles have stem (Qal) and voice (active or passive). Like an adjective, they have gender and number. Participles do not have person.

2. The Qal active Participle paradigm for the strong verb must be memorized. The inflectional endings are the same as those that you have memorized for adjectives and nouns (except for the irregular feminine singular form קֹטֶלֶת).

	Active Participle		**Inflectional Endings**	
	Singular	*Plural*	*Singular*	*Plural*
Masculine	קֹטֵל	קֹטְלִים		ـִים
Feminine	קֹטֶ֫לֶת	קֹטְלוֹת	ـֶת	וֹת
Feminine	קֹטְלָה		ـָה	

3. The Holem-Tsere vowel pattern is distinctive of the masculine singular Qal active Participle.

4. The only class of Qal active Participles without the Holem vowel is the Biconsonantal weak verb class. These weak verbs have a Qamets throughout (22.4.5).

5. The Qal passive Participle paradigm for the strong verb must be memorized. The inflectional endings are the same as those you have memorized for adjectives and nouns.

	Passive Participle		**Inflectional Endings**	
	Singular	*Plural*	*Singular*	*Plural*
Masculine	קָטוּל	קְטוּלִים		ـִים
Feminine	קְטוּלָה	קְטוּלוֹת	ـָה	וֹת

6. The diagnostic feature for the Qal passive Participle is the Shureq stem vowel in every form, though you must memorize the Qamets-Shureq vowel pattern of the masculine singular form.

7. Most weak verbs inflect like the strong verb in the active and passive Participle. However, III-הׇ weak verbs exhibit a number of irregularities. In both active and passive forms, the final root consonant (הׇ) has been lost. Both paradigms must be memorized.

	Active Participle		Passive Participle	
	Singular	*Plural*	*Singular*	*Plural*
Masculine	בֹּנֶה	בֹּנִים	בָּנוּי	בְּנוּיִים
Feminine	בֹּנָה	בֹּנוֹת	בְּנוּיָה	בְּנוּיוֹת
Feminine	בֹּנִיָּה			

8. The three uses of the Participle (active and passive) are attributive, predicative, and substantive.

   a. *Attributive Use.* In the attributive use, the Participle follows the noun that it modifies and agrees in gender, number and definiteness.

   b. *Predicative Use.* In the predicative use, the Participle either precedes or follows the noun that it modifies and agrees in gender and number only (not definiteness).

   c. *Substantive Use.* These Participles are used independently as nouns, indicating the "one who" performs a certain action. When a Participle is used substantively, it behaves just like a noun and may take the definite article, prepositional prefixes, or pronominal suffixes.

22.13 Vocabulary.

Verbs

אָרַר	to curse (64)
בּוֹשׁ	to be ashamed (125)
גָּדַל	to grow up, be(come) great, become strong, wealthy or important (117)
חָשַׁב	to think, consider, devise, plan, value, esteem, reckon (124)
יָטַב	to be well with, go well with, be pleasing (117)
לָכַד	to take, capture, catch, seize (121)
נָגַשׁ	to draw near, come near, approach (125)

קָבַץ	to collect, gather, assemble (127)
קָבַר	to bury (133)
שָׁכַן	to settle, abide, reside, dwell, inhabit (130)
שָׁפַךְ	to pour (out), spill, shed (blood) (117)

Nouns

חוֹמָה	wall (133)
חֹק	statute, appointed time, portion (131)
כֶּבֶשׂ	lamb, sheep (107)

22.14 Double Trouble.[2] "'Comfort, comfort my people,' says your God." So reads Isa 40:1, and in the next verse there appear (after the introductory clauses "speak kindly to Jerusalem and proclaim to her") three parallel statements (each beginning with כִּי) regarding the fulfillment of Israel's period of punishment. The first two are as follows:

מָלְאָה צְבָאָהּ   Her [assigned term of] service is completed.

נִרְצָה עֲוֹנָהּ   [The debt of] her iniquity has been paid.

The last of the three parallel statements reads as follows:

לָקְחָה מִיַּד יְהוָה   She has received from the hand of the Lord

כִּפְלַיִם בְּכָל־חַטֹּאתֶיהָ   for all her sins.

The dual noun כִּפְלַיִם (lexical form כֶּפֶל) in this last statement is usually translated "double" (so, e.g., NIV, KJV, RSV, ESV, NASB). Such a translation runs the risk, however, of obscuring the divine justice, for it could be understood as asserting that Yahweh employed imbalanced scales to judge Israel, paying out twice the amount of punishment deserved by her sin. This problem disappears, though, when we recognize that כִּפְלַיִם in this context should not be translated "double," but rather "equivalent" or "matching payment."

---

[2] The present essay is a summary of an article of the same name written by Meredith G. Kline and published in *Journal of the Evangelical Theological Society* (32.2 [June 1989]: 171-79). Dr. Kline (my grandfather) has kindly granted me permission to summarize his arguments and to borrow freely from his language without acknowledging the many cases where my mode of expression imitates his. Because space constraints allow only the conclusions of the original article to be presented here with limited supporting evidence, the reader is advised to consult the original article (subsequently referred to as *Double Trouble*) for a fuller treatment of the present discussion.

The first two of the three parallel clauses in Isa 40:2 speak of punishment commensurate with (not exceeding) the crimes committed, and this must therefore be the meaning of the third clause as well. What is more, an examination of the biblical uses of the noun כֶּפֶל (as well as the cognate verb כָּפַל) reveals that the word rarely (if ever) means "double" in the sense of "twofold." Instead, it means "double" in the sense, as we suggested above, of "equivalent" or "matching image."

In Exod 28:16 and 39:9, for example, a form of the verb כָּפַל is used to refer to the fact that the cloth material of the priestly breastpiece was "doubled," that is, doubled over, folded in half – not doubled in quantity. Similarly, Exod 26:9 speaks of the "doubling" (כָּפַל) of the sixth curtain at the front of the tabernacle. What is envisioned here is not that the curtain was doubled with respect to its size (all eleven of the tabernacle's curtains were the same size), but that it was folded over in some way.

Ezek 21:19 [English 21:14] contains a command to clap the hands (in which "symbolic act one hand meets its mate in a duplicating sort of process, producing a matching pair"[3]), and then proceeds to speak of the "doubling" (כָּפַל), i.e., replicating or multiplying, of a sword of judgment, the producing of another sword to match the original. In Job 41:5 [English 41:13] the noun כֶּפֶל refers to the "pair" of leviathan's jaws, and in Job 11:6 כֶּפֶל is a poetic synonym for lips (cf. v. 5).

"What we find," then, "is that the meaning definitely required in most passages is, for the noun כֶּפֶל, 'duplicate, twin, matching equivalent' and, for the verb כָּפַל, 'produce a duplicate or duplex,' or, with respect to an action, 'repeat,' while the idea of a double amount is not clearly demanded in any passage."[4]

Like Isa 40:2, Jer 16:18 and 17:18 contain statements that might appear to describe twofold retribution. The critical word in these passages in Jeremiah is not כֶּפֶל/כָּפַל, but מִשְׁנֶה, a word that sometimes does in fact have the meaning "double" with respect to quantity (see, e.g., Exod 16:5, 22; Job 42:10). Uses of מִשְׁנֶה elsewhere indicate, however, that it may sometimes be translated, as כֶּפֶל may in Isa 40:2, "equivalent." For example, in Deut 17:18 מִשְׁנֶה denotes the "copy" of the Deuteronomic treaty, and in Deut 15:18 the word refers to a hired servant's wages commensurate with his time of service.

---

[3] *Double Trouble*, 175.
[4] *Double Trouble*, 174.

Thus Jer 16:18 (which we mentioned above) may be translated as follows:

וְשִׁלַּמְתִּי   [And] I will repay [them with punishment]

מִשְׁנֵה עֲוֺנָם וְחַטָּאתָם   *equivalent to* their iniquity and their sin.

And the petitioner's plea against his foes in Jer 17:18 may be rendered:

וּמִשְׁנֶה שִׁבָּרוֹן שָׁבְרֵם   With a *matching* destruction destroy them.

The concept of "equivalent" punishment also appears in the New Testament, expressed by the verb διπλόω and the adjective διπλοῦς. These terms appear, for example, in Rev 18:6, which the NIV translates, "Pay her back double (διπλώσατε τὰ διπλᾶ) for what she has done. Mix her a double portion (διπλοῦν) from her own cup." As with כֶּפֶל in Isa 40:2, the translation "double" here contradicts the context, for surrounding the text quoted from Rev 18:6 are statements stressing punishment commensurate with the measure of Babylon's sins. What is more, in its two other occurrences in the New Testament διπλοῦς has the meaning "equivalent" (Matt 23:15; 1 Tim 5:17).

"On closer scrutiny," therefore, "all the Biblical data customarily cited as evidence of the teaching of a double divine punishment for sin dissolves with the discovery that the key Hebrew and Greek terms either never mean 'double' or do not have that meaning in the relevant passages."[5]

In Isa 40, God proclaims to his people Israel that their seventy years of exile have constituted a complete recompense for their iniquity. "Isaiah is prophetically assuring the new covenant beneficiaries of all ages that their debt of sin has been paid and the divine justice perfectly satisfied. This is accomplished by the suffering of that Servant of the Lord whom Isaiah proceeds to set forth in the following chapters. On this One the Lord lays the iniquity of the many, and he endures the curse due to them, making atonement for them (52:13–53:12). . . . [I]n that Israel's completion of the allotted time of punishment, the seventy years of captivity, did constitute a full payment, a recompense commensurate with their sins, it could provide a figurative groundwork for the gospel pronouncement of 40:2. Comfort my people: In Christ they have received the hell punishment, the eternal seventy years of banishment from the

---

[5] *Double Trouble*, 178.

divine Presence, the just wages, the full equivalent payment that matches and cancels their debt of sin."[6]

J. Bergman Kline
M.A., Biblical Languages
Gordon-Conwell Theological Seminary
South Hamilton, Massachusetts

---

[6] *Double Trouble,* 173-74.

Chapter 23

Issues of Sentence Syntax

23.1 **Introduction**. Before we move on to study the derived stems, we will pause to treat the issue of normal word order in verbal sentences along with a selection of other issues relating to sentence syntax. The point of the following discussion is to organize and clarify many issues of verbal syntax[1] with which you should already be familiar from your study of the Qal stem.

In English, normal word order is subject-verb-object. For example, in the sentence "Jacob loved Rachel," *Jacob* is the subject of the verb because his name precedes the verb. Additionally, *Rachel* is the object of the verb because her name follows the verb. If the sentence read "Rachel loved Jacob," then *Rachel* would be the subject and *Jacob* the object because of their positions in the sentence. In Hebrew, normal word order for a verbal sentence is *verb-subject-object*. The following examples illustrate this basic and general guideline.

וַיִּזְכֹּר אֱלֹהִים אֶת־נֹחַ

(And) God remembered Noah (Gen 8:1).

וַיַּחֲלֹם יוֹסֵף חֲלוֹם

(And) Joseph dreamed a dream (Gen 37:5).

In the above examples, the verbs are in the first position, the subjects are in second position, and the objects are last (verb-subject-object). It is not uncommon, however, to encounter variations from this pattern, especially in poetic material. You can also expect certain particles, prepositional phrases or other sentence components to occur regularly in the midst of the basic verb-subject-object pattern.

---

[1] The study of Hebrew generally falls into three categories: phonology (the study of the sounds of the language), morphology (the study of how words are formed), and syntax (the study of sentence structure and the ordering of words into meaningful semantic units). All three are important for a working knowledge of the language, but syntax is often the area of study that produces the most fruit in terms of exegetical insight.

23.2 **The Syntax of the Verb**. In the syntax of the verbal sentence, the verb is normally at the beginning. In the following examples, the verb is in the first position.

וַיָּקָם מֶלֶךְ־חָדָשׁ עַל־מִצְרָיִם

(And) a new king *arose* over Egypt (Ex 1:8).

שִׁירוּ לַיהוָה שִׁיר חָדָשׁ

Sing to the LORD a new song (Ps 96:1).

While the verb usually stands first in a sentence or clause, it may also be preceded by an adverb of time, an adverbial phrase, the word הִנֵּה (behold), a temporal modifier (וַיְהִי or וְהָיָה), an expression that provides circumstantial information, or an independent personal pronoun. A negated verb will be preceded by a negative particle. These are only some of the more common exceptions to verb-first word order.

1. The verb may be preceded by an adverb (see 23.14).

עַתָּה יָדַעְתִּי כִּי־גָדוֹל יְהוָה מִכָּל־הָאֱלֹהִים

Now I know that the LORD is greater
than all gods (Ex 18:11).

2. The verb may be preceded by an expression that provides context, circumstantial information, or a connection with the preceding clause or verse.

עַל־כֵּן יַעֲזָב־אִישׁ אֶת־אָבִיו וְאֶת־אִמּוֹ

Therefore, a man shall leave his father
and his mother (Gen 2:24).

3. The verb may be preceded by הִנֵּה (behold).

וְהִנֵּה נָפְלוּ אֲבוֹתֵינוּ בֶּחָרֶב

And *behold*, our fathers have fallen
by the sword (2 Chr 29:9).

4. The verb may be preceded by a *temporal clause* beginning with וַיְהִי or וְהָיָה. The example below illustrates the frequent use of the Infinitive Construct following a temporal modifier.

וַיְהִי בִּהְיוֹתָם בַּשָּׂדֶה וַיָּקָם קַיִן אֶל־הֶבֶל אָחִיו וַיַּהַרְגֵהוּ

When they were in the field, Cain rose up against
Abel his brother and he killed him (Gen 4:8).

5. The verb may be preceded by a negative particle.

לֹא־אִירָא רָע

I will *not* fear evil (Ps 23:4).

6. The verb may be preceded by an independent personal pronoun.

וְאַתֶּם תִּהְיוּ־לִי מַמְלֶכֶת כֹּהֲנִים

And *you* will be to me a kingdom of priests (Ex 19:6).

7. The verb may be preceded by a number of other modifiers or grammatical constructions.

אֵלִי אֵלִי לָמָה עֲזַבְתָּנִי

My God, my God, why have you
forsaken me? (Ps 22:2 [1]).

23.3 **The Syntax of the Subject.** Perfect, Imperfect, and Imperative verbs have an implied subject (12.3). This means that you will not always need an explicit subject to complete a sentence in Hebrew. When you do have an explicit subject, however, it will normally follow the verb.

1. In the syntax of the verbal sentence, the verb is normally followed immediately by its subject if one is specified.

וַיֹּאמֶר הַנָּחָשׁ אֶל־הָאִשָּׁה

The serpent said to the woman (Gen 3:4).

וַיִּשְׁכֹּן כְּבוֹד־יְהוָה עַל־הַר סִינַי

The glory of the LORD dwelt upon Mount Sinai (Ex 24:16).

2. The verb may be preceded by its subject.

יְהוָה יִמְלֹךְ לְעֹלָם וָעֶד

The LORD will reign forever and ever (Ex 15:18).

וְנֹחַ מָצָא חֵן בְּעֵינֵי יְהוָה

And *Noah* found favor in the eyes of
the LORD (Gen 6:8).

23.4 **The Syntax of the Object.** There are a number of different types of "objects" in Hebrew. For this discussion, the most important are the indirect (dative) and the direct (accusative) objects.

1. The indirect object is the person or thing that is indirectly affected by the action of the verb. It is usually marked with either the preposition לְ (to, for) or אֶל־ (to, for) and may either precede or follow the direct object (if any).

יָדַעְתִּי כִּי־נָתַן יְהוָה לָכֶם אֶת־הָאָרֶץ

I know that the LORD has given *to you* the land (Josh 2:9).

וַיִּקְרָא מֹשֶׁה אֶל־כָּל־יִשְׂרָאֵל

(And) Moses called *to all Israel* (Deut 5:1).

2. A direct object (if any) will frequently stand immediately after the verb or its subject. A direct object may precede or follow an indirect object.

בָּרָא אֱלֹהִים אֵת הַשָּׁמַיִם וְאֵת הָאָרֶץ

God created *the heavens and the earth* (Gen 1:1).

וְיִתֶּן־לְךָ מִשְׁאֲלֹת לִבֶּךָ

(And) he will give to you *the desires of your heart* (Ps 37:4).

3. The verb may be preceded by its object.

אֶת־יְהוָה אֱלֹהֶיךָ תִּירָא

The LORD your God you shall fear (Deut 10:20).

אֶת־הַצַּדִּיק וְאֶת־הָרָשָׁע יִשְׁפֹּט הָאֱלֹהִים

The righteous and the wicked God will judge (Eccl 3:17).

23.5 **Syntax of the Perfect.** In addition to the general discussion of word order above, it is helpful to understand that the type of verb that appears in a clause (for example, Perfect or Imperfect) and the use of that verb (for example, Imperfect, consecutive Imperfect, volitional Imperfect) contributes to the issue of word order.

1. **Perfect.** When a Perfect verb is used to describe a completed action, it is normally not the first word in its clause, though there are exceptions (see 17.6.4). The following examples illustrate this usage. Note that in each example, the Perfect verb is not the first word in its clause.

בַּיּוֹם הַהוּא כָּרַת יְהוָה אֶת־אַבְרָם בְּרִית

In that day, the LORD *made (cut)* a covenant
with Abram (Gen 15:18).

בְּרֵאשִׁית בָּרָא אֱלֹהִים אֵת הַשָּׁמַיִם וְאֵת הָאָרֶץ

In the beginning, God *created* the heavens
and the earth (Gen 1:1).

2. **Consecutive Perfect.** A consecutive Perfect verb is normally the first word in its clause. The following examples illustrate this usage. Note that in each example, the consecutive Perfect is the first word in its clause.

וְאָהַבְתָּ אֵת יְהוָה אֱלֹהֶיךָ

And *you will love* the Lord your God (Deut 6:5).

וְזָכַרְתִּי אֶת־בְּרִיתִי

And *I will remember* my covenant (Gen 9:15).

23.6 **Syntax of the Imperfect.** You have learned that the Imperfect is used to express an incomplete *action* normally translated by the English future tense. You have also studied the consecutive Imperfect used in past tense narrative sequences and the volitional Imperfect used to express some type of command, wish, or desire.

1. **Imperfect.** The regular Imperfect verb does not normally appear as the first word in its clause. The following examples illustrate this use. Note that in each example, the Imperfect verb is not the first word of the clause.

הוּא יְשׁוּפְךָ רֹאשׁ וְאַתָּה תְּשׁוּפֶנּוּ עָקֵב

He *will crush* you on the head and
you *will crush* him on the heel (Gen 3:15).

יְהוָה יִמְלֹךְ לְעֹלָם וָעֶד

The Lord *will reign* forever and ever (Exod 15:18).

2. **Consecutive Imperfect.** The consecutive Imperfect verb is always first in its clause. The following examples illustrate this use.

וַיִּקַּח יְהוּדָה אִשָּׁה לְעֵר בְּכוֹרוֹ

And Judah *took* a wife for Er, his firstborn (Gen 38:6).

וַתַּהַר לֵאָה וַתֵּלֶד בֵּן וַתִּקְרָא שְׁמוֹ רְאוּבֵן

And Leah *conceived* and she *bore* a son
and she *called* his name Reuben (Gen 29:32).

3. **Volitional Imperfect.** Volitional Imperfects are also called Cohortative (first person) and Jussive (third person). The volitional Imperfect is normally the first word in its clause, though there are exceptions.

יִשְׁפֹּט יְהוָה בֵּינִי וּבֵינֶיךָ

May (let) the LORD *judge* between me and you (Gen 16:5).

נַעֲשֶׂה אָדָם בְּצַלְמֵנוּ

Let us make man in our image (Gen 1:26).

23.7 **Important Sequences with Volitional Conjugations.** There are many important sequences involving the volitional conjugations (Imperative, Cohortative, Jussive). Three of the more important sequences are described below.

1. Several Imperative verbs may occur in succession. They may or may not be linked with the conjunction וְ. In this construction, context will determine whether or not they are related consequentially or sequentially.

עֲלֵה וּקְבֹר אֶת־אָבִיךָ

Go up and *bury* your father (Gen 50:6).

זֹאת עֲשׂוּ וִחְיוּ

Do this and *you will live* (Gen 42:18).

2. An Imperative may be followed by a consecutive Perfect. In this sequence, the Perfect verb may carry the full force of the preceding Imperative in its translation. In such cases, the Perfect verb with Waw Consecutive and the preceding Imperative are related in terms of consecution of action.

לֵךְ וְאָמַרְתָּ אֶל־עַבְדִּי

Go and *say* to my servant (2 Sam 7:5).

וַיֹּאמֶר צֵא וְעָמַדְתָּ בָהָר לִפְנֵי יְהוָה

And he said, "*Go out* and *stand* on the mountain before the LORD" (1 Kgs 19:11).

3. An Imperative may be followed by an Imperfect or Cohortative, a construction that will create a purpose or result clause. In this

sequence, the Imperfect will be marked with the conjunction וְ
(not Waw Consecutive) and may be translated as "so that."

רְדוּ־שָׁמָּה וְשִׁבְרוּ־לָנוּ מִשָּׁם וְנִחְיֶה

Go down there and *buy grain* for us from
there *so that we might live* (Gen 42:2).

בֹּא הֵנָּה וְאֶשְׁלְחָה אֹתְךָ אֶל־הַמֶּלֶךְ

Come here *so that I may send* you to the king (2 Sam 14:32).

23.8   Conditional Clauses.[2] A conditional sentence consists of two units.
The first clause states the condition and is called the *protasis* (the "if-
clause"). The second clause states the consequence of the condition and
is called the *apodosis* (the "then-clause"). The protasis of a conditional
sentence will often begin with אִם (if), as in the following example.

וַיֹּאמֶר אֵלֶיהָ בָּרָק אִם־תֵּלְכִי עִמִּי וְהָלָכְתִּי וְאִם־לֹא תֵלְכִי עִמִּי לֹא אֵלֵךְ

Barak said to her, "*If* you will go with me, *then* I will go;
but *if* you will not go with me, (*then*) I will not go" (Judg 4:8).

Condition (Protasis)	*Consequence (Apodosis)*
"if (אִם) you will go"	"then I will go"
"but if (אִם) you will not go"	"(then) I will not go"

In addition to אִם, the *protasis* may begin with כִּי, הֵן or אֲשֶׁר followed
by a Perfect, Imperfect, or Participle.[3] The *apodosis* will often begin with
the conjunction וְ. Finally, note that in rare circumstances, both the
protasis and apodosis may be unmarked. The following examples
illustrate a number of different types of conditional clauses.

אִם־יֶשְׁךָ מְשַׁלֵּחַ אֶת־אָחִינוּ אִתָּנוּ נֵרְדָה וְנִשְׁבְּרָה לְךָ אֹכֶל
וְאִם־אֵינְךָ מְשַׁלֵּחַ לֹא נֵרֵד

If you send our brother with us, (*then*) we will go down
and buy food for you; but *if* you do not send (him),
(*then*) we will not go down (Gen 43:4-5).

---

2   For a more detailed study of conditional sentences and other clause sequences,
    see B. K. Waltke and M. O'Connor, *An Introduction to Biblical Hebrew Syntax* (Winona
    Lake: Eisenbrauns, 1990) 632-46.

3   Though less frequent, there is another type of conditional sentence (clause)
    that may begin with לוּ (if) or לוּלֵי (if not). For examples, see Num 14:2 and Ps
    119:92.

כִּי־תַעֲלֶה בָבֶל הַשָּׁמַיִם וְכִי תְבַצֵּר מְרוֹם עֻזָּהּ מֵאִתִּי יָבֹאוּ שֹׁדְדִים לָהּ

If Babylon were to reach up to heaven and *if* she were to fortify
the height of her strength, (then) destroyers would come from me
upon (to) her (Jer 51:53).

וְעָזַב אֶת־אָבִיו וָמֵת

If he leaves his father, *then* he (his father)
will die (Gen 44:22).

23.9   Additional Clause Types. There are many types of Hebrew clauses.
The following types are common.

1.   A *causal clause* indicates what causes another clause to happen.
     Causal clauses often begin with כִּי (because, for) or אֲשֶׁר (because,
     for).

לֹא נֵרֵד כִּי־הָאִישׁ אָמַר אֵלֵינוּ

We will not go down *because the man spoke to us* (Gen 43:5).

קְדֹשִׁים תִּהְיוּ כִּי קָדוֹשׁ אָנִי

You will be holy *because I am holy* (Lev 19:2).

2.   A *purpose clause* indicates the purpose of another clause; it states
     the goal that the subject of another clause hopes to achieve or
     avoid by means of that other clause. Purpose clauses often begin
     with לְמַעַן (so that), בַּעֲבוּר (so that), אֲשֶׁר (so that), לְבִלְתִּי (so
     that … not), לְמַעַן לֹא (so that not), or פֶּן (lest). Purpose clauses
     can also begin with וְ followed by an Imperative, Cohortative, or
     Jussive verb (see 23.7.3 above).

וְשָׁמַרְתָּ לַעֲשׂוֹת אֲשֶׁר יִיטַב לְךָ

And you will be careful to do *so that*
it will go well with you (Deut 6:3).

נַעֲשֶׂה־לָּנוּ שֵׁם פֶּן־נָפוּץ עַל־פְּנֵי כָל־הָאָרֶץ

Let us make a name for ourselves *lest we become scattered*
over the face of all the earth (Gen 11:4).

3.   A *result clause* states something that is true or happens because
     of another clause. Result clauses often begin with a Waw
     Consecutive verb or with כִּי (so, that).

מִי אָנֹכִי כִּי אֵלֵךְ אֶל־פַּרְעֹה

Who am I *that I can go to Pharaoh*! (Exod 3:11)

וַיֹּאמֶר יוֹאָב יָקֻמוּ וַיָּקֻמוּ

And Joab said, "Let them arise!"
So they arose (2 Sam 2:14-15).

4. A *concessive clause* states something that might be thought to prevent another clause, but it in fact does not. The other clause occurs in spite of the concessive clause. Concessive clauses are often marked with אִם, גַּם, גַּם כִּי, וְ, כִּי, or עַל, all of which can be translated "although" or "even though" when they are used to mark a concessive clause.

גַּם כִּי־אֵלֵךְ בְּגֵיא צַלְמָוֶת לֹא־אִירָא רָע

Even though I walk through the valley of the shadow
of death, I will not fear evil (Ps 23:4).

23.10 Disjunctive Waw. Even a casual exposure to biblical Hebrew will yield the striking impression that sentences are often composed of numerous clauses connected by a form of the conjunction וְ. You have probably noticed by now that this conjunction should not be translated as "and" in every occurrence. In Hebrew, there are two different types of the conjunction, identified as *conjunctive* and *disjunctive*. The conjunctive Waw is usually prefixed to a verb and links clauses sequentially, temporally, logically, and often consequentially. You have had some exposure to this usage in chapter 17 (Waw Consecutive).[4] The disjunctive Waw is prefixed to a non-verbal form and is non-sequential; that is, it introduces some kind of a break or interruption in the narrative. The disjunctive Waw may be used in a number of different ways. Four of the major uses are described below: parenthetical, circumstantial, contrastive, and introductory.

1. *Parenthetical*. In this use, the disjunctive clause interrupts the narrative flow in order to provide some explanatory information that is important for understanding the narrative.

---

[4] For an in-depth study of the conjunctive Waw, see B. K. Waltke and M. O'Connor, *An Introduction to Biblical Hebrew Syntax* (Winona Lake: Eisenbrauns, 1990) 519-63, 647-73.

וְהֵם לֹא יָדְעוּ כִּי שֹׁמֵעַ יוֹסֵף כִּי הַמֵּלִיץ בֵּינֹתָם

Now they did not know that Joseph was understanding
(them) because there was an interpreter between
them (Gen 42:23).

The disjunctive Waw on the independent personal pronoun
(וְהֵם) introduces a parenthetical comment that explains why
Joseph's brothers spoke openly with one another.

2. *Circumstantial*. In this use, the disjunctive clause introduces or
identifies circumstantial information that relates to the main
action of the narrative. These disjunctive clauses are often helpful
for understanding or visualizing the action of the narrative. As
the following example illustrates, the distinction between the
parenthetical and circumstantial uses can be subtle.

וַיְהִי כְּהַיּוֹם הַזֶּה וַיָּבֹא הַבַּיְתָה לַעֲשׂוֹת מְלַאכְתּוֹ
וְאֵין אִישׁ מֵאַנְשֵׁי הַבַּיִת שָׁם בַּבָּיִת

(And) one day, he went into the house to do his work
and none of the household servants were there
in the house (Gen 39:11).

The disjunctive Waw on אֵין (וְאֵין) introduces a circumstantial
comment that is important by way of setting up the attempted
seduction of Joseph by Potiphar's wife.

3. *Contrastive*. In this use, the disjunctive Waw introduces a
contrastive idea and is often translated as "but."

וַיִּשַׁע יְהוָה אֶל־הֶבֶל וְאֶל־מִנְחָתוֹ
וְאֶל־קַיִן וְאֶל־מִנְחָתוֹ לֹא שָׁעָה

The Lord looked favorably on Abel and his offering
but on Cain and his offering he did not look
favorably (Gen 4:4b-5a).

The disjunctive Waw on אֶל־קַיִן (וְאֶל־קַיִן) contrasts the Lord's
response to the two men and their offerings.

4. *Introductory*. In this use, the disjunctive Waw may begin a new
narrative or introduce a new idea or theme within a narrative.

וְהַנָּחָשׁ הָיָה עָרוּם מִכֹּל חַיַּת הַשָּׂדֶה
אֲשֶׁר עָשָׂה יְהוָה אֱלֹהִים

Now the serpent was more crafty than any
creature that the Lord God had made (Gen 3:1).

The disjunctive Waw on הַנָּחָשׁ (וְהַנָּחָשׁ) introduces the temptation
narrative of Adam and Eve. One could also view this disjunctive
Waw as introducing a "parenthetical" comment that is essential
for understanding the serpent's question that follows (Did God
really say ...?). Again, the various uses of the disjunctive Waw
will often overlap.

23.11 Summary.

1. The normal word order for a Hebrew verbal sentence is verb-
   subject-object. Note, however, that neither an explicit subject
   nor an object is required in every instance. Conversely, a verbal
   clause may have multiple subjects or objects.

2. The verb may be preceded by an adverb of time, an adverbial
   phrase, the word הִנֵּה (behold), a temporal clause, an expression
   that provides context or circumstantial information, or an
   independent personal pronoun for emphasis. A verb that is
   negated will be preceded immediately by a negative particle.

3. It is not uncommon for either the subject or the object to precede
   the verb. In such cases, the element placed before the verb is
   usually emphatic, though there are other reasons for this type of
   variation.

4. A conditional sentence consists of two clauses: (1) the first clause
   states the condition (*protasis* or "if-clause") and (2) the second
   clause states the consequence of the condition (*apodosis* or "then-
   clause"). The protasis will often begin with אִם (if).

5. An adverb is a word that is used to modify, describe, limit, or
   qualify a verb, adjective, or another adverb. Adverbs are generally
   divided into four categories: adverbs of time, place, degree, and
   manner.

6. A disjunctive Waw is prefixed to a non-verbal form and is non-
   sequential; that is, it introduces some kind of break or interruption
   in the narrative. Four of the major uses of disjunctive Waw are
   parenthetical, circumstantial, contrastive, and introductory.

23.12 Vocabulary.

Nouns

אוֹר	light, daylight, sunshine (120)
בְּכֹר	firstborn (120); also as בְּכוֹר
חֵמָה	wrath, heat, poison (125)
חֲצִי	half, middle (125)
כֹּחַ	strength, power (126)
נְחֹשֶׁת	copper, bronze (139)
נָשִׂיא	chief, leader, prince (130)
עֶרֶב	evening, sunset (134)
עֶצֶם	bone, skeleton (126)
פְּרִי	fruit, offspring (119)
קָהָל	assembly, community, crowd (123)
רֶכֶב	chariot, (coll) chariots or chariot riders, upper millstone (120)
לָשׁוֹן	tongue, language (117)
תּוֹעֵבָה	abomination, abhorrence, offensive thing (118)

23.13 We Have Not Come To an End.

חַסְדֵי יְהוָה כִּי לֹא־תָמְנוּ כִּי לֹא־כָלוּ רַחֲמָיו

The steadfast love of the LORD never ceases,
his mercies never come to an end.
Lam 3:22 (RSV)

Most of us are familiar with this English translation of Lam 3:22. Frequently, commentators and scholars have suggested that this text, as it presently stands, has suffered corruption in the history of its transmission. The first half of the verse does not seem straightforward, and the form תָמְנוּ (Qal Perfect 1cp of תָּמַם) is difficult because the root is both Geminate *and* stative. Many emend תָמְנוּ (Qal Perfect 1cp) to תָּמּוּ (Qal Perfect 3cp) on the basis of parallelism with כָלוּ (Qal Perfect 3cp) in the second half of the verse.[5] The second half of the verse is clear and may be translated "for his mercies have not come to an end." The emended line of text is translated "the steadfast love of Yahweh does not cease" (cf. RSV, NRSV, NJPS). Thus חַסְדֵי יְהוָה is considered the subject of the verb and כִּי is either considered emphatic or ignored. It is possible to consider that if חַסְדֵי יְהוָה is the subject, then it has been removed from the כִּי clause and placed at the front of the verse for emphasis. The dislocation of clause elements, or fronting, is not normal, however, in a כִּי clause (i.e., embedded sentence).

Is it possible to make sense of the text by reading the verb as it currently stands? A function of כִּי that is standard is to nominalize its clause, i.e., reduce the entire clause to the level of a nominal (functioning as a noun). We would then have a verbless clause in which the construct phrase חַסְדֵי יְהוָה is the subject and the nominalized clause כִּי לֹא־תָמְנוּ is the predicate. Taken this way, it would be translated "The steadfast love of Yahweh is that we have not come to an end." This makes better sense of כִּי and the order of the words in the text. The argument to emend the text on the basis of parallelism is not strong; even when parallelism is synonymous, the parallel lines may say something slightly different from each other.

The text is saying something more powerful than that the steadfast love of the Lord never ceases. It is saying that it is due to the steadfast love of the Lord that we, the people of God, do not come to an end and, in this way, his mercies never fail. It is always better to patiently study the text as it stands than to rashly assume a corrupt text and emend it.

Peter J. Gentry
Professor of Old Testament Interpretation
The Southern Baptist Theological Seminary
Louisville, Kentucky

---

[5] Whether we read תָּמְנוּ or תַּמּוּ, it must be noted that either form is pausal (see 36.3) and so the expected Pathach has been lengthened to Qamets. The non-pausal form תַּמְנוּ is attested elsewhere twice (Num 17:28 and Ps 64:7) and is clearly Qal Perfect 1cp.

23.14 **Advanced Information: Adverbs.** An adverb is a word that is used to modify, describe, limit, or qualify a verb, adjective, or another adverb. In the example, "he *continually* seeks the Lord," the adverb "continually" modifies the verb "seeks." In the example, "the king seemed *genuinely* pleased," the adverb "genuinely" modifies the adjective "pleased." Adverbs are generally divided into four categories: adverbs of time (then, now), place (here, there), degree (very, extremely), and manner (swiftly, gently). For the purpose of illustration, a few Hebrew adverbs are categorized below with examples.

1. *Adverbs of Time.*[6]

   עַתָּה (now)

   עַתָּה יָדַעְתִּי כִּי־יְרֵא אֱלֹהִים אַתָּה

   Now I know that you fear God (Gen 22:12).

   אָז (then, at that time)

   אָז יַקְהֵל שְׁלֹמֹה אֶת־זִקְנֵי יִשְׂרָאֵל

   Then Solomon assembled the elders of Israel (1 Kgs 8:1).

   טֶרֶם (before, not yet)[7]

   וַיָּלִנוּ שָׁם טֶרֶם יַעֲבֹרוּ

   They camped there *before* they crossed over (Josh 3:1).

2. *Adverbs of Place.*

   פֹּה (here)

   וַיֹּאמֶר שְׁבוּ־פֹה וַיֵּשֵׁבוּ

   And he said, "Sit *here*," and they sat (Ruth 4:2).

   הֵנָּה (here)

   וַיֹּאמֶר יְהוֹשֻׁעַ אֶל־בְּנֵי יִשְׂרָאֵל גֹּשׁוּ הֵנָּה וְשִׁמְעוּ

   And Joshua said to the people of Israel, "Approach *here* and listen" (Josh 3:9).

---

[6] It is important to note that certain adverbs of time, such as אָז (then, at that time) and טֶרֶם (before, not yet), may be followed by an Imperfect verb that should be translated as a Perfect. The examples above, following אָז and טֶרֶם, illustrate this special use of these adverbs with the Imperfect conjugation.

[7] This adverb will also appear with the preposition בְּ (בְּטֶרֶם) with the same meaning.

שָׁם (there)

וַיָּשֶׂם שָׁם אֶת־הָאָדָם אֲשֶׁר יָצָר

And he placed *there* the man whom he had formed (Gen 2:8).

חוּץ (outside)

וְשַׂמְתָּ אֶת־הַשֻּׁלְחָן מִחוּץ[8]

You will place the table *outside* (Ex 26:35).

3. *Adverbs of Degree.*

מְאֹד (very)

וַיַּרְא אֱלֹהִים אֶת־כָּל־אֲשֶׁר עָשָׂה וְהִנֵּה־טוֹב מְאֹד

And God saw everything that he had made and, behold, (it was) *very* good (Gen 1:31).

עוֹד (again)

וַתַּהַר עוֹד וַתֵּלֶד בֵּן

And she conceived *again* and bore a son (Gen 29:33).

תָּמִיד (continually)

עֵינַי תָּמִיד אֶל־יְהוָה

My eyes are *continually* on the Lord (Ps 25:15).

4. *Adverbs of Manner.*

יַחְדָּו (together)

וַיַּעֲנוּ כָל־הָעָם יַחְדָּו

And all the people answered *together* (Ex 19:8).

פִּתְאֹם (suddenly)

וַיָּבֹא אֲלֵיהֶם יְהוֹשֻׁעַ פִּתְאֹם

And Joshua came upon them *suddenly* (Josh 10:9).

---

[8] חוּץ = מִחוּץ with the preposition מִן

Chapter 24

The Niphal Stem - Strong Verbs

24.1 **Introduction.** Having studied the Qal stem, you are now equipped to identify over sixty-nine percent of all verb forms in the Hebrew Bible. It is now time to begin our study of the derived stems and their conjugations. You will find it helpful to review the introduction to verbal stems in 12.5-10. The good news is that no further paradigm memorization is required. The "diagnostic" approach to the derived stems does assume, however, that you have mastered the Qal stem and all of its paradigms.

24.2 **The Meaning of the Niphal Stem.** The Niphal stem is used to express *simple* action with either a *passive* or *reflexive* voice.[1] Frequently, whatever a verb means in the Qal stem, it becomes passive or reflexive in the Niphal stem. For example, שָׁמַע in the Qal stem is translated "he heard," while נִשְׁמַע in the Niphal stem is translated as either "he *was* heard" (passive) or "he heard *himself*" (reflexive). The Niphal may also be used with a reciprocal meaning as in נִשְׁמְעוּ, "they heard *one another*."[2] The name "Niphal" (נִפְעַל) *will remind you* that every verb in the Niphal stem takes a נ prefix. This prefix is unique to the Niphal stem and so distinguishes it from the other verbal stems.

24.3 **The Conjugations of the Niphal Stem.** In the Niphal paradigms throughout this chapter, you will notice that a נ is present in the verbal stem of every form. This is the נ of the Niphal. In the Perfect, Participle, and one form of the Infinitive Absolute, this prefixed נ makes identification of the Niphal stem easy. In the Imperfect, Imperative, Infinitive Construct, and the other Infinitive Absolute form, however, the נ prefix assimilates into the first consonant of the verbal root and remains as a Daghesh

---

[1] The Niphal stem occurs 4,138 times in the Hebrew Bible. It occurs in the Perfect 1,426 times, Imperfect 1,544 times, Imperative 118 times, Infinitive Construct 205 times, Infinitive Absolute 37 times, and Participle 808 times.

[2] Though infrequent by comparison with its passive, reflexive, or reciprocal uses, the Niphal may also be used to express a "middle" meaning. The middle nuance describes an action where agency is not specified. That is, the object of the action is also remotely the subject of the action. For example, the Niphal as passive is translated "the gate was opened," whereas the Niphal as middle is translated "the gate opened," where "gate" is both the subject and object of the verbal idea.

Forte. In other words, the prefixed נ of the Niphal will be present either as the actual consonant or as a Daghesh Forte representing the assimilation of that נ. We will study the various conjugations of the Niphal stem with the strong verb קָטַל (to kill) even though it will produce some awkward translations in selected forms. The following Niphal strong verb paradigms are presented with the corresponding Qal paradigms for the purpose of comparison. Please note that you are not required to memorize any of these Niphal paradigms. You must, however, memorize the diagnostic points of spelling for each of the Niphal conjugations.

24.4 Niphal Perfect. The Niphal Perfect is formed with the Niphal prefix (נִ), the verbal stem, and the Perfect sufformatives. For now, translate the Niphal Perfect passively with a form of the helping verb "to be," as in "he *was* killed."

	Qal	Niphal	Translation
3ms	קָטַל	נִקְטַל	he was killed
3fs	קָטְלָה	נִקְטְלָה	she was killed
2ms	קָטַׁלְתָּ	נִקְטַׁלְתָּ	you were killed
2fs	קָטַלְתְּ	נִקְטַלְתְּ	you were killed
1cs	קָטַׁלְתִּי	נִקְטַׁלְתִּי	I was killed
3cp	קָטְלוּ	נִקְטְלוּ	they were killed
2mp	קְטַלְתֶּם	נִקְטַלְתֶּם	you were killed
2fp	קְטַלְתֶּן	נִקְטַלְתֶּן	you were killed
1cp	קָטַׁלְנוּ	נִקְטַׁלְנוּ	we were killed

24.5 Niphal Perfect Diagnostics.

1. נִ prefix in every form. This is the נ of the Niphal stem, and it will enable you to distinguish between the Niphal Perfect and the Qal Perfect. This prefix will also distinguish the Niphal Perfect from all other derived stem Perfects.

2. Pathach stem vowel in all forms, except the 3fs (נִקְטְלָה) and 3cp (נִקְטְלוּ). The inflection of these two forms exhibits a Vocal Shewa in the stem vowel position. This vocalization is occasioned by the fact that these forms have a sufformative that either begins with a vowel or consists of a vowel.

*Niphal Perfect
Strong Verb*

נִקְטַל

24.6 **Niphal Imperfect.** The Niphal Imperfect is formed with the Imperfect preformatives, the verbal stem with assimilated נ of the Niphal, and the Imperfect sufformatives. It must be emphasized that with the Imperfect, the נ of the Niphal will assimilate into the first consonant of the verbal root and be represented by a Daghesh Forte. Translate the Niphal Imperfect passively with a form of the helping verb "to be," as in "he will *be* killed."

	Qal	Niphal	Translation
3ms	יִקְטֹל	יִקָּטֵל	he will be killed
3fs	תִּקְטֹל	תִּקָּטֵל	she will be killed
2ms	תִּקְטֹל	תִּקָּטֵל	you will be killed
2fs	תִּקְטְלִי	תִּקָּטְלִי	you will be killed
1cs	אֶקְטֹל	אֶקָּטֵל	I will be killed
3mp	יִקְטְלוּ	יִקָּטְלוּ	they will be killed
3fp	תִּקְטֹלְנָה	תִּקָּטַלְנָה	they will be killed
2mp	תִּקְטְלוּ	תִּקָּטְלוּ	you will be killed
2fp	תִּקְטֹלְנָה	תִּקָּטַלְנָה	you will be killed
1cp	נִקְטֹל	נִקָּטֵל	we will be killed

24.7 **Niphal Imperfect Diagnostics.**

1. Hireq preformative vowel in all forms, except the 1cs (אֶקָּטֵל) which has Seghol like the Qal.

2. Daghesh Forte in the first consonant of the verbal root (יִקָּטֵל). This is the נ of the Niphal but it has been assimilated into the first consonant of the verbal root. Note that this assimilation also occurs in the Imperative, Infinitive Construct, and one form of the Infinitive Absolute.

3. Qamets under the first consonant of the verbal root in every Imperfect form. Note that the stem vowel is not considered to be diagnostic.

4. Be careful not to confuse the Qal Imperfect 1cp form (נִקְטֹל) with the Niphal Imperfect 1cp form (נִקָּטֵל).

*Niphal Imperfect
Strong Verb*

יִקָּטֵל

24.8 **Niphal Imperative.** The Niphal Imperative and Infinitive Construct forms may be studied together in terms of their diagnostics because their basic forms are identical. The Niphal Imperative is formed with a ה prefix, verbal stem with assimilated נ of the Niphal, and the Imperative sufformatives. It must be emphasized again that the נ prefix of the Niphal will assimilate into the first consonant of the verbal root. For now, translate the Niphal Imperative passively with a form of the helping verb "to be," as in *"be* killed!"[3]

	Qal	Niphal	Translation
2ms	קְטֹל	הִקָּטֵל	be killed!
2fs	קִטְלִי	הִקָּטְלִי	be killed!
2mp	קִטְלוּ	הִקָּטְלוּ	be killed!
2fp	קְטֹלְנָה	הִקָּטַלְנָה	be killed!

24.9 **Niphal Infinitive Construct.** The masculine singular Imperative (הִקָּטֵל) and the basic Infinitive Construct form (הִקָּטֵל) are identical.

24.10 **Niphal Imperative and Infinitive Construct Diagnostics.**

1. ה prefix in every form of the Imperative and in the Infinitive Construct.

2. Daghesh Forte in the first consonant of the verbal root. This is the assimilated נ of the Niphal stem.

---

[3] The translation value of the Niphal Imperative will often lose the passive nuance as in הִשָּׁמֶר לְךָ פֶּן־תִּשְׁכַּח אֶת־יְהוָה "take heed to yourself lest you forget the Lord" (Deut 6:12).

3. Qamets under the first consonant of the verbal root in every form of the Imperative and in the Infinitive Construct.

4. The stem vowel is variable in both the Imperative and Infinitive Construct forms but it is not considered to be diagnostic.

Niphal Imperative/
Inf Construct

הִקָּטֵל

24.11 Niphal Infinitive Absolute. There are two forms for the Niphal Infinitive Absolute. The first form preserves the נ of the Niphal in the spelling. The second form has the ה prefix and assimilates the נ of the Niphal into the first consonant of the verbal root.

Qal	Niphal
קָטוֹל	נִקְטוֹל
	הִקָּטוֹל

24.12 Niphal Infinitive Absolute Diagnostics.

1. The Niphal Infinitive Absolute occurs only thirty-seven times in the Hebrew Bible. The two forms (נִקְטוֹל and הִקָּטוֹל) are evenly attested.

2. Both forms preserve the Holem Waw stem vowel, like the Qal Infinitive Absolute. The Holem Waw may also be written defectively as Holem (הִקָּטֹל). Frequently, the stem vowel is Tsere (הִקָּטֵל) and thus identical in form to the 2ms Imperative and Infinitive Construct forms.

Niphal Inf Absolute
Strong Verb

נִקְטוֹל
הִקָּטוֹל

24.13 Niphal Participle. The Niphal Participle is formed with the Niphal prefix (נִ), the verbal stem, and the same inflectional endings that were seen on the Qal Participle. Remember that Participles are verbal adjectives and inflect for gender and number but not for person.

	Qal	Niphal	Translation
ms	קֹטֵל	נִקְטָל	being killed
fs	קֹטֶלֶת	נִקְטֶלֶת[4]	being killed
mp	קֹטְלִים	נִקְטָלִים	being killed
fp	קֹטְלוֹת	נִקְטָלוֹת	being killed

24.14 Niphal Participle Diagnostics.

1. נִ prefix in all forms of the Participle.

2. Qamets stem vowel in all forms, except one form of the feminine singular (נִקְטֶלֶת).

3. Note that the only difference between the Niphal Perfect 3ms (נִקְטַל) and the masculine singular Niphal Participle (נִקְטָל) is the stem vowel. It is Pathach in the Perfect and Qamets in the Participle.

Niphal Participle
Strong Verb

נִקְטָל

24.15 Summary. At this point in the grammar, chapter summaries will consist primarily of diagnostic reviews. It is very important that you memorize the basic diagnostic features of each conjugation since this will prevent having to memorize numerous paradigms.

1. The Niphal stem is used to express *simple action* with either a *passive* or *reflexive* voice. It may also express a *reciprocal* type of action.

---

[4] Like the Qal Participle, the Niphal Participle also occurs with the ה ending as in נִקְטָלָה.

2. In the Niphal stem, the נ prefix is added to every form of every conjugation. In the Perfect, Participle, and one form of the Infinitive Absolute (נִקְטוֹל), the נ appears as a consonant in the spelling. In the Imperfect, Imperative, Infinitive Construct, and one form of the Infinitive Absolute (הִקָּטוֹל), the נ assimilates into the first consonant of the verbal root and remains as a Daghesh Forte.

3. It is not necessary that you memorize the paradigms in this chapter. Rather, you should memorize the diagnostic features of spelling that are presented in the following summary chart for each conjugation.

Niphal Stem - Strong Verb

Perfect		Imperfect	Imperative	Infinitive Construct	Infinitive Absolute	Participle
נִקְטַל	יִקָּטֵל		הִקָּטֵל	הִקָּטֵל	נִקְטוֹל הִקָּטוֹל	נִקְטָל
נִקְטַל		יִקָּטֵל	הִקָּטֵל	הִקָּטֵל	נִקְטוֹל	נִקְטָל
נִקְטְלָה		תִּקָּטֵל	הִקָּטְלִי		הִקָּטוֹל	נִקְטֶלֶת
נִקְטַלְתָּ		תִּקָּטֵל	הִקָּטְלוּ			נִקְטָלִים
נִקְטַלְתְּ		תִּקָּטְלִי	הִקָּטַלְנָה			נִקְטָלוֹת
נִקְטַלְתִּי		אֶקָּטֵל				
נִקְטְלוּ		יִקָּטְלוּ				
נִקְטַלְתֶּם		תִּקָּטַלְנָה				
נִקְטַלְתֶּן		תִּקָּטְלוּ				
נִקְטַלְנוּ		תִּקָּטַלְנָה				
		נִקָּטֵל				

24.16 Vocabulary. Note that translation values for verbal stems other than the Niphal have been included in the vocabulary, even though you have not yet studied the other derived stems in depth (12.7). This practice will continue in subsequent chapters. Entries for which the verbal stem is not specified are Qal.

Verbs

אָמַן	(Niphal) to be reliable, be faithful, be trustworthy (97)
יָשַׁע	(Niphal) to be delivered, be victorious, receive help (205)
יָתַר	(Niphal) to be left over, remain (106)
כּוּן	(Niphal) to be established, be steadfast, be ready (219)
לָחַם	(Niphal) to fight, do battle with (171)
מָלַט	(Niphal) to escape, flee to safety (94)
נָחַם	(Niphal) to be sorry, regret, have compassion (108)
נָכָה	(Hiphil) to strike, smite, beat, strike dead, destroy, injure (501)
נָצַב	(Niphal) to stand (firm), take one's stand (74)
נָצַל	(Niphal) to be rescued, be delivered (213)
סָתַר	(Niphal) to be hidden, hide oneself (82)
פָּלָא	(Niphal) to be extraordinary, be wonderful, be too difficult (71)
רוּץ	to run (104)
שָׁחַת	(Piel, Hiphil) to ruin, destroy, spoil, annihilate (152)
שָׁמַד	(Niphal) to be exterminated, be destroyed, be annihilated (90)

24.17 Hebrew Reading: The Call and Commission of Moses at the Burning Bush. The narrative of Moses' call at the burning bush (Ex 3) is mesmerizing and captures the imagination. In the mountainous desert of the Sinai, God identifies himself to the fearful shepherd in this way (Ex 3:6).

וַיֹּאמֶר אָנֹכִי אֱלֹהֵי אָבִיךָ אֱלֹהֵי אַבְרָהָם אֱלֹהֵי יִצְחָק וֵאלֹהֵי יַעֲקֹב

וַיַּסְתֵּר מֹשֶׁה פָּנָיו כִּי יָרֵא מֵהַבִּיט אֶל־הָאֱלֹהִים

As Moses hides his face, the Lord speaks (Ex 3:7-8).

7 וַיֹּ֣אמֶר יְהוָ֗ה רָאֹ֥ה רָאִ֛יתִי אֶת־עֳנִ֥י עַמִּ֖י אֲשֶׁ֣ר בְּמִצְרָ֑יִם וְאֶת־צַעֲקָתָ֤ם שָׁמַ֙עְתִּי֙ מִפְּנֵ֣י נֹֽגְשָׂ֔יו כִּ֥י יָדַ֖עְתִּי אֶת־מַכְאֹבָ֑יו 8 וָאֵרֵ֞ד לְהַצִּיל֣וֹ מִיַּ֣ד מִצְרַ֗יִם וּֽלְהַעֲלֹתוֹ֮ מִן־הָאָ֣רֶץ הַהִוא֒ אֶל־אֶ֤רֶץ טוֹבָה֙ וּרְחָבָ֔ה אֶל־אֶ֛רֶץ זָבַ֥ת חָלָ֖ב וּדְבָֽשׁ

The converted Imperfect verb וָאֵרֵד (and so I have come down) at the beginning of 3:8 reveals that God has witnessed the dire plight of his people in Egypt and he now acts to meet their need in faithfulness to the covenant promises that he made to the patriarchal fathers (Ex 2:24). For his part, Moses now learns that he will play a prophet's role in God's deliverance (Ex 3:10).

וְעַתָּ֣ה לְכָ֔ה וְאֶֽשְׁלָחֲךָ֖ אֶל־פַּרְעֹ֑ה וְהוֹצֵ֛א אֶת־עַמִּ֥י בְנֵֽי־יִשְׂרָאֵ֖ל מִמִּצְרָֽיִם

Moses poses a question that betrays his sense of inadequacy and lack of credentials for the mission to which God has called him, though some have suggested that his question is prompted out of a sense of humility (Ex 3:11).

וַיֹּ֤אמֶר מֹשֶׁה֙ אֶל־הָ֣אֱלֹהִ֔ים מִ֣י אָנֹ֔כִי כִּ֥י אֵלֵ֖ךְ אֶל־פַּרְעֹ֑ה וְכִ֥י אוֹצִ֛יא אֶת־בְּנֵ֥י יִשְׂרָאֵ֖ל מִמִּצְרָֽיִם

The reluctant prophet is given divine assurance that he will not be on his own: אֶהְיֶה עִמָּךְ (Ex 3:12). In the early stages of his call to this seemingly impossible mission, Moses' greatest fear is the prospect that the people will believe neither the message nor the divine messenger (Ex 3:13).

וַיֹּ֤אמֶר מֹשֶׁה֙ אֶל־הָ֣אֱלֹהִ֔ים הִנֵּ֤ה אָנֹכִי֙ בָ֣א אֶל־בְּנֵ֣י יִשְׂרָאֵ֔ל וְאָמַרְתִּ֣י לָהֶ֔ם אֱלֹהֵ֥י אֲבוֹתֵיכֶ֖ם שְׁלָחַ֣נִי אֲלֵיכֶ֑ם וְאָֽמְרוּ־לִ֣י מַה־שְּׁמ֔וֹ מָ֥ה אֹמַ֖ר אֲלֵהֶֽם

In asking for the deliverer's name, the people are seeking to understand his character, authority, and credential to accomplish their release from bondage. Is the God of the patriarchal fathers (Ex 2:24; 3:6) up to the task of confronting the god-king of Egypt and a pantheon of many gods? After all, Egypt is not the desert region of Abraham, Isaac, and Jacob with its provincial gods but one of the world empires of the day with cosmic deities. In order to convince Israel to listen and Pharaoh to obey, Moses needs to give the people a name but, more importantly, the character and authority behind it.

It is in the context of the call of Moses and his commission to mediate Israel's release from bondage in Egypt that the divine name and the character behind it are revealed afresh to the prophet and to the oppressed nation. In its fullest scope within the book of Exodus, the divine self-revelation is contained in three texts (3:13-15; 6:2-8; 34:5-7). Each of these texts will be the subject of a brief study in the coming chapters.

Gary D. Pratico
Professor of Old Testament
Gordon-Conwell Theological Seminary
South Hamilton, Massachusetts

Chapter 25

The Niphal Stem - Weak Verbs

25.1 **Introduction.** We will now study weak verbs in the Niphal stem. The study of weak verb diagnostics will build upon your familiarity with strong verb diagnostics. For this reason, you will need to have memorized the Niphal strong verb diagnostics in the previous chapter before working through this chapter. Remember, you should be memorizing diagnostics and *not paradigms*. You should also note that many weak verbs in the Niphal will preserve the diagnostics of the Niphal strong verb. For example, III-ח/ע verbs exhibit all of the Niphal strong verb diagnostics.

25.2 **III-א Verbs: Diagnostics and Paradigms.**

Perfect	Imperfect	Imperative	Infinitive Construct	Infinitive Absolute	Participle
נִמְצָא	**יִמָּצֵא**	**הִמָּצֵא**	**הִמָּצֵא**	**נִמְצוֹא**	**נִמְצָא**
נִמְצָא	יִמָּצֵא	הִמָּצֵא	הִמָּצֵא	נִמְצוֹא	נִמְצָא
נִמְצְאָה	תִּמָּצֵא	הִמָּצְאִי			נִמְצָאָה[1]
נִמְצֵאת	תִּמָּצֵא	הִמָּצְאוּ			נִמְצָאִים
נִמְצֵאת	תִּמָּצְאִי	הִמָּצֶאנָה			נִמְצָאוֹת
נִמְצֵאתִי	אֶמָּצֵא				
נִמְצְאוּ	יִמָּצְאוּ				
נִמְצֵאתֶם	תִּמָּצֶאנָה				
נִמְצֵאתֶן	תִּמָּצְאוּ				
נִמְצֵאנוּ	תִּמָּצֶאנָה				
	נִמָּצֵא				

---

[1] An alternative form, נִמְצֵאת, occurs only two times. While the form נִמְצָאָה is more frequent, it only occurs four times.

25.3   **III-א Verbs: Notes**. Most of the diagnostics for the Niphal strong verb are retained in the III-א Niphal forms. The diagnostics are identical in the Imperfect, Imperative, Infinitive Construct, and Infinitive Absolute. The diagnostics of the Perfect and Participle, however, exhibit only minor changes.

1. The נ prefix, characteristic of the Niphal stem, remains in both the Perfect and Participle. No other stem has this prefix and it is a sure indicator of the Niphal stem.

2. In the Perfect, it is the stem vowel that has changed compared to the strong verb. In the strong verb, the stem vowel is normally Pathach as in נִקְטַל. In III-א forms, however, the stem vowel is Qamets as in נִמְצָא. It should be noted, however, that the Qamets stem vowel occurs only in the 3ms form. It is more frequently Tsere as in נִמְצֵאתִי and Vocal Shewa in the 3fs and 3cp forms. These minor changes in the stem vowel should not pose any great difficulty. Your knowledge of the strong verb diagnostics should be sufficient for identification of most III-א Niphal forms.

25.4   **III-ה Verbs: Diagnostics and Paradigms**.

Perfect	Imperfect	Imperative	Infinitive Construct	Infinitive Absolute	Participle
נִבְנָה נִבְנֵית	יִבָּנֶה	הִבָּנֵה	הִבָּנוֹת	נִבְנֹה הִבָּנֵה	נִבְנֶה
נִבְנָה	יִבָּנֶה	הִבָּנֵה	הִבָּנוֹת	נִבְנֹה	נִבְנֶה
נִבְנְתָה	תִּבָּנֶה	הִבָּנִי		הִבָּנֵה	נִבְנָה
נִבְנֵיתָ	תִּבָּנֶה	הִבָּנוּ			נִבְנִים
נִבְנֵית	תִּבָּנִי	הִבָּנֶינָה			נִבְנוֹת
נִבְנֵיתִי	אֶבָּנֶה				
נִבְנוּ	יִבָּנוּ				
נִבְנֵיתֶם	תִּבָּנֶינָה				
נִבְנֵיתֶן	תִּבָּנוּ				
נִבְנֵינוּ	תִּבָּנֶינָה				
	נִבָּנֶה				

25.5 **III-ה Verbs: Notes.** Once again, the majority of the diagnostics for the Niphal strong verb are retained in the III-ה forms of the Niphal. The diagnostics are the same in every conjugation, except the Perfect and Participle.

1. The stem vowel of the Perfect varies between Qamets in the 3ms form (נִבְנָה) and Tsere Yod in the remaining forms (נִבְנֵיתָ), except in the 3fs and 3cp forms as usual. The stem vowel of the masculine singular Participle is Seghol. The reason for this is explained in the next point.

2. In the chart of Niphal III-ה diagnostics (25.4), you should note the endings that are highlighted in dark gray. With the exception of the Infinitive Construct, all of the other conjugations end with the consonant ה. You will recall from your study of Qal III-ה verbs that this is not the third consonant of the verbal root but a vowel letter. The shading of these vowel letters (and their associated vowels) is for the purpose of identifying them as unique and diagnostic endings of the III-ה class of verbs. These endings are not diagnostic, however, of the various stems because they are attested in all stems (Qal through Hithpael). The following chart lists the III-ה endings for your review (see also page 465).

Diagnostic Endings for III-ה
Verbs in All Stems

Conjugation	*Ending*
Perfect	הָ
Imperfect	הֶ
Imperative	הֵ
Infinitive Construct	וֹת
Participle	הֶ

You will also need to remember that these endings do not appear in verb forms with sufformatives. For example, the הֵ ending of the Imperative appears only in the masculine singular form because all other Imperative forms have a sufformative. Similarly, the הֶ ending of the Participle will occur only in the masculine singular because the other Participle forms have inflectional endings.

25.6   I-Guttural Verbs: Diagnostics and Paradigms.

Perfect	Imperfect	Imperative	Infinitive Construct	Infinitive Absolute	Participle
נֶעֱזָב	יֵעָזֵב *(no dagesh)*	הֵעָזֵב	הֵעָזֵב	נַעֲזוֹב / הֵעָזוֹב	נֶעֱזָב
נֶעֱזַב	יֵעָזֵב	הֵעָזֵב	הֵעָזֵב	נַעֲזוֹב	נֶעֱזָב
נֶעֶזְבָה	תֵּעָזֵב	הֵעָזְבִי		הֵעָזוֹב	נֶעֱזֶבֶת
נֶעֱזַבְתָּ	תֵּעָזֵב	הֵעָזְבוּ			נֶעֱזָבִים
נֶעֱזַבְתְּ	תֵּעָזְבִי	הֵעָזַבְנָה			נֶעֱזָבוֹת
נֶעֱזַבְתִּי	אֵעָזֵב				
נֶעֶזְבוּ	יֵעָזְבוּ				
נֶעֱזַבְתֶּם	תֵּעָזַבְנָה				
נֶעֱזַבְתֶּן	תֵּעָזְבוּ				
נֶעֱזַבְנוּ	תֵּעָזַבְנָה				
	נֵעָזֵב				

25.7   I-Guttural Verbs: Notes. The changes that occur in the Niphal forms of I-Guttural verbal roots, while appearing drastic at first, are explained by rules that you have already learned.

1. With those forms where the נ of the Niphal normally assimilates into the first consonant of the verbal root (Imperfect, Imperative, Infinitive Construct, and one form of the Infinitive Absolute), the guttural consonant rejects the Daghesh Forte associated with the assimilating נ. This results in *compensatory lengthening* of the prefix vowel, Hireq to Tsere in every form of these conjugations. Remember that in the rules of compensatory lengthening, Hireq lengthens to Tsere. For example, in the Imperfect form יֵעָזֵב (3ms), the presence of the Tsere under the Imperfect preformative is due to the fact that the ע has rejected the Daghesh Forte of the assimilating נ and caused the Hireq preformative vowel to lengthen to Tsere. Note that the diagnostic Qamets under the first consonant of the verbal root is preserved in each of these conjugations (Imperfect, Imperative, Infinitive Construct, and one form of the Infinitive Absolute).

2. Memorizing the diagnostic forms of the Niphal Perfect and Participle should be easy since you are already familiar with the pattern. The Perfect and Participle forms of Niphal I-Guttural verbs behave just like the I-Guttural forms of the Qal Imperfect of חָזַק (16.8). Compare the diagnostics below.

Qal Imperfect	Niphal Perfect	Niphal Participle
יֶחֱזַק	נֶעֱזַב	נֶעֱזָב

In every form of the Niphal Perfect and Participle, the prefix vowel is Seghol. In most forms, this is followed by the Hatef Seghol under the guttural that is the first consonant of the verbal root. In the Niphal Perfect forms, the stem vowel is Pathach (except in the 3fs and 3cp). In the Niphal Participle, the stem vowel is Qamets, except in the feminine singular form.

25.8   I-נ Verbs: Diagnostics and Paradigms.

Perfect	Imperfect	Imperative	Infinitive Construct	Infinitive Absolute	Participle
נִצַּל	יִנָּצֵל	הִנָּצֵל	הִנָּצֵל	הִנָּצֵל נִצּוֹל	נִצָּל
נִצַּל	יִנָּצֵל	הִנָּצֵל	הִנָּצֵל	הִנָּצֵל	נִצָּל
נִצְּלָה	תִּנָּצֵל	הִנָּצְלִי		נִצּוֹל	נִצֶּלֶת
נִצַּלְתָּ	תִּנָּצֵל	הִנָּצְלוּ			נִצָּלִים
נִצַּלְתְּ	תִּנָּצְלִי	הִנָּצַלְנָה			נִצָּלוֹת
נִצַּלְתִּי	אֶנָּצֵל				
נִצְּלוּ	יִנָּצְלוּ				
נִצַּלְתֶּם	תִּנָּצַלְנָה				
נִצַּלְתֶּן	תִּנָּצְלוּ				
נִצַּלְנוּ	תִּנָּצַלְנָה				
	נִנָּצֵל				

25.9   **I-נ Verbs: Notes.** All of the diagnostics for the Niphal strong verb are retained in the Niphal I-נ conjugations.

1. Our concern for the I-נ Niphal forms relates not to the diagnostics but rather to the need for recognizing the assimilation of the first root consonant in the Perfect, one form of Infinitive Absolute (נִצּוֹל), and the Participle forms. The נ that appears at the beginning of each form in these three conjugations is the נ of the Niphal stem and not the נ that is the first consonant of the verbal root. The נ of the verbal root has assimilated into the second root consonant and remains as a Daghesh Forte.

2. In the Imperfect, Imperative, Infinitive Construct, and one form of the Infinitive Absolute (הִנָּצֵל), the נ of the verbal root is retained while the נ of the Niphal stem has assimilated into the first consonant of the verbal root. This is the regular pattern of assimilation characteristic of the Niphal stem. Knowing when a נ is part of the I-נ verbal root or part of the Niphal stem is essential for the proper identification of the stem and verbal root. Carefully study each paradigm of 25.8 and be certain that you understand which נ has assimilated, the first consonant of the verbal root or the נ of the Niphal stem.

25.10   I-י Verbs: Diagnostics and Paradigms.

Perfect	Imperfect	Imperative	Infinitive Construct	Infinitive Absolute[2]	Participle
נוֹשַׁב	יִוָּשֵׁב	הִוָּשֵׁב	הִוָּשֵׁב		נוֹשָׁב
נוֹשַׁב	יִוָּשֵׁב	הִוָּשֵׁב	הִוָּשֵׁב	נוֹשָׁב
נוֹשְׁבָה	תִּוָּשֵׁב	הִוָּשְׁבִי			נוֹשֶׁבֶת
נוֹשַׁבְתָּ	תִּוָּשֵׁב	הִוָּשְׁבוּ			נוֹשָׁבִים
נוֹשַׁבְתְּ	תִּוָּשְׁבִי	הִוָּשַׁבְנָה			נוֹשָׁבוֹת
נוֹשַׁבְתִּי	אִוָּשֵׁב				
נוֹשְׁבוּ	יִוָּשְׁבוּ				
נוֹשַׁבְתֶּם	תִּוָּשַׁבְנָה				
נוֹשַׁבְתֶּן	תִּוָּשְׁבוּ				
נוֹשַׁבְנוּ	תִּוָּשַׁבְנָה				
	נִוָּשֵׁב				

---

[2] The Niphal Infinitive Absolute is not attested in I-י verbs.

25.11 I-ʾ Verbs: Notes. While the vowel changes in the above diagnostics and paradigms appear drastic at first glance, most of the Niphal strong verb diagnostics are still evident.

1. Most of the verbs that we now identify as I-ʾ were originally I-ו. In the conjugations of the Niphal stem, this original ו reappears and replaces the ʾ that is in the first root position. In the Imperfect, Imperative, and Infinitive Construct, the Waw appears as the first root consonant with the Daghesh Forte (וּ),[3] representing the assimilated נ of the Niphal stem. Knowing this, the diagnostics of the Imperfect, Imperative, and Infinitive Construct forms are identical to the strong Niphal diagnostics.

2. In the Perfect and Participle forms, the original ו appears as a Holem Waw (וֹ). The נ of the Niphal stem is still present and the stem vowel of each form is also unchanged from the strong diagnostics (Pathach in the Perfect and Qamets in the Participle). In other words, the only change in diagnostics in the Perfect and Participle forms of I-ʾ verbs is the presence of the Holem Waw prefix vowel rather than the Hireq of the strong verb.

3. The difficulty with I-ʾ verbs is not the recognition of diagnostics but rather the identification of the verbal root. In order to correctly identify these verbs, you will need to remember that I-ʾ verbs were originally I-ו and that the original ו consonant reappears in the Niphal stem as either a consonant (Imperfect, Imperative, and Infinitive Construct) or a vowel (Perfect and Participle).

25.12 Other Weak Forms. There are several other weak verb classes that are attested in the Niphal stem. The diagnostics of III-ה/ע weak verbs are identical to the strong verb. Biconsonantal, Geminate, and various doubly weak forms occur infrequently and do not warrant attention here. Mastery of the diagnostics for the strong and weak verbs already presented should be sufficient to enable you to successfully identify these more infrequent weak forms of the Niphal stem.

---

[3] You must understand that this is the consonant Waw with a Daghesh Forte (וּ) and not the vowel Shureq (וּ).

25.13 Summary: Niphal Diagnostics.

	Perfect	Imperfect	Imperative	Infinitive Construct	Infinitive Absolute	Participle
Strong	נִקְטַל	יִקָּטֵל	הִקָּטֵל	הִקָּטֵל	נִקְטוֹל / הִקָּטוֹל	נִקְטָל
III-א	נִמְצָא	יִמָּצֵא	הִמָּצֵא	הִמָּצֵא	נִמְצוֹא	נִמְצָא
III-ה	נִבְנָה / נִבְנֵיתָ	יִבָּנֶה	הִבָּנֵה	הִבָּנוֹת	נִבְנֹה / הִבָּנֵה	נִבְנֶה
I-Gutt	נֶעֱזַב	יֵעָזֵב	הֵעָזֵב	הֵעָזֵב	נַעֲזוֹב / הֵעָזוֹב	נֶעֱזָב
I-נ	נִצַּל	יִנָּצֵל	הִנָּצֵל	הִנָּצֵל	הִנָּצֵל / נִצּוֹל	נִצָּל
I-י	נוֹשַׁב	יִוָּשֵׁב	הִוָּשֵׁב	הִוָּשֵׁב		נוֹשָׁב

25.14 Vocabulary.

Verbs

הָפַךְ	to turn, overturn, overthrow, destroy (95)
זָנָה	to commit fornication, be a harlot (prostitute), be unfaithful (60)
חָרָה	to be(come) hot, burn with anger, become angry (93)
רָעַע	to be bad, be evil, be displeasing (98)
שָׂבַע	to be satisfied, be satiated, eat or drink one's fill (97)
שָׁכַח	to forget (102)
שָׁמֵם	to be deserted, be uninhabited, be desolated (92)

Nouns

זָכָר	male, man	(82)
חֹשֶׁךְ	darkness	(80)
מִגְרָשׁ	open land, pasture	(114)
מַמְלָכָה	kingdom, dominion, reign	(117)
נָהָר	river, stream	(119)
צֶדֶק	righteousness, equity	(123)
רֹעֶה	shepherd	(84)

25.15 **What Is His Name?** Exodus 3:13-15 is the first of three biblical texts that are essential for a provisional understanding of the revelation and meaning of God's personal name, יהוה, the name that defines his relationship as covenant Lord of his people. In Ex 3:13, Moses asks God how he is to respond to the community in bondage when they ask about the name and authority of the one in whose name Moses mediates the message of deliverance.

הִנֵּה אָנֹכִי בָא אֶל־בְּנֵי יִשְׂרָאֵל וְאָמַרְתִּי לָהֶם אֱלֹהֵי אֲבוֹתֵיכֶם
שְׁלָחַנִי אֲלֵיכֶם וְאָמְרוּ־לִי מַה־שְּׁמוֹ מָה אֹמַר אֲלֵהֶם

> Suppose I go to the people of Israel and I say to them,
> "The God of your fathers has sent me to you," and they ask me, "What
> is his name?" Then what shall I say to them?

This verse makes clear the intention of Moses to identify the God of Exodus events with the God of the patriarchal fathers. This is how God revealed himself to Moses at the burning bush (Ex 3:6), in the context of his self-revelation in this text (Ex 3:15-16), in the preparation of Moses for his mission (Ex 4:5), and in the reiteration of his promise of deliverance (Ex 6:2, 8). In fact, the destination of the delivered people will be the land promised to the fathers (Ex 6:8).

וְהֵבֵאתִי אֶתְכֶם אֶל־הָאָרֶץ אֲשֶׁר נָשָׂאתִי אֶת־יָדִי לָתֵת אֹתָהּ לְאַבְרָהָם
לְיִצְחָק וּלְיַעֲקֹב וְנָתַתִּי אֹתָהּ לָכֶם מוֹרָשָׁה אֲנִי יְהוָה

The narrative is burdened to establish the unbroken continuity and identity between the God of the fathers and the God of Exodus events.

The question of the people in Ex 3:13 (מַה־שְּׁמוֹ) is supremely theological. In its Old Testament usage, and especially in 3:13 and 6:3, the noun שֵׁם (name) often communicates immeasurably more than a simple label by which one is known. The concept of a personal name includes personhood, character, reputation, and authority. The concept of a name can signify and encompass the whole person. A name can express theological meaning or signify one's hopes or expectations for a person. This explains the significance of naming and name changes in the Old Testament (Gen 17:5, 15; 32:28; 35:10; Isa 8:3; Hos 1:2-8). In some contexts, the name of God is tantamount to his being (Ex 20:24; 23:21; Deut 12:5). In their question, the people are seeking to know the character, authority, and reputation of the divine messenger behind the message. God identifies himself to Moses and instructs him how to respond to the people (Ex 3:14).

וַיֹּאמֶר אֱלֹהִים אֶל־מֹשֶׁה אֶהְיֶה אֲשֶׁר אֶהְיֶה וַיֹּאמֶר כֹּה תֹאמַר לִבְנֵי
יִשְׂרָאֵל אֶהְיֶה שְׁלָחַנִי אֲלֵיכֶם

Here God declares that his name is אֶהְיֶה אֲשֶׁר אֶהְיֶה (traditionally, "I am who I am"). The two verbs are Qal Imperfect 1cs from הָיָה with the relative pronoun אֲשֶׁר between them. This construction allows for "I am who/what I am" or "I will be who/what I will be." Moses is further instructed in 3:14 to identify the God of their fathers as אֶהְיֶה ("I am" or "I will be"). The context clearly links the אֶהְיֶה אֲשֶׁר אֶהְיֶה with God's statement to Moses in Ex 3:12 (אֶהְיֶה עִמָּךְ) and also with the *tetragrammaton* in 3:15. The divine self-revelation continues in 3:15, creating a seamless connection between the God of the fathers (3:13, 15), אֶהְיֶה אֲשֶׁר אֶהְיֶה (3:14a), אֶהְיֶה (3:14b), and the *tetragrammaton* (3:15), which also derives from היה (originally הוה).

How, then, does this divine self-revelation answer the people's question in 3:13, validating the mission of Moses and disclosing the authority of the divine deliverer? The answer is in the verb "to be" (הָיָה), which floods this narrative. Clearly, the use of this verb in Ex 3:10-15 implies more than just ontological being. The use of הָיָה in the context of God's mighty and miraculous deliverance of Israel from Egypt and the exercise of his judgment on the oppressing nation implies both his dynamic presence and his dynamic activity. The arena of human history is about to experience a dynamic intrusion of the divine.[4]

Gary D. Pratico
Professor of Old Testament
Gordon-Conwell Theological Seminary
South Hamilton, Massachusetts

---

[4] This study will continue in 26.15.

Chapter 26

The Piel Stem - Strong Verbs

26.1 **Introduction.** In this chapter, we will study the second of the derived stems, the Piel.[1] As in your study of the Niphal stem, paradigm memorization is not required for the Piel stem. Rather, you will study certain diagnostic points of spelling that are unique to the Piel stem. The most important diagnostic features include: (1) Vocal Shewa under all Imperfect and Participle preformatives and prefixes; (2) Pathach under the first root consonant of every conjugation, except the Perfect; and (3) Daghesh Forte in the second root consonant of every form.

26.2 **The Meaning of the Piel Stem.**[2]

1. *Intensive.* The Piel stem is used to express an *intensive* type of action with an *active* voice.[3] In other words, the simple action of the Qal stem will take on some type of intensive nuance in the Piel stem. For example, the verb שָׁבַר means "he broke" in the Qal stem. The Piel form, however, is שִׁבֵּר and means "he smashed" or "he shattered." This intensive type of action, however, is only one of several different types of "intensive" action denoted by the Piel stem. Some of the more common types of action are detailed below.

2. *Factitive.* The factitive use of the Piel makes an intransitive Qal verb transitive. In other words, if a Qal verb is intransitive (does not take a direct object), it will become transitive (can take a direct object) in the Piel stem. The following examples illustrate how an intransitive Qal verb becomes transitive in the Piel.

---

[1] The Piel stem occurs 6,473 times in the Hebrew Bible. It appears in the Perfect 2,120 times, Imperfect 2,446 times, Imperative 436 times, Infinitive Construct 708 times, Infinitive Absolute 84 times, and Participle 679 times.

[2] Some Piel verbs do not fall into any of the following categories. You will need to consult a standard lexicon when you are not certain of a verb's meaning in a given derived stem.

[3] We recognize the difficulty of characterizing the varieties of action denoted by the Piel stem (also Pual and Hithpael) with a single designation like "intensive." Such a designation is a helpful starting point, however, for the beginning student. Additionally, it is legitimate to think of the factitive and iterative as "types" of intensive action.

Qal (Intransitive)		*Factitive Piel (Transitive)*
קָדַשׁ to be holy	➤	קִדֵּשׁ to sanctify
אָבַד to perish	➤	אִבֵּד to destroy
טָמֵא to be unclean	➤	טִמֵּא to defile

3. *Denominative.* Verbs that are derived from a noun or adjective are often inflected in the Piel stem, not the Qal. When this occurs, the type of verbal action is simple and not intensive.

Noun		*Denominative Piel*
דָּבָר word	➤	דִּבֶּר to speak
כֹּהֵן priest	➤	כִּהֵן to serve as priest
עָפָר dust	➤	עִפַּר to throw dirt

4. *Iterative.* The iterative action of the Piel expresses the nuance of repeated action. This use occurs primarily with verbs that express physical movement, effort, or voice projection. This type of action is often difficult to translate into English.

Qal		*Iterative Piel*
הָלַךְ to go, walk	➤	הִלֵּךְ to pace, walk around
צָעַק to cry	➤	צֶעֵק to weep over and over, keep crying

26.3 **Piel Perfect.** It is the vocalization (vowel pattern) that will distinguish the Piel stem from the Qal stem. In the Piel Perfect, the distinguishing features are a Hireq under the first root consonant and a Daghesh Forte in the second root consonant.

	Qal	Piel	Translation[4]
3ms	קָטַל	קִטֵּל	he slaughtered
3fs	קָטְלָה	קִטְּלָה	she slaughtered
2ms	קָטַ֫לְתָּ	קִטַּ֫לְתָּ	you slaughtered
2fs	קָטַלְתְּ	קִטַּלְתְּ	you slaughtered
1cs	קָטַ֫לְתִּי	קִטַּ֫לְתִּי	I slaughtered
3cp	קָטְלוּ	קִטְּלוּ	they slaughtered
2mp	קְטַלְתֶּם	קִטַּלְתֶּם	you slaughtered
2fp	קְטַלְתֶּן	קִטַּלְתֶּן	you slaughtered
1cp	קָטַ֫לְנוּ	קִטַּ֫לְנוּ	we slaughtered

26.4 Piel Perfect Diagnostics.

1. Hireq under the first consonant of the verbal root.

2. Daghesh Forte in the second consonant of the verbal root.

3. The stem vowel is variable between <u>Tsere and Pathach</u>, except in the 3fs and 3cp, where the expected Vocal Shewa is present. Note that the Tsere stem vowel occurs only in the 3ms.

Piel Perfect
Strong Verb
קִטֵּל

26.5 Piel Imperfect. Once again, it is the vowel pattern that will distinguish the Piel Imperfect from the Qal Imperfect. In the Piel Imperfect, the distinguishing features include: Vocal Shewa under the preformative, Pathach under the first root consonant, and Daghesh Forte in the second root consonant.

---

[4] The verb קָטַל is not attested in the Piel stem. The translation "to slaughter" would be the intensive rendering of the Qal, meaning "to kill."

	Qal	Piel	Translation
3ms	יִקְטֹל	יְקַטֵּל	he will slaughter
3fs	תִּקְטֹל	תְּקַטֵּל	she will slaughter
2ms	תִּקְטֹל	תְּקַטֵּל	you will slaughter
2fs	תִּקְטְלִי	תְּקַטְּלִי	you will slaughter
1cs	אֶקְטֹל	אֲקַטֵּל	I will slaughter
3mp	יִקְטְלוּ	יְקַטְּלוּ	they will slaughter
3fp	תִּקְטֹלְנָה	תְּקַטֵּלְנָה	they will slaughter
2mp	תִּקְטְלוּ	תְּקַטְּלוּ	you will slaughter
2fp	תִּקְטֹלְנָה	תְּקַטֵּלְנָה	you will slaughter
1cp	נִקְטֹל	נְקַטֵּל	we will slaughter

26.6   Piel Imperfect Diagnostics.

1.   Vocal Shewa under the Imperfect preformative (Hateph Pathach in the 1cs since gutturals cannot take Vocal Shewa).

2.   Pathach under the first consonant of the verbal root. This is the most important diagnostic feature since it occurs in every other Piel conjugation, except the Perfect. Note that the stem vowels are not considered to be diagnostic, though it is helpful to observe the presence of Tsere throughout the conjugations of the Piel (see summary chart in 26.13).

3.   Daghesh Forte in the second consonant of the verbal root.

*Piel Imperfect
Strong Verb*

יְקַטֵּל

26.7   Piel Imperative, Infinitive Construct, and Infinitive Absolute. These forms may be studied together in terms of their diagnostics because their basic forms are identical. There are two diagnostic features that characterize all three forms.

1. Pathach under the first consonant of the verbal root.

2. Daghesh Forte in the second consonant of the verbal root.

*Piel Imperative/
Infinitive Construct
and Absolute*

קַטֵּל

26.8 **Piel Imperative.** As in the Qal, all four forms of the Piel Imperative are derivable from their corresponding Imperfect forms by simply removing the Imperfect preformatives. When studying the Piel Imperative paradigm, note the similarity between the Imperative forms and the corresponding forms of the Imperfect.

	Piel Imperfect	Piel Imperative	Translation
2ms	תְּקַטֵּל	קַטֵּל	(you) slaughter!
2fs	תְּקַטְּלִי	קַטְּלִי	(you) slaughter!
2mp	תְּקַטְּלוּ	קַטְּלוּ	(you) slaughter!
2fp	תְּקַטֵּלְנָה	קַטֵּלְנָה	(you) slaughter!

26.9 **Piel Infinitive Construct.** The basic form of the Piel Infinitive Construct is identical to the 2ms form of the Piel Imperative. The following chart compares the Qal and Piel Infinitive Construct forms.

	Qal	*Piel*	*Translation*
	קְטֹל	קַטֵּל	to slaughter, slaughtering

26.10 **Piel Infinitive Absolute.** The Piel Infinitive Absolute of קָטַל is קַטֵּל. The Qal and Niphal forms of the Infinitive Absolute normally exhibit an o-class stem vowel, Holem or Holem Waw. In the Piel, Hiphil and Hithpael stems, however, an e-class stem vowel is present, usually Tsere (but sometimes Tsere Yod or Seghol).[5]

---

[5] In six instances, the Piel Infinitive Absolute will have an o-class stem vowel (Holem Waw or Holem).

26.11 Piel Participle. The Piel Participle is formed with a מ prefix and has diagnostics similar to those of the Piel Imperfect. Remember that Participles are verbal adjectives and inflect for gender and number but not person.

	Qal	Piel	Translation
ms	קֹטֵל	מְקַטֵּל	slaughtering
fs	קֹטֶלֶת	מְקַטֶּלֶת⁶	slaughtering
mp	קֹטְלִים	מְקַטְּלִים	slaughtering
fp	קֹטְלוֹת	מְקַטְּלוֹת	slaughtering

26.12 Piel Participle Diagnostics.

1. מְ prefix. A מ prefix will characterize the Participles of the Piel, Pual, Hiphil, and Hophal stems. In the Piel and Pual Participles, this prefix appears with Shewa (מְ).

2. Pathach under the first consonant of the verbal root.

3. Daghesh Forte in the second consonant of the verbal root.

*Piel Participle
Strong Verb*

מְקַטֵּל

26.13 Summary.

1. The most important diagnostic features for the strong verb of the Piel stem include: (1) Daghesh Forte in the second root consonant of every form; (2) Pathach under the first root consonant of every conjugation, except the Perfect; and (3) Vocal Shewa under all Imperfect and Participle preformatives and prefixes. Though not considered to be diagnostic, it is helpful to note the Tsere stem vowel throughout the conjugations.

2. Looking ahead, note that the Daghesh Forte in the second consonant of the verbal root will also characterize the strong verb inflections of the Pual and Hithpael stems.

---

⁶ Like the Qal Participle, the Piel Participle may also end in ָה as in מְקַטְּלָה.

3. Note the distinctive מ prefix in the forms of the Piel Participle. This same prefix also occurs with the Participles of the Pual, Hiphil, and Hophal stems.

Piel Stem - Strong Verbs

Perfect	Imperfect	Imperative	Infinitive Construct	Infinitive Absolute	Participle
קִטֵּל	יְקַטֵּל	קַטֵּל	קַטֵּל	קַטֵּל	מְקַטֵּל
קִטֵּל	יְקַטֵּל	קַטֵּל	קַטֵּל	קַטֵּל	מְקַטֵּל
קִטְּלָה	תְּקַטֵּל	קַטְּלִי			מְקַטֶּלֶת
קִטַּלְתָּ	תְּקַטֵּל	קַטְּלוּ			מְקַטְּלִים
קִטַּלְתְּ	תְּקַטְּלִי	קַטֵּלְנָה			מְקַטְּלוֹת
קִטַּלְתִּי	אֲקַטֵּל				
קִטְּלוּ	יְקַטְּלוּ				
קִטַּלְתֶּם	תְּקַטֵּלְנָה				
קִטַּלְתֶּן	תְּקַטְּלוּ				
קִטַּלְנוּ	תְּקַטֵּלְנָה				
	נְקַטֵּל				

26.14 Vocabulary.

Verbs

בָּקַשׁ   (Piel) to seek, search for, discover, demand, require (225)

דָּבַר   (Piel) to speak (1,136)

הָלַל   (Piel) to praise, sing hallelujah (146)

יָדָה   (Hiphil) to thank, praise, confess (111)

כָּסָה   to cover, conceal, hide; (Piel) cover (up), clothe (153)

מָהַר   (Piel) to hasten, hurry, go or come quickly (81)

נָבָא   (Niphal) to prophesy, be in a state of prophetic ecstasy (115)

נָבַט   (Piel) to look (at), gaze, behold (70)

סָגַר   to shut, close (91)

צָוָה	(Piel) to command, give an order, charge (496)
קַטֵּר	(Piel) to make a sacrifice go up in smoke, offer (a sacrifice) by burning (115)
שִׁיר	to sing (88)
שִׁית	to set, put, place (86)
שָׁרַת	(Piel) to minister, serve, attend to the service of God (98)

26.15 Hebrew Reading: I Am the Lord. Exodus 6:2-8 is the second text that is essential for understanding the revelation and meaning of God's covenant name (יהוה). It complements Ex 3:13-15, repeating some aspects of the earlier divine self-revelation but adding new elements. The intervening narrative is devoted to Moses' resistance to God's call with God's continued encouragement and equipping of the reluctant prophet (4:1-17). In Ex 5:1-23, we witness the initial failures of Moses' mission before both Pharaoh and the deliverer's own people.

Moses demands (Ex 5:1):

וְאַחַר בָּאוּ מֹשֶׁה וְאַהֲרֹן וַיֹּאמְרוּ אֶל־פַּרְעֹה כֹּה־אָמַר יְהוָה אֱלֹהֵי
יִשְׂרָאֵל שַׁלַּח אֶת־עַמִּי וְיָחֹגּוּ לִי בַּמִּדְבָּר

Pharaoh responds (Ex 5:2):

וַיֹּאמֶר פַּרְעֹה מִי יְהוָה אֲשֶׁר אֶשְׁמַע בְּקֹלוֹ לְשַׁלַּח אֶת־יִשְׂרָאֵל לֹא
יָדַעְתִּי אֶת־יְהוָה וְגַם אֶת־יִשְׂרָאֵל לֹא אֲשַׁלֵּחַ

Pharaoh's statement is both profound and amusing. With his declaration (לֹא יָדַעְתִּי אֶת־יְהוָה), he is about to embark on a graduate-level education. This deficiency in his cosmopolitan schooling is about to be remedied. Initially, neither the message nor the messenger are accorded any respect by the god-king of Egypt but, with time, Pharaoh will come to know, fear, and obey the God of Moses.

Early on, Moses' greatest fears are realized. Deliverance is not immediately forthcoming and his first efforts only increase the burden of his people. He complains to God (Ex 5:22-23).

22 וַיָּשָׁב מֹשֶׁה אֶל־יְהוָה וַיֹּאמַר אֲדֹנָי לָמָה הֲרֵעֹתָה לָעָם הַזֶּה לָמָּה זֶּה
שְׁלַחְתָּנִי 23 וּמֵאָז בָּאתִי אֶל־פַּרְעֹה לְדַבֵּר בִּשְׁמֶךָ הֵרַע לָעָם הַזֶּה וְהַצֵּל
לֹא־הִצַּלְתָּ אֶת־עַמֶּךָ

The promise of deliverance is reiterated (Ex 6:1).

וַיֹּאמֶר יְהוָה אֶל־מֹשֶׁה עַתָּה תִרְאֶה אֲשֶׁר אֶעֱשֶׂה לְפַרְעֹה כִּי בְיָד חֲזָקָה
יְשַׁלְּחֵם וּבְיָד חֲזָקָה יְגָרְשֵׁם מֵאַרְצוֹ

Notice the use of verbs and verbal stem. Pharaoh won't just "let them go" (יְשַׁלְּחֵם Piel Imperfect 3ms of שָׁלַח with 3mp pronominal suffix); "he will drive them from his land" (יְגָרְשֵׁם Piel Imperfect 3ms of גֵּרֵשׁ with 3mp pronominal suffix). The divine declaration אֲנִי יְהוָה (I am Yahweh) is used like bookends in Ex 6:2-8. The passage begins and ends with this divine self-identification and it occurs twice more within the passage. Throughout the text, the divine name is connected with a torrent of verbs and phrases that describe the Lord's redemptive activity on behalf of his people.

אֲנִי שָׁמַעְתִּי אֶת־נַאֲקַת בְּנֵי יִשְׂרָאֵל
I have heard …

וָאֶזְכֹּר אֶת־בְּרִיתִי
I have remembered …

וְהוֹצֵאתִי אֶתְכֶם מִתַּחַת סִבְלֹת מִצְרַיִם
I will bring you out …

וְהִצַּלְתִּי אֶתְכֶם מֵעֲבֹדָתָם
I will deliver you …

וְגָאַלְתִּי אֶתְכֶם בִּזְרוֹעַ נְטוּיָה
I will redeem you …

In fulfillment of his promises to the fathers (Ex 3:6, 13, 15, 16; 4:5; 6:3, 8), God will mightily, dynamically, and miraculously break into human history for the purpose of redeeming his people from bondage and creating with them an intimate relationship (Ex 6:7).[7]

וְלָקַחְתִּי אֶתְכֶם לִי לְעָם וְהָיִיתִי לָכֶם לֵאלֹהִים וִידַעְתֶּם כִּי אֲנִי יְהוָה
אֱלֹהֵיכֶם הַמּוֹצִיא אֶתְכֶם מִתַּחַת סִבְלוֹת מִצְרָיִם

Gary D. Pratico
Professor of Old Testament
Gordon-Conwell Theological Seminary
South Hamilton, Massachusetts

---

[7] This study will continue in section 27.14.

26.16 Advanced Information: Loss of Daghesh Forte. There are a number of circumstances in which an expected Daghesh Forte is lost. You have already encountered this phenomenon (5.5) when, for example, the definite article is prefixed to words that begin with יְ or מְ as in הַיְלָדִים (the boys) or הַמְרַגְּלִים (the spies). Similarly, the consonants יְ, וְ, לְ, מְ, נְ, קְ and שְׁ, שְׂ, סְ, צְ (the sibilants) will frequently lose an expected Daghesh Forte when a Vocal Shewa occurs under that consonant. Note that this phenomenon is especially common with the Piel stem, as the following examples illustrate.

הַמְדַבֵּר — Piel Participle ms with the definite article. The expected Daghesh Forte of the definite article is lost because the syllable begins with מְ.

וַיְדַבֵּר — Piel Imperfect 3ms with Waw Consecutive. The expected Daghesh Forte of the Waw Consecutive is lost because the syllable begins with יְ.

וַיְקַנְאוּ — Piel Imperfect 3mp with Waw Consecutive. The expected Daghesh Forte of the Waw Consecutive is lost because the syllable begins with יְ. Additionally, the expected Daghesh Forte in the second root consonant of the Piel stem is absent because נ is one of the consonants that may give up a Daghesh Forte when occurring with Vocal Shewa (נְ).

מִלְאוּ — Piel Perfect 3cp. The expected Daghesh Forte in the second root consonant of the Piel stem is lost because the ל occurs with Vocal Shewa (לְ).

26.17 Advanced Information: Conjunctive Daghesh. A Conjunctive Daghesh is a *Daghesh Forte that has been placed in the initial consonant of a word* to connect it to the previous word in order to smooth out the pronunciation. The use of the Conjunctive Daghesh often takes place when the first word ends in an unaccented הָ or הֶ and the following word begins with an accented syllable. Two examples include וְזֶה־שְּׁמוֹ (and this is his name) and לְכָה־נָּא (come then). The Daghesh Forte in the שׁ of שְׁמוֹ and in the נ of נָּא is the Conjunctive Daghesh.

Chapter 27

The Piel Stem - Weak Verbs

27.1 **Introduction**. Most weak verbs in the Piel stem maintain the diagnostic features of the strong verb. It is only II-Guttural weak verbs that exhibit any major changes.

27.2 **Weak Verbal Roots with Strong Diagnostic Features**. The following four weak verb classes (III-ח/ע, III-א, III-ה and Geminate) are given for your study and observation but not for memorization.

27.3 **III-ח/ע Verbs: Diagnostics and Paradigms**. The paradigm verb שָׁלַח is translated "to send off, send away" in the Piel stem. Note that the Tsere stem vowel of the Piel strong verb is replaced by a Pathach stem vowel in this weak verb class. This change is due to the fact that gutturals prefer a-class vowels. With the exception of this stem vowel change, all of the diagnostics of the Piel strong verb are present.

Perfect	Imperfect	Imperative	Infinitive Construct	Infinitive Absolute	Participle
שִׁלַּח	יְשַׁלַּח	שַׁלַּח	שַׁלַּח¹	שַׁלֵּחַ	מְשַׁלֵּחַ
שִׁלַּח	יְשַׁלַּח	שַׁלַּח	שַׁלַּח	שַׁלֵּחַ	מְשַׁלֵּחַ
שִׁלְּחָה	תְּשַׁלַּח	שַׁלְּחִי			מְשַׁלַּחַת
שִׁלַּחְתָּ	תְּשַׁלַּח	שַׁלְּחוּ			מְשַׁלְּחִים
שִׁלַּחַתְּ	תְּשַׁלְּחִי	שַׁלַּחְנָה			מְשַׁלְּחוֹת
שִׁלַּחְתִּי	אֲשַׁלַּח				
שִׁלְּחוּ	יְשַׁלְּחוּ				
שִׁלַּחְתֶּם	תְּשַׁלַּחְנָה				
שִׁלַּחְתֶּן	תְּשַׁלְּחוּ				
שִׁלַּחְנוּ	תְּשַׁלַּחְנָה				
	נְשַׁלַּח				

---

¹ Even though the stem vowel is not diagnostic, a Tsere stem vowel occurs with the same frequency as Pathach.

27.4   **III-א Verbs: Diagnostics and Paradigms.** In the paradigm verb מָצָא, note that the stem vowel in the Perfect is Tsere and not Pathach. Nevertheless, all of the Piel strong verb diagnostics are present in this weak verb class.

Perfect	Imperfect	Imperative	Infinitive Construct	Infinitive Absolute	Participle
מָצֵא	יְמָצֵא	מָצֵא	מָצֵא	מָצֵא²	מְמַצֵּא
מִצֵּא	יְמַצֵּא	מַצֵּא	מַצֵּא	מַצֵּא	מְמַצֵּא
מִצְּאָה	תְּמַצֵּא	מַצְּאִי			מְמַצֵּאת
מִצֵּאתָ	תְּמַצֵּא	מַצְּאוּ			מְמַצְּאִים
מִצֵּאת	תְּמַצְּאִי	מַצֶּאנָה			מְמַצְּאוֹת
מִצֵּאתִי	אֲמַצֵּא				
מִצְּאוּ	יְמַצְּאוּ				
מִצֵּאתֶם	תְּמַצֶּאנָה				
מִצֵּאתֶן	תְּמַצְּאוּ				
מִצֵּאנוּ	תְּמַצֶּאנָה				
	נְמַצֵּא				

27.5   **III-ה Verbs: Diagnostics and Paradigms**. The paradigm verb גָּלָה is translated "to uncover," "disclose," or "make known" in the Piel. All of the Piel strong verb diagnostics are present in this weak verb class. Note, however, the stem vowels in the Piel Perfect (Qamets and Hireq Yod). Additionally, note the III-ה diagnostic endings that are highlighted in dark gray. These are the same III-ה endings that appear in all stems, Qal through Hithpael.

---

² The Piel Infinitive Absolute form of III-א verbs occurs only four times: one time with the Tsere stem vowel (טַמֵּא) and three times with the Holem stem vowel (קַנֹּא and רַפֹּא). Nevertheless, the stem vowel is not considered to be diagnostic.

Perfect	Imperfect	Imperative	Infinitive Construct	Infinitive Absolute	Participle
גָּלָה	יְגַלֶּה	גַּלֵּה	גַּלּוֹת	גַּלֵּה	מְגַלֶּה
גִּלָּה	יְגַלֶּה	גַּלֵּה	גַּלּוֹת	גַּלֵּה	מְגַלֶּה
גִּלְּתָה	תְּגַלֶּה	גַּלִּי			מְגַלָּה
גִּלִּיתָ	תְּגַלֶּה	גַּלּוּ			מְגַלִּים
גִּלִּית	תְּגַלִּי	גַּלֶּינָה			מְגַלּוֹת
גִּלִּיתִי	אֲגַלֶּה				
גִּלּוּ	יְגַלּוּ				
גִּלִּיתֶם	תְּגַלֶּינָה				
גִּלִּיתֶן	תְּגַלּוּ				
גִּלִּינוּ	תְּגַלֶּינָה				
	נְגַלֶּה				

27.6 Geminate Verbs: Diagnostics and Paradigms. The paradigm verb הָלַל is translated "to praise" in the Piel. All of the Piel strong verb diagnostics are present in this weak verb class. Note the absence of the Daghesh Forte in selected forms of the Perfect (3fs, 3cp), Imperfect (2fs, 3mp, 2mp), and Imperative (fs, mp).

Perfect	Imperfect	Imperative	Infinitive Construct	Infinitive Absolute	Participle
הַלֵּל	יְהַלֵּל	הַלֵּל	הַלֵּל	הַלֵּל	מְהַלֵּל
הִלֵּל	יְהַלֵּל	הַלֵּל	הַלֵּל	הַלֵּל	מְהַלֵּל
הִלְלָה	תְּהַלֵּל	הַלְלִי			מְהַלֶּלֶת
הִלַּלְתָּ	תְּהַלֵּל	הַלְלוּ			מְהַלְלִים
הִלַּלְתְּ	תְּהַלְלִי	הַלֵּלְנָה			מְהַלְלוֹת
הִלַּלְתִּי	אֲהַלֵּל				
הִלְלוּ	יְהַלְלוּ				
הִלַּלְתֶּם	תְּהַלֵּלְנָה				
הִלַּלְתֶּן	תְּהַלְלוּ				
הִלַּלְנוּ	תְּהַלֵּלְנָה				
	נְהַלֵּל				

27.7   **II-Guttural Verbs.** With the previous weak verbal roots, the strong verb diagnostics are retained. In the Piel stem, only II-Guttural verbs exhibit any major changes compared to the diagnostics of the strong verb. These changes occur because the guttural consonant in second root position rejects the Daghesh Forte of the Piel stem, and this results in either virtual doubling or compensatory lengthening (see 5.4 for a review of these concepts). With virtual doubling, the guttural consonant rejects the Daghesh Forte but the preceding vowel is *not* lengthened. With compensatory lengthening, the guttural consonant rejects the Daghesh Forte and the preceding vowel is lengthened. The following graphic illustrates these two patterns with the Piel Perfect 3ms.

Strong Verb	*II-Guttural Virtual Doubling*	*II-Guttural Compensatory Lengthening*
קִטֵּל	בִּעֵר	מֵאֵן

In the form בִּעֵר the ע rejects the Daghesh Forte but the preceding vowel is *not* lengthened. In the form מֵאֵן the א rejects the Daghesh Forte and the Tsere under the מ is the result of compensatory lengthening. In the patterns of compensatory lengthening, the vowel Hireq lengthens to Tsere. Most verbs exhibit either virtual doubling or compensatory lengthening. Some verbs, however, may exhibit both patterns.

27.8   **II-Guttural Verbs with Virtual Doubling: Diagnostics and Paradigms.** The paradigm verb נָחַם is translated "to comfort" or "to console" in the Piel. This verb exhibits virtual doubling in the Piel conjugations.

Perfect	Imperfect	Imperative	Infinitive Construct	Infinitive Absolute	Participle
נִחַם	יְנַחֵם	נַחֵם	נַחֵם	נַחֵם	מְנַחֵם
נִחַם	יְנַחֵם	נַחֵם	נַחֵם	נַחֵם	מְנַחֵם
נִחֲמָה	תְּנַחֵם	נַחֲמִי			מְנַחֶמֶת
נִחַמְתָּ	תְּנַחֵם	נַחֲמוּ			מְנַחֲמִים
נִחַמְתְּ	תְּנַחֲמִי	נַחֵמְנָה			מְנַחֲמוֹת
נִחַמְתִּי	אֲנַחֵם				
נִחֲמוּ	יְנַחֲמוּ				
נִחַמְתֶּם	תְּנַחֵמְנָה				
נִחַמְתֶּן	תְּנַחֲמוּ				
נִחַמְנוּ	תְּנַחֵמְנָה				
	נְנַחֵם				

27.9 **II-Guttural Verbs with Virtual Doubling: Notes**. All of the Piel strong verb diagnostics are present in this weak class, except the Daghesh Forte in the second root consonant.

1. You should now understand that when the Daghesh Forte is rejected by the guttural consonant in the second root position and the preceding vowel is *not* lengthened, it is called *virtual doubling*.

2. In the II-Guttural class of weak verbs in the Piel, the stem vowel may be either Tsere (בֵּעֵר) or Pathach (נִחַם). Though it is important to be aware of this distinction, the stem vowel is not considered to be a diagnostic feature of the Piel stem.

27.10 **II-Guttural Verbs with Compensatory Lengthening: Diagnostics and Paradigms**. The paradigm verb בָּרַךְ is translated "to bless" in the Piel. This verb exhibits compensatory lengthening in the Piel conjugations.

Perfect	Imperfect	Imperative	Infinitive Construct	Infinitive Absolute	Participle
בֵּרֵךְ	יְבָרֵךְ	בָּרֵךְ	בָּרֵךְ	בָּרֵךְ	מְבָרֵךְ
בֵּרֵךְ	יְבָרֵךְ	בָּרֵךְ	בָּרֵךְ	בָּרֵךְ	מְבָרֵךְ
בֵּרְכָה	תְּבָרֵךְ	בָּרְכִי			מְבָרֶכֶת
בֵּרַכְתָּ	תְּבָרֵךְ	בָּרְכוּ			מְבָרְכִים
בֵּרַכְתְּ	תְּבָרְכִי	בָּרֵכְנָה			מְבָרְכוֹת
בֵּרַכְתִּי	אֲבָרֵךְ				
בֵּרְכוּ	יְבָרְכוּ				
בֵּרַכְתֶּם	תְּבָרֵכְנָה				
בֵּרַכְתֶּן	תְּבָרְכוּ				
בֵּרַכְנוּ	תְּבָרֵכְנָה				
	נְבָרֵךְ				

27.11 II-Guttural Verbs with Compensatory Lengthening: Notes. In the verb בָּרַךְ (to bless), the consonant ר in second root position is functioning like a guttural in that it rejects the Daghesh Forte of the Piel. The result is compensatory lengthening of the preceding vowel. In the Perfect, Hireq is lengthened to Tsere under the first root consonant (בֵּרֵךְ). In all other conjugations, Pathach is lengthened to Qamets under the first root consonant (יְבָרֵךְ). Be certain that you understand where compensatory lengthening takes place in each conjugation.

27.12 Summary: Piel Diagnostics. Once again, the major diagnostic features of the Piel stem include: (1) Daghesh Forte in the second root consonant; (2) Pathach under the first consonant of the verbal root in every conjugation, except the Perfect; and (3) Vocal Shewa under all Imperfect and Participle preformatives and prefixes. The only weak verbs to experience any significant change in these diagnostics are II-Guttural weak verbs. The following chart summarizes all Piel stem diagnostics, both strong and weak.

	Perfect	Imperfect	Imperative	Infinitive Construct	Infinitive Absolute	Participle
Strong	קִטֵּל	יְקַטֵּל	קַטֵּל	קַטֵּל	קַטֵּל	מְקַטֵּל
III-ח/ע	שִׁלַּח	יְשַׁלַּח	שַׁלַּח	שַׁלַּח	שַׁלֵּחַ	מְשַׁלֵּחַ
III-א	מִצֵּא	יְמַצֵּא	מַצֵּא	מַצֵּא	מַצֵּא	מְמַצֵּא
III-ה	גִּלָּה	יְגַלֶּה	גַּלֵּה	גַּלּוֹת	גַּלֵּה	מְגַלֶּה
Geminate	הִלֵּל	יְהַלֵּל	הַלֵּל	הַלֵּל	הַלֵּל	מְהַלֵּל
II-Gutt[3]	נִחַם	יְנַחֵם	נַחֵם	נַחֵם	נַחֵם	מְנַחֵם
II-Gutt[4]	בֵּרַךְ	יְבָרֵךְ	בָּרֵךְ	בָּרֵךְ	בָּרֵךְ	מְבָרֵךְ

27.13 Vocabulary.

Verbs

גּוּר	to sojourn, dwell as a foreigner or alien (82)
יָעַץ	to advise, counsel, plan, decide (80)
לָמַד	to learn; (Piel) teach (87)
מָשַׁל	to rule, reign, govern, have dominion (81)
מָכַר	to sell, hand over (80)
עָזַר	to help, assist, come to the aid of (82)
עָנָה	(Piel) to afflict, oppress, humiliate, violate (79)
קָלַל	to be small, be insignificant, be swift; (Niphil, Piel) declare cursed (82)
קָנָה	to get, acquire, buy (85)
רָכַב	to mount and ride, ride (78)
שָׁחַט	to slaughter (81)

---

[3] II-Guttural verbs with virtual doubling

[4] II-Guttural verbs with compensatory lengthening

Nouns

אָחוֹת	sister, relative, loved one (119); feminine
כָּנָף	wing, edge, extremity (111)
עַמּוּד	pillar, column, tent pole (112)
שֶׁקֶר	lie, deception, falsehood (113)

27.14 But By My Name Yahweh. Few verses in the Old Testament have generated the scholarly attention received by Ex 6:2-3.

וַיְדַבֵּר אֱלֹהִים אֶל־מֹשֶׁה וַיֹּאמֶר אֵלָיו אֲנִי יְהוָה 2

וָאֵרָא אֶל־אַבְרָהָם אֶל־יִצְחָק וְאֶל־יַעֲקֹב בְּאֵל שַׁדָּי 3
וּשְׁמִי יְהוָה לֹא נוֹדַעְתִּי לָהֶם

2 God said to Moses, "I am Yahweh.
3 I appeared[5] to Abraham, to Isaac and to Jacob as El Shaddai[6]
but by my name Yahweh I did not make myself known to them."[7]

Based on these verses, many scholars deny to the patriarchs any knowledge of the divine name (יהוה), contrary to its appearance nearly 170 times in the book of Genesis and the first three chapters of Exodus. In dozens of instances, the name יהוה is spoken by the patriarchs or used by God and others in speaking to the fathers. It is argued, nevertheless, that the patriarchal fathers worshiped El Shaddai and had no knowledge of the name יהוה. On this view, the name יהוה was first revealed in the setting of these Exodus events.[8] In its most extreme expression, this understanding of Ex 6:2-3 severs the historical and theological continuity between the religion of the patriarchal fathers and that of Moses and early Israel at the time of the Exodus. This disjuncture has important implications for one's understanding of early Israelite origins and the composition of the early biblical writings.

Contrary to this view is the interpretation that does not deny knowledge of the name יהוה to the patriarchs, as is clearly suggested by the narratives of Genesis and early Exodus. The fathers knew the name but they did

---

[5] וָאֵרָא (Niphal Imperfect 1cs of רָאָה with Waw Conversive) may also be translated with the reflexive nuance (I revealed myself).

[6] El Shaddai (אֵל שַׁדָּי) is traditionally translated "God Almighty," but its etymology is uncertain.

[7] נוֹדַעְתִּי is the Niphal Perfect 1cs of יָדַע (to know). In the Niphal stem, the verb means "to make oneself known."

[8] Proponents of this view argue that the name יהוה was written into the text of Genesis anachronistically.

not understand the fullness of its revelation of the divine character. Ex 6:2-8 is not a new revelation of the name; it is a nuanced revelation of the name. The name is now being revealed afresh in the setting of God's dynamic and miraculous intrusion into human history for the primary purpose of redeeming his people from bondage in Egypt. Understanding the use of the noun שֵׁם (name) as detailed earlier, Ex 6:2 may be interpretively translated as follows.

> I appeared to Abraham, to Isaac, and to Jacob as El Shaddai,
> but in the character expressed by my name Yahweh
> I did not make myself known to them.[9]

With regard to the etymology of the tetragrammaton (יהוה), there is general agreement that it derives from the verb "to be" (הָיָה originally הָוָה) and that it is also associated with an Imperfect 3ms form. Uncertainty and disagreement abound, however, as to whether the name derives from the Qal or Hiphil stem or whether the Imperfect derivation should be translated by the present or future tense. Though some will protest, an analysis of historical and textual context will contribute more to an understanding of the name than etymological analysis. The context of Ex 3:14-15 would appear to favor the Qal derivation. But whether translated by the present or future, this much is clear. The name is not metaphysical but dynamic. The "new" revelation of the divine character is that of dynamic activity. Mightily and miraculously (Ex 7:3), the Lord intervenes in time and space in order to effect his redemptive purposes for his covenant people and brings judgment on Egypt and its gods in the process. Ex 3:13-15 and 6:2-8 record a new stage in the progressive self-revelation of God's name and character to his people. One cannot help but recall that in the sacramental setting of Jesus' last meal with his disciples, he said, "I have manifested your name" (John 17:6). Implicit in "your name" is the person, character, authority, and the redemptive work of God.[10]

Gary D. Pratico
Professor of Old Testament
Gordon-Conwell Theological Seminary
South Hamilton, Massachusetts

---

[9] J. A. Motyer, *The Revelation of the Divine Name* (London: Tyndale, 1959) 11-17.

[10] This study will continue in section 28.11.

27.15 Advanced Information: The Polel Stem. In chapter 12, you were introduced to the seven "major" stems of the Hebrew verbal system (Qal and the six derived stems). There are, however, a number of additional stems that are considered "minor" because of their relative infrequency. In this grammar, we will cover four of the "minor" verbal stems in certain "Advanced Information" sections. These stems include the Polel, Polal (29.13), Hithpolel, (35.13) and Hishtaphel (35.14).[11]

Biconsonantal verbs occur infrequently in the Piel, Pual, and Hithpael stems. Instead, they occur in the Polel, Polal, and Hithpolel stems. Geminate roots may also appear in these stems. In general, the meaning of the Piel corresponds to the meaning of the Polel, the Pual to the Polal, and the Hithpael to the Hithpolel. With Biconsonantal verbs, these stems are characterized by a Holem Waw after the first consonant and the duplication of the second root consonant. For your reference, the Polel forms of the verb רוּם (to exalt, lift up) are presented below.

Perfect	Imperfect	Imperative	Infinitive Construct	Infinitive Absolute	Participle
רוֹמֵם	יְרוֹמֵם	רוֹמֵם	רוֹמֵם		מְרוֹמֵם
רוֹמְמָה	תְּרוֹמֵם	רוֹמְמִי			מְרוֹמֶמֶת
רוֹמַ֫מְתָּ	תְּרוֹמֵם	רוֹמְמוּ			מְרוֹמְמִים
רוֹמַמְתְּ	תְּרוֹמְמִי	רוֹמֵ֫מְנָה			מְרוֹמְמוֹת
רוֹמַ֫מְתִּי	אֲרוֹמֵם				
רוֹמְמוּ	יְרוֹמְמוּ				
רוֹמַמְתֶּם	תְּרוֹמֵ֫מְנָה				
רוֹמַמְתֶּן	תְּרוֹמְמוּ				
רוֹמַ֫מְנוּ	תְּרוֹמֵ֫מְנָה				
	נְרוֹמֵם				

---

[11] There are several other "minor" verbal stems found in the Hebrew Bible. For a more thorough discussion, see B. K. Waltke and M. O'Connor, *Introduction to Biblical Hebrew Syntax* (Winona Lake: Eisenbrauns, 1990) 359-361.

Chapter 28

The Pual Stem - Strong Verbs

28.1 **Introduction.** In this chapter, we will study the Pual stem.[1] It is the passive counterpart of the Piel stem. Once again, paradigm memorization is not required in this chapter. Instead, the diagnostic features of the Pual stem are presented for study. The most significant diagnostic features of the Pual stem include: (1) Vocal Shewa under all Imperfect and Participle preformatives and prefixes; (2) Qibbuts under the first root consonant of every form; and (3) Daghesh Forte in the second root consonant of every form. Note that the first and third diagnostic features are identical to the Piel stem. Therefore, it is the second diagnostic feature (Qibbuts under the first root consonant) that will distinguish Pual forms from Piel forms. Given the infrequency of certain Pual forms, we will study only the Perfect, Imperfect, and Participle.

28.2 **The Meaning of the Pual Stem.** The Pual stem is the passive counterpart of the Piel stem. The Pual stem is used, therefore, to express an *intensive* type of action with a *passive* voice. For example, the Piel Perfect verb שִׁבֵּר means "he smashed." The Pual form, however, would be שֻׁבַּר and it would be translated "he (it) *was* smashed." Notice how a form of the English verb "to be" (was) is used to make the translation passive.

---

[1] The Pual stems occurs 423 times in the Hebrew Bible: 146 times in the Perfect, 85 times in the Imperfect, 1 time in the Infinitive Construct, 1 time in the Infinitive Absolute, and 190 times in the Participle.

28.3 **Pual Perfect**. In the following paradigms, the Pual Perfect is listed with the Piel Perfect for comparison. The vowel under the first root consonant of each form will distinguish the Pual from the Piel. Translate the Pual Perfect passively with a form of the helping verb "to be," as in "he (it) *was* slaughtered."

	Piel	Pual	Translation
3ms	קִטֵּל	קֻטַּל	he (it) was slaughtered
3fs	קִטְּלָה	קֻטְּלָה	she (it) was slaughtered
2ms	קִטַּלְתָּ	קֻטַּלְתָּ	you were slaughtered
2fs	קִטַּלְתְּ	קֻטַּלְתְּ	you were slaughtered
1cs	קִטַּלְתִּי	קֻטַּלְתִּי	I was slaughtered
3cp	קִטְּלוּ	קֻטְּלוּ	they were slaughtered
2mp	קִטַּלְתֶּם	קֻטַּלְתֶּם	you were slaughtered
2fp	קִטַּלְתֶּן	קֻטַּלְתֶּן	you were slaughtered
1cp	קִטַּלְנוּ	קֻטַּלְנוּ	we were slaughtered

28.4 **Pual Perfect Diagnostics**.

1. The important diagnostic is a Qibbuts under the first consonant of the verbal root. This feature distinguishes the Pual Perfect from the Piel Perfect. The Piel Perfect has a Hireq under the first root consonant.

2. As in the Piel, there is a Daghesh Forte in the second consonant of the verbal root. As noted above, this diagnostic feature is characteristic of the Piel, Pual and Hithpael stems. Though not diagnostic, the stem vowel is a Pathach (except in the 3fs and 3cp).

Pual Perfect
Strong Verb

קֻטַּל

28.5   **Pual Imperfect.** The vowel under the first root consonant will distinguish the Pual Imperfect from the Piel Imperfect. Translate the Pual Imperfect passively with a form of the helping verb "to be," as in "he (it) will *be* slaughtered."

	Piel	*Pual*	*Translation*
3ms	יְקַטֵּל	יְקֻטַּל	he (it) will be slaughtered
3fs	תְּקַטֵּל	תְּקֻטַּל	she (it) will be slaughtered
2ms	תְּקַטֵּל	תְּקֻטַּל	you will be slaughtered
2fs	תְּקַטְּלִי	תְּקֻטְּלִי	you will be slaughtered
1cs	אֲקַטֵּל	אֲקֻטַּל	I will be slaughtered
3mp	יְקַטְּלוּ	יְקֻטְּלוּ	they will be slaughtered
3fp	תְּקַטֵּלְנָה	תְּקֻטַּלְנָה	they will be slaughtered
2mp	תְּקַטְּלוּ	תְּקֻטְּלוּ	you will be slaughtered
2fp	תְּקַטֵּלְנָה	תְּקֻטַּלְנָה	you will be slaughtered
1cp	נְקַטֵּל	נְקֻטַּל	we will be slaughtered

28.6   **Pual Imperfect Diagnostics.**

1. Vocal Shewa under the Imperfect preformative as in the Piel Imperfect.

2. Qibbuts under the first consonant of the verbal root. This diagnostic feature distinguishes the Pual Imperfect from the Piel Imperfect. The Piel has a Pathach under the first root consonant.

3. Daghesh Forte in the second consonant of the verbal root as in the Piel.

Pual Imperfect
Strong Verb

יְקֻטַּל

28.7   **Pual Participle**. Like the Piel, the Pual Participle is formed with a מְ prefix. Translate the Pual Participle passively with a form of the helping verb "to be," as in *"being* slaughtered."

	Piel	*Pual*	*Translation*
ms	מְקַטֵּל	מְקֻטָּל	being slaughtered
fs	מְקַטֶּלֶת	מְקֻטֶּלֶת²	being slaughtered
mp	מְקַטְּלִים	מְקֻטָּלִים	being slaughtered
fp	מְקַטְּלוֹת	מְקֻטָּלוֹת	being slaughtered

28.8   **Pual Participle Diagnostics**.

1.   As with the Piel, the Pual Participle has the מְ prefix. As noted above, a מְ prefix is used with the Piel, Pual, Hiphil, and Hophal Participles.

2.   Qibbuts under the first consonant of the verbal root. This diagnostic feature distinguishes the Pual Participle from the Piel Participle. The Piel has a Pathach under the first root consonant.

3.   Daghesh Forte in the second consonant of the verbal root.

*Pual Participle
Strong Verb*

מְקֻטָּל

28.9   **Summary**. The following chart summarizes the Pual strong verb diagnostics studied in this chapter. Be sure that you understand the diagnostic feature that will distinguish a Pual strong verb from a Piel strong verb, namely, the Qibbuts under the first consonant of the verbal root.

---

² The Pual Participle may also end in ה‍ָ as in the form מְקֻטָּלָה.

Pual Stem - Strong Verbs

Perfect	Imperfect	Participle
קֻטַּל	יְקֻטַּל	מְקֻטָּל
קֻטַּל	יְקֻטַּל	מְקֻטָּל
קֻטְּלָה	תְּקֻטַּל	מְקֻטֶּלֶת
קֻטַּלְתָּ	תְּקֻטַּל	מְקֻטָּלִים
קֻטַּלְתְּ	תְּקֻטְּלִי	מְקֻטָּלוֹת
קֻטַּלְתִּי	אֲקֻטַּל	
קֻטְּלוּ	יְקֻטְּלוּ	
קֻטַּלְתֶּם	תְּקֻטַּלְנָה	
קֻטַּלְתֶּן	תְּקֻטְּלוּ	
קֻטַּלְנוּ	תְּקֻטַּלְנָה	
	נְקֻטַּל	

28.10 Vocabulary.

Verbs

אָסַר	to tie, bind, fetter, imprison (73)
זָעַק	to cry (out), call for help, summon (73)
חָזָה	to see, behold, perceive (55)
חָלָה	to be(come) weak or tired, be(come) sick (75)
חָנַן	to be gracious to, show favor to, favor (77)
מָאַס	to refuse, reject, despise (74)
עוּר	to be awake, stir up (80)
עָרַךְ	to lay out, set in rows, arrange, stack (wood), draw up a battle formation (75)
רָחַץ	to wash, bathe (72)
שָׂכַל	(Hiphil) to understand, comprehend, have insight, make wise, have success (60)

Nouns

מַרְאֶה	vision, sight, appearance (103)
נֶגֶב	south, Negev (112)
עָפָר	dust, dry earth (110)
פַּעַם	foot, pace, time (118); feminine

28.11 The Lord Proclaimed. By the hand of Moses, God performed signs and wonders in the land of Egypt (Ex 7:3; Ps 78:42-51; 105:26-36), and by his chosen prophet, God led his people like a flock through the wilderness (Ps 77:11-20; 78:52-54). The psalmist remembered (Ps 77:14-16, 21 [English 77:13-15, 20]):

14 אֱלֹהִים בַּקֹּדֶשׁ דַּרְכֶּךָ מִי־אֵל גָּדוֹל כֵּאלֹהִים

15 אַתָּה הָאֵל עֹשֵׂה פֶלֶא הוֹדַעְתָּ בָעַמִּים עֻזֶּךָ

16 גָּאַלְתָּ בִּזְרוֹעַ עַמֶּךָ בְּנֵי־יַעֲקֹב וְיוֹסֵף

21 נָחִיתָ כַצֹּאן עַמֶּךָ בְּיַד־מֹשֶׁה וְאַהֲרֹן

Moses was truly a remarkable figure in Old Testament history. Between the Nile and Nebo, he wore many mantles, but perhaps none was more important for the people of Israel than that of intercessor (Ps 106:23). It is in the context of Israel's faithlessness and Moses' intercession on behalf of God's delivered people that we encounter the third text that is essential for understanding the meaning of the name יהוה and the character behind it (Ex 34:5-7).

Even God's "signs and wonders" in Egypt were not sufficient to ensure Israel's faithfulness in the wilderness of Sinai. While still on the sacred mountain, Moses receives this instruction from God (Ex 32:7-8).

7 וַיְדַבֵּר יְהוָה אֶל־מֹשֶׁה לֶךְ־רֵד כִּי שִׁחֵת עַמְּךָ אֲשֶׁר הֶעֱלֵיתָ מֵאֶרֶץ

מִצְרָיִם 8 סָרוּ מַהֵר מִן־הַדֶּרֶךְ אֲשֶׁר צִוִּיתִם עָשׂוּ לָהֶם עֵגֶל מַסֵּכָה

וַיִּשְׁתַּחֲווּ־לוֹ וַיִּזְבְּחוּ־לוֹ וַיֹּאמְרוּ אֵלֶּה אֱלֹהֶיךָ יִשְׂרָאֵל אֲשֶׁר הֶעֱלוּךָ

מֵאֶרֶץ מִצְרָיִם

Note the use of the 2ms pronominal suffix on עַם in 32:7 (your people). Addressing Moses, God here refers to this people as Moses' people (עַמְּךָ). In the intimate language of covenant relationship, God always uses a language construction that claims Israel as his own (Ex 6:7; Lev 26:12; Jer 7:23; Ezek 11:20). God then declares his intention to consume this stiff-necked people and make a great nation through Moses (Ex 32:10). Moses intercedes (Ex 32:11, 13).

11 וַיְחַל מֹשֶׁה אֶת־פְּנֵי יְהוָה אֱלֹהָיו וַיֹּאמֶר לָמָה יְהוָה יֶחֱרֶה אַפְּךָ
בְּעַמֶּךָ אֲשֶׁר הוֹצֵאתָ מֵאֶרֶץ מִצְרַיִם בְּכֹחַ גָּדוֹל וּבְיָד חֲזָקָה

13 זְכֹר לְאַבְרָהָם לְיִצְחָק וּלְיִשְׂרָאֵל עֲבָדֶיךָ אֲשֶׁר נִשְׁבַּעְתָּ לָהֶם בָּךְ
וַתְּדַבֵּר אֲלֵהֶם אַרְבֶּה אֶת־זַרְעֲכֶם כְּכוֹכְבֵי הַשָּׁמָיִם וְכָל־הָאָרֶץ הַזֹּאת
אֲשֶׁר אָמַרְתִּי אֶתֵּן לְזַרְעֲכֶם וְנָחֲלוּ לְעֹלָם

The people are spared but at heavy cost (Ex 32:19; 30-35; 36:1-6). In the midst of this narrative, we are given a special glimpse of Moses' stature before the Lord (Ex 33:11).

וְדִבֶּר יְהוָה אֶל־מֹשֶׁה פָּנִים אֶל־פָּנִים כַּאֲשֶׁר יְדַבֵּר אִישׁ אֶל־רֵעֵהוּ

With this background, we now come to one of the most remarkable texts in the Old Testament (Ex 34:5-7). The Lord declares his intention to show his glory and to proclaim the name יהוה (Ex 33:18-19). Moses is instructed to return to the mountain with a new set of tablets, and then we read in 34:5-6:

5 וַיֵּרֶד יְהוָה בֶּעָנָן וַיִּתְיַצֵּב עִמּוֹ שָׁם וַיִּקְרָא בְשֵׁם יְהוָה
6 וַיַּעֲבֹר יְהוָה עַל־פָּנָיו וַיִּקְרָא יְהוָה יְהוָה אֵל רַחוּם וְחַנּוּן
אֶרֶךְ אַפַּיִם וְרַב־חֶסֶד וֶאֱמֶת

Inherent in the repeated declaration of the name יהוה in verse 6 are those dynamic aspects of the divine character that have already been revealed in Ex 3:13-15 and 6:2-8. But then, almost by way of apposition, we read: אֵל רַחוּם וְחַנּוּן אֶרֶךְ אַפַּיִם וְרַב־חֶסֶד וֶאֱמֶת. With these words, God himself reveals those attributes of his character that define his relationship with his chosen people. With rare exception, the word רַחוּם (compassionate, merciful) is used only of God and refers to his deep compassion and mercy. The essential quality of this divine attribute is perhaps best understood with reference to a mother's tender love for her child. The word חַנּוּן (gracious) is used only with reference to God and in most of its occurrences it appears in combination with רַחוּם. In terms of the relationship between divine grace and divine mercy, grace is that aspect of God's character that gives what is not deserved; mercy withholds what is deserved. In other words, in his grace God gives redemption to those who don't deserve it. In his mercy, he does not give the judgment that is deserved. The construct אֶרֶךְ אַפַּיִם (literally, "long of nose") is used in the majority of its occurrences with reference to God; only four times in connection with man. The phrase is usually translated "longsuffering" or "slow to anger" and refers to God's seemingly inexhaustible patience. His patience is demonstrated principally with reference to his mercy. It is the "not yet" timing of the dispensing of his judgment. God's חֶסֶד is all of the above and so much more. With reference to God, it is a divine love that is forgiving, redeeming, and relentless in its pursuit of those to whom it is to be given. The word חֶסֶד has been translated "lovingkindness," "steadfast love," "unfailing love," "mercy," and more. Some have attempted to associate the term with fidelity and loyalty to covenant obligation. No single word in English encompasses the range or complexity of its nuances in biblical usage. In the context of Ex 34:6, God's faithfulness (אֱמֶת) carries the underlying certainty and assurance that the attributes of this divine self-revelation will never fail.

Moses responds to the Lord's revelation with worship, and he again intercedes for the people (Ex 34:9).

וַיֹּאמֶר אִם־נָא מָצָאתִי חֵן בְּעֵינֶיךָ אֲדֹנָי יֵלֶךְ־נָא אֲדֹנָי בְּקִרְבֵּנוּ כִּי עַם־קְשֵׁה־עֹרֶף הוּא וְסָלַחְתָּ לַעֲוֺנֵנוּ וּלְחַטָּאתֵנוּ וּנְחַלְתָּנוּ

Moses asks that the Lord will manifest his presence in the midst of this undeserving people. The Lord promises to do wonders on their behalf, wonders never done before in any nation in all of the world (34:10). The book of Exodus now concludes (Ex 35-40) with the building of the tabernacle, the portable tent-shrine that represented the earthly dwelling of יהוה in the midst of his people during their wilderness sojourn. Little wonder that the Lord's own revelation of his name and his character will echo throughout later Old Testament history (Neh 9:17; Ps 103:8; 145:8; Joel 2:13; Jonah 4:2) as, for example, in Ps 86:15:

וְאַתָּה אֲדֹנָי אֵל־רַחוּם וְחַנּוּן אֶרֶךְ אַפַּיִם וְרַב־חֶסֶד וֶאֱמֶת

Gary D. Pratico
Professor of Old Testament
Gordon-Conwell Theological Seminary
South Hamilton, Massachusetts

Chapter 29

The Pual Stem - Weak Verbs

29.1 **Introduction**. Before studying weak verbs in the Pual stem, be certain that you have mastered the Pual strong verb diagnostics in the previous chapter.

29.2 **Weak Verbal Roots with Strong Diagnostic Features**. Like the Piel, most weak verbal roots in the Pual stem maintain the strong verb diagnostics. Only II-Guttural verbs exhibit significant changes in the Pual. The following III-א and III-ה paradigms are given for your study and observation but not for memorization. Both of these weak verb classes maintain all of the Pual strong verb diagnostics. Those diagnostics will not be repeated below. Be certain, however, that you can identify each diagnostic feature.

29.3 **III-א Verbs: Diagnostics and Paradigms**. The paradigm verb מָצָא is translated "to be found" in the Pual.

Perfect	*Imperfect*	*Participle*
מֻצָּא	יְמֻצָּא	מְמֻצָּא
מֻצָּא	יְמֻצָּא	מְמֻצָּא
מֻצָּאָה	תְּמֻצָּא	מְמֻצָּאָה
מֻצֵּאתָ	תְּמֻצָּא	מְמֻצָּאִים
מֻצֵּאת	תְּמֻצְּאִי	מְמֻצָּאוֹת
מֻצֵּאתִי	אֲמֻצָּא	
מֻצְּאוּ	יְמֻצְּאוּ	
מֻצֵּאתֶם	תְּמֻצֶּאנָה	
מֻצֵּאתֶן	תְּמֻצְּאוּ	
מֻצֵּאנוּ	תְּמֻצֶּאנָה	
	נְמֻצָּא	

29.4 **III-ה Verbs: Diagnostics and Paradigms**. As you know, the final ה that is present in selected forms below is not the ה of the verbal root but rather a vowel letter or *mater lectionis*. Here, as above, the identification of these vowel letters with dark gray text recognizes that this is a unique feature of III-ה verbs. This is something that you are already familiar with from your study of III-ה roots in the Qal, Niphal, and Piel stems. The paradigm verb גָּלָה is translated "to be uncovered," "disclosed," or "made known" in the Pual. All of the strong verb diagnostics are present in every form of each conjugation.

Perfect	*Imperfect*	*Participle*
גֻּלָּה	יְגֻלֶּה	מְגֻלֶּה
גֻּלָּה	יְגֻלֶּה	מְגֻלָּה
גֻּלְּתָה	תְּגֻלֶּה	מְגֻלָּה
גֻּלֵּיתָ	תְּגֻלֶּה	מְגֻלִּים
גֻּלֵּית	תְּגֻלִּי	מְגֻלּוֹת
גֻּלֵּיתִי	אֲגֻלֶּה	
גֻּלּוּ	יְגֻלּוּ	
גֻּלֵּיתֶם	תְּגֻלֶּינָה	
גֻּלֵּיתֶן	תְּגֻלּוּ	
גֻּלֵּינוּ	תְּגֻלֶּינָה	
	נְגֻלֶּה	

29.5 **II-Guttural Verbs**. Only II-Guttural verbs exhibit any significant changes in the Pual stem. These changes occur because the guttural consonant in second root position rejects the Daghesh Forte of the Pual stem and this results in either virtual doubling or compensatory lengthening. The following graphic illustrates these two patterns with the Pual Perfect 3ms.

Strong Verb	*II-Guttural Virtual Doubling*	*II-Guttural Compensatory Lengthening*
קֻטַּל	נֻחַם	בֹּרַךְ

In the patterns of compensatory lengthening, the vowel Qibbuts lengthens to Holem. In the form בֹּרַךְ, the Holem is the result of compensatory lengthening.

29.6 **II-Guttural Verbs with Virtual Doubling: Diagnostics and Paradigms.** The paradigm verb נָחַם is translated "to be comforted" or "to be consoled" in the Pual.

Perfect	Imperfect	Participle
נֻחַם	יְנֻחַם	מְנֻחָם
נֻחַם	יְנֻחַם	מְנֻחָם
נֻחֲמָה	תְּנֻחַם	מְנֻחֶמֶת
נֻחַׄמְתָּ	תְּנֻחַם	מְנֻחָמִים
נֻחַמְתְּ	תְּנֻחֲמִי	מְנֻחָמוֹת
נֻחַׄמְתִּי	אֲנֻחַם	
נֻחֲמוּ	יְנֻחֲמוּ	
נֻחַמְתֶּם	תְּנֻחַׄמְנָה	
נֻחַמְתֶּן	תְּנֻחֲמוּ	
נֻחַׄמְנוּ	תְּנֻחַׄמְנָה	
	נְנֻחַם	

29.7 **II-Guttural Verbs with Virtual Doubling: Notes.** All of the Pual strong verb diagnostics are present in this weak verb class, except the Daghesh Forte in the second root consonant. This verb exhibits virtual doubling.

29.8 **II-Guttural Verbs with Compensatory Lengthening: Diagnostics and Paradigms.** The paradigm verb בָּרַךְ is translated "to be blessed" in the Pual.

Perfect	*Imperfect*	*Participle*
בֹּרַךְ	יְבֹרַךְ	מְבֹרָךְ
בֹּרַךְ	יְבֹרַךְ	מְבֹרָךְ
בֹּרְכָה	תְּבֹרַךְ	מְבֹרֶכֶת
בֹּרַ֫כְתָּ	תְּבֹרַךְ	מְבֹרָכִים
בֹּרַכְתְּ	תְּבֹרְכִי	מְבֹרָכוֹת
בֹּרַ֫כְתִּי	אֲבֹרַךְ	
בֹּרְכוּ	יְבֹרְכוּ	
בֹּרַכְתֶּם	תְּבֹרַ֫כְנָה	
בֹּרַכְתֶּן	תְּבֹרְכוּ	
בֹּרַ֫כְנוּ	תְּבֹרַ֫כְנָה	
	נְבֹרַךְ	

29.9 **II-Guttural Verbs with Compensatory Lengthening: Notes**. This verb exhibits compensatory lengthening because the ר rejects the Daghesh Forte of the Pual. As noted above, in the patterns of compensatory lengthening, the vowel Qibbuts lengthens to Holem. In the Pual Perfect, Imperfect, and Participle of בֹּרַךְ, the Holem vowel with the first consonant of the verbal root is the result of compensatory lengthening.

29.10 **Summary: Pual Diagnostics**. Once again, the diagnostic features of the Pual stem include: (1) Qibbuts under the first root consonant of every form; (2) Daghesh Forte in the second root consonant of every form; and (3) Vocal Shewa under all Imperfect and Participle preformatives and prefixes. Remember that the Qibbuts under the first root consonant distinguishes the Pual from the Piel. Also, like the Piel, only II-Guttural weak verbs exhibit any significant changes in the Pual. The following chart summarizes the Pual stem diagnostics studied in this chapter.

	Perfect	Imperfect	Participle
Strong	קֻטַּל	יְקֻטַּל	מְקֻטָּל
III-א	מֻצָּא	יְמֻצָּא	מְמֻצָּא
III-ה	גֻּלָּה	יְגֻלֶּה	מְגֻלֶּה
II-Gutt[1]	נֻחַם	יְנֻחַם	מְנֻחָם
II-Gutt[2]	בֹּרַךְ	יְבֹרַךְ	מְבֹרָךְ

29.11 Vocabulary.

Verbs

לִין	to remain overnight, spend the night, stay, dwell (71)
מָשַׁח	to smear, anoint (70); מָשִׁיחַ anointed one, Messiah (38)
נָצַר	to keep watch, watch over, guard, protect, preserve (63)

Nouns

גֵּר	stranger, sojourner, alien (92)
חַיָּה	animal, beast (96)
חֵלֶב	fat; (metaphorically) best, choice part (92)
חֲמוֹר	donkey (96)
יֶתֶר	rest, remainder, excess (97)
עוֹר	skin, hide, leather (99)
עֹז	strength, power, might (76)
פֶּשַׁע	transgression, rebellion, crime (93)
קָצֶה	end, border, outskirts (92)
שִׂמְחָה	joy, gladness (94)
תָּמִים	blameless, perfect, honest, devout (91)

---

[1] II-Guttural with virtual doubling

[2] II-Guttural with compensatory lengthening

29.12 Hebrew Reading: Jonah and the Character of God.[3] Contrary to how Jonah is often preached, this book is not about the prophet. It is not about a great fish. It is about God and the character of God. Jonah's first commission (1:1-2) provided him with the opportunity to be, in the tradition of the patriarchs, a mediator of blessing and, in the tradition of the prophets, a conduit for the word of God. The recipient of both was to be Nineveh, the capital of the world empire of Assyria (Jonah 1:1-2).

וַיְהִי דְּבַר־יְהוָה אֶל־יוֹנָה בֶן־אֲמִתַּי לֵאמֹר 2 קוּם לֵךְ אֶל־נִינְוֵה הָעִיר 1
הַגְּדוֹלָה וּקְרָא עָלֶיהָ כִּי־עָלְתָה רָעָתָם לְפָנָי

Jonah would have been pleased to deliver Nahum's message of divine judgment against Assyria (Nahum 3:1-7), but he was a century and a half too early. His commission was to proclaim God's word with a view to repentance. His resistance to the possibility that this hated nation would be the recipient of divine blessing was so great that he fled even from the presence of the Lord, or so he thought (Jonah 1:3).

וַיָּקָם יוֹנָה לִבְרֹחַ תַּרְשִׁישָׁה מִלִּפְנֵי יְהוָה וַיֵּרֶד יָפוֹ וַיִּמְצָא אֳנִיָּה בָּאָה
תַרְשִׁישׁ וַיִּתֵּן שְׂכָרָהּ וַיֵּרֶד בָּהּ לָבוֹא עִמָּהֶם תַּרְשִׁישָׁה מִלִּפְנֵי יְהוָה

His flight from the presence of the Lord (מִלִּפְנֵי יְהוָה) is a point of emphasis (1:3, 10). In fact, flight and disobedience were his very first thought. That is the implication of קִדַּמְתִּי לִבְרֹחַ (I was quick to flee) in 4:2. The prophet did indeed understand the gracious and merciful character of God (4:2). That was why he fled, because he understood the qualities of divine grace. Given this divine character, repentance and redemption for this hated enemy just might be a possibility. But escape was impossible because God is present even "in the uttermost parts of the sea" (Ps 139:7-9). Jonah's God is the Creator and Lord of the sea (Gen 1:10; Ex 14:21), and he pursues his prophet in a great windstorm. Jonah's fellow-passengers suspect that he is the cause of their plight (Jonah 1:8-10, 15).

וַיֹּאמְרוּ אֵלָיו הַגִּידָה־נָּא לָנוּ בַּאֲשֶׁר לְמִי־הָרָעָה הַזֹּאת לָנוּ 8
מַה־מְּלַאכְתְּךָ וּמֵאַיִן תָּבוֹא מָה אַרְצֶךָ וְאֵי־מִזֶּה עַם אָתָּה 9 וַיֹּאמֶר
אֲלֵיהֶם עִבְרִי אָנֹכִי וְאֶת־יְהוָה אֱלֹהֵי הַשָּׁמַיִם אֲנִי יָרֵא אֲשֶׁר־עָשָׂה
אֶת־הַיָּם וְאֶת־הַיַּבָּשָׁה 10 וַיִּירְאוּ הָאֲנָשִׁים יִרְאָה גְדוֹלָה וַיֹּאמְרוּ אֵלָיו

---

[3] All biblical references in Jonah refer to the numbering of the Hebrew text.

מַה־זֹּאת עָשִׂיתָ כִּי־יָדְעוּ הָאֲנָשִׁים כִּי־מִלִּפְנֵי יְהוָה הוּא בֹרֵחַ
כִּי הִגִּיד לָהֶם

15 וַיִּשְׂאוּ אֶת־יוֹנָה וַיְטִלֻהוּ אֶל־הַיָּם וַיַּעֲמֹד הַיָּם מִזַּעְפּוֹ

There is a dimension to Jonah's call that is unique (Jonah 2:1-2).

1 וַיְמַן יְהוָה דָּג גָּדוֹל לִבְלֹעַ אֶת־יוֹנָה וַיְהִי יוֹנָה בִּמְעֵי הַדָּג שְׁלֹשָׁה
יָמִים וּשְׁלֹשָׁה לֵילוֹת 2 וַיִּתְפַּלֵּל יוֹנָה אֶל־יְהוָה אֱלֹהָיו מִמְּעֵי הַדָּגָה

Jonah's psalm of thanksgiving and celebration of the Lord's deliverance
and mercy in 2:3-10 is a literary jewel in the Old Testament.

The prophet is commissioned a second time (Jonah 2:11; 3:1-3).

11 וַיֹּאמֶר יְהוָה לַדָּג וַיָּקֵא אֶת־יוֹנָה אֶל־הַיַּבָּשָׁה

1 וַיְהִי דְבַר־יְהוָה אֶל־יוֹנָה שֵׁנִית לֵאמֹר 2 קוּם לֵךְ אֶל־נִינְוֵה הָעִיר
הַגְּדוֹלָה וּקְרָא אֵלֶיהָ אֶת־הַקְּרִיאָה אֲשֶׁר אָנֹכִי דֹּבֵר אֵלֶיךָ 3 וַיָּקָם יוֹנָה
וַיֵּלֶךְ אֶל־נִינְוֵה כִּדְבַר יְהוָה

Jonah's first and worst fear was realized (Jonah 3:5, 10).

5 וַיַּאֲמִינוּ אַנְשֵׁי נִינְוֵה בֵּאלֹהִים וַיִּקְרְאוּ־צוֹם וַיִּלְבְּשׁוּ שַׂקִּים מִגְּדוֹלָם
וְעַד־קְטַנָּם

10 וַיַּרְא הָאֱלֹהִים אֶת־מַעֲשֵׂיהֶם כִּי־שָׁבוּ מִדַּרְכָּם הָרָעָה וַיִּנָּחֶם הָאֱלֹהִים
עַל־הָרָעָה אֲשֶׁר־דִּבֶּר לַעֲשׂוֹת־לָהֶם וְלֹא עָשָׂה

Jonah wasn't just displeased at the success of his preaching. He was
outraged, morally outraged and angry at the enemy's response (Jonah
4:1-3).

1 וַיֵּרַע אֶל־יוֹנָה רָעָה גְדוֹלָה וַיִּחַר לוֹ 2 וַיִּתְפַּלֵּל אֶל־יְהוָה וַיֹּאמַר אָנָּה
יְהוָה הֲלוֹא־זֶה דְבָרִי עַד־הֱיוֹתִי עַל־אַדְמָתִי עַל־כֵּן קִדַּמְתִּי לִבְרֹחַ
תַּרְשִׁישָׁה כִּי יָדַעְתִּי כִּי אַתָּה אֵל־חַנּוּן וְרַחוּם אֶרֶךְ אַפַּיִם וְרַב־חֶסֶד
וְנִחָם עַל־הָרָעָה 3 וְעַתָּה יְהוָה קַח־נָא אֶת־נַפְשִׁי מִמֶּנִּי
כִּי טוֹב מוֹתִי מֵחַיָּי

God's lifeline to Nineveh was a noose around the neck of the prophet
(4:3). Jonah was outraged that the compassion of the Lord was not
provincial but that it stretched far beyond the boundaries of his world
and that it embraced even his worst enemy. The text does not disclose

the resolution of Jonah's anger but, after all, this book is not about Jonah. It is not about a great fish. It is about God and the character of God (Jonah 4:2).

> That is why I was so quick to flee to Tarshish.
> I knew that you are a gracious and merciful God,
> slow to anger and abounding in steadfast love.

Gary D. Pratico
Professor of Old Testament
Gordon-Conwell Theological Seminary
South Hamilton, Massachusetts

29.13 **Advanced Information: The Polal Stem.** The Polal stem is the passive counterpart of the Polel stem (27.15). It is the equivalent of the Pual stem for certain Biconsonantal (and Geminate) verbal roots. With Biconsonantal verbs, you will recall that these stems are characterized by a Holem Waw after the first consonant and the duplication of the second root consonant. For your reference, the Polal forms of the verb רום (to raise, lift up, exalt) are presented below. In the Perfect, note that the forms of the Polal are identical to the Polel, except in the 3ms (רוֹמַם). In the Imperfect, there are also a number of identical forms (2fs, 3mp, 2mp).

Perfect	*Imperfect*	*Participle*
רוֹמַם	יְרוֹמַם	מְרוֹמָם
רוֹמְמָה	תְּרוֹמַם	מְרוֹמֶ֫מֶת
רוֹמַ֫מְתָּ	תְּרוֹמַם	מְרוֹמָמִים
רוֹמַמְתְּ	תְּרוֹמְמִי	מְרוֹמָמוֹת
רוֹמַ֫מְתִּי	אֲרוֹמַם	
רוֹמְמוּ	יְרוֹמְמוּ	
רוֹמַמְתֶּם	תְּרוֹמַ֫מְנָה	
רוֹמַמְתֶּן	תְּרוֹמְמוּ	
רוֹמַ֫מְנוּ	תְּרוֹמַ֫מְנָה	
	נְרוֹמַם	

Chapter 30

The Hiphil Stem - Strong Verbs

30.1 **Introduction.** In this chapter, we will study the Hiphil stem. The Hiphil stem occurs more frequently than any other derived stem.[1] As you know by now, the name "Hiphil" (הִפְעִיל) preserves certain diagnostic features of the Hiphil Perfect (הִ prefix and the Hireq Yod stem vowel).

30.2 **The Meaning of the Hiphil Stem.**

1. *Causative.* The Hiphil stem is used to express a *causative* type of action with an *active* voice. For example, the verb מָלַךְ means "he was king" or "he reigned" in the Qal stem. The Hiphil form is הִמְלִיךְ and it means "he *caused* to reign" or "he *made* (someone) king." Notice how the key words "caused" and "made" are used to express the causative action of the Hiphil stem. Study the following additional examples that illustrate how a Qal verb takes on a causative nuance in the Hiphil stem.

Qal Stem		*Hiphil Stem*	
זָכַר	he remembered	הִזְכִּיר	he caused to remember he reminded
שָׁמַע	he heard	הִשְׁמִיעַ	he caused to hear he proclaimed
קָרַב	he approached	הִקְרִיב	he caused to approach he presented

In the translation of the Hiphil forms above, notice that there are both literal (he caused to remember) and then more idiomatic translations (he reminded). In terms of good English style, the more idiomatic translation is to be preferred. At first, however, you might want to use the more literal type of translation in order to reinforce the causative nuance of the Hiphil stem. In addition to causative action, the Hiphil stem may also express other types of action.

---

[1] The Hiphil stem occurs 9,496 times in the Hebrew Bible. It appears in the Perfect 2,684 times, Imperfect 4,063 times, Imperative 740 times, Infinitive Construct 951 times, Infinitive Absolute 223 times, and Participle 835 times.

2. *Simple Action.* Some verbs in the Hiphil stem can preserve the simple action of the Qal stem. In this case, the Hiphil verb would be translated like a Qal verb. This is frequently the case with verbal roots that are common in the Hiphil stem but are not attested (or rarely attested) in the Qal stem. The following examples illustrate this usage.

Qal Stem	Hiphil Stem	Translation
שָׁכַם	הִשְׁכִּים	he arose early
שָׁלַךְ	הִשְׁלִיךְ	he threw (down)
שָׁמַד	הִשְׁמִיד	he exterminated

3. *Declarative.* Hiphil verbs sometimes carry a declarative nuance, meaning that the subject of the verb declares someone (or something) to be in a certain condition or state of being. For example, the verb רָשַׁע means "to be guilty" in the Qal stem. In the Hiphil stem, however, it means "to declare guilty" or "to pronounce guilty."

4. *Factitive.* Like the Piel stem, the Hiphil stem may be used to make an intransitive verb into a transitive verb. That is, if a Qal verb is intransitive (does not take a direct object), it will become transitive (can take a direct object) in the Hiphil stem. For example, the verb גָּדַל means "to be great" in the Qal stem. In the Hiphil stem, however, it means "to make someone (something) great."

There are a few other categories of verbal meaning in the Hiphil stem, such as denominative and permissive, but these are infrequent. Additionally, the meaning of some Hiphil verbs cannot be categorized. In such cases, you will need to check the lexicon in order to determine meaning.

30.3 **Hiphil Perfect.** The Hiphil Perfect is formed with the Hiphil prefix (הַ), the verbal root (with a stem vowel that is variable between Hireq Yod and Pathach), and the Perfect sufformatives.

	Qal	*Hiphil*	*Translation*
3ms	קָטַל	הִקְטִיל	he caused to kill[2]
3fs	קָטְלָה	הִקְטִילָה	she caused to kill
2ms	קָטַלְתָּ	הִקְטַלְתָּ	you caused to kill
2fs	קָטַלְתְּ	הִקְטַלְתְּ	you caused to kill
1cs	קָטַלְתִּי	הִקְטַלְתִּי	I caused to kill
3cp	קָטְלוּ	הִקְטִילוּ	they caused to kill
2mp	קְטַלְתֶּם	הִקְטַלְתֶּם	you caused to kill
2fp	קְטַלְתֶּן	הִקְטַלְתֶּן	you caused to kill
1cp	קָטַלְנוּ	הִקְטַלְנוּ	we caused to kill

30.4 **Hiphil Perfect Diagnostics.**

1. הַ prefix in every form.

2. The stem vowel is variable between Hireq Yod (הִקְטִיל) and Pathach (הִקְטַלְתָּ). All third person forms have Hireq Yod and all first and second person forms have Pathach.

Hiphil Perfect Strong Verb

הִקְטִיל
הִקְטַלְתָּ

3. Remember that the הַ prefix also characterizes the Niphal Imperative and Infinitive Construct (הִקָּטֵל). These forms should not be confused, however, because the vowel pattern of each is

---

[2] Though these translations are awkward, the intention is to reinforce the essential causative nuance of the Hiphil stem with our standard paradigm verb קָטַל.

distinctive. Note especially the assimilated נ of the Niphal stem in the Niphal Imperative and Infinitive Construct forms. In fact, the הָ prefix is the only feature that these two forms have in common.

	Niphal Imperative/ Infinitive Construct	Hiphil Perfect 3ms
	הִקָּטֵל	הִקְטִיל

30.5 Hiphil Imperfect. The Hiphil Imperfect is formed with the Imperfect preformatives, the verbal root (with Hireq Yod stem vowel), and the Imperfect sufformatives.

	Qal	Hiphil	Translation
3ms	יִקְטֹל	יַקְטִיל	he will cause to kill
3fs	תִּקְטֹל	תַּקְטִיל	she will cause to kill
2ms	תִּקְטֹל	תַּקְטִיל	you will cause to kill
2fs	תִּקְטְלִי	תַּקְטִׁילִי	you will cause to kill
1cs	אֶקְטֹל	אַקְטִיל	I will cause to kill
3mp	יִקְטְלוּ	יַקְטִׁילוּ	they will cause to kill
3fp	תִּקְטֹׁלְנָה	תַּקְטֵׁלְנָה	they will cause to kill
2mp	תִּקְטְלוּ	תַּקְטִׁילוּ	you will cause to kill
2fp	תִּקְטֹׁלְנָה	תַּקְטֵׁלְנָה	you will cause to kill
1cp	נִקְטֹל	נַקְטִיל	we will cause to kill

30.6 Hiphil Imperfect Diagnostics.

1. Pathach preformative vowel in every form. This same preformative vowel also occurs in the I-Guttural (Type 2) Qal Imperfect verbs (יַעֲמֹד). In such cases, the stem vowel will distinguish between the Qal (Holem stem vowel) and Hiphil (Hireq Yod stem vowel).

2. Hireq Yod stem vowel in every form, except the 3fp and 2fp forms, in which it is Tsere (תַּקְטֵׁלְנָה).

3. Note that when prefixed with Waw Consecutive, the stem vowel is usually Tsere and not Hireq Yod. For example, the 3ms form יַקְטִיל is spelled וַיַּקְטֵל when prefixed with Waw Consecutive.

Hiphil Imperfect Strong Verb

יַקְטִיל

30.7 Hiphil Imperative. The Hiphil Imperative is formed with the Hiphil prefix (הַ), the verbal root (with a stem vowel that is variable between Tsere and Hireq Yod), and the Imperative sufformatives.

	Qal	*Hiphil*	*Translation*
2ms	קְטֹל	הַקְטֵל	cause to kill!
2fs	קִטְלִי	הַקְטִילִי	cause to kill!
2mp	קִטְלוּ	הַקְטִילוּ	cause to kill!
2fp	קְטֹלְנָה	הַקְטֵלְנָה	cause to kill!

30.8 Hiphil Imperative Diagnostics.

1. הַ prefix in every form. This same prefix is also used with the Hiphil Infinitive Construct and Infinitive Absolute (30.9-12).

2. The stem vowel is either Tsere (2ms, 2fp) or Hireq Yod (2fs, 2mp). Those forms with sufformatives consisting of a vowel take the Hireq Yod stem vowel.

Hiphil Imperative Strong Verb

הַקְטֵל
הַקְטִילִי

30.9 Hiphil Infinitive Construct. The Hiphil Infinitive Construct is formed with the Hiphil prefix (הַ) and the verbal root (with a Hireq Yod stem vowel). There are no sufformatives because the Infinitive Construct is not an inflected form. Remember, however, that an Infinitive Construct can take pronominal suffixes, as in הַקְטִילִי (Hiphil Infinitive Construct with 1cs suffix).

Qal	Hiphil	Translation
קְטֹל	הַקְטִיל	to cause to kill, killing

30.10 Hiphil Infinitive Construct Diagnostics.

1. הַ prefix.

2. Hireq Yod stem vowel. It is the stem vowel that will distinguish the Infinitive Construct (הַקְטִיל) from the Hiphil Imperative ms (הַקְטֵל).

Hiphil Infinitive Construct

הַקְטִיל

30.11 Hiphil Infinitive Absolute. The Infinitive Absolute is formed with the Hiphil prefix (הַ) and the verbal root (with Tsere stem vowel). The stem vowel will distinguish the Infinitive Absolute (הַקְטֵל) from the Infinitive Construct (הַקְטִיל).

30.12 Hiphil Infinitive Absolute Diagnostics.

1. הַ prefix.

2. Tsere stem vowel. Note that the masculine singular Imperative and the Infinitive Absolute forms are identical. Context should enable you to identify the form correctly.

Hiphil Infinitive Absolute

הַקְטֵל

30.13 Hiphil Participle. The Hiphil Participle is formed with the Participle prefix (מַ), the verbal root (with a Hireq Yod stem vowel), and the inflectional endings of the Participle.

	Qal	Hiphil	Translation
ms	קֹטֵל	מַקְטִיל	causing to kill
fs	קֹטֶלֶת	מַקְטֶלֶת [3]	causing to kill
mp	קֹטְלִים	מַקְטִילִים	causing to kill
fp	קֹטְלוֹת	מַקְטִילוֹת	causing to kill

30.14 Hiphil Participle Diagnostics.

1. מַ prefix in every form. Remember that a מַ prefix characterizes the Participle in the Piel, Pual, Hiphil, and Hophal stems.

2. Hireq Yod stem vowel throughout, except in one of the feminine singular forms (מַקְטֶלֶת).

Hiphil Participle Strong Verb

מַקְטִיל

30.15 Summary.

1. The Hiphil stem is used to express *causative* action with an *active* voice. The key words "cause" and "make" may be used to change the simple action of the Qal into the causative action of the Hiphil. Oftentimes, however, the more idiomatic translations are to be preferred.

2. The most important diagnostic features of the Hiphil stem include: (1) ה prefix in all conjugations, except the Imperfect and Participle; (2) Pathach under all preformatives and prefixes, except in the Perfect, where it is Hireq; (3) Hireq Yod or Tsere stem vowel in all forms, except the second and first person forms of the Perfect, where it is Pathach.

---

[3] Like the Qal Participle, the Hiphil Participle may also end in ה as an alternative form (מַקְטִילָה).

Hiphil Stem - Strong Verbs

Perfect	Imperfect	Imperative	Infinitive Construct	Infinitive Absolute	Participle
הִקְטִיל הִקְטַלְתְּ	יַקְטִיל הַקְטִילִי	הַקְטֵל הַקְטִילִי	הַקְטִיל	הַקְטֵל	מַקְטִיל
הִקְטִיל	יַקְטִיל	הַקְטֵל	הַקְטִיל	הַקְטֵל	מַקְטִיל
הִקְטִילָה	תַּקְטִיל	הַקְטִילִי			מַקְטֶלֶת
הִקְטַלְתָּ	תַּקְטִיל	הַקְטִילוּ			מַקְטִילִים
הִקְטַלְתְּ	תַּקְטִילִי	הַקְטֵלְנָה			מַקְטִילוֹת
הִקְטַלְתִּי	אַקְטִיל				
הִקְטִילוּ	יַקְטִילוּ				
הִקְטַלְתֶּם	תַּקְטֵלְנָה				
הִקְטַלְתֶּן	תַּקְטִילוּ				
הִקְטַלְנוּ	תַּקְטֵלְנָה				
	נַקְטִיל				

30.16 Vocabulary.

חָלַל   (Niphal) to be defiled, defile oneself; (Piel) profane, defile; (Hiphil) let something be profaned, begin (135)

נָגַד   (Hiphil) to tell, announce, report, declare, inform (371)

שָׁבַע   (Niphal) to swear, take an oath; (Hiphil) plead with someone (186)

שָׁלַךְ   (Hiphil) to send, throw (down, into or away), cast (125)

Nouns

דַּעַת   knowledge, understanding, ability (88); feminine

דֶּלֶת   door (88); feminine

הָמוֹן   multitude, crowd, sound, roar (85)

זְרוֹעַ   arm, forearm; (metaphorically) strength or power (91); feminine

כְּרוּב   cherub (91)

כֶּרֶם   vineyard (94)

מַלְכוּת   kingdom, dominion, royal power (91)

עֵצָה   counsel, plan, advice (87)

Other

חָלָל   pierced, slain, defiled (94)

טָמֵא   unclean (88)

30.17 The Promises to the Fathers. God's promises to Abraham, Isaac, and Jacob are central to the book of Genesis. One aspect of these promises is that Abraham will have many descendants. They will be "as numerous as the stars of the heaven and the sand of the seashore." Yet ironically, the wife of Abraham is barren (Gen 11:30). Isaac's wife, Rebekah, is also barren (Gen 25:21), and so is Rachel, the wife of Jacob (Gen 29:31). The infertility of Sarah, Rebekah, and Rachel highlights an important theological truth: that God himself will bring about what he has promised. Thus God provides a son for Sarah, in spite of her barrenness and old age (Gen 21:1-2); Rebekah gives birth to twins in answer to the prayer of Isaac (Gen 25:21-26); and God opens Rachel's womb, which previously had produced no "fruit" (Gen 30:22-24). The theological truth that God himself will accomplish what he has promised is clearly reflected in the common use of the Hiphil verbal stem in the context of God's promises.

This theological truth is not only seen in the patriarchal narratives but also in the grammar, since it is the Hiphil verb form that is commonly used in God's promises. The Hiphil stem is important in this context because it expresses "causative" action. Let us consider, for example, the verb פָּרָה (to be fruitful) and רָבָה (to multiply). God said to Abraham, "I will multiply you exceedingly" (Gen 17:2) and "I will cause you to be exceedingly fruitful" (Gen 17:6). The Hiphil forms of רָבָה and פָּרָה in these two passages can be translated: "I will *cause* you to multiply exceedingly" and "I will *cause* you to be exceedingly fruitful." Notice that in both cases, God is the subject of the verbs.

We also read that God appeared to Jacob and said to him, "I will multiply your descendants as the stars of the heavens" (Gen 26:4). Toward the end of Jacob's life, he recalled the promise that God had made to him: "I will *make* you fruitful and *make* you numerous" (Gen

48:4). The Hiphil verbal forms in these two texts, with God as the subject, once again underscore the causative action of God. The book of Genesis then concludes with Jacob's descendants numbering seventy when they entered Egypt (Gen 46:27; Ex 1:5).

Yet when the Israelites left Egypt, they numbered in the thousands! Moses acknowledges that it was God who brought this to pass, recalling his covenant with Abraham: "The Lord your God has multiplied you, and behold, you are this day as the stars of heaven for a multitude" (Deut 1:10). The Hiphil form of רָבָה once again highlights that God caused Israel to multiply in Egypt (cf. Ps 105:23-24). God brought to fruition his promise of increase! In the New Testament, we read that God continues to bring forth children, for we, like Isaac, are children of promise (Gal 4:28).

Carol M. Kaminski
Assistant Professor of Old Testament
Gordon-Conwell Theological Seminary
Boston, Massachusetts

Chapter 31

The Hiphil Stem - Weak Verbs

31.1 **Introduction.** In this chapter, we will study weak verbs in the Hiphil stem. Before working through this chapter, however, be certain that you have first mastered the strong verb diagnostics of the Hiphil stem. By way of review, the diagnostics for the strong verb of the Hiphil stem include: (1) ה prefix in all conjugations, except the Imperfect and Participle; (2) Pathach under all preformatives and prefixes, except in the Perfect, where it is Hireq; (3) Hireq Yod or Tsere stem vowel in all forms, except the second and first person forms of the Perfect, where it is Pathach.

31.2 **I-Guttural Paradigms and Diagnostics.**

Perfect	Imperfect	Imperative	Infinitive Construct	Infinitive Absolute	Participle
הֶעֱמִיד הֶעֱמַׂדְתָּ	יַעֲמִיד	הַעֲמֵד הַעֲמִׂידִי	הַעֲמִיד	הַעֲמֵד	מַעֲמִיד
הֶעֱמִיד	יַעֲמִיד	הַעֲמֵד	הַעֲמִיד	הַעֲמֵד	מַעֲמִיד
הֶעֱמִׂידָה	תַּעֲמִיד	הַעֲמִׂידִי			מַעֲמֶׂדֶת[1]
הֶעֱמַׂדְתָּ	תַּעֲמִיד	הַעֲמִׂידוּ			מַעֲמִידִים
הֶעֱמַׂדְתְּ	תַּעֲמִׂידִי	הַעֲמֵׂדְנָה			מַעֲמִידוֹת
הֶעֱמַׂדְתִּי	אַעֲמִיד				
הֶעֱמִׂידוּ	יַעֲמִׂידוּ				
הֶעֱמַדְתֶּם	תַּעֲמֵׂדְנָה				
הֶעֱמַדְתֶּן	תַּעֲמִׂידוּ				
הֶעֱמַׂדְנוּ	תַּעֲמֵׂדְנָה				
	נַעֲמִיד				

---

[1] The alternate form מַעֲמִידָה is also attested.

31.3   I-Guttural Notes.

1. In every conjugation, except the Perfect, the strong verb
    diagnostics of the Hiphil stem are preserved in this weak verb
    class.

2. The Perfect has a Seghol prefix vowel (הֶעֱמִיד) rather than the
    Hireq of the strong verb (הִקְטִיל). You have encountered this
    same vowel pattern in both the Qal Imperfect (יֶחֱזַק) and Niphal
    Perfect (נֶעֱזַב) of I-Guttural verbs (16.8-9; 25.6-7).

3. While it is not diagnostic, it is helpful to note that the guttural
    consonant in first root position takes a reduced vowel in every
    form of every conjugation: Hateph Seghol in the Perfect and
    Hateph Pathach in all other conjugations.

31.4   III-ח/ע Paradigms and Diagnostics.

Perfect	Imperfect	Imperative	Infinitive Construct	Infinitive Absolute	Participle
הִשְׁלִיחַ הִשְׁלַחְתְּ	יַשְׁלִיחַ	הַשְׁלַח הַשְׁלִיחִי	הַשְׁלִיחַ	הַשְׁלֵחַ	מַשְׁלִיחַ
הִשְׁלִיחַ	יַשְׁלִיחַ	הַשְׁלַח	הַשְׁלִיחַ	הַשְׁלֵחַ	מַשְׁלִיחַ
הִשְׁלִיחָה	תַּשְׁלִיחַ	הַשְׁלִיחִי			מַשְׁלַחַת
הִשְׁלַחְתָּ	תַּשְׁלִיחַ	הַשְׁלִיחוּ			מַשְׁלִיחִים
הִשְׁלַחַתְּ	תַּשְׁלִיחִי	הַשְׁלַחְנָה			מַשְׁלִיחוֹת
הִשְׁלַחְתִּי	אַשְׁלִיחַ				
הִשְׁלִיחוּ	יַשְׁלִיחוּ				
הִשְׁלַחְתֶּם	תַּשְׁלַחְנָה				
הִשְׁלַחְתֶּן	תַּשְׁלִיחוּ				
הִשְׁלַחְנוּ	תַּשְׁלַחְנָה				
	נַשְׁלִיחַ				

31.5   III-ח/ע Notes.

1. Most of the Hiphil strong verb diagnostics are preserved in this
    weak verb class. The only variations are in the stem vowel of a
    few forms.

2. In the Imperfect 3fp and 2fp (תִּשְׁלַחְנָה), the stem vowel is Pathach rather than Tsere. This minor change is occasioned by the fact that gutturals prefer a-class vowels.

3. In the Imperative 2ms (הַשְׁלַח) and 2fp (הַשְׁלַחְנָה), the stem vowel is also Pathach rather that Tsere, just like the forms of the Imperfect mentioned above. Such minor variations should not present any difficulty in terms of identifying these Hiphil forms.

31.6 III-א Paradigms and Diagnostics.

Perfect	Imperfect	Imperative	Infinitive Construct	Infinitive Absolute	Participle
הִמְצִיא הִמְצֵאת	יַמְצִיא	הַמְצֵא הַמְצִיאִי	הַמְצִיא	הַמְצֵא	מַמְצִיא
הִמְצִיא	יַמְצִיא	הַמְצֵא	הַמְצִיא	הַמְצֵא	מַמְצִיא
הִמְצִיאָה	תַּמְצִיא	הַמְצִיאִי			מַמְצֵאת
הִמְצֵאתָ	תַּמְצִיא	הַמְצִיאוּ			מַמְצִיאִים
הִמְצֵאת	תַּמְצִיאִי	הַמְצֶאנָה			מַמְצִיאוֹת
הִמְצֵאתִי	אַמְצִיא				
הִמְצִיאוּ	יַמְצִיאוּ				
הִמְצֵאתֶם	תַּמְצֶאנָה				
הִמְצֵאתֶן	תַּמְצִיאוּ				
הִמְצֵאנוּ	תַּמְצֶאנָה				
	נַמְצִיא				

*[handwritten margin note: * likes i-class vowels]*

31.7 III-א Notes.

1. Most of the Hiphil strong verb diagnostics are preserved in this weak verb class. All prefix and preformative consonants and vowels follow the pattern of the Hiphil strong verb. The stem vowel variations that do occur should be familiar to you as changes characteristic of the III-א weak verb class.

2. In all second and first person forms of the Perfect, the stem vowel is Tsere (הִמְצֵאתָ). The stem vowel of the Hiphil strong verb is Pathach (הִקְטַלְתָּ).

3. In the Imperfect, the stem vowel in the 3fp and 2fp forms is Seghol (תִּמְצֶׂאנָה) rather than Tsere (תִּקְטֹׁלְנָה). This same variation also occurs in the Imperative 2fp form (הִמְצֶׂאנָה).

31.8   III-ה Paradigms and Diagnostics.

Perfect	Imperfect	Imperative	Infinitive Construct	Infinitive Absolute	Participle
הִגְלָה הִגְלִיתָ	יַגְלֶה	הַגְלֵה	הַגְלוֹת	הַגְלֵה	מַגְלֶה
הִגְלָה	יַגְלֶה	הַגְלֵה	הַגְלוֹת	הַגְלֵה	מַגְלֶה
הִגְלְתָה	תַּגְלֶה	הַגְלִי			מַגְלָה
הִגְלִיתָ	תַּגְלֶה	הַגְלוּ			מַגְלִים
הִגְלִית	תַּגְלִי	הַגְלֶינָה			מַגְלוֹת
הִגְלֵיתִי	אַגְלֶה				
הִגְלוּ	יַגְלוּ				
הִגְלִיתֶם	תַּגְלֶינָה				
הִגְלִיתֶן	תַּגְלוּ				
הִגְלִינוּ	תַּגְלֶינָה				
	נַגְלֶה				

31.9   III-ה Notes.

1. In Hiphil III-ה verbs, all prefix and preformative consonants and vowels retain the Hiphil strong verb diagnostics. Variation from the strong verb diagnostics occurs mainly in the stem vowels of the various conjugations. In most instances, however, the distinctive preformatives and prefixes should be sufficient for identifying Hiphil III-ה verbs.

2. Note the III-ה diagnostic endings that are highlighted in gray in the above chart (31.8). These are the same endings that appear on all III-ה verbs in the Qal and derived stems.

3. In the Perfect, the Hireq Yod stem vowel may also occur as Tsere Yod (הִגְלֵיתָ).

4. In the Imperfect, the Hireq Yod stem vowel of the Hiphil strong verb does not occur in any form. Note, however, that the הֶ ending is characteristic of Imperfect III-ה forms that do not take a sufformative.

5. As expected in III-ה verbs, the Infinitive Construct has the וֹת ending.

31.10 I-נ Paradigms and Diagnostics.

Perfect	Imperfect	Imperative	Infinitive Construct	Infinitive Absolute	Participle
הִצִּיל יַצִּיל	הַצֵּל	הַצִּיל	הַצֵּל	מַצִּיל	
הִצַּלְתָּ		הַצִּילִי			

Perfect	Imperfect	Imperative	Infinitive Construct	Infinitive Absolute	Participle
הִצִּיל	יַצִּיל	הַצֵּל	הַצִּיל	הַצֵּל	מַצִּיל
הִצִּילָה	תַּצִּיל	הַצִּילִי			מַצֶּלֶת
הִצַּלְתָּ	תַּצִּיל	הַצִּילוּ			מַצִּילִים
הִצַּלְתְּ	תַּצִּילִי	הַצֵּלְנָה			מַצִּילוֹת
הִצַּלְתִּי	אַצִּיל				
הִצִּילוּ	יַצִּילוּ				
הִצַּלְתֶּם	תַּצֵּלְנָה				
הִצַּלְתֶּן	תַּצִּילוּ				
הִצַּלְנוּ	תַּצֵּלְנָה				
	נַצִּיל				

31.11 I-נ Notes.

1. All Hiphil strong verb diagnostics are preserved in this weak verb class.

2. The difficulty with I-נ Hiphil verbs is not with the recognition of stem diagnostics but rather with the identification of the verbal root. This difficulty is due to the fact that in every form of every conjugation above, the first root consonant (נ) has assimilated into the second root consonant (צ) and remains as a Daghesh Forte. In order to correctly identify the verbal root, you will need to recognize that the Daghesh Forte in the צ represents the assimilated נ of the verbal root.

31.12 I-י Paradigms and Diagnostics.

Perfect	Imperfect	Imperative	Infinitive Construct	Infinitive Absolute	Participle
הוֹשִׁיב הוֹשַׁבְתָּ	יוֹשִׁיב	הוֹשֵׁב הוֹשִׁיבִי	הוֹשִׁיב	הוֹשֵׁב	מוֹשִׁיב
הוֹשִׁיב	יוֹשִׁיב	הוֹשֵׁב	הוֹשִׁיב	הוֹשֵׁב	מוֹשִׁיב
הוֹשִׁיבָה	תּוֹשִׁיב	הוֹשִׁיבִי			מוֹשֶׁבֶת
הוֹשַׁבְתָּ	תּוֹשִׁיב	הוֹשִׁיבוּ			מוֹשִׁיבִים
הוֹשַׁבְתְּ	תּוֹשִׁיבִי	הוֹשֵׁבְנָה			מוֹשִׁיבוֹת
הוֹשַׁבְתִּי	אוֹשִׁיב				
הוֹשִׁיבוּ	יוֹשִׁיבוּ				
הוֹשַׁבְתֶּם	תּוֹשֵׁבְנָה				
הוֹשַׁבְתֶּן	תּוֹשִׁיבוּ				
הוֹשַׁבְנוּ	תּוֹשֵׁבְנָה				
	נוֹשִׁיב				

31.13 I-י Notes. Recall from your study of the Niphal stem that most I-י verbs were originally I-ו (25.10-11). In the Niphal, Hiphil, Hophal, and Hithpael stems, the original ו will reappear as either a vowel letter (Holem Waw or Shureq) or as a consonant, replacing the י in first root position.

1. In each of the above forms, note that the י in first root position has been replaced with Holem Waw. In every conjugation, this Holem Waw follows the prefix or preformative consonant. As in the Niphal Perfect and Participle, this Holem Waw represents the reappearance of the ו that was originally in first root position. Knowing that this Holem Waw is indicative of the I-י verb class will enable you to correctly identify the verbal root.

2. Apart from the presence of the Holem Waw discussed above, all of the other Hiphil strong verb diagnostics are preserved in the Hiphil stem of I-י verbs. The preformative and prefix consonants are exactly the same as in the strong verb, and the stem vowels are as expected in all conjugations.

31.14 Biconsonantal Paradigms and Diagnostics.

Perfect	Imperfect	Imperative	Infinitive Construct	Infinitive Absolute	Participle
הֵקִים הֲקִימֹ֫ותָ	יָקִים הָקִ֫ימִי	הָקֵם	הָקִים	הָקֵם	מֵקִים

Perfect	Imperfect	Imperative	Infinitive Construct	Infinitive Absolute	Participle
הֵקִים	יָקִים	הָקֵם	הָקִים	הָקֵם	מֵקִים
הֵקִ֫ימָה	תָּקִים	הָקִ֫ימִי			מְקִימָה
הֲקִימֹ֫ותָ	תָּקִים	הָקִ֫ימוּ			מְקִימִים
הֲקִימֹות	תָּקִ֫ימִי	הָקֵ֫מְנָה			מְקִימֹות
הֲקִימֹ֫ותִי	אָקִים				
הֵקִ֫ימוּ	יָקִ֫ימוּ				
הֲקִימֹותֶם	תְּקִימֶ֫ינָה²				
הֲקִימֹותֶן	תָּקִ֫ימוּ				
הֲקִימֹ֫ונוּ	תְּקִימֶ֫ינָה				
	נָקִים				

31.15 Biconsonantal Notes.

1. As you know, there are three Biconsonantal verb classes, each distinguished by their medial vowel letter. These classes are represented by the verbs קוּם (with Shureq), שִׂים (with Hireq Yod), and בוֹא (with Holem Waw). In the Hiphil stem, however, Biconsonantal verbs exhibit the diagnostic Hireq Yod stem vowel in most forms, regardless of the Biconsonantal verb class. For example, the Hiphil Imperfect 3ms form for each class is יָקִים (קוּם), יָשִׂים (שִׂים), and יָבִיא (בוֹא). Notice how each Imperfect form takes the Hireq Yod stem vowel, regardless of its original medial vowel letter. For this reason, the diagnostics for קוּם will suffice for all three classes of Biconsonantal verbs.

2. In the Perfect, the prefix vowel is variable between Tsere in the third person forms and Hateph Pathach in the second and first person forms. There is also a Holem Waw "connecting" vowel between the verbal root and Perfect sufformatives in all second and first person forms (הֲקִימֹ֫ותָ). You have already encountered

---

² The spelling תָּקֵ֫מְנָה is also attested.

this same connecting vowel in the Qal Perfect forms of Geminate verbs (סַבֹּ֫ותָ 2ms from סָבַב). You should also note, however, that the Holem Waw connecting vowel also appears simply as Holem. For example, הֲקִימֹ֫ותִי is spelled defectively as הֲקִימֹתִי.

3. In the Imperfect, Imperative, Infinitive Construct, and Infinitive Absolute, the prefix and preformative vowels are Qamets rather than the Pathach of the strong verb pattern. You should also note that the prefix vowel for the Participle is variable between Tsere (masculine singular) and Vocal Shewa.

4. The inflection of Hiphil Biconsonantal verbs can exhibit further variation. Due to the relative infrequency of these variant spellings, however, they will not be studied.

31.16 Summary: Hiphil Diagnostics. With weak verbs of the Hiphil stem, most of the strong verb diagnostics are retained. These should be sufficient for the identification of Hiphil weak verbs.

	Perfect	*Imperfect*	*Imperative*	*Infinitive Construct*	*Infinitive Absolute*	*Participle*
Strong	הִקְטִיל הִקְטַֽלְתָּ	יַקְטִיל	הַקְטֵל הַקְטִֽילִי	הַקְטִיל	הַקְטֵל	מַקְטִיל
I-Gutt	הֶעֱמִיד הֶעֱמַֽדְתָּ	יַעֲמִיד	הַעֲמֵד הַעֲמִֽידִי	הַעֲמִיד	הַעֲמֵד	מַעֲמִיד
III-ע/ח	הִשְׁלִיחַ הִשְׁלַחְתְּ	יַשְׁלִיחַ	הַשְׁלַח הַשְׁלִֽיחִי	הַשְׁלִיחַ	הַשְׁלֵחַ	מַשְׁלִיחַ
III-א	הִמְצִיא הִמְצֵֽאתָ	יַמְצִיא	הַמְצֵא הַמְצִֽיאִי	הַמְצִיא	הַמְצֵא	מַמְצִיא
III-ה	הִגְלָה הִגְלִֽיתָ	יַגְלֶה	הַגְלֵה	הַגְלוֹת	הַגְלֵה	מַגְלֶה
I-נ	הִצִּיל הַצַּֽלְתָּ	יַצִּיל	הַצֵּל הַצִּֽילִי	הַצִּיל	הַצֵּל	מַצִּיל
I-י	הוֹשִׁיב הוֹשַֽׁבְתָּ	יוֹשִׁיב	הוֹשֵׁב הוֹשִֽׁיבִי	הוֹשִׁיב	הוֹשֵׁב	מוֹשִׁיב
Bicon	הֵקִים הֲקִימֹֽותָ	יָקִים	הָקֵם הָקִֽימִי	הָקֵם	הָקֵם	מֵקִים

31.17 Vocabulary.

אָוֶן	iniquity, wickedness, evildoer (81)
אוֹצָר	treasure, treasury, storehouse (79)
אוֹת	sign, mark, pledge (79)
גּוֹרָל	lot, portion, allotment (77)
יְשׁוּעָה	salvation, help, deliverance (78)
מִקְנֶה	cattle, livestock, property (76)
מִשְׁמֶרֶת	watch, guard, responsibility (78); feminine
נֶגַע	mark, plague, affliction (78)
צַר	adversary, enemy (72)
קֶדֶם	east, ancient times (61)
קָרְבָּן	gift, offering (80)
שֶׁקֶל	measurement of weight, shekel (88)

31.18 Abram's Amen.[3] Ensuant upon the Lord's promises to give Abram a great reward and to make his descendants as numerous as the stars (Gen 15:1, 4-5) is the following statement (Gen 15:6):

| וְהֶאֱמִן בַּיהוָה | He [Abram] declared "Amen" in Yahweh['s name], |
| וַיַּחְשְׁבֶהָ לּוֹ צְדָקָה | And he [Yahweh] reckoned it to him as righteousness. |

The first half of this verse is usually understood to indicate that Abram gave mental-volitional assent to Yahweh's promises ("He [Abram] believed (in) the Lord" [so, e.g., NIV, KJV, RSV, ESV, NASB]), and the second half of the verse is accordingly taken to mean that Yahweh credited this inner assent to Abram as righteousness.

The Hiphil of אָמַן (henceforth referred to by the Perfect form הֶאֱמִין) has traditionally been analyzed sometimes as causative, though more

---

[3] The present essay is a summary of an article of the same name written by Meredith G. Kline and published in *The Westminster Theological Journal* (31 [1968/69]: 1-11). Dr. Kline (my grandfather) has kindly granted me permission to summarize his arguments and to borrow freely from his language without acknowledging the many cases where my mode of expression imitates his. Because space constraints allow only the conclusions of the original article to be presented here with limited supporting evidence, the reader is advised to consult the original article (subsequently referred to as *Abram's Amen*) for a fuller treatment of the present discussion.

often as declarative-estimative or intransitive/internal-transitive, or a mix of the last two categories. Recent research has indicated, however, that there exists in biblical Hebrew a kind of verb known as "delocutive," which "is intended to denote the phenomenon of a spoken formula or stock phrase that has been verbalized."[4] A survey of the biblical usages of הֶאֱמִין indicates that a delocutive meaning is in fact present in many (though not all) instances. Gen 15:6 most likely contains such an instance, and this fact is apparent both from the verse's context and from the similarity of its use of הֶאֱמִין to delocutive uses of הֶאֱמִין elsewhere.

The covenantal setting of Gen 15:6 commends a delocutive understanding of הֶאֱמִין: "Genesis 15 is the account of a solemn covenant ritual and an 'Amen' response by the covenant vassal in such ceremonies is attested in the records of both biblical and extra-biblical covenants."[5] Reinforcing such an understanding of הֶאֱמִין here is the fact that "the verb חָשַׁב, 'reckon,' is employed for the rendering of decisions in cultic-judicial process (cf. Lev 7:18; 17:4; Num 18:27). And the substance of the divine reckoning, 'righteousness,' points to the judicial locution, 'You are in the right.'"[6]

The delocutive use of הֶאֱמִין appears elsewhere in the Bible. Some passages in which הֶאֱמִין appears "describe occasions when Israel was confronted with signs or marvelous divine acts in response to which a formal attestation to their divine origin was in order (Exod 4:31; Isa 7:9; 28:16; Hab 1:5)."[7] In other passages "הֶאֱמִין is closely connected with verbs of saying (Job 29:24; cf. v. 22; 39:24; cf. v. 25; Ps 116:10)."[8] And it may be that the clause וְלֹא־הֶאֱמִין סִיחוֹן אֶת־יִשְׂרָאֵל in Judg 11:20 is best translated, "Sihon did not declare 'Amen' with Israel."[9]

On other occasions, הֶאֱמִין is associated with commands. "Response to commands is in terms of assent and obedience, not directly in terms of trust and credence, which are appropriate rather to reports and promises. Agreeably, in the passages under discussion (see Deut 9:23; 2 Kgs 17:14; Pss 106:24; 119:66) הֶאֱמִין is actually found in series with verbs not of trust but of obedience."[10]

---

4 *Abram's Amen*, 2.

5 *Abram's Amen*, 3.

6 *Abram's Amen*, 3.

7 *Abram's Amen*, 6.

8 *Abram's Amen*, 6.

9 *Abram's Amen*, 5.

10 *Abram's Amen*, 6.

"It would appear, therefore, that a delocutive use of הֶאֱמִין in Genesis 15:6 would not be an isolated phenomenon but part of a fairly widely attested usage that points to a delocutive origin of the *hiph'il* of אָמַן."[11] What Gen 15:6 states explicitly, therefore, is not "that Abram's inner attitude was one of faith but that Abram voiced his 'Amen' (אָמֵן) in audible response to the word of God."[12] While most of the quotations of Gen 15:6 in the New Testament (Rom 4:3, 22-24; Gal 3:6) do not make this delocutive, confessional character of הֶאֱמִין overt, an understanding of "the confessional nature of justifying faith"[13] nevertheless appears at various points in the New Testament, particularly in the statements of Paul and James (cf. Rom 10:8-10; James 2:23-24). The reality of the justifying nature of believing assent to God's gospel promises – a faith that begins in the heart and mind and issues in confession through word and deed – is given voice perhaps most vividly in 2 Cor 1:20, which "sounds like the faith-witness of Abram's 'Amen' transposed into a New Testament key":[14]

"For all the promises of God find their Yes in him. That is why we utter the Amen through him, to the glory of God." (RSV)

J. Bergman Kline
M.A., Biblical Languages
Gordon-Conwell Theological Seminary
South Hamilton, Massachusetts

---

[11] *Abram's Amen*, 6-7.

[12] *Abram's Amen*, 2-3.

[13] *Abram's Amen*, 10.

[14] *Abram's Amen*, 11.

31.19 Advanced Information: יָדָה. The verb יָדָה (to thank, praise) is well-attested in the Hiphil stem (100 times), especially in the Psalms (67 times). Given that this verb is doubly weak, both I-י and III-ה, certain of its forms merit special attention. Note that as a I-י verb in the Hiphil stem, the original ו will reappear as Holem Waw, replacing the י root consonant. You will also want to remember that III-ה verbs have their own distinctive endings. Some of the more common forms of this verb are presented below.

Perfect	הוֹדִינוּ	1cp	we give thanks
	הוֹדוּ	3cp	they give thanks
Imperfect	אוֹדֶה	1cs	I will give thanks
	יוֹדוּ	3mp	they will give thanks
Imperative	הוֹדוּ	2mp	(you) give thanks!
Inf Construct	הוֹדוֹת[15]		to give thanks
Participle	מוֹדֶה	ms	giving thanks

A few biblical examples with the Hiphil of יָדָה are presented below.

טוֹב לְהֹדוֹת לַיהוָה

(It is) good *to give thanks* to the LORD.
(Ps 92:2 [English 92:1])

הוֹדוּ לַיהוָה כִּי־טוֹב כִּי לְעוֹלָם חַסְדּוֹ

Give thanks to the LORD, for he is good;
for his steadfast love endures forever!
(Ps 118:1)

אוֹדֶה יְהוָה בְּכָל־לִבִּי

I will give thanks to the LORD with all my heart.
(Ps 9:2 [English 9:1])

---

[15] This form is most often spelled defectively as הֹדוֹת.

Chapter 32

The Hophal Stem - Strong Verbs

32.1 **Introduction.** In this chapter, we will study the Hophal stem. The Hophal stem occurs less frequently than any other derived stem.[1] Because certain forms of the Hophal stem occur with such infrequency, we will study only the Perfect, Imperfect, and Participle in this chapter. The stem name "Hophal" (הָפְעַל) preserves certain diagnostic features of the Perfect (הָ prefix with Qamets Hatuf and Pathach stem vowel). In this case, the prefix vowel and the stem vowel will distinguish the Hophal from most Hiphil forms. In modern Hebrew, the name of this stem is spelled "Huphal," denoting the frequent presence of a u-class vowel with either the prefix or preformative in certain verbs.

32.2 **The Meaning of the Hophal Stem.** For the most part, the Hophal is the passive of the Hiphil. The Hophal stem, therefore, is used to express *causative* action with a *passive* voice. For example, the Hiphil verb הִמְלִיךְ means "he made (someone) king." The Hophal form is הָמְלַךְ and it is translated, "he *was* made king."

32.3 **Hophal Perfect.** The Hophal Perfect of a strong verb may occur with either a Qibbuts (u-class) or Qamets Hatuf (o-class) prefix vowel, though Qamets Hatuf is more frequent in the strong verb.[2] For this reason, two Hophal Perfect paradigms are given below, each with a different prefix vowel. The Hophal Perfect is formed with the Hophal prefix (הָ), the verbal stem (with Pathach stem vowel), and the Perfect sufformatives. Translate the Hophal Perfect passively with a form of the helping verb "to be," as in "he *was* made king."

---

[1] The Hophal stem occurs 396 times in the Hebrew Bible. It appears in the Perfect 109 times, Imperfect 163 times, Imperative 2 times, Infinitive Construct 8 times, Infinitive Absolute 6 times, and Participle 108 times.

[2] In Hophal weak verbs, u-class vowels are more frequent. The Hophal occurs 109 times in the Perfect (strong and weak verbs). In only 37 instances does the o-class vowel appear under the הָ prefix. In the remaining 72 instances, the u-class vowels Qibbuts or Shureq are present with the הַ. With the Hophal Imperfect, the o-class vowel occurs only 10 out of the 163 total occurrences.

	Hophal u-class	Hophal o-class
3ms	הָקְטַל	הָקְטַל
3fs	הָקְטְלָה	הָקְטְלָה
2ms	הָקְטַׄלְתָּ	הָקְטַׄלְתָּ
2fs	הָקְטַלְתְּ	הָקְטַלְתְּ
1cs	הָקְטַׄלְתִּי	הָקְטַׄלְתִּי
3cp	הָקְטְלוּ	הָקְטְלוּ
2mp	הָקְטַלְתֶּם	הָקְטַלְתֶּם
2fp	הָקְטַלְתֶּן	הָקְטַלְתֶּן
1cp	הָקְטַׄלְנוּ	הָקְטַׄלְנוּ

32.4   Hophal Perfect Diagnostics.

1. הֻ (u-class) or הָ (o-class) prefix in every form of their respective paradigms.

2. Pathach stem vowel in both classes, except in the 3fs and 3cp forms.

Hophal Perfect
Strong Verb

הֻקְטַל

הָקְטַל

32.5   Hophal Imperfect. The Hophal Imperfect is formed with Imperfect preformatives, the verbal stem (with a Pathach stem vowel), and the Imperfect sufformatives. Like the Perfect above, the Imperfect preformative vowel is variable between Qibbuts and Qamets Hatuf. Translate the Hophal Imperfect passively with a form of the verb "to be," as in "he will *be* made king."

	Hophal u-class	Hophal o-class
3ms	יָקְטֵל	יָקְטַל
3fs	תָּקְטַל	תָּקְטַל
2ms	תָּקְטַל	תָּקְטַל
2fs	תָּקְטְלִי	תָּקְטְלִי
1cs	אָקְטַל	אָקְטַל
3mp	יָקְטְלוּ	יָקְטְלוּ
3fp	תָּקְטַֿלְנָה	תָּקְטַֿלְנָה
2mp	תָּקְטְלוּ	תָּקְטְלוּ
2fp	תָּקְטַֿלְנָה	תָּקְטַֿלְנָה
1cp	נָקְטַל	נָקְטַל

32.6   Hophal Imperfect Diagnostics.

1.   Qibbuts preformative vowel (u-class) as in יָקְטַל or Qamets Hatuf preformative vowel (o-class) as in יָקְטַל in their respective paradigms.

2.   Pathach stem vowel in both classes, except in those forms with sufformatives that consist of a vowel (2fs, 3mp, 2mp).

32.7   Hophal Participle. The Hophal Participle is formed with the Participle prefix (מ), the verbal stem (with Qamets stem vowel), and the inflectional endings of the Participle. Once again, both prefix vowels, Qibbuts and Qamets Hatuf, are attested in the Participle. Translate the Hophal Participle passively with a form of the verb "to be," as in *"being* made king."

	Hophal u-class	Hophal o-class
ms	מׇקְטָל	מׇקְטָל
fs	מׇקְטֶלֶת	מׇקְטֶלֶת
mp	מׇקְטָלִים	מׇקְטָלִים
fp	מׇקְטָלוֹת	מׇקְטָלוֹת

32.8 Hophal Participle Diagnostics.

1. מֻ or מׇ prefix. You will recall that the Piel, Pual, Hiphil, and Hophal Participles have a מ prefix. The Piel and Pual have a Vocal Shewa under the prefix (מְ). The Hiphil has a Pathach under the prefix (מַ).

2. Qamets stem vowel in every form with the exception of the feminine singular.

Hophal Participle Strong Verb

מֻקְטָל

מׇקְטָל

32.9 Summary.

1. The Hophal stem is used to express *causative* action with a *passive* voice. In most of its occurrences, the Hophal is the passive of the Hiphil.

2. The Hophal conjugations are distinguished from other derived stem conjugations by their prefix or preformative vowels, Qibbuts or Qamets Hatuf. It is perhaps best to think of the Hophal prefix vowels in terms of vowel class rather than particular vowels. As such, you should learn that the Hophal prefix vowel is variable between u-class and o-class vowels. With u-class vowels, Qibbuts appears most frequently, but Shureq also occurs in many weak verbs (e.g., 33.8, 10, 12). With o-class vowels, Qamets Hatuf occurs most frequently but Holem and Holem Waw also appear.

Thinking of the Hophal prefix vowel in terms of vowel classes will prevent confusion when you encounter variation, especially in the weak verb forms.

3. In the Perfect and Imperfect conjugations, the stem vowel is Pathach, except in those forms with sufformatives that begin with or consist of a vowel. In the Participle, the stem vowel is Qamets, except in the feminine singular.

Hophal Stem - Strong Verbs

Perfect u-class	*Perfect o-class*	*Imperfect u-class*	*Imperfect o-class*	*Participle u-class*	*Participle o-class*
הֻקְטַל	הָקְטַל	יֻקְטַל	יָקְטַל	מֻקְטָל	מָקְטָל
הֻקְטַל	הָקְטַל	יֻקְטַל	יָקְטַל	מֻקְטָל	מָקְטָל
הֻקְטְלָה	הָקְטְלָה	תֻּקְטַל	תָּקְטַל	מֻקְטֶלֶת	מָקְטֶלֶת
הֻקְטַלְתָּ	הָקְטַלְתָּ	תֻּקְטַל	תָּקְטַל	מֻקְטָלִים	מָקְטָלִים
הֻקְטַלְתְּ	הָקְטַלְתְּ	תֻּקְטְלִי	תָּקְטְלִי	מֻקְטָלוֹת	מָקְטָלוֹת
הֻקְטַלְתִּי	הָקְטַלְתִּי	אֻקְטַל	אָקְטַל		
הֻקְטְלוּ	הָקְטְלוּ	יֻקְטְלוּ	יָקְטְלוּ		
הֻקְטַלְתֶּם	הָקְטַלְתֶּם	תֻּקְטַלְנָה	תָּקְטַלְנָה		
הֻקְטַלְתֶּן	הָקְטַלְתֶּן	תֻּקְטְלוּ	תָּקְטְלוּ		
הֻקְטַלְנוּ	הָקְטַלְנוּ	תֻּקְטַלְנָה	תָּקְטַלְנָה		
		נֻקְטַל	נָקְטַל		

32.10 Vocabulary.

Nouns

אֶרֶז	cedar (73)
צוּר	rock, boulder (73)
קֶרֶן	horn (76); feminine
קֶשֶׁת	bow, weapon (76); feminine

32.11 A Word Is Worth a Thousand Pictures. One of the great benefits of learning to read biblical Hebrew is that you will be able to do "word studies" in the original language in order to determine precisely what a given term means in a particular passage. Although many wonderful English translations are available, doing your own word studies on key terms in a passage often provides you with tremendous insight into a text's meaning that cannot be gained from the English alone. In the context of Ps 137:1-9, let's look at verses 5-6 as an example.

> **5** If I forget you, O Jerusalem, may my right hand wither.
> **6** May my tongue cling to the roof of my mouth,
> if I do not remember you,
> if I do not exalt Jerusalem above my chief joy.

What does it mean to "forget" Jerusalem? Why do many English translations render verse 5b as "may my right hand *forget its skill*" and why does the author refer to malfunctioning body parts in verses 5-6? A word study on שָׁכַח (to forget) reveals that while this term can mean simply a temporary or permanent lapse of memory, it can also refer to abandonment. Biblically, to forget God is to abandon him (Isa 49:14), to pervert one's ways (Jer 3:21), and to commit idolatry (Deut 4:23; Judg 3:7; Ps 44:17). In essence, to forget God is to break the covenant (for example, see Deut 8:2). This is precisely what is meant in verse 5. To forget Jerusalem would be to assimilate into Babylonian culture into which Judah had been exiled and to adopt her pagan religion.

Second, why do many English translations render verse 5b as "may my right hand forget its skill" rather than "may my right hand wither," as it has been translated above? This is where knowing Hebrew is particularly useful. The text of verse 5b reads תִּשְׁכַּח יְמִינִי with the verb שָׁכַח (to forget). Some argue, however, that a scribal mistake known as "graphic confusion" occurred, where כָּחַשׁ (to grow lean, wither) was mistaken for the previous verb in verse 5, שָׁכַח (to forget), and that the original text actually read תִּכְחַשׁ יְמִינִי ("may my right hand grow lean" or "may my right hand wither"). The Greek version of the Old Testament, the Septuagint, also attests to the confusion by rendering the active Hebrew verb with a passive Greek verb. How is one to determine the correct reading?

One possible interpretation, and the one followed here, is based on the context of Ps 137:5-6 and the author's reference to a malfunctioning tongue as a consequence of "forgetting" Jerusalem. Again, a brief word study on terms in the Old Testament, not only for "tongue" but also for body parts generally (eye, ear, tongue, hand, nose, etc.), demonstrates that mute tongues, dim eyes, deaf ears, and withering hands are often linked to idol worship! This is the message of Ps 115:4-8.

4   Their idols are silver and gold,
    The work of man's hands.
5   They have mouths, but they cannot speak;
    They have eyes, but they cannot see;
6   They have ears, but they cannot hear;
    They have noses, but they cannot smell;
7   They have hands, but they cannot feel;
    They have feet, but they cannot walk;
    They cannot make a sound with their throat.
8   Those who make them will become like them,
    Everyone who trusts in them. (NASB)

The operative principle here is that you are what you worship! Thus the translation, "may my right hand wither" in Ps 137:5 better fits the context of idolatry in Ps 137. It also complements the following verse, "may my tongue cling to the roof of my mouth," with which it stands in parallel. In other words, the psalmist is saying, "may I become like an immobile and mute idol if I worship one ever again!"

While much can be learned by reading Ps 137 in English, without a knowledge of biblical Hebrew, textual problems like the one above cannot be examined. Additionally, by studying the text in English only, the reader may fail to see the connections between malfunctioning body parts and idolatry and, therefore, miss the force of the author's message.

Catherine Beckerleg
PhD Candidate
Harvand University
Cambridge, Massachusetts

32.12 Advanced Information: Verbal Hendiadys. Hebrew can express a single concept or idea by using two independent words that are connected by the conjunction וְ (and). An example of this type of construction in English is the expression "nice and warm" to communicate the single idea of extreme comfort. This coordination of two independent words with the conjunction is called *hendiadys*.[3] It is especially common with verbs, as the following examples illustrate.

וּמִהַרְתֶּם וְהוֹרַדְתֶּם אֶת־אָבִי הֵנָּה

And you will *quickly (soon) bring* my
father *down* here (Gen 45:13).

The coordination in the above example is with the verbs מָהַר (Piel: to do something quickly or in a hurry) and יָרַד (Hiphil: to bring down).

וַיּוֹסִפוּ עוֹד שְׂנֹא אֹתוֹ

And they *hated* him even *more* (Gen 37:5).

In the above example, the two verbs יָסַף (Hiphil: to increase, enhance) and שָׂנֵא (to hate) are linked.

וַיְמַהֲרוּ וַיַּשְׁכִּימוּ וַיֵּצְאוּ אַנְשֵׁי־הָעִיר לִקְרַאת־יִשְׂרָאֵל לַמִּלְחָמָה

The men of the city *went out quickly, early in the morning,*
to meet Israel in battle (Josh 8:14).

In this example, the coordination is with the three verbs מָהַר (Piel: to do something quickly or in a hurry), שָׁכַם (Hiphil: to arise or do something early), and יָצָא (to go out).

וַיֹּאכַל וַיֵּשְׁתְּ וַיָּשָׁב וַיִּשְׁכָּב

And he ate and he drank and (then) he *lay
down again* (1 Kgs 19:6).

The last two verbs in this example are coordinated with the conjunction: שׁוּב (to do something again) and שָׁכַב (to lay down).

In each of the above examples, the verbs are not translated independently but are coordinated in translation with the use of an adverb (quickly, more, again). In these constructions, the second verb usually expresses

---

[3] This is a Greek term meaning "one (ἕν) through (διά) two (δύο)," that is, the expression of one idea through two words.

the main idea with the first verb translated adverbially. Verbs commonly used in this type of construction include:

מִהַר	to do something quickly (Piel)
יָסַף	to do something again, increase (Hiphil)
שׁוּב	to do something again (Qal)
שָׁכַם	to do something early (Hiphil)
רָבָה	to do something many times (Hiphil)

Chapter 33

The Hophal Stem - Weak Verbs

33.1   Introduction. The weak verb forms of the Hophal stem occur much more frequently than the strong verb forms. In fact, there are only about fifty Hophal strong verb forms in the Hebrew Bible, compared to about 250 weak verb forms. In spite of this fact, however, you must first master the strong verb diagnostics before studying Hophal weak verbs. Having memorized the strong verb diagnostics, you will be prepared to understand the weak verb variations of the Hophal stem. Once again, due to the infrequency of certain forms, only the Perfect, Imperfect, and Participle of selected weak verbs will be studied.

33.2   I-Guttural Paradigms and Diagnostics.

Perfect	*Imperfect*	*Participle*
הָעֳמַד	יָעֳמַד	מָעֳמָד
הָעֳמַד	יָעֳמַד	מָעֳמָד
הָעֳמְדָה	תָּעֳמַד	מָעֳמֶדֶת
הָעֳמַדְתָּ	תָּעֳמַד	מָעֳמָדִים
הָעֳמַדְתְּ	תָּעֳמְדִי	מָעֳמָדוֹת
הָעֳמַדְתִּי	אָעֳמַד	
הָעֳמְדוּ	יָעֳמְדוּ	
הָעֳמַדְתֶּם	תָּעֳמַדְנָה	
הָעֳמַדְתֶּן	תָּעֳמְדוּ	
הָעֳמַדְנוּ	תָּעֳמַדְנָה	
	נָעֳמַד	

33.3   I-Guttural Notes.

1. I-Guttural verbs in the Hophal stem prefer the Qamets Hatuf (o-class) prefix or preformative vowel. However, Qibbuts (u-class) is also attested (7 times).

377

2. I-Guttural verbs maintain all strong verb diagnostics. Based on your study of I-Guttural verbs in the Qal and other derived stems, the presence of a reduced vowel (Hateph Qamets) under the guttural in first root position is expected (see 16.8-9).

33.4   III-ה Paradigms and Diagnostics.

Perfect		Imperfect	Participle
הָגְלָה	הָגְלֵי	יָגְלֶה	מֻגְלֶה
הָגְלָה		יָגְלֶה	מֻגְלֶה
הָגְלְתָה		תָּגְלֶה	מֻגְלָה
הָגְלֵיתָ		תָּגְלֶה	מֻגְלִים
הָגְלֵית		תָּגְלִי	מֻגְלוֹת
הָגְלֵיתִי		אָגְלֶה	
הָגְלוּ		יָגְלוּ	
הָגְלֵיתֶם		תָּגְלֶינָה	
הָגְלֵיתֶן		תָּגְלוּ	
הָגְלֵינוּ		תָּגְלֶינָה	
		נָגְלֶה	

33.5   III-ה Notes.

1. Like I-Guttural verbs above, III-ה verbs in the Hophal stem prefer the o-class (Qamets Hatuf) prefix or preformative vowel.

2. Remember that the verbs of this weak class will drop the final ה in the Perfect, Imperfect, and Participle. In those forms that do show a final ה, it is the *mater lectionis* and not the final consonant of the verbal root.

33.6   I-נ Paradigms and Diagnostics.

Perfect	*Imperfect*	*Participle*
הֻצַּל	יֻצַּל	מֻצָּל
הֻצַּל	יֻצַּל	מֻצָּל
הֻצְּלָה	תֻּצַּל	מֻצֶּלֶת
הֻצַּלְתָּ	תֻּצַּל	מֻצָּלִים
הֻצַּלְתְּ	תֻּצְּלִי	מֻצָּלוֹת
הֻצַּלְתִּי	אֻצַּל	
הֻצְּלוּ	יֻצְּלוּ	
הֻצַּלְתֶּם	תֻּצַּלְנָה	
הֻצַּלְתֶּן	תֻּצְּלוּ	
הֻצַּלְנוּ	תֻּצַּלְנָה	
	נֻצַּל	

33.7   I-נ Notes.

1. I-נ Hophal verbs prefer the u-class prefix or preformative vowel, Qibbuts.

2. In verbs of this weak class, the נ in first root position assimilates into the second root consonant and remains as a Daghesh Forte. With only two root consonants remaining, the Daghesh Forte is your clue for the identification of the I-נ verbal root.

33.8   I-ʾ Paradigms and Diagnostics.

Perfect	*Imperfect*	*Participle*
הוּשַׁב	יוּשַׁב	מוּשָׁב
הוּשַׁב	יוּשַׁב	מוּשָׁב
הוּשְׁבָה	תּוּשַׁב	מוּשֶׁבֶת
הוּשַׁבְתָּ	תּוּשַׁב	מוּשָׁבִים
הוּשַׁבְתְּ	תּוּשְׁבִי	מוּשָׁבוֹת
הוּשַׁבְתִּי	אוּשַׁב	
הוּשְׁבוּ	יוּשְׁבוּ	
הוּשַׁבְתֶּם	תּוּשַׁבְנָה	
הוּשַׁבְתֶּן	תּוּשְׁבוּ	
הוּשַׁבְנוּ	תּוּשַׁבְנָה	
	נוּשַׁב	

33.9   I-ʾ Notes.

1. The last three weak verb classes to be studied in the Hophal stem are I-ʾ, Biconsonantal and Geminate. Each of these weak verb types prefers the u-class vowel (frequently Shureq but sometimes Qibbuts) in the various conjugations of the Hophal. In the I-ʾ paradigms above, note that Shureq appears as the prefix or preformative vowel in each of the conjugations (see also 33.10 and 33.12 below).

2. Remember that most I-ʾ verbs were originally I-ו. In the Hophal stem, the original ו reappears as the vowel letter Shureq (וּ) in the Perfect (הוּשַׁב), Imperfect (יוּשַׁב), and Participle (מוּשָׁב). Since only two root consonants remain, it is important that you are able to recognize the Shureq as diagnostic of the I-ʾ class of verbs. You will recall from previous chapters that the original ו also reappears in the Niphal (25.10-11) and Hiphil (31.12-13) stems.

33.10 Biconsonantal Paradigms and Diagnostics.

Perfect	*Imperfect*	*Participle*
הוּקַם	יוּקַם	מוּקָם
הוּקַם	יוּקַם	מוּקָם
הוּקְמָה	תּוּקַם	מוּקֶּמֶת
הוּקַמְתָּ	תּוּקַם	מוּקָמִים
הוּקַמְתְּ	תּוּקְמִי	מוּקָמוֹת
הוּקַמְתִּי	אוּקַם	
הוּקְמוּ	יוּקְמוּ	
הוּקַמְתֶּם	תּוּקַמְנָה	
הוּקַמְתֶּן	תּוּקְמוּ	
הוּקַמְנוּ	תּוּקַמְנָה	
	נוּקַם	

33.11 Biconsonantal Notes.

1. Shureq prefix or preformative vowel in every form (33.9.1).

2. The medial vowel letters of the Biconsonantal verb classes do not appear in the Hophal stem. The Perfect and Imperfect have a Pathach stem vowel, except in those forms that have sufformatives that begin with or consist of a vowel. The Participle has a Qamets stem vowel, except in the feminine singular form.

33.12 Geminate Paradigms and Diagnostics.

Perfect	Imperfect	Participle
הוּסַב	יוּסַב	מוּסָב
הוּסַב	יוּסַב	מוּסָב
הוּסַבָּה	תּוּסַב	מוּסֶבֶת
הוּסַבּוֹתָ	תּוּסַב	מוּסַבִּים
הוּסַבּוֹת	תּוּסַבִּי	מוּסַבּוֹת
הוּסַבּוֹתִי	אוּסַב	
הוּסַבּוּ	יוּסַבּוּ	
הוּסַבּוֹתֶם	תּוּסַבֶּינָה	
הוּסַבּוֹתֶן	תּוּסַבּוּ	
הוּסַבּוֹנוּ	תּוּסַבֶּינָה	
	נוּסַב	

33.13 Geminate Notes.

1. Shureq prefix or preformative vowel in every form (33.9.1), though some Geminate forms do show a Qibbuts prefix vowel.

2. With the Hophal forms of this weak class, only two root consonants are present because only one Geminate consonant is preserved. In some forms, however, the Daghesh Forte in the remaining Geminate consonant will aid in your identification of this weak verbal root. Additionally, the Holem Waw connecting vowel in the Perfect is another indicator of the Geminate class (14.10-11).

33.14 Summary: Hophal Diagnostics. In the following summary chart, observe that five weak verb classes preserve only two root consonants. With III-ה verbs, the final ה is lost. With I-נ verbs, the נ assimilates into the second root consonant and remains as a Daghesh Forte. With I-י verbs (originally I-ו), the vowel letter Shureq replaces the י as the prefix or preformative vowel in the Perfect, Imperfect, and Participle. With Geminate verbs, only one Geminate consonant is preserved, though it is represented as a Daghesh Forte in some forms. With Biconsonantal verbs, both root consonants remain and the prefix or preformative vowel is Shureq in every form of the Perfect, Imperfect, and Participle.

	Perfect	*Imperfect*	*Participle*
Strong (u-class)	הָקְטַל	יָקְטַל	מֻקְטָל
Strong (o-class)	הָקְטַל	יָקְטַל	מָקְטָל
I-Guttural	הָעֳמַד	יָעֳמַד	מָעֳמָד
III-ה	הָגְלָה	יָגְלֶה	מָגְלֶה
I-נ	הֻצַּל	יֻצַּל	מֻצָּל
I-י	הוּשַׁב	יוּשַׁב	מוּשָׁב
Biconsonantal	הוּקַם	יוּקַם	מוּקָם
Geminate	הוּסַב	יוּסַב	מוּסָב

33.15 Vocabulary.

בֶּטֶן	belly, stomach, womb (72); feminine
הֶבֶל	vanity, futility, breath (73)
חֶרְפָּה	reproach, disgrace, shame (73)
מִזְרָח	east, sunrise (74)

33.16 Marry a Prostitute?

לֵךְ קַח־לְךָ אֵשֶׁת זְנוּנִים וְיַלְדֵי זְנוּנִים כִּי־זָנֹה תִזְנֶה הָאָרֶץ מֵאַחֲרֵי יְהוָה

Go marry a woman of prostitution and have children of prostitution
because the land is completely committing prostitution
away from Yahweh (Hos 1:2).

In Hos 1, we are confronted with an interpretational question: Did God actually command Hosea to marry a prostitute? Some commentators have answered in the affirmative, even suggesting that Hosea's wife probably turned to prostitution sometime after their marriage, and Hosea, looking back at his past at a later point when he was seeking an analogy for Israel's unfaithfulness to Yahweh, recast the story of his marriage as if he had been commanded to marry a prostitute in the first place. However, these interpreters do not necessarily have Hebrew grammar on their side.

There are three words for "prostitute" in Hebrew: קְדֵשָׁה (cult prostitute), זֹנָה (common prostitute), and כֶּלֶב (male prostitute). None of the three is used here. Instead, a special *construct* term appears: the word אִשָּׁה (construct אֵשֶׁת) for a woman or wife is used in combination with a governing noun in the masculine plural, זְנוּנִים. In Hebrew, the masculine plural is the standard way to convey abstraction – in this case, not "prostitute" but the concept of "prostitution," i.e., in theological contexts, the opposite of "faithfulness." Moreover, a noun in the construct is often related logically to its governing noun in the manner of "something characterized by" so that אֵשֶׁת זְנוּנִים would tend to mean "a woman characterized by [the abstract concept of] prostitution" rather than literally "a prostitute." Further, Hosea's children are called יַלְדֵי זְנוּנִים, "children of prostitution" in a precisely parallel Hebrew construct, i.e., "children characterized by [the abstract concept of] prostitution" rather than "children of a prostitute." Additionally, the verse goes on to say that the land (of Israel) זָנֹה תִזְנֶה, "is completely committing prostitution."

Thus the same thing is being said about Hosea's wife, about his future children, and about the land of Israel in general – and in no case is the literal meaning apparently related to actually selling sex. All of this fits in well with the way that the Hebrew root in question, זנה, is used elsewhere in Hosea (and other prophetical contexts, especially Ezekiel), to convey the sense of "ultimate [religious] unfaithfulness" to Yahweh. In other words, Hos 1:2 is conceptually parallel to Isa 64:4 or Ps 14:2-3 (cf. Rom 3:10-12). It makes the point, not that Hosea actually married a prostitute, but that in his day, all Israel has abandoned Yahweh's covenant, so that even Hosea's wife and children – no matter whom he married – would be tainted by the same unfaithfulness that "the land" in general displayed.

Douglas Stuart
Professor of Old Testament
Gordon-Conwell Theological Seminary
South Hamilton, Massachusetts

Chapter 34

The Hithpael Stem - Strong Verbs

34.1   **Introduction.** The Hithpael is the easiest of the derived stems to recognize because of the distinctive preformatives and prefixes in each of the conjugations.[1] The diagnostic features of the Hithpael stem include: (1) a distinctive prefix in all of the conjugations (for example, הִתְ in the Perfect); (2) Pathach under the first consonant of the verbal root; and (3) Daghesh Forte in the second consonant of the verbal root. With expected variations, these diagnostic features appear in every conjugation of the Hithpael strong verb. At this point, it is helpful to recall that Piel, Pual, and Hithpael verbs have a Daghesh Forte in the second consonant of the verbal root.

34.2   **The Meaning of the Hithpael Stem.**

   1.   The Hithpael stem is used to express an *intensive* type of action with a *reflexive* voice. The reflexive voice is used when the subject of the verb performs the verbal action upon itself. For example, the verb קָדַשׁ means "he was holy" in the Qal. The Hithpael form is הִתְקַדֵּשׁ and it means "he sanctified *himself*." Notice how the reflexive pronoun "himself" is used to render the reflexive nuance of the Hithpael. Other examples of English reflexive pronouns include: (singular) herself, yourself, myself and (plural) themselves, yourselves, ourselves. When translating Hithpael verbs with a reflexive nuance, the verbal subject and the reflexive pronoun must agree in both gender, number, and person. In addition to the reflexive nuance, the Hithpael stem may also express the reciprocal or iterative types of action.

   2.   *Reciprocal.* This type of action expresses the notion of reciprocity. For example, "they looked *at each other*" is an illustration of reciprocal action. The notion of "at each other" indicates that the action of looking by one party was returned or reciprocated by the other party.

---

[1] The Hithpael stem occurs 842 times in the Hebrew Bible. It appears in the Perfect 137 times, Imperfect 420 times, Imperative 64 times, Infinitive Construct 93 times, Infinitive Absolute 3 times, and Participle 123 times.

הִתְרָאוּ they looked *at each other*
(Hithpael Perfect 3cp from רָאָה)

הִתְקַשְּׁרוּ they conspired *with each other*
(Hithpael Perfect 3cp from קָשַׁר)

3. *Iterative.* The iterative expresses the notion of repeated action. For example, "he walked *back and forth*" is an illustration of iterative action. The notion of "back and forth" expresses the fact that the action of the verb occurred repeatedly.

הִתְהַלֵּךְ he walked *back and forth*
(Hithpael Perfect 3ms from הָלַךְ)

הִתְהַפֵּךְ he turned *this way and that*
(Hithpael Perfect 3ms from הָפַךְ)

4. It must also be noted that the Hithpael, in some instances, is translated just like the Qal, simple action with an active voice.

הִתְפַּלֵּל he prayed
(Hithpael Perfect 3ms from פָּלַל)

הִתְיַצֵּב he stood firm
(Hithpael Perfect 3ms from יָצַב)

34.3 **Hithpael Perfect**. The Hithpael Perfect is formed with the Hithpael prefix (הִתְ), the verbal stem (with a Daghesh Forte in the second root consonant), and the Perfect sufformatives.

	Qal	Hithpael	Translation
3ms	קָטַל	הִתְקַטֵּל	he killed himself[2]
3fs	קָטְלָה	הִתְקַטְּלָה	she killed herself
2ms	קָטַ֫לְתָּ	הִתְקַטַּ֫לְתָּ	you killed yourself
2fs	קָטַלְתְּ	הִתְקַטַּלְתְּ	you killed yourself
1cs	קָטַ֫לְתִּי	הִתְקַטַּ֫לְתִּי	I killed myself
3cp	קָטְלוּ	הִתְקַטְּלוּ	they killed themselves
2mp	קְטַלְתֶּם	הִתְקַטַּלְתֶּם	you killed yourselves
2fp	קְטַלְתֶּן	הִתְקַטַּלְתֶּן	you killed yourselves
1cp	קָטַ֫לְנוּ	הִתְקַטַּ֫לְנוּ	we killed ourselves

34.4 **Hithpael Perfect Diagnostics**.

1. הִתְ prefix in every form. This prefix is hard to miss and makes identification of the Hithpael Perfect an easy matter.

2. Pathach under the first consonant of the verbal root.

3. Daghesh Forte in the second consonant of the verbal root.

Hithpael Perfect Strong Verb

הִתְקַטֵּל

---

[2] The rationale for preserving the paradigm verb קָטַל (despite the awkward translations) has been explained in sections 30.3 and 32.3.

34.5 **Hithpael Imperfect.** The Hithpael Imperfect is formed with the Hithpael Imperfect preformatives (יִת/תִּת/אֶת/נִת), the verbal stem (with a Daghesh Forte in the second root consonant), and the Imperfect sufformatives.

	Qal	*Hithpael*	*Translation*
3ms	יִקְטֹל	יִתְקַטֵּל	he will kill himself
3fs	תִּקְטֹל	תִּתְקַטֵּל	she will kill herself
2ms	תִּקְטֹל	תִּתְקַטֵּל	you will kill yourself
2fs	תִּקְטְלִי	תִּתְקַטְּלִי	you will kill yourself
1cs	אֶקְטֹל	אֶתְקַטֵּל	I will kill myself
3mp	יִקְטְלוּ	יִתְקַטְּלוּ	they will kill themselves
3fp	תִּקְטֹלְנָה	תִּתְקַטֵּלְנָה	they will kill themselves
2mp	תִּקְטְלוּ	תִּתְקַטְּלוּ	you will kill yourselves
2fp	תִּקְטֹלְנָה	תִּתְקַטֵּלְנָה	you will kill yourselves
1cp	נִקְטֹל	נִתְקַטֵּל	we will kill ourselves

34.6 **Hithpael Imperfect Diagnostics.**

1. The preformatives for the Imperfect are יִת, תִּת, אֶת and נִת. These Hithpael Imperfect preformatives are unique and easy to identify.

2. Pathach under the first consonant of the verbal root.

3. Daghesh Forte in the second consonant of the verbal root.

Hithpael Imperfect
Strong Verb

יִתְקַטֵּל

34.7 **Hithpael Imperative.** The Hithpael Imperative, Infinitive Construct, and Infinitive Absolute may be studied together because the diagnostics for these three forms are identical (הִתְקַטֵּל). In fact, their diagnostics are the same as those for the Hithpael Perfect. Because the spelling of these four basic forms is identical, you will need to rely on context for correct identification. The Hithpael Imperative is formed with the Hithpael prefix (הִת), the verbal stem (with a Daghesh Forte in the second root consonant), and the Imperative sufformatives.

	Qal	*Hithpael*	*Translation*
2ms	קְטֹל	הִתְקַטֵּל	kill yourself!
2fs	קִטְלִי	הִתְקַטְּלִי	kill yourself!
2mp	קִטְלוּ	הִתְקַטְּלוּ	kill yourselves!
2fp	קְטֹלְנָה	הִתְקַטֵּלְנָה	kill yourselves!

34.8 **Hithpael Infinitive Construct and Infinitive Absolute.**[3] The Infinitive Construct and Infinitive Absolute are identical (הִתְקַטֵּל) and are formed with the Hithpael prefix (הִת) and the verbal stem (with a Daghesh Forte in the second root consonant).

34.9 **Hithpael Imperative, Infinitive Construct, and Infinitive Absolute Diagnostics.** As noted above, these same diagnostic features are also present in the Hithpael Perfect.

1. הִת prefix in every form.

2. Pathach under the first consonant of the verbal root.

3. Daghesh Forte in the second consonant of the verbal root.

Hithpael Imperative, Infinitive Construct and Absolute

הִתְקַטֵּל

34.10 **Hithpael Participle.** The Hithpael Participle is formed with the Hithpael Participle prefix (מִת), the verbal stem (with a Daghesh Forte in the second root consonant), and the inflectional endings of the Participle.

---

[3] The Hithpael Infinitive Absolute appears only three times in the Hebrew Bible.

	Qal	*Hithpael*
ms	קָטֵל	מִתְקַטֵּל
fs	קֹטֶ֫לֶת	מִתְקַטֶּ֫לֶת
mp	קֹטְלִים	מִתְקַטְּלִים
fp	קֹטְלוֹת	מִתְקַטְּלוֹת

34.11 Hithpael Participle Diagnostics.

1. מִתְ prefix in every form. This unique prefix makes identification of the Hithpael Participle an easy matter.

2. Pathach under the first consonant of the verbal root.

3. Daghesh Forte in the second consonant of the verbal root.

Hithpael Participle Strong Verb

מִתְקַטֵּל

34.12 Metathesis. It has been emphasized that the Hithpael stem is easy to recognize with few exceptions. For the most part, these exceptions are occasioned by a phenomenon known as metathesis. *Metathesis* is a term used to describe *the transposition of two contiguous (side-by-side) consonants* in order to smooth out a word's pronunciation. In Hebrew, whenever the תְ of the Hithpael prefix or preformative precedes verbal roots beginning with ס, שׂ, שׁ or צ (sibilant or "s" sound consonants), the two consonants will switch places. For example, we would expect the Hithpael Perfect 3ms form of שָׁמַר to be הִתְשַׁמֵּר. Because of metathesis, however, the Hithpael Perfect 3ms form of שָׁמַר is הִשְׁתַּמֵּר. Notice how the תְ of the Hithpael prefix has switched places with the שׁ of the verbal root. Once again, this switching of the two consonants is called metathesis. You will need to be familiar with this phenomenon in order to correctly reconstruct the verbal root in those verbs in which metathesis occurs. Note the following additional examples.

סָתַר	he hid	הִסְתַּתֵּר	he hid himself
שָׂכַר	he hired	הִשְׂתַּכֵּר	he hired himself (earned wages)
צָדֵק	he is just	הִצְטַדֵּק[4]	he justified himself

---

[4] When the first consonant of the verbal root is צ (3 times), the תְ of the Hithpael

34.13 Assimilation of ת. When the first consonant of a verbal root is ז, ד, ט or ת, the ת of the Hithpael preformative or prefix will assimilate into the first consonant of the verbal root and remain as a Daghesh Forte.

דִּבֶּר he spoke   הִדַּבֵּר he spoke with

טָמֵא he was unclean   הִטַּמֵּא he became unclean

34.14 Summary.

1. In every form of every Hithpael strong verb conjugation, there is a Pathach under the first consonant of the verbal root and a Daghesh Forte in the second consonant of the verbal root. In the Perfect, Imperative, Infinitive Construct, and Infinitive Absolute, the prefix is הִת. The preformatives for the Imperfect are תִת, יִת, אֶת or נִת and the prefix for the Participle is מִת. These distinctive preformatives and prefixes make the Hithpael stem easy to identify with most verbs.

2. *Metathesis* is a term used to describe the transposition of two contiguous (side-by-side) consonants in order to smooth out a word's pronunciation. Whenever the ת of a Hithpael prefix or preformative precedes verbal roots beginning with ס, שׁ, שׂ or צ (sibilant or "s" sound consonants), the two consonants will switch places. Additionally, with ז, ד, ט or ת, the ת of the Hithpael preformative or prefix will assimilate into the first consonant of the verbal root and remain as a Daghesh Forte.

---

prefix will switch places with the first consonant of the verbal root. Additionally, the ת of the Hithpael prefix will change to ט (הִצְטַדֵּק ◄ הִתְצַדֵּק).

Hithpael Stem - Strong Verb

Perfect	Imperfect	Imperative	Infinitive Construct	Infinitive Absolute	Participle
הִתְקַטֵּל	יִתְקַטֵּל	הִתְקַטֵּל	הִתְקַטֵּל	הִתְקַטֵּל	מִתְקַטֵּל
הִתְקַטֵּל	יִתְקַטֵּל	הִתְקַטֵּל	הִתְקַטֵּל	הִתְקַטֵּל	מִתְקַטֵּל
הִתְקַטְּלָה	תִּתְקַטֵּל	הִתְקַטְּלִי			מִתְקַטֶּלֶת
הִתְקַטַּלְתָּ	תִּתְקַטֵּל	הִתְקַטְּלוּ			מִתְקַטְּלִים
הִתְקַטַּלְתְּ	תִּתְקַטְּלִי	הִתְקַטֵּלְנָה			מִתְקַטְּלוֹת
הִתְקַטַּלְתִּי	אֶתְקַטֵּל				
הִתְקַטְּלוּ	יִתְקַטְּלוּ				
הִתְקַטַּלְתֶּם	תִּתְקַטֵּלְנָה				
הִתְקַטַּלְתֶּן	תִּתְקַטְּלוּ				
הִתְקַטַּלְנוּ	תִּתְקַטֵּלְנָה				
	נִתְקַטֵּל				

34.15 Vocabulary.

מִקְדָּשׁ	sanctuary (75)
עוֹף	flying creatures, birds, insects; עוּף to fly (71)
עֵז	goat, goat's hair (74)
פָּלַל	(Hithpael) to pray, make intercession (84)
קִיר	wall (73)
שׁוֹפָר	trumpet, ram's horn (72)

34.16 In the Lord His God. Prepositional phrases can sometimes provide important information. In the Amalekite raid against David's town of Ziklag in 1 Sam 30, the prepositional phrase in verse 6, בַּיהוָה אֱלֹהָיו (in the Lord his God), may serve as an illustration.

The attack against Ziklag has left David and his band of men in complete despair. The settlement is destroyed and their possessions are gone but, more devastatingly, wives and children have been taken captive. Matters get worse as David's band of discontented wanderers (1 Sam 22:2) turn against him and are ready to stone him. David has been in tight spots before, but now the end seems imminent. However, this climactic catalogue of misfortune is abruptly interrupted by the declaration, "but David strengthened himself *in the* LORD *his God*" (30:6). We are not told specifically how David regained control of his troops, but this sentence may be regarded as the turning point of the narrative. Hereafter, David gradually gains the initiative and eventually recovers completely from his loss (30:18).

The verb חָזַק (Hithpael, "to strengthen oneself") has for a general range of meaning "political strength," "military strength," or "courage." In 1 Sam 30:6, the definition "courage" seems to fit the context best. The phrase יְהוָה plus אֱלֹהִים plus pronominal suffix is quite common in the Hebrew Bible and occurs frequently in the covenantal context of Deuteronomy. The frequency drops significantly, however, when the phrase is found in association with a preposition. With the preposition בְּ, it is attested either in a positive context: "Believe in the LORD your God" (בַּיהוָה אֱלֹהֵיכֶם [2 Chr 20:20]) or negative: "Against the LORD your God you have transgressed" (בַּיהוָה אֱלֹהָיִךְ [Jer 3:13]).

The text of 1 Sam 30:6 is noteworthy because it is the only instance where the verb, "to strengthen oneself" is modified by the phrase "in the LORD his God." By way of contrast, even close parallels fail to convey the same relationship between the verb and the prepositional phrase. Solomon "strengthened himself [חָזַק in the Hithpael] with regard to his kingdom, and the LORD his God was with him" (2 Chr 2:1). And, Jonathan "strengthened [חָזַק in the Piel] his hand in God" (1 Sam 23:16). Thus it seems "in the LORD his God" takes on an important function. It determines precisely the nature of the strength that David found: it was not a martial courage found deep within himself; it was not a regaining of emotional composure; instead, it was a personal courage grounded in covenantal trust and loyalty to his God.

Tom Petter
Assistant Professor of Old Testament
Gordon-Conwell Theological Seminary
South Hamilton, Massachusetts

Chapter 35

The Hithpael Stem - Weak Verbs

35.1 **Introduction**. In this chapter, we will study selected weak verb classes (Geminate, III-ה, and II-Guttural) in the Hithpael stem. It is important to observe that most of the strong verb diagnostics are retained in Geminate and III-ה verbs. It is only the II-Guttural class of weak verbs that exhibits significant variation from the strong verb diagnostics. This variation is due to the fact that the guttural in second root position cannot take the Daghesh Forte of the Hithpael stem. Your study of II-Guttural verbs in the Piel (27.7-11) and Pual (29.5-9) will have prepared you for this study of Hithpael II-Guttural verbs.

35.2 **Geminate Paradigms and Diagnostics**.

Participle	Infinitive Absolute	Infinitive Construct	Imperative	Imperfect	Perfect
מִתְפַּלֵּל	הִתְפַּלֵּל	הִתְפַּלֵּל	הִתְפַּלֵּל	יִתְפַּלֵּל	הִתְפַּלֵּל
מִתְפַּלֵּל	הִתְפַּלֵּל	הִתְפַּלֵּל	הִתְפַּלֵּל	יִתְפַּלֵּל	הִתְפַּלֵּל
מִתְפַּלֶּלֶת			הִתְפַּלְלִי	תִּתְפַּלֵּל	הִתְפַּלְלָה
מִתְפַּלְלִים			הִתְפַּלְלוּ	תִּתְפַּלֵּל	הִתְפַּלַּלְתָּ
מִתְפַּלְלוֹת			הִתְפַּלֵּלְנָה	תִּתְפַּלְלִי	הִתְפַּלַּלְתְּ
				אֶתְפַּלֵּל	הִתְפַּלַּלְתִּי
				יִתְפַּלְלוּ	הִתְפַּלְלוּ
				תִּתְפַּלֵּלְנָה	הִתְפַּלַּלְתֶּם
				תִּתְפַּלְלוּ	הִתְפַּלַּלְתֶּן
				תִּתְפַּלֵּלְנָה	הִתְפַּלַּלְנוּ
				נִתְפַּלֵּל	

35.3 Geminate Notes.

1. Most Geminate verbs retain all of the Hithpael strong verb diagnostics.

2. With the Geminate verb פָּלַל (to pray), however, there is one minor exception. Note that the Daghesh Forte in the second consonant of the verbal root may be given up when this consonant is followed by Shewa, as in the Perfect 3cp (הִתְפַּלְלוּ). In light of the fact that all other strong verb diagnostics are retained, this minor variation should not present any significant difficulty.

35.4 III-ה Paradigms and Diagnostics.

Perfect		Imperfect	Imperative	Infinitive Construct	Infinitive Absolute	Participle
הִתְגַּלֶּה		יִתְגַּלֶּה	הִתְגַּלֵּה	הִתְגַּלּוֹת		מִתְגַּלֶּה
הִתְגַּלָּה		יִתְגַּלֶּה	הִתְגַּלֵּה	הִתְגַּלּוֹת		מִתְגַּלֶּה
הִתְגַּלְּתָה		תִּתְגַּלֶּה	הִתְגַּלִּי			מִתְגַּלָּה
הִתְגַּלִּיתָ		תִּתְגַּלֶּה	הִתְגַּלּוּ			מִתְגַּלִּים
הִתְגַּלִּית		תִּתְגַּלִּי	הִתְגַּלֶּינָה			מִתְגַּלּוֹת
הִתְגַּלִּיתִי		אֶתְגַּלֶּה				
הִתְגַּלּוּ		יִתְגַּלּוּ				
הִתְגַּלִּיתֶם		תִּתְגַּלֶּינָה				
הִתְגַּלִּיתֶן		תִּתְגַּלּוּ				
הִתְגַּלִּינוּ		תִּתְגַּלֶּינָה				
		נִתְגַּלֶּה				

35.5 III-ה Notes.

1. All of the strong verb diagnostics are retained in the Hithpael forms of this weak verb class.

2. The endings that are present on these III-ה Hithpael conjugations are precisely the same ones that were seen on the Qal and all of the other derived stems previously studied.

35.6   **II-Guttural Paradigms and Diagnostics: Virtual Doubling.** You know
that a Daghesh Forte in the second consonant of the verbal root is a
diagnostic feature of the Piel, Pual, and Hithpael. A guttural in the
second root position, however, will reject this Daghesh Forte. In your
study of Piel and Pual II-Guttural verbs, you learned that the guttural's
rejection of the Daghesh Forte results in either virtual doubling or
compensatory lengthening. Hithpael II-Guttural verbs respond in the
same way. The following II-Guttural verb exhibits virtual doubling.

Perfect	*Imperfect*	*Imperative*	*Infinitive Construct*	*Infinitive Absolute*	*Participle*
הִתְנַחֵם	יִתְנַחֵם	הִתְנַחֵם	הִתְנַחֵם	הִתְנַחֵם	מִתְנַחֵם
הִתְנַחֵם	יִתְנַחֵם	הִתְנַחֵם	הִתְנַחֵם	הִתְנַחֵם	מִתְנַחֵם
הִתְנַחֲמָה	תִּתְנַחֵם	הִתְנַחֲמִי			מִתְנַחֶמֶת
הִתְנַחַׁמְתָּ	תִּתְנַחֵם	הִתְנַחֲמוּ			מִתְנַחֲמִים
הִתְנַחַמְתְּ	תִּתְנַחֲמִי	הִתְנַחַׁמְנָה			מִתְנַחֲמוֹת
הִתְנַחַׁמְתִּי	אֶתְנַחֵם				
הִתְנַחֲמוּ	יִתְנַחֲמוּ				
הִתְנַחַמְתֶּם	תִּתְנַחַׁמְנָה				
הִתְנַחַמְתֶּן	תִּתְנַחֲמוּ				
הִתְנַחַׁמְנוּ	תִּתְנַחַׁמְנָה				
	נִתְנַחֵם				

35.7   **II-Guttural Notes: Virtual Doubling.**

1. With the exception of the Daghesh Forte in the second consonant
   of the verbal root, all of the other strong verb diagnostics are
   retained.

2. The guttural consonant in second root position rejects the Daghesh
   Forte of the Hithpael stem. II-Guttural verbs with virtual doubling
   retain the diagnostic Pathach under the first root consonant.

35.8 II-Guttural Paradigms and Diagnostics: Compensatory Lengthening.

Perfect	Imperfect	Imperative	Infinitive Construct	Infinitive Absolute	Participle
הִתְבָּרֵךְ	יִתְבָּרֵךְ	הִתְבָּרֵךְ	הִתְבָּרֵךְ	הִתְבָּרֵךְ	מִתְבָּרֵךְ
הִתְבָּרֵךְ	יִתְבָּרֵךְ	הִתְבָּרֵךְ	הִתְבָּרֵךְ	הִתְבָּרֵךְ	מִתְבָּרֵךְ
הִתְבָּרְכָה	תִּתְבָּרֵךְ	הִתְבָּרְכִי			מִתְבָּרֶכֶת
הִתְבָּרַכְתָּ	תִּתְבָּרֵךְ	הִתְבָּרְכוּ			מִתְבָּרְכִים
הִתְבָּרַכְתְּ	תִּתְבָּרְכִי	הִתְבָּרֵכְנָה			מִתְבָּרְכוֹת
הִתְבָּרַכְתִּי	אֶתְבָּרֵךְ				
הִתְבָּרְכוּ	יִתְבָּרְכוּ				
הִתְבָּרַכְתֶּם	תִּתְבָּרֵכְנָה				
הִתְבָּרַכְתֶּן	תִּתְבָּרְכוּ				
הִתְבָּרַכְנוּ	תִּתְבָּרֵכְנָה				
	נִתְבָּרֵךְ				

35.9 II-Guttural Notes: Compensatory Lengthening.

1. In this II-Guttural (ר) paradigm with compensatory lengthening, only the distinctive prefixes and preformatives of the strong verb diagnostics remain.

2. The ר in second root position rejects the Daghesh Forte of the Hithpael stem and causes the preceding Pathach to undergo compensatory lengthening. Compared to the Hithpael strong verb diagnostics, there is neither the Daghesh Forte in the second consonant of the verbal root nor is there the Pathach beneath the first root consonant. Despite these significant changes, the distinctive preformatives and prefixes in the various conjugations should make stem identification easy.

35.10 Summary: Hithpael Diagnostics.

	Perfect	*Imperfect*	*Imperative*	*Infinitive Construct*	*Infinitive Absolute*	*Participle*
Strong	הִתְקַטֵּל	יִתְקַטֵּל	הִתְקַטֵּל	הִתְקַטֵּל	הִתְקַטֵּל	מִתְקַטֵּל
Geminate	הִתְפַּלֵּל	יִתְפַּלֵּל	הִתְפַּלֵּל	הִתְפַּלֵּל	הִתְפַּלֵּל	מִתְפַּלֵּל
III-ה	הִתְגַּלָּה	יִתְגַּלֶּה	הִתְגַּלֵּה	הִתְגַּלּוֹת		מִתְגַּלֶּה
II-Gutt[1]	הִתְנֶחָם	יִתְנֶחָם	הִתְנֶחָם	הִתְנֶחָם	הִתְנֶחָם	מִתְנֶחָם
II-Gutt[2]	הִתְבָּרֵךְ	יִתְבָּרֵךְ	הִתְבָּרֵךְ	הִתְבָּרֵךְ	הִתְבָּרֵךְ	מִתְבָּרֵךְ

35.11 Vocabulary.

Nouns

בַּרְזֶל	iron (76)
עֵד	witness (69)
צָרָה	distress, anxiety, trouble (70)
שׁוֹר	ox, bull, cow (79)
שֻׁלְחָן	table (71)
תְּפִלָּה	prayer (77)

35.12 In the Cool of the Day? Our knowledge of Hebrew is not complete, and may never be. But study of other, sister languages in the ancient Near East (cognate studies) can sometimes increase our understanding of biblical Hebrew. A case in point is Gen 3:8, a verse that has long been mistranslated and misunderstood. Cognate studies can sweep away the guesswork that has long characterized translations of this verse

---

[1] II-Guttural with virtual doubling

[2] II-Guttural with compensatory lengthening

and give us an accurate translation that also makes more sense theologically.

The *crux interpretum* has been the Hebrew phrase, לְרוּחַ הַיּוֹם. The traditional English translation has been "in the cool of the day" or something of that sort. This translation is based on a guess made by the Septuagint translators, who thought that רוּחַ meant "wind" and יוֹם meant "day." Hence, the sense would be something like "in the windy or breezy part of the day." St. Jerome followed suit in his Latin (Vulgate) translation, and so the standard interpretation was established.

Now רוּחַ can certainly mean "wind," and יוֹם can certainly mean "day." But anyone who knows Hebrew and reads the phrase in question finds the whole expression rather odd. It is odd enough to raise the question, Can't there be some other way to translate this phrase? And there is.

Cognate studies, specifically in Akkadian, have revealed a cognate word for the Hebrew יוֹם (day). It is the Akkadian word, *umu*, which also means "day." We call this *umu*[1] because studies have revealed a homonym, or an *umu*[2] in Akkadian, that means "storm." The question naturally arises, What if there is a cognate word in Hebrew, a יוֹם[2] that means not "day" but "storm"? There is such a Hebrew cognate, rarely used in the Hebrew Bible, but attested nevertheless. Holladay notes it in his lexicon, although not in Gen 3:8.[3]

On this understanding, the translation of Gen 3:8 changes significantly. It now reads: "Then the man and his wife heard the thunderous voice of Yahweh God as he was going back and forth in the garden in the *wind of the storm* and they hid from Yahweh God among the trees of the garden."

Yahweh has come to judge his disobedient servants. So he comes in the first storm theophany, a manner of coming later associated in the Old Testament with the "Day of Yahweh." Since he comes in stormy glory, other terms in the verse merit an altered translation. "Voice" (קוֹל) now becomes "thunderous voice," as at Sinai (Ex 19:16). "Walking" (מִתְהַלֵּךְ) now becomes "going back and forth" like the lightning flashes of Ps 77:17-19.

---

[3] W. L. Holladay, *A Concise Hebrew and Aramaic Lexicon of the Old Testament* (Grand Rapids: Eerdmans, 1971) 131.

We can now translate accurately and sensibly a verse that has long seemed puzzling. More than one sermon has portrayed God and Adam walking together in the garden "in the cool of the day," as though they were taking a pleasant after-dinner stroll. The linguistic clarification brings with it greater theological clarity. Yahweh God is coming in storm theophany to judge his disobedient servants as he will come again on the day of Yahweh – as Jesus puts it, on the clouds with great power and glory – to judge a disobedient world.[4]

Jeffrey J. Niehaus
Professor of Old Testament
Gordon-Conwell Theological Seminary
South Hamilton, Massachusetts

35.13 Advanced Information: The Hithpolel Stem. The Hithpolel is the equivalent of the Hithpael stem for certain Biconsonantal (and Geminate) verbs. Like the Polel (27.15) and Polal (29.13), the Hithpolel of Biconsonantal verbs is characterized by a Holem Waw after the first consonant and the duplication of the second root consonant. Finally, note that the Hithpolel is distinguished from the Polel only by its distinctive prefixes (for example, הִת).

Perfect	Imperfect	Imperative	Infinitive Construct	Infinitive Absolute	Participle
הִתְרוֹמֵם	יִתְרוֹמֵם	הִתְרוֹמֵם	הִתְרוֹמֵם	הִתְרוֹמֵם	מִתְרוֹמֵם
הִתְרוֹמְמָה	תִּתְרוֹמֵם	הִתְרוֹמְמִי			מִתְרוֹמֶּמֶת
הִתְרוֹמַֿמְתָּ	תִּתְרוֹמֵם	הִתְרוֹמְמוּ			מִתְרוֹמְמִים
הִתְרוֹמַמְתְּ	תִּתְרוֹמְמִי	הִתְרוֹמַֿמְנָה			מִתְרוֹמְמוֹת
הִתְרוֹמַֿמְתִּי	אֶתְרוֹמֵם				
הִתְרוֹמְמוּ	יִתְרוֹמְמוּ				
הִתְרוֹמַֿמְתֶּם	תִּתְרוֹמַֿמְנָה				
הִתְרוֹמַמְתֶּן	תִּתְרוֹמְמוּ				
הִתְרוֹמַֿמְנוּ	תִּתְרוֹמַֿמְנָה				
	נִתְרוֹמֵם				

---

[4] For a fuller discussion of the verse and its theological significance, see J. J. Niehaus, *God at Sinai* (Grand Rapids: Zondervan, 1995) 155-59.

35.14 Advanced Information: The Verb חָוָה. The verb חָוָה (to bow down, worship) appears 173 times in the Hebrew Bible and requires special attention because it occurs only in a stem called the Hishtaphel.[5] These verbal forms are easy to identify because of the distinctive prefixes and preformatives of the Hishtaphel stem (for example, הָשְׁתַּ in the Perfect). Note also that חָוָה is a III-ה verb and will exhibit the distinctive endings of this weak verb class, inflecting quite regularly. The following chart lists the prefixes of the Hishtaphel stem along with some of the more common forms of this verb. This chart is followed by a number of biblical examples.

Perfect	הָשְׁתַּ		
	הָשְׁתַּחֲוָה	3ms	he worshiped
	הָשְׁתַּחֲווּ	3cp	they worshiped
	הָשְׁתַּחֲוִיתֶם	2mp	you worshiped
Imperfect	יִשְׁתַּ		
	יִשְׁתַּחֲוֶה	3ms	he will worship
	וַיִּשְׁתַּחוּ	3ms	he worshiped (Waw Consecutive)
	תִּשְׁתַּחֲוֶה	2ms	you will worship
	אֶשְׁתַּחֲוֶה	1cs	I will worship
	יִשְׁתַּחֲווּ	3mp	they will worship
Imperative	הָשְׁתַּ		
	הָשְׁתַּחֲווּ	2mp	(you) worship!
Inf Construct	הָשְׁתַּ		
	הָשְׁתַּחֲוֹת		to worship, bow down
Participle	מָשְׁתַּ		
	מָשְׁתַּחֲוֶה	ms	worshiping, bowing down
	מָשְׁתַּחֲוִים	mp	worshiping, bowing down

וְהִשְׁתַּחֲווּ לַיהוָה בְּהַר הַקֹּדֶשׁ

(And) they will worship the Lord on the holy mountain.
(Isa 27:13)

---

[5] Some older lexical sources identify the verbal root as שָׁחָה and the stem as Hithpalel.

וַיִּשְׁתַּחוּ אַבְרָהָם לִפְנֵי עַם הָאָרֶץ

(And) Abraham bowed down before the people of the land.

(Gen 23:12)

וְנִשְׁתַּחֲוֶה וְנָשׁוּבָה אֲלֵיכֶם

(And) we will worship and we will return to you.

(Gen 22:5)

נָפְלוּ לִפְנֵי יְהוָה לְהִשְׁתַּחֲוֺת לַיהוָה

(They) fell down before the LORD to worship the LORD.

(2 Chr 20:18)

Chapter 36

Introduction to the Hebrew Bible

36.1   **The Masoretic Text and *BHS*.** At this point in your study of Hebrew, you have translated (both in the grammar and in the workbook) a few hundred biblical phrases and verses from various sections of the Hebrew Bible. The text that you have been translating is called the Masoretic Text (abbreviated MT). The term "Masoretic" is derived from the Hebrew word מָסוֹרָה (tradition) and refers to the textual tradition of Jewish scholars known as Masoretes. These scholars labored in the preservation of the biblical text between the sixth and tenth centuries A.D.

The Masoretes perfected a system of vowel pointing that was added to the consonantal text, thereby graphically representing the vowel tradition that had been transmitted orally until that time. You will recall that Hebrew, in its earliest stages, did not have a written vowel system (2.1). Additionally, the Masoretes developed a system of symbols to mark word accents in order to assist in the reading and recitation of the text. They also collected and prepared an elaborate set of notes that accompanied the text in the top, bottom, and side margins. These laborious efforts (vowel pointing, a system of accents and notes) helped to ensure the accurate transmission of the biblical text.

This Tiberian[1] Masoretic text was regarded by early scholars as authoritative and is similarly accepted by modern scholarship. It is the textual tradition that is used for what is now the standard edition of the Hebrew Bible, entitled *Biblia Hebraica Stuttgartensia*.[2] The text of *BHS*, as it is commonly abbreviated, is a copy of the Leningrad Codex, an eleventh century A.D. manuscript located in the Leningrad Public Library. Your first exposure to the pages of *BHS* can be a bit intimidating with its myriad of marks, symbols, and enigmatic entries that surround the Hebrew text. In the following discussion, we will identify and briefly explain some of the major features located on the pages of your

---

[1]   The term "Tiberian" refers to the city of Tiberias, on the western shore of the Sea of Galilee, where the Masoretes lived and worked. The standard Masoretic text is also known as the Ben Asher text, named after the family of Tiberian scholars who completed the final editing.

[2]   K. Elliger and W. Rudolph, eds., *Biblia Hebraica Stuttgartensia* (New York: American Bible Society, 1987).

Hebrew Bible. For your reference, the first page of the book of Genesis is printed below. Additionally, in the left margin, we have identified some of the basic *BHS* page components.

Book Title

Masorah Parva (Mp)

Masorah Magna (Mm) Register

Textual Apparatus

36.2 **Looking at *BHS*.** Open your Hebrew Bible to Gen 1:1. Remember to open it from the right. After several pages of introduction, you will locate the first page of the Hebrew Scriptures at the beginning of Genesis (page 1 of *BHS*).

1. *Book Title.* The main body of the page is given to the biblical text in Hebrew. At the top of the page, the book is identified as Genesis with the Hebrew word בראשית in bold characters to

the right. This is the Hebrew name of the book. You will notice that Gen 1:1 begins with this same word but it is vocalized בְּרֵאשִׁית (in the beginning). Ancient literary works were frequently titled by the first word or phrase of the composition. Similarly, the book of Exodus is titled ואלה שמות at the top of page 86, and the first verse begins וְאֵלֶּה שְׁמוֹת (these are the names of). Within the Pentateuch (Torah), the books of Leviticus (page 158) and Deuteronomy (page 283) are also named in this way. The book of Numbers (page 209), however, does not take its Hebrew name from the first word or phrase of the book. It is called במדבר (בְּמִדְבַּר, in the wilderness), the fifth Hebrew word in the first verse. Many books, especially the prophetical works (and others), are named after the main character. You should be able to identify the Hebrew titles for most Old Testament books.

2. *Chapter and Verse.* Like most English Bibles, the text of the Hebrew Bible is divided into chapters and verses. There was no such numbering system in the original Hebrew texts. This was the work of Christian scholars in the thirteenth century and later. You should also note that the chapter and verse divisions of the Hebrew Bible do not always correspond with the divisions of our English Bibles. This phenomenon is especially common in the book of Psalms. The elements of English punctuation (such as a comma, period, semicolon, question mark, exclamation point, etc.) do not appear in the Hebrew Bible. The end of each verse is marked, however, with what looks like a large colon (׃). This symbol is called Sof Pasuq and means "end of verse" in Hebrew. The Sof Pasuq is the equivalent of a period in English punctuation.[3] In Gen 1:1, this symbol occurs after the ץ of the last word (הָאָרֶץ׃).

3. *Accent Marks.* On any page of *BHS*, you will see a number of symbols (placed either above or beneath words) that you do not recognize. Most of these symbols are accent marks.[4] Imposed

---

[3] Though the Sof Pasuq designates the end of a verse, its presence does not always mark the end of a sentence. See, for example, the use of Sof Pasuq at the end of Gen 22:16.

[4] There are two systems of accent used in the Hebrew Bible, though there is some overlap between the two. The books of Psalms, Proverbs, and Job employ an accent system that differs from the other books. Some accents are placed after the stressed syllable (postpositive) and others are placed before the stressed syllable (prepositive), but most accent marks appear on the stressed syllable.

upon the text is a complex system of conjunctive and disjunctive accents that serves to mark the stress in individual words and, more importantly, to facilitate the reading, recitation, and understanding of the text by marking logical units of thought.[5]

The disjunctive accents are the most important of the two types because they usually divide a verse into two or more units of thought. The use of the major disjunctive accents is comparable to using a comma, semicolon, or period in an English sentence. It is important to be able to identify the major disjunctive accents in order to more easily recognize a verse's primary units of thought.

The two major disjunctive accents are Athnak and Silluq. The Athnak marks the end of the first major division in a verse. In Gen 1:1, this accent mark occurs under the ה in אֱלֹהִים (God). The Silluq marks the end of the second major division in a verse and usually appears under the accented syllable of the last word in a verse. In Gen 1:1, this accent mark occurs under the א in הָאָרֶץ (the earth). Note that the Silluq is similar in appearance to the Metheg (3.7). In the recitation of the text, these are the major points of pause. The conjunctive accents do not divide semantic units. They appear on words between the disjunctive accents and serve to mark some kind of close syntactical connection to the next word. For now, become familiar with the major disjunctive accents noted above.[6]

36.3 **Pausal Forms.** It was noted above that the accents Athnak and Silluq mark the two major points of pause in the recitation of the text. Words that occur at these major points of verse division are said to be "in pause" because of the reader's inclination to pause or break the stride of recitation at these points. Words that are "in pause" will often show slight changes in their spelling. The following are some of the most common changes.

1. Pathach will change to Qamets. For example, קָטַל (he killed) will become קָטָל and עַם (people) will become עָם.

---

[5] Accents are also closely related to the musical rendition of the Hebrew text called "cantillation."

[6] For a full discussion of Hebrew accents, consult W. R. Scott, *A Simplified Guide to BHS* (Berkeley: BIBAL, 1987) 23-34 or P. Joüon, *A Grammar of Biblical Hebrew* (Rome: Pontifical Biblical Institute, 1996) 61-74.

2. Seghol will change to Qamets in some Segholate nouns. For example, אֶרֶץ (earth, land) will become אָרֶץ.

3. The Shewa connecting vowel of the 2ms pronominal suffix will change to Seghol. For example, סוּסְךָ (your horse) will become סוּסֶךָ.

4. Words that are accented on the ultima may undergo an accent shift to the penultima with resulting vowel change. For example, the Shewa of the Qal Perfect 3fs (כָּתְבָה) may become Qamets (כָּתָבָה) when in pause because of the retraction of the accent. In this example, a Vocal Shewa is changed to a full vowel. Similarly, אֲנִי (with accent on the ultima) becomes אָנִי when in pause. Here, a Hateph vowel is changed to a full vowel.

36.4 **The Masorah of *BHS*.** As noted above, one of the important and interesting contributions of the Masoretes was their system of marginal notes. These notes are called the Masorah and are traditionally categorized into two main groups: the marginal Masorah and the final Masorah. The category of marginal Masorah is further divided into the Masorah parva (small Masorah) in the outer side margins and the Masorah magna (large Masorah), traditionally located in the top and bottom margins of the text. The Masorah parva consists of word-use statistics, similar documentation for expressions or certain phraseology, observations on full or defective writing, references to the Kethiv-Qere readings (see 36.5), and more. Though some of this information seems trivial and inconsequential to the modern reader, these observations are the result of a passionate zeal to safeguard the accurate transmission of the sacred text.

The Masorah magna, in measure, is an expanded Masorah parva. Oftentimes, the notations simply provide greater depth or specificity beyond those in the Masorah parva. Traditionally, the Masorah magna was recorded in the top and bottom margins of the text. Though the Masorah magna is not printed in *BHS*, there is a register of notations (located between the last line of Hebrew text and the lowest register of textual variants) that provides access to this information that has been published in separate volumes. Given that the Masorah magna is abbreviated Mm, this is sometimes called the "Mm register."

The final Masorah is located at the end of biblical books or after certain sections of the text, such as at the end of the Torah. The final Masorah contains information and statistics regarding the number of words in a book or section, the middle word of a book, or even the middle consonant of a book. For example, after the conclusion of Deuteronomy, we learn that the book has 955 verses and that the precise midpoint falls on עַל־פִּי in Deut 17:10. Additionally, we learn that the Torah has 5,845 verses, 79,856 words and 400,945 letters. The purpose for this statistical information was to ensure accuracy in the transmission of the text with the production of subsequent copies that were done by hand.

36.5   **The Kethiv-Qere**. The most important of the Masoretic notes are those that detail the Kethiv-Qere that are located in the Masorah parva in the outside margins of *BHS*. Given that the Masoretes would not alter the sacred consonantal text, the Kethiv-Qere notes were a way of "correcting" or commenting on the text for any number of reasons (grammatical, theological, aesthetic, etc.) deemed important by the copyist. The consonantal (uncorrected) wording of the text is the Kethiv, a term that is a transliteration of the Aramaic כְּתִיב ("what is written"). The Kethiv is the reading that comes literally from the consonantal text. The reading that is suggested for "correction" by the Masorete is the Qere, a term that is a transliteration of the Aramaic קְרֵי ("what is to be read").

The Qere is signaled by a small circle that is written above the word in the text. This circle refers the reader to a marginal note where the consonants to be read are given. The vowel points of the Qere were placed under the consonants in the text. In the Masorah parva, in the outside margin, the Qere is noted with the consonant ק, over which is located a dot (קֹ), an abbreviation for Qere. The word(s) to be read in the margin are printed above this symbol (for example, see היצא in the outside margin at Gen 8:17). There are hundreds of Kethiv-Qere notations in the Hebrew Bible of varying significance.

A few common words are always read differently than the reading suggested by the consonantal text. This phenomenon is known as a "perpetual Kethiv-Qere." Perhaps the most important example is the divine name יהוה which was never pronounced out of reverence. The consonantal spelling (Kethiv) is יהוה but the perpetual Qere is אֲדֹנָי. The vowels of אֲדֹנָי were superimposed on the four consonants of the divine name, producing יְהֹוָה or יְהוָה.[7] Because of its frequency, this Qere reading was not written in the margin with every occurrence. In this case, the vowels of אֲדֹנָי with the consonants of the divine name served as a reminder to ensure reverence.[8]

---

[7] In some instances, the Qere reading tells the reader to pronounce אֱלֹהִים.

36.6 **The Textual Apparatus of *BHS* and Textual Criticism**. At the bottom of each page of *BHS*, below the Mm register, there is a collection of editorial notes in what is called the *textual apparatus*. In these notes, the editors of *BHS* have assembled a selection of important readings, textual variants, and (conjectural) emendations that do not appear in the Leningrad Codex (the text of your Hebrew Bible). The textual apparatus of *BHS* provides students with a point of entry into the exegetical discipline of textual criticism.

In the study of biblical (textual) criticism, the term "autograph" refers to the original copy of an author's writing, such as that produced by the prophet Isaiah. The original copy of every book of the Bible has been lost; that is, no autograph of any biblical book has survived or is known at the present time. All known biblical manuscripts are only later copies of the original autographs. From ancient times and until the invention of the printing press, biblical manuscripts were copied by hand with the inevitable result that textual corruptions or errors were introduced into the text, despite the painstaking efforts of scribes to preserve the accuracy of the text. Some books and sections of the Old Testament are relatively free of textual problems (the Pentateuch, Judges, Jonah). Other sections present the reader with an array of textual difficulties (Samuel-Kings, Psalms, Job, Ezekiel, Zechariah).

Textual problems are generally categorized as either unintentional or intentional. Unintentional errors in the copying of a manuscript include the confusion of letters that look alike, the confusion of letters that sound alike, the accidental omission of a letter(s) or a word(s), the accidental repeating of a letter(s) or a word(s), incorrect word division, and a number of other similar errors. Intentional errors in the copying of a manuscript include the altering of a text because the scribe deemed the wording to be disrespectful to God, the substitution of a euphemism for a word or expression that the scribe deemed to be indelicate or offensive, and lastly, the introduction of glosses into the text for the purpose of clarification or explanation.[9] Because of these kinds of errors, most scholars acknowledge the need to do textual criticism in order to

---

[8] Other examples of perpetual Qere include הוא (Kethiv) for הִיא (Qere) and יְרוּשָׁלַם (Kethiv) for יְרוּשָׁלַיִם (Qere).

[9] For an excellent discussion of scribal errors with illustrative examples, see E. R. Brotzman, *Old Testament Textual Criticism* (Grand Rapids: Baker, 1994) 107-21; Paul D. Wegner, *A Student's Guide to Textual Criticism of the Bible* (Downers Grove: InterVarsity, 2006) 44-57.

restore what is considered to be a more original reading of the text. To this end, the discipline of textual criticism has two primary purposes: (1) to reconstruct the biblical text as close to its original wording as can be established in light of existing manuscript evidence and (2) to document and better understand the transmission of the text through time.

In its fullest dimension, textual criticism involves the task of assembling and translating the full range of ancient manuscript evidence, discerning all the known variant readings, evaluating the quality of each ancient witness, evaluating the quality of each reading, determining the most original reading, and sometimes even the conjectural emendation of the text. The *BHS* textual apparatus has done a good deal of this work already, though neither exhaustively nor perfectly. There are a number of works currently available that explain the layout, symbols, and use of this apparatus.[10]

As a postscript to this brief introduction to textual criticism, it is important to emphasize that the text of the Old Testament has been transmitted with remarkable care and accuracy. The need for textual criticism should not undermine, in any measure, our belief in the inspiration and authority of the Old Testament or our confidence in its providential preservation through the centuries.

36.7   **The Ordering of the Books of the Hebrew Bible.** The Hebrew Bible is composed of twenty-four books arranged in three major divisions: the Law (תּוֹרָה), the Prophets (נְבִיאִים), and the Writings (כְּתוּבִים). The Hebrew Scriptures are sometimes referred to as the Tanak (also Tanach), an acronym derived from the initial letters of the names of the three divisions. The Law is composed of the books of Genesis, Exodus, Leviticus, Numbers and Deuteronomy. The remaining two divisions of the Hebrew Bible have a different ordering and numbering of books compared to the various Christian Bibles. The Prophets comprise eight books: the former Prophets, consisting of Joshua, Judges, 1 and 2 Samuel (counted as one book), 1 and 2 Kings (also counted as one book); and

---

[10] The most important and helpful resources are E. R. Brotzman, *Old Testament Textual Criticism* (Grand Rapids: Baker, 1994); W. R. Scott, *A Simplified Guide to BHS* (Berkeley: BIBAL, 1987); R. Wonnenberger, *Understanding BHS: A Manual for the Uses of Biblia Hebraica Stuttgartensia* (Rome: Pontifical Biblical Institute, 1984); P. Rüger, *An English Key to the Latin Words and Abbreviations and Symbols of Biblia Hebraica Stuttgartensia* (Stuttgart: German Bible Society, 1985); E. Würthwein, *The Text of the Old Testament* (Grand Rapids: Eerdmans, 1979).

the four Latter Prophets, containing Isaiah, Jeremiah, Ezekiel, and the Twelve (the Minor Prophets counted as one). The Writings number eleven books that are ordered in various ways.[11] The sequential ordering in *BHS* is Psalms, Job, Proverbs, Ruth, Song of Songs (Canticles), Ecclesiastes (Qoheleth), Lamentations, Esther, Daniel, Ezra-Nehemiah (counted as one book), and 1 and 2 Chronicles (also counted as one book). You should become familiar with the arrangement and sequential ordering of the biblical books in *BHS*.

36.8 Selected Resources for Further Study.

1. **Hebrew Bibles.**

Dotan, A., ed. *Biblia Hebraica Leningradensia*. Peabody: Hendrickson, 2001.

Elliger, K., and W. Rudolph, eds. *Biblia Hebraica Stuttgartensia*. New York: American Bible Society, 1997 (now available in paperback, 2001).

2. **Reference Grammars.**

Gesenius' Hebrew Grammar. Edited and enlarged by E. Kautzsch. Revised by A. E. Cowley. Oxford: Oxford University Press, 1910.

Joüon, P. *A Grammar of Biblical Hebrew*. 2 vols. Translated and revised by T. Muraoka. Rome: Pontifical Biblical Institute, 1996.

Waltke, B. K., and M. O'Connor. *An Introduction to Biblical Hebrew Syntax*. Winona Lake: Eisenbrauns, 1990.

3. **Hebrew Lexicons.**

Brown, F., S. R. Driver, and C. A. Briggs. *The New Brown-Driver-Briggs-Gesenius Hebrew and English Lexicon*. Peabody: Hendrickson, 1979.

Holladay, W. L. *A Concise Hebrew and Aramaic Lexicon of the Old Testament*. Grand Rapids: Eerdmans, 1988.

---

[11] The study of the development and ordering of the Hebrew canon is an interesting and complex topic, especially for the Writings. For a helpful introduction, see R. K. Harrison, *Introduction to the Old Testament* (Grand Rapids: Eerdmans, 1969) 260-88.

Köhler, L., W. Baumgartner, and J. Stamm. *The Hebrew and Aramaic Lexicon of the Old Testament*. Study Edition. 2 vols. Translated and edited by M. E. J. Richardson. Boston: Brill, 2001.

4. **Understanding and Using *BHS* for Old Testament Exegesis.**

Brotzman, E. R. *Old Testament Textual Criticism: A Practical Introduction*. Grand Rapids: Baker, 1994.

Kelly, P. H., D. S. Mynatt, and T. G. Crawford. *The Masorah of Biblia Hebraica Stuttgartensia*. Grand Rapids: Eerdmans, 1998.

Scott, W. R. *A Simplified Guide to BHS*. Berkley: BIBAL, 1987.

Soulen, R. N. *Handbook of Biblical Criticism*. Altanta: John Knox, 1981.

Stuart, D. *Old Testament Exegesis: A Primer for Students and Pastors*. Philadelphia: Westminster, 2001.

Van Pelt, Miles V., and Gary D. Pratico. *Graded Reader of Biblical Hebrew : A Guide to Reading the Hebrew Bible*. Grand Rapids: Zondervan, 2006.

Wegner, Paul D. *A Student's Guide to Textual Criticism of the Bible*. Downers Grove: InterVarsity, 2006.

Wonneberger, R. *Understanding BHS: A Manual for the Users of Biblia Hebraica Stuttgartensia*. Rome: Pontifical Biblical Institute, 1984.

Würthwein, E. *The Text of the Old Testament*. Grand Rapids: Eerdmans, 1979.

5. **Vocabulary Resources.**

Van Pelt, Miles V., and Gary D. Pratico. *The Vocabulary Guide to Biblical Hebrew*. Grand Rapids: Zondervan, 2003.

Van Pelt, Miles V., and Gary D. Pratico. *Old Testament Hebrew Vocabulary Cards*. Grand Rapids: Zondervan, 2004.

Van Pelt, Miles V., and Gary D. Pratico. *Basics of Biblical Hebrew Vocabulary Audio*. Read by Jonathan T. Pennington. Grand Rapids: Zondervan, 2006.

6. **Electronic Resources.**

> Mac platform: *Accordance Bible Software*. Developed by OakSoft Software, Inc. (www.accordancebible.com)

> PC platform: *Greek and Hebrew Library 6.0*. Developed by Zondervan. Powered by Pradis. (www.zondervan.com)

> PC platform: *BibleWorks*. Developed by Hermeneutika (www.bibleworks.com)

> PC platform: *Logos Bible Software*. (www.logos.com)

36.9   **A Still Small Voice?** The prophet Elijah has a famous triumph over the prophets of Baal on Mt. Carmel (1 Kgs 18:17-40). The Lord shows who is truly God by answering the prophet's prayer with fire. For a time, God's people seem to repent. But in the next chapter, in a move of questionable courage, Elijah flees Queen Jezebel when she threatens to have him killed in retaliation. With angelic aid, he makes it to Mt. Horeb, where he encounters Yahweh in storm theophany, much as Moses had long before. When Moses and Israel encountered Yahweh, he came in a dark cloud with "thunderous sounds" (קֹלֹת, Ex 19:16), such that the mountain trembled – as did the people! Now, however, Elijah meets God and hears, according to the traditional translations, "a still small voice" (קוֹל, KJV) or a "gentle whisper" (קוֹל, NIV). What is wrong with this picture?

Whenever Yahweh appears in storm theophany in the Old Testament, the Hebrew word קוֹל is properly and logically translated "thunder," "thunderous voice," or the like. The translation in 1 Kgs 19:12 should be the same. The storm theophany genre leads us to expect it, and a study by J. Lust vindicates this expectation. Lust has shown that the key terms of the phrase, קוֹל דְּמָמָה דַקָּה (traditionally translated "still small voice" or the like) carry a very different meaning from that to which we are accustomed.[12] The Hebrew קוֹל, of course, can mean "voice," "sound," "thunder," "thunderous voice," etc., depending on context. The theophanic context here would lead us to choose "thunderous voice." But what about the other terms? Lust has argued that דְּמָמָה comes from the root דמם[2] (to roar). Likewise, דַקָּה comes from דקק (to crush, grind small). Traditionally, the adjective דַקָּה was interpreted figuratively, i.e., "made small, gentle." Lust, however, suggests the sense, "crushing." So, instead of a "still, small voice," Elijah hears a "roaring, crushing sound." Or, I would suggest, a "roaring, crushing, thunderous voice."[13]

Here is a case in which either translation is possible. But genre considerations make the new translation preferable. If it is to be adopted, the quality of Yahweh's voice makes perfect sense. His voice always sounds thunderous in storm theophany. But his voice is not merely thunder. God speaks words. And this one fact distinguishes him from Baal in a passage that is partly anti-Baal polemic. We read that Elijah encountered wind, earthquake, and fire, but that Yahweh was not in any of these. We would translate, "not yet." The Lord is not yet in any of these cosmic phenomena because they only precede and announce his coming, just as they did at Mt. Sinai (Ex 19:16-19). On the other hand, such phenomena are all that a Baal worshiper might ever expect of Baal, because Baal was himself the storm! What a difference: between worshiping the storm and the Maker of the storm – between worshiping the creature and the Creator!

Jeffrey J. Niehaus
Professor of Old Testament
Gordon-Conwell Theological Seminary
South Hamilton, Massachusetts

---

[12] J. Lust, "A Gentle Breeze or a Roaring, Thunderous Sound?" *Vetus Testamentum* 25 (1975) 110-15.

[13] Cf. discussion in J. J. Niehaus, *God at Sinai* (Grand Rapids: Zondervan, 1995) 247-48.

Appendix

Strong and Weak Verb Paradigms
Diagnostics At-A-Glance
Summary of Endings on III-ה Verbs

Strong Verbs

Handwritten annotations: "Stems", "causative", "active", "passive"; Qal — "simple active / basic active / undefined"; Niphal — "passive verb"; Piel — "active / intensive"; Pual — "passive / intensive"; Hiphil — "active / causative"; Hophal — "passive / reflexive".

Perfect

	Qal	Niphal	Piel	Pual	Hiphil	Hophal (1)	Hophal (2)	Hithpael
3ms	קָטַל	נִקְטַל	קִטֵּל	קֻטַּל	הִקְטִיל	הָקְטַל	הֻקְטַל	הִתְקַטֵּל
3fs	קָטְלָה	נִקְטְלָה	קִטְּלָה	קֻטְּלָה	הִקְטִילָה	הָקְטְלָה	הֻקְטְלָה	הִתְקַטְּלָה
2ms	קָטַלְתָּ	נִקְטַלְתָּ	קִטַּלְתָּ	קֻטַּלְתָּ	הִקְטַלְתָּ	הָקְטַלְתָּ	הֻקְטַלְתָּ	הִתְקַטַּלְתָּ
2fs	קָטַלְתְּ	נִקְטַלְתְּ	קִטַּלְתְּ	קֻטַּלְתְּ	הִקְטַלְתְּ	הָקְטַלְתְּ	הֻקְטַלְתְּ	הִתְקַטַּלְתְּ
1cs	קָטַלְתִּי	נִקְטַלְתִּי	קִטַּלְתִּי	קֻטַּלְתִּי	הִקְטַלְתִּי	הָקְטַלְתִּי	הֻקְטַלְתִּי	הִתְקַטַּלְתִּי
3cp	קָטְלוּ	נִקְטְלוּ	קִטְּלוּ	קֻטְּלוּ	הִקְטִילוּ	הָקְטְלוּ	הֻקְטְלוּ	הִתְקַטְּלוּ
2mp	קְטַלְתֶּם	נִקְטַלְתֶּם	קִטַּלְתֶּם	קֻטַּלְתֶּם	הִקְטַלְתֶּם	הָקְטַלְתֶּם	הֻקְטַלְתֶּם	הִתְקַטַּלְתֶּם
2fp	קְטַלְתֶּן	נִקְטַלְתֶּן	קִטַּלְתֶּן	קֻטַּלְתֶּן	הִקְטַלְתֶּן	הָקְטַלְתֶּן	הֻקְטַלְתֶּן	הִתְקַטַּלְתֶּן
1cp	קָטַלְנוּ	נִקְטַלְנוּ	קִטַּלְנוּ	קֻטַּלְנוּ	הִקְטַלְנוּ	הָקְטַלְנוּ	הֻקְטַלְנוּ	הִתְקַטַּלְנוּ

Imperfect

	Qal	Niphal	Piel	Pual	Hiphil	Hophal (1)	Hophal (2)	Hithpael
3ms	יִקְטֹל	יִקָּטֵל	יְקַטֵּל	יְקֻטַּל	יַקְטִיל	יָקְטַל	יֻקְטַל	יִתְקַטֵּל
3fs	תִּקְטֹל	תִּקָּטֵל	תְּקַטֵּל	תְּקֻטַּל	תַּקְטִיל	תָּקְטַל	תֻּקְטַל	תִּתְקַטֵּל
2ms	תִּקְטֹל	תִּקָּטֵל	תְּקַטֵּל	תְּקֻטַּל	תַּקְטִיל	תָּקְטַל	תֻּקְטַל	תִּתְקַטֵּל
2fs	תִּקְטְלִי	תִּקָּטְלִי	תְּקַטְּלִי	תְּקֻטְּלִי	תַּקְטִילִי	תָּקְטְלִי	תֻּקְטְלִי	תִּתְקַטְּלִי
1cs	אֶקְטֹל	אֶקָּטֵל	אֲקַטֵּל	אֲקֻטַּל	אַקְטִיל	אָקְטַל	אֻקְטַל	אֶתְקַטֵּל
3mp	יִקְטְלוּ	יִקָּטְלוּ	יְקַטְּלוּ	יְקֻטְּלוּ	יַקְטִילוּ	יָקְטְלוּ	יֻקְטְלוּ	יִתְקַטְּלוּ
3fp	תִּקְטֹלְנָה	תִּקָּטַלְנָה	תְּקַטֵּלְנָה	תְּקֻטַּלְנָה	תַּקְטֵלְנָה	תָּקְטַלְנָה	תֻּקְטַלְנָה	תִּתְקַטֵּלְנָה
2mp	תִּקְטְלוּ	תִּקָּטְלוּ	תְּקַטְּלוּ	תְּקֻטְּלוּ	תַּקְטִילוּ	תָּקְטְלוּ	תֻּקְטְלוּ	תִּתְקַטְּלוּ
2fp	תִּקְטֹלְנָה	תִּקָּטַלְנָה	תְּקַטֵּלְנָה	תְּקֻטַּלְנָה	תַּקְטֵלְנָה	תָּקְטַלְנָה	תֻּקְטַלְנָה	תִּתְקַטֵּלְנָה
1cp	נִקְטֹל	נִקָּטֵל	נְקַטֵּל	נְקֻטַּל	נַקְטִיל	נָקְטַל	נֻקְטַל	נִתְקַטֵּל

Imperative	2ms	קְטֹל	הִקָּטֵל	קַטֵּל		הַקְטֵל
	2fs	קִטְלִי	הִקָּטְלִי	קַטְּלִי		הַקְטִילִי
	2mp	קִטְלוּ	הִקָּטְלוּ	קַטְּלוּ		הַקְטִילוּ
	2fp	קְטֹלְנָה	הִקָּטַלְנָה	קַטֵּלְנָה		הַקְטֵלְנָה
Infinitive Construct		קְטֹל	הִקָּטֵל	קַטֵּל		הַקְטִיל
Infinitive Absolute		קָטוֹל	הִקָּטֹל נִקְטֹל	קַטֵּל		הַקְטֵל
Active Participle	ms	קֹטֵל		קַטֵּל		מַקְטִיל
	fs	קֹטֶלֶת		מְקַטֶּלֶת		מַקְטֶלֶת
	mp	קֹטְלִים		מְקַטְּלִים		מַקְטִילִים
	fp	קֹטְלוֹת		מְקַטְּלוֹת		מַקְטִילוֹת
Passive Participle	ms	קָטוּל	נִקְטָל	מְקֻטָּל		מַקְטָל
	fs	קְטוּלָה	נִקְטָלָה	מְקֻטָּלָה		מָקְטֶלֶת
	mp	קְטוּלִים	נִקְטָלִים	מְקֻטָּלִים		מָקְטָלִים
	fp	קְטוּלוֹת	נִקְטָלוֹת	מְקֻטָּלוֹת		מָקְטָלוֹת

I-Guttural Verbs

		Qal (1)	Qal (2)	Niphal	Hiphil	Hophal
Perfect	3ms	עָמַד	חָזַק	נֶעֱמַד	הֶעֱמִיד	הָעֳמַד
	3fs	עָמְדָה	חָזְקָה	נֶעֶמְדָה	הֶעֱמִידָה	הָעֳמְדָה
	2ms	עָמַדְתָּ	חָזַקְתָּ	נֶעֱמַדְתָּ	הֶעֱמַדְתָּ	הָעֳמַדְתָּ
	2fs	עָמַדְתְּ	חָזַקְתְּ	נֶעֱמַדְתְּ	הֶעֱמַדְתְּ	הָעֳמַדְתְּ
	1cs	עָמַדְתִּי	חָזַקְתִּי	נֶעֱמַדְתִּי	הֶעֱמַדְתִּי	הָעֳמַדְתִּי
	3cp	עָמְדוּ	חָזְקוּ	נֶעֶמְדוּ	הֶעֱמִידוּ	הָעֳמְדוּ
	2mp	עֲמַדְתֶּם	חֲזַקְתֶּם	נֶעֱמַדְתֶּם	הֶעֱמַדְתֶּם	הָעֳמַדְתֶּם
	2fp	עֲמַדְתֶּן	חֲזַקְתֶּן	נֶעֱמַדְתֶּן	הֶעֱמַדְתֶּן	הָעֳמַדְתֶּן
	1cp	עָמַדְנוּ	חָזַקְנוּ	נֶעֱמַדְנוּ	הֶעֱמַדְנוּ	הָעֳמַדְנוּ
Imperfect	3ms	יַעֲמֹד	יֶחֱזַק	יֵעָמֵד	יַעֲמִיד	יָעֳמַד
	3fs	תַּעֲמֹד	תֶּחֱזַק	תֵּעָמֵד	תַּעֲמִיד	תָּעֳמַד
	2ms	תַּעֲמֹד	תֶּחֱזַק	תֵּעָמֵד	תַּעֲמִיד	תָּעֳמַד
	2fs	תַּעַמְדִי	תֶּחֶזְקִי	תֵּעָמְדִי	תַּעֲמִידִי	תָּעֳמְדִי
	1cs	אֶעֱמֹד	אֶחֱזַק	אֵעָמֵד	אַעֲמִיד	אָעֳמַד
	3mp	יַעַמְדוּ	יֶחֶזְקוּ	יֵעָמְדוּ	יַעֲמִידוּ	יָעֳמְדוּ
	3fp	תַּעֲמֹדְנָה	תֶּחֱזַקְנָה	תֵּעָמַדְנָה	תַּעֲמֵדְנָה	תָּעֳמַדְנָה
	2mp	תַּעַמְדוּ	תֶּחֶזְקוּ	תֵּעָמְדוּ	תַּעֲמִידוּ	תָּעֳמְדוּ
	2fp	תַּעֲמֹדְנָה	תֶּחֱזַקְנָה	תֵּעָמַדְנָה	תַּעֲמֵדְנָה	תָּעֳמַדְנָה
	1cp	נַעֲמֹד	נֶחֱזַק	נֵעָמֵד	נַעֲמִיד	נָעֳמַד

Imperative	2ms	קְטֹל	חֲזַק	הִבָּנֵה	הַקְטֵל
	2fs	קִטְלִי	חִזְקִי	הִבָּנִי	הַקְטִילִי
	2mp	קִטְלוּ	חִזְקוּ	הִבָּנוּ	הַקְטִילוּ
	2fp	קְטֹלְנָה	חֲזַקְנָה	הִבָּנֶינָה	הַקְטֵלְנָה
Infinitive Construct		קְטֹל	חֲזַק	הִבָּנוֹת	הַקְטִיל
Infinitive Absolute		קָטוֹל	חָזוֹק	הִבָּנֹה / נִבְנֹה	הַקְטֵל
Active Participle	ms	קֹטֵל	חָזָק		
	fs	קֹטֶלֶת	חֲזָקָה		
	mp	קֹטְלִים	חֲזָקִים		
	fp	קֹטְלוֹת	חֲזָקוֹת		
Passive Participle	ms	קָטוּל	חָזוּק	נִבְנֶה	מַקְטִיל
	fs	קְטוּלָה	חֲזוּקָה	נִבְנָה	מַקְטִילָה
	mp	קְטוּלִים	חֲזוּקִים	נִבְנִים	מַקְטִילִים
	fp	קְטוּלוֹת	חֲזוּקוֹת	נִבְנוֹת	מַקְטִילוֹת

I-א Verbs

	Qal (1)	Qal (2)	Qal (2)
Perfect			
3ms	אָמַר	אָכַל	אָמַר
3fs	אָמְרָה	אָכְלָה	אָמְרָה
2ms	אָמַרְתָּ	אָכַלְתָּ	אָמַרְתָּ
2fs	אָמַרְתְּ	אָכַלְתְּ	אָמַרְתְּ
1cs	אָמַרְתִּי	אָכַלְתִּי	אָמַרְתִּי
3cp	אָמְרוּ	אָכְלוּ	אָמְרוּ
2mp	אֲמַרְתֶּם	אֲכַלְתֶּם	אֲמַרְתֶּם
2fp	אֲמַרְתֶּן	אֲכַלְתֶּן	אֲמַרְתֶּן
1cp	אָמַרְנוּ	אָכַלְנוּ	אָמַרְנוּ
Imperfect			
3ms	יֹאמַר	יֹאכַל	יֹאמַר
3fs	תֹּאמַר	תֹּאכַל	תֹּאמַר
2ms	תֹּאמַר	תֹּאכַל	תֹּאמַר
2fs	תֹּאמְרִי	תֹּאכְלִי	תֹּאמְרִי
1cs	אֹמַר	אֹכַל	אֹמַר
3mp	יֹאמְרוּ	יֹאכְלוּ	יֹאמְרוּ
3fp	תֹּאמַרְנָה	תֹּאכַלְנָה	תֹּאמַרְנָה
2mp	תֹּאמְרוּ	תֹּאכְלוּ	תֹּאמְרוּ
2fp	תֹּאמַרְנָה	תֹּאכַלְנָה	תֹּאמַרְנָה
1cp	נֹאמַר	נֹאכַל	נֹאמַר

Imperative	2ms	אֱמֹר	אֱמֹל	אֱמֹר
	2fs	אִמְרִי	אִמְלִי	אִמְרִי
	2mp	אִמְרוּ	אִמְלוּ	אִמְרוּ
	2fp	אֱמֹרְנָה	אֱמֹלְנָה	אֱמֹרְנָה
Infinitive Construct		אֱמֹר	אֱמֹל	אֱמֹר
Infinitive Absolute		אָמוֹר	אָמוֹל	אָמוֹר
Active Participle	ms	אֹמֵר	אֹמֵל	אֹמֵר
	fs	אֹמֶרֶת	אֹמֶלֶת	אֹמֶרֶת
	mp	אֹמְרִים	אֹמְלִים	אֹמְרִים
	fp	אֹמְרוֹת	אֹמְלוֹת	אֹמְרוֹת
Passive Participle	ms	אָמוּר	אָמוּל	אָמוּר
	fs	אֲמוּרָה	אֲמוּלָה	אֲמוּרָה
	mp	אֲמוּרִים	אֲמוּלִים	אֲמוּרִים
	fp	אֲמוּרוֹת	אֲמוּלוֹת	אֲמוּרוֹת

II-Guttural Verbs

		Qal	Niphal	Piel (vd)	Piel (cl)	Pual (vd)	Pual (cl)	Hithpael (vd)	Hithpael (cl)
Perfect	3ms	בָּחַר	נִבְחַר	נִחַם	בֵּרַךְ	נֻחַם	בֹּרַךְ	הִתְנַחֵם	הִתְבָּרֵךְ
	3fs	בָּחֲרָה	נִבְחֲרָה	נִחֲמָה	בֵּרֲכָה	נֻחֲמָה	בֹּרֲכָה	הִתְנַחֲמָה	הִתְבָּרֲכָה
	2ms	בָּחַרְתָּ	נִבְחַרְתָּ	נִחַמְתָּ	בֵּרַכְתָּ	נֻחַמְתָּ	בֹּרַכְתָּ	הִתְנַחַמְתָּ	הִתְבָּרַכְתָּ
	2fs	בָּחַרְתְּ	נִבְחַרְתְּ	נִחַמְתְּ	בֵּרַכְתְּ	נֻחַמְתְּ	בֹּרַכְתְּ	הִתְנַחַמְתְּ	הִתְבָּרַכְתְּ
	1cs	בָּחַרְתִּי	נִבְחַרְתִּי	נִחַמְתִּי	בֵּרַכְתִּי	נֻחַמְתִּי	בֹּרַכְתִּי	הִתְנַחַמְתִּי	הִתְבָּרַכְתִּי
	3cp	בָּחֲרוּ	נִבְחֲרוּ	נִחֲמוּ	בֵּרֲכוּ	נֻחֲמוּ	בֹּרֲכוּ	הִתְנַחֲמוּ	הִתְבָּרֲכוּ
	2mp	בְּחַרְתֶּם	נִבְחַרְתֶּם	נִחַמְתֶּם	בֵּרַכְתֶּם	נֻחַמְתֶּם	בֹּרַכְתֶּם	הִתְנַחַמְתֶּם	הִתְבָּרַכְתֶּם
	2fp	בְּחַרְתֶּן	נִבְחַרְתֶּן	נִחַמְתֶּן	בֵּרַכְתֶּן	נֻחַמְתֶּן	בֹּרַכְתֶּן	הִתְנַחַמְתֶּן	הִתְבָּרַכְתֶּן
	1cp	בָּחַרְנוּ	נִבְחַרְנוּ	נִחַמְנוּ	בֵּרַכְנוּ	נֻחַמְנוּ	בֹּרַכְנוּ	הִתְנַחַמְנוּ	הִתְבָּרַכְנוּ
Imperfect	3ms	יִבְחַר	יִבָּחֵר	יְנַחֵם	יְבָרֵךְ	יְנֻחַם	יְבֹרַךְ	יִתְנַחֵם	יִתְבָּרֵךְ
	3fs	תִּבְחַר	תִּבָּחֵר	תְּנַחֵם	תְּבָרֵךְ	תְּנֻחַם	תְּבֹרַךְ	תִּתְנַחֵם	תִּתְבָּרֵךְ
	2ms	תִּבְחַר	תִּבָּחֵר	תְּנַחֵם	תְּבָרֵךְ	תְּנֻחַם	תְּבֹרַךְ	תִּתְנַחֵם	תִּתְבָּרֵךְ
	2fs	תִּבְחֲרִי	תִּבָּחֲרִי	תְּנַחֲמִי	תְּבָרֲכִי	תְּנֻחֲמִי	תְּבֹרֲכִי	תִּתְנַחֲמִי	תִּתְבָּרֲכִי
	1cs	אֶבְחַר	אֶבָּחֵר	אֲנַחֵם	אֲבָרֵךְ	אֲנֻחַם	אֲבֹרַךְ	אֶתְנַחֵם	אֶתְבָּרֵךְ
	3mp	יִבְחֲרוּ	יִבָּחֲרוּ	יְנַחֲמוּ	יְבָרֲכוּ	יְנֻחֲמוּ	יְבֹרֲכוּ	יִתְנַחֲמוּ	יִתְבָּרֲכוּ
	3fp	תִּבְחַרְנָה	תִּבָּחַרְנָה	תְּנַחֵמְנָה	תְּבָרֵכְנָה	תְּנֻחַמְנָה	תְּבֹרַכְנָה	תִּתְנַחֵמְנָה	תִּתְבָּרֵכְנָה
	2mp	תִּבְחֲרוּ	תִּבָּחֲרוּ	תְּנַחֲמוּ	תְּבָרֲכוּ	תְּנֻחֲמוּ	תְּבֹרֲכוּ	תִּתְנַחֲמוּ	תִּתְבָּרֲכוּ
	2fp	תִּבְחַרְנָה	תִּבָּחַרְנָה	תְּנַחֵמְנָה	תְּבָרֵכְנָה	תְּנֻחַמְנָה	תְּבֹרַכְנָה	תִּתְנַחֵמְנָה	תִּתְבָּרֵכְנָה
	1cp	נִבְחַר	נִבָּחֵר	נְנַחֵם	נְבָרֵךְ	נְנֻחַם	נְבֹרַךְ	נִתְנַחֵם	נִתְבָּרֵךְ

Imperative	2ms
	2fs
	2mp
	2fp
Infinitive Construct	
Infinitive Absolute	
Active Participle	ms
	fs
	mp
	fp
Passive Participle	ms
	fs
	mp
	fp

III-ה/ע Verbs

Perfect	Qal	Niphal	Piel	Pual	Hiphil	Hophal
3ms	שָׁלַח	נִשְׁלַח	שִׁלַּח	שֻׁלַּח	הִשְׁלִיחַ	הָשְׁלַח
3fs	שָׁלְחָה	נִשְׁלְחָה	שִׁלְּחָה	שֻׁלְּחָה	הִשְׁלִיחָה	הָשְׁלְחָה
2ms	שָׁלַחְתָּ	נִשְׁלַחְתָּ	שִׁלַּחְתָּ	שֻׁלַּחְתָּ	הִשְׁלַחְתָּ	הָשְׁלַחְתָּ
2fs	שָׁלַחַתְּ	נִשְׁלַחַתְּ	שִׁלַּחַתְּ	שֻׁלַּחַתְּ	הִשְׁלַחַתְּ	הָשְׁלַחַתְּ
1cs	שָׁלַחְתִּי	נִשְׁלַחְתִּי	שִׁלַּחְתִּי	שֻׁלַּחְתִּי	הִשְׁלַחְתִּי	הָשְׁלַחְתִּי
3cp	שָׁלְחוּ	נִשְׁלְחוּ	שִׁלְּחוּ	שֻׁלְּחוּ	הִשְׁלִיחוּ	הָשְׁלְחוּ
2mp	שְׁלַחְתֶּם	נִשְׁלַחְתֶּם	שִׁלַּחְתֶּם	שֻׁלַּחְתֶּם	הִשְׁלַחְתֶּם	הָשְׁלַחְתֶּם
2fp	שְׁלַחְתֶּן	נִשְׁלַחְתֶּן	שִׁלַּחְתֶּן	שֻׁלַּחְתֶּן	הִשְׁלַחְתֶּן	הָשְׁלַחְתֶּן
1cp	שָׁלַחְנוּ	נִשְׁלַחְנוּ	שִׁלַּחְנוּ	שֻׁלַּחְנוּ	הִשְׁלַחְנוּ	הָשְׁלַחְנוּ

Imperfect	Qal	Niphal	Piel	Pual	Hiphil	Hophal
3ms	יִשְׁלַח	יִשָּׁלַח	יְשַׁלַּח	יְשֻׁלַּח	יַשְׁלִיחַ	יָשְׁלַח
3fs	תִּשְׁלַח	תִּשָּׁלַח	תְּשַׁלַּח	תְּשֻׁלַּח	תַּשְׁלִיחַ	תָּשְׁלַח
2ms	תִּשְׁלַח	תִּשָּׁלַח	תְּשַׁלַּח	תְּשֻׁלַּח	תַּשְׁלִיחַ	תָּשְׁלַח
2fs	תִּשְׁלְחִי	תִּשָּׁלְחִי	תְּשַׁלְּחִי	תְּשֻׁלְּחִי	תַּשְׁלִיחִי	תָּשְׁלְחִי
1cs	אֶשְׁלַח	אֶשָּׁלַח	אֲשַׁלַּח	אֲשֻׁלַּח	אַשְׁלִיחַ	אָשְׁלַח
3mp	יִשְׁלְחוּ	יִשָּׁלְחוּ	יְשַׁלְּחוּ	יְשֻׁלְּחוּ	יַשְׁלִיחוּ	יָשְׁלְחוּ
3fp	תִּשְׁלַחְנָה	תִּשָּׁלַחְנָה	תְּשַׁלַּחְנָה	תְּשֻׁלַּחְנָה	תַּשְׁלַחְנָה	תָּשְׁלַחְנָה
2mp	תִּשְׁלְחוּ	תִּשָּׁלְחוּ	תְּשַׁלְּחוּ	תְּשֻׁלְּחוּ	תַּשְׁלִיחוּ	תָּשְׁלְחוּ
2fp	תִּשְׁלַחְנָה	תִּשָּׁלַחְנָה	תְּשַׁלַּחְנָה	תְּשֻׁלַּחְנָה	תַּשְׁלַחְנָה	תָּשְׁלַחְנָה
1cp	נִשְׁלַח	נִשָּׁלַח	נְשַׁלַּח	נְשֻׁלַּח	נַשְׁלִיחַ	נָשְׁלַח

		Qal	Niphal	Piel	Pual
Imperative	*2ms*	קְטֹל	הִקָּטֵל	קַטֵּל	
	2fs	קִטְלִי	הִקָּטְלִי	קַטְּלִי	
	2mp	קִטְלוּ	הִקָּטְלוּ	קַטְּלוּ	
	2fp	קְטֹלְנָה	הִקָּטַלְנָה	קַטֵּלְנָה	
Infinitive Construct		קְטֹל	הִקָּטֵל	קַטֵּל	
Infinitive Absolute		קָטוֹל	נִקְטוֹל / הִקָּטֹל	קַטֹּל	קֻטֹּל
Active Participle	*ms*	קֹטֵל	נִקְטָל	מְקַטֵּל	
	fs	קֹטֶלֶת	נִקְטָלָה	מְקַטֶּלֶת	
	mp	קֹטְלִים	נִקְטָלִים	מְקַטְּלִים	
	fp	קֹטְלוֹת	נִקְטָלוֹת	מְקַטְּלוֹת	
Passive Participle	*ms*	קָטוּל			מְקֻטָּל
	fs	קְטוּלָה			מְקֻטֶּלֶת
	mp	קְטוּלִים			מְקֻטָּלִים
	fp	קְטוּלוֹת			מְקֻטָּלוֹת

III-א Verbs

		Qal	Niphal	Piel	Pual	Hiphil	Hophal	Hithpael
Perfect	3ms	מָצָא	נִמְצָא	מִצֵּא	מֻצָּא	הִמְצִיא	הֻמְצָא	הִתְמַצֵּא
	3fs	מָצְאָה	נִמְצְאָה	מִצְּאָה	מֻצְּאָה	הִמְצִיאָה	הֻמְצְאָה	הִתְמַצְּאָה
	2ms	מָצָאתָ	נִמְצֵאתָ	מִצֵּאתָ	מֻצֵּאתָ	הִמְצֵאתָ	הֻמְצֵאתָ	הִתְמַצֵּאתָ
	2fs	מָצָאת	נִמְצֵאת	מִצֵּאת	מֻצֵּאת	הִמְצֵאת	הֻמְצֵאת	הִתְמַצֵּאת
	1cs	מָצָאתִי	נִמְצֵאתִי	מִצֵּאתִי	מֻצֵּאתִי	הִמְצֵאתִי	הֻמְצֵאתִי	הִתְמַצֵּאתִי
	3cp	מָצְאוּ	נִמְצְאוּ	מִצְּאוּ	מֻצְּאוּ	הִמְצִיאוּ	הֻמְצְאוּ	הִתְמַצְּאוּ
	2mp	מְצָאתֶם	נִמְצֵאתֶם	מִצֵּאתֶם	מֻצֵּאתֶם	הִמְצֵאתֶם	הֻמְצֵאתֶם	הִתְמַצֵּאתֶם
	2fp	מְצָאתֶן	נִמְצֵאתֶן	מִצֵּאתֶן	מֻצֵּאתֶן	הִמְצֵאתֶן	הֻמְצֵאתֶן	הִתְמַצֵּאתֶן
	1cp	מָצָאנוּ	נִמְצֵאנוּ	מִצֵּאנוּ	מֻצֵּאנוּ	הִמְצֵאנוּ	הֻמְצֵאנוּ	הִתְמַצֵּאנוּ
Imperfect	3ms	יִמְצָא	יִמָּצֵא	יְמַצֵּא	יְמֻצָּא	יַמְצִיא	יֻמְצָא	יִתְמַצֵּא
	3fs	תִּמְצָא	תִּמָּצֵא	תְּמַצֵּא	תְּמֻצָּא	תַּמְצִיא	תֻּמְצָא	תִּתְמַצֵּא
	2ms	תִּמְצָא	תִּמָּצֵא	תְּמַצֵּא	תְּמֻצָּא	תַּמְצִיא	תֻּמְצָא	תִּתְמַצֵּא
	2fs	תִּמְצְאִי	תִּמָּצְאִי	תְּמַצְּאִי	תְּמֻצְּאִי	תַּמְצִיאִי	תֻּמְצְאִי	תִּתְמַצְּאִי
	1cs	אֶמְצָא	אֶמָּצֵא	אֲמַצֵּא	אֲמֻצָּא	אַמְצִיא	אֻמְצָא	אֶתְמַצֵּא
	3mp	יִמְצְאוּ	יִמָּצְאוּ	יְמַצְּאוּ	יְמֻצְּאוּ	יַמְצִיאוּ	יֻמְצְאוּ	יִתְמַצְּאוּ
	3fp	תִּמְצֶאנָה	תִּמָּצֶאנָה	תְּמַצֶּאנָה	תְּמֻצֶּאנָה	תַּמְצֶאנָה	תֻּמְצֶאנָה	תִּתְמַצֶּאנָה
	2mp	תִּמְצְאוּ	תִּמָּצְאוּ	תְּמַצְּאוּ	תְּמֻצְּאוּ	תַּמְצִיאוּ	תֻּמְצְאוּ	תִּתְמַצְּאוּ
	2fp	תִּמְצֶאנָה	תִּמָּצֶאנָה	תְּמַצֶּאנָה	תְּמֻצֶּאנָה	תַּמְצֶאנָה	תֻּמְצֶאנָה	תִּתְמַצֶּאנָה
	1cp	נִמְצָא	נִמָּצֵא	נְמַצֵּא	נְמֻצָּא	נַמְצִיא	נֻמְצָא	נִתְמַצֵּא

		Qal	Niphal	Piel	Pual	Hiphil
Imperative	2ms	מְצָא	הִמָּצֵא	מַצֵּא		הַמְצֵא
	2fs	מִצְאִי	הִמָּצְאִי	מַצְּאִי		הַמְצִיאִי
	2mp	מִצְאוּ	הִמָּצְאוּ	מַצְּאוּ		הַמְצִיאוּ
	2fp	מְצֶאנָה	הִמָּצֶאנָה	מַצֶּאנָה		הַמְצֶאנָה
Infinitive Construct		מְצֹא	הִמָּצֵא	מַצֵּא		הַמְצִיא
Infinitive Absolute		מָצוֹא	נִמְצֹא	מַצֹּא		הַמְצֵא
Active Participle	ms	מֹצֵא	נִמְצָא	מְמַצֵּא	מְמֻצָּא	מַמְצִיא
	fs	מֹצֵאת	נִמְצֵאת	מְמַצֵּאת	מְמֻצֵּאת	מַמְצִיאָה
	mp	מֹצְאִים	נִמְצָאִים	מְמַצְּאִים	מְמֻצָּאִים	מַמְצִיאִים
	fp	מֹצְאוֹת	נִמְצָאוֹת	מְמַצְּאוֹת	מְמֻצָּאוֹת	מַמְצִיאוֹת
Passive Participle	ms	מָצוּא				
	fs	מְצוּאָה				
	mp	מְצוּאִים				
	fp	מְצוּאוֹת				

III-ה Verbs

		Qal	Niphal	Piel	Pual	Hiphil	Hophal	Hithpael
Perfect	3ms	גָּלָה	נִגְלָה	גִּלָּה	גֻּלָּה	הִגְלָה	הָגְלָה	הִתְגַּלָּה
	3fs	גָּלְתָה	נִגְלְתָה	גִּלְּתָה	גֻּלְּתָה	הִגְלְתָה	הָגְלְתָה	הִתְגַּלְּתָה
	2ms	גָּלִיתָ	נִגְלֵיתָ	גִּלִּיתָ	גֻּלֵּיתָ	הִגְלִיתָ	הָגְלֵיתָ	הִתְגַּלִּיתָ
	2fs	גָּלִית	נִגְלֵית	גִּלִּית	גֻּלֵּית	הִגְלִית	הָגְלֵית	הִתְגַּלִּית
	1cs	גָּלִיתִי	נִגְלֵיתִי	גִּלִּיתִי	גֻּלֵּיתִי	הִגְלֵיתִי	הָגְלֵיתִי	הִתְגַּלִּיתִי
	3cp	גָּלוּ	נִגְלוּ	גִּלּוּ	גֻּלּוּ	הִגְלוּ	הָגְלוּ	הִתְגַּלּוּ
	2mp	גְּלִיתֶם	נִגְלֵיתֶם	גִּלִּיתֶם	גֻּלֵּיתֶם	הִגְלִיתֶם	הָגְלֵיתֶם	הִתְגַּלִּיתֶם
	2fp	גְּלִיתֶן	נִגְלֵיתֶן	גִּלִּיתֶן	גֻּלֵּיתֶן	הִגְלִיתֶן	הָגְלֵיתֶן	הִתְגַּלִּיתֶן
	1cp	גָּלִינוּ	נִגְלֵינוּ	גִּלִּינוּ	גֻּלֵּינוּ	הִגְלִינוּ	הָגְלֵינוּ	הִתְגַּלִּינוּ
Imperfect	3ms	יִגְלֶה	יִגָּלֶה	יְגַלֶּה	יְגֻלֶּה	יַגְלֶה	יָגְלֶה	יִתְגַּלֶּה
	3fs	תִּגְלֶה	תִּגָּלֶה	תְּגַלֶּה	תְּגֻלֶּה	תַּגְלֶה	תָּגְלֶה	תִּתְגַּלֶּה
	2ms	תִּגְלֶה	תִּגָּלֶה	תְּגַלֶּה	תְּגֻלֶּה	תַּגְלֶה	תָּגְלֶה	תִּתְגַּלֶּה
	2fs	תִּגְלִי	תִּגָּלִי	תְּגַלִּי	תְּגֻלִּי	תַּגְלִי	תָּגְלִי	תִּתְגַּלִּי
	1cs	אֶגְלֶה	אֶגָּלֶה	אֲגַלֶּה	אֲגֻלֶּה	אַגְלֶה	אָגְלֶה	אֶתְגַּלֶּה
	3mp	יִגְלוּ	יִגָּלוּ	יְגַלּוּ	יְגֻלּוּ	יַגְלוּ	יָגְלוּ	יִתְגַּלּוּ
	3fp	תִּגְלֶינָה	תִּגָּלֶינָה	תְּגַלֶּינָה	תְּגֻלֶּינָה	תַּגְלֶינָה	תָּגְלֶינָה	תִּתְגַּלֶּינָה
	2mp	תִּגְלוּ	תִּגָּלוּ	תְּגַלּוּ	תְּגֻלּוּ	תַּגְלוּ	תָּגְלוּ	תִּתְגַּלּוּ
	2fp	תִּגְלֶינָה	תִּגָּלֶינָה	תְּגַלֶּינָה	תְּגֻלֶּינָה	תַּגְלֶינָה	תָּגְלֶינָה	תִּתְגַּלֶּינָה
	1cp	נִגְלֶה	נִגָּלֶה	נְגַלֶּה	נְגֻלֶּה	נַגְלֶה	נָגְלֶה	נִתְגַּלֶּה

	Qal	Niphal	Piel	Pual	Hiphil	Hophal	Hithpael
Imperative 2ms	בְּנֵה	הִבָּנֵה	בַּנֵּה		הַבְנֵה		הִתְבַּנֵּה
2fs	בְּנִי	הִבָּנִי	בַּנִּי		הַבְנִי		הִתְבַּנִּי
2mp	בְּנוּ	הִבָּנוּ	בַּנּוּ		הַבְנוּ		הִתְבַּנּוּ
2fp	בְּנֶינָה	הִבָּנֶינָה	בַּנֶּינָה		הַבְנֶינָה		הִתְבַּנֶּינָה
Infinitive Construct	בְּנוֹת	הִבָּנוֹת	בַּנּוֹת		הַבְנוֹת		הִתְבַּנּוֹת
Infinitive Absolute	בָּנֹה	נִבְנֹה / הִבָּנֹה	בַּנֹּה		הַבְנֵה		
Active Participle ms	בֹּנֶה	נִבְנֶה	מְבַנֶּה		מַבְנֶה		מִתְבַּנֶּה
fs	בֹּנָה	נִבְנָה	מְבַנָּה		מַבְנָה		מִתְבַּנָּה
mp	בֹּנִים	נִבְנִים	מְבַנִּים		מַבְנִים		מִתְבַּנִּים
fp	בֹּנוֹת	נִבְנוֹת	מְבַנּוֹת		מַבְנוֹת		מִתְבַּנּוֹת
Passive Participle ms	בָּנוּי			מְבֻנֶּה		מָבְנֶה	
fs	בְּנוּיָה			מְבֻנָּה		מָבְנָה	
mp	בְּנוּיִם			מְבֻנִּים		מָבְנִים	
fp	בְּנוּיוֹת			מְבֻנּוֹת		מָבְנוֹת	

I-נ Verbs

		Qal (1)	Qal (2)	Qal (Irreg.)	Niphal	Hiphil	Hophal
Perfect	3ms	נָפַל	נָסַע	נָתַן	נִפַּל	הִפִּיל	הֻפַּל
	3fs	נָפְלָה	נָסְעָה	נָתְנָה	נִפְּלָה	הִפִּילָה	הֻפְּלָה
	2ms	נָפַלְתָּ	נָסַעְתָּ	נָתַתָּ	נִפַּלְתָּ	הִפַּלְתָּ	הֻפַּלְתָּ
	2fs	נָפַלְתְּ	נָסַעַתְּ	נָתַתְּ	נִפַּלְתְּ	הִפַּלְתְּ	הֻפַּלְתְּ
	1cs	נָפַלְתִּי	נָסַעְתִּי	נָתַתִּי	נִפַּלְתִּי	הִפַּלְתִּי	הֻפַּלְתִּי
	3cp	נָפְלוּ	נָסְעוּ	נָתְנוּ	נִפְּלוּ	הִפִּילוּ	הֻפְּלוּ
	2mp	נְפַלְתֶּם	נְסַעְתֶּם	נְתַתֶּם	נִפַּלְתֶּם	הִפַּלְתֶּם	הֻפַּלְתֶּם
	2fp	נְפַלְתֶּן	נְסַעְתֶּן	נְתַתֶּן	נִפַּלְתֶּן	הִפַּלְתֶּן	הֻפַּלְתֶּן
	1cp	נָפַלְנוּ	נָסַעְנוּ	נָתַנּוּ	נִפַּלְנוּ	הִפַּלְנוּ	הֻפַּלְנוּ
Imperfect	3ms	יִפֹּל	יִסַּע	יִתֵּן	יִנָּפֵל	יַפִּיל	יֻפַּל
	3fs	תִּפֹּל	תִּסַּע	תִּתֵּן	תִּנָּפֵל	תַּפִּיל	תֻּפַּל
	2ms	תִּפֹּל	תִּסַּע	תִּתֵּן	תִּנָּפֵל	תַּפִּיל	תֻּפַּל
	2fs	תִּפְּלִי	תִּסְּעִי	תִּתְּנִי	תִּנָּפְלִי	תַּפִּילִי	תֻּפְּלִי
	1cs	אֶפֹּל	אֶסַּע	אֶתֵּן	אֶנָּפֵל	אַפִּיל	אֻפַּל
	3mp	יִפְּלוּ	יִסְּעוּ	יִתְּנוּ	יִנָּפְלוּ	יַפִּילוּ	יֻפְּלוּ
	3fp	תִּפֹּלְנָה	תִּסַּעְנָה	תִּתֵּנָּה	תִּנָּפַלְנָה	תַּפֵּלְנָה	תֻּפַּלְנָה
	2mp	תִּפְּלוּ	תִּסְּעוּ	תִּתְּנוּ	תִּנָּפְלוּ	תַּפִּילוּ	תֻּפְּלוּ
	2fp	תִּפֹּלְנָה	תִּסַּעְנָה	תִּתֵּנָּה	תִּנָּפַלְנָה	תַּפֵּלְנָה	תֻּפַּלְנָה
	1cp	נִפֹּל	נִסַּע	נִתֵּן	נִנָּפֵל	נַפִּיל	נֻפַּל

Appendix 1: Verb Paradigms

		Qal	Niphal	Piel	Pual	Hiphil
Imperative	2ms	קְטֹל	הִקָּטֵל	קַטֵּל		הַקְטֵל
	2fs	קִטְלִי	הִקָּטְלִי	קַטְּלִי		הַקְטִילִי
	2mp	קִטְלוּ	הִקָּטְלוּ	קַטְּלוּ		הַקְטִילוּ
	2fp	קְטֹלְנָה	הִקָּטַלְנָה	קַטֵּלְנָה		הַקְטֵלְנָה
Infinitive Construct		קְטֹל	הִקָּטֵל	קַטֵּל	קֻטַּל	הַקְטִיל
Infinitive Absolute		קָטוֹל	נִקְטֹל	קַטֹּל	קֻטֹּל	הַקְטֵל
Active Participle	ms	קֹטֵל	נִקְטָל	מְקַטֵּל		מַקְטִיל
	fs	קֹטֶלֶת	נִקְטֶלֶת	מְקַטֶּלֶת		מַקְטֶלֶת
	mp	קֹטְלִים	נִקְטָלִים	מְקַטְּלִים		מַקְטִילִים
	fp	קֹטְלוֹת	נִקְטָלוֹת	מְקַטְּלוֹת		מַקְטִילוֹת
Passive Participle	ms	קָטוּל			מְקֻטָּל	
	fs	קְטוּלָה			מְקֻטֶּלֶת	
	mp	קְטוּלִים			מְקֻטָּלִים	
	fp	קְטוּלוֹת			מְקֻטָּלוֹת	

I-ʾ Verbs

	Qal (1)	Qal (2)	Niphal	Hiphil	Hophal
Perfect					
3ms	אָכַל	אָמַר	נֶאֱכַל	הֶאֱכִיל	הָאֳכַל
3fs	אָכְלָה	אָמְרָה	נֶאֶכְלָה	הֶאֱכִילָה	הָאֳכְלָה
2ms	אָכַלְתָּ	אָמַרְתָּ	נֶאֱכַלְתָּ	הֶאֱכַלְתָּ	הָאֳכַלְתָּ
2fs	אָכַלְתְּ	אָמַרְתְּ	נֶאֱכַלְתְּ	הֶאֱכַלְתְּ	הָאֳכַלְתְּ
1cs	אָכַלְתִּי	אָמַרְתִּי	נֶאֱכַלְתִּי	הֶאֱכַלְתִּי	הָאֳכַלְתִּי
3cp	אָכְלוּ	אָמְרוּ	נֶאֶכְלוּ	הֶאֱכִילוּ	הָאֳכְלוּ
2mp	אֲכַלְתֶּם	אֲמַרְתֶּם	נֶאֱכַלְתֶּם	הֶאֱכַלְתֶּם	הָאֳכַלְתֶּם
2fp	אֲכַלְתֶּן	אֲמַרְתֶּן	נֶאֱכַלְתֶּן	הֶאֱכַלְתֶּן	הָאֳכַלְתֶּן
1cp	אָכַלְנוּ	אָמַרְנוּ	נֶאֱכַלְנוּ	הֶאֱכַלְנוּ	הָאֳכַלְנוּ
Imperfect					
3ms	יֶאֱסֹר	יֹאכַל	יֵאָכֵל	יַאֲכִיל	יָאֳכַל
3fs	תֶּאֱסֹר	תֹּאכַל	תֵּאָכֵל	תַּאֲכִיל	תָּאֳכַל
2ms	תֶּאֱסֹר	תֹּאכַל	תֵּאָכֵל	תַּאֲכִיל	תָּאֳכַל
2fs	תֶּאֶסְרִי	תֹּאכְלִי	תֵּאָכְלִי	תַּאֲכִילִי	תָּאֳכְלִי
1cs	אֶאֱסֹר	אֹכַל	אֵאָכֵל	אַאֲכִיל	אָאֳכַל
3mp	יֶאֶסְרוּ	יֹאכְלוּ	יֵאָכְלוּ	יַאֲכִילוּ	יָאֳכְלוּ
3fp	תֶּאֱסֹרְנָה	תֹּאכַלְנָה	תֵּאָכַלְנָה	תַּאֲכֵלְנָה	תָּאֳכַלְנָה
2mp	תֶּאֶסְרוּ	תֹּאכְלוּ	תֵּאָכְלוּ	תַּאֲכִילוּ	תָּאֳכְלוּ
2fp	תֶּאֱסֹרְנָה	תֹּאכַלְנָה	תֵּאָכַלְנָה	תַּאֲכֵלְנָה	תָּאֳכַלְנָה
1cp	נֶאֱסֹר	נֹאכַל	נֵאָכֵל	נַאֲכִיל	נָאֳכַל

Imperative	2ms	שֻׁב	שׁוּב	הִשָּׁב	הָשֵׁב
	2fs	שֻׁבִּי	שׁוּבִי	הִשָּׁבִי	הָשִׁיבִי
	2mp	שֻׁבוּ	שׁוּבוּ	הִשָּׁבוּ	הָשִׁיבוּ
	2fp	שֹׁבְנָה	שֹׁבְנָה	הִשָּׁבְנָה	הָשֵׁבְנָה
Infinitive Construct		שֻׁוֹב	שׁוּב	הִשָּׁב	הָשִׁיב
Infinitive Absolute		שָׁוֹב	שׁוֹב	הִשּׁוֹב	הָשֵׁב
Active Participle	ms	שָׁב	שָׁב	נָשׁוֹב	מֵשִׁיב
	fs	שָׁבָה	שָׁבָה	נְשׁוֹבָה	מְשִׁיבָה
	mp	שָׁבִים	שָׁבִים	נְשׁוֹבִים	מְשִׁיבִים
	fp	שָׁבוֹת	שָׁבוֹת	נְשׁוֹבוֹת	מְשִׁיבוֹת
Passive Participle	ms			מוּשָׁב	מוּשָׁב
	fs			מוּשֶׁבֶת	מוּשָׁבָה
	mp			מוּשָׁבִים	מוּשָׁבִים
	fp			מוּשָׁבוֹת	מוּשָׁבוֹת

Biconsonantal Verbs

Perfect

	Qal (ו-class)	Qal (י-class)	Qal (ו-class)	Hiphil	Hophal
3ms	קָם	שָׂם	בָּא	הֵקִים	הוּקַם
3fs	קָמָה	שָׂמָה	בָּאָה	הֵקִימָה	הוּקְמָה
2ms	קַמְתָּ	שַׂמְתָּ	בָּאתָ	הֲקִימוֹתָ	הוּקַמְתָּ
2fs	קַמְתְּ	שַׂמְתְּ	בָּאת	הֲקִימוֹת	הוּקַמְתְּ
1cs	קַמְתִּי	שַׂמְתִּי	בָּאתִי	הֲקִימוֹתִי	הוּקַמְתִּי
3cp	קָמוּ	שָׂמוּ	בָּאוּ	הֵקִימוּ	הוּקְמוּ
2mp	קַמְתֶּם	שַׂמְתֶּם	בָּאתֶם	הֲקִימוֹתֶם	הוּקַמְתֶּם
2fp	קַמְתֶּן	שַׂמְתֶּן	בָּאתֶן	הֲקִימוֹתֶן	הוּקַמְתֶּן
1cp	קַמְנוּ	שַׂמְנוּ	בָּאנוּ	הֲקִימוֹנוּ	הוּקַמְנוּ

Imperfect

	Qal (ו-class)	Qal (י-class)	Qal (ו-class)	Hiphil	Hophal
3ms	יָקוּם	יָשִׂים	יָבוֹא	יָקִים	יוּקַם
3fs	תָּקוּם	תָּשִׂים	תָּבוֹא	תָּקִים	תּוּקַם
2ms	תָּקוּם	תָּשִׂים	תָּבוֹא	תָּקִים	תּוּקַם
2fs	תָּקוּמִי	תָּשִׂימִי	תָּבוֹאִי	תָּקִימִי	תּוּקְמִי
1cs	אָקוּם	אָשִׂים	אָבוֹא	אָקִים	אוּקַם
3mp	יָקוּמוּ	יָשִׂימוּ	יָבוֹאוּ	יָקִימוּ	יוּקְמוּ
3fp	תְּקוּמֶינָה	תְּשִׂימֶינָה	תָּבוֹאנָה	תְּקִימֶינָה	תּוּקַמְנָה
2mp	תָּקוּמוּ	תָּשִׂימוּ	תָּבוֹאוּ	תָּקִימוּ	תּוּקְמוּ
2fp	תְּקוּמֶינָה	תְּשִׂימֶינָה	תָּבוֹאנָה	תְּקִימֶינָה	תּוּקַמְנָה
1cp	נָקוּם	נָשִׂים	נָבוֹא	נָקִים	נוּקַם

Imperative	2ms	קוּם	שׂים	בּוֹא	קוֹמֵם
	2fs	קוּמִי	שׂימִי	בּוֹאִי	קוֹמְמִי
	2mp	קוּמוּ	שׂימוּ	בּוֹאוּ	קוֹמְמוּ
	2fp	קֹמְנָה	שֵׂמְנָה	בֹּאנָה	קוֹמֵמְנָה
Infinitive Construct		קוּם	שׂוּם	בּוֹא	קוֹמֵם
			שִׂים		
Infinitive Absolute		קוֹם	שׂוֹם	בּוֹא	קוֹמֵם
Active Participle	ms	קָם	שָׂם	בָּא	מְקוֹמֵם
	fs	קָמָה	שָׂמָה	בָּאָה	מְקוֹמֶמֶת
	mp	קָמִים	שָׂמִים	בָּאִים	מְקוֹמְמִים
	fp	קָמוֹת	שָׂמוֹת	בָּאוֹת	מְקוֹמְמוֹת
Passive Participle	ms	קוּם		בּוּא	מְקוֹמָם
	fs				מְקוֹמֶמֶת
	mp				מְקוֹמָמִים
	fp				מְקוֹמָמוֹת

Geminate Verbs

Perfect

	Qal (1)	Qal (2)	Niphal	Piel	Hiphil	Hophal	Hithpael
3ms	סָבַב	תַּם	נָסַב	גִּלֵּל	הֵסֵב	הוּסַב	הִתְגַּלֵּל
3fs	סָבְבָה	תַּמָּה	נָסַבָּה	גִּלְּלָה	הֵסֵבָּה	הוּסַבָּה	הִתְגַּלְּלָה
2ms	סַבּוֹתָ	תַּמּוֹתָ	נְסַבּוֹתָ	גִּלַּלְתָּ	הֲסִבּוֹתָ	הוּסַבּוֹתָ	הִתְגַּלַּלְתָּ
2fs	סַבּוֹת	תַּמּוֹת	נְסַבּוֹת	גִּלַּלְתְּ	הֲסִבּוֹת	הוּסַבּוֹת	הִתְגַּלַּלְתְּ
1cs	סַבּוֹתִי	תַּמּוֹתִי	נְסַבּוֹתִי	גִּלַּלְתִּי	הֲסִבּוֹתִי	הוּסַבּוֹתִי	הִתְגַּלַּלְתִּי
3cp	סָבְבוּ	תַּמּוּ	נָסַבּוּ	גִּלְּלוּ	הֵסֵבּוּ	הוּסַבּוּ	הִתְגַּלְּלוּ
2mp	סַבּוֹתֶם	תַּמּוֹתֶם	נְסַבּוֹתֶם	גִּלַּלְתֶּם	הֲסִבּוֹתֶם	הוּסַבּוֹתֶם	הִתְגַּלַּלְתֶּם
2fp	סַבּוֹתֶן	תַּמּוֹתֶן	נְסַבּוֹתֶן	גִּלַּלְתֶּן	הֲסִבּוֹתֶן	הוּסַבּוֹתֶן	הִתְגַּלַּלְתֶּן
1cp	סַבּוֹנוּ	תַּמּוֹנוּ	נְסַבּוֹנוּ	גִּלַּלְנוּ	הֲסִבּוֹנוּ	הוּסַבּוֹנוּ	הִתְגַּלַּלְנוּ

Imperfect

	Qal (1)	Qal (2)	Niphal	Piel	Hiphil	Hophal	Hithpael
3ms	יָסֹב	יֵתַם	יִסַּב	יְגַלֵּל	יָסֵב	יוּסַב	יִתְגַּלֵּל
3fs	תָּסֹב	תֵּתַם	תִּסַּב	תְּגַלֵּל	תָּסֵב	תּוּסַב	תִּתְגַּלֵּל
2ms	תָּסֹב	תֵּתַם	תִּסַּב	תְּגַלֵּל	תָּסֵב	תּוּסַב	תִּתְגַּלֵּל
2fs	תָּסֹבִּי	תֵּתַמִּי	תִּסַּבִּי	תְּגַלְּלִי	תָּסֵבִּי	תּוּסַבִּי	תִּתְגַּלְּלִי
1cs	אָסֹב	אֵתַם	אֶסַּב	אֲגַלֵּל	אָסֵב	אוּסַב	אֶתְגַּלֵּל
3mp	יָסֹבּוּ	יֵתַמּוּ	יִסַּבּוּ	יְגַלְּלוּ	יָסֵבּוּ	יוּסַבּוּ	יִתְגַּלְּלוּ
3fp	תְּסֻבֶּינָה	תְּתַמֶּינָה	תִּסַּבֶּינָה	תְּגַלֵּלְנָה	תְּסִבֶּינָה	תּוּסַבֶּינָה	תִּתְגַּלֵּלְנָה
2mp	תָּסֹבּוּ	תֵּתַמּוּ	תִּסַּבּוּ	תְּגַלְּלוּ	תָּסֵבּוּ	תּוּסַבּוּ	תִּתְגַּלְּלוּ
2fp	תְּסֻבֶּינָה	תְּתַמֶּינָה	תִּסַּבֶּינָה	תְּגַלֵּלְנָה	תְּסִבֶּינָה	תּוּסַבֶּינָה	תִּתְגַּלֵּלְנָה
1cp	נָסֹב	נֵתַם	נִסַּב	נְגַלֵּל	נָסֵב	נוּסַב	נִתְגַּלֵּל

	Qal	Niphal	Polel	Hiphil	Hophal	Hitpolel
Imperative 2ms	קוּם	הִקּוֹם	קוֹמֵם	הָקֵם		הִתְקוֹמֵם
2fs	קוּמִי	הִקּוֹמִי	קוֹמְמִי	הָקִימִי		הִתְקוֹמְמִי
2mp	קוּמוּ	הִקּוֹמוּ	קוֹמְמוּ	הָקִימוּ		הִתְקוֹמְמוּ
2fp	קֹמְנָה	הִקּוֹמֶינָה	קוֹמֵמְנָה	הָקֵמְנָה		הִתְקוֹמֵמְנָה
Infinitive Construct	קוּם	הִקּוֹם	קוֹמֵם	הָקִים	הוּקַם	הִתְקוֹמֵם
Infinitive Absolute	קוֹם	הִקּוֹם		הָקֵם		
Active Participle ms	קָם		מְקוֹמֵם	מֵקִים		מִתְקוֹמֵם
fs	קָמָה		מְקוֹמֶמֶת	מְקִימָה		מִתְקוֹמֶמֶת
mp	קָמִים		מְקוֹמְמִים	מְקִימִים		מִתְקוֹמְמִים
fp	קָמוֹת		מְקוֹמְמוֹת	מְקִימוֹת		מִתְקוֹמְמוֹת
Passive Participle ms					מוּקָם	
fs					מוּקֶמֶת	
mp					מוּקָמִים	
fp					מוּקָמוֹת	

Strong Verb Diagnostics
At-A-Glance

	Perfect	Imperfect	Imperative	Infinitive Construct	Infinitive Absolute	Participle
Qal	קָטַל קָטֹל	יִקְטֹל	קְטֹל	קְטֹל	קָטוֹל	קֹטֵל
Niphal	נִקְטַל נִקְטָל	יִקָּטֵל	הִקָּטֵל	הִקָּטֵל	נִקְטוֹל הִקָּטוֹל	נִקְטָל
Piel	קִטֵּל קִטַּל	יְקַטֵּל	קַטֵּל	קַטֵּל	קַטֵּל	מְקַטֵּל
Pual	קֻטַּל	יְקֻטַּל				מְקֻטָּל
Hiphil	הִקְטִיל הִקְטַלְתְּ	יַקְטִיל	הַקְטֵל הַקְטִילִי	הַקְטִיל	הַקְטֵל	מַקְטִיל
Hophal	הָקְטַל הֻקְטַל	יָקְטַל יֻקְטַל				מָקְטָל מֻקְטָל
Hithpael	הִתְקַטֵּל	יִתְקַטֵּל	הִתְקַטֵּל	הִתְקַטֵּל	הִתְקַטֵּל	מִתְקַטֵּל

Niphal Diagnostics
At-A-Glance

	Perfect	Imperfect	Imperative	Infinitive Construct	Infinitive Absolute	Participle
Strong	נִקְטַל נִקְטְל	יִקָּטֵל	הִקָּטֵל	הִקָּטֵל	נִקְטוֹל הִקָּטוֹל	נִקְטָל
III-א	נִמְצָא נִמְצָא	יִמָּצֵא	הִמָּצֵא	הִמָּצֵא	נִמְצוֹא	נִמְצָא
III-ה	נִבְנָה נִבְנֵיתָ	יִבָּנֶה	הִבָּנֵה	הִבָּנוֹת	נִבְנֹה הִבָּנֵה	נִבְנֶה
I-Gutt	נֶעֱזַב נֶעֱזָב	יֵעָזֵב	הֵעָזֵב	הֵעָזֵב	נַעֲזוֹב הֵעָזוֹב	נֶעֱזָב
I-נ	נִצַּל נִצַּל	יִנָּצֵל	הִנָּצֵל	הִנָּצֵל	הִנָּצֵל נִצּוֹל	נִצָּל
I-י	נוֹשַׁב נוֹשַׁב	יִוָּשֵׁב	הִוָּשֵׁב	הִוָּשֵׁב		נוֹשָׁב

Piel Diagnostics
At-A-Glance

	Perfect		Imperfect	Imperative	Infinitive Construct	Infinitive Absolute	Participle
Strong	קִטֵּל	קַטֵּל	יְקַטֵּל	קַטֵּל	קַטֵּל	קַטֵּל	מְקַטֵּל
III-ח/ע	שִׁלַּח	שַׁלַּח	יְשַׁלַּח	שַׁלַּח	שַׁלַּח	שַׁלֵּחַ	מְשַׁלֵּחַ
III-א	מִצֵּא	מַצֵּא	יְמַצֵּא	מַצֵּא	מַצֵּא	מַצֵּא	מְמַצֵּא
III-ה	גִּלָּה	גָּלָה	יְגַלֶּה	גַּלֵּה	גַּלּוֹת	גַּלֵּה	מְגַלֶּה
Geminate	הִלֵּל	הַלֵּל	יְהַלֵּל	הַלֵּל	הַלֵּל	הַלֵּל	מְהַלֵּל
II-Gutt[1]	נִחַם	נַחֵם	יְנַחֵם	נַחֵם	נַחֵם	נַחֵם	מְנַחֵם
II-Gutt[2]	בֵּרֵךְ	בֵּרַךְ	יְבָרֵךְ	בָּרֵךְ	בָּרֵךְ	בָּרֵךְ	מְבָרֵךְ

---

[1] II-Guttural verbs with virtual doubling
[2] II-Guttural verbs with compensatory lengthening

Pual Diagnostics
At-A-Glance

	Perfect	Imperfect	Participle
Strong	קֻטַּל קֻטְּל	יְקֻטַּל	מְקֻטָּל
III-א	מֻצָּא מֻצָּא	יְמֻצָּא	מְמֻצָּא
III-ה	גֻּלָּה גֻּלָּה	יְגֻלֶּה	מְגֻלֶּה
II-Gutt[1]	נֻחַם נֻחַם	יְנֻחַם	מְנֻחָם
II-Gutt[2]	בֹּרַךְ בֹּרַךְ	יְבֹרַךְ	מְבֹרָךְ

---

[1] II-Guttural with virtual doubling
[2] II-Guttural with compensatory lengthening

Hiphil Diagnostics
At-A-Glance

	Perfect	Imperfect	Imperative	Infinitive Construct	Infinitive Absolute	Participle
Strong	הִקְטִיל הִקְטַלְתָּ	יַקְטִיל	הַקְטֵל הַקְטִילִי	הַקְטִיל	הַקְטֵל	מַקְטִיל
I-Gutt	הֶעֱמִיד הֶעֱמַדְתָּ	יַעֲמִיד	הַעֲמֵד הַעֲמִידִי	הַעֲמִיד	הַעֲמֵד	מַעֲמִיד
III-ח/ע	הִשְׁלִיחַ הִשְׁלַחְתָּ	יַשְׁלִיחַ	הַשְׁלַח הַשְׁלִיחִי	הַשְׁלִיחַ	הַשְׁלֵחַ	מַשְׁלִיחַ
III-א	הִמְצִיא הִמְצֵאתָ	יַמְצִיא	הַמְצֵא הַמְצִיאִי	הַמְצִיא	הַמְצֵא	מַמְצִיא
III-ה	הִגְלָה הִגְלִיתָ	יַגְלֶה	הַגְלֵה	הַגְלוֹת	הַגְלֵה	מַגְלֶה
I-נ	הִצִּיל הִצַּלְתָּ	יַצִּיל	הַצֵּל הַצִּילִי	הַצִּיל	הַצֵּל	מַצִּיל
I-י	הוֹשִׁיב הוֹשַׁבְתָּ	יוֹשִׁיב	הוֹשֵׁב הוֹשִׁיבִי	הוֹשִׁיב	הוֹשֵׁב	מוֹשִׁיב
Bicon	הֵקִים הֲקִימֹות	יָקִים	הָקֵם הָקִימִי	הָקִים	הָקֵם	מֵקִים

Hophal Diagnostics
At-A-Glance

	Perfect		Imperfect	Participle
Strong (u)	הָקְטַל		יָקְטַל	מָקְטָל
Strong (o)	הָקְטַל		יָקְטַל	מָקְטָל
I-Guttural	הָעֳמַד		יָעֳמַד	מָעֳמָד
III-ה	הָגְלָה		יָגְלֶה	מָגְלֶה
I-נ	הֻצַּל		יֻצַּל	מֻצָּל
I-י	הוּשַׁב		יוּשַׁב	מוּשָׁב
Bicon	הוּקַם		יוּקַם	מוּקָם
Geminate	הוּסַב		יוּסַב	מוּסָב

Hithpael Diagnostics
At-A-Glance

	Perfect	Imperfect	Imperative	Infinitive Construct	Infinitive Absolute	Participle
Strong	הִתְקַטֵּל	יִתְקַטֵּל	הִתְקַטֵּל	הִתְקַטֵּל	הִתְקַטֵּל	מִתְקַטֵּל
Geminate	הִתְפַּלֵּל	יִתְפַּלֵּל	הִתְפַּלֵּל	הִתְפַּלֵּל	הִתְפַּלֵּל	מִתְפַּלֵּל
III-ה	הִתְגַּלָּה	יִתְגַּלֶּה	הִתְגַּלֵּה	הִתְגַּלּוֹת		מִתְגַּלֶּה
II-Gutt[1]	הִתְנַחֵם	יִתְנַחֵם	הִתְנַחֵם	הִתְנַחֵם	הִתְנַחֵם	מִתְנַחֵם
II-Gutt[2]	הִתְבָּרֵךְ	יִתְבָּרֵךְ	הִתְבָּרֵךְ	הִתְבָּרֵךְ	הִתְבָּרֵךְ	מִתְבָּרֵךְ

---

[1] II-Guttural with virtual doubling
[2] II-Guttural with compensatory lengthening

Summary of Endings on III-ה Verbs
Qal and Derived Stems

Ending	Qal	Niphal	Piel	Pual	Hiphil	Hophal	Hithpael
Perfect ה ָ	בָּנָה	נִבְנָה	גִּלָּה	גֻּלָּה	הִגְלָה	הָגְלָה	הִתְגַּלָּה
Imperfect ה ֶ	יִבְנֶה	יִבָּנֶה	יְגַלֶּה	יְגֻלֶּה	יַגְלֶה	יָגְלֶה	יִתְגַּלֶּה
Imperative ה ֵ	בְּנֵה	הִבָּנֵה	גַּלֵּה		הַגְלֵה		הִתְגַּלֵּה
Inf Construct וֹת	בְּנוֹת	הִבָּנוֹת	גַּלּוֹת		הַגְלוֹת		הִתְגַּלּוֹת
Participle ה ֶ	בֹּנֶה	נִבְנֶה	מְגַלֶּה	מְגֻלֶּה	מַגְלֶה	מָגְלֶה	מִתְגַּלֶּה

Hebrew-English Lexicon

Hebrew words occurring fifty times or more, including less frequently occurring words that appear in the grammar and workbook. The number located to the left of some Hebrew words indicates the chapter in which the vocabulary item is presented.

א

3 אָב — father; אָבוֹת (plural); אֲבִי (ms construct)

17 אָבַד — to perish; (Piel) destroy; (Hiphil) exterminate

אָבָה — to be willing, consent, agree

אֶבְיוֹן — poor, oppressed

אֲבִימֶלֶךְ — Abimelech

אֵבֶל — mourning

אֲבָל — truly, indeed, however

10 אֶבֶן — stone (fs)

אַבְנֵר — Abner

אַבְרָהָם — Abraham

אַבְרָם — Abram

אַבְשָׁלוֹם — Absalom

אֵד — fresh water, surface water (mist?)

אֱדוֹם — Edom; אֲדוֹמִי Edomite(s)

4 אָדוֹן — lord, master, Lord (see אֲדֹנָי)

3 אָדָם — man, Adam

10 אֲדָמָה — ground, land

אֶדֶן — pedestal, socket

אֲדֹנָי — Lord

17 אָהַב — to love, like

אַהֲבָה — love

8 אֹהֶל — tent; אֹהֶל מוֹעֵד tent of meeting

אַהֲרוֹן — Aaron

9 אוֹ — or

אוּלַי — perhaps

31 אָוֶן — wickedness, iniquity

31 אוֹצָר — supply, storehouse, treasure

23 אוֹר — light

אוֹר — (Hiphil) to give light, shine

31 אוֹת — sign; אֹתוֹת (plural)

15 אָז — then, formerly, since; (מִן + אָז) מֵאָז from then, from that time

אָזַן — (Hiphil) to listen

15 אֹזֶן — ear (fs); אָזְנֵי (dual construct)

4 אָח — brother; אַחִים (plural); אֲחִי (ms construct)

אַחְאָב — Ahab

7 אֶחָד — one (ms)

אָחוֹר — back, behind

27 אָחוֹת — sister (fs)

20 אָחַז — to seize, hold fast

	אֲחֻזָּה	property, possession
6	אַחַר	after, behind (more frequently as אַחֲרֵי)
8	אַחֵר	another; אַחֶרֶת (fs)
	אַחֲרוֹן	behind, last
	אַחֲרִית	end, outcome (fs)
11	אַחַת	one (fs)
	אֵי־מִזֶּה	from what place
10	אֹיֵב	enemy; אוֹיֵב (full spelling)
	אַיֵּה	where?
	אִיּוֹב	Job
8	אֵיךְ	how?
	אֵיכָה	how? where?
15	אַיִל	ram
	אִילָם	porch, vestibule (spelling varies as אוּלָם or אֵלָם)
	אֵימָה	fear, terror, dread
9	אַיִן	there is not, there are not; אֵין (construct)
	אֵיפֹה	where?
4	אִישׁ	man, husband; אֲנָשִׁים (plural); אַנְשֵׁי (mp construct)
12	אַךְ	only, surely
12	אָכַל	to eat, devour
	אֹכֶל	food
	אָכְלָה	food
3	אֵל	God, mighty one, god
6	אֶל	to, toward, unto
12	אַל	no, not

8	אֵלֶּה	these
3	אֱלֹהִים	God, gods; אֱלֹהֵי (mp construct)
	אַלּוּף	tribal chief
	אֵלִיָּה	Elijah; also as אֵלִיָּהוּ
	אֱלִישָׁע	Elisha
	אָלַם	(Piel) to bind sheaves
	אֲלֻמָּה	sheaf
	אַלְמָנָה	widow
	אֶלְעָזָר	Eleazar
8	אֶלֶף	thousand, tribe, clan
11	אֵם	mother (fs)
12	אִם	if, then, or
	אָמָה	female slave
11	אַמָּה	forearm, cubit
	אֱמוּנָה	steadiness, firmness
24	אָמַן	(Niphal) to be steady, firm, trustworthy, faithful; (Hiphil) believe
	אָמַץ	to be strong, brave
12	אָמַר	to say
	אֱמֹרִי	Amorite(s)
17	אֱמֶת	trustworthiness, stability, truth (fs)
	אַמְתַּחַת	sack; אַמְתְּחֹת (plural)
	אֱנוֹשׁ	man, men (collective)
8	אֲנַחְנוּ	we
8	אֲנִי	I
8	אָנֹכִי	I (alternate form of אֲנִי)
	אֲנָשִׁים	men, husbands (plural of אִישׁ); אַנְשֵׁי (mp construct)
	אָסָא	Asa

	אָסִיר	prisoner
17	אָסַף	to gather, assemble
28	אָסַר	to bind; (Niphal, Pual) be fettered, imprisoned
	אֶסְתֵּר	Esther
9	אַף	nose, nostril, anger
15	אַף	also, even
	אֶפְרַיִם	Ephraim; אֶפְרָתִי Ephraimite
	אֵצֶל	beside, near, next to
	אַרְבַּע	four; אַרְבָּעָה (fs)
12	אָרוֹן	ark, chest (with definite article הָאָרוֹן)
	אָרוּר	accursed
32	אֶרֶז	cedar
	אֹרַח	way, path
	אֲרִי	lion
	אַרְיֵה	lion (alternate of אֲרִי)
	אֹרֶךְ	length
	אֲרָם	Aram, Syria; אֲרַמִּי Aramean(s), Syrian(s)
3	אֶרֶץ	earth, land (fs); אֲרָצוֹת (plural); אַרְצוֹת (construct)
	אַרְצָה	toward the earth, to the ground (אֶרֶץ with directional ending ה ָ)
22	אָרַר	to curse
5	אֵשׁ	fire (fs)
4	אִשָּׁה	woman, wife; אֵשֶׁת (fs construct); נָשִׁים (plural); נְשֵׁי (construct)
	אִשֶּׁה	offering by fire

	אַשּׁוּר	Assyria
	אָשֵׁם	to be guilty; also אָשַׁם
8	אֲשֶׁר	who, which, that
6	אֵת/אֶת־	with, beside; אִתִּי (with 1cs suffix)
6	אֵת/אֶת־	definite direct object marker (not translated); אֹתִי (with 1cs suffix)
8	אַתְּ	you (2fs)
8	אַתָּה	you (2ms)
	אָתוֹן	female donkey (fs)
8	אַתֶּם	you (2mp)
	אֶתְמוֹל	yesterday
8	אַתֵּן	you (2fp)
8	אַתֵּנָה	you (2fp)

בּ

6	בְּ	in, against
	בְּאֵר	well, pit (fs)
	בָּבֶל	Babylon (Babel)
11	בֶּגֶד	garment
	בִּגְלַל	(בְּ + גְּלָל) on account of
8	בְּהֵמָה	cattle, animal(s)
14	בּוֹא	to go in, enter, come; (Hiphil) to bring, carry
	בּוֹר	pit, cistern
22	בּוֹשׁ	to be ashamed
	בָּחוּר	young man; בַּחוּרִים (plural)
18	בָּחַר	to choose
19	בָּטַח	to trust
33	בֶּטֶן	belly, womb (fs)

18	בִּין	to understand, perceive
6	בֵּין	between
	בִּינָה	understanding, intelligence
3	בַּיִת	house; בָּתִּים (plural); בֵּית (ms construct); בָּתֵּי (mp construct)
	בֵּית־אֵל	Bethel
19	בָּכָה	to weep, mourn
23	בְּכֹר	firstborn; בְּכוֹר (full spelling)
	בַּל	not (mostly in poetry)
20	בִּלְתִּי	not, except (negates Infinitive Construct); frequently as לְבִלְתִּי
21	בָּמָה	high place, funerary installation; בָּמוֹת (plural)
3	בֵּן	son; בָּנִים (plural); בֶּן־ (ms construct); בְּנֵי (mp construct)
14	בָּנָה	to build
	בִּנְיָמִין	Benjamin
	בַּעֲבוּר	because of, for the sake of
18	בַּעַד	distance, behind, through; בְּעַד (construct)
	בְּעֵינֵי	in the eyes of, in the opinion of
18	בַּעַל	owner, husband, Baal
17	בָּעַר	to consume, burn
	בָּקַע	to split, break open
9	בָּקָר	cows, herd(s), cattle

9	בֹּקֶר	morning
26	בָּקַשׁ	(Piel) to seek
	בָּרָא	to create
	בָּרָד	hail
35	בַּרְזֶל	iron
	בָּרַח	to run away, flee
10	בְּרִית	covenant (fs)
13	בָּרַךְ	(Piel) to bless, kneel
9	בְּרָכָה	blessing; בִּרְכַּת (construct)
10	בָּשָׂר	flesh
	בָּשָׁן	Bashan
4	בַּת	daughter (fs); בָּנוֹת (plural)
6	בְּתוֹךְ	in the midst of
	בְּתוּלָה	virgin

ג

16	גָּאַל	to redeem
	גָּבַהּ	to be high, exalted
	גָּבֹהַּ	high; גְּבֹהִים (plural)
10	גְּבוּל	boundary, territory, border
15	גִּבּוֹר	warrior, mighty man (גִּבּוֹר חַיִל mighty warrior)
	גְּבוּרָה	strength
	גִּבְעָה	hill, (cultic) high place; גְּבָעוֹת (plural)
	גָּבַר	to excel, swell, rise
	גֶּבֶר	young man, strong man
	גָּד	Gad; גָּדִי Gadite(s)

22	גָּדַל	to be(come) strong, great; (Piel) bring up, let grow, nourish; (Hiphil) to make great, magnify
7	גָּדוֹל	great
4	גּוֹי	people, nation
27	גּוּר	to sojourn, stay as a foreigner
31	גּוֹרָל	lot, allotment
17	גָּלָה	to reveal, uncover, depart, go into captivity
	גָּלַל	to roll, roll away
	גָּלָל	on account of (frequently with inseparable preposition, בִּגְלַל)
	גִּלְעָד	Gilead; גִּלְעָדִי Gileadite(s)
8	גַּם	also, indeed
	גָּמַל	to wean
	גָּמָל	camel; גְּמַלִּים (plural)
	גַּן	garden; גָּן (alternate spelling)
	גָּנַב	to steal
	גַּנָּה	vineyard, garden
	גָּעַר	to rebuke
	גֶּפֶן	vine (fs)
29	גֵּר	stranger, sojourner, alien
	גֹּרֶן	threshing-floor
	גֵּרַשׁ	(Piel) to drive away
	גַּת	winepress (fs)

ד

	דָּבַק	to stick, cling to, cleave
26	דָּבַר	(Piel) to speak
3	דָּבָר	word, matter, thing; דִּבְרֵי (mp construct)
	דְּבַשׁ	honey
	דָּג	fish
	דָּוִד	David; דָּוִיד (full spelling)
	דּוֹד	beloved, lover
19	דּוֹר	generation, lifetime, lifespan; דּוֹרוֹת (plural)
	דִּין	to judge
7	דַּל	poor
30	דֶּלֶת	door (fs)
8	דָּם	blood; דָּמִים (plural); דַּם (ms construct); דְּמֵי (mp construct)
	דָּמַם	to be astonished, silent
	דָּן	Dan; דָּנִי Danite(s)
	דָּנִיֵּאל	Daniel
30	דַּעַת	knowledge (fs)
4	דֶּרֶךְ	way, road (ms, fs)
18	דָּרַשׁ	to seek

ה

5	הַ	the (with Daghesh Forte in the following consonant)
8	הֲ	interrogative particle (not translated)

33	הֶבֶל	breath, vanity, idol
	הֶבֶל	Abel
8	הוּא	he, that
8	הוּא	she (alternate form of the 3fs independent personal pronoun הִיא)
8	הִיא	she, that
12	הָיָה	to be, happen, become
5	הֵיכָל	palace, temple
12	הָלַךְ	to go, walk
26	הָלַל	(Piel) to praise; (Hithpael) boast
8	הֵם	they (3mp)
8	הֵמָּה	they (3mp)
30	הָמוֹן	tumult, turmoil, multitude
9	הֵן	behold, if
8	הֵן	they (3fp)
8	הֵנָּה	they (3fp); those (fp)
	הֵנָּה	here, to this place
9	הִנֵּה	behold! lo!; הִנְנִי or הִנֵּנִי (with 1cs suffix)
25	הָפַךְ	to turn, overturn, destroy
	הֲפֵכָה	destruction
4	הַר	mountain, mountain range; הָרִים (plural)
18	הָרַג	to kill
	הָרָה	to conceive, become pregnant

ו

5	וְ	and, or, also, even

ז

8	זֹאת	this (fs)
21	זָבַח	to slaughter, sacrifice
15	זֶבַח	sacrifice
8	זֶה	this (ms)
5	זָהָב	gold
	זַיִת	olive, olive tree
25	זָכָר	man, male
13	זָכַר	to remember; (Hiphil) to summon, recall, make known
	זֵכֶר	remembrance, memorial
	זָנָב	tail (as of a snake)
25	זָנָה	to commit fornication, be a harlot
	זֵעָה	sweat; זֵעַת (fs construct)
28	זָעַק	to cry out; (Niphal) called to arms; (Hiphil) send out a call to arms
	זְקוּנִים	old age
13	זָקֵן	to be(come) old
7	זָקֵן	(adjective) old; (noun) old man, elder; זְקַן (construct)
	זָר	strange, different, illicit
30	זְרוֹעַ	arm, forearm, power, strength (fs)
	זָרַע	to sow, scatter seed

11	זֶ֫רַע	seed, descendant
	זָרַק	to sprinkle, scatter

ח

	חֶבְרוֹן	Hebron
	חָג	procession, feast, festival; חַג (alternate spelling)
	חָדַל	to cease, desist, stop
	חָדָשׁ	new, fresh
10	חֹ֫דֶשׁ	new moon, month; חֲדָשִׁים (plural)
	חָוָה	(Hishtaphel) to bow down, worship
	חַוָּה	Eve
22	חוֹמָה	wall
19	חוּץ	outside; חוּצָה (חוּץ with directional ending) to the outside
28	חָזָה	to see, perceive
	חִזָּיוֹן	vision; חֶזְיֹנוֹת (plural)
13	חָזַק	to be(come) strong; (Hiphil) seize, grasp
	חָזָק	hard, strong
	חִזְקִיָּה	Hezekiah; חִזְקִיָּ֫הוּ (alternate spelling)
16	חָטָא	to miss (a mark), sin
9	חַטָּאת	sin, sin-offering, expiation (fs); חַטָּאוֹת (plural); חַטַּאת (fs construct)
5	חַי	life, lifetime; (adjective) living, alive

15	חָיָה	to live, be (stay) alive
29	חַיָּה	(wild) animal, living thing
	חַיִּים	life, lifetime (see חַי above)
	חִיל	to be in labor, pain
10	חַ֫יִל	strength, wealth, army; חֵיל (ms construct)
	חֵיק	bosom
	חָכַם	to be(come) wise
7	חָכָם	wise
6	חָכְמָה	experience, shrewdness, wisdom
29	חֵ֫לֶב	fat
	חָלָב	milk
28	חָלָה	to be(come) weak, tired, sick
	חֲלוֹם	dream; חֲלוֹמוֹת (plural)
30	חָלָל	(adjective) slain
30	חָלַל	(Niphal) to be defiled; (Piel) pollute, profane; (Hiphil) begin
	חָלַם	to dream
	חָלַק	to divide, apportion; (Piel) scatter
	חֵ֫לֶק	part, portion
23	חֵמָה	heat, rage, wrath, poison
29	חֲמוֹר	(male) ass, donkey
	חָמָס	violence, wrong
11	חָמֵשׁ	five; חֲמִשָּׁה (fs)
11	חֲמִשִּׁים	fifty
	חֵן	favor, grace

21	חָנָה	to encamp
28	חָנַן	to be gracious to, favor; (Hithpael) implore favor or compassion
10	חֶסֶד	loyalty, kindness, devotion, steadfast love
	חָסָה	to seek refuge
	חָסִיד	one who is faithful, devout
18	חָפֵץ	to please, delight, take pleasure
	חָפַשׂ	to search out; (Piel) look; (Hithpael) disguise oneself
	חֵץ	arrow
23	חֲצִי	half
11	חָצֵר	permanent settlement, court, enclosure
22	חֹק	statute, prescription, rule, ordinance; חֻקִּים (plural)
21	חֻקָּה	statute, prescription; חֻקּוֹת (plural)
5	חֶרֶב	sword (fs)
	חֹרֵב	Horeb
25	חָרָה	become hot, burning, angry
	חָרַם	to devote to the ban, consecrate
33	חֶרְפָּה	reproach, disgrace
	חָרַשׁ	to be deaf
	חָשַׂךְ	to withhold

22	חָשַׁב	to account, regard, value, think; (Piel) calculate, plan, think about
	חָשַׁךְ	to be(come) dim, dark
25	חֹשֶׁךְ	darkness
	חֵת	Heth; חִתִּי Hittite(s)
	חֹתֵן	father-in-law
	חָתַת	to be shattered, filled with terror

ט

	טָבַח	to slaughter
8	טָהוֹר	clean, pure
17	טָהֵר	to be clean, pure
18	טוֹב	to be good, pleasant (cf. יָטַב)
7	טוֹב	good
20	טָמֵא	(verb) to be unclean
30	טָמֵא	(adjective) unclean
	טַף	children
	טֶרֶם	not yet, before, frequently as בְּטֶרֶם with the same meaning

י

	יְאֹר	Nile river, river
	יָבֵשׁ	to be dry, dry up
10	יָד	hand (fs); יָדוֹת (plural); יַד (fs construct); יָדַיִם (dual); יְדֵי (dual construct)

26	יָדָה	(Piel) to throw, cast; (Hiphil, Hithpael) thank, praise, confess
13	יָדַע	to know, notice; (Hiphil) to teach, declare, make known
	יְהוּדָה	Judah; יְהוּדִי Judahite, Judean
3	יְהוָה	Yahweh, the Lord; יָהּ or יָה (shortened, often poetic forms)
	יְהוֹיָדָע	Jehoiada
	יְהוֹנָתָן	Jonathan
	יְהוֹשֻׁעַ	Joshua
	יְהוֹשָׁפָט	Jehoshaphat
	יוֹאָב	Joab
	יוֹאָשׁ	Joash
3	יוֹם	day; יָמִים (plural); יְמֵי (mp construct)
	יוֹמָם	in the daytime, by day
	יוֹסֵף	Joseph
20	יַחַד	(noun) community; (adverb) together, at the same time (frequently spelled יַחְדָּו with the same meaning)
20	יַחְדָּו	see יַחַד above
22	יָטַב	to be good; (Hiphil) treat kindly, graciously
20	יַיִן	wine
	יָכַח	(Niphal) to dispute; (Hiphil) reprove, give judgment, settle quarrels
15	יָכֹל	to be able

14	יָלַד	to bring forth, bear; (Piel) help at birth, serve as midwife
5	יֶלֶד	male child, boy
	יַלְדָּה	girl
5	יָם	sea, west; יַמִּים (plural)
	יָמָּה	westward (יָם with directional ending הָ)
21	יָמִין	right hand (side), south (fs)
16	יָסַף	to add, continue to do more or again; (Hiphil) enhance, increase
18	יַעַן	on account of, because
	יַעַן אֲשֶׁר	because
27	יָעַץ	to give counsel, advice
	יַעֲקֹב	Jacob
	יַעַר	thicket
7	יָפֶה	beautiful, handsome
12	יָצָא	to go (come) out, go (come) forth; (Hiphil) make come out, lead out
	יִצְחָק	Isaac
	יָצַק	to dish up (food), pour out (liquid)
20	יָצַר	form, shape, fashion
	יָקַץ	to wake up
	יָקָר	precious
14	יָרֵא	to fear, be afraid
14	יָרַד	to go down; (Hiphil) bring down, throw down
	יַרְדֵּן	Jordan

	יָרָה	(Hiphil) to instruct, teach
3	יְרוּשָׁלַם	Jerusalem; also spelled יְרוּשָׁלַיִם
	יָרֵחַ	moon
	יְרִיעָה	curtain, tent (fabric)
	יָרֵךְ	thigh; יֶרֶךְ (construct)
	יִרְמְיָה	Jeremiah; יִרְמְיָהוּ (alternate spelling)
16	יָרַשׁ	to inherit, subdue, possess, dispossess, tread; (Hiphil) drive out, take possession of
3	יִשְׂרָאֵל	Israel
9	יֵשׁ	there is (are)
12	יָשַׁב	to sit, dwell
31	יְשׁוּעָה	deliverance, salvation
	יִשְׁמָעֵאל	Ishmael; יִשְׁמְעֵאלִי Ishmaelite
24	יָשַׁע	(Niphal) to be saved, receive help; (Hiphil) save, help, rescue
	יֵשַׁע	salvation, help (יִשְׁעִי with 1cs suffix)
7	יָשָׁר	straight, right, upright, just
	יָתוֹם	orphan
24	יָתַר	(Niphal, Hiphil) be left, remain
29	יֶתֶר	remainder, remnant

כ

6	כְּ	as, like, according to כָּמוֹנִי (with 1cs suffix)
8	כַּאֲשֶׁר	as, when
13	כָּבֵד	(verb) to be heavy, honored
	כָּבֵד	(adjective) heavy
9	כָּבוֹד	glory, honor, possessions
	כָּבַס	(Piel) to wash (clothes)
22	כֶּבֶשׂ	young ram, lamb
	כִּבְשָׂה	ewe-lamb
5	כֹּה	thus, so
	כָּהַן	(Piel) to perform the duties of a priest
4	כֹּהֵן	priest
	כּוֹכָב	star; כּוֹכָבִים (plural)
24	כּוּן	(Niphal) to be firm, established; (Polel) establish; (Hiphil) establish, set up
23	כֹּחַ	strength, power
8	כִּי	because, for, that, when, but, indeed, truly
	כַּיּוֹם	today, this day (הַיּוֹם + כְּ)
	כָּכָה	so, thus
	כִּכָּר	that which is round, i.e., loaf of bread, talent, region, proper name
6	כֹּל	all, each, every, whole; כָּל־ (construct)

17	כָּלָה	to cease, come to an end, finish, complete
9	כְּלִי	vessel, utensil; כֵּלִים (plural); כְּלֵי (construct)
9	כְּמוֹ	as, like (cf. כְּ above)
7	כֵּן	thus, so
	כָּנַע	(Niphal) to be subdued, humbled
	כְּנַעַן	Canaan; כְּנַעֲנִי Canaanite
27	כָּנָף	wing, corner, edge
17	כִּסֵּא	seat, throne; כִּסְאוֹת (plural)
26	כָּסָה	(Piel) to cover, conceal
8	כְּסִיל	stupid, dull, foolish, insolent
5	כֶּסֶף	silver, money
	כָּעַס	to be irritated, angry; (Hiphil) provoke, insult, offend
16	כַּף	hand, palm (fs)
16	כָּפַר	to cover; (Piel) expiate
30	כְּרוּב	cherub
30	כֶּרֶם	vineyard
15	כָּרַת	to cut (off), make a covenant
	כַּשְׂדִּים	Chaldea, Chaldeans
	כָּשַׁל	to stumble, totter
13	כָּתַב	to write
	כֻּתֹּנֶת	tunic (also as כְּתֹנֶת)
	כָּתֵף	shoulder (fs)

ל

6	לְ	to, toward, for
12	לֹא	no, not
	לֵאמֹר	saying (used to introduce a direct quote)
4	לֵב	heart, mind, will
4	לֵבָב	heart, mind, will (alternate spelling of לֵב)
9	לְבַד	alone, besides (בַד with לְ prefix)
	לַבָּה	flame; לַבַּת (construct)
	לְבִלְתִּי	not, except (negates Infinitive Construct); see בִּלְתִּי
	לָבָן	Laban
19	לָבַשׁ	to put on, clothe
	לֶהָבָה	flame
	לוּחַ	tablet; לוּחוֹת (plural)
	לֵוִי	Levi, Levite(s)
24	לָחַם	(Niphal) to fight
9	לֶחֶם	bread, food
	לָחַץ	to crowd, press, oppress, torment
	לַחַץ	oppression, affliction
11	לַיְלָה	night
29	לִין	to spend the night, lodge
22	לָכַד	to seize, capture
11	לָכֵן	therefore
27	לָמַד	to learn; (Piel) teach
8	לָמָּה	why; לָמֶה (alternate spelling)

6	לְמַ֫עַן	for the sake of, on account of, in order that
6	לִפְנֵי	before, in the presence of
14	לָקַח	to take, lay hold of, seize
	לִקְרַאת	toward, over against, opposite
23	לָשׁוֹן	tongue

מ

7	מְאֹד	very, exceedingly
11	מֵאָה	one hundred
	מְא֫וּמָה	anything
	מֵאָז	from then, from that time (מִן + אָז)
	מֵאַ֫יִן	from where? (מִן + אַ֫יִן)
	מָאֵן	(Piel) to refuse
28	מָאַס	to reject, refuse
11	מָאתַ֫יִם	two hundred
	מַבּוּל	flood, deluge
	מִבְטָח	trust, confidence
	מִגְדָּל	tower
	מָגֵן	shield
	מַגֵּפָה	stroke, plague
25	מִגְרָשׁ	pasture, pasture-land
10	מִדְבָּר	pasturage, wilderness, steppe
	מִדְבָּ֫רָה	toward the wilderness (מִדְבָּר with directional ending ָה)
	מָדַד	to measure
	מִדָּה	measure

8	מַדּוּעַ	why?
	מִדְיָן	Midian; מִדְיָנִי Midianite
8	מָה	what? how?
26	מָהַר	(Piel) to hasten, hurry, do something quickly or in a hurry
	מוֹאָב	Moab; מוֹאָבִי Moabite(s)
	מוֹלֶ֫דֶת	descendants, offspring, (with 3ms suffix מוֹלַדְתּוֹ)
	מוּסָר	chastening, correction
11	מוֹעֵד	appointed place, appointed time, season
14	מוּת	to die; (Hiphil) kill, have executed
10	מָ֫וֶת	death; מוֹת (construct)
5	מִזְבֵּחַ	altar; מִזְבְּחוֹת (plural)
	מִזְמוֹר	psalm
33	מִזְרָח	sunrise, east
	מָחָה	to wipe out, annihilate
	מַחֲזֶה	vision
	מַחֲלָה	sickness
11	מַחֲנֶה	camp, army; מַחֲנִים and מַחֲנוֹת (plural); מַחֲנֵה (construct)
	מָחָר	tomorrow
	מַחֲשָׁבָה	thought, idea
10	מַטֶּה	rod, staff, tribe
	מַטְמוֹן	treasure
	מָטָר	rain
8	מִי	who?
4	מַ֫יִם	water; מֵי (construct)
27	מָכַר	to sell

13	מָלֵא	(verb) to be full; (Piel) fill, fulfill
	מָלֵא	(adjective) full
11	מַלְאָךְ	messenger, angel
19	מְלָאכָה	work
	מָלוֹן	lodging place
9	מִלְחָמָה	war, battle; מִלְחֶמֶת (construct)
24	מָלַט	(Niphal) to escape; (Piel) save, deliver
13	מָלַךְ	to reign, be king; (Hiphil) make someone king
3	מֶלֶךְ	king; מַלְכֵי (mp construct)
	מַלְכָּה	queen; מְלָכוֹת (plural)
30	מַלְכוּת	dominion, kingdom, reign (fs)
6	מִלִּפְנֵי	from before, from the presence of, on account of
25	מַמְלָכָה	kingdom; מַמְלֶכֶת (construct)
	מִמַּעַל	above, on top of (מֵעַל with מִן)
	מָן	manna
6	מִן	from
12	מִנְחָה	gift, offering
	מָנַע	to retain, hold back, withhold
17	מִסְפָּר	number
7	מְעַט	a few, a little
6	מַעַל	upwards, above
11	מַעֲשֶׂה	work, deed, act

6	מִפְּנֵי	from before, from the presence of, on account of
13	מָצָא	to find
	מַצֵּבָה	standing-stone
	מַצָּה	unleavened bread; מַצּוֹת (plural)
6	מִצְוָה	commandment; מִצְוֹת (plural)
	מִצְרִי	Egyptian (gentilic of מִצְרַיִם)
3	מִצְרַיִם	Egypt; מִצְרִי Egyptian; מִצְרִים Egyptians
34	מִקְדָּשׁ	sanctuary
5	מָקוֹם	place; מְקוֹמוֹת (plural)
31	מִקְנֶה	possession (of land or cattle); מִקְנֵה (construct)
	מַר	bitter
28	מַרְאֶה	sight, appearance; מַרְאֵה (construct)
	מְרַגֵּל	spy
	מָרוֹם	height
	מֶרְכָּבָה	chariot; מֶרְכֶּבֶת (construct)
	מִרְעֶה	pasture
	מָרַר	to be bitter
	מַשָּׂא	burden, message
3	מֹשֶׁה	Moses
29	מָשַׁח	to anoint
	מָשִׁיחַ	anointed one; מְשִׁיחַ (construct)
21	מִשְׁכָּן	dwelling, tabernacle

27	מָשַׁל	to govern, rule
	מִשְׁמָר	jail, place of confinement
31	מִשְׁמֶרֶת	guard, obligation, service (fs)
9	מִשְׁפָּחָה	family, clan; מִשְׁפַּחַת (construct)
5	מִשְׁפָּט	judgment, custom, justice
	מִשְׁתֶּה	banquet
	מֵת	dead
6	מִתּוֹךְ	from the midst of

נ

18	נָא	please, now (used after volitional conjugations and often untranslated)
5	נְאֻם	utterance, declaration (נְאֻם יְהוָה declares the Lord)
	נְאָקָה	groan, groaning
26	נָבָא	(Niphil, Hithpael) to prophesy
	נָבוֹן	intelligent, discerning
26	נָבַט	(Piel, Hiphil) to look at, regard
4	נָבִיא	prophet
30	נָגַד	(Hiphil) to make known, report, tell
28	נֶגֶב	dry country, south, Negev
16	נֶגֶד	opposite, before, in front of
	נָגִיד	chief, leader, prince

20	נָגַע	to touch, reach
31	נֶגַע	blow, assault, plague
	נָגַף	to strike, smite
	נָגַשׂ	to beat, drive, force; taskmaster (Participle)
22	נָגַשׁ	to draw near, approach
	נָדַח	(Niphal) to be scattered, go astray
	נָדַר	to vow
	נֶדֶר	vow; נֵדֶר (alternate spelling)
25	נָהָר	river, stream; נְהָרוֹת and rarely נְהָרִים (plural)
	נָוֶה	pasturage, abode, residence
21	נוּחַ	to rest, settle down, make quiet; (Hiphil) lay, deposit
20	נוּס	to flee, escape
	נָחַל	to obtain, receive property
21	נַחַל	stream, small river, wadi
11	נַחֲלָה	inheritance, property, possession
24	נָחַם	(Niphal) to be sorry, repent; (Piel) comfort, console
	נָחָשׁ	snake
23	נְחֹשֶׁת	copper, bronze
16	נָטָה	to turn, stretch out, spread out
	נָטַע	to plant

24	נָכָה	(Niphal) to be hit; (Hiphil) to smite
	נָכַר	(Niphal) to pretend; (Hiphil) investigate, recognize
	נָסָה	(Niphal) to put someone to the test
	נֶסֶךְ	libation, drink-offering; נֵסֶךְ (alternate spelling)
21	נָסַע	to depart
	נַעַל	shoe, sandal
11	נַעַר	youth, young man
	נַעֲרָה	young girl
	נְפִילִים	giants; נְפִלִים (alternate spelling)
14	נָפַל	to fall
4	נֶפֶשׁ	life, soul (fs)
24	נָצַב	(Niphal) to take one's stand, be stationed; (Hiphil) establish
	נָצַח	(Piel) to lead, supervise
24	נָצַל	(Niphal) to be delivered; (Hiphil) snatch away
29	נָצַר	to watch, guard
	נְקֵבָה	female
	נָקַם	to take revenge, vengeance
14	נָשָׂא	to lift up, bear, carry
	נָשַׂג	(Hiphil) to overtake
23	נָשִׂיא	prince, chief
	נָשִׁים	women, wives (plural of אִשָּׁה); נְשֵׁי (construct)
	נָשַׁק	to kiss

12	נָתַן	to give
	נָתָן	Nathan
	נָתַשׁ	to uproot, tear up, pull up

ס

20	סָבַב	to turn around, go around, surround
9	סָבִיב	all around, surrounding, neighborhood
	סְגֻלָּה	personal property
26	סָגַר	to shut, close; (Hiphil) deliver up
3	סוּס	horse
	סוּסָה	mare
15	סוּר	to turn aside; (Hiphil) take away, remove, get rid of
	סִינַי	Sinai
	סֻכָּה	booth, hut
	סֶלָה	selah (unexplained technical term of music or recitation)
	סֹלֶת	fine wheat, flour
	סְנֶה	bush, thorny shrub
	סְעָרָה	heavy windstorm, gale
20	סָפַר	to write, count, number; (Piel) recount, report, enumerate
4	סֵפֶר	scroll, book
	סֹפֵר	scribe, writer
	סָרִיס	eunuch, officer

24	סָתַר	(Niphal) to conceal, hide; (Hiphil) hide

עָ

15	עָבַד	to serve, work, till, cultivate
3	עֶבֶד	servant
20	עֲבוֹדָה	work, labor, service; עֲבֹדָה (alternate spelling)
14	עָבַר	to pass over, transgress
	עֵבֶר	side, region, opposite side
	עִבְרִי	Hebrew
	עֲגָלָה	wagon; עֲגָלוֹת (plural)
	עֶגְלָה	heifer
35	עֵד	witness
6	עַד	to, unto, as far as (spatial); until, while (temporal)
20	עֵדָה	congregation, assembly, testimony, witness
	עֵדוּת	warning sign, reminder, precept, commandment (fs); עֵדֹת (plural)
	עֵדֶן	Eden
	עֵדֶר	flock, herd
	עוּד	(Hiphil) to warn, admonish
10	עוֹד	yet, still, again
5	עוֹלָם	remote time, forever, eternity, everlasting; לְעֹלָם וָעֶד) forever and ever)

11	עָוֹן	transgression, iniquity, guilt
34	עוֹף	flying creatures, birds, insects
28	עוּר	to arouse, awake
29	עוֹר	skin, leather
34	עֵז	goat (fs)
29	עֹז	strength, power, might
16	עָזַב	to leave, forsake, abandon
27	עָזַר	to help, assist
	עֵזֶר	help, assistance
4	עַיִן	eye, fountain (fs); עֵין (construct)
4	עִיר	city (fs); עָרִים (plural)
6	עַל	on, upon, against, over
6	עַל־דְּבַר	on account of, because of
	עַל־כֵּן	therefore
6	עַל־פְּנֵי	on the surface of, in front of, before
	עֹל	yoke
14	עָלָה	to go up
10	עֹלָה	burnt offering; עֹלוֹת (plural)
	עֶלְיוֹן	Most High, upper
	עָלַץ	to rejoice
9	עַם	people; עַמִּים (plural)
6	עִם	with
14	עָמַד	to stand
	עֹמֶד	place where one stands or is stationed
27	עַמּוּד	pillar, column

	עַמּוֹן	Ammon; עַמּוֹנִי Ammonite
	עָמָל	distress, trouble, effort
	עֵמֶק	valley
15	עָנָה	to answer
27	עָנָה	to bend down, be afflicted, humble; (Piel) oppress, humiliate
8	עָנִי	afflicted, poor
	עֳנִי	misery, affliction
5	עָנָן	cloud(s)
28	עָפָר	dirt, dust
9	עֵץ	tree; עֵצִים (plural)
30	עֵצָה	advice, counsel
	עָצוּם	mighty, vast
	עָצַם	to be mighty, vast, numerous
23	עֶצֶם	bone (fs)
23	עֶרֶב	evening
	עֲרָבָה	desert, plain
	עֶרְוָה	nakedness, shame
	עָרוּם	clever, subtle, shrewd
28	עָרַךְ	to arrange, set in order
	עֹרֶף	neck, back of neck
	עֵשֶׂב	grass, green plants, vegetation
12	עָשָׂה	to do, make; (Piel) press, squeeze
	עֵשָׂו	Esau
17	עֶשֶׂר	ten, decade
11	עֶשְׂרִים	twenty (plural of עֶשֶׂר)
	עָשִׁיר	rich, wealthy

10	עֵת	time (fs)
7	עַתָּה	now

פ

	פֵּאָה	side, rim, corner
	פָּגַע	to meet, encounter
	פֶּגֶר	corpse, carcass
	פָּדָה	to buy (off), ransom, redeem
6	פֶּה	mouth; פִּי (construct)
14	פֹּה	here; פּוֹ or פֹּא (alternate spellings)
	פוּץ	to scatter, disperse
	פָּחַד	to tremble
	פַּחַד	trembling, terror
24	פָּלָא	(Niphal) to be extraordinary, wonderful
34	פָּלַל	(Hithpael) to pray
	פְּלִשְׁתִּי	Philistine; פְּלֶשֶׁת Philistia; פְּלִשְׁתִּים Philistines
15	פֶּן־	lest
21	פָּנָה	to turn about, turn aside
10	פָּנִים	face; פְּנֵי (construct)
	פֶּסֶל	idol, image
	פָּעַל	to do, make
28	פַּעַם	foot, step, time (fs)
	פַּעֲמַיִם	twice
13	פָּקַד	to visit, number, appoint, miss, take care of, muster

19	פַּר	young bull
	פָּרַד	(Niphal) to divide, branch off; (Hiphil) separate
	פָּרָה	heifer, cow
23	פְּרִי	fruit
3	פַּרְעֹה	Pharaoh
	פָּרַץ	to make a breach, burst out
	פָּרַר	(Hiphil) to break out, burst forth, shake
	פָּרַשׂ	to spread out, flaunt
	פָּרָשׁ	horseman, rider, horse
	פָּשַׁט	to take off, strip off
29	פֶּשַׁע	rebellion, revolt, transgression
21	פָּתַח	to open; (Piel) loosen, free
19	פֶּתַח	gate, opening, entrance

צ

10	צֹאן	flock, small herd of sheep and / or goats
	צָבָא	(verb) to serve in war
4	צָבָא	(noun) host, army; צְבָאוֹת (plural)
7	צַדִּיק	righteous, just
	צָדֵק	to be right, just, righteous; (Hiphil) give justice
25	צֶדֶק	righteousness, what is right, just
15	צְדָקָה	righteousness

26	צָוָה	(Piel) to command, order, direct
32	צוּר	rock, boulder, cliff
	צִיּוֹן	Zion
	צֵל	shadow, shade, protection
	צָלַח	to be strong, effective, succeed
	צֶלֶם	image, likeness
	צֵלָע	rib, side (fs)
	צָמַד	(Niphal) to commit oneself to, attach oneself to
	צֶמַח	growth, sprout, bud
	צָעַק	to cry out
	צְעָקָה	outcry, wailing, call for help
	צָעַר	to be trifling, insignificant
15	צָפוֹן	north (fs)
	צָפוֹנָה	northward (צָפוֹן with directional ending הָ)
31	צַר	adversary, foe
35	צָרָה	distress
	צָרַף	to smelt gold, refine
	צָרַר	to wrap up, be hostile toward

ק

22	קָבַץ	to gather
22	קָבַר	to bury
	קֶבֶר	grave

	קָדַד	to bow down, kneel down
7	קָדוֹשׁ	holy
	קָדִים	east side, east
	קָדַם	to be in front, walk at the head
31	קֶדֶם	east, in front, east(ward); קֵדֶם (alternate spelling)
	קֵדְמָה	eastward (קֵדֶם with directional ending הָ)
18	קָדַשׁ	to be holy; (Piel) make holy, consecrate, sanctify; (Hiphil) consecrate, designate as holy
7	קֹדֶשׁ	(noun) holy, holy thing
23	קָהָל	assembly, congregation
4	קוֹל	voice, sound
14	קוּם	to rise, arise, stand
	קָטַל	to kill
7	קָטֹן	small, insignificant
26	קָטַר	(Piel) to send an offering up in smoke; (Hiphil) make smoke, make a sacrifice go up in smoke
	קְטֹרֶת	smoke (of sacrifice), incense
	קִיא	to vomit
	קַיִן	Cain
34	קִיר	wall
27	קָלַל	to be slight, trifling, swift; (Piel) declare cursed; (Hiphil) make light
	קְלָלָה	curse; קִלְלַת (construct)

	קָנָא	(Piel) to be jealous of, be zealous for
27	קָנָה	to acquire, buy
	קָנֶה	(measuring) reed, tube
	קֵץ	end, limit, boundary
29	קָצֶה	end, border, extremity; קְצֵה (construct)
14	קָרָא	to call, read aloud, summon, proclaim
	קָרָא	to happen, encounter, meet, befall
16	קָרַב	to draw near, approach; (Hiphil) bring, bring near
11	קֶרֶב	inward part, midst, in the midst of (also spelled בְּקֶרֶב with the same meaning)
31	קָרְבָּן	offering, gift
	קָרָה	to meet, encounter, befall
7	קָרוֹב	near, imminent
32	קֶרֶן	horn
	קָרַע	to tear up, away
	קֶרֶשׁ	plank, board
7	קָשֶׁה	difficult
32	קֶשֶׁת	bow (weapon), rainbow (fs)

ר

12	רָאָה	to see; (Niphal) appear
4	רֹאשׁ	head, chief, top

11	רִאשׁוֹן	first; רִישׁוֹן (alternate spelling); רִאשֹׁנִים or רִאשֹׁנוֹת (plural)
	רֵאשִׁית	beginning, first
19	רֹב	multitude, abundance
7	רַב	much, many, great, numerous
16	רָבָה	to be(come) numerous, be great; (Hiphil) multiply, make many
11	רְבִיעִי	fourth, one-fourth
	רָגַל	(Piel) to spy out
10	רֶגֶל	foot (fs)
21	רָדַף	to pursue, persecute
5	רוּחַ	wind, spirit (fs)
17	רוּם	to be(come) high, exalted; (Hiphil) raise, lift up, exalt
24	רוּץ	to run
	רֹחַב	breadth, width
	רַחוּם	compassionate
7	רָחוֹק	far, distant, distance
28	רָחַץ	to wash (off), bathe
	רָחַק	be(come) far (away), distant
	רִיב	(verb) to contend, quarrel, dispute, conduct a lawsuit
	רִיב	(noun) contention, lawsuit, legal speech
	רִיבָה	contention, lawsuit, legal speech (see רִיב above)

	רֵיחַ	odor, scent
27	רָכַב	to ride, mount
23	רֶכֶב	chariot, chariotry
	רְכוּשׁ	property; רְכֻשׁ (alternate spelling)
	רָנַן	to shout (for joy)
16	רֵעַ	friend, fellow, companion
7	רַע	evil, bad; רָע (alternate spelling)
21	רָעָב	hunger, famine
	רָעֵב	to be(come) hungry; (adjective) hungry
18	רָעָה	to feed, graze, tend (flocks)
25	רֹעֶה	shepherd
25	רָעַע	to be wicked, evil
	רָפָא	to heal (someone)
	רָפָה	to relax, become slack, desist; (Hiphil) abandon, forsake
	רָצָה	to be pleased with, like
	רָצוֹן	pleasure, favor
	רָצַח	to kill
11	רַק	only
	רֵשִׁית	beginning (see רֵאשִׁית above)
	רָשַׁע	to be(come) guilty
7	רָשָׁע	guilty, wicked

שׂ

25	שָׂבַע	to satisfy, be satiated
6	שָׂדֶה	open field; שָׂדוֹת (plural)
	שֶׂה	lamb
	שֵׂיבָה	old age, gray-headedness
14	שִׂים	to set, place, put
28	שָׂכַל	to have success, prosper; (Hiphil) cause to consider, teach
	שְׂמֹאל	left (side), left hand
20	שָׂמַח	to rejoice; (Piel) gladden
29	שִׂמְחָה	joy, rejoicing
21	שָׂנֵא	to hate
	שָׂעִיר	male goat, demon
19	שָׂפָה	lip, shore, bank
	שַׂק	sackcloth; שַׂקִּים (plural)
5	שַׂר	official, leader, prince; שָׂרִים (plural)
	שָׂרָה	Sarah
	שָׂרַי	Sarai
19	שָׂרַף	to burn
	שָׂרָף	seraph, fiery serpent; שְׂרָפִים (plural)

שׁ

	שָׁאוּל	Saul
	שְׁאוֹל	Sheol, underworld (fs)
18	שָׁאַל	to ask (for), demand
	שְׁאֹלָה	to Sheol (שְׁאוֹל with directional ending הָ)

	שְׁאֵלָה	request
21	שָׁאַר	to remain; (Niphal, Hiphil) be left over
	שְׁאֵרִית	remainder, remnant, what is left
	שָׁבָה	to take captive
	שְׁבוּעָה	oath
18	שֵׁבֶט	rod, staff, tribe
11	שְׁבִיעִי	seventh
30	שָׁבַע	(Niphil, Hiphil) to swear
11	שֶׁבַע	seven; שִׁבְעָה (fs)
20	שָׁבַר	(I) to break; (II) buy grain; (Hiphil) to sell grain
	שֶׁבֶר	grain
12	שָׁבַת	to cease, rest
12	שַׁבָּת	Sabbath, rest
	שָׁדַד	to devastate, lay waste, overpower
	שָׁוְא	worthless(ness), in vain, vainly
14	שׁוּב	to turn, return; (Hiphil) bring back, lead back
34	שׁוֹפָר	ram's horn, trumpet
35	שׁוֹר	bull(ock), steer
27	שָׁחַט	to slaughter, kill
24	שָׁחַת	(Niphal) to be corrupt, spoiled; (Piel) spoil, wipe out, ruin; (Hiphil) destroy
26	שִׁיר	(verb) to sing
7	שִׁיר	(noun) song
	שִׁירָה	song (see שִׁיר above)

26	שִׁית	to put, set, place
13	שָׁכַב	to lie down, have sexual intercourse
25	שָׁכַח	to forget
	שָׁכַם	(Hiphil) to rise early
22	שָׁכַן	to dwell, settle
	שָׁכֵן	neighbor; שְׁכֵנוֹת (plural)
	שָׁכַר	to be(come) drunk
	שֵׁכָר	intoxicating drink (perhaps a kind of beer)
11	שָׁלוֹם	peace, health
13	שָׁלַח	to stretch out, let go, send
35	שֻׁלְחָן	table
	שְׁלִישִׁי	third, one-third
30	שָׁלַךְ	(Hiphil) to throw, throw down, cast
	שָׁלַל	to plunder
	שָׁלָל	plunder, booty
19	שָׁלֵם	to be whole, complete; (Piel) repay; (Hiphil) make peace with
	שֶׁלֶם	peace offering; שְׁלָמִים (plural); שַׁלְמֵי (mp construct)
	שְׁלֹמֹה	Solomon
11	שָׁלֹשׁ	three; שְׁלֹשָׁה (fs)
3	שֵׁם	name; שֵׁמוֹת (plural)
11	שָׁם	there
24	שָׁמַד	(Niphal) to be destroyed, exterminated; (Hiphil) exterminate
	שָׁמָּה	there, to that place

	שְׁמוּאֵל	Samuel
5	שָׁמַיִם	heaven(s), sky
25	שָׁמֵם	to be astonished, be desolate, be appalled
8	שֶׁמֶן	oil
	שְׁמֹנָה	eight; שְׁמֹנָה (fs)
12	שָׁמַע	to hear, heed (with אֶל or לְ), to obey (with בְּקוֹל or לְקוֹל)
13	שָׁמַר	to keep, guard, watch, observe; (Niphal) be careful, be on one's guard
	שֹׁמְרוֹן	Samaria
17	שֶׁמֶשׁ	sun
	שֵׁן	tooth, crag (fs)
3	שָׁנָה	year; שָׁנִים (plural)
11	שֵׁנִי	second
11	שְׁנַיִם	two (masculine)
	שְׁנָתַיִם	two years
5	שַׁעַר	gate
	שִׁפְחָה	female slaveloyalty
17	שָׁפַט	to judge, enter into controversy; (Niphal) plead, go to court
8	שֹׁפֵט	judge
22	שָׁפַךְ	to pour out, spill, shed
	שָׁקָה	(Hiphil) to give drink to
31	שֶׁקֶל	shekel (unit of weight)
27	שֶׁקֶר	lie, falsehood, deception
26	שָׁרַת	(Piel) to minister, serve
11	שֵׁשׁ	six; שִׁשָּׁה (fs)

16	שָׁתָה	to drink
11	שְׁתַּיִם	two (also as שְׁנַיִם)

ת

	תֹּאַר	form, appearance
	תְּהִלָּה	glory, praise
6	תָּוֶךְ	midst, middle, within, through; בְּתוֹךְ in the midst, in the middle
	תּוֹלְדוֹת	line of descendants, generation; תּוֹלְדוֹת (construct)
23	תּוֹעֵבָה	abomination
4	תּוֹרָה	teaching, law, Torah
6	תַּחַת	beneath, below, under, instead of
	תֵּימָן	south
	תֵּימָנָה	southward (תֵּימָן with directional ending ה ָ)

	תְּלֻנֹּת	complaining, grumbling; תְּלוּנֹת (alternate spelling)
	תְּמוּנָה	image, form, shape
11	תָּמִיד	continually, regularly
29	תָּמִים	whole, entire, blameless
16	תָּמַם	to be complete, finished
	תָּעָה	to wander off, stagger, be confused
	תִּפְאֶרֶת	ornament, decoration (fs)
35	תְּפִלָּה	prayer
	תָּפַשׂ	to seize, take hold of, capture
	תִּקְוָה	hope, expectation
	תָּקַע	to drive, thrust, strike
	תְּרוּמָה	tribute, contribution
11	תֵּשַׁע	nine; תִּשְׁעָה (fs)

Subject Index

The items listed in this index refer to section numbers, not page numbers.

Basics of Biblical Hebrew Workbook

Second Edition

Gary D. Pratico and Miles V. Van Pelt

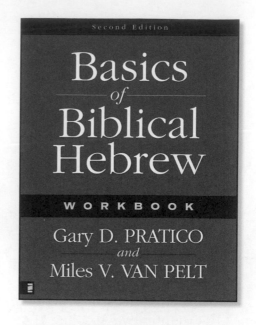

The *Basics of Biblical Hebrew Workbook* is intended to function as a workbook along with the *Basics of Biblical Hebrew Grammar*. Students begin from day 1 to translate from the Hebrew Bible. This workbook has just gotten better. In order to keep students from becoming discouraged, especially in the beginning stages, the authors have decided to give more vocabulary aid, so students do not have to spend their time trying to look up words in a dictionary. Many of the minor changes in this workbook have come as a result of professor and student feedback.

Basics of Biblical Hebrew Video Lectures

A Complete Course for the Beginner

Miles V. Van Pelt

Basics of Biblical Hebrew Video Lectures provides 36 easy-to-follow lessons (6 DVDs) introducing the grammar and language of the Hebrew Bible. Integrated for use with *Basics of Biblical Hebrew Grammar*, it is an ideal resource for traditional students in need of additional instruction; for professors, who can now utilize precious classroom time for discussion and exercises — and have students watch lectures at home; and for self-learners and homeschoolers with an interest in learning Hebrew on their own.

Each lesson is approximately half an hour and is taught by experienced teacher Miles V. Van Pelt using a logical and simple method of learning biblical Hebrew, an approach he's refined over more than 20 years of studying and instructing students in biblical languages. Focused on the structural pattern of biblical Hebrew instead of tedious memorization, each video session will give students in formal language classes and self-learners alike the basic understanding they need to begin studying the Hebrew Scriptures.

Available in stores and online!

Graded Reader of Biblical Hebrew

A Guide to Reading the Hebrew Bible

Miles V. Van Pelt and Gary D. Pratico

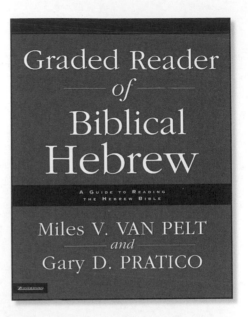

This *Graded Reader of Biblical Hebrew* is the ideal next-step resource for the student who has completed a year of elementary Hebrew, or it can be used as a refresher for the pastor or scholar whose language skills have diminished through lack of use. Immersion in the language is the best way to reinforce what you have already learned and to gain greater proficiency in using the language for exegesis and preaching. *Graded Reader of Biblical Hebrew* is a structured introduction to the reading of biblical Hebrew texts.

Through these readings, you will be able to review basic Hebrew grammar, become familiar with issues of intermediate grammar, and gain confidence in handling the Hebrew text. The readings chosen for inclusion, which are arranged generally in order of increasing difficulty, span the whole of the Old Testament and represent some of the most important Old Testament texts from the standpoint of biblical history, theology, and exegesis.

The many notes that accompany the text include information on grammar, exegetically significant constructions, vocabulary words, idioms, bibliographic information, and more. Parsing exercises are included with each reading, and there is room for you to write your own English translation.

Charts of Biblical Hebrew

Miles V. Van Pelt and Gary D. Pratico

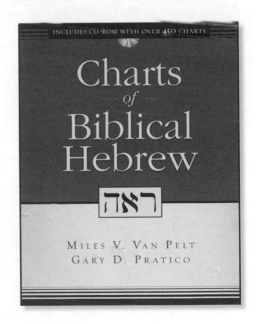

Charts of Biblical Hebrew provides students of biblical Hebrew with a unique study aid. This innovative language resource contains 130 of the most vital charts in print for instant access. The included CD-ROM provides access to a complete collection of over 450 charts.

Featuring two color design, *Charts of Biblical Hebrew* is cross-referenced to Pratico and Van Pelt's *Basics of Biblical Hebrew Grammar* and may be used with other first-year biblical Hebrew textbooks as well. The charts are also an ideal means of review for advanced students.

Available in stores and online!

Biblical Hebrew Survival Kit

Gary D. Pratico and Miles V. Van Pelt

Equip your students for success in first year Hebrew, and save them money! Assign the *Biblical Hebrew Survival Kit* as a supplemental "text" for your course and give your students the tools they need. This value-priced kit ($8 less than items purchased separately) includes:

- *Old Testament Hebrew Vocabulary Cards* — this set contains all words occurring in the Hebrew OT more than 30 times.
- *Basics of Biblical Hebrew Vocabulary Audio CD* (also in mp3 format) — with all the words contained in *Basics of Biblical Hebrew*, in chapter order.
- *Zondervan Get an A! Study Guides: Biblical Hebrew* — all the noun and verb paradigms you need to know all in one handy place.

Old Testament Hebrew Vocabulary Cards

Miles V. Van Pelt

Features:

- Keyed to four leading Hebrew grammars (Pratico/Van Pelt, Futato, Ross, Seow)
- Frequency numbers on every card
- Unusual forms included
- Cards numbered for easy assignment
- Cards 1–979 contain all words that occur 30 or more times (except proper names)
- Cards 980–1,000 contain select proper names and words occurring less than 30 times

Old Testament Hebrew Vocabulary Cards is part of the Zondervan Vocabulary Builder Series. *Basics of Biblical Greek Vocabulary Cards* is also available, keyed to Mounce.

Available in stores and online!

The Vocabulary Guide to Biblical Hebrew

Miles V. Van Pelt and Gary D. Pratico

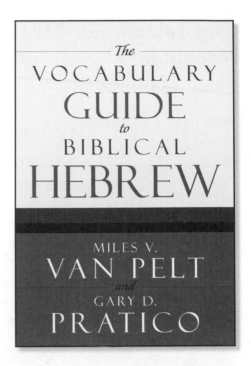

A guide for mastering basic Hebrew vocabulary

This guide helps seminary and Christian college students develop in their knowledge of Hebrew vocabulary. A special feature of the guide is that it groups the vocabulary in three basic sections:

- All words occurring ten times or more in the Hebrew Bible in descending order of frequency
- Primary roots and all words derived from roots occurring ten times or more
- Unusual and difficult word lists, such as proper names, adjectives, prepositions, pronouns, particles, and verbs

Old Testament Hebrew Vocabulary Cards App

Miles V. Van Pelt

The *Old Testament Hebrew Vocabulary Cards App* is tailor-made to meet the study needs of nearly every biblical Hebrew student.

Features include:

- Over 1,000 of the most common biblical Hebrew words
- Cards linked to 7 popular Hebrew grammars
- Sortable in various ways, including by chapter (in related grammars), by parts of speech, and by frequency
- Viewable alphabetically, by frequency, or randomly
- Test your knowledge with a "Quiz Mode" that tracks your progress
- Pronunciation mode automatically pronounces the word when each new card appears or upon request
- And much more

Go to *zndr.vn/hebrewapp* for more details

Available in stores and online!

Old Testament Hebrew Vocabulary

Learn on the Go

Jonathan T. Pennington

These two audio CDs with a booklet enable a person who is taking biblical Hebrew to work on, by ear as well as through the eyes, all vocabulary words that occur in the Old Testament 20 times or more and all the names of people in the Old Testament that occur 100 times or more. A forty-page booklet containing the entire word list and glosses accompanies the CDs. Read by Jonathan T. Pennington.

Biblical Hebrew Laminated Sheet

Gary D. Pratico and Miles V. Van Pelt

Students of biblical Hebrew may not know everything they need to know, but they do know there's a lot they need to know! Whether studying for exams or translating passages of Scripture, students need critical information at their fingertips. Instead, it's usually scattered throughout textbooks, self-made crib sheets, and sticky-notes on their computer monitor. Now there's a better way! The Zondervan Get an A! Study Guide to Biblical Hebrew is a handy, at-a-glance study aid ideal for last minute review, a quick overview of grammar, or as an aid in translation or sermon preparation. Each sheet contains four information-packed sheets that are laminated and three-hole-punched, making them both durable and portable.

Available in stores and online!

Biblical Hebrew: A Compact Guide

Miles V. Van Pelt

Biblical Hebrew: A Compact Guide offers a one-stop guide for those who have taken first-year Hebrew to refresh the memory on language forms, grammar, and word meanings. Students who are in second-year Hebrew courses can use this reference resource to assist them in the identification of words in the biblical text and the way they are used in sentences. Ultimately, this inexpensive reference gives the most important information on biblical Hebrew grammar.

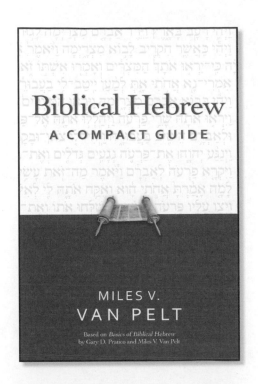

English Grammar to Ace Biblical Hebrew

Miles V. Van Pelt

English Grammar to Ace Biblical Hebrew enables students of biblical Hebrew to grasp the basic concepts of English grammar that are needed in order to be able to transfer these concepts to biblical Hebrew. One of the biggest problems students encounter learning biblical languages, especially Hebrew, is that they have either forgotten or simply do not know their English grammar. Concepts such as verb tense and voice, relative pronouns, antecedents, adjectival substantives, and the like, sound like familiar terms, but may seem foreign when it's time to put them to practice.

   With chapters such as, "To Be or Not To Be, that is the Infinitive" and "Pronouns: Grammatical Stunt Doubles," this book is both clever and engaging. All Hebrew students will become better translators---and ultimately better pastors and leaders---with the help of this book. Tips for studying Hebrew, a glossary, and a list of additional Hebrew resources is also provided. This book is a companion to *English Grammar to Ace New Testament Greek* by Samuel Lamerson.